Echoes of the Times in Philosophy

Collected Works of Zhao Jianying

Authored by Zhao Jianying
Translated by Chen Fengjiao

Warmly and affectionately dedicated to the memory of my parents

Contents

Preface 1

Issues of Practice

A Historical Examination of Conceptual Connotations and Forms of Practice 9
On Contemporary Development of Forms of Human Practice... 31
Changes in Forms of Intercourse and New Characteristics of Contemporary Society 45
On the Role of Quantitative Thinking in Scientific Cognition... 64
Thinking Modes of Practical Subject and the Execution of Practical Activity...................... 73
On Logic of Practice.. 81
China's Construction of Socialism from the Perspective of Purposive Operation Mode....... 91
Contradictions Between Norm and Innovation in Practice and Their Solutions 105
On Operating Mechanism of Practical Activity 111
Restrictive Effect of Practice Object: Standardized Operation Mechanism of
    Practical Activity 121
Ethical Requirements for Transformation of Contemporary Social Form........................... 125

Contemporary Development of Marxist Philosophy

From Value Criticism to Scientific Criticism: Establishment of Marx's Method of
    Value Criticism and Historical Materialism 137
Historical Science on Proletariat and Human Emancipation: On Unity of
    Scientificity and Value of Marxist Philosophy 145
Historical Meditation on Theoretical Basis of Historical Materialism 151
On the Principle of Marxist Subjectivity and Its Practical Significance.............................. 165

Social Transformation and Trend of Chinese Philosophy in the 21st Century 178
Radically Changing World and Mission of Contemporary Marxist Philosophy 194
On Construction of Forms of Marxist Philosophy in China Today 205
On Connotations of Adapting of Marxist Philosophy to the Chinese Context 233
Main Trends and Issues of Current Studies of Marxist Philosophy in China 242

Cultural Issues and Theory of Chinese Socialist Culture

Status and Value of Humanities 269
Exploring a New World of Value in Conflicts and Changes: Mentality and
    Orientation of the Youth in Contemporary China 274
Modernity and Chinese People's Cultural Identity Crisis and Reconstruction
    in Modern Times 285
The Crisis of Cultural Identity and the Urgency of Constructing Basic Social Values 304
From New-democratic Culture to Socialist Culture with Chinese Characteristics:
    How the CPC Inherits and Innovates Chinese Culture 316
An Outlook on Development of Chinese Socialist Culture 333
Supportive Role of Philosophy and Social Sciences in Construction of
    Cultural Fronts 354
Basic Connotations of the Theory of Chinese Socialist Culture 362
Giving Full Play to the Role of Chinese Socialist Culture: Study Important
    Remarks by Xi Jinping About Cultural Issues 395

The Theory of Socialism with Chinese Characteristics

From Decline to Rejuvenation: China's Century-long Pursuit and Prospect
    of Modernization 407
Theoretical Attribute, Philosophical Basis and Cultural Essence of the Important Thought
    of the Three Represents 428
On Characteristics of a Progressive Theory: Unity of Zeitgeist, Regularity and
    Affinity to the People 437
Unity of Development of Productive Forces and Free, Well-rounded Development
    of People: Reflections on Philosophical Connotations of Scientific
    Outlook on Development 444

Only Through Reform and Opening Up Can We Develop China, Socialism and
    Marxism: Studying the Report to the 17th National Congress of the CPC 463
Unswervingly Take the Path of Chinese Socialism: Study the Report to the 18th
    CPC National Congress 467
On Necessity and Innovation of the Path of Chinese Socialism 473
Chinese Socialism as a New Social Form: its Value and Significance 490
A Comprehensive and Incisive Interpretation of Marxism: Study Important Remarks
    by General Secretary Xi Jinping on Marxism 507

Postscript 519

Preface

It has been 40 years since I started my research on philosophy. In August 1982, I was admitted to the Philosophy Department of Renmin University of China (hereinafter referred to as RUC). My favorite department; my favorite university. In July 1986, I was recommended for admission to the same university as an exam-exempted postgraduate working on dialectical and historical materialism. The seven years of learning at this university has not only enriched my knowledge of philosophy but also cultivated my strong interest in philosophy, particularly Marxist philosophy.

The young people who managed to go to universities in the early 1980s were unusually lucky. The first reason is that it was just the beginning of China's reform and opening up, for the Third Plenary Session of the 11th Central Committee of the Communist Party of China (hereinafter referred to as CPC), held from Dec 18 to 22, 1978, witnessed a historical turning point and heralded a historical revolution of contemporary China. This great revolution started with the heated discussion on the philosophical concept that "Practice is the sole criterion for testing truth." To set right the philosophic thoughts and liberate philosophy became the philosophical premise on which contemporary China would overcome those mistakes made during the Cultural Revolution (1966-1976) and get out of the "political mire" of ultra-leftism. By 1982, under the principle put forward by Deng Xiaoping of "emancipating the mind, seeking truth from facts and uniting as one and looking to the future", the entire Party membership and the community at large had done lots of work to set things right, "concentrating to make up for the lost time" and working tirelessly to realize the four modernizations[①], and thus China embarked upon the path towards advancing reform and opening up and revitalizing the nation. The whole society, under the guidance of the new philosophical and political lines and with the new developing

---

① the modernization of agriculture, industry, national defense, and science and technology. —Tr.

goals, has achieved unprecedented solidarity.

The great practice of reform and opening up called for liberation of philosophy and liberated philosophy. Humanities and Social Sciences were also facing the mission of theoretical innovation demanded earnestly by the times. It was in such a historical context that I started my Philosophy studies in RUC.

The second reason why I am among those who are lucky is that it was the Department of Philosophy of RUC that I was admitted to. It was the philosophical hub of China. At that time, our department was a place where the Chinese philosophy masters congregated, particularly those working the Marxist Philosophical circles, which had been at its heyday, with many brilliant philosophy professors, such as Xiao Qian (肖前), Li Xiulin (李秀林), Chen Xianda (陈先达), etc. Later on, Prof. Xia Zhentao (夏甄陶) was transferred from the Philosophy Institute of the Chinese Academy of Social Sciences, which further boosted the strength of the Philosophy Department of RUC. Shi Jun (石峻), Fang Litian (方立天) and Zhang Liwen (张立文) and many others devoted themselves to studying Chinese philosophy while Miao Litian (苗力田), Pang Jingren (庞景仁) and Zhong Yuren (钟宇人) and others turned to studying Western philosophy. Li Deshun (李德顺) and Guo Zhan (郭湛), the first two who managed to earn their doctorates in Marxist philosophy in China, also have distinguished themselves in this academic field before my admission to RUC.

In the early 1980s, emancipating the mind, academic contending, and making bold innovation became common practices among the then university students. The ideal spirit of endeavoring to learn more knowledge to rejuvenate the Chinese nation, the spirit of freedom in debating issues, and the truth-seeking spirit have rendered themselves as the most sonorous voices of the era. Having been deeply infected by such spirits, I have been intoxicated with burrowing deep in the field of philosophy.

In the early 1980s, the Chinese researchers on Marxist philosophy mainly focused on the following themes: (1) the influence on human society of the development of natural science technology; (2) humanity, humanitarianism and alienation; (3) reflections on the role of traditional culture; (4) Marxist philosophy reform and the construction of a new philosophical system. During my days on campus, I read a great many relevant philosophy books and articles, all contributing to the discussion of such themes. In my junior year, I wrote an article entitled "On the Role of Quantitative Thinking in Scientific Cognition" which was published by a national research journal *Chinese Philosophical Trends* (now *Philosophical Trends*) in its third issue in 1986, which explores the content, features and objective evidences of quantitative thinking method and the role it plays in scientific cognition. That was my first published article, which not only sharpened my writing skills but also injected confidence and courage into my life, which has supported me to keep at my academic research ever since.

The article entitled "From Value Critique to Scientific Critique" probes into the positive role of the method of value critique played in the forming of the historical materialism by Marx. Later on, having done further pondering over and delving into the nature and theoretical forms of Marxist philosophy, I proposed that Marxist philosophy is a historical science on the liberation of the proletariat and mankind, and that the realization of the free and well-rounded development of everyone is one of its highest value goals, which reflects human society's eternal pursuit. All these efforts were further addressed in my articles: "Historical Science on Proletariat and Human Emancipation", "On Constructing Forms of Sinicized Marxist Philosophy in Contemporary Society", "Radically Changing World and Mission of Contemporary Marxist Philosophy".

The concept of practice is the theoretical foundation of Marxist philosophy and it is through establishing a rational concept of practice that Marx revolutionized Western philosophy. I wrote a series of articles with the word "practice" in the titles, which are my theoretical explanations on the concept of practice in Marxist philosophy. Since the 1990s, along with the development of globalization, IT application and networking, the form of human society and its operation and development mechanisms have undergone profound changes. Therefore, during that period, I discussed the contemporary development of practice form. For example, in "On Contemporary Development of Forms of Human Practice", I hold that knowledge practice has become the most important form of practice and the powerful motivator for human production and social progress.

Since the 1990s, along with the establishment and development of socialist market economy, the decaying social morality as represented by money worship and utilitarianism have prevailed silently. At that time, the intellectuals in China were on such low incomes and in such poor living conditions that academic research, particularly academic research in humanities, was not valued or even was overlooked. In the face of such reality, I considered over the position and role of the humanities. I am one of the earliest to suggest that great importance be attached to the construction of the humanities and the humanistic spirit, pointing out that the development of the humanities is an important indicator of a nation's level of theoretical thinking and its people's quality, but also of its consciousness and maturity in dealing with human itself and the relationship between human and nature, and that economic determinism, utilitarianism and pragmatism are extremely unilateral and detrimental. What I thought at that time in this regard are reflected in "Status and Value of the Humanities Sciences" and other discussions on values.

It is at the turn of the century that I turned my academic attention to the retrospect and introspection of the modernization of China in the last century, and to the issues of modernity and the Chinese people's cultural identity. By reflecting on the Chinese people's century-long arduous pursuit of modernization, I have gained a deep understanding of the urgency and historical necessity in hope of the great rejuvenation of the Chinese nation in the 21st century. What I have thought can be read in "From Decline to Rejuvenation: China's Century-long Pursuit and Prospect of Modernization" "Modernity and Chinese People's Cultural Identity Crisis and Reconstruction in Modern Times" makes a historical exploration and realistic introspection over China's modernity and cultural identity from the perspectives of cultural exchange and collision between China and Western countries. Following the path of building socialism with Chinese characteristics, we have been responding to modernity and cultural identity crisis with a positive attitude of integrating the essence of ancient and modern Chinese and foreign cultures, that is, through the interpretation and inheritance of the connotation of cultural traditions, the use of Chinese discourse to describe the principles of international relations that reflect the basis of Chinese values, so as to do our utmost to enhance national cohesion and promote national spirit.

As a theoretician, I have laid special emphasis on studying innovative theoretical achievements that the Party has made in unswervingly pushing forward reform and opening and advancing the cause of building socialism with Chinese characteristics, and learned a lot from Deng Xiaoping Theory, the important thought of the Three Represents and the Scientific Outlook on Development, on which I have published a few articles. In particular since the Eighteenth National Congress of CPC, convened from Nov 8 to 14, 2012, the Central Committee of the CPC headed by General Secretary Xi Jinping has been putting continuous efforts into and laying much emphasis on theoretical innovation, which have enriched and adapted Marxism to the conditions of the 21st-century China. My understanding of Xi Jinping's important speeches can be further explored in my essays like "On Necessity and Innovation of the Path of Chinese Socialism", "Giving Full Play to the Role of Chinese Socialist Culture" and "A Comprehensive and Incisive Interpretation of Marxism: Study Important Remarks by General Secretary Xi Jinping on Marxism".

For over four decades, along with the great journey of China's reform and opening up and development of socialism with Chinese characteristics, I have allowed myself to navigate the vast ocean of Marxist philosophy. If one wants to gain something from what he or she has been thinking, the key lies in "To know the commonness is to achieve changes" and "To do as one sees fit". Here, commonness refers to the general laws of the development of nature, human society and thinking, which are revealed by Marxist Philosophy. Only when we know commonness, can we make changes. As is said in *Yi*（《易》）, "Loss or gain? Full moon or crescent? To do as one sees fit." Only when we have had a grip of the "key" to the true spirit of Marxist philosophy and "do as one sees fit", can we keep up with the pace of the times and contribute our wisdom to the construction of philosophy and social sciences with Chinese features and thus further advance the cause of building socialism with Chinese characteristics.

The essays collected in this anthology are all testimony to my theoretical reflection and response toward the changes of the times and the transformation of society, as well as a summary of what I have acquired in my past decades of academic research. I sincerely hope to have the honor to receive comments and suggestions to sharpen my thinking.

Zhao Jianying
2023

Issues of Practice

A Historical Examination of Conceptual Connotations and Forms of Practice*

Practical activity is the objective activity of mankind, and mutual objectivity is an essential stipulation of practice. Any realistic, sensuous activity that constitutes objectivity is practical activity. Marx's concept of practice has unraveled the mystery of Nature, social history, and human existence and development, making ontology, the concept of social history and epistemology take on a completely new form, thus achieving a great revolutionary change in the history of philosophy.

Human practical activity manifests itself as various historical forms evolving continuously, with different characteristics and connotations in different historical stages. Human history, in a certain sense, is a history in which the form of practice has been constantly evolving.

One of the outstanding manifestations of the new development of human practice forms in the contemporary era is the rise of the form of knowledge practice. Knowledge practice (knowledge production and knowledge labor) has become an important form of practice and a powerful motive force for human production and social progress.

In Marxist philosophy, practice is the fundamental and leading philosophical category. It is through the creation of a rational concept of practice that Marx brought a great change to the history of Western philosophy. Therefore, to correctly understand and grasp the scope of practice is of great theoretical and practical significance. Besides, practice is also a very controversial concept. This article, therefore, attempts to make a historical investigation of the concept of practice, and

---

* Originally published in Li Deshun 李德顺, Sun Weiping 孙伟平, Zhao Jianying 赵剑英: *Research on Categories of Marxist Philosophy*《马克思主义哲学范畴研究》, Beijing: China Social Science Press, 2009. This essay was independently written by Zhao Jianying.

comprehensively elaborate the meanings of the category of practice.

I. Concept of practice: a brief historical examination

In a certain sense, it can be said that the history of Western philosophy revolves around the understanding of "practice" and the solution to the problems concerning the relationship between thinking and existence. Generally speaking, the philosophies before the emergence of Marxist philosophy did not understand that practice is human objective material activity which is not only purposive, conscious but also perceptual, objective; that practice is not only a way of satisfying the needs of human life and material desires, but also a creative activity of human beings; and that such activity is the basis for the survival and development of human society. Rather, they put practical activity opposite to theoretical activity, and to material production activity (labour).

What is practice? The philosophers of different times hold different interpretations, so practice assumes utterly different roles in different philosophical systems. The philosophical thoughts which had existed before Marxist philosophy made its appearance, on the whole, had not yet developed themselves into any rational concept of practice, though there were some valuable ideas in which there were some reasonable factors.

The original meaning of "practice" in the Western philosophical tradition focuses on being human, rather than acting. In ancient Greece, "practice" initially referred to the most general way in which living things deport themselves.[①] Aristotle is generally believed to be the founder of Western philosophy of practice, in which people "make choices" in their life activities, that is, "the activities related to the meaning and value of life". He holds that practice relates to the meaning and value of life while production only cares about the satisfaction of human desires and demands; that the object of practice is human beings and things while the object of production is objects; and that practice and action refer specifically to the ways people behave or act whereas production and technology are the means in which people act on nonhuman things, with the former involving putting forward purposes against some standard or benchmark and the latter referring merely to the realization of specific

---

① See in Zhang Rulun 张汝伦: *History and Practice*《历史与实践》, Shanghai: Shanghai People's Publishing House, 1995, p. 215.

purposes.[1]

In his *Metaphysics*, Aristotle speaks of the fundamental difference between the two forms of practice. Practice is a process of movement to an end and in itself (e.g., building, learning, or moving for an end), that is, the acting for an end (e.g., living, happiness, watching, contemplation, and thinking)[2], which separates acting from making and producing. In his view, only correct action is the ultimate end of human beings. The "correct action" mentioned here is the practice that constitutes an end in itself. It is related to the well-being of another and society. It is a good action that pursues happiness. Labor distinguishes between human ethical and political action. This is the basic meaning of "practice". In Aristotle's view, the ultimate meaning of life is free activity, moral action originates from a free way of life, and freedom itself originates from politics.[3] Theoretical life and political activity are the ends in themselves in the final sense, so they are the highest practice.[4] Aristotle distinguishes practice from theory and production, and in fact he limits practice to only referring to interpersonal relationships and actions that have value and moral significance, that is, ethical and moral action.

The concept of practice of John Duns Scotus, a medieval Scottish philosopher, also has had a significant impact on the thoughts of later generations. In his view, neither vegetative actions nor sensuous actions can be attributed to the concept of practice, moreover and above all, even rational actions *per se* cannot be understood as practice. And rather, practice is nothing other than the action which is induced by the will. "To put it more accurately, it is the purely intrinsic action of will itself that originally and actually constitutes of the essence of practice, and, at the same time, the bidden action of the will, namely, the extrinsic action, is called as practice just accidentally and for the sake of the intrinsic action mentioned above, that is, just because it is in actuality dependent upon and subordinate to the prior action, because if, on the one hand, practice is the action of the will which is prepared through virtue and will become possible only through virtue; on the other hand, the right choice of

---

[1] Quoted in Zhang Rulun 张汝伦: History and Practice 《历史与实践》, Shanghai: Shanghai People's Publishing House, 1995, p.216.

[2] Aristotle: *Metaphysics*, Chin. ed., tran. by Wu Shoupeng, Beijing: Commercial Press, 1983, p.178-179.

[3] Quoted in Zhang Rulun 张汝伦: History and Practice 《历史与实践》, Shanghai: Shanghai People's Publishing House, 1995, p. 215.

[4] Aristotle: *Metaphysics*, Chin. ed., tran. by Wu Shoupeng, Beijing: Commercial Press, 1983, p.248.

the will takes virtue as its premise and requires it, such choice of the will *per se*, as the action that directly stems from virtue—as in contrast with extrinsic action—is necessarily practice in the real sense of the word, and the latter therefore deserves to have a true (formal) 'moral goodness', while in the bidden practice, 'moral goodness' is only in terms of substance."[1]

Kant was opposed to an expanded *concept* of practice in which such things as the ability to govern a country, national economy, housekeeping routine, rules of communication, regulations, welfare and daily life, whether in physical or mental aspects, are regarded as the content of practical philosophy. In such a program concerning practical philosophy, the concept of practice has been close to that of activity in general. Instead, he defined practice as a special form of activity. What distinguishes practice from other forms of activity—such as political "practical activity"—or forms of "labor" —is freedom. Everything that is made possible through freedom is practice. Another element of his concept of practice is manifested in his contrast of it with the concept of theory, in which such theories as virtue theory and law theory, in their own right, is practical, for they, based on 'practical rationality', explain the principles of moral behaviors and of life in a country or society. Such rationality is not merely concerned with the possible application of its concept in practice, but it is also in itself acting... Ethics, a theory which is applied in life practice different from it, holds that morality, as the totality of the orders upon which we are supposed to act unconditionally, is itself a kind of practice in an objective sense.[2]

Friedrich Hegel's concept of practice is beyond Aristotelian tradition. Practice is no longer opposite to but includes productive or technical (technics) activities. Practice refers to man's positive relationship with the external world. In the stage of subjective spirit, practice manifests itself as "will, the practical spirit", which realizes its "purpose and interest"[3] in the external nature. The practical spirit is not an act or an activity. Practical spirit dose not manifest itself as action or activity, but as the destination; action or activity can enter the realm of objective spirit only through

---

[1] Quoted from Sun Zhouxing 孙周兴: "Sorrows of Practical Philosophy"《实践哲学的悲哀》, *China Reading Weekly*, 2000-3-29 (5).
[2] Ibid.
[3] Hegel: *Phenomenology of Spirit*, Vol. 1, Chin. ed., tran. by He Lin & Wang Taiqing, Beijing: Commercial Press, 1983, p. 146-151.

"concrete, general ... volition of intention".① In essence, Hegel stressed the active role of labor in the formation of man in *The Phenomenology of Mind*, but he regarded the actual labor (the practice of material production) as a certain stage of Absolute's self-consciousness and self-awareness. The labor, in his understanding, is a mental work.②

Ludwig Andreas Feuerbach disaffected Hegel's "abstract thinking"—self-movement of absolute spirit, and then resorted to "sensuous contemplation".③ He tried to degrade Hegel's "spirit" to the human domain and regard human existence as the Object of contemplation. It can be said that this is where Feuerbach was right, which is enlightening and contributes to the formation of Marx's concept of practice. However, Feuerbach conceived and defined practice only in its dirty-Jewish form of appearance [*Erscheinungs form*]. In Chapter 12 of his book *The Essence of Christianity* [*Das Wesen des Christenthums*], he expounded on the concept of practice, believing that the relation of human practice to the world, as evidenced by the doctrine of the Creation of Judaism, was rooted in egoism. "The doctrine of the Creation in its characteristic significance arises only on that stand-point where man in practice makes Nature merely the servant of his will and needs…."④ Egoism guides people to imagine an Almighty God who is able to cross the abyss between the desire and the realization of it. In this sense, God is the will of divine egoism, so that as long as he wants to fulfill the desire, the desire will be able to be harmonized; i.e., the subject only contemplates free Nature, rather than seeking to change it. And the only possible relationship between them is the practical relationship to make Nature merely the servant of narrow-minded, subjective, utilitarian needs. "When man places himself only on the practical standpoint and looks at the world from thence, making the practical standpoint the theoretical one also, he is in disunion with Nature; he makes Nature the abject vassal of his selfish interest, of his practical egoism."⑤

It can be seen that for Feuerbach, practice is not only a useful activity, but also an utilitarian activity in the narrowest and most peevish sense. The basis of Judaism and

---

① Hegel: *Phenomenology of Spirit*, Vol. 1, Chin. ed., tran. by He Lin & Wang Taiqing, Beijing: Commercial Press, 1983, p. 152-153.
② Ibid., p. 146-151.
③ Marx, K. & F. Engels: *Selected Works of Marx and Engels*, Vol. 1. Chin. ed., Beijing: People's Publishing House, 1995, p. 56.
④ Feuerbach: *The Essence of Christianity*, Chin, ed., tran. by Rong Zhenhua 荣震华, Beijing: the Commercial Press, 1984, p. 159-160.
⑤ Ibid., p.161.

religion in general is precisely this subjective and practical standpoint. Among Jews, egoism takes the form of religion: "Utilism and utility constitute the essential principle of Judaism." "Their principle and their God constitute the most practical principle in the world." "To the Jews, Nature was a mere means towards achieving the end of egoism, a mere object of will."① This practice has not only failed to exalt humanity to complete humanity or to humanize Nature, but also has completely exposed corruptive selfishness of humanity as the subject. Thus, in Feuerbach's view, one can only prove himself or herself in practice at an arbitrary and selfish level. However, theory makes Nature a thought-object while practice makes it an object of utilism and utility.

By briefly examining the history of understanding of the concept of practice by some of leading philosophers in the history of Western philosophy, we see the ambiguity and complexity of the concept of practice. In a certain sense, the history of Western philosophy is based on the understanding of practice and the solution to the problem of the relationship between thinking and existence.

Aristotle's understanding of practice does not render clear the relationship between the practice which he thought is of the same kind as its end, productive activity and theoretical activity. Later, all philosophers who insisted on Aristotle's differentiation of "praxis", actually all regarded practice as interpersonal behavior and theoretical activity, which belong to authentically human activity.

Kant followed the tradition of Aristotle's concept of practice, neither did he regard material practice such as labor as a field of activity suitable for free men, but limited his practice to "moral-practical" action. For him, it is only "moral-practical" action and "technological-practical" action in particular contexts that are morally worthwhile activity, and both are conscious activities.

For the first time, Hegel included human labor in the concept of practical activity, emphasizing the positive role of labor in the formation of mankind. As Lukacs pointed out, this is related to his emphasis and study on the thought of labor by other classical economists such as Adam Smith. "Of all German philosophers, Hegel most profoundly and most completely understood the French Revolution and the nature of the Napoleonic period. He was also the only German thinker who was earnestly devoted to delving into the problems caused by the industrial revolution in England at

---

① Feuerbach: *The Essence of Christianity*, Chin, ed., tran. by Rong Zhenhua 荣震华, Beijing: the Commercial Press, 1984, p.161,163,164.

that time and the only thinker who linked the problems of British classical economics with the problems of philosophy and dialectics."①

However, though he greatly enriched the thinking of Adam Smith and other classical economists who regarded labor only as a category of economy, he regarded human labor as a phase and a manifestation of self-awareness of "absolute spirit". That is, he boiled labor down to a form of mental activity, which mystifies and reverses the concept of realistic, material productive labor.

The main defect of Feuerbach's concept of practice "is that the Object [*der Gegenstand*], actuality, sensuousness, are conceived only in the form of the object [*Objekts*], or of contemplation [*Anschauung*], but not as human sensuous activity, practice [*Praxis*]". Hence, he does not grasp the significance of "revolutionary", of "practical-critical", activity.② He did not recognize the role of production and human labor in social life. He regarded practice as a mere consumption activity that satisfies the direct, natural needs of humanity. As productive activity, practice is transforming nature in the process of transforming human beings. In his view, of top priority is theoretical activity, instead of revolutionary practice devoted to transforming social relations. From his point of view, since human estrangement occurs at the level of consciousness, the means and methods to overcome this alienation must also be sought in consciousness. Therefore, it is theoretical activity, instead of practical activity, that is important for this process of overcoming. This is why he failed to develop theory into revolutionary activity. He still stayed at the level of "the human essence" which is in consciousness and which is lost or acquired through consciousness, without social historical reality involved.

Feuerbach's narrow, utilitarian understanding of practice prevented him from recognizing that practice is the foundation of cognition. Since practical activity is excluded from the relationship between the subject and the object, which are in an external relationship; that is, the subject confronts the object in a passive way while the object serves only as nothing but the Object of contemplation. This ability of cognition or contemplation is immutable. No matter what effect the development of social practice itself has on the subject or the object in the cognitive relationship, it

---

① See Lukács, G: "The Young Hegel", quoted from Sánchez Vázquez, Adolfo: *Filosofía de la praxis* (Mexico, D.F.: Grijalbo,1967), Chin. ed., tran. by Bai Yaguang 白亚光. Heilongjiang: Heilongjiang People's Publishing House, 1987, p.50.
② Marx, K. & F. Engels: *Selected Works of Marx and Engels*, Vol. 1, Chin. ed., Beijing: People's Publishing House, 1995, p.54.

will not change. Feuerbach emphasized the role of the senses and regarded the feeling as a starting point. From this, people can acquire scientific cognition through reason. However, in his view, whether sensuous activity or rational activity, as well as the Object of the subject thinking, their development has nothing to do with people's practical activity.

Generally speaking, all the hitherto existing philosophies before Marx's philosophy did not realize that practical activity is human material activity which is not only purposive, conscious but also sensuous and objective; they did not realize that practice is not only a way of satisfying people's needs of life and their desire for material but also a kind of creative human activity; they did not realize that such activity is the basis for existence and development of human society, that there should be no opposite relationship between practical activity and theoretical activity and between practical activity and material production activity (labor), that material labor is neither a low activity (even an activity suitable only for slaves), nor an abject activity of egoism, and that practice cover more activities than those that reflect human essence of freedom, the meaning and value of life, such as theoretical activity, political activity, and ethical life.

II.Marx: practice is sensuous objective activity unique to man

Through practical activity, people have not only changed the objective in the external world, but also changed themselves. Practice and Nature, practice and society, or practice and history, form an indivisible unity. Nature, society, history, human cognition and existence must be viewed from the perspective of practice. It is such concept of practice that Marx summed up and expounded in These on Feuerbach and German Ideology. It is due to the profound understanding of practice that Marx's concept of practice has uncovered mysteries of Nature, social history, as well as human existence and development, making ontology, social conception of history and epistemology gain a completely new form, thus achieving a great revolutionary change in the history of philosophy. The rational concept of practice is the core concept of Marxist philosophy. Marx's concept of practice is the core concept that distinguishes Marxist philosophy from other philosophies, and that is based on critically absorbing Hegel's concept of "labor" and Feuerbach's thinking of existence of perceptual object, and that is judiciously expounded in *Theses on Feuerbach* and *German Ideology*. As mentioned above, the philosophies that antedate Marxist philosophy understood practice either as creative mental activity or as material activity that is indistinguishable from the activity of animals, failing to unify the initiative and materiality of practice according to their inherent relationship mainly as a result of understanding of practice without considering productive labor. Marx found that productive labor is the most basic human practical activity, and productive labor not only embodies the active, creative nature of human beings but also belongs to perceptual material activities. It is precisely through regarding the practice of labor production as the basis of all human practical activity that Marx can unify the two opposing natures of practice so as to establish the rational concept of practice.

Marxist philosophy regards practice as the basic form of human existence and development and as the objective sensuous activity unique to humanity, which, first of all, includes the initiative, material activity which man, in order to meets his living needs, uses certain tools and takes certain measures to transform the external world.

The concept of practice in Marxist philosophy has the following basic characteristics:

First, practice is the basic way of human existence and development, and is human sensuous activity of objective reality. According to Marx, "we must begin by stating the first premise of all human existence and, therefore, of all history, the premise, namely, that men must be in a position to live in order to be able to 'make history.' But life involves before everything else eating and drinking, a habitation, clothing and many other things. The first historical act is thus the production of the means to satisfy these needs, the production of material life itself."[1] Marx pointed out that "So much is this activity, this unceasing sensuous labour and creation, this production, the basis of the whole sensuous world."[2] Productive practice not only created mankind, but also provided the foundation for mankind to exist and develop. Practice is the embodiment of essence of man.

Second, practice is objective, sensuous and perceptual activity. Practice is a realistic activity in which the subject and the object are mutually obejctificated. Without mutually objective relationship, practical activity will not take place. Marx does not regard practice as an isolated and abstract self-movement of man, or merely a one-way process of imposing one's own will on Nature and society. In Marx's view, "The coincidence of the changing of circumstances and of human activity or self-

---

[1] Marx, K. & F. Engels: *Selected Works of Marx and Engels*, Vol. 1, Chin. ed., Beijing: People's Publishing House, 1995, p.78-79.
[2] Ibid., p.77.

change can be conceived and rationally understood only as revolutionary practice."[1] In the process of practice, people regard the external world as the object of cognition and transformation, while the external world also remoulds man. As the main part of practice, human beings are the object of existence. "It is not objectively related. Its being is not objective. A being which has no object outside itself is not an objective being. A being which does not have its nature outside itself is not a natural being, and plays no part in the system of nature. Therefore it does not mean that it shifts from its own 'pure activity' to the creation of the object, but its objective production merely confirms its objective activity, and that its activities are objective and natural being's activities."[2] That is, practical activity is human objective activity, and mutual objectivity is an essential stipulation of practice.

There is one point that should be pointed out: The distinction between sensuous objective practical activity and conceptual activity is relative. The difference between the two is only established in the epistemological sense of "which is primary?" "Which acts as the basis?" In this sense, practice is by no means pure conceptual activity. Although it includes conceptual activity, it cannot be equated with conceptual activity, which by its very nature, is subjective activity that, by itself, cannot go beyond the limits of the human's brain and therefore cannot directly change the objective reality. However, once it goes beyond the meaning, the sensuous realistic activity, which constitutes the relation of objectivity, can be called practical activity. Practical activity turns thoughts and concepts into object existence of direct reality. The reason why man can turn conceptual existence into actual existence is because he acts as a perceptual entity to relate to perceptual entities and produce actual perceptible changes. In the process of practice, the subject of practice has objectivity, reality and materiality; the means and methods of practice also have objective materiality; and the result of practice is also an objective existence. Therefore, human social practice is a special, objective material activity. As Marx clearly pointed out, practice is "realistic, sensuous activity", that is, "objective activity".[3]

Third, practice is a conscious and purposeful creative activity of man. The

---

[1] Marx, K. & F. Engels: *Selected Works of Marx and Engels*, Vol. 1, Chin. ed., Beijing: People's Publishing House, 1995, p.55.
[2] Marx, K.: *Economic and Philosophic Manuscripts of 1844*, Chin. ed., tran. by Liu Pikun 刘丕坤, Beijing: People's Publishing House, 1979, p.120.
[3] Marx, K. & F. Engels: *Selected Works of Marx and Engels*, Vol. 1, Chin. ed., Beijing: People's Publishing House, 1995, p. 54.

activities of animals also have "sensuous" objectivity, but it is not practice, given that it is instinctual activity without guidance of any thought or purpose. Instinctual activity is a sort of activity in which people just obey nature, for they just adapt themselves to the external environment in a passive manner and cannot change the environment purposefully. Humans are thinking and rational animals and the purpose of their activities is to make the objective world transformed according to man's will and needs so that the object becomes "a thing for me" that satisfies human needs. In labor, man not only changes the form of the object, but also realizes his own purpose in the object.

Fourth, practice is social historical activity. The practical power of mankind is formed and developed historically. People in every era can only start their own activities on the basis of inheriting the achievements of their predecessors' practice. Each generation brings the practical power of their previous generation into their own activities and expands their practical ability. Therefore, although practice can be manifested as activities of individuals, people always rely on the power of man (to form a certain historical development of social relations) with Nature to engage in practical activity. This is the social and historical practice.

To sum up, practice, as a unique way of human existence, is the basis and bond of distinguishing human beings from animals and establishing a higher-calibre unity and connection between man and nature; of bringing people together and building social contact and forming a whole society; and of realizing mutual transformation between material things and conceptual things and thereby fostering and strengthening the subjective and objective relations. Practical activity not only reflects the restriction of the object to man, but also demonstrates human autonomy and initiative to the object. Through practical activity, man has not only changed the objective in the external world, but also changed himself. Practice and Nature, practice and society, or practice and history, form an indivisible unity. Nature, society, history, human cognition, and human existence itself must be viewed from the perspective of practice. It is the concept of practice that Marx summed up and expounded in *These on Feuerbach* and *German Ideology*. It is due to such profound understanding of practice that Marx's concept of practice has uncovered mysteries of Nature, social history as well as human existence and development, making ontology, concept of social history and epistemology gain a completely new form, thus achieving a great revolutionary change in the history of philosophy. The rational concept of practice is the core concept of Marxist philosophy.

III. Historical form of practical activity

Human practical activity manifests itself as various evolving historical forms. According to Marx's thoughts on practical forms, the forms of human practice mainly include the following aspects: material production, intellectual production, human production, management activity, communication activity. Delving into the new development and new features of these practical forms in the present era is an important task of current philosophical innovation.

Human practical activity manifests itself as various evolving historical forms. According to Marx's thought of the mode of production of the society formed by the unification of the productive forces and the relations of production in certain stages of social history, I think that the form of practice refers to the way in which people transform Nature and the way of social activity and the unification of the relation structure formed in such activity. Simply put, the form of practice is the unity of the way of practice and the internal relationship within practice.

1. Three main forms of social production: material production, intellectual production, human production

K.Marx and F. Engels, in German Ideology, respectively called "the production of life of one's own" (the production of means of human material life), "the production of fresh life" and "the production of ideas, conceptions and consciousness". According to this, I think that there are three forms of productive practice in a broad sense: production of material life (material production), human production and intellectual production. Productive practice, in a narrow sense, refers only to material productive activity.

Material production refers to the activities and processes of the human's creating material life products. It is the most basic form of human practice and the foundation for the existence of human society. It is also the fundamental motive force for the development of human history. In *German Ideology*, Marx states: "we must begin by stating the first premise of all human existence and, therefore, of all history, the premise, namely, that men must be in a position to live in order to be able to 'make history.' But life involves before everything else eating and drinking, a habitation, clothing and many other things. The first historical act is thus the production of the means to satisfy these needs, the production of material life itself."[1] "By producing

---

[1] Marx, K. & F. Engels: *Selected Works of Marx and Engels*, Vol. 1, Chin. ed., Beijing: People's Publishing House, 1995, p.78-79.

their means of subsistence men are indirectly producing their actual material life."①

The productive practice is the only way for men to obtain material means of subsistence. Their means of subsistence needs to be created by material productive practice. Men's material production, and the means of reproduction also need to be created by material productive practice. Marx said, "So much is this activity, this unceasing sensuous labour and creation, this production, the basis of the whole sensuous world as it now exists, that, were it interrupted only for a year, Feuerbach would not only find an enormous change in the natural world, but would very soon find that the whole world of men and his own perceptive faculty, nay his own existence, were missing."②

Material productive practice is the original activity of humanity. It provides material and time for men to engage in other activities, and the level of material productive practice determines the extent to which other political activities, scientific activities, and artistic activities develop.

Material productive practice is the decisive factor restricting the social structure, character and outlook. "All social life is essentially practical."③ "The mode of production of material life restricts the entire process of social life, political life and mental life."④ Material production practice determines social life, as well as social structure and social outlook. The economic, political and cultural structure of a society and its development are all directly or indirectly constrained by the mode of material production; that is, it is subjected to the practice of material production.

The practice of material production is the fundamental force of social development, which created human social civilization and promoted unceasing development of social civilization. The various elements and aspects of society have a role to play in promoting change and alternation in social form. However, the most fundamental force is the practice of material production in society. The high development of material production is the fundamental condition for the complete emancipation of mankind. In this sense, the history of the development of material productive practice is also the history of human development, and human history is the history of material productive practice .

---

① Marx, K. & F. Engels: *Selected Works of Marx and Engels*, Vol. 1, Chin. ed., Beijing: People's Publishing House, 1995, p.67.
② Ibid., p.77.
③ Ibid., p.56.
④ Ibid., p.32.

There are many different types of material production in the development of human history, which can be classified according to different standards. For example, according to the different nature of products, material production can be divided into two basic types: the production of means of living and the production of means of production; according to the characteristics of the production process, it can also be divided into two types: biological production (plantation, animal husbandry and fishery, brewing industry, etc.) and abiotic production (extractive industries, smelting industry, machinery manufacturing industry, electronics industry, chemical industry, etc.); according to the stages of industrial revolution, it can be divided into primary industry (agricultural production), secondary industry (industrial production) and tertiary industries (production of social service industry and information industry).

Regarding the intellectual production, K. Marx and F. Engels have focused elaboration in "German Ideology": "The production of ideas, of conceptions, of consciousness, is at first directly interwoven with the material activity and the material intercourse of men, the language of real life. Conceiving, thinking, the mental intercourse of men, appear at this stage as the direct efflux of their material behaviour. The same applies to intellectual production as expressed in the language of politics, laws, morality, religion, metaphysics, etc. of a people."[1] "Division of labour only becomes truly such from the moment when a division of material and mental labour appears. From this moment onwards consciousness can really flatter itself that it is something other than consciousness of existing practice, that it really represents something without representing something real; from now on consciousness is in a position to emancipate itself from the world and to proceed to the formation of 'pure' theory, theology, philosophy, ethics, etc."[2]

Marx also expounds on the intellectual production in his "Capital" and "Theory of Surplus Value": "The development of the productive power of labour in any one line of production, e.g., the production of iron, coal, machinery, in architecture, etc., which may again be partly connected with progress in the field of intellectual production, notably natural science and its practical application."[3]

Marx also holds that art is a special form of production. In *A Contribution to the*

---

[1] Marx, K. & F. Engels: *Selected Works of Marx and Engels*, Vol. 1, Chin. ed., Beijing: People's Publishing House, 1995, p. 72.
[2] Ibid., p.82.
[3] Marx, K. & F. Engels: *Marx and Engels: Collected Works*, Vol. 46, Chin. ed., Beijing: People's Publishing House, 2003, p. 96.

Critique of Political Economy, he comprehensively expounds on the relationship of ideology with the relations of production and of intercourse, and when talking about "the unequal development of material production and, e.g., that of art", he formally put forward the concept of artistic production.[①] In "Capital", artistic production has become one of the issues that must be explored and elucidated in the study of the laws of production. K. Marx studied the characteristics of men's "process of labor in general," the difference between productive labor and non-productive labor in the production of art, the status of art producers under the commodity system, the contradiction between capitalist production relations and real artistic production, especially in "theory of surplus value", the issue of "artistic production" is discussed more specifically.

The "Bakunin Abstracts of *Statism and Anarchy*", which was written in late 1874 and early 1875, also raised the issue of "intellectual productivity" and language, literature and technology were included in such productivity.

In their exposition given above, K. Marx and F. Engels directly put forward the concepts of intellectual production and intellectual productivity, and essentially revealed the connotation of intellectual production, namely, the activity with the creation of intellectual and cultural products as its direct purpose. In the strict sense of the term, intellectual production refers mainly to the productive activity in which the producers in the sector of intellectual production consciously and purposefully create various forms of social consciousness(such as science, art, education, morality, religion, politics, laws, etc.) and the concept of practice (policies, planning programs, etc.), and the distribution, exchange, and consumption of intellectual products, that is, the relations and processes of intellectual intercourse. The subject of intellectual production is mainly but not limited to mental workers, for some manual workers are also engaged in intellectual production.

Intellectual production distinguishes itself from material productive practice in a certain stage of the development of material production and then forms a relatively independent production line. In primitive society, intellectual production was integrated with material production without differentiation. K.Marx and F. Engels pointed out, "The production of ideas, of conceptions, of consciousness, is at first directly interwoven with the material activity and the material intercourse of

---

① Marx, K. & F. Engels: *Selected Works of Marx and Engels*, Vol. 2, Chin. ed., Beijing: People's Publishing House, 1995, p. 28.

men, the language of real life. Conceiving, thinking, the mental intercourse of men, appear at this stage as the direct efflux of their material behaviour. The same applies to intellectual production as expressed in the language of politics, laws, morality, religion, metaphysics, etc. of a people."[1] In the final stage of primitive society, with the advent of social division of labor, that is, the separation of material labor and mental work, intellectual production became a relatively independent area of production, bringing about the people who specialized in mental labor and the area which is devoted to the production of the forms of social consciousness. Intellectual production is differentiated from material production to become an independent production line, marking the development of productive practice and social progress.

As for the status and role of the creative activity of intellectual culture in social production and social life, Marx said incisively that all productive forces are material productive forces and intellectual productive forces. In the contemporary society in which science and technology have become "primary productive forces", Marx's thought has increases its appeal to the people. At present, people's intellectually and culturally creative activities are not only an element of material productivity, but also have become an independent and important form of productive practice. The activities of intellectual and cultural creation not only play an irreplaceable role in creating intellectual life products and satisfying the intellectual life needs of people, but also become a powerful driving force for creating and developing the productive forces, promoting economic development and social progress. Obviously, we can no longer regard intellectual and cultural activity and their functions as a subordinate factor of material production (or material productive forces) to understand the role of spirit and its activities and the relationship between material and intellectual production. Material production is the basis for the existence and development of human society and certainly the foundation for the intellectual and cultural creation and the possible existence of intellectual production. It is unshakable and absolute. However, aside from this perspective, we can say that the intellectual and cultural creation (intellectual production) highlights the essence of man as a free and conscious creative existence. It is increasingly becoming an important field of human productive activity, becoming the form of advanced practice that people tirelessly and actively pursue.

The production of life of one's own, or the generation of children refers to

---

[1] Marx, K. & F. Engels: *Selected Works of Marx and Engels*, Vol. 1, Chin. ed., Beijing: People's Publishing House, 1995, p.72.

the propagation of human species, including the generation of offspring and their cultivation and education. It is not only the production of population but also the cultivation and shaping of human qualities, that is, the inheritance and reproduction of human culture. The ultimate goal of material production and intellectual production is to satisfy the human needs of material and intellectual life, to satisfy the needs of human existence and development. Both are unified into the generation of children. Because mankind is not only a natural being, but also a social being. Thus, the generation of children is not merely the production of natural life, but must be the production of human intellectual life and overall quality. If there is only the former, without the latter, there is no human progress, and no difference from production of animals in general. Both the generation of children and the production of material production must be carried out. F. Engels pointed out: "According to the materialistic conception, the decisive element of history is pre-eminently the production and reproduction of life and its material requirements. This implies, on the one hand, the production of the means of existence (food, clothing, shelter and the necessary tools); on the other hand, the generation of children, the propagation of the species. The social institutions, under which the people of a certain historical period and of a certain country are living, are dependent on these two forms of production; partly on the development of labor, partly on that of the family."[1]

The generation of children is the basic premise and necessary condition for social existence and development. Society is made up of people. "The first premise of all human history is, of course, the existence of living human individuals."[2] Without the multiplication of human germlines and the absence of a certain number of people, there can be neither the existence of human society nor the development. Man is the subject of productive activity. The conditions of the population, such as the number and quality, the growth rate and the distribution of the population, all directly restrict and affect the development of material production and other aspects of society, from different angles. The generation of children also affects the ecological balance between man and nature. Practice has proved that population, resources and environment must be developed in a well-coordinated way.

Material production, intellectual production, and the generation of children are

---

[1] Marx, K. & F. Engels: *Selected Works of Marx and Engels*, Vol. 4, Chin. ed., Beijing: People's Publishing House, 1995, p.2.
[2] Marx, K. & F. Engels: *Selected Works of Marx and Engels*, Vol. 1, Chin. ed., Beijing: People's Publishing House, 1995, p.67.

not isolated in the system of social production, but are interpenetrated, restricted, interacting and inextricably linked. Material production is the basis for the existence and development of human society, which determines the nature and content of intellectual production and restricts the form, structure and development of the generation of children. Intellectual production also respectively plays a significant impact on the other two kinds of production. And so does the generation of children. Only by coordinating the development of these three kinds of production can we push the entire system of social production toward stability. This is the main idea of Marxist philosophy on the three kinds of social production.

2. Management activity is an important form of human practice

People's practice of transforming nature and society is always carried out in certain social relations. How shall we deal with and coordinate the relationship between people and between man and nature in practical activity, and to adjust and solve all kinds of contradictions so that people can more effectively transform nature and society? It is the tasks that have to be confronted in management activity. Under the situation of hand workshop production, due to the small scale of production, producers are fully capable of assuming all issues concerning production, sales and management, so the importance and status of management are not yet outstanding. With the advent of machinery industry, the socialization of production has been greatly enhanced, the scale of production and enterprises have become larger and larger, the division of labor within the enterprise has become finer and lesser, and the emphasis on organizational management took on greater urgency. In particular with the rapid development of modern technology, higher requirements are placed on management.[1] Management of labor is no longer manual work and mental work in general, but even more advanced mental work. Just as Marx said, "All combined labour on a large scale requires, more or less, a directing authority, in order to secure the harmonious working of the individual activities, and to perform the general functions that have their origin in the action of the combined organism, as distinguished from the action of its separate organs. A single violin player is his own conductor; an orchestra requires a separate one."[2] "A greater number of labourers working together, at the same time, in one place (or, if you will, in the same field

---

[1] See Chen Zheng: "New Characteristics of Contemporary Labor", *Guangming Daily*, 2001-7-17.
[2] Marx, K. & F. Engels: *Marx and Engels: Collected Works*, Vol. 23, Chin. ed., Beijing: People's Publishing House, 1972, p.367.

of labour), in order to produce the same sort of commodity under the mastership of one capitalist, constitutes, both historically and logically, the starting-point of capitalist production."① Marx also pointed out: "The labour of supervision and management is naturally required wherever the direct process of production assumes the form of a combined social process, and not of the isolated labour of independent producers." "All labour in which many individuals co-operate necessarily requires a commanding will to co-ordinate and unify the process, and functions which apply not to partial operations but to the total activity of the workshop, much as that of an orchestra conductor. This is a productive job, which must be performed in every combined mode of production."② Labor manifests itself no longer as being included in the process of production as it was before, but, on the contrary, as man's entering into the relationship with the process of production itself as the supervisor and regulator of the process.③ For the modern enterprise, various management activities such as planning, organizing, directing, regulating and controlling the production and operation of the enterprise are all aspects of the enterprise that ensure the coordinated operation in every aspect. It serves as an integral part of the enterprise's entire production process. The success of modern business management, in addition to rely on technological innovation and introduce new products, is closely related to whether managers understand judicious management. A manager who does not know how to manage or a mistake in the management can lead to the bankruptcy of a business; a capable entrepreneur who is good at management can bring a bankrupt company back to life. In the history of the development of modern enterprises, the enterprise system experienced a "managers' revolution" and thereby there emerged a "class of professional managers". This highlights the important position and role of judicious management activity in contemporary economic development and social progress. This shows that management activity has become an important form of human practice.

3. Social intercourse is an important form of practice

Practice is not only the interaction between the subject and the object, but also the

---

① Marx, K. & F. Engels: *Marx and Engels: Collected Works*, Vol. 23, Chin. ed., Beijing: People's Publishing House, 1972, p.358.
② Marx, K. & F. Engels: *Marx and Engels: Collected Works*, Vol. 25, Chin. ed., Beijing: People's Publishing House, 1974, p.431.
③ Marx, K. & F. Engels: *Selected Works of Marx and Engels*, Vol. 2, Chin. ed., Beijing: People's Publishing House, 2012, p.783.

interaction between people. Marx pointed out: "In the process of production, human beings work not only upon nature, but also upon one another. They produce only by working together in a specified manner and reciprocally exchanging their activities. In order to produce, they enter into definite connections and relations to one another, and only within these social connections and relations does their influence upon nature operate–i.e., does production take place."[1] In *German Ideology*, the meaning of communication (*Verkehr*) is very wide. It includes the material and intellectual intercourse between individuals, between social groups, and between states. Material intercourse is the interaction of people in the process of production, which is the foundation of any other kind of intercourse. Regarding the role of intercourse, Marx paid a great deal of attention:

First, intercourse restricts the development of people and of the nation. Marx said: "Men are the producers of their conceptions, ideas, etc. —real, active men, as they are conditioned by a definite development of their productive forces and of the intercourse corresponding to these, up to its furthest forms."[2] He added: "The relations of different nations among themselves depend upon the extent to which each has developed its productive forces, the division of labour and internal intercourse. This statement is generally recognised. But not only the relation of one nation to others, but also the whole internal structure of the nation itself depends on the stage of development reached by its production and its internal and external intercourse."[3]

Second, intercourse is an important perspective for understanding the nature of human beings correctly. In analyzing and criticizing Feuerbach's intuitive materialism, Marx profoundly pointed out: "He realises how man too is an 'object of the senses'. But apart from the fact that he only conceives him as an 'object of the senses', not as sensuous activity', because he still remains in the realm of theory and conceives of men not in their given social connection, not under their existing conditions of life, which have made them what they are."[4] Marx states in "Theses on Feuerbach" that "The essence of man is no abstraction inherent in each single

---

[1] Marx, K. & F. Engels: *Selected Works of Marx and Engels*, Vol. 1, Chin. ed., Beijing: People's Publishing House, 1995, p.344.
[2] Ibid., p.72.
[3] Ibid., p.68.
[4] Ibid., p.77-78.

individual. In reality, it is the ensemble of the social relations."[1] Intercourse, as a way of the existence of people's social relations, is one of essential characteristics of humanity.

Finally, the expansion of intercourse must inevitably promote the development of the productive forces. Marx said: "Manufacture and the movement of production in general received an enormous impetus through the extension of commerce which came with the discovery of America and the sea-route to the East Indies."[2] He added:"The further the separate spheres, which interact on one another, extend in the course of this development, the more the original isolation of the separate nationalities is destroyed by the developed mode of production and intercourse and the division of labour between various nations naturally brought forth by these, the more history becomes world history."[3] Intercourse is also a condition for keeping the existing productive forces inherited. "It depends purely on the extension of commerce whether the productive forces achieved in a locality, especially inventions, are lost for later development or not. As long as there exists no commerce transcending the immediate neighbourhood, every invention must be made separately in each locality, and mere chances such as irruptions of barbaric peoples, even ordinary wars, are sufficient to cause a country with advanced productive forces and needs to have to start right over again from the beginning. In primitive history every invention had to be made daily anew and in each locality independently. How little highly developed productive forces are safe from complete destruction, given even a relatively very extensive commerce. Only when commerce has become world commerce and has as its basis large-scale industry, when all nations are drawn into the competitive struggle, is the permanence of the acquired productive forces assured."[4]

Marx also revealed the relationship between the forms of intercourse and the productive forces: "In the place of an earlier form of intercourse, which has become a fetter, a new one is put, corresponding to the more developed productive forces and, hence, to the advanced mode of the self-activity of individuals—a form which in its turn becomes a fetter and is then replaced by another. Since these conditions

---

[1] Marx, K. & F. Engels: *Selected Works of Marx and Engels*, Vol. 1, Chin. ed., Beijing: People's Publishing House, 1995, p.110.
[2] Ibid., p.60.
[3] Ibid., p.88.
[4] Ibid., p.107-108.

correspond at every stage to the simultaneous development of the productive forces, their history is at the same time the history of the evolving productive forces taken over by each new generation, and is, therefore, the history of the development of the forces of the individuals themselves."[1]

It can be seen from the above that the "form of intercourse" and "relationship of intercourse" which contained the concept of productive relation that Marx formed at that time. Therefore, the structure of the intercourse relationship should have the following levels:

(1) The most fundamental is the relations of production, the core of which is the relationship between people's possession of material or not.

(2) Management relations is affected by the relations of production, but not entirely dependent on the nature of the relations of production; that is, the interrelationship in people's productive activities in a certain organizational structure

(3) Various forms of material and intellectual relationships in daily life.

According to Marx's ideas of social practice and the development of contemporary human practice, it is reasonable to think that there are mainly the following aspects in human practice: material production, intellectual production, the generation of children, intercourse and management. Studying the new development and new features of such forms of practice, especially the current form of people's knowledge production, is an important task to achieve philosophical innovation. And it will be discussed on another occasion.

---

[1] Marx, K. & F. Engels: *Selected Works of Marx and Engels*, Vol. 1, Chin. ed., Beijing: People's Publishing House, 1995, p.124.

On Contemporary Development of Forms of Human Practice*

A notable feature of human practice in the 20th century is that the rapid development of science and technology and its wide application in social life have made it a decisive factor of economic and social progress. The development level of knowledge production is not only an important indicator to measure the development level of the productive forces, but also an important symbol of human civilization progress. Knowledge production is an extremely important field in social production practice, reflecting the current "*zeitgeist*", that is, knowledge becomes a mode of human living activity. Therefore, it can be said that science and technology is increasingly being an important form of practical activity, having a significant impact on the practice of material production. Human practical activity is taken on various new features and forms.

I. Contemporary scientific and technological revolution and rise of knowledge industry

The development of contemporary science and technology has a significant impact on human social production and life, one manifestation of which is the rise of knowledge industry. Therefore, the study of the forms of human practice in contemporary era must proceed from the development of contemporary science and technology and its impact on human social production and life.

In a certain sense, the entire history of human social labor is a history of the development from the transformation of traditional industries to the formation of new industries. In 1935, Allan G.B. Fisher pointed out in *The Clash of Progress and Security* that the development of human productive activities can be divided

---

* Originally published in *Philosophical Researches*, 2002 (11).

into three stages. In the primary stage, agricultural and pastoral occupations are the most important; in the secondary stage, priority is given to the development of the industry; and in the tertiary stage, the development of the service industry is taken as the principal thing. In early 20th century, Western Europe, the United States, Australia, Japan and other countries entered the third stage. In 1940, Colin G. Clark, British economist and statistician, classified in *Conditions of Economic Progress* the industrial structure into three sectors: the first sector is mainly dominated by agriculture. The second, manufacturing industry and the rest of economic activities fall into the third sector, namely, the service industry. Since then, the Western countries mostly adopt Clark's three-sector classification when they classify the industrial structure.

In 1962, as American economist Fritz Machlup calculated, 29% of the U.S. Gross National Product (GNP) came from the knowledge industry in 1958, and that the average annual growth rate of the knowledge industry was 10.6% from 1947 to 1958, twice the average annual growth rate of GNP for the corresponding period. In 1959, the labor force engaged in the knowledge industry in the United States accounted for 31.6% of the total workforce. Therefore, the important concept of "Knowledge Industry" was proposed, which was defined by Machlup, including: (1) education; (2) research and development; (3) communication industry; (4) information equipment; (5) information services.

After Machlup advocated the concept of "knowledge industry", no great progress had been made in this area for quite a long time. In the 1970s and 1980s, the new technological revolution was thriving, leading to the major breakthrough made in high-tech industry groups with a great momentum of development. All of these elements have made the separation of the knowledge industry from the tertiary industry become an inevitable result. In the contemporary era, knowledge industry has become an independent industry, which will surely become the leading industry in the 21st century.

The first significant change has taken place in the product structure, in which knowledge has become the main product.

Digital electronic information products, based on digitization and network and featured by multimedia, have become the leading part in the product structure. In 1996, the annual sales volume of electronic computers in the world exceeded the sales volume of automobiles, the typical products in the industrial age, and increased substantially year by year. The total number of computers currently used in the world is over 300 million, including more than 100 million in the United States. The digital products connected with the computer are communication. The current integrated services digital network will gradually take the place of ordinary optical fiber lines and program-controlled exchangers. Such replacement will result in an order of magnitude increase in transmission capacity and such network will constitute the main line of the information highway in the future. In terms of consumer electronics, digital high-tech televisions and digital broadcasts will replace the current analog televisions and broadcast equipment.

It is particularly noteworthy that, based on digitalization, multimedia devices that integrate computers, televisions, telephones, fax machines, and stereos will enter homes, offices, enterprises, and various fields of society, replacing the existing scattered office electronics and household electronics. As some experts predicted, the market capacity of digital information products at the beginning of the 21st century will reach the level of several trillions or even tens of trillion U.S. dollars, becoming a huge family of new electronic products and the commanding point of market competition.

The second significant change has taken place in the industrial structure. The knowledge industry with the information industry as its main content has become a pillar industry.

The major trend of the change in the industrial structure that contemporary scientific and technological revolution leads to is the high-tech and informatization of the industrial structure. The information industry will become the leading industry while the electronic information industry and other high-tech industries will permeate all areas of the primary, secondary, and tertiary industries. The wide application of biotechnology will result in the change in the "landscape" of agriculture, significantly increasing the quantity and quality of agricultural products and improving the diet structure. High-tech and high value-added industries such as electronic information equipment will become the leading industries in the secondary industry. Moreover, the grafting of electronic information technology into the traditional industries will promote the industrial upgrading and automation and accelerate the entire process of IT application, which now has been breaking down the division of labor between the communications industry, the computer industry and the film and television media industry, making the public telephone network, the data communication network and the radio and television network intertwined into a whole, greatly reducing the cost of communication infrastructure and improving efficiency. Networking integrates data processing, information communication, information resource services, financial services, consumer services, and public media services into one system. The large collection of various data brings unlimited prospects of technological development and opportunities of business. As the statistical data from the World Bank shows, the information industry, together with its closely related industries, accounts for 60% to 70% of its added value in developed countries. The modern tertiary industry supported by electronic information technology has taken the place of the manufacturing industry as the largest industry. In 2000, the output value of the industry that transmitted various data through computer networks exceeded $ 1000 billion. In the 21st century, the employed population in the information service industry and other tertiary industries in the United States will account for 90% of the total labor force, which requires higher and higher technological and cultural qualities of laborers. The impact of the change in the industrial structure and employment structure far exceeds that of transformation from agriculturalization to industrialization ever since the industrial revolution in the 18th century.

In today's developed countries, tertiary industry such as information industry, education, scientific research and development, consulting, services, sports, and culture has sprung up and has become the pillar industry in the industrial structure.

The third significant change is that knowledge and intelligence have become the foundation and driving force of the knowledge industry, achieving a qualitative leap in human economic form.

The scientific and technological revolution has made the contribution of knowledge to economic growth more and more significant, and knowledge has become the primary resource. After World War II, among the factors that have contributed to the economic growth in developed countries, the share of scientific and technological progress was as high as 60%-70%. With the rise of the new scientific and technological revolution, the economic development relies more and more on the accumulation and innovation of knowledge. The contribution of technological progress to economic growth has risen to the first productive factor among various productive factors, and its stability has been greatly improved; the transformation process of "internalization" has been gradually realized, and the economies in developed countries has depended on the production, diffusion and application of knowledge more than ever before.

According to statistics, more than half of the gross domestic product (GDP) of the major OECD[①] member countries has been now produced by knowledge-based

---

[①] Organization for Economic Co-operation and Development. –Tr.

enterprises. Both the share of high-tech industries in the manufacturing industry and the share of exports in developed countries are increasing substantially. At the same time, investment is tilting toward technological goods and services, especially in the field of information and communication technology, and the amount of investment in research and development, education and training is also large. The major OECD member countries spend about 2.3% of GDP on research and development, about 12% of government expenditures on average on education, and about 2.5% of GDP on vocational training. [1]

In short, knowledge has been increasingly playing a fundamental and pivotal role in the economic process. As the famous American economist Theodore W. Schultz pointed out, the future of mankind does not entirely depend on space, energy and arable land, but on the development of human wisdom. In the knowledge economy, high-tech industries have grown rapidly, and knowledge-based industries have gradually risen to the leading industries in society. The proportion of employment in technology-intensive and intelligence-intensive industries has risen significantly, employment opportunities tend to be more intelligently distributed, and economic distribution is also mainly based on the possession of knowledge. Human resources have become the most important strategic resources, and their quantity and quality are the key factors for economic growth and social development.

The rise of knowledge industry and the great adjustment of industrial structure caused by high-tech revolution are of profound philosophical and historical significance.

II. From knowledge industry to knowledge practice

Traditionally, industrial structure is an economic concept. Then, to delve from the perspective of philosophy, most notably from the perspective of historical materialism, into the question of what the trend of industrialization of science and technology or knowledge means, is what philosophers should do. They are expected to think about it, carry out in-depth study and then offer an answer. For my part, the major changes in the industrial structure of human society caused by the rise of the knowledge industry and the huge and profound impact on economic development and social progress have brought revolutionary changes to human production modes,

---

[1] See Li Jingwen 李京文: *Knowledge Economy: The New Economic Form in the 21st Century*《知识经济：21世纪的新经济形态》, Beijing: Social Sciences Academic Press, 1998, p. 16-17.

lifestyles, ways of thinking, and values. All these cannot only be valued in economic terms. The knowledge industry itself and its huge effect is an issue with profound philosophical meanings.

Through the explanation given above, it is not difficult to confirm that the industrialization of knowledge activity and the increasing technologization and intellectualization of material production activity and social life have become an important fact and trend in contemporary society. A team that specializes in the study, invention, and dissemination of knowledge production has grown in strength and has had a significant impact on the development of social economy and culture. Knowledge production activity has been separated from material production and intellectual production, and has made great difference on the practice of material production and intellectual production. The philosophical significance of the characteristics and trends in this important era lies in the fact that knowledge has become the way of human existence and the core motive force of social progress. This is exactly the core basis and mark of knowledge practice. In the contemporary era, the study and invention of science and technology, and the promotion and application of its achievements have formed an organic chain, constituting the entire process of knowledge practice. The first manifestation is that the system of knowledge production has been getting improved; the second is the number of the links of knowledge production and its scale have been getting larger and larger; and the third is that the transformation and application of knowledge achievements in production and other social practices (such as management) has been getting faster and faster. This form of practice occupies an increasingly important position in the system of human practical activity and has become the form of practice that is in the leading position and has a significant impact on other forms of practice. In the contemporary era, the ascendant of knowledge industry is the actual confirmation of the form of knowledge practice.

What is knowledge practice? I think that it is a new form of human practice which has been emerging under the historical conditions of modern scientific and technological revolution and information society. It is the unity of knowledge production and knowledge labor, the former referring to the research and innovation of knowledge while the latter referring to the labor which transforms knowledge into main content. Knowledge practice is a new main form lately differentiated in the development of human practice, as the result of the continuous innovation and development of science and technology and the widespread penetration and application in social life, reflecting the current *Zeitgeist*, that is, knowledge being the mode of human subsistence.

The main reasons for putting forward the concept of knowledge practice are as follows:

(1) Since the 1970s and 1980s, the new scientific and technological revolutions that have flourished around the world have exerted a most extensive and profound impact ever in history, which not only have greatly promoted the development of the productive forces and social progress, but also have deeply changed people's understanding of the world situation. Knowledge production and knowledge activity have brought huge and profound changes in the production methods, lifestyles, thinking modes, and values of human society. Therefore, we cannot figure out the significance of industrialization of knowledge only in economic terms. We must realize the problems of the knowledge industry from the perspective of philosophy, particularly from the perspective of the historical materialism. Only in this way can we truly and profoundly reflect the problems of knowledge industry in theoretical terms.

(2) The historical Materialism believes that practice is the most fundamental driving force and the ultimate source of the development of human history. Putting forward the concept of knowledge practice, developing knowledge industry as an important aspect of human practice to what it is now today, can greatly improve the understanding of the impact of knowledge industry on the development of human society, and provide a good theoretical analysis tool for penetratingly revealing the great and far-reaching significance of knowledge production and knowledge industry, for, by dint of the concept of knowledge practice, the economic, social and cultural significance of knowledge industry as a whole can be reflected, thereby the historical significance of knowledge industry highlighted.

(3) Industry is a form of human economic activity, which is essentially a matter of human material production practice, so industry can be said to be a concrete manifestation of the connotation and form of human practice. The state and history of industry can confirm the development of human practice. Investigating the evolution of human industrial structure is an indispensable and important perspective to correctly understand the history of the development of human practice.

(4) Through putting forward the concept of knowledge practice, it is possible to correctly reflect the reality of the continuous differentiation of human practice, the new characteristics and new forms of human practice developed in the contemporary

era, and enrich and development the concept of practice.

(5) Understanding knowledge industry from the perspective of knowledge practice can enable us to pay more attention, both in cognition and in practice, to the production, innovation, dissemination and application of knowledge, and to intellectuals and various talents, and to carry out reform and innovation of the relevant systems and institutions.

(6) The concept of knowledge practice is more comprehensive, holistic and dominating than the concepts of knowledge production and knowledge industry. It is more abstract and broader in connotation. It is a concept that unifies the production, innovation, dissemination and application of knowledge.

Since scientific and technological knowledge is the main part of human knowledge, the basic form of knowledge production is scientific work, which includes not only the accumulation and summarization of a large amount of practical experience, the work involved in the process of scientific discovery, invention, creation, development and learning and inheritance, but also the work involved in the process of application practice, namely the transformation of science into technology and then into production.[1] "Scientific and technological activities are important practical activities for mankind to understand and transform nature and society,"[2] which means science is not just a system of knowledge, but actually a process of knowledge production, the essence of which is exploration and innovation. In a static sense, science and technology is the product of creative human work and the wisdom of understanding and transforming the world. From a dynamic perspective, science and technology itself is creative activity. Therefore, what knowledge practice is can be understood as follows: First, it is the creative (innovative) knowledge production itself, that is, creative activities of research, exploration, discovery and invention of science and technology, which requires a large amount of living labor and materialized labor, and which needs long-term accumulation; second, it mainly applies scientific and technological knowledge to carry out the labor of material production, which thereby is rendered scientificized, knowledgeablized and informatized.

Marx once thought that science was a revolutionary force that played a driving role in history; due to the limitations of science and technology and social

---

[1] See Chen Zheng 陈征: New Characteristics of Contemporary Labor《当代劳动的新特点》, *Guangming Daily*, 2001-7- 17.
[2] Jiang Zemin: *On Science and Technology*, Beijing: Central Party Literature Press, 2001, p. 96.

development at the time, however, he did not and could not develop such thinking into such conclusion as "Science and technology is the primary productive forces", a remarkable assertion later proposed by Deng Xiaoping according to the reality of rapid development of science and technology since the Second World War and its great influence on economic and social development, which is a great contribution to Marxist theory. And, now, based on the new characteristics of the scientific and technological revolution and the profound changes caused by it in all aspects of human society, I think it is possible to further deepen our understanding of Deng's assertion in theoretical terms, proposing that knowledge practice with knowledge production and knowledge labor as its important content has become an important form of human practice, and has become the most basic driving force for economic development and human social progress.

Regarding the profound economic and social significance of knowledge production and knowledge industry, Jiang Zemin has made a profound exposition from the viewpoint of philosophical history, which has extremely important enlightenment for us to further study this issue.

On January 11, 1999, Jiang Zemin pointed out in his speech at a financial seminar, attended by officials at provincial/ministerial level: "At present, economy of some developed countries is developing in the direction of relying mainly on knowledge innovation and creative application of knowledge. This trend must arouse our close attention."[①] On August 23, 1999, Jiang Zemin pointed out in his speech at the National Technological Innovation Conference: "It can be expected that scientific and technological innovation will further become the leading force in economic and social development in the 21st century. New scientific theories and technological inventions, especially the continuous innovation and industrialization of high technology, will have an even greater and more profound impact on global competition, the improvement of overall national strength, the development of the world, and the progress of human civilization. Social production modes and industrial structure, productive factors such as production tools and labor quality, as well as people's lifestyles and ideas, will all undergo revolutionary changes." He also pointed out incisively that "At the core of the competition for the overall national strength of various countries in the world today is knowledge innovation and high-tech industrialization." "Scientific and technological innovation has increasingly

---

① Jiang Zemin: *On Science and Technology*, Beijing: Central Party Literature Press, 2001, p. 121.

become the main foundation and symbol of the liberation and development of the productive forces and has increasingly determined the process of the development of a country and a nation."[1] In a speech at the Central Economic Work Conference held on November 15, 1999, scientific and technological innovation was regarded as the decisive force for social development. He pointed out: "Scientific and technological progress and innovation are the determinants of the development of the productive forces and the leading force in economic and social development."[2] In the speech at the opening ceremony of the 16th World Computer Congress on August 28, 2000, the concept of "knowledge production" was put forward for the first time in the official documents of the central authorities and it was pointed out that "With the continuous advancement of knowledge innovation and technological innovation, the combination of material production and knowledge production, the combination of hardware manufacturing and software manufacturing, and the combination of traditional economy and information network technology will form a powerful impetus for economic and social development in the 21st century."[3]

Jiang Zemin's afore-mentioned assertions have actually clarified the comprehensive significance of economic, political, cultural, and social progress of knowledge production as a whole, and contains the perspective of historical materialism. I think, from the viewpoint of historical philosophy, further proposing the concept of knowledge practice provides a very good theoretical analysis tool for more profoundly revealing the important and far-reaching significance of knowledge production and knowledge industry, for the concept of "knowledge practice" can reflect as a whole the economic, social and cultural significance of the concept of knowledge industry.

III. Characteristics of knowledge practice

In order to grasp profoundly the connotation of knowledge practice, it is necessary to analyze the meaning and characteristics of knowledge production, because it is knowledge production that constitutes the concept of knowledge practice.

Compared with material production, knowledge production has its own characteristics.

---

[1] Jiang Zemin: *On Science and Technology*, Beijing: Central Party Literature Press, 2001, p.145-146.
[2] Ibid., p. 171.
[3] Ibid., p. 221.

First, knowledge production is a labor that mainly consumes mental labor. Although the activity of knowledge production also relies on necessary physical means (such as ink, paper, instruments and equipment, etc.) and materials (such as the materials for investigation and experiment) and a certain amount of physical labor, it is in essence the consumption of brain power realized by human conscious activity. A new discovery, a new theory and a new method cannot be made mainly through physical activity, but through active, creative thinking. Computer software is the most important and valuable product of knowledge production (information product) in modern times. Production of computer software must rely on physical means such as compact discs and tapes, but such production is fundamentally an activity of mental creation on the part of the producer. The production, storage and utilization of software has become the most important industry in modern social production. Computer software can be said to be an unalloyed brain product and the main added value source as far as the world wealth is concerned. Some people now say that wealth does not belong to the rulers of slaves, but belongs to the pioneers of human creativity; no longer to the conqueror of land, but to the emancipators of the mind.[1] These words fully show the outstanding role of creative mind and thought in contemporary times. Thus, it can be seen that the activity of creating ideas and thoughts is in a decisive position and plays a key role in the production of knowledge, which is the most prominent feature of knowledge production.

Second, the essential feature of knowledge production is innovativity. What is produced by knowledge production must be new thoughts, new ideas and new works that did not exist in the past or are different from those which existed in the past, and which cannot be simply repeated or imitated. Otherwise, knowledge practice loses its meaning. As far as knowledge productive activity is concerned, its eternal pursuit is the commitment to generating new discoveries and innovations by dint of arduous thinking and exploring. Of course, the products of knowledge production cannot be separated from the scientific and cultural achievements that mankind has accumulated. It requires the creation of the predecessors as the prerequisite, through critical inheritance and innovative reference, rather than fully incorporating and absorbing. In the dissemination of knowledge products, it is often necessary to carry out a certain amount of repetitive production, such as printing and distributing books, copying artworks, and repeating artistic performances, etc., but these are nothing

---

[1] See Hu Yongwen 胡咏文: *Sanlian Life Week*《三联生活周刊》(Magazine), 2001(20).

but the representation of the mental products that have been created and objectified (actually they belong to the category of material production), and it does not reflect the nature of knowledge production.①

Third, knowledge production is characterized by autonomy and freedom. In the knowledge products, the original insights and discoveries of the producers are also clearly manifested. With the increasing socialization of production today, knowledge products are often completed by many people through collaboration, but in this collaborative work, the most basic form of knowledge production is the free and independent exploration of the participants of knowledge production, such as scientists. In this sense, we can say that knowledge production is an "autonomous production" or "free production".②

Fourth, knowledge production should be carried out based on material production, but the latter cannot be separated from the former. With the development of human creativity, material production is increasingly guided by the result of knowledge production in its content, methods and means. Those who engage in material production must increasingly arm themselves with the result of knowledge production. The level of the result of knowledge production is not synchronized with the level of the development of material production; it often appears above or below the level of material production.

Now in the information society and knowledge society in which the contemporary scientific and technological revolution is highly socialized, the position of material production and knowledge production in human social and economic activities has undergone major changes. If it is said that in the industrial economy, capital determines the scale, speed and direction of knowledge production and application, then in the knowledge economy, the situation is just the opposite. The direction and scale of capital investment are determined by knowledge. Questions such as what to produce, how to produce, and in what scale of production were decided by capital owners in the age of industrial economy, but now are decided by the experts who have garnered various scientific knowledge. Because the direction, speed and scale of the development of scientific and technological knowledge, to a large extent, directly determine the direction, speed and scale of development of material production

---

① Jiang Xuemo 蒋学模: "On Socialist Intellectual production, Mental Labor and Mental Products"《论社会主义的精神生产、精神劳动和精神产品》, *Academic Monthly*, 1984(4).
② See Wang Dong 王东 & Sun Chengshu 孙承叔: "The Source of Value and Charm"《价值和魅力的深刻源泉》, *Teaching and Research*, 1988(1).

activities material production, which, in a sense, has become the natural extension of human exploration of scientific knowledge. People have been investing more and more in the production and distribution of knowledge and thereby gaining huge benefits from its consumption.①

In short, in the contemporary era, the level of development of knowledge production is an important indicator not only of the level of development of the productive forces, but also of the degree of progress of human civilization. Knowledge production plays an extremely important role in social production.

What is the relation between knowledge production and intellectual production? In my opinion, in general, knowledge production belongs to the category of intellectual production. In Marx's thoughts of the forms of practice, the creation and invention of scientific theories and techniques are also mentioned in the category of intellectual production.

There are many forms of intellectual production, which can be categorized differently from different perspectives. According to the interrelationship between product and consumption, Marx divided it into two basic forms: the first form, the product of which "has a form independent of the producer and the consumer, and therefore, can exist in the period between its production and consumption," such as books, paintings, film copies, videos and records; the second form, the product of which "cannot be separated from the act of producing, as is the case with all performing artists, orators, actors, teachers, physicians, priests, etc.", and which is consumed by consumers while the production of intellectual value is not yet completed;② it can also be divided, according to the content and function of products, into the production of scientific knowledge, that of literary arts, that of philosophical theories, and that of institutional codes. The characteristics of knowledge production, such as creativity, autonomy and freedom, in principle, also can be applied to intellectual production. The difference between the two is that the style of intellectual production is more individual and unique than that of knowledge production. For example, the most valuable but most difficult part in the artists' creation of paintings, music pieces, and literary works is to form their own unique "style", which is the

---

① See Wang Chunfa 王春法: the preface of *The Road of Science and Technology Competition under the Background of Economic Globalization* 《经济全球化背景下的科技竞争之路》, Beijing: Economic Science Press, 2000, p.4.
② Marx, K. & F. Engels: *Marx and Engels: Collected Works*, Vol. 48, Chin. ed., Beijing: People's Publishing House, 1985, p. 61-62.

greatest success of artistic creation.

Just intellectual production was separated from material production and became an independent sector of production when material productivity was promoted, now science and technology is in a position high enough for us to draw the conclusion that knowledge production has become a huge, extremely important and relatively independent sector of production in the system of intellectual production, which is clearly different, in terms of characteristic and function, from the labor of intellectual production in general. In order to correctly understand and reflect the important position of knowledge production in economic development and social progress of humanity which regards scientific and technological research, innovation, communication and application as its main contents, I think it is necessary to differentiate knowledge production from intellectual production in theoretical terms : knowledge production is identified as an important form of human practice; intellectual production refers specifically to the activity which produces and inherits humanistic spirit and provides people with intellectual products which satisfy their intellectual and mental needs in human development, mainly including intellectual and cultural activities such as arts and literature, say, music, paintings, fictions, poetry and calligraphy, religions, philosophy and psychology.

Intellectual production provides people with ideals and convictions, theoretical concepts, value orientation, code of conduct, etc. Therefore, it is an important condition for realizing and improving the consciousness, initiative and creativity of human activities. Intellectual production satisfies the needs of human mental life, thereby vigorously promote the development of material production, so it is an extremely important field of social practice, has an important role in the existence and development of society, and is an important indicator of the progress of human civilization.

The above study enables us to say that human practical activity manifests itself as various forms of history which are evolving continuously, with different characteristics and connotations in different historical stages; that, in a certain sense, human history can be regarded as the history of the continuous development of the forms of practice. A prominent manifestation of the new pattern of human practice in contemporary history is the emergence of the form of knowledge practice (knowledge production and knowledge labor), which has become an important form of practice and a powerful driving force for human production and social progress.

Changes in Forms of Intercourse and New Characteristics of Contemporary Society*

Since the 1990s, the most salient and far-reaching features of human society have been undoubtedly globalization, IT application and intellectualization. It can be thus said that great changes have taken place in the forms of human society and its operation and development mechanisms. This is a major research issue in today's Marxist philosophy. This article attempts to make some exploration from the perspective of modern development of the forms of intercourse.

What is globalization? Even if opinions differ group to group in academic circles around the world, there is now a consensus that globalization is a historical concept which has undergone three historical stages: first, the "great geographical discovery" in the 15th century, which Marx called "the transition from history to world history"; second, the industrial revolution in the 18th century that promoted the formation of a "world market"; third, the development of information technology in the latter half of the 20th century, particularly the rapid development of Internet technology after the 1990s, which has greatly deepened world integration. Globalization is a process of constant transformation from national history to world history.

The accelerating of globalization is based on the development of information technology, which refers to the technology that fulfills the functions of acquiring, transmitting, processing, reproducing and utilizing information, including technologies of computerization, communications and control, and information-collection technology. It is the core and forerunner of the world's new technological revolution, and extensively permeates all other high-tech fields, thus becoming the basic basis and the important means for their development. The rapid development of information technology has accelerated the IT application in modern society. The

---

* Originally published in *Philosophical Researches*, 2003 (11).

IT application will inevitably lead to networking, thereby making data processing, information communication, information resources services, financial services, consumer services and public media services all incorporated into computer systems.

The development of modern information technology and the tendency of globalization of human activities have led to the IT application and networking of the means and the modes of intercourse, which have revolutionized the content and the modes of human intercourse. They are not only the important features of changes and developments in human intercourse but also will have a significant impact on the mode and tendency of human intercourse. Mankind has really entered the era of universal intercourse—what Marx called "world history". New elements have emerged in all dimensions of human intercourse; profound changes have taken place in the concept of time and space of intercourse; the connectivity, closeness and instability of intercourse have greatly increased, thus making human intercourse taking on a new form.

I. Changes in the form of intercourse subject

In modern societies, in addition to the traditional national states, communities, companies, schools, individuals and a large number of non-governmental organizations, there has emerged important new forms of intercourse subject.

(1) As an important subject of economic globalization, transnational corporations have been developing rapidly, playing an increasingly important role in the intercourse between national states.

At present, more than 60,000 transnational corporations are in control of more than 500,000 branches in the world. Transnational corporations and companies have run beyond the borders, with the output of the former now accounting for about 40% of the world's gross output. The world market has expanded unprecedentedly in both capacity and scope. In the world, the import and export trade markets, the foreign exchange market, and the investment market have greatly opened up. What's more, the development of information technology, especially the promotion of economic information resources by the Internet, has created good conditions for the global flow of capital and goods.[①]

[①] Yu Yongding 余永定: "Trends of World Economic Development in the 21st Century"《21世纪世界经济发展趋势》, *International Economic Review*, 2000(1-2).

Economic globalization is an intensification of the interdependence of all nations in all types of productive activities and marketization, which propels the cross-border movement of manpower, capital, goods, services, and technology and thus optimizes the allocation of various elements of production and resources. The economic strength of many transnational corporations has exceeded that of some medium-sized nations, the activities of transnational corporations have been a great part and the force of economic globalization, so that the view has sprung up that transnational corporations, instead of sovereign states, have come to act as the organizers of socialized production in the world. Transnational corporations have, as the most important foundation and the carrier of economic globalization, pushed the wave of globalization all over the world.

(2) Formation of global interests and increasing importance of non-governmental international organizations

Globalization has given rise to all the states' highly-connective economic, political and cultural life. As a result, there have arisen such problems as ecological destruction, depletion of resources, and epidemics, which have affected humans' survival and safety, and which have hereupon become global problems. Some political scientists, therefore, have put forward a new series of political concepts such as world civil rights, world civil society, world state, and global governance, which have made a wide range of impacts. The meanings and intentions of these concepts vary from one another, some of which are worthy of further discussion, but we can be positive that in the era when economic globalization is increasing substantially, the role of international organizations will be further consolidated, with international regulation and cooperation becoming more and more important. For example, in today's world, the IMF, WTO and the World Bank have apparently played a very important role in the world's financial, trade and economic development and the maintenance of the world's economic order and will play an increasingly pivotal role, and so do others such as the World Health Organization (WHO) and the International Atomic Energy Agency (IAEA). It is positive that with economic globalization deepening substantially, with the integration of the world market making its appearance, and with the world economic organizations establishing their niches in handling world economic affairs, the role of the supranational world economic organizations will be further consolidated and sovereign states are supposed to be subjected to the arrangements and regulations of international organizations. The statuses, natures and capabilities of the states in the international system are under change, national sovereignty is increasingly undermined, the ways and means of pursuing national interests are being transformed, and the concourse of national affairs with international affairs and many functions of a state are gradually being socially organized.[①] The traditional provincialism, conceptions of nation and state, as well as people's modes of thinking, have been hard hit by globalization.

At the same time, the Internet enables non-governmental organizations to disseminate their ideas and expand their influence at an extremely low cost, breaking totally the monopoly of information by government and traditional media, and thereby affecting the governance of all states and the public opinion.

(3) With the intensification of globalization and the emergence of transnational or globalizational problems, global governance has come into the consideration of many scholars and statesmen, and there has emerged what is called "primary actors of global governance". The "global governance" refers to the solution to such problems as global conflicts, ecology, human rights, immigration, drugs, smuggling and infectious diseases through binding international regimes in order to maintain a normal international political and economic order. The values of global governance are the ideal goals that the advocates of global governance aim to achieve all over the world. These values should be the universal values of all humans, regardless of country, race, religion, ideology and the level of economic development. The "primary actors of global governance" refers to the organization that formulates and implements global regulations. In a nutshell, there are mainly three types of "primary actors of global governance": first, governments, government departments and sub-national government authorities; second, formal international organizations such as the UN, the World Bank, the World Trade Organization, the International Monetary Fund, etc.; third, informal social organizations of global citizens. All these three types of organizations have been playing an important role in global governance. Some scholars believe that the European Community is a model for global governance. It has gradually shifted its path from government governance to governance without government. As the well-known expert on governance of the European Union Beate

---

① Yu Yongding 余永定: "Trends of World Economic Development in the 21st Century," 《21世纪世界经济发展趋势》 *International Economic Review*, 2000(1-2); Ye Jiang 叶江: "On the Relationship between Economic Globalization and the State," 《论经济全球化与国家的关系》 *World Economics and Politics*, 1998(1).

Kohler-Koch states, "The European Community is a polity *sui generis*, a political system which is far more than an international organization and yet does not conform with other models of state or political organisation, in particular those of a federation or confederation. European integration has, indeed, taken us beyond a national state in two different ways: first, by extending the political domain beyond the borders of the once sovereign national states; second, by shaping a political system which is not now a state and, will not be in the foreseeable future also. One of the most quintessential features of this '*sui generis* system' is that it is governed without government."[①]

II. IT Application and Digitalization of Communication Objects

With the extensive application of information technologies, IT application have increasingly been promoted about the objects and environment of their production and living, thus entering an information society. The so-called "IT application" means that information technologies and information industries play an increasingly active role in economic and social development. IT application has three main interrelated aspects: the development of information technology itself and its industrialization; the development of information-technology-based information industry (including information equipment manufacturing, information transmission and information services); third, the wide application of information technologies in economic and social arenas. To put it briefly, not only people's productive activities but also their lives have been increasingly involved in cyberspace.[②]

There are two facts that can best show informatization and digitization of human practices: one is the emergence of the Digital Earth and its application; the other is the advent of digital libraries.

The earth on which humans live is increasingly digitalized. The Digital Earth is also the IT application earth, which is a kind of IT application earth model, a complete information model set up through collecting all kinds of information from every corner of the earth and then processing them according to the geographical coordinates on the earth, on the base of which multimedia data can be utilized to help go beyond

---

① Yu Keping 俞可平: "Capitalism in the Era of Globalization: Comments on Several Theories of New Changes of Contemporary Capitalism by Western Left-wing Scholars,"《全球化时代的资本主义—西方左翼学者关于当代资本主义新变化若干理论的评析》, *Marxism and Reality*, 2003(1), p. 75.

② Wang Xiangdong 汪向东: *Informatization: China's choice in the 21st Century*《信息化：中国21世纪的选择》, Beijing: Social Science Literature Press, 1998, p.8.

the limits of time and space, providing not only a detailed knowledge of every corner of the earth from a microscopic point of view but also an overall picture of the earth from macro-scopic point of view. The Digital Earth contains high-resolution satellite imagery, digitalized maps and social, economic and demographic information, which, if utilized well, can help achieve sustainable development in education, agriculture, etc., help to carry out land-use planning, work on the most pressing problems and generate a wide range of social and economic benefits. It not only can promptly respond to man-made or natural disasters, and rally the people all over the world to hold together to respond to environmental challenges, but also can provide information systems whose geographic coordinates can be of great service if anyone wants to roam and search in any place of the earth. In short, as an important object for people to cognize, the Digital Earth will play an increasingly active role in people's understanding and transforming the world in a more rational, reasonable and effective manner.[①]

Reading and learning are the important foundation for people to know about the world and engage themselves in practical activities. However, the objects of learning, that is, the expression of knowledge is more and more digitalized, which is indicated by the advent of the digital library, an information system in which information is stored and processed in digital form, that is, stored and transmitted in bit (a portmanteau of binary digit) after being encoded in binary, then providing electronic network retrieval and services by the aid of computerization, communication and multi-media technologies, so that users can spread, copy or transmit on the Internet, anytime, anywhere. The digital library has two important characteristics: first, virtualization of space. The digital library is an open information system that is a ubiquitous virtual library, which utilizes modern network technologies to link information resources to the same system, or to retrieve relevant information online and to localize off-site resources through its retrieval function;second, intellectualization of functions. In addition to its traditional functions, the digital library, an exchange station or node of the global information network, is a highly-responsive service division capable of retrieving a great amount of highly-indexed information, which breaks the retrieval limitations of the common websites whose retrieval of the information resources are restricted due to just indexing the topics and

---

① Chen Yousong 陈幼松: "Digital Earth: Understanding Our Planet in 21st Century" 《数字地球——认识21世纪我们这颗地球》, *Encyclopedic Knowledge*, 1999(1).

the titles. Instead, through precisely indexing the content of resources, it can manage to help readers carry out cross-database search, and thus quickly and comprehensively collect the information they need.① It can be seen that "digital library" will fundamentally change the *status quo* of scattered information on the internet. Seen in this light, the object of human practice and awareness activities will increasingly be replaced by "digital existence" and "living via IT application". Some people think that the Internet is still only a "child" in that the digitization and internetization of human life has just made their debut. It is in the 21st century when people will truly enter the era of digitalized living.②

III. Intellectualization of Intercourse Modes and Means

The Internet, which consists of computers and global communications networks, has become a basic and indispensable communications tool in people's work and life. The meaning of computer systems has undergone tremendous changes: a computer system refers to the network structure of the computer, the computer system being the networking computer. The experts have predicted that the scale and capacity of the global Internet may expand several times, or even hundreds of times, in the 21st century. Every computer will become an intelligent subject in the whole network system. The application of multi-agent and distributed technology will make people awash in the sea of information. In the information society, one of the basic contents of people's cognition and practice is to deal with and screen useful information and make correct decisions. Whether nowadays or in the future, it is impossible for all human activities to be carried out without information. People's daily work and life will depend on the collection, processing and handling of information in computer networks. In the near future, the electronic computer will be gradually eliminated and replaced by one or more different types of computers, such as three-dimensional computers, DNA computers, optical computers and quantum computers. Thanks to the maturity of artificial intelligence technology, there will be a robot that does not have any difference from human beings in such aspects as thinking mode, feeling and emotion.

Economic intercourse is the basic content of human intercourse. Thanks

---

① Ding Ke 丁珂 & Yang Mingfang 杨明方: "*How Fay Is the Digital Library away from Us*"《数字图书馆离我们多远》, *People's Daily*, 2000-08-27.
② Fang Zhouzi 方舟子: "The Real Digital Future"《真实的数字化未来》, *China Reading Weekly*, 1999-12-19.

to the development of information technology, especially the development and popularization of Internet commercialization, electronic commerce has achieved a milestone transformation in economic intercourse. E-commerce is a generic term for various commodity-exchange-centered activities in the modern society with highly-developed technology and economy, in which people savvy about information technologies and business rules carry out their business with high efficiency and at low cost by systematically using electronic tools—that is, it is via computer networks that people go through with a series of commercial activities such as transaction of commodity or products and payment settlement, as well as a whole set of procedures for handling the administrative work, such as online shopping, online stock trading, e-trading, e-banking, online tax payment, and online declaration. It is characterized by low payment, low cost, low price, the wide range of users, no limitations in space or time and direct interaction with users, and so forth. In addition, with no intermediary of traditional industries, the warehouses, shelves and stores will all be virtualized, thus greatly reducing the cost and cycle of the production and distribution chain and improving production efficiency.① As is universally agreed, e-commerce can be divided into two categories: business-to-business (B2B) and business-to-customer (B2C). In addition, there is government-to-enterprise e-commerce and government-to-consumer e-commerce. E-commerce will at last bring people into the information society characterized by cyber economy.

In the information society or knowledge society, it is far from enough for enterprises to engage in production and operation activities solely by traditional means. Improving management, developing new markets and enhancing the competitiveness of corporations by means of electronic commerce and by the aid of the Internet has been considered by large corporations all over the world as a lowest-cost but most efficient way. The rapid development of economic intercourse in the form of e-commerce will bring great changes to the lifestyle and production mode of human society.

IV. Great Changes in Space-time Concept Concerning Intercourse

The high-capacity, high-speed modern transportation and communications tools provided by the modern scientific and technological revolution have enabled people

---

① Zhang Zhou 张周: "E-commerce is Coming to Us"《电子商务向我们走来》, *People's Daily*, 1999-5-12.

to break geographical barriers and exponentially expand their world market. They use modern tools to engage in social activities simultaneously in regional markets, domestic markets and the world market.

According to British scholar Ralf Drendorf, it is the ecological crisis of the 1970s and the nuclear debate in the 1980s (especially after the Chernobyl Nuclear Power Plant Accident) that have given rise to global awareness. The information revolution has made the entire world of humankind a real space, and the development from telephone to computer to the Internet presents the people's social and economic communication to the whole world beyond the limitations of space, something that no previous technological development could do.①

According to Ulrich Beck, a German sociologist, "What globality describes is such a state that from now on, all the things that have taken place on our planet have lost their geographical limitations and all findings, victories and disasters are closely related to the entire world. Our organizations and institutions are redirected and reorganized within local-global coordinates." So how has "globality" come? There are many causes as follow:

    1. The geographical expansion and ever greater density of international trade, as well as the global networking of finance markets and the growing power of transnational corporations.

    2. The ongoing revolution of information and communications technology.

    3. The universal demands for human rights - the (lip service paid to the) principle of democracy.

    4. The stream of images from the global culture industries.

    5. The emergence of a postnational, polycentric world politics, in which transnational actors (corporations, non-governmental organizations, United Nations) are growing in power and number alongside governments.

    6. The question of world poverty.

    7. The issue of global environmental destruction.

    8. Transcultural conflicts in one and the same place.

"Globalization means that borders become markedly less relevant to everyday behavior in the various dimensions of economics, information, ecology, technology,

---

① Zhang Shipeng 张世鹏: "What is Globalization," *Europe*, 2000(1). Ralph Darrendorf: "On Globalization," ed. by Ulrich Baker: *Prospects of the World Society*, Zurkam Press, Frankfurt am Main, 1998, p. 41.

cross-cultural conflict and civil society...So does globalization conjure away distance. It means that people are thrown into transnational lifestyles that they often neither want nor understand-or, following Anthony Giddens's definition, it means acting and living (together) over distance, across the apparently separate worlds of national states, religions, regions and continents."[1]

Ryuhei Hatsuse, a professor at Kobe University in Japan, believes that globalization includes at least five meanings:

(1) Human activities, especially economic activities, are increasing worldwide or globally in many fields;

(2) It brings different parts of the world closer to each other.

(3) The same or a similar lifestyle prevails throughout the world;

(4) The world becomes smaller and smaller as people's mobility increases;

(5) These changes have built a new international system in some specific ways.

Ryuhei believes one of the features of globalization is that "the world is being compressed in space and time". Thanks to the revolutions of telecommunications and transportation, our lives has been depending more on the activities of others and our connection with the outside world is thus much closer, whether in temporal or spatial term.[2]

Marx made incisive assertion on the significance of intercourse brought about by the capital globalization and the exploitation of the world market: "The bourgeoisie has through its exploitation of the world market given a cosmopolitan character to production and consumption in every country. [...] In place of the old local and national seclusion and self-sufficiency, we have intercourse in every direction, universal inter-dependence of nations. ...In a word, it creates a world after its own image."[3]

The above-mentioned views on globalization are not totally alike, but they are completely unanimous in that the impact of globalization has infiltrated the politics, philosophy, values, lifestyles and the relations between nation-states. People's

---

[1] Zhang Shipeng: "What is Globalization," *Europe*, 2000(1). Ralph Darrendorf: "On Globalization," ed. by Ulrich baker: *Prospects of the World Society*, Zurkam Press, Frankfurt am Main, 1998, p.20.
[2] Hatsuse, Ryuhei: "The Historical Process of Globalization and its Impact on Asia," Chin. ed., *World Economy and Politics*, 2000(6).
[3] Marx, K. & F. Engels: *Selected Works of Marx and Engels*, Vol. 1, Chin. ed., Beijing: People's Publishing House, 1995, p.276.

perception space and activity space have become internationalized and globalized, so that concepts such as "the earth getting smaller", "global village" and "world society" have emerged. This shows that globalization has gone beyond geographical limits and that the space for human intercourse has been greatly expanded, creating a "flowing survival space".

The first cause for this kind of space is economic globalization, which is mainly manifested in capital globalization, product globalization and communication globalization. Increasingly, these modern economic elements are required to break the barriers of nation-states so that they can flow freely to the maximum extent possible on a global scale and require a corresponding globally mobile space, namely, the world market or the global market. According to Newcastle, information development mode of new communication system and new information technology has brought about a shift from places to flows and channels, which means eliminating the impact of place on the process of production and consumption. He believes that the information network of enterprises will consolidate the expansion and integration of the capitalist world system and may turn the world assembly line into reality so as to open up a real global market. We are moving towards a world order which is largely unaffected by geography, and which is linked to a small number of "concentrated centres for production of knowledge and storage of information as well as centres for emission of images and information, nerve centres in the cybernetic grids, command and control headquarters of the world financial and industrial system".[1]

The second cause is that, due to the extensive use of the Internet, network communication has become a new lifestyle for human beings. Apart from physical space, human beings have opened up new existence space, that is, cyberspace or virtual space. The world is truly being compressed in time and space, and thus there has come into being globalized and close intercourse. The world has witnessed the rapid formation of global communications empires, such as those of Murdoch, Berlusconi or Bertelsmanne. Co-financed and co-produced products are made on a global assembly line by these giant corporations and are aimed at world markets, hereby shaping a global space of image flows. This globalisation of image flows and spaces is fundamentally transforming spatiality and the sense of space and place. As a result, the psychic world is as colonised as the physical world by the whole

---

[1] Morley, D. & Robins. K. *Spaces of Identity: Global Media, Electronic Landscapes and Cultural Boundaries*, Chin. ed., trans. by Si Yan, Nanjing: Nanjing University Press, 2001. p.39.

image industry. The world, therefore, has entered a world in which the image reigns supreme, a "civilisation of the Image".① "The maintenance of national sovereignty and identity [is] becoming increasingly difficult as the unities of economic and cultural production and consumption become increasingly transnational."② Fredric Jameson believes that "the puzzle about existence in this 'new space of post-modernity'" is a kind of "culture in which anyone fails to orientate themselves".③

Thanks to modern means of information transmission and transport, communication has rapidly sped up, which means that greatly shortening of the time for communication, great acceleration of its pace of communication, and the dramatic increase in its frequency. New communication technologies make it possible to move money on an unprecedented scale. The interconnected stock market operates around the clock. Money moves at the speed of light from one end of the earth to the other for profit.

V. New Features of Modern Society Seen from New Changes in Forms of Intercourse

1. New Changes in Social Operation Mechanism and the Formation of Risk Society

The rapid development of globalization based on information technology has greatly enhanced the efficiency of human intercourse in terms of immediacy, connectivity, interactivity, and openness. The efficiency of intercourse has been greatly enhanced while the cost of communication has been greatly reduced. It can be said that the information movement has become a basic mode of material and social movement, which will further promote the complementary and mutually reinforcing effects of human production, circulation and consumption as well as the improvement of their respective efficiency, as an indicator of social progress.

However, the other side cannot be ignored, either. That is, since the information movement has become the basic mode of material movement and social movement, IT application, digitization and networking of human intercourse, the connectivity, interactivity, openness and immediacy among various social subjects and things have

---

① Morley, D. & Robins. K. *Spaces of Identity: Global Media, Electronic Landscapes and Cultural Boundaries*, Chin. ed., trans. by Si Yan, Nanjing: Nanjing University Press, 2001, p.50.
② Ibid., p.43.
③ Ibid., p.50.

been greatly enhanced. As a result, uncertainty and vulnerability of the state of human society have also increased. For example, the development of information technology has made it possible to facilitate the flow of financial capital with IT application. The flow of bank capital and securities capital is expanding in space and increasing in speed, which can promote rational allocation of resources all over the world and make financial capital more liberalized and globalized, which also means globalization of financial speculation and of financial risk, which have greatly increased the instability of the international financial system. Evidence is given by the financial turmoils that have taken place in various regions and the ensuing serious economic crises and social unrest. In other words, the international financial crises have "contagion effect" and in this sense we can say that the world economy and politics have become very vulnerable.[1] As Peter Drucker argues, a labor organization unique to a knowledge society will become a "destabilizing factor". First of all, the stability of corporation is greatly challenged. In the era when knowledge and technology are constantly innovated, the behaviors of corporation must change accordingly, otherwise they are bound to be threatened with collapse; and their management tends to depend on their ability to respond to the changes instead of improving their static structure. And corporations, as such, become "chameleon-style organization", so to speak. In such situation, those organizations have to struggle to keep stability, and so does the community compose of a large number of such organizations. The organizations of a knowledge society "thus continue to undermine the community, making it chaotic and unstable".[2]

The uncertainty of the contemporary society comes from two aspects. First, that social interaction depends more and more on information technology and network. For various reasons, it may cause, at any time, problems concerning cyber-security and information security. For example, paralysis caused by hackers' attacking the network will result in disruption of economic or political communication and among others, which will lead to serious consequences; second, that as a result of tremendous changes in technology base and mechanism of information movement and diffusion in contemporary society, the connectivity, interactivity and integrity of the communication have been enhanced while the contagion effect of risk is not only fast,

---

[1] Yu Yongding: "Trends of World Economic Development in the 21st Century," *International Economic Review*, 2000(1-2).
[2] Drucker, Peter: *Post-capitalist Society*, Chin. ed., Shanghai: Shanghai Translation Publishing House, 1998, p.63.

but also more magnified. For example, even in traditional social conditions, in case of any unexpected incident, the information would be disseminated in an unimaginable speed and scope, let alone at present, when it is most likely to cause the turmoil or even the collapse of a certain social subsystem or even the entire social system.

With regard to the uncertainty of contemporary society, some Western thinkers have been keenly concerned. Some of their statements should be very enlightening.

In 1992, Baker published one of his classic works on the theory of risk society—*The Risk Society: Toward a New Modernity*, and for the first time proposed the notion of the "risk society". In the book, he pointed out that the Western developed countries are moving from the "industrial society" to the "risk society". The risk society is a society fraught with uncertainty, increasingly obvious individualism and the fundamental changes in social forms. Giddens emphasized the impact of globalization on a risk society: globalization and the ensuing risk society have "brought about other forms of risks and uncertainties" that have made the world more and more out of control, becoming 'a runaway world.' Scott Rush believes that the contemporary sociations are "are characteristically risk culture (unlike communitarian traditional bodies, which are not risk, but 'security cultures' in that there is a chronic uncertainty, a continual questioning, an openness to innovation built into them. They dealt with risk, with identity-risks and ecological risks". "Risk sub-politics will be dealing with a whole new set of unintended consequences, no longer from material good-producing industry but from the information sectors, from bio-technology, form the communications and software sectors, generating new, for example, financial and existential risks." He sharply pointed out: "While technology will ultimately meet the needs of humankind to a greatest extent, its negative effects are also increasingly revealed. The various existential risks due to technology will be the primary issue to be studied and addressed in the era of risk culture."[①]

In fact, the globalized and IT application society is a technicalized society. With the social intercourse and the structure of social organizations constructed on the base of information, satellites and telecommunications technologies, emergent high technologies applied in social production and social life in an extensive and in-depth manner, the risk contained in a contemporary society is inevitable and tremendous. The financial turmoil sweeping the globe at the end of the 20th century and the

---

① Lash, Scott: *Risk Society and Risk Culture*, Wang Wulong (tran.), in Li Huibin(ed.), *Globalization and Civil Society*, Guangxi: Guangxi Normal University Press, 2003, p. 318-319.

ensuing series of unexpected crises in the new century such as the "September 11", SARS outbreak, and the collapse of the U.S. power grid system have left profound, far-reaching and fast-spread impacts, which were unprecedented throughout history. These are enough to show the high relevance and dependence characteristic of contemporary society, the high efficiency and immediacy of contagion effect, as well as extreme vulnerability and instability, revealing the distinct features of contemporary society.

2. Expansion of the International Social Space of Super-nation-state

The traditional conceptions of sovereignty and state governance have been hit hard by the emergence of many global problems, highlighting the importance of international organizations and global governance, which will inject new dynamism into the maintenance of the world's political and economic orders. At the same time, however, globalization and the Internet have posed challenges to the philosophy of governance and the approach of traditional nation-states. As Baker argues, "Globalization calls into question *a basic premise of the first modernity*: the conceptual figure that A.D. Smith calls "methodological nationalism", according to which the contours of society largely coincide with those of the national state. With multidimensional globalization, it is not only a new set of connections and cross-connections between states and societies which comes into being. Much more far-reaching is the breakdown of the basic assumptions whereby societies and states have been conceived, organized and experienced as territorial units separated from one another. Globality means that the unity of national state and national society comes unstuck; new relations of power and competition, conflict and intersection, take shape between, on the one hand, national states and actors, and on the other hand, transnational actors, identities, social spaces, situations and processes." With the help of the low-cost linkages and coordination of the Internet, non-governmental organizations have become an active force in international politics. Reister said: "The information revolution has increased individual rights and has broken the hierarchical organizational structure so that the three pillars of a world order born in the industrial age-state sovereignty and the country's economy and military forces-face severe challenges."[1] The "network" was included in the world market without the political

---

[1] Wriston, Walter: "Bits, Bytes, and Diplomacy," *United States Foreign Affairs* (bimonthly), Sep. - Oct., 1997.

restrictions of any country. "For the first time in history, political and economic space are not linked together."[1] Esther Dyson believes that the widespread development of the Internet, multinational corporations, airlines and telecommunications will lead to the ebb and flow of sovereign nation states, but that does not mean that the nation-states will die out, "but that power is falling into the hands of other forces, that is, to the multinationals, the public media, and the small businesses that can be globally operated online. Overall, power is shifting from nation states to commercial entities."[2]

Given the challenges posed by economic globalization to the territory, sovereignty and citizenship of nation-states, some scholars directly defined the process of globalization as the process of "non-nationalization", arguing that globalization is eliminating the economic and political space consistency. The disappearance of this consistency has invalidated the rule of the nation-state. Such "non-nationalization" is becoming a feature of our times. "The non-nationalization of society, namely, the expansion of the economic, ecological, cultural and military connection in terms of action and function is rapidly moving forward and the creation of a political management body in the super-nation state is a process of real importance but with a very slow progress."[3] Some scholars even pointed out that globalization is undermining the nation-state's autonomy, and the world of states is being replaced by a world of societies and "the nation-state is about to vanish".[4] James N. Rosinau said that we are now in an era characterized and marked by "transnational migration, the restructuring of authority, the decline of nation states and the proliferation of non-governmental organizations (NGOs) at the regional, national, international and global levels". "Where it is necessary to cease to focus all attention on the state but to admit that a large number of non-governmental actors are to be the subject of analysis, in consequence the state should not be regarded as the top priority any longer, but as nothing more than an important actor in a world characterized by gradual diversion

---

[1] Benoit, Alain: *Globalization and the World*, compiled by Wang Lie & Yang Xuedong, Beijing: Central Compilation & Translation Press, 1998, p. 12.
[2] Dyson, Esther: *Release 2.0: A Design for Living in the Digital Age*, Chin. ed., Hainan: Hainan Publishing House, 1998, p. 101.
[3] See Baker, Ulrich & Habermas, et al.: *Globalization and Politics*, p. 162, 171, quoted from Yu Keping: *An Introduction to Global Governance*, ed. by Li Huibin, *Globalization and Civil Society*, Guangxi: Guangxi Normal University Press, 2003, p. 83-84.
[4] See Dittgen, Helbert. *"The Borderless World*, quoted from Yu Keping: *An Introduction to Global Governance,"* ed. by Li Huibin, *Globalization and Civil Society*. Guangxi: Guangxi Normal University Press, 2003, p. 84.

of authority and disappearance of gradualization. The state, of course, still has sovereignty, but the range in which such rights can be exercised is being shrinking in the world characteristic of interdependence and the ambiguity of the borders between the states of the world. With the acceleration of the diversion of authority, the states, in face of increasingly complex challenges, will no longer manage to protect their own interests by relying on sovereignty."[1]

Surely, we cannot agree some of the above-mentioned ideas, for they are radical and exaggerated. However, under the historic situation in which globalization cannot be surpassed, the functions of the states, the ways state sovereignty is exercised, and how to handle the relations between state sovereignty, global interests and the international community, have been new issues that cannot be evaded and need to be seriously considered by nation-states.

3. Reflection upon Humans' Existence from the Perspective of Changes in the Communication Mode

The expansion of communication space, the acceleration of communication speed and the saving of communication time essentially mean the increase of people's freedom, which makes people move towards a freer realm, and thus allows them to be liberated to a greater extent. However, the non-presence and detachedness characteristic of the internet-based communication makes the originally glorified human nature "virtualized", so the brilliance and warmth of the sensuousness of humanity have been on wane, while its evil is wantonly released. The co-presence of "angels" and "devils" has now become the reality of human existence.

Changes in the mode of communication not only affect the degree of actualization of human nature, but also means different ways to constitute the subject. According to Mark Post, an American scholar, communication practices in the era of in electronically mediated communication (what he calls "the mode of information") constitute subjects as unstable, multiple and diffuse, different from identities as autonomous and (instrumentally) rational elicited by patterned practices of postmodernity or in the mode of information.[2] Print culture constitutes the individual

---

[1] See *"Toward an Ontology for Global Governance, quoted from Yu Keping: An Introduction to Global Governance,"* ed. by Li Huibin, *Globalization and Civil Society.* Guangxi: Guangxi Normal University Press, 2003, p. 84.
[2] Poster, Mark: *The Second Media Age,* Chin. ed., tran. by Fan Jinghua, Nanjing: Nanjing University Press, 2001, p. 45.

as a subject, as transcendent to objects, as stable and fixed in identity, while the emergence of electronically-mediated communications system and decentralization of the network of communications elicit the individual's unstable identity.① The referential anchor of the individual recedes in social prominence as global communication networks (Lyotard) and human/machine combinations (Haraway) replace older figures of man versus nature and individual versus society.②

Mark Post also believes that in the era of electronically-mediated cultural communication, that is, in the information age, the community consisted of face-to-face individuals in the hitherto existing modern society will also transpire. In modern society, a community of face-to-face individuals is definable,(…) but the dramatic spread of electronic communication systems which will undoubtedly rise even more precipitously once the computer, the telephone and the television are systematically integrated toll the end of community in any shape it has hitherto been imagined. Relations of mind to body, person to person, humanity to nature are undergoing such profound reconfiguration that images of community are presented if at all only in science fiction books and films.③

The contemporary communication based on information and communications technology (ICT) and modern transport means are undoubtedly the greatest transformation in the history of human communication and are a major emancipation of the relations between the productive forces and the production relations. However, we cannot therefore fail to see its impact on human existence. As Habermas profoundly pointed out, the unchecked spread of technological rationality and its continuous spread into the life of humans resulted in the colonialization of the lifeworld, namely, the constant technicalization and institutionalization of the lifeworld. In his view, "In the lifeworld, communicative action operates according to a non-instrumental principle(…) without the imperatives of the system for profit, control, efficiency."④ Watching movies, listening to the radio, watching TV, using

---

① Poster, Mark: *The Second Media Age,* Chin. ed., tran. by Fan Jinghua, Nanjing: Nanjing University Press, 2001, p.84-85.
② Ibid., p. 75. Lyotard's *The Inhuman* and Haraway's *Simians, Cyborgs and Women* register the depths of postmodern culture in a recognition of an emerging "inhuman" or transhuman social order.
③ Poster, Mark: *The Second Media Age,* Chin. ed., tran. by Fan Jinghua, Nanjing: Nanjing University Press, 2001, p.4.
④ Poster, Mark: *The Second Media Age,* Chin. ed., tran. by Fan Jinghua, Nanjing: Nanjing University Press, 2001, p.65.

computers or fax machines to transmit information, making phone calls, etc. are derogatory and trampling on communication rationality, all of which are examples of the system colonizing the lifeworld. The relation of person to person and individuals' life tend to be subjected to technologization, instrumentalization and legalization, with their daily life increasingly under the imperatives for technology, control, legality. The colonization of the lifeworld by technological rationality has been undermining normal and harmonious interpersonal communication, individuals' free space being constantly eroded, social and humanistic environment being deteriorated severely, and the humanistic connotation of the lifeworld being on the wane.[①]

In short, globalization and IT application appear to be where the elements of production such as capital, technology and products (which can manifest themselves as information) flow, but what is behind, as a matter of fact, is the multi-factorial interaction between people and their social relations, indicating the cyberization and enrichment of human relations. It can be said that globalization and IT application are the latest stages in the development of human communication, which represent the changes in and new forms of contemporary human communication, that is, the subjects of intercourse change from simplification to stratification, diversification and multi-dimensionalization, the objects from substantiation to informatization and virtualization, the means of communication from mechanization to electronization and intelligentization, the space for communication from territorialization to mobilization and globalization, the content of communication from economy- and-trade orientation to comprehensive communication in the fields such as economy, politics, culture, art, science and technology, education, talents and so on. Today's society is a IT-supported and network-based globalized digital society. It is a "risk society" of instability and uncertainty; it is a transnational community where the sovereignty of the nation-state is being undermined whereas the world's public social sphere is opening up. The hitherto existing humans are increasingly becoming "humans in the world history" that is "decentralized" and "de-territorialized", namely, "global citizens". All these show a new pattern of human communication in the early 21st century and show that profound changes have taken place in the formation of human society. Thus, it is high time that we introspected the question of whether we have made corresponding adjustment in the concepts, system and approach to policy-making that have taken shape for a long time.

---

① Habermas, Jurgen & Michael Hall: *The Past as Future*, Chin. ed., tran. by Zhang Guofeng, Hangzhou: Zhejiang People's Publishing House, 2001, p.182.

On the Role of Quantitative Thinking in Scientific Cognition*

I

Quantitative reasoning is a methodology through which the subject of knowledge, from the perspective of the quantitative attributes of things, investigate the objects through recording, computing, and deducing the objects' quantities, changes in quantities, and the relationship between quantities, so as to obtain a more accurate and profound understanding of the essence of things. The quantity of objects has a variety of attributes and forms. In the process of obtaining a profound understanding, there are many different forms of quantity, including quality, energy, effect size, amount of electricity, amount of heat, the magnitude of value, and information volume. From the property of quantity, it can be described as continuous quantities and discrete quantities, infinitesimals and infinite quantities, constants and variables. From philosophical methodology, quantity is divided into scalar, vector, and ordinal quantity. A scalar, also known as quantity, is of or relating to a directionless magnitude (such as mass or speed etc.), a vector is of or relating to a directional magnitude, and ordinal quantity is of or relating to a magnitude which represents orderliness of universal association between things, such as structure, relationship, rank, etc. Moreover, from the perspective of the relationship between quantity and quality, it can be divided into external and internal. The external quantity shows the external extension, size and shape of a thing, and the internal quantity shows the internal form, structure of a thing. The former can be directly perceived, while the latter is hard for us to grasp. The forms of quantity are various, so quantitative reasoning actually is a general term of various quantitative methods, and it also has various forms, such as quantitative observation, quantitative test, and quantitative analysis. Besides, it has information methods, cybernetic methods, systems

---

* Originally published in *Philosophical Studies*, 2003(11).

theory methods, computer methods, model methods. Despite their differences, with different emphasis, these quantitative methods have something in common, whether in content or in characteristic. As far as content is concerned, they all, from the perspective of the quantitative attributes, describe things, understand the qualities of things, and the resultant digitalization and symbolization of the language system which can be used to describe things. As far as characteristic is concerned, they are all accruable and reliable, at height of formalization and abstraction, and of high logical diversity and accuracy.

Quantitative thinking exerts its influence in the process of understanding things because it has its own objective bases. The first basis is that all things are the unity of quality and quantity, in which the prescriptive of the quality of a thing is always demonstrated via that of its quantity, and changes as the latter does. In addition, the relationship between different quantities and the essence of a thing differentiates in level. Some quantities, such as internal quantity, represent the inner structure of a thing and the relationship between the internal elements of the thing, which, to a large extent, directly reflect the intrinsic quality, and via which the essence of a thing and the laws involved can be grasped. Therefore, in order to understand the essence of a thing, we can and should make quantitative observation of it.

II

The content, characteristics and objective basis of quantitative thinking determined its role in scientific cognitive activities.

1. Quantitative thinking has become an important opportunity and lever for the creation and development of new scientific theories

Scientific theories are the crystallization of human knowledge. Throughout the history of modern science, scientific developments are achieved mainly as the result of the improvement of mathematics and its application. Thanks to the improvement and application of quantitative thinking methods, astronomy, classical mechanics and classical physics have been established made as rigorous theoretic systems, based on a range of theoretical developments, from Copernicus's proposal of the theory of the solar system to Kepler's elaboration, in precise mathematical forms, of laws of the motions of the planets and their changes; from Galileo's empirical and qualitative description of the motion of falling objects to Newton's enunciation of the three laws of motion quantitatively in mathematical form; from Faraday's proposal of the concept of field which reveals the relationship between electricity and magnetism to Maxwell's establishment of Maxwell's equations composed of four calculus equations. Other disciplines such as biology, meteorology, chemistry, are have been developed from being empirical descriptions to being exact sciences also because they have adopted quantitative analysis. Nowadays, with the rapid development of science, quantitative methods are widely employed in various disciplines and fields, and their importance has become increasingly prominent. Therefore, it can be seen that the development of science follows a path from qualitative knowledge to quantitative knowledge, which is the law of scientific progress and the law of human knowledge development. It can be said that quantitative thinking is a golden key to scientific mystery.

2. Quantitative thinking penetrates all stages of cognition, so as to complete a whole and accurate process of cognition

First, let's look into the significance and role of quantitative thinking in the epistemological stage. Due to space limitations, only the observation and experiment are dealt with here. Observation marks the beginning of cognition. In the early stage of human cognition, observation is largely manifested in a kind of sensuous contemplation, through which the cognizance of things was so superficial that only the question of whether something has a certain attribute can be made clear, and thus can be regarded as qualitative cognition. But in the sensuous contemplation there also involved contemplation of the quantity (external quantity) of things. Take the contemplation of a table as an example: when a general result of cognition is made about a table, it included the contemplation of such quantitative attributes as appearance, height, and size. Those quantitative attributes are, of course, the observation of the first phase of human cognition. Since then, the method of observation has gradually developed. For instance, in modern times, astronomical observation has developed itself into observing the quantity of celestial bodies and the changes in their motion, from which Kepler's three laws and Newton's law of universal gravitation were discovered. In contemporary times, it can be concluded that any observation is the combination of qualitative and quantitative observation, the latter being the main one, so as to reflect quality.

An experiment means creating a man-made environment for experimental subjects, introduce controllable changes, record and explain the process and result of change, through observation which is done for the cognitive purpose. In scientific experiments, there are also qualitative experiments and quantitative experiments.

Generally, it is enough for us to carry out qualitative experiments if the purpose is to discover new facts or to provide preliminary proofs for new theories. This is a lower level of cognition. However, if the purpose is to make in-depth research, then it is necessary to carry out quantitative experiments, determining the quantity of experimental subjects, the relationship between quantity and quantity, and the changes in quantity of the thing during the experiment. Actually, in this process, the change of the experimental subjects and the results should be quantitatively measured and recorded, and the degree of control should also be adjusted based on that of change in quantity. In short, scientific experiments cannot be carried out without quantitative methods.

By sorting, processing and abstracting perceptual knowledge, knowledge enters the stage of rational knowledge. There are two forms of abstraction: one is quantitative abstraction, reflecting the relationship between the quantity of a thing; the other is qualitative abstraction, reflecting the aspects which constitute the essence of a thing. Qualitative attributes are often manifested by quantitative attributes. Therefore, comparatively speaking, quantitative abstraction is what reflects an objective thing in a more specific and direct way, and conceptual abstraction of quality is often premised on quantitative abstraction, and is a general description of the quality of a thing reflected by the relationship of quantity. There are many aspects involved in abstraction, and what the present article mainly deals with is the role of quantitative abstraction in analysis, synthesis, induction, and deduction.

In the analysis and synthesis, the employment of quantitative methods can sort out the relationship between things and between internal elements and makes it easier to grasp the essence of things and their laws, as is the case with the biological cognition of genetic variation. The explanations of genetic variation and its mechanisms have been vague and speculative till Mendel succeeded in unraveling this mystery of nature. In his hybridization experiments on pea plants, Mendel conducted a great deal of accurate counting and mathematical analysis of hybrids and their progeny via mathematical statistics, then, based on the categorization in accordance with agronomical traits, regrouped them in different ways according to different traits, and thereby found out its distribution frequency, and then conducted quantitative research by applying combinatorics. It is on this basis that Mendel discovered the three laws of genetic variation. The use of quantitative analysis and statistical methods in analyzing and synthesizing the order is precisely the reason for Mendel's success.

Induction is the inference of general conclusions and concepts from a great number of empirical facts. In inductive logic, modern inductive logic is the combination of induction and probability theory. In the 1930s, logical positivists Carnap and Leibach linked induction and mathematical theory of stochastic processes, and as a result, the concept of probability of logic is introduced. The more experimental facts which can prove a conclusion, the greater the probability of a hypothesis. This kind of inductive process and its conclusion can be described and measured by quantity. This development direction of inductive reasoning is called mathematical induction, and the results of its preliminary development, namely, statistical reasoning and probabilistic reasoning have now been widely used in all disciplines.

Deduction is the inference of some particular conclusions from a general principle or concept. Deriving conclusions to be tested from hypotheses (which is the general model of scientific development) is a complex process of deduction, and mathematical methods are an important tool for deductive reasoning. Because this tool is characteristics of formalization and abstraction, it carries out reasoning by taking aside all the other features of the objective object, leaving only the quantity of the thing, and using a symbolized and formalized language. In this way, on one hand, it can make inference more rigorous, logically necessary, precise and axiomatic; on the other hand, it can generalize, in concise statement, many common laws and natures of things, which can greatly simplify and speed up thinking process. Nowadays, mathematical logic has revealed the relatively complex laws of deductive method and sought to express in mathematical forms. This has provided possibility for electronic calculators to simulate the schema of deductive thinking and thereby greatly promoted the development of modern science.

3.Quantitative thinking plays a decisively leading role in comprehending things

Given the particularity and complexity of things, it is hard or sometimes even impossible to study some of them and their motion via direct observation, which puts quantitative thinking which shifts the focus directly from quantity to quality play a decisively leading role in comprehending such things. It is the case with cognition of the cosmos. For a long time, there has been different opinions on the explanation of the universe. Albert Einstein conducted a new exploration based on his predecessors. He first proposed his basic proposition that gravitation theory is the metric theory. This means that physical problems can be expressed in purely geometric quantities, and can be quantitated. Based on this, Einstein made use of whatever was regarded as relatively advanced mathematical theories at that time to make assumption and deduction, and eventually constructed the mathematic model that contains the relationship between the matter in which exists gravitation field and geometric metric, namely the well-known Einstein field equations, which can be applied to explain the universe, thus a universe model was proposed, which is static, finite in time, and boundless in space. And the model is later proved to be basically correct. Both Einstein's assumed premise and the deductive process, are obviously the assumption about the relationships between pure and abstract quantities and their transformation and derivation. The results of derivation are the generalization of the essences and laws of the universe, which shows clearly the power of quantitative thinking which shifts the focus directly from quality to quantity. In modern times, it is this method that carves out a way for scientific cognition and plays a leading role in studying the complex phenomena in the real world. The employment of this method to cognize things can greatly reduce the complicated links of cognition, and reduce repetitions. At the same time, it can also break through the limitations of human senses and cognize those things that cannot be observed directly.

4.Quantitative thinking is conducive to foreseeing what can be cognized about things, leading people to generate new theories

When a mathematical model is constructed to observe and cognize things, because a model is not only the general, concise and clear reflection of the relationship between various internal elements of objective objects, but also contains parameters, which have coherence with the objects' essence and laws of development, we can, based on parameters, these changes which reflect the quantities of objects, foresee the essence of objects and their development. In addition, if the relationship of the signs of a mathematical model has such characteristics as conciseness, clarity and symmetry, it may inspire people to seek new approaches to scientific research and new well-conceived goals. It may offer new interesting experiments, new ways to analyze or explain off-the-shelf data, or new means of conceptual expression.

5.Quantitative thinking endows cognition with depth and accuracy while eliminating its subjectiveness and arbitrariness

No matter how accurate human cognizance of objective objects may be, at most, it is approximate, there being some distance between "authenticity" and "duplication". This distance is flexible and can be large or small, its elasticity coefficient to some extent depending on how much man has grasped the quantities of the objects.

III

Since the 1940s, due to the establishment of systems theory, information theory and cybernetics, and the extensive application of electronic computers, quantitative thinking has been greatly developed, and its importance and application are increasing day by day.

The so-called great development of quantitative thinking means that computer methods closely linked with SCI (Systemics, Cybernetics and Informatics) have become the main form of quantitative thinking. Since the twentieth century, the development of the productive forces has offered many new technical means for human social practice and greatly broadened the scope of human practice. This also means that the flow of information the world sends to people has been expanded. In scientific and cultural field, the information on human scientific knowledge has increased by geometric progression, new scientific discoveries have been constantly emerging, information and knowledge have been proliferating, and we have entered the era of "explosion of knowledge". In social lives, with the development of social production, social interactions among people become more frequent and complex, resulting in dramatic increase in social information. In short, the object of human cognition is a sea of information, which is diverse, complicated, huge and changeable. On the other hand, as the subject of cognition, human beings are physiologically limited, whether in terms of the efficiency of information processing and reorganization, in terms of accuracy and reliability of cognition, or in terms of space of activity. This has led to a contradiction between expanded information flows and limited human capacity to cognize. Fortunately, the advent of electronic computers eased this contradiction. This equipment is an electronic machine that simulates partial thinking function of human brain, and can process information automatically and efficiently. It is composed of five units: input unit, memory unit, arithmetic and logical unit, control unit, and output unit. The task or questions that requires the computer to complete, the data and the operational program are entered, through input devices, in a form which can be accepted by the computer, and then such data is stored in the storage unit, a memory device which holds a large amount of data and calculation programs. Then, the arithmetic unit and control unit carry out complicated numerical calculation and logic judgment, and finally solve the problems. Because the computer's receiving and processing the information is characteristic of automation, high speed, huge amount and precision, it has been widely used in practice. And as the main form of quantitative thinking, the computer method has become an important method of carrying out scientific cognitive activities and played a significant role in scientific cognition.

First of all, with the aid of electronic computers, cognition can be greatly speeded up, and be optimized. As the information theory shows, the process of human cognition involves information input, storage, processing, output (interventive practice) and feedback, and such information can also be quantitatively expressed in mathematical language and with mathematical tools through encoding. So every step of cognition can be quantitatively represented. If, based on the concept of feedback and according to the views and ideas of cybernetics, via the computer method, it is possible to systematically analyze the information output, calculate its volume of information involved, and then have the best control over all steps of the cognitive process, and even to characterize the truth of cognition by the coincidence rate of the feedback information with the expected goal. In addition, the computer's processing information is characteristic of high speed, huge amount and accuracy. In this way, it is possible to shorten the period of information being stranded in each link, and thereby greatly speed up cognition and achieve an optimized cognition.

Secondly, by virtue of the electronic computer method, the field of human cognition has been greatly expanded. In modern scientific research, it is with the help of electronic computers that can quickly and accurately process information and then quantitatively carve out the essence and laws of things that human beings have broken through the limitations of cognition brought about by human sensory limitations and broaden the horizon of human cognition, as big as the universe which is 10^{28} centimeters in length and 10^{16} years in time, as small as the basic particle world which is 10^{-15} centimeters in length and 10^{-23} second in time.

Thirdly, with the aid of the electronic computers, it is possible to promptly handle those complex systems and mega-systems by processing a large amount of data and information, and make the judgment of the possible complicated situations of the systems, and thereby overcome the limitations of human brain which can be slow, inefficient and prone to err when handling such complex systems.

Finally, computer can be used in numerical calculation, character recognition and scene recognition, natural language understanding, and the rediscovery of scientific laws and proof of mathematical theorems. The famous problem in the history of mathematics – the proof of the four color map theorem is one example of computer application.

In conclusion, the computer method which is closely related to the SCI (Systemics, Cybernetics and Informatics) has been increasingly becoming a major form of quantitative thinking, which has been playing a significant role in scientific cognitive activities. This is a great development of quantitative thinking and is in keeping with the high development of science and technology and the characteristics of social practice. It can be believed that quantitative thinking will gain more popularity in scientific cognition and the prospects of its practical benefit is seductive.

Thinking Modes of Practical Subject and the Execution of Practical Activity*

Practice, as the conscious activity of humans reforming and transforming the objects, must be accompanied with their intellectual and perceptual activities. In the actual practical activities, the material activity of transforming objects is unified in the same process with the intellectual and perceptual activities of practical subjects. The intellectual and perceptual activities of practical subjects can never be independent from practical activities. On the contrary, practical activities are carried out under the guidance of subjects' thinking mode. The orientation, mode, process and result of the operation of practical activity, are limited absolutely by such factors as the structures, attributes and characteristics of practical objects. But to a large extent, they are controlled and regulated by subjects' thinking mode.

The thinking mode is a relatively stable, stereotyped thinking style in which the subject just conceptually grasps the object. From a functional point of view, the thinking mode is the conceptual starting point from which the subject recognizes the object, and serves as an internal yardstick for the subject to grasp the object. From a structural point of view, it includes experience, knowledge, values, emotions, will, and etc. These factors, intertwined and integrated, play an important guiding, controlling and regulating role in practice. And practical activity includes the following three steps in terms of its process, namely, determination of purpose and plans, execution of plans, and evaluation of the result, which are interconnected and interdependent, constituting the whole practical activity, and which are respectively the indispensable steps of practical activity. And the restriction on practical activity imposed by the subjects' thinking mode is mainly manifested in the following three aspects:

---

* Originally published in *Philosophical Trends*, 1989（11）.

I. Decision-maker's Thinking Mode affect the orientation of a practice

First, the values and value-orientation in decision makers' thinking mode can restrict significantly the orientation of a practice. As we all know, the need of the subject is the power house of practical activity, while the goal of the subject guides and regulates its progress. It needs to be pointed out that there are a series of intermediate steps to develop a need into a real practical activity, within which the values and value orientation of the subject have a direct and profound effect on the purpose of the practice. Values and value orientation reflect a constant tendency and "habit-set" of the subject's needs for the object. Once the concept of value is formed, it plays a selective role in the needs of the subject. According to a certain concept of value, a certain need will be selected, and then a certain needed object will be selected, a certain practical goal and a specific plan to achieve this goal will be determined, thus there coming into being practical activities of different directions and different nature. For example, decision-makers with different values always have different selections of action when there is a conflict between an individual's interests and another's or the collective interests, between partial interests and global interests, between short-term interests and long-term interests. The action of a decision-maker (including a specific individual or group) holding the values of collectivism is always premised on not undermining another's, the collective and the state interests. However, a policy-maker who is seriously greedy or "departmentalist", always satisfies their own self-interest at the expense of others, the collective and the state. Different values of the decision-making subjects will lead to different directions and natures of practice activity. In short, the subject's concept of value not only restricts the establishment of the purposes of practice, but also affect the formulation of the plan of practice, to a large extent, regulating and standardizing the nature and direction of practical activity.

Second, knowledge and experience which constitute the decision-maker's thinking mode is of relevance to the direction of practical activity. Knowledge stands for human achievements in the cognition of the objective world. And there are two levels of knowledge: empirical knowledge and scientific knowledge. The former is a kind of direct feeling and grasp of the characteristics and relationships of objective things, which people accumulate in practice, a kind of non-standard and unsystematic knowledge, usually directly related to the individual's practical activity and life experience; the latter is the revelation and summarization of the essential features and internal relations between objective things, and therefore is systematic and universally applicable. Both of them make up the basic elements of the subject's thinking mode and specifically play an important role in the subject' practice of transforming the object. In general, the more extensive knowledge the subject has, the more likely it is to make a sound and rational decision and ensure that the practical activity is carried out in accordance with its purpose. Because the more scientific knowledge and experience the subject has, the more information he or she can accept and understand, and therefore it is more likely for the subject to broaden the horizon of mind and to find and analyze the problems if there are. In the contemporary era, social practice takes on the characteristics of large-scale, complication and networking. And a single social practice sometimes involves various aspects, such as politics, economy, military, ecological environment and health care.

Undoubtedly, rich knowledge in social science and natural science is necessary for setting goals and strategies, namely, making decisions about practical activities. In this case, in order to enhance the correctness and reliability of decision making, and thus improve the success rate of practical activities, one needs to apply more profound knowledge, rather than depending on narrow experience, for, despite that it can provide some direct guidance on practical activities, it is still far from being as "powerful" as profound knowledge in terms of breadth and depth. As profound knowledge reveals and summarizes the essential features and inherent laws of objective things, it has abstract universality. Therefore, the subject can not only understand and grasp many essential characteristics of similar things through exploring profound knowledge, but also foresee the trend of development through grasping the laws, so as to minimize the loss inflicted by blind decision making. In reality, the large number of decision-making and advisory bodies and think tanks emerging at home and abroad are the most powerful evidence for a significant role of scientific knowledge in practical decision making.

II. The executive subject's thinking mode, particularly knowledge and skills, affect practical activity style

Practical activity style is a scope to mark how practice proceeds. For one thing, it depends on the purpose; for another, it relies on the material means of practice, namely the tools of practice. It can be said that it is the difference among the means of practice that result in the difference among the practices of different kinds and their outcomes. It is self-evident that the purpose of practice has constraint on the formation of a certain practice. Here, I would like to emphasize that tools of practice also play an important role in the formation of a certain practice. It can be said that the differences between practices are always characterized by the differences in the tools of practice. Different tools of practice lead to different methods of practice. The tools of human practice have gone through three major forms of development, from traditional hand-made tools to common machines in general, and to automatic or intelligent machines (both being developed based on electronic computer). Correspondingly, significant changes have taken place in human practice. In the contemporary era, the extensive application of automatic and intelligent machines in social practice has brought more and more modernization in human practice and demonstrated a tremendous power of practice. What kind of tool to be used for a practical activity not only determines how the activity goes, but also is directly related to the effectiveness of the practical activity. In reverse, what tool of practice to be chosen for a practical activity and how to operate or apply it is also largely dependent on the subject's knowledge and skill. People who lack basic scientific knowledge can only use traditional hand-made tools for labor and production; those who have little knowledge of modern science and technology can only use simple, traditional machines to carry out practical operations and are not eligible for modern tools. As we all know, in the practical activity carried out by hand tools, what the subject needs to pay is mainly the "energy" — physical strength, with some daily experience involved at most; in the labor where a common machine is required, what the subject needs to pay is also mainly human physical strength, with only ordinary technical knowledge needed; in the practical activity where modern tools of practice such as automatic and intelligent machines are necessary, such machines can not only replace human physical labor, but also partially replace and implement human intelligent activities, the main function of the subject being not to pay his or her physical strength, but to carry out intelligent activities such as information identification, comprehension, programming and transformation of information forms. In such case, if the subject is not equipped with necessary modern scientific knowledge and certain technical qualifications, he or she would not be capable of using those tools. This knowledge-based requirement for the practical subject is an inevitable result of the fast development in science and technology in contemporary times and the increasing technologization of society. If the practical subject does not have updated and advanced skills and knowledge, he or she can only adopt traditional means to carry out practice, in which practice will not be carried out efficiently.

III. Non-rational factors in the practical subject's thinking mode affect and adjusting the process of practical activity

So far, we have discussed the effect of a practical subject's values, knowledge and skills on the orientation and means of a practical activity, and thereby on the benefit of practice, which is only one aspect of this issue. And the other aspect cannot be neglected, namely the important role of a practical subject's non-rational factors, such as feelings, emotion and will, in regulating practical activities.

Emotion is a special form of human response to the objective world, is the psychological state (such as attitude, feeling, experience) which the subject entertains in the process of cognizing and transforming the object, with regard to whether it satisfies his or her need. Human emotion is an extremely complex and dynamic system. By nature, emotions can be divided into active and inactive ones, affirmative and negative ones; in terms of form, it has different levels, such as mood, enthusiasm, passion, morality, reason and aesthetics. The effects of human emotion on human activity have long been pointed out by many philosophers. Even "absolute" rationalists such as Hegel acknowledge the effects of human emotion and will. As he said, "Nothing great was ever achieved without enthusiasm." And he claimed that "ideas" and "human passion" are intertwined as the "longitude and latitude of world history".[1] As Marx said, "Passion is the essential power of man energetically bent on its object."[2] Lenin also pointed out: "There is no man's pursuit of truth without human affections."[3] Emotion is an indispensable factor in the motivation mechanism of the subject's practical activities. If the subject's knowledge, skills and tools are the "hardware" through which the practice is run, then emotion is a kind of "software" that appears to be a "lubricant", without which the activity cannot be initiated or normally carried out. Only by triggering human emotions and arousing their enthusiasm can practical activities be started and maintained. In a sense, emotion is an internal driving force behind the practice of the subject, which motivates people to move and help them overcome obstacles and difficulties in their activities. Human emotions largely determine the power of practical activities, affecting their speed and

---

[1] The teaching and Research Office of foreign philosophy history, Department of philosophy, Peking University (Compiled): *German philosophy from the end of the 18th century to the beginning of the 19th century*, Beijing: Commercial Press, 1975, p. 477.
[2] Marx, K. & F. Engels: *Marx and Engels: Collected Works*, Vol. 42, Chin. ed., Beijing: People's Publishing House, 1979, p. 169.
[3] *Lenin's Collected Works*, Vol. 20, Chin. ed., Beijing: Publishing House, 1958, p. 255.

duration. The stronger and the richer the emotions of the practical subject, the more powerful the motive power of practice, and thus the more likely it is to accelerate the progress of practical activities. Positive and healthy emotions, good emotional environment, can stimulate people's creative thinking, which is an indispensable factor for people to carry out creative practice. There are ample examples of such scientific activities. Negative and humble feelings will interfere with and hinder the normal operation of practical activities, and even directly lead to negative, destructive activities. An individual who has lost enthusiasm and lacked sense of responsibility will not only fail to devote himself or herself into social practice in a proactive manner, but also fail to be motivated by any positive goal in his own life.

Emotion is a kind of psychological phenomenon specific to mankind. It relates to people's direct experiences of the surroundings and their inner feelings, such as happiness, pleasure, anger, sorrow, sadness, anxiety, nervousness, distress and so on. Either the constant psychological backdrop or the temporary state of mind, formed by the experiences of emotion, has an impact on the current activities of information processing. Emotion is prompt response and signal according to which it can be judged whether the practical activity of the subject is going smoothly, and whether the needs of the subject are satisfied. Positive and good emotions can coordinate social interaction and interpersonal relations. It is an indispensable "soft" environment to facilitate the operation of practical activities. On the contrary, negative and obstructive emotions will hinder the enthusiasm of the subject.

Will is a psychological process in which the subject consciously adjusts his or her own behavior to overcome difficulties in order to achieve some desired purpose, and it is the transformation of the subject's internal intention or desire to the external objective reality. The role of will in the subject's practical activities is mainly manifested in the following two aspects:

First, the strength of the subject's will is an important factor that determines the success or failure of practical activities. A practical activity may not necessarily go smoothly even if the decision is made correctly. Just as Lenin said, the objective world goes in its own way, and what humans confront in their practice is this objective world, so if they want to attain their goals, they have to overcome the obstacles accompanied thereby.[1] In practical activities, they will not only encounter the object's resistance (such as the complexity of the object, arduousness, riskiness

---

[1] *Lenin's Collected Works*, Vol. 38, Chin. ed., Beijing: People's Publishing House, 1959, p. 231.

and long duration of the process), but also the subject's resistance (such as opposite motive, negative emotion, laziness, and etc.). In such case, if they are tenacious and patient enough, they can withstand and eventually overcome the obstacles until they achieve their desired goals. On the contrary, if they are weak-willed, hesitative, or give up halfway, practical activities can never go smoothly.

Second, humans control and regulate the initiation and proceeding of practical activities through efforts of will. Practical activities can go smoothly only when they satisfy the needs of the subjects and are in line with the latter's emotions. However, the needs and emotions of the subject are characteristic of fertility, diversity and volatility, so, if the practical activity is at the mercy of the needs and emotions, the chances of its success of may be slim. The practical activity can satisfy the needs of the practical subject and be carried out orderly and continuously unless those needs which are not realistic, not urgent or even negative are controlled, those impulses that are harmful to the reality are suppressed, and those negative emotions or moods which interfere with and obstruct the current practice of the subject are excluded, with the most basic and urgent needs selected, the favorable emotions which are beneficial to the current practical activity retained and consolidated.

In short, emotions, moods, will and other non-rational factors determine the subject's state of mind, which is the "powerhouse" to facilitate a practical activity, which determines the extent to which the subject exerts his or her initiative in an activity, and which affects the final outcome of the practice.

Through the above analysis, we can conclude that in the practice to reform and transform the object, the thinking mode of the practical subject always plays a guiding, controlling and regulative role. Whether a practical activity is "running smoothly" or how efficiently it runs, is closely related to the subject's thinking mode. This is what the subjective effect of practical activity is. From this, it can be seen that it is one-sided and incorrect to advocate that the purpose, thinking and cognition of the practical subject should be excluded from the connotation of practice, and that practice should be attributed only to the sensuous material activity of the subject reforming and transforming the object. In fact, in any practical activity, the material activity in which the subject reforms and transforms the object and the subject's cognition are inseparable. A practical activity is inherently the unity of the forementioned two aspects. Purposively and consciously reforming and transforming the objective world is exactly the essential characteristic of human practice.

The relationship between the thinking mode of a practical subject and the implementation of a practical activity also suggests that the objective effect cannot be underestimated in a practical activity, but the subjective effect is more significant and active than the objective effect. Therefore, the subject of a practical activity should pay more attention to the subjective effect. No matter what the results of the practical activity, the practical subject should first explore the "roots of subjectivity", reflect on his or her own behaviors, and then sum up experience of success or lessons from failure. Only by continually strengthening his or her quality, increasing his or her practical ability and exerting initiative and creativity to the maximum, can the practical subject more consciously choose and grasp the correct direction of a practical activity, so as to accelerate the practical operation and maximize the benefit of practice.

On Logic of Practice*

The purposive operation of a practical activity has its inherent logic. It is of great significance to recognize such logic from the concept of thinking, which helps us to do our utmost to minimize the twists and turns during the operation of a practical activity, to avoid the anti-purpose practical activity and to increase the probability of success of the practical activity. Here, an elaboration will be made on the concrete content of practical logic from the following six aspects:

I: Purposiveness and Regularity of Making Decisions for Practice

As we all know, making decisions for practice (including the establishment of purposes and the plans of practice) is directly related to the success or failure of a practical activity. In order to ensure the success of a practical activity, one of the most important premises is that the decisions about a practical activity must adhere to the dual scales of "purposiveness" and "regularity".

The purposiveness of decision-making means that the decision making must be done based on the actual needs of the practical subject, in line with and conducive to his or her overall development. Logically speaking, a practical activity is a purposive and conscious human activity, which is carried out to satisfy the needs of the subject. People tend to set different practical goals of according to different needs and form different practical activities. Therefore, if the goal of the practical activity does not reflect or deviate from the actual needs of the practical subject, then it is incompatible with the inherent nature of the practical activity, and this kind of activity is obviously not a positive motivation for starting or fully launching the dynamic mechanism of a practical activity. Even if it is launched—in some way, it can only be undertaken in a low-efficiency or negative-benefit state which lacks internal motivation. This has

---

* Originally published in *Academic Monthly*, 1990 (03).

been evidenced by China's practice of socialist construction.

Worthy of specific mention, due to the multiple forms and levels of practice subject, each individual subject has his or her own needs and there are many different needs even for the same subject. Therefore, on the surface, although every concrete practice of different subjects and of different natures is based on their needs, a certain conflict or contradiction is bound to emerge among them. Then, how shall we measure and understand the "purposiveness" of practical activities? We think that "purposiveness" should not just refer to satisfying the subject's needs at a certain level, nor to satisfying the short-term needs of a particular subject, but refer to satisfying the subject's actual needs at the highest-level cognition and practice.

All kinds of practical activity carried out by humans are interrelated and influencing each other. A certain purpose of practice and its corresponding practical activity which are suitable for the subject of a specific form and at a certain level may have some opposite effects on the subjects of other forms and at other levels. That is to say, a practical activity which is in line with the short-term needs of the subject, is harmful to his or her long-term interests.

Therefore, before making decisions about practical activities, particularly before carrying out large-scale and significant practical activities, the practical subjects must have an integrated and strategic vision to give full consideration to and balance the overall efficiency of practical activities. It is necessary to consider the economic benefits, but also fully evaluate the social benefits of practical activities and the possible consequences to Nature. We should not only think about immediate interests, but also give deliberation to long-term interests. We should take into consideration the overall interests as well as the partial interests. We should make accurate and feasible decisions after repeatedly weighing and balancing in justification. That means we must oppose the practice of obtaining a certain one-way interest or satisfying a single individual's need at the expense of other multiple needs or overall interests. When there arises a conflict between multiple needs and multiple-way interests, we should follow the overarching principle of practice that practice must be conducive to the well-rounded development of people. This is the theoretical consciousness that every decision-maker should bear in mind.

The laws of decision-making mean that the decision-making for practical activity must, as far as possible, correctly and comprehensively reflect the multiple attributes, internal relations and essential characteristics of the objective things involved, which is the basic premise for making judicious decisions. As Lenin explicitly pointed out, in fact, people's purposes are the result of the objective world, and exist based on it;① the laws of the external world or the laws of nature which can be significantly separated into the laws of machinery and the laws of chemistry, is the foundation of purposive activities of human beings, who confront the objective world in their own practical activities, rely on it, and regulate their own activities with it.② The need of a person always points to a certain object, and the realization of the need is the objectification of the need which manifests itself as the result of some transformation of the object by the subject. Therefore, when setting practical goals and developing practical solutions, that is, when making practical decisions, we must first and foremost fully assess the various attributes, characteristics, and prescribed effects of such objects, and the changes in the relations between them. Then, it is necessary to fully assess the interaction and mutual influence of such objects with other related things. A feasible and realistic decision can be made only after we have conducted thorough analysis and synthesis of the object' different aspects, made deep, concrete and meticulous postulation, inference and judgement concerning such aspects of the purpose of decision-making as the nature, quantity, time and range, and carried out a series of feasibility analysis and quantitative calculation; otherwise, if we just takes into account our own needs while scorning the objective dimensions of the object itself, and does not make necessary quantitative analysis and forecasting, we will make decisions simply based on desire and passion, which will end up with the punishment of the laws concerning the object. The implementation of a practical activity must be premised on the cognition of the objectivity of the practical object. This is a truth that has been repeatedly proved by human beings, and is virtually a common sense.

In short, the needs of the subject provide the necessity for constructing practical decisions, while the adequate understanding of the object provides the possibility for making correct decisions. The unity of the needs of the subject and the deep understanding of the object constitutes the primary logic that guarantees the purposive implementation of a practical activity.

II: Conducting typical experiment before a decision is implemented

Unlike scientific experimentation, social practice tends to be non-repeatable. The

---

① *Lenin's Collected Works*, Vol.38, Beijing: People's Publishing House, 1959, p.201.
② Ibid., p.200.

correctness and effect of the practical goals and solutions can only be indicted by a certain outcome obtained through specific implementation of practice, for which the subject needs to pay large price, involving large consumption of the energy of the subject. Particularly in the contemporary era, those large-scale and complex practical activities require a major investment in human and material resources. Even a slightest of negligence or mistake in the process of decision-making (that is, establishing practical goals and solutions) may result in heavy losses. So, it is unquestionably necessary that before a social practical activity of significant importance is carried out, the practical decision can be conducted in a small-scale manner; that is, a pilot test is supposed to be carried out to further measure and demonstrate the correctness and rationality of the decision-making and make it more rational and reasonable, from which, at the same time, the subject can also explore certain experience and methods. Then a large-scale practical activity can be more consciously and effectively carried out, so as to avoid major losses caused by mistakes in decision-making.

The pilot test is a well-conceived method to solve the issues concerning the relations between an abstract theory and a concrete practice, between the general and the individual, which, from the perspective of the cybernetic principles, belongs to a "feed-forward device" for ensuring the smooth and effective operation of the system. When it comes to the practical system, the pilot test is essentially a "feed-forward" which can guarantee the smooth and effective operation of the system. It can eliminate the mistakes which may exist in the decision-making before the implementation of a practical activity. It is a rational and economical approach.

III: Normalization of practical activity implementation

In order to achieve the practical goal, the practical subject must construct and follow a certain norm to carry out an activity. Here "norm" refers to the totality of the code of conduct, the standard and procedure that the practical subject should abide by in order to achieve his or her intended purpose. In order to ensure the efficiency of the practical activity, the subject who implements the activity must, in principle, accurately understand and accept the directives of the decision and stringently implement them. Implementation activity, as the name implies, is the activity that implements the directives, not the arbitrary activity of the subject who implements the activity; otherwise, implementation activity will inevitably deviate partly or even entirely from the practice as a whole. Such activity may also be beneficial to part of subjects or some individual subjects, but as far as the benefit of practical activity as a whole is concerned, it tends to be interference or disruption, only to bring about an opposite effect. Such situation often crops up in practical activities. The obstructions, selfish departmentalism, short term conducts and other undesirable actions that we have confront when carrying out the policy of reform, are all non-normative behaviors that have deviated from the overall objective of the reform.

Second, the subject of the implementation activity should also construct and follow certain rules or procedures, which should be made in accordance with on the directives of the decision, which stipulate and guarantee that the implementation activity be performed toward the goal of practice, and which have double functions: to protect and guide the purposive practice; at the same time, to prevent and reject any conduct which deviates from or is detrimental to the practice. If these norms were lacking or not obeyed at all, the implementation activity would be inevitably thrown into a chaotic and disorderly state, and be reduced to a divergent oscillating activity, partially or entirely deviating from the goal of practice. Moreover, since norms and rules are the condensation or formalization of empirical knowledge from the practical subject's creative activity, they provide the subject with the procedures and methods through which a certain practical activity is carried out under normal circumstances. Therefore, the development of uniform rules, procedures and norms for specific implementation activity enables the practical activity to be conducted in an orderly and coordinated manner, thereby boosting the efficiency and effectiveness of performing an implementation activity. For example, textile workers must follow certain procedures, rules and models to produce cotton cloth products that are qualified; otherwise, the lack of uniform specifications and certain operation procedures will end up with chaotic production activity and more defective products, inefficiency and low benefits.

Here, it is particularly necessary to point out the significance of the legal norms to the purposive and efficient implementation of practical activities. The legal norms are the mandatory norms that reflect the will of the sovereign subject of social management, namely the people, which safeguard the basic interests of society and, correspondingly, those of every single individual, and which thereby regulate individual or collective conducts. As long as we look into the status quo of our social practice, it is not hard to find that one of the most important reasons for the chaos and low efficiency in political, economic activities and other social activities in China is the lack of necessary norms, especially legal norms, while implementing these activities.

As practice has proved, without strict or sound norms, no matter how good the goal of practice may be, it would not necessarily be achieved as intended. No matter how rational a program of practice may be, it would not necessarily be implemented as designed.

IV: Overseeing the making of practical decisions and the implementation of practice

After the norms of activities are established, the key is whether or not they can be followed. Norms can function only when the subjects follow them in actual activities. However, in practice, the subjects often cannot follow consciously for this or that reason, including the fact that the subjects have their own interests. This requires a functional department that is independent from the executive system to oversee the implementation of the norms; otherwise, norms cannot really play their role. Supervision is to observe and check whether the results of decision-making are accurately and promptly implemented, and whether the corresponding norms are followed in the activities. Efficient supervision manifests itself in the following aspects: First, the supervisor and the supervisee should be functionally separated and independent from each other, and the two cannot be combined into a single role. For only self-supervision is not likely to be efficient. Second, the supervision subject must issue clear supervisory directives to the implementation subject, the content of which include: (1) the purpose of supervision. The implementation subject should be informed of the value and necessity of the practical activity, particularly the consistency with his or her own interests, so as to urge him or her to consciously cooperate with the supervisor. (2) the content of supervision. The implementation subject should be informed of the basic guidelines for the activity. Third, the feedback about how the implementation subjects carry out the activity. It must be made promptly. The supervision subject, based on the feedback about the actual performance of the implementation subject, issues new directives to correct the deviations, if they arise in the process of implementation, so as to ensure that the activity is implemented in accordance with the norms of implementation. The process of supervision, in essence, involves a process of feedback.

V: Establish a sensitive and effective system of information feedback for a practical activity

A practical activity is a dynamic system and a process of information flow.

Establishing a system of information feedback about the implementation of a practice is a necessary requirement for the smooth running of a practical activity. In order to make a practical activity run in a purposive and highly efficient manner, it is also indispensable to make proper use of a mechanism of negative feedback on system operation and establish a sensitive and efficient feedback system of information about the implementation of practical activities.

Firstly, the directives made by the decision-making system, that is, the practical goals and solutions, must be clear, and sometimes require quantitative criteria. Otherwise, the relevant information is ambiguous, against which the outcomes of a certain phase of the practice cannot be measured, tested, modified and improved, nor conducive to practical operation.

Secondly, the speed of feedback should be high. In a practical activity, not only the object but also the subject itself is constantly changing. The source sends new or some "mutation" information. If the feedback speed is too low, and the relevant information is not garnered and used promptly, it is impossible to correctly and effectively adjust the direction and steps of the practice, only to leave the practical goal remain unachieved or unrealized. Therefore, the feedback agency of practical activities must be agile and capable enough to garner information promptly and accurately, conduct comparison, analysis and research, and make timely judgment to transmit information to the decision-making body so that it can, as soon as possible, make corresponding adjustments. To speed up the feedback, a necessary condition is that the feedback path be short, with less intermediate links. The tree-structured feedback loop (such as adjustment mode of a highly centralized planned economy) has many levels, subordinate relations, and a special feedback path, in which, therefore, the feedback information stays in each link for a long time, feedback efficiency is low and the subject fails to act promptly and effectively. On the contrary, a net-structured feedback loop (such as market regulation mechanism of economic activity) has few intermediate links, and its feedback path is short, and therefore, fast, which can reduce or avoid the distortion of feedback information due to too many intermediary links.

Thirdly, while the subject accurately and promptly conducts the actual adjustment activity to all feedback loops, it is also necessary to try to avoid excessive feedback. In the actual practical activity, if the theories guiding the practice or the purposes or plans of practice are found unreasonable and wrong, the corresponding revision is naturally expected. However, if excessive feedback occurs during the revision, that is, too much revision of the decision-making of practice, the goal of practical activity may also remain unrealized. Therefore, during the process of feedback-based regulation, the subject should pay attention to this kind of easily emerging "over-correction". Such excessiveness or inadequacy should be minimized. Also, such tendency should be noticed as soon as possible, and timely new feedback-based regulation should be activated, until the purposes of practice are eventually realized.

VI: Autonomy, consciousness and wisdom of the subject: ultimate source of purposive implementation of a practical activity

If we say that the afore-mentioned five points constitutes a set of longitudinal logic for the purposive implementation of practical activities, then there is such a "general term" in this longitudinal logic chain: autonomy, self-consciousness and wisdom on the part of the practical subject. The reason why they are called "general terms" is that they are indispensable for the purposive implementation of a practical activity, and they are contained in its every aspect.

A necessary premise for the purposive implementation of a practical activity is that the practical subject should abound with initiative, creativity and enthusiasm. For this, the practical subject must have full freedom in the activity. The decision-making subject has the power and freedom to control the direction of a practical activity. The implementation subject should have the power and freedom to correct the specific steps of the implementation according to actual situations and circumstances. The supervision subject should have power and freedom to supervise the activities of decision-makers and actual operators, which should not result in any intervention. In such implementation, the subject of decision-making resides at the core of the structure of practical organization.

As social psychology studies show, people's attitude towards or their sense of responsibility for an organization (group) which they belong to, depends on their status and existential value in the organization. As the functional subjects of a practical activity, they have their own specific substantive power and freedom as the subjects, and their status and dignity as the subjects are affirmed in the organization, which inevitably arouses their sense of responsibility because the power and freedom they have in their hands enable them to realize that they are not nobody, but an inseparable part of the organization. Respect for and affirmation of one's status, personality and dignity will ensure that they engage in the organization's activities with the awareness that they are the masters of their own affairs and so actively and proactively undertake their work and take responsibility in realizing the goals of practice for which they have participating the decision-making. Only in this way the practical subject becomes a conscious subject, thus greatly enhancing the solidarity for the implementation of a practical activity. Such cohesiveness is the representation of the potential energy of practice. If it is strong, then the practical activity will acquire a greater drive force, which can enable the subject to overcome numerous obstacles and greatly enhance the efficiency of the practical activity.

The autonomy and self-awareness of the practical subject provides good conditions and strong motivation for creative practice, which also depends critically on the subject's wisdom.

Wisdom, I think, includes two aspects: first, the scientific knowledge and practical experience; second, a way of thinking concerning how to apply knowledge in a flexible manner. Even if the practical subject has autonomy in the activity and an active and conscious attitude, but has no necessary wisdom, it is still impossible to carry out creative activities. Rich and profound knowledge is necessary for creative practice. The more knowledge and experience the subjects have, the more they can broaden their horizons, open avenues, and come up with various solutions and provide more alternative programs when a problem arises. Different natures of practice require different knowledge. Different functionary subjects should have the corresponding knowledge structures. At a time when modern science and technology are highly developed and increasingly socialized, it is hard to live without knowledge. If decision -makers and leaders do not have a certain amount of knowledge of economics and management methods, and the necessary knowledge on judicious organization and decision-making, such as knowledge of histology, psychology, decision-making theory and SCI (systemics, cybernetics and informatics), it is impossible for them to make judicious and effective decisions and it is difficult for enterprises to survive in the fierce competition. As for the workers, if they do not possess certain scientific and technical knowledge, they cannot operate and control the machines and will be eliminated by the machines. Even if they are not squeezed out by them, the efficiency of a productive activity will be reduced. Therefore, in order to gain the benefits of practical activities, improving the scientific and cultural qualities of the practical subjects is the primary foundation.

Of course, knowledge is not directly equivalent to creativity, which requires not only adequate knowledge but also scientific thinking mode and good quality of thinking on the part of practical subjects. Specifically speaking, first, they should be courageous to break new ground, they should be equipped with a strong sense of innovation, not conservative, not rigidly conventional; second, they should be resolute in decision making; third, they should be responsive to external information and good at flexibly revising the programs or steps of practical activities based on ever-changing information. In fact, the development of human society, from low level to high level, from low efficiency to relatively high efficiency, is the very process of human thinking constantly sublating and increasingly optimizing itself.

China's Construction of Socialism from the Perspective of Purposive Operation Mode*

The past 40 years has witnessed China's remarkable achievements in socialist construction which have been acknowledged by the whole world, but it has also witnessed many twists and turns that China has gone through. It is an urgent need to ensure the smooth operation of China's cause of building socialism by soberly and consciously reflecting on the road we have travelled, in hope to find the deep-rooted causes of the mistakes and summarize the valuable lessons and experiences. The present article attempts to analyze the dynamic structure of practical activities and propose a basic model for the purposive operation of practical activities. Thus, it will reflect on the mistakes that have occurred in the practice of socialist construction in China.

I. Dynamic structure of practice and Purposive operation mode of practice

It is a common view that practice is a three-factor structure composed of the subject, the instrument and the object. In my opinion, this only reveals the static structure of practice. A practical activity surely will manifest itself as a dynamic process, which is practice itself. It is a system containing many activities at different levels and with different functions.

One of the links, the theoretical activity with "seeking truth" as its own mission, is the primary logical prerequisite for a practical activity. Fundamentally, practice is the source of theory (cognition). However, at the same time, we must realize that the antagonism between practice and theory is relative, and in a certain sense, they are mutually inclusive, for the concrete practical activities are always carried out under the guidance of certain theoretical understanding of the subject. Resorting to

---

* Originally published in *Seeking Truth* (《求是学刊》), 1992(3).

theoretical guidance, whether consciously or initiatively, is the fundamental sign that distinguished human practical activities from animal instinct activities. Moreover, in human practical activities, the level of scientificity and the richness of the theory represents the level of development of practical activities. The more ancient human practice, the simpler its structure and the smaller its scope of effect. Why modern practice has developed itself in richness, complexity, scale, and effect scope? The fundamental reason lies in the increasingly powerful infiltration of the wisdom of the subject and a more and more important role that theory plays in practice, which indicates that the level of self-consciousness in practice is getting higher and higher, and human beings are farther and farther away from the animal kingdom. Therefore, the maturity and richness of theory which exhibit themselves in practice is an important yardstick of human progress. The theoretical activity is the primary internal link of the practical activity, and theory is the precursor of practice. Such a statement does not in the least belittle the role of practice, but is precisely a correct understanding of the dialectical relationship between practice and theory.

The second link is the decision-making activity of establishing the practical goal and plan in accordance with the theoretical understanding derived from the situation of the practical subject and object. It is necessary to understand the subject's actual needs, quality and ability, and the object's structure, characteristics, attributes, and laws of development. This is a prerequisite for carrying out practical activities. In order to concretely and effectively carry out the practice, it is necessary to establish a certain goal of practice according to the theoretical understanding that has ever been acquired. Practice without any purpose can only be a disorderly and chaotic conduct, which is not enough for practice in its original sense, and which must result in inefficiency or even negative effect. After the practical goal is made clear, we have to find an effective way to realize the goal, and design a plan or project to guide practice. Without plan, the practical activity will become chaotic and disorderly without rules to follow, often resulting in practices that rely solely on experience, subjective will, and feeling—a hammer in the east, a wooden club in the west. Usually, in order to ensure the success of a practical activity and to try to avoid or reduce mistakes in practice, it is often necessary to design several alternative plans and schemes, from which we can, through the analysis and prediction of the feasibility and benefit, choose the better one and put it into practice. This link of practical activity is mainly in the form of a large number of investigation and research, collection and analysis of information about the object. It is an intellectual activity mainly based on brain expenditure. As a result, some researchers exclude from the practical content the activities which are aimed at establishing objectives and programs. This view not only does not accord with the internal operation logic of a practical activity, but also deviates from the characteristics and trends of contemporary practice. With the development of science and technology and with the intensification of information technology in modern society, the scale of practical activities has expanded, showing the characteristics of multiple links and levels. Different from the simple traditional transformation activities, which mainly devote physical strength and which directly affect the target object, the intelligence-based or information-based activities which involve processing, analyzing and operating the information of the object have become more and more important forms of contemporary practical activities.

The third link is the implementation activity, which aims at the implementation of the practical program. As the name suggests, the implementation activity is the activity of carrying out and implementing according to the directives of the decision-making organs, not the arbitrary activity of the executor or operator himself. This link is the stage in which the practical subject carries out the actual transformation on the object by means of tools. Without this link, the subject's goal and the program of practice would just stay in mind or on paper. Only when the subject mobilizes and invests a certain amount of human and material resources, can the practical goal and program break away from its conceptual state and constitute a realistic practical activity and causing some change in the object.

The key issue in the implementation activities is whether the subject who carries out the operation follows the relevant directives. In fact, due to the fact that the subject objectively has its own relatively independent interests and other reasons, there often occurs deviation or even departure from the directives and execution norms. This requires a functional subject independent of the execution system to supervise the situation of execution and compliance. Supervision is the activity of observing and checking whether the decision is accurately and promptly implemented and the corresponding norms have been complied with in the actual practical activities; it not only refers to the implementation activities, but also refers to the decision-making activities—supervising whether the decision is made judiciously according to due procedures, whether it is made on the basis of fully promoting democracy, and whether it satisfies the actual needs of the people, etc. Modern practice has proved that supervision is an indispensable part of practical activity. Without supervision, it is very hard for any practical activity to go on smoothly towards its intended goal.

In summary, the practical activity is represented by a dynamic structure, which can be graphically represented as follows:

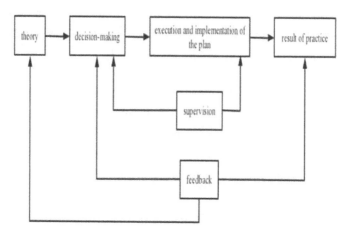

This complete closed-loop system constitutes the practical activity itself. Based on the dynamic structure of practice, I thought, the operation mode of practical activity is:

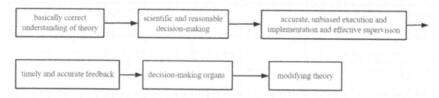

That is to say, if a practical activity attempts to go smoothly as intended, the necessary and sufficient condition is the complete closed-loop system made up of the links mentioned above, any one of which is indispensable, and any "failure" of which will affect the smooth operation of the whole practice.

II. "Mode" analysis of China's practice of building socialism

Let us examine and analyze the causes of the mistakes that have occurred in China's construction of socialist modernization from the perspective of purposive mode of operation.

1. Theory on socialism construction

The establishment of socialist system in China is an inevitable product of the development of Chinese history and world history into the 20th century. However, building socialism in a country that is quite backward in the productive forces is a new historical topic that needs to be constantly explored in practice. Although, in the initial stage of socialism construction, the Party and Mao Zedong also realized that "We must learn the good experience of all countries, whether it is from a socialist country or a capitalist country."① "We should integrate the universal truth of Marxism with China's particular conditions."② However, in the concrete practice of socialism construction, these correct ideas and viewpoints were not implemented well, and the correct theories and viewpoints which could guide our construction were not formulated based on deeply grasping China's particular conditions and the objective laws of economic development; instead, the Soviet mode was copied. Let me give the first instance: New China founded in 1949, which was just founded from the ruins of a semi-colonial and semi-feudal society, was quite backward in terms of the productive forces. In order to strengthen the country and develop economy, public ownership should be taken as the leading factor while the existence of various other economic forms should be allowed to exist. However, in actual work, socialist industrialization and the socialist transformation of agriculture, handicrafts and capitalist industry and commerce were basically accomplished in roughly three years, a single socialist ownership system was established by employing more administrative orders. Give another instance: After the socialist transformation, the exploiting class was eliminated, so the large-scale stormy class struggle should be ended, and the focus of work should be shifted from class struggle to economic construction. However, in the then guiding principle of the supreme decision-maker, there existed the concept that class struggle was the ultimate driving force for the development of social history and thus was still regarded as the main contradiction of China's socialist society. It was thought that grasping class struggle and engaging in political movement could promote the development of the productive forces. The third instance: The commodity economy is an insurmountable stage of social development, and China, a country with backward economy, should bring prosper economy, increase the strength of economy, and enrich the lives of the people. However, at that time, the Party did not fully realize this point, and just thought that a socialist society could only be a single planned economy and there should

---

① Mao Zedong: *On the United Front by Mao Zedong*, Chin. ed., Beijing: People's Publishing House, 1988, p. 347.
② *Historical Documents Since the Thirteenth National Congress of the CPC* (2), Beijing: People's Publishing House, 1991, p.1430.

be no commodity economy, as the classic writers of Marxism imagined. All these understandings and practices are divorced from China's particular national conditions and the inherent objective laws of China's socialism construction, which, to a greater extent, is a kind of subjective will, willingness and a certain established principle.

After the Third Plenary Session of the 11th CPC Central Committee in December 18-22, 1978, the Party re-established the thought route of seeking truth from facts, brought order out of chaos, criticized various non-Marxist theoretical viewpoints that were divorced from China's particular conditions, and proposed a series of important theories suited to China's particular national conditions by learning from the past mistakes and from the new practice and exploration. For example, the Party has established the basic line of persisting in focusing on economic construction, adhering to "the Four Cardinal Principles"[①], and reform and opening up; it has advocated that we must always work for material progress and at the same time for cultural and ethical progress; it has established the important viewpoint that the socialist economy is public-ownership-based planned commodity; the coexisting economic system with public ownership as the mainstay of multiple economic forms, the multiple forms of distribution with the principle of distribution according to work as the mainstay, and the economic operation mode that combines planned economy (macro-control) and market regulation, etc. have become the policies and guidelines we are implementing. All these theoretical achievements show that our understanding of the national conditions and the laws of economic development has become more and more in-depth, and, theoretically speaking, we have become more and more conscious. As a result, the practice of reform and opening up for more than 10 years[②] has achieved unprecedented results. However, it should be admitted that the mistakes that have taken place during this period also show that our understanding and grasp of China's national conditions and the laws of socialist construction are still far away from reaching a more comprehensive and in-depth state of consciousness and sobriety. Even some of the existing correct theoretical viewpoints have not truly and firmly become the guiding principle for practical work. On the contrary, there was always shows vacillation and deviation in concrete implementation. Regarding the

---

① This refers to keeping to the socialist road and upholding the people's democratic dictatorship, the leadership of the CPC, and Marxism-Leninism and Mao Zedong Thought. The Four Cardinal Principles are the foundation of the state, and the political cornerstone for the survival and development of the Party and the state. –Tr.
② 1978-1992.—Tr.

relationship between planned economy and market regulation, between macro control and micro invigoration, and between the central and local governments, etc., are all difficult problems that need to be explored for China's socialism construction.

In short, China's socialist construction has taken so many detours and made so many mistakes, which is closely related to our lack of systematic and correct theory derived from China's particular national conditions and the objective laws of socialist construction. Without the knowledge of the realm of necessity of objective laws, and without a clear and conscious theoretical understanding, blindness, as well as mistakes and setbacks, cannot be avoided in our actions. Therefore, enough attention should be paid to each step of practice, practical experience should be reflected on seriously and promptly, and theories should be extracted from what is regular. All these are required judiciously according to true Marxism.

2. Conversion of theory to decision-making

The inadequate understanding of the laws of socialist construction and the wrong tendency of voluntarism and subjectivism in decision-making practice are closely related to each other and are a reciprocal causation. Looking back on the course of China's socialist construction, it is not difficult to find that voluntarism, subjectivism, and dogmatism resulting from departure from objective reality often occur in the decision-making practice. This is mainly reflected in the lack of practice-based criticism and reflection on the theory itself as the basis for decision-making and the lack of analysis and argumentation of the scientific nature and practical feasibility of the theory. The theories that guide decision-making are often formed according to the subjective wishes of certain decision-makers, or are constrained to certain viewpoints and expositions of classic Marxist writers. For instance, the transition from New Democracy to socialism had been originally expected to take 10 to 15 years or even longer, but it was announced that it had entered the climax of socialism shortly after the beginning of the transition. The socialist industrialization and the socialist transformation of agriculture, handicrafts and capitalist industry and commerce were announced to be basically accomplished in roughly three years. In the late 1950s, quick success was more anxiously pursued and integrity was blindly sought, so the "Great Leap Forward" was launched, with "people's communes" coming into being and "Run into communism" called for. From that period of historical practice, it can be seen that socialist construction seemed to be taken as nothing but a process of individual leaders imposing their subjective wills, in which the political passion and enthusiasm of the people could be agitated to promote social and economic development, just as in war mobilization. Take another example: a highly centralized central planning system was established and implemented for a long time, based on the Marxist founders' theoretical assumption that the socialist economy is a single public ownership and planned economy, with the commodity economy and the market repelled and terminated as capitalist things. This dogmatic approach, which departed from China's particular national conditions (rather low productivity) and the laws of economic development, brought about extremely slow development of China's economy, and the loss of the vitality of the socialist economy. This kind of error resulting from subjectivism and dogmatism was manifested in the practice of reform and opening up as random ambition, experience-based decision-making and blind introduction of technology and equipment, even the political and economic theories of the Western capitalist countries.

The prevalence of voluntarism, subjectivism, and dogmatism in decision-making practice will inevitably lead to the rejection of correct claims and viewpoints that reflect the objective realities and the objective laws of economic development, and cannot be transformed into judicious and rational decision-making.

In the more than 40 years of construction practice, the number of such kind of regrettable and tragic incidents seems not small at all. Typical examples include the theory of population control proposed by Ma Yinchu(马寅初), the views proposed by Sun Yefang(孙冶方) that a socialist society cannot avoid the stage of commodity economic development and that changes in the production relations must conform to the level of productivity development, and the right proposals of Peng Dehuai (彭德怀)and other Party members that exaggeration should be opposed and that the practice of being too hasty and going too "Left" in economic construction should be opposed. All these have not been adopted by decision makers and turned into implementable decisions. Thus, it can be seen that the transformation from theory to decision-making is an extremely complex epistemological and sociological issue. A correct theoretical proposition cannot be always transformed into decision-making, but a wrong theoretical viewpoint that is essentially derived from subjective will can often be transformed into decision-making through the power in the hands of decision-makers. It also can be seen that attaching importance to the analysis, criticism, and feasibility demonstration of theories and preventing wrong and one-sided theoretical propositions from turning into decision-making is an important issue in practice. In recent years, the democratization and scientification of decision-making has received more and more attention from decision-makers and all the people. This is precisely a response to the objective requirements of realistic practice.

3. Implementation of decision-making

The life of decision-making lies in its movement to practice and its being well implemented in practice. The high prestige of the CPC in revolution and construction has allowed the Party and the country to enable the policy directives (including principles and policies) to be implemented in practice (here, for present, regardless of whether the goals of decision-making are judicious and reasonable and whether the practical effects are beneficial). However, it should be noted that in our practice, some of the macroeconomic policies and principles of the Party and the state were often deviated or even distorted in the course of implementation, and the overall and expected results cannot be achieved. There were orders that did not work; there were prohibitions that were not implemented; there were openly violation of the Central decisions or commands; there was over-emphasis on the "particularity" of the unit or the area they belong to, with the people involved adapting the policies, developing other countermeasures, or doing whatever they wanted to do on their own accord; or there were such acts as double-dealing, following their bigoted course; and so on. Such acts disrespect the decisions and commands of the Central government and the State, and will inevitably cause disorder and chaos in the economic and political operation of the society, and interfere with and undermine the realization of the overall strategic goal of socialist modernization.

Such deviation and distortion in the implementation of decisions and policies are closely related to the ineffective macro-control of the highest decision-making organ and the lack of necessary systematic specifications. Besides this, more importantly, since all levels of implementation entities have their own interest orientation and choices, they will often consciously or unconsciously make choices and adaptations that are beneficial to them when expected to follow decisions and commands. Judging from the current situation of practice, it is indeed an urgent task to strengthen and improve various laws and regulations, and to regulate the corresponding responsibilities and rights of the subjects at all levels of implementation.

4. Issues concerning supervision and feedback in the practice of socialist construction

In the past, we did not regard supervision as one of the internal links of practical activity, so we paid insufficient attention to the important role of supervision in socialist construction in actual work, which is manifested in the following aspects: the imperfect supervision institutions; monotonous forms of supervision in political and economic activities; top-down supervision being the main form while the bottom-up internal supervision and the horizontal external supervision being not sound enough to give due play. Therefore, in order to achieve the overall goal and prevent the subjects who held partial interests from misconducting, it is necessary to set up some supervision organs to carry out effective supervision by administrative and economic means.

If there is no feedback about the practice, the practice is unsustainable, through which the expected objective is hard to achieve; if there is distorted information in the feedback, the practical activity will end up with failure. In the practice of socialist construction in China, the function of timely and accurate feedback has not been well brought into play. First of all, much information from the sources is not objective and accurate. For example, in the practice of socialist construction, there exist such undesirable phenomena as false reporting, grandiose reporting, incomplete reporting, and pompous reporting, only to distort the source information. The people involved are essentially deceiving their superiors and deluding their subordinates, driven by certain interests. Secondly, there are a pitifully few paths of feedback while there involve various levels of feedback, which affects the speed of information transmission and increases information loss. In the past, economic management system was highly centralized, in which there was a clear-cut affiliation hierarchy, multiple intermediate feedback links, monotonous forms of feedback, basically in a "tree-like" style of information transmission. Since the reform and opening-up, market adjustment mechanism has been introduced, which means that, from the perspective of information theory, multi-faceted and horizontal information feedback and adjustment channels have been opened up. From the perspective of the practice of socialist construction, however, the function of information feedback, especially the accuracy and efficiency of feedback, needs to be strengthened urgently.

So far, we have investigated the practice of Chinese socialist construction from the perspective of the purposive operation mode of practice, from which we can find that it is precisely because there arose the "malfunctions" in the above-mentioned links of socialist construction that the phenomenon of deviation or departure from the intended purpose has inevitably occurred.

III. Issues that need to be highly valued

Reflecting on the road we have traveled in the past 40 plus years①, especially on the practice of reform and opening up in the past 10 plus years②, I think the following issues are urgently needed to be concerned about in the future practice.

1. Correctly exert the functions of theory

To derive theory and decision according to the objective situation of a practice is the highest rational principle that a successful practice must adhere to, namely Marxist principle of practical objectivity. According to this principle, we must resolutely oppose and abandon the so-called theory that simply rigidly sticks to books and rules, which is essentially nothing more than the speculation utterly divorced from reality. It is strange that such theory could be adopted by the decision-makers without causing confusion. In my opinion, at present, the primary task of the theory is to self-criticize the *status quo* of theory itself. We are not opposed to absorbing all advanced thoughts and theories, but when we apply these thoughts and theories, we should adapt them to China's particular national conditions.

The critique function of theory not only points to theory itself, but also to practice. As to the practice that does harm to the overall interests and that is neither well-conceived nor in line with the needs of all the people, and the kind of vulgar practice that only satisfies the purposes and interests of a small number of individuals, theory should "step forward" and exert its critique function, revealing the drawbacks and harms of such practice, and correcting their direction.

The real theoretical critique should be constructive. While rectifying erroneous theories and vulgar practices, it is supposed to offer the prediction and guidance concerning how to operate practical activities in a purpose-oriented manner and in the correct direction. In recent years, theory has gained a bad reputation. One of the important reasons is that it has not well performed its exploring and guiding functions. On the contrary, it has more often reduced itself to being a footnote to the will of some decision-makers, or a defense tool for a vulgar practice. Indeed, there is some decision-makers who do neglect the predicting and guiding functions of theory, often make decision based on their own will or experience, and then work out a "theory" to further strengthen the argument to show the "correctness" of the decision. It should be seriously

---

① 1949-1992. —Tr.
② 1978-1992. —Tr.

pointed out that such neglect of theory and of judiciousness and democracy of decision-making is an extremely irresponsible attitude towards the development of the entire country and nation, and it can even be said to be malfeasance. The mistakes that have occurred in the practice of building socialism in China warn us again that the neglect of theory is the inevitable result of empiricism, subjective volitionism, bureaucracy and pragmatism. These "illnesses" inevitably have an inherent and interlinked connection. The causes of these "illnesses" are based on lack of cognizance, but to a greater extent, they stem from the unreasonable concept of interest.

2. Correctly employ interest mechanism and its norms and orientation

After all, human practice is carried out to satisfy the needs of their own survival and development. Interest is manifested by the activities which are aimed at satisfying certain needs in a particularly strong and lasting way, and in which people do their utmost to pursue the goal in a tenacious manner. Interest can be general or specific, broad or narrow, long-term or immediate. Long-term and general interests reflect the nature of the production relations which are of vital importance in any society. Marxism generally believes that need and interest are the most important and direct driving forces of historical development, but it maintains that only the interests of all the people which satisfy and represent the trend of human progress to the greatest extent are legitimate and reasonable interests. Such concept of interest is obviously opposed to the interest concept of backward and narrow-minded small-scale producers and of the selfish bourgeois that only satisfy the interests of a certain class or group. When there is a conflict between the understanding of inevitability and the interests, people are prone to act against this understanding; in particular for those people who represent a certain group's interests or local interests, this seems to be an "inevitable instinct". In China whose level of productivity was still relatively backward, with deeply-rooted small-scale production traditions, unreasonable concepts of interest had especially conspicuously interfered and deviated profound understanding. In fact, some mistakes which occurred in practical activities were not caused by the people's ignorance of historical laws (including economic laws), but by the kind of unreasonable and narrow-minded concept of self-interest, namely selfish departmentalism.

Before the introduction of the reform and opening-up policy, under the "big-pot" distribution system[①], local interests, enterprises' interests and individual interests

---

① egalitarian practice of "everybody eating from the same big pot". –Tr.

were ignored and curbed, only to seriously dampen the enthusiasm of the people for creativity and lead to the loss of vitality of socialist economy. Since the launch of reform and opening up, the implementation of economic reforms focusing on power decentralization and delegation, interest concession, and the breaking of "big-pot" distribution system, have rendered local governments at all levels, enterprises, and individual industrial and commercial households relatively independent subjects of economic activity, to varying degrees. These micro-economic subjects generally consider the issues concerning effectiveness from the angle of their own interests. Therefore, when confronted with the conflict between the overall interests and their own interests, they are apt to protect their own interests. As a result, short-term corporate behaviors often occur, and local governments are keen to compete for investment and projects, in pursuit of "small-scale but all-inclusive" local economy. In fact, the deepest contradictions encountered in the reform are the ones between the local interests of various micro-economic subjects and the overall macro-economic interests of the country, and between immediate interests and long-term interests. Just as some economists incisively point out, the conflict between overall interests and partial interests is an important reason why it is no easy to integrate planning with the market. If local interests and immediate interests were allowed to arbitrarily pursued, utterly regardless of the overall interests, then economy would inevitably be thrown in chaos and disorder, and the entire society would not be able to move forward in a coordinated and stable manner. Therefore, in the practice of reform, we should never slacken macro-control. This does not mean that we must turn back to a highly centralized traditional economic system, but that the state must take a series of economic means and necessary administrative means to regulate and adjust the behaviors of micro-economic subjects so as to optimize the pattern of interests and correctly handle the relationship between the interests of the central government, the local government, enterprises and individuals. At the same time, it is necessary to strengthen the education of the decision-makers in various micro-economic entities so that they can think in terms of the general picture, take all relevant factors into consideration when they make an overall plan.

3. Establishing a Whole Set of Orderly Action Logic

On the premise of obtaining a basically correct understanding of the situation of the practical subject and object, we are faced a problem of vital importance: how to judiciously and reasonably set the goal of practice, and how to achieve it, that is, how to clarify "what should be done" and "what should not be done". Mao Zedong put it eloquently: "It is not enough to set tasks; we must also solve the problem of the methods for carrying them out. If our task is to cross a river, we cannot cross it without a bridge or a boat. Unless the bridge or boat problem is solved, it is idle to speak of crossing the river. Unless the problem of method is solved, talk about the task is useless."[1] Reviewing the mistakes that we made in China's previous stage of socialist construction, we can find that an important experience and lesson is that in the process of realizing the goal of practice, we must work out a series of methods and means to ensure the realization of this goal: an experiment with a typical case should be done before the implementation of a practice scheme; extensive and in-depth publicity should be carried out to the general public, so as to obtain their understanding and mobilize their enthusiasm and creativity; the boundaries of responsibilities, rights and interests of the subjects of the implementation should be clarified; corresponding measures should be formulated; the agencies responsible for oversighting and feedbacking should be gradually established and improved, etc.; and above all, the leading decision-makers must master rational thinking methods and working methods. This is what we consider from the perspective of vertical implementation of a practical activity. Considering from the perspective of the horizontal relationship involved in a practical activity, we must also pay attention to the mutual coordination and support between practical activities. In the previous period of reform, there was a situation in which the plans were not matched or even contradicted each other, which made it difficult for the plans to be implemented, which also made it possible for some players who still need develop their conscious morality to "take undue advantage of the loopholes", and which will eventually lead to the destruction of the overall benefits of the reform and the deviation of the expected goals. In order to make practical activity go smoothly to the destination, we must attach great importance to the close connection of each link in the vertical implementation of the practice and the horizontal matching with other practical activities. This is another valuable lesson that the actual building of socialism has provided us.

---

[1] *Selected Works of Mao Zedong*, Vol.1, Chin. ed., Beijing: People's Publishing House, 1991, p.139.

Contradictions Between Norm and Innovation in Practice and Their Solutions*

In general, human practical activities always follow certain norms. However, upon examining the history of human practice, we can find that every progress and development achieved in practical activities is the result of constantly breaking through some existing norms and constructing new ones. The breakthrough of the old norms and the construction of new norms are the creative performance of human activity. The history and reality of human practice show that norm and innovation are a pair of conflicts that exist objectively in human practice. Whether this contradiction can be judiciously solved is directly related to whether a practical activity can succeed or not. The present article will make a preliminary discussion of this contradiction.

I. Normative System and Functions of Practical Activities

What is a norm? A norm is the sum of some principles, rules, standards, etc. that are formed by refining and summarizing the experience which has been repeatedly proved to be reasonable and valid in practice. There involves a hierarchy of levels, according which norms include legal norms, policy norms, disciplinary norms, procedures and the norms for specific operational activities, ethical norms, and so on. Some of these norms are highly mandatory while others are principled and belong to "soft constraints". Specifically speaking, a norm at least has the following characteristics: First, it should be mandatory. Once a norm has been formulated, people are duty-bound to abide by it and act within the framework it sets up. Generally speaking, no violation or rejection is allowed. Some norms are applicable to all practical activities and should not be overstepped optionally, such as legal norms. Second, it should have a certain degree of universality. The norms at a certain level

---

* Originally published in *Philosophical Studies*(《哲学研究》), 1993(11).

or in a certain area are applicable to the corresponding subjects of practice and can be promoted. Third, it should have guidance. A norm needs to provide the direction, way and method for the practical activity of a certain subject, marking out the boundaries between what one should do and what one should not do, between what one can do and what one cannot do, and providing the basis, measure and standard for a practical activity. These features are interrelated. And the above-mentioned features displayed by the norms at different levels have difference in degree.

Certain practical activities are always subjected to the corresponding normative system. This system is generally composed of the following factors: from the perspective of internal structure of practical activity, the first factor, is the guidance and control of practical purpose; the second is the influence that the values and theoretical conceptions of practical subject have on practical activity; and the next one is the restriction of the structures, characteristics and rules of practical object on practical activity. From perspective of the external environment of practical activity, the first factor is legal norms, which represent and protect the interests of individuals, the public, nations and even all human beings and which any practical activities must follow; the second is policies, guidelines, directives and disciplines, which reflect the overall and national interests, and which activities in certain areas are supposed to implement such as economic activities, political activities, theoretical activities, press and publication activities; and the next one is the specific procedures which are needed to be followed during the implementation of the practice; the last is the public morality, that is, the social ethics that must be followed when practical activity has a relationship with society, and the ecological ethics that must be followed when it has a relationship with nature.

All these factors combined constitute the normative system of practical activity. So, what functions does this system have? First of all, generally speaking, it can help or ensure the realization of the purpose of the practical subject. Secondly, it has the "economic" function of improving the efficiency of practical activities. Since the norms are the extraction and summarization of the experience that the people have gained in their past, then, if activities can be carried out directly in accordance with these norms, unnecessary exploration can be avoided and a lot of manpower and material resources can be saved. Thirdly, it plays a role in maintaining the normal order in the operation of practical activities, thereby enabling the steady development of practical activities. If there is no norm or no sound norms, any practical activity will inevitably be thrown into a chaotic and disorderly state, and thus the practice cannot be carried out. Instead of achieving the practical goal, serious actual losses may occur. For example, recently, China was thought to have been confronting financial disorder in recent times, primarily because the macroeconomic regulation and control system still needs to be improved in its transition to a market economy, and the primary economic operators lack an effective regulatory and restraint mechanism and risk responsibility mechanism. Therefore, it is necessary to formulate and improve various market laws and regulations to ensure the healthy and orderly operation of the market economy.

II. Limitations of norms and necessity of innovation

Since norm is summarized and refined based on the experience proved repeatedly by past practice, then, judging from the dimension of time, it is not progressive or dynamic, but static. In addition, judging from the dimension of space, it is the basis and scale for evaluating things and the rationality of human activities: things that conform to norms and do not go beyond norms are rational, otherwise they are irrational. This means that norms are exclusive in that they cannot accommodate non-standard and unconventional things. In this sense, norms necessarily have its limitation: unreceptivity.

Needless to say, norms do have an important role in directing the course of practice. However, the problem is that the activities carried out within the norms are prone to be routine and repetitive while the objective things are constantly changing and developing, and space-time conditions for them are constantly changing, not to mention that there are differences between different things in nature, state, characteristics and space-time conditions. Therefore, if you recognize or evaluate merely within the existing norms the things that have changed and developed, and analyze other things which are quite different, you will inevitably reject them as "outsiders". Such situation often occurs in human scientific activities and social practices. For example, the theory of China's revolutionary road of using rural areas to encircle the cities, which Mao Zedong proposed based on China's specific national conditions and the international political and economic environment, was regarded as narrow empiricism that violates the basic principles of Marxism-Leninism by Wang Ming and other theorists who over-confidently thought they had mastered Marxist-Leninist orthodoxy. Here in this case, they are guilty of rigid dogmatism as evidenced by unconditionally universalizing, singularizing, or ossifying a certain theory or norm.

If people's activities are confined to routines at any time and in any space and dare not surpass them, human society will not progress, and will be trapped in identicality and monotony and thereby lose its vitality. In fact, for the things, phenomena or situations that are not standard, analysis should be made from two sides. On the one hand, such things, phenomena or situations are indeed detrimental to achieving the practical goal, or they are beneficial to achieving the goal of a certain practical subject but harmful to achieving the goals of others as well as the overall and long-term interests of the country and the nation, which should naturally be criticized and rejected; on the other hand, however, these non-standard and beyond-normative things, phenomena or situations may contain new opportunities for further development of things. Therefore, if they are ignored or even rejected, or if we just follow the beaten track, the development of things will be delayed or obstructed, and the opportunities for them to develop faster and better will be lost. In this case, we must muster the boldness and the courage to face up to the new situations and phenomena that have emerged in the change and development of things, to identify the problems in the bud, and to break through norms, that is, to carry out innovative or creative practical activities. Therefore, innovative practical activities have revolutionary significance for the development of things and the progress of society. We must treat norms dialectically.

III. Grasp the unity of norms and innovation

As mentioned above, people cannot fail to follow the norms necessary in their practical activities; on the other hand, innovative activities marked by transcending norms are revolutionary opportunities for the development of practice, which indeed constitutes a major contradiction in human practice. In real life, we often encounter such contradictions. However, one thing we must point out is that although innovative activities are inevitably marked by transcending existing norms, not any activity that transcends or breaks norms is an innovative activity. In the real social practice, there exist such people who know the regulations but do not comply, know the rules but do not abide, and know the bans but do not act accordingly. Instead, they intentionally distort the policies and take countermeasures; they attempt to maintain their narrow local and departmental interests in the name of innovation. Then, how shall we confirm the true meaning of innovative activities? How shall we define the boundaries between norms and innovative activities. That is, what standards should be adopted to decide whether or not to follow the norms and whether or not to surpass or break the norms? The answer to such question has important methodological significance for realistic practices. I think that, in order to judiciously and reasonably solve the contradiction between standardization and innovation and to achieve the dialectical unity of them in practice, we should follow the following criteria:

First, rationality. Should we follow norms in specific practices? Should we break norms? We should make judgment, based on the rationality of practical basis of the norms. That is, we must examine whether the nature, status and characteristics of things, on which the norms depend, have undergone stage-specific or global change in quality. Due to the change of the same thing in time, space and other conditions, the expression form and characteristics of the law of things will change correspondingly, and some new characteristics and new trends will appear; different things have their own particularities due to differences in factors such as region and culture. In this case, the general applicability, guidance, and interpretative function will be restricted, its rationality will be weakened, and it may even move towards the reverse orbit of the special laws of things. Under such circumstances, the practical subject should, based on the changed situation, be brave to revise and surpass certain norms that obviously have not been conducive any longer to the exercise of the subject's own initiative and the improvement of activity benefits. Whoever acts as an outstanding leader and practitioner is always keenly aware of the signs of new life as well as the characteristics of the things which are outside the norms. When the existing norms constrain practical subjects' ability to give full play to their creative wisdom and enthusiasm, it is necessary to break the norms.

Second, interests-orientation. The norms that reflect the overall and long-term interests of the entire nation must be followed, since these norms themselves have innovative value. In the ultimate sense, the value of innovative activities is nothing more than being conducive to promoting social progress, meeting the needs of the majority of the people and pursuing their interests to a large extent. In this regard, these norms and innovations are essentially unified. For example, human activities cannot pollute the environment and undermine the ecological balance, so the laws of natural ecology should be followed and the interests-orienting norms in this regard have their rationality at any time and have an eternal indicative value. For another example, the legal norms and the policy directives that represent the overall interests of the nation, and the public ethics that regulate the interest relations among people must also be followed, and should not be broken or violated. Otherwise, although the interests of some people may be satisfied, the overall and long-term interests will be destroyed, and the losses will outweigh the gains in the end, with the existing interests damaged. At no time can the dialectics of nature and the dialectics of society be violated. Any activity that violates these norms merely by looking at the present or immediate interests but which is claimed self-righteously to be "flexible" and "innovative" is fundamentally a devastating activity that should be truly excluded, constrained and punished according to these norms. In this regard, every builder and decision-maker of China's socialist modernization should have a clear understanding and a high degree of practical self-consciousness.

On Operating Mechanism of Practical Activity*

Practical activity is a purposive and conscious human activity. The process of practical activity is nothing more than a process in which the practical subject pursues and realizes the practical goal. In general, the operation of practical activities includes three basic steps: (a) to establish the practical purposes and programs, (b) to implement the operation of practical programs, and (c) to check and evaluate the practical results. Then, how is practical activity as a dynamic system or process carried out? what is its operation mechanism? Obviously, theoretically answering this question will undoubtedly help us more consciously operate practical activities, grasp the correct direction of practical activities and improve the efficiency of practical activities. This article will intend to make some discussions on this issue.

Objectification and Actualization of the Subject's Needs: Dynamic Mechanism of Practical Activity

For a human being as a unity of natural being and social being, need is their internal and natural inevitability.[①] As natural being—a living organism with complicated organization, he or she need intake the material energy and information from the external environment, which is the most basic condition for survival and continuation. In this sense, need means life. All living organisms have their needs. No need, no life. The direct need for material objects always means human life. "The first premise of all human history is, of course, the existence of living human individuals. Thus, the first fact to be established is the physical organization of these

---

* Originally published in *Philosophical Studies*, 1989(12).
① Marx, K. & F. Engels: *Marx and Engels: Collected Works*, Vol. 1, Beijing: People's Publishing House, 1956, p. 439.

individuals and their consequent relation to the rest of nature."[1] Here, K. Marx and F. Engels clearly revealed that human need is the ultimate motive to drive people to work. But K. Marx did not believe that the need that drives human labor is merely to satisfy the physical needs for materials. Human beings are conscious social beings, always in certain social relations to carry out their activities. Therefore, human needs attributes a lot to sociality. In addition to satisfying material needs for survival, there are other needs such as social interaction, love and free creation. Material needs are different from the unalloyed physiological needs of animals. Obviously, the contents and ways of satisfying human material needs have social characteristics. Human beings generate more needs in their activities and treat such activity itself as a need, and pursue free creative activities, all these constituting the essential feature which distinguished human needs from animal needs. In this sense, we can say that human needs reflect the essence of humanity. K. Marx once vehemently criticized the capitalist society for making human labor only a means to satisfy physical needs, and pointed out that comprehensiveness and richness of human needs will be fully realized in a communist society. Are human needs used to explain human activities? F. Engels regards this question as the basic criterion for distinguishing historical materialism from historical idealism. Historical idealism holds that the ultimate cause of historical development is mental driving force, instead of investigating what is behind them and what is the motive force of these forces. As F. Engels said, "Men became accustomed to explain their actions as arising out of thought instead of their needs." "and so in the course of time there emerged that idealistic world outlook."[2] However, historical materialism holds that human needs are the most general nature, which actually implies some kind of "difference" or contradictory relation between human beings and the external material world—the overcoming of such difference and the resolution of such contradiction are manifested as human practical activities—human beings, through material power, makes some changes in external material objects, so as to achieve the purposes of satisfying their own needs.

Then, how does human need play its role as a driving force? It mainly manifests itself in the following aspects:

First, it is human need which produces the motive behind practical activity.

---

[1] Marx, K. & F. Engels: *Marx and Engels: Collected Works*, Vol. 3, Chin. ed., Beijing: People's Publishing House, 1960, p. 23.
[2] Marx, K. & F. Engels: *Selected Works of Marx and Engels*, Vol. 3, Chin. ed., Beijing: People's Publishing House, 1972, p. 515.

Need, as the objective nature of humanity, is infinitely abundant and diverse. When a need hits upon a human, is recognized by him or her, develops itself into a certain intention or desire and even has a specific thing as the material object, the motive behind human activity is thus formed. If human need is the ultimate motive for human activity, such motive is the direct motive of actual human activity. Just as F. Engels said, "All the driving forces of the actions of any individual person must pass through his brain, and transform themselves into motives of his will in order to set him into action."[①] From a psychological point of view, motive is a tensile state of deprivation and insecurity, which inevitably will generate some driving force, so as to resort to and launch a certain action to make up for the deprivation and drive away anxiety and tension, unfetter and then alleviate the driving force, thereby bringing about the rectification of the imbalance between people's physiology and psychology. Thus, it can be seen that motive plays its role in motivating activities, and that there is no activity not motivated by motives. At the same time, psychology reveals that the nature of motive can constrain the way of activity to a large extent. Only those motives that are consistent with the actual relationship between the subject and the object can have a strong priming effect. On the contrary, those motives that are not consistent will weaken the energy of the activity, only to hinder the subject from action out of his or her will.

Second, human need generates motives which transform themselves into practical purposes. When the subject thinks that the object pointed out by the motive can satisfy a certain need and has the conditions for realization, the motive will display itself as a purpose in the subject's mind. As we know, practical activity is activity that starts directly with a purpose, guided by it and goes for it. The purpose which directly guides an activity is nothing more than a need which has been identified and pursued by the subject of practice and which has certain conditions for its achievement.

Third, the operation of practical activity is shown as in the diagram given below:

It is obvious from the diagram that the relationship between the subject's needs and the nature of the results of practice and the way of distribution and possession is the key to a practical activity continuing to run smoothly. If the results of practice do not satisfy the subject's needs and largely deviate from the intended purpose of the subject, or the subject cannot obtain the results of practice that should be possessed

---

① Marx, K. & F. Engels: *Marx and Engels: Collected Works*, Vol. 21, Chin. ed., Beijing: People's Publishing House, 1965, p. 345.

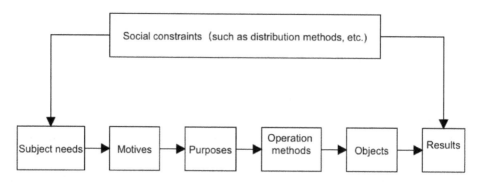

and enjoyed, it would mean that the feedback loop from "results" to "subject's needs" is cut off. In this case, the integrity of practical activity as a closed-loop system is destroyed, the subject's enthusiasm for further activities has been dampened, and the energy for further activities has shrunk, making it difficult to sustain practical activities. On the contrary, if the results of practice meet the subject's expected purpose and make the subject get the due satisfaction, then this will prompt the practical subject to burst into higher enthusiasm, stimulate huge energy, and invest more in re-activities. In this way, practical activities can continue to run smoothly.

Thus, it can be seen that need is the ultimate motive for practical activity which is nothing more than the "unfolding" of the subject's needs, that is, the objectification and actualization of the subject's needs. The intrinsic and essential connection between human needs and human activities provide us the following insight: Activities that do not meet human needs are dehumanizing activities and thus cannot be tolerated by human beings. Such activities cannot provide motive, so they are unsustainable. Practical activities can only be carried out in accordance with the subject's needs—not only material needs, but more importantly human mental needs, such as respect for personality, trust, care, and autonomous and conscious creative activities, etc. Sufficient satisfaction means sufficient and inexhaustible internal motivation to enable the practice activities to run smoothly and even speed up.

Orientation and Operation of Subject's Thinking Mode: Control and Adjustment Mechanism of Practical Activity

Practical activities are purposive and conscious human activities, which must be accompanied with the thinking and cognitive activities of human beings as practice subjects. In actual practical activities, the thinking activities and cognitive activities of the subjects of the material activities and practical activities which can transform the objects are always unified in the same process. Thinking activities and cognitive activities of practical subjects can never be separated from practical activities. On the contrary, practical activities are developed and carried out and even guided, controlled and regulated by the thinking modes of the subjects.

1. Thinking modes of decision-making subjects affect directions of practical activities

First of all, value concept and value orientation in the thinking mode of the decision-making subject have an important restrictive effect on the choice of the direction of the entire practice activity. There are a series of intermediate links from needs to the formation of practical purposes, among which the subject's value concept and value-orientation have a direct and profound effect on the determination of practical purposes. Value concept and value-orientation reflect a constant tendency and habitual fixation about the subject's needs for the object. Once a certain concept of value is formed, it will play a role in the subject choosing the needs, in choosing a certain required object, and in determining a certain practical goal and a specific program to achieve this goal, which leads to practical activities in different directions and different natures. For example, when personal interests conflict with others' or collective interests, when local interests conflict with overall interests, when short-term interests conflict with long-term interests, the decision makers with different value concepts will choose different behaviors. A decision-maker (including a certain individual or group) with the collectivistic concept of value, always acts on the premise of not harming the interests of others, the community and the country, whereas the one driven by profit or with serious selfishness always chooses to meet his own personal interests at the expense of the interests of others, the community and the country. In short, the value concept of a decision-maker not only restricts the establishment of practical purposes, but also affects the formulation of practical plans, and to a large extent directs and regulates the nature and direction of a practical activity.

Second, knowledge and experience which constitute the thinking mode of the decision-maker have an important coherent effect on the choice of the direction of a practical activity. Knowledge is the result of human understanding of the objective world, including two levels of knowledge: empirical knowledge and scientific knowledge, each of which plays a vital role in the subject's transforming the object. In general, the more deeply learned the subjects are, the more likely it is for them to make judicious and rational decisions and to ensure the operation of a practical activity in accordance with the purposes. Because the richer the scientific knowledge and experience, the more information the subjects can acquire and understand, then, the broader the decision-maker's thinking horizon can be so that they can be better at identifying and analyzing problems. A factory director or manager who does not understand economic management, modern market economy, and lacks the necessary modern scientific knowledge and methods can hardly guarantee that he can make judicious decisions. In the contemporary era, social practice is characterized by large scale, complexity and networking. More often than not, a social practice involves politics, economy, military, eco-environment, health care and other aspects. There is no doubt that a wealth of knowledge in social sciences and natural sciences is necessary for establishing the goals and plans of practical activities, that is, making decisions about practical activities. Here, using more scientific knowledge, rather than relying on narrow experience, one can enhance the correctness and reliability of decision-making and improve the success rate of practical activities. This is because scientific knowledge is the revelation and generalization of the essential characteristics and internal laws of objective things; and compared with non-systematic narrow empirical knowledge, scientific knowledge is abstract and universal. Therefore, through learning scientific knowledge, the subject can not only understand and master the essential characteristics of many similar things, but also can predict the development trend of things by grasping the laws, so as to minimize possible losses due to the blindness of decision-making in practical activities. Nowadays, with science and technology highly developed and increasingly socialized, a practical decision-maker should arm his or her mind with extensive knowledge and a rational thinking mode. It is an urgent and important task.

2. Subject's Thinking Mode, especially knowledge and skill, affect choice of mode of practical activity

The mode of practice is the category which marks how a practical activity is carried out. It first and foremost depends on the purpose of practice; and it also depends on the material means of practice, namely, the tool of practice. It is self-evident that the purpose of practice is restrictive to the formation of a certain mode of practice, and the effect of the tool of practice on the formation of a certain mode of practice also cannot be dismissed. It can be said that the difference among the modes of practice always manifests itself as the difference in the characteristics of the tools of practice. The use of different tools of practice means the formation of different modes of practice. As far as human production is concerned, since production tools have experienced the three major development forms—traditional hand tools; general machines; automatic and intelligent machines (all using electronic computers as basic components), correspondingly, human practices have also undergone major changes. In modern times, the widespread application of automatic and intelligent machines in social practice has made human practice more and more modernized, showing great practical power. What kind of tools are used for practical activities not only determines the aspects of the practical activities, but also directly affects their efficiencies. Which tools of practice to choose for practice and whether they can be operated and used depends to a large extent on the level of knowledge and skill of the practical subject. The science illiterates, those who are short of common scientific knowledge, can only use traditional hand tools for labor and production. Those who lack knowledge of modern science and technology can only use the traditional simple machine for the operation of practice instead of modernized tools of practice. Nowadays, modern tools of practice—automatic and intelligent machines—are increasingly used in social practice. As automatic and intelligent machines not only do what was ever done by human physical labor, but also partially implement the function of human intellectual activities. Thus, the function of the practical subject is no longer to pay physical strength, but to perform intelligent activities such as the identification, understanding and programming of information and the transformation of information forms, etc. This requires the subject to have the necessary modern scientific knowledge and certain technical qualities. If the practical subjects just have obsolescent sci-tech knowledge, they can only practice in traditional modes of practice, and in this case, they cannot implement practical activities effectively.

Now take human management activities again. The different methods of management result in different effects. The top-down centralized management is convenient for unifying and directing the activities of who are managed, for implementing the will of the manager, and sometimes convenient for bringing about high efficiency, but it is not conducive for the managed people to fully and freely exert their creativity and wisdom, thus necessarily affecting the efficiency of the activities. By contrast, the democratic management with democratic centralism as its guiding principle brings about concentration on the basis of the managed people freely expressing their will and opinions, so the activities are inevitably fruitful. Obviously, different methods of management are related to the degree and focus of the managers' understanding of the characteristics, features of who are managed, and the structure in which they are, including the understanding of human nature and psychology.

In political activities, a series of legal systems, guidelines and policies are indispensable intermediaries and means for achieving certain political goals. Regardless of the nature and actual effects of these systems, guidelines, and policies, their formulation must be subjected to a variety of other factors, but they cannot but admit that they are inseparable from the thinking mode of decision-makers in political activities.

3.Emotion, will and other irrational factors in the thinking mode of practical subject affect and regulate the process of practical activity

We have discussed the impact of the value concept, knowledge and skills of the practical subject on the direction and modes of practice activities and then on the effectiveness. This is just one aspect of the issue. The other aspect cannot be ignored, that is, emotion, will and other irrational factors of the practical subject also play an important role in regulating the operation of practical activities.

Emotion is what the subject holds in the process of recognizing and transforming the object in terms of whether the object meets his needs or not—his attitude, feeling, experience and other aspects of his psychological state. Human emotion is an extremely complex and changeable system. In terms of nature, it can be divided into positive and negative emotion. In terms of form, it has different levels: mood, enthusiasm, passion, senses of reason, of morality, and of beauty, etc. The effect of human emotion on human activity has long been known to many philosophers. Even "absolute" rationalists such as Hegel acknowledge the effects of human emotions and will. He said, "Without enthusiasm, all great undertakings in the world will not succeed," claiming that ideas and human enthusiasm are intertwined into the latitude and longitude of World History.[①] As Marx said, passion is the essential power of man energetically bent on its object.[②] Lenin also pointed out that "There never have been anyone's pursuit of truth without human emotion."[③] Emotion is an indispensable factor in the motive mechanism of the subject's practical activities. If the subject's knowledge, skills and tools are the "hardware", through which the practice can run,

---

[①] The Department of Philosophy of Peking University (Compiled): *German Philosophy from the late 18th century to early 19th century.* Beijing: The Commercial Press, 1975, p. 477.
[②] Marx, K. & F. Engels: *Collected Works of Marx and Engels*, Vol. 42, Chin. ed., Beijing: People's Publishing House, 1979, p. 169.
[③] *Lenin's Collected Works*, Vol.20, Chin. ed., Beijing: People's Publishing House, 1958, p. 255.

then emotion is a kind of "software", which seems to be a "lubricant", without which practical activities cannot be launched or normally run. Only through provoking human emotions and arousing enthusiasm can practical activities be initiated and maintained. In a sense, emotion is the internal driving force to push the subject to carry out practical activities. It urges man to take part in activities and helps him to overcome the obstacles and difficulties they confront in carrying out the activities. Human emotion largely determines the powerfulness of the energy of practical activities and thereby influences and regulates the speed and duration of practical activities. The stronger and richer the emotion of the practical subject, the more sufficient and powerful the motive power of practice, and the more possible it is to speed up the process of practical activities. Positive and sound emotions and good emotional environment can stimulate human creative thinking. It is an indispensable factor for man to carry out creative practice. This is no shortage of examples in scientific activities. Negative and humble emotions will interfere with and hinder the normal operation of practical activities, and even directly lead to negative and destructive activities. Those who have lost their enthusiasm and lacked responsibility would not only fail to devote themselves into social practice in a proactive manner, but also have no positive goals even for his own life practice.

Will is a psychological process where the subject consciously adjusts his behavior to overcome the difficulties so as to achieve some intended purpose. The role of will in the subject's practical activities mainly manifests itself in two aspects:

First of all, the powerfulness of the subject's will is an important factor in determining the success or failure of practical activities. Even if the decision is correct, practical activities may not be automatically successful. This is because the "objective world" "walks its own path", and "what people faces in practice is this objective world, so the 'realization' of goals will encounter 'difficulties'."[1] In the process of practice, you will not only encounter resistance from the object (such as the complexity of the object, the arduousness of the practice process, risk, and long duration, etc.), but also that from the subject (such as motivation conflict, negative emotions, laziness of the subject, etc.) At this point, if the subjects have a strong will and endurance, they will be able to withstand and eventually overcome obstacles and achieve the intended goals. On the contrary, if the subject is weak in willpower and hesitates to move forward, practical activities may be abandoned halfway.

---

[1] *Lenin's Collected Works*, Vol.38, Chin. ed., Beijing: People's Publishing House, 1959, p.231.

In addition, willpower controls and regulates the initiation and implementation of practical activities. Only when they meet the needs of the subject and are affirmed by the subject's emotions can practical activities happen. However, the needs and emotions of the subject are rich, diverse and volatile. If the practical activity is completely subjected to the needs and emotions, then the chance of success may be very slim. How can we enable practical activities not only to meet the subject's needs, but also to be carried out in an orderly and continuous manner? We can make it only through willpower controlling those unrealistic, imperative or even negative needs for the subject, transforming and eliminating those negative emotions and moods that interfere and hinder the subject's current practical activities, choosing a certain kind of need that is the most basic and the most urgent for the subject at present, and retaining and consolidating those emotions that are beneficial to the practical activity that the subject is currently carrying out.

In a word, the inner soul of practical activity is the thinking mode of the practical subject, which not only leads and dominates the practice but also is the energy source of practice, and which has an extremely great influence on the process and result of practical activity.

Restrictive Effect of Practice Object: Standardized Operation Mechanism of Practical Activity

Practical activity is a conscious activity of the subject transforming the object, and its operation is not only deeply influenced by the subject but also restricted by many aspects of the object. When talking about historical activity, F. Engels emphasized many times, "Men make their history themselves, only in given surroundings which condition it and on the basis of actual relations already existing," and "or even in a definitely defined, given society".[①] As Lenin also clearly pointed out, "In fact, the purpose of man is produced by the objective world and is based on it." and "The distinction between the external world, the laws of nature, the laws of machinery and the laws of chemistry... is the basis of human purposive activities. People face the objective world in their own practical activities, rely on it, and use it to define their own activities."[②] These statements of the classical Marxist authors correctly reveal the reality that practical activity is by no means an arbitrary activity of the subject, but is restricted by the object and its laws of development.

First of all, when the practical purpose should be established, on the one hand, it must be based on the needs of the subject; on the other hand, it must reflect the nature, state and development laws of the object. If a practical purpose is established through relying only on the subject's will, regardless of the actual situation and conditions of the object, it is purely subjective and arbitrary, and is destined to lead to the failure of the actual practical activity. Only in this way can the proposed purpose of practice be both reasonable and practicable. Otherwise, solely on the willpower and intentions of the subject but regardless of the actual conditions and real conditions of the

---

① *Marx, K. & F. Engels: Selected Works of Marx and Engels*, Vol. 4, Chin. ed., Beijing: People's Publishing House, 1972, p. 506, 477-478.
② *Lenin's Collected Works*, Vol.38, Chin. ed., Beijing: People's Publishing House, 1959, p. 200-201.

subject, the practical purposes hitherto established are purely subjective and arbitrary that is doomed to lead to the failure of actual practical activities. For example, in a war, making right strategic decisions requires analyzing the strengths of both sides (including manpower, equipment and logistics), the support of the people, the geographical environment and even the climatic conditions. If the strength of both sides and the environment change, strategic goals and policies should be changed accordingly. The reason why the Chinese Communists headed by Mao Zedong were able to lead the people of the whole country to victory in the new democratic revolution was precisely because they had a profound grasp of the objective laws of the Chinese Revolutionary War and formulated correct strategies, tactics, and policies accordingly. In the practice of socialist construction, we made many "leftist" mistakes and one of the important epistemological roots is that we were divorced from the actual national conditions of the country, that is, the stage of development and the laws of development of our society, proposing some social development goals which were too high to realize for lack of certain conditions. As a result, it brought about serious damage to the cause of building socialism. The experience and lessons in this field are profound. Practical purpose is possible to be achieved only when it is rooted in the correct understanding of the nature, characteristics and development laws of the object.

Secondly, the proposal of the practical purpose is subjected to the restriction of the object, therefore, so is the choice or formulation of the practical methods and steps. To change and transform different objects requires the subject to adopt different practical tools, means, and methods. Even for the same practical object, different practical modes and steps should be adopted in different stages of development and in different states. This is what we often highlight, that is, "prescribing the right medicine" and "treating everything from actual conditions".

We point out the restriction of the practical object on practical activity, which does not mean the negation of the role that subjective mechanism plays in the operation of practical activity. In practice, the subject plays an active and creative role. However, the creation of the subject must be premised on acknowledging the objectivity of the object's restrictive and regulative role. Acknowledging this is not a contempt for the subject's initiative (or dynamic role), but to make it possible for the subject to exert creativity more fully. Recognizing and obeying the objective standards of the object is a necessary prerequisite for the implementation of practical activities. To adhere to this point is to adhere to the most basic materialist attitude in practical activities.

Feedback Adjustment in Practical Activity: Correction and Error-Correcting Mechanism of Practical Activity

When a practical activity is implementated by the subject according to a certain goal and plan, it does not always go off smoothly, and there emerge some difficulties and obstacles, and unexpected situations. This may make the progress of practical activities unsatisfactory, resulting in the phenomenon that the practical results deviate from the expected purpose. In such case, we must rely on feedback adjustments to make practical activities run smoothly.

What is feedback? In cybernetics, it is the process in which the results produced after the information sent out by the system is applied to the controlled object and then sent back to affect the re-output of the system's information. There are two forms of feedback. Generally, the feedback approaching the target is called negative feedback, and the feedback that deviates from the target and breaks the original stable state is called positive feedback. Practical feedback means that the practical subject compares, with a certain result, some new information and changes in practice, the established practical goal and plan, and then finds out the reasons, so as to adjust and modify the implementation of practical activity. Norbert Wiener, one of the founders of cybernetics, repeatedly pointed out that an effective action must obtain information through some kind of feedback process so as to know whether its purpose has been achieved.[①] If there is no feedback on the practical activities, it will become "a wild horse running off the rein", which can only be blindly and disorderly tossing, only to cause huge losses. Practical feedback of (strictly speaking, the negative feedback) is so important because of the following three points: Firstly, the practical purpose and plan are based on the subject's knowledge of the nature and laws of the object; in fact, human knowledge is always incomplete and inaccurate, and it is difficult to grasp the essential characteristics of the objective matters at once and recognize the law of development of things. Therefore, the practical plan formulated is likely to be incomplete and imprecise. Secondly, even though the practical purpose and plan are correct, certain deviations are unavoidable in the specific implementation of the practical plan. Thirdly, in a practical activity, the subject, the object and

---

① See Wiener, Norbert: *The Human Use of Human Beings: Cybernetics and Society*, tran. by Chen Bu, Beijing: The Commercial Press, 1978, p. 44, 46.

the environment of practice are constantly changing and developing, which will inevitably produce a certain new situation and new information. Therefore, in the re-implementation of a practical activity, it is necessary to make some response to the new situations and new information. Based on the practical feedback, we can adjust unscientific and non-procedural practical operations; correct the practical plan to more accurately and strictly reflect the practical purpose; or adjust or change the practical purpose to make it more judicious and reasonable, which not only meets the needs of the subject, but also is realistic and feasible. In short, the feedback-based adjustment in practical activities can correct the errors and deviations that may occur in all aspects of practical activities and revise some imperfections and inaccuracies so as to make a practical activity run smoothly and purposefully.

Practical feedback is an important mechanism for the implementation of practical activities. The use of feedback-based adjustment in any specific practical activity requires a serious and rational attitude. The practical subject must carry out a pragmatic investigation and analysis of the implementation of practice, the practical plan, the practical purpose and the theoretical understanding that guides and forms the practical purpose, so as to find out the objective defects and make targeted corrections and adjustments.

Through the analysis of the implementation mechanism of practical activities, we have a clearer understanding of the "interaction between the subject and the object" in practical activities. What is more significant is that the correct understanding of the implementation mechanism of practical activities is a prerequisite for us to carry out practical activities consciously and effectively. How to use these understandings to guide the implementation of practical activities and make them run purposefully and efficiently is obviously an issue of more practical meaning, which needs further special exploration.

Ethical Requirements for Transformation of Contemporary Social Form*

I. Introduction

Since the 1990s, the most distinctive and far-reaching characteristics of human society have undoubtedly been globalization, informatization and networking. Thus, we can say that great changes have taken place in the form and development mechanism of human society. Some people summarize the contemporary society as "global society", "information society", "network society", and "post-modern society". Manuel Castells, writes in his book *The Power of Identity* (1997) that "Contemporary world and our lives are being shaped by the conflicting trends of globalization and identity. The reconstruction of the information technology revolution and capitalism has induced a new form of society— the network society, a new form of social organization that, with its global presence, has spread to the entire world, as has been the case in the industrial capitalism of the twentieth century and its twin enemy—industrialism, shook the system, transformed the culture, created wealth and triggered poverty, stimulated greed, innovation and hope, while adding to suffering and instilling despair. But it is indeed a new world, whether beautiful or not."[①] As Anthony Giddens said, we are in a period of dramatic change and confusion, and perhaps this represents a profound evolution of social patterns.

In today's world, we find it is undergoing change on a scale unseen in a century and it can anticipate hopes and opportunities as well as risks and challenges. Since the 20th century, dramatic and profound changes have taken place in human society. Mankind has created brilliant achievements in civilization, but it is at the same time

---

* This article is an academic speech delivered by the author at the Sino-German Engineering Ethics Symposium held at the Technical University of Berlin in 2003.

[①] Custer, Manuel: *The Power of Identity*, Beijing: Social Sciences Academic Press, 2002.

facing a serious crisis of existence. Global issues such as environmental pollution, ecological imbalances, ethnic conflicts, regional wars, terrorism, the thermonuclear threat, cultural conflicts, and the gap between the rich and the poor, have cast a deep shadow on human survival and development in the 21st century. The predicament of survival and development is actually a crisis of the concept of human existence and development, essentially reflecting the crisis of human civilization, in other words, the crisis of modernity.

How to deal with and resolve such crises and establish a fair and reasonable order of human life is not only a subject that thinkers and politicians from all over the world are struggling to explore, but also a practice at which the global citizens who care about the destiny of mankind have been working hard. The massive anti-globalization movement, green movement, feminist movement, and even the successive terrorist activities and local wars are actually the direct manifestations of human crisis and the different ways of resolving the crisis. However, various kinds of postmodern philosophical ideas which can be exemplified by universal ethics, universal value, communicative rationality, intercultural understanding and dialogue, returning to the life-world, the existential philosophy ontology, justice ethics, which are in pursuit of difference, marginalization, pluralism as academic interest, which are in opposition to enlightenment rationality, centralism, essentialism and fundamentalism, are all the manifestations of ideological construction through which philosophy responds to the problems of the times and manages to resolve the crisis, are all the philosophical responses to modern civilization crisis, and are therefore the embodiment of human wisdom.. The transformation of social form requires not only new ideas and norms of the relationship between man and nature, but also new norms of human activities. Especially in present society, the rapid development of science and technology, on the one hand, has created favorable conditions for mankind to transform nature and benefit itself; on the other hand, science and technology often rid themselves of human control and thereby exert a negative impact on human life, increase the possibility of endangering human survival, and exacerbate the negative impact of mankind on the nature. Science and technology, while bringing well-being to mankind, may cause harm if they are misused without control and guidance. If nuclear weapons were possessed and used by terrorists, it is unimaginable what detriment to mankind it would cause. In this case, it is urgently needed that ethical spirit should get involved in science, that the construction of scientific ethics and morality should be strengthened, and that people should observe sci-tech ethics. The ultimate goal of sci-tech research should benefit mankind.

II. Network society calls for network ethics

The rapid development of information technology-based globalization has enabled information communication to become the fundamental pattern of human intercourse. The information movement has become the basic mode of material movement and social movement. The rapidity, interconnectivity, interactivity, and openness of human intercourse, are greatly enhanced, and so is its efficiency, while the cost of intercourse is greatly reduced. This will further enhance the complementation and mutual promotion between human production, circulation and consumption, and so will be their respective efficiencies, all these indicating the progress of society.

However, the other side cannot be ignored either. That is, as information movement has become the basic mode of material movement and social movement, human intercourse has been characterized by IT application, digitization and networking, the connectivity, interactivity, openness and immediacy between various social subjects, between various social things and between various social subjects and things, have been greatly enhanced, and the uncertainty and vulnerability of the state of human society have thereby increased. Such new changes in social operating mechanism have led to the coming into being of risk society.

For example, the development of information technology has made the flow of financial capital informatized, and the flow of bank capital and securities capital is expanding in space and accelerating in speed. It can promote the rational allocation of resources in the global scope, thus promoting the more liberalization and globalization of financial capital. On the other hand, it also means the globalization of financial speculation and risks, which have greatly increased the instability of international financial system. Evidence is given by the financial turmoil that has taken place in various regions and the consequent serious economic crisis and social unrest. In other words, the international financial crisis has the "contagious effect" and in this sense it can be said that the world economy and politics have become very vulnerable. Peter Drucker argues that the labor organization peculiar to knowledge society will become "a destabilizing factor". First of all, the stability of the enterprise has been greatly challenged. In the era of continuous innovation in knowledge and technology, corporate behavior must change with the changes in knowledge and technology, otherwise it will perish, and the management of enterprises will increasingly become a response to change, rather than improving the static structure of the enterprise, which renders enterprises a "organizational chameleon". In such situation where the stability of organizations cannot be guaranteed, the community and society composed of a large number of such organizations will fail to guarantee stability. The organization of knowledge society thus continues to undermine the community, making it chaotic and unstable.[①]

The uncertainty in contemporary society comes from two aspects. First, social interaction depends more and more on information technology and network, but the problems of cybersecurity and information security may arise at any time for various reasons. For example, the paralysis caused by hacker attacks in the network will the interruption of various economic and political exchanges and leads to serious consequences; second, due to the tremendous changes in the information movement and the technical basis and mechanism of communication in contemporary society, the interconnectivity, interactivity, and integrity of communication has been strengthened, so the contagious effect of risk is not only rapid, but also will be more magnified. For instance, the speed of information transmission and the wide impact of an emergency are unimaginable under the traditional social conditions, and now it is likely to cause instability or even collapse of a certain subsystem of society or even the social system.

In fact, a globalized and IT application society is a technological society. Because the structure system of social communication and organization is built with information, satellite, telecommunications and other technologies as the means and foundation, and because the high-tech has been applied in a very extensive and in-depth manner in social production and social life, the risks inherent in contemporary society are inevitable and huge. The financial turmoil sweeping through the world at the end of the 20th century and the ensuing series of unexpected crises in the new century, such as the outbreak of "September 11", "SARS" and the collapse of the U.S. power grid system, were unprecedented in history in the breadth and depth of impact and in the speed of transmission. These are enough to show the high interconnectivity and dependence of contemporary society, the high efficiency and instantaneity of the transmission effect, as well as the extreme fragility and instability, and show the distinctive characteristics of contemporary society.

---

① Drucker, Peter: *Post-capitalist Society*, Chin. ed., Shanghai: Shanghai Translation Publishing House, 1998.

It is estimated that now there are about 500 million netizens in the world and more than 68 million in China (as of June 30, 2003). Computer network hackers, viruses and other problems emerged one after another, and inflicted huge losses. The situation in recent years shows that most of the threats to the network come from information network personnel. According to relevant information in 1999, there was a hacking incident almost every 20 seconds around the world that year. The economic losses inflicted by hacking in the United States exceeded 10 billion U.S. dollars and the losses on the Chinese Internet network reached hundreds of millions of *yuan*. Information network security and ethical issues have aroused widespread concern.[①]

Therefore, the ethics of computer professionals must be strengthened. Information technology personnel should work together with all the rest of society to rationally and responsibly use information networks to promote economic development and social progress; oppose the spread of computer viruses, spam, various illegal or harmful information by using network, and oppose intrusion, interfere with or attack other people's information systems, steal national and trade secrets, infringe other people's privacy.

III. Humanistic observation and examination of science and technology

The rapid development of contemporary science and technology has a profound impact on the ways and circumstances of the existence of contemporary people. The contemporary modes of intercourse based on information and communication technologies and modern means of transportation are undoubtedly a huge leap in the history of human communication and intercourse, and a great liberation of the relations of human productivity and the production relations. However, we cannot therefore lose sight of its impact on people's life-world and existence. Juergen Habermas profoundly pointed out that the proliferation of technological rationality and the continuous expansion of people have resulted in the "colonization" of the "life-world", namely, the constant technicalization and institutionalization of "life-world". In his view, communicative action in the daily life-world operates according to a non-instrumental principle, and there is no necessity to meet the mandatory requirements of the system such as profit, control and efficiency. Watching movies, listening to the radio, watching television, using computers or fax machines to

---

① Zhang Qiyao 张其瑶: "A Summary of Symposium on Science and Technology Ethics and Its Social Impact"《科技伦理问题及其社会影响研讨会综述》, *Science Times*, 2002-7-26.

transmit information, making phone calls, etc. are derogatory and trampling on the communicative rationality, and they are all examples of the colonization of the life-world by the system. The relationship between people and between people's lives are becoming more and more technicalized, instrumentalized, and legalized, and personal daily life is increasingly subjected to external mandatory requirements, control and supervision such as technology, management norms, and laws. The "colonization" of technical rationality on the life world has destroyed the normal and harmonious state of interpersonal intercourse, personal free space has been eroded, the social and humanistic living environment has deteriorated severely, and the humanistic connotation of the life-world has become increasingly weak.[1]

The expansion of communication space, the acceleration of communication rhythm and the saving of communication time, in essence, mean the increase of people's freedom, make people move towards a freer realm, and thus achieve a greater degree of liberation. However, the absentness and detachedness of communication realized via the Internet has made the originally strong virtualization, sensibility and warmth of human nature are increasingly weakened or even lost while the evil aspects of human nature are freely released, the mutual emergence of "angels" and "monsters" becoming the reality of human existence today.

The change in the way of intercourse not only affects the degree of realization of human nature, but also means the difference in the way the subject is constructed. According to Mark Poster, an American scholar, the communication practice in the era of electronic communication—what he also calls the information society — constitutes an unstable, multiple and diffuse subject, whose identities are different from those elicited by the "patterned practices" signified by "modernity or the modern mode of production" as autonomous and (instrumental) rational.[2] Print culture constitutes the individual as a subject, as transcendent to objects, as stable and fixed in identity while with the emergence of the electronically mediated systems of communication, the decentralization of communications network promotes the individual as an unstable identity. The print culture constructs the individual as a subject, a subject that is transparent to the object, and a subject that has a stable and fixed identity; however, the advent of electronic communication system has made

---

[1] See Habermas, J. & M. Haller: *The Past as Future*, Chin. ed., Hangzhou: Zhejiang People's Publishing Press, 2002.
[2] Post, Mark: *The Second Media Age*, Chin. ed., Nanjing: Nanjing University Press, 2000, p.45.

the "decentralization" of the communication network elicit the individual's unstable identity.[1] "The referential anchor of the individual recedes in social prominence as global communication networks (Lyotard) and human/machine combinations (Haraway) replace older figures of man versus nature and individual versus society."[2] Lyotard's *The Inhuman* and Haraway's *Simians, Cyborgs and Women* register the depths of postmodern culture in a recognition of an emerging "inhuman" or transhuman social order.

Mark Poster also argues that in the age of electronic culture and communication, which is also called the age of information, the community of face-to-face individuals in the hitherto existing modern society will disappear. In modern society, a community of face-to-face individuals is definable and the dramatic spread of electronic communication systems will "toll the end of community in any shape it has hitherto been imagined." "Relations of mind to body, person to person, humanity to nature are undergoing such profound reconfiguration that images of community are presented if at all only in science fiction books and films."[3]

In my opinion, we should pay much attention to the application of science and technology from the perspective of humanistic rationality, surpassing the cognitive rationality of science and the instrumental rationality of technology. Science is not omnipotent, but limited. Science should leave a place for human values, mental freedom and space, that is, people's daily life world.

IV. Construction of environmental ethics

Mankind is facing a paradoxical and embarrassing situation. On the one hand, relying on technological progress, mankind has mastered an unprecedented ability to transform nature, creating and enjoying huge material wealth. On the other hand, technological progress has also greatly aggravated the generation of alien forces that are not good for mankind, and its negative effects are increasing day by day and becoming more obvious. Especially since the middle of the 20th century, the human living environment has generally deteriorated and the ecosystem has been in a state of crisis resulting from comprehensive impact. The ecological crisis is not the fault of technology, but the negative consequences or effects of technology inflicted by

---

[1] Post, Mark: *The Second Media Age*, Chin. ed., Nanjing: Nanjing University Press, 2000, p.84-85.
[2] Ibid., p.75.
[3] Ibid., p.74.

people's improper utilization of it.

Respect and be kind to nature, esteem all life species, value the harmony and stability of the natural ecology, etc. Whether it may be government decision-making, corporate behavior or personal behavior, the issue of environmental ethics should be examined. Scientific and technical personnel should regard protecting resources and the environment, preventing environmental pollution, and ensuring sustainable development as the goal of their researches, the overall interests and long-term interests as the criteria for research and development, and establishing a correct environmental ethics and a high sense of responsibility for society as the foundation of being a good scientist.

In the construction of environmental ethics, scientists should assume certain moral and social responsibilities. They have the responsibility to popularize and educate their work groups so that policy makers and the public can understand, respect and protect nature. In scientific research activities, including reviewing and evaluating research projects, they should take into consideration the impact of ecology and the environment. In order to survive and develop, they are prone to be utilitarian in tackling with the problems related to environment and development, unaware that some activities may lead to environmental degradation. They should seek truth from facts and tell the truth from an objective perspective and in accordance with objective laws.

It should be advocated that the mode of development at the expense of increasing consumption of natural resources and environmental degradation should be rooted out through the re-understanding of the value objectives of human society and a correct understanding of the ethical relationship between people and the environment, and that the orderly human activities that adapt to the laws of nature should be carried out in order to establish a new ethical relationship between man and nature.[1]

V. Conclusion

To sum up, I agree with Lu Yongxiang (路甬祥), General Secretary of the Chinese Academy of Sciences, that the progress of science and technology should serve all mankind, the noble cause of advancing world peace, development and progress, and should not endanger mankind itself. The construction of scientific ethics and morality

---

[1] Zhang Qiyao: "A Summary of Symposium on Science and Technology Ethics and Its Social Impact," *Science Times*, 2002-7-26.

requires that natural sciences should be tightly integrated with humanities and social sciences, and that great importance should be attached to science and technology from the height of humanistic rationality, beyond the cognitive rationality of science and the instrumental rationality of technology. All these will ensure that science and technology have always been in the sound development along the right track of serving mankind.

The subjects of scientific and technological activities are scientists and the ethical issues of scientific and technological activities and the application of scientific and technological achievements are always closely related to scientists. Since science and technology contains values and ethical characteristics, it should not be separated from ethics and should be subjected to certain regulations. The contemporary experts in science and technology should exert their initiative and creativity in the practice of science and technology ethics, follow the basic ethical principles of objectivity, fairness and public-interest priority, and establish an effective buffer mechanism between science and technology and the social ethical value system. Remember, science should leave a place for human values, and for the nature and space of human spiritual freedom. Science is not a panacea, and it should still have its limits, which need to be examined from the humanistic perspective.

Contemporary Development
of Marxist Philosophy

From Value Criticism to Scientific Criticism: Establishment of Marx's Method of Value Criticism and Historical Materialism*

In any theoretical research, the researcher has a certain way of thinking that runs through its main part. The major leap from theoretical research to scientific truth is often the result of a change in his or her theoretical thinking method. This is clearly reflected by the creation of historical materialism. Looking at Marx's road of theoretical exploration leading to historical materialism, we can find a change in Marx's theoretical thinking method, namely the change from abstract value critique to concrete and rational analysis and abstraction of experience. Then, what is the method of value criticism? Does it play any role in the formation of historical materialism? What role? What is the intrinsic mechanism of the transition from value criticism to rational analysis? The researches for these questions are still lacking, so this article attempts to make a brief discussion on them.

I

The path of Marx's theoretical exploration of historical materialism has many twists and turns. If *German Ideology* is regarded as the mark of the emergence of historical materialism, then taking it as a boundary marker, the development of Marx's thoughts can be divided into two stages, namely the gestation stage of historical materialism in the early period, and the maturity and development stage of historical materialism in the later period. Studying Marx's earlier works, we can find that in his theoretical exploration of historical materialism there is a method of value criticism, that is, the method based on a certain value judgment, taking an abstract

---

* Originally published in *Teaching and Research*, 1989(2).

concept as the theoretical starting point, so as to review and criticize reality (and theories). Specifically, this method has the following three characteristics:

1.Abstract speculativity: contradictory thinking of "essentiality" and "reality"

This is mainly manifested in Marx's inability to get rid of such a way of thinking when he explained and enunciated historical and practical problems: to measure, examine and criticize reality with a certain fictional scale of rationality and ideal obligation. On the path to historical materialism, Marx respectively stopped and stayed in "self-consciousness", "rationality", "freedom", and "(abstract) essence of man", take them as the starting point of his theory, and built the theoretical battle-fortress. In his "Doctoral Dissertation", Marx uses "self-consciousness" as the central concept, expounds the interaction between philosophy and reality, people and the environment, and emphasizes that philosophy must embody "self-consciousness", and that philosophy which embodies "self-consciousness" must conquer the world and impose marks on phenomena.[1] During the period of "Rhineland", focusing on the censorship of books and newspapers and the freedom of the press and related material interests, Marx, from the viewpoint that "rationality determines the world", reduced the country to philosophy and rationality, and then condemned the irrationality of the authoritarian system of the Prussian state, trying to find in philosophical rationality a basis to explain and transform the real country. In the Kroznach period, although Marx put forward the important ideas that civil society determines the state and that private property determines the political state, but he also believes that private property is determined by people's civic characteristics, that there exists a rational and free country, and that democracy is a true state system, starts from people rather than from "abstract ideas", and is the product of freedom. During the period of "Yearbook of Germany and France", the idea of political alienation in modern countries was put forward. The so-called political alienation refers to the separation of human existence and essence. In *Economic and Philosophic Manuscripts of 1844*, Marx believed that labor is the essence of humanity, and realized that "the entire so-called history of the world is nothing but the creation of man through human labor,"[2] but his understanding of labor is abstract, and labor is understood as a kind

---

[1] Marx, K. & F. Engels: *Collected Works of Marx and Engels*, Vol.40, Chin. ed., Beijing: People's Publishing House, 1982, p.136, 258.
[2] Marx, K. & F. Engels: *Collected Works of Marx and Engels*, Vol. 42, Chin. ed., Beijing: People's Publishing House, 1979, p.131.

of human "real labor" (that is, completely free and conscious labor). Using this "real labor" to measure labor in real society, Marx believes that labor in a real capitalist society is a kind of alienated labor. Therefore, the emancipation of the proletariat and the realization of a communist society are the historical process of eliminating alienated labor and restoring free and conscious nature of man. Even in his book The Holy Family, Marx started to explain the essence and history of humankind with the material living conditions on which human beings depend, but at the same time, he still proceeded from the perspective of assuming that human beings have a trans-historical nature and believed that "The property-owning class and the class of the proletariat represent the same human self-alienation". When analyzing the historical status of the proletariat, Marx mainly focused on the living conditions in which they had in the capitalist society and which violated humanity, and on the contradiction between their living conditions and the human nature.

In short, Marx's criticism of reality, his elucidation of history, his demonstration of the proletariat's historical status and mission, and the communist society always base their theories on such concepts as "self-consciousness", "rationality" and "freedom", set them as the essential and ideal nature of human beings, as opposed to the *status quo* of human beings in the real society, and make them serve as the theoretical basis for criticizing and transforming the real society. However, the resulting contradiction between the "essential" human nature and the actual human existence is not an objective and realistic contradiction, but a product of humanistic thinking logic.

2.Passionate criticalness: establish "critique" as theoretical starting point of speculation

The theoretical starting point of this speculation is the weapon to criticize reality. Marx's early thoughts are full of a kind of passionate criticism. In his *Doctoral Dissertation*[1], Marx expresses an idea as follows: Just as Prometheus started to build a house on the ground after he stole the fire from the sky, philosophy rose to oppose the world of phenomena after grasping the whole world. He thought that his philosophy should be like Prometheus, to "steal fire" for the real world and become "a light to guide" to lacerate the darkness and change unreasonable reality of society.

---

[1] Marx, K. & F. Engels: *Collected Works of Marx and Engels*, Vol. 42, People's Publishing House, 1982, p.136.

In the "Yearbook of Germany and France", Marx declared: "We must cruelly criticize everything that exists."① In the *Introduction to Critique of Hegel's Philosophy of Right*, Marx issued a gladiatorial declaration: "War on the German state of affairs! By all means!... In the struggle against that state of affairs, criticism is no passion of the head, it is the head of passion. It is not a lancet, it is a weapon. Its object is its enemy, which it wants not to refute but to exterminate...Its essential pathos is indignation, its essential work is denunciation."② These words, full of "gunpowder smell", are enough to show the passionate criticalness of Marx's early days to the fullest. The essential meaning of this criticalness is to "rearrange the real world".

3.Distinct value orientation

The purpose of Marx's "all-out relentless criticism" is to condemn the authoritarian politics in Germany at the time, exposing irrational social reality and "human essence" crying for the suffering of the working people and the proletariat and establishing a humane society where everyone lives in a rational, free and conscious manner. From the beginning of Marx's theoretical activities, he consciously stood on the side of the toiling people. During the "Rheinland" period, focusing on the issue of newspaper inspections and press freedom, the theft of trees, and the conditions of farmers in the Mosser region, Marx stood on the standpoint of "rationality" and "right" and condemned exploitation and oppression of the working people by the Prussian authoritarian system and landlord bourgeoisie. In the Introduction *to Critique of Hegel's Philosophy of Right*, Marx made clear his philosophical position: "As philosophy finds its material weapon in the proletariat, so the proletariat finds its mental weapon in philosophy."③ It thereby proclaims that his philosophical mission is to liberate the proletariat. It can be said simply that an important turning point in promoting Marx's theoretical research and then incessantly deepening his theory is to reveal the reasons for inequality in the real society, to scream and fight for the suffering of the people, and to remold the real society through his philosophy so that the proletariat will be liberated. In fact, Marx's theoretical work in all his life did not deviate from this purpose.

---

① Marx, K. & F. Engels: *Collected Works of Marx and Engels*, Vol. 1, Chin. ed., Beijing: People's Publishing House, 1956, p. 416.
② Ibid., p. 455.
③ Marx, K. & F. Engels: *Collected Works of Marx and Engels*, Vol. 1, Chin. ed., Beijing: People's Publishing House, 1956, p. 467.

As the survey and analysis aforementioned show, the method of value critique exists objectively in the Marx's theoretical exploration of historical materialism.

In our opinion, the method of value critique undoubtedly plays a significant role in the formation of historical materialism. This role and its action mechanism mainly is manifested in the following aspects:

First, the method of value critique is the "mother womb" of historical materialism, which breeds the continuous growth of historical materialism, and which is the "bridge" that leads Marx to the historical materialism.

Historical materialism did not emerge from the ether, all of sudden, but after some gestational work, which, in our opinion, is undertaken by value critique method. For example, Marx regarded "self-consciousness" as the starting point of philosophy and clarified the interaction between philosophy and the external world, between theory and reality. In particular, he proposed "worldization of philosophy", namely the great idea that philosophy must step out of the mental world and transform the real world, taking transforming the external real world as the highest mission of philosophy. Here, although Marx's understanding of philosophy is idealistic (that is, understanding of philosophy of self-consciousness), his clarification of the mission of philosophy is extremely correct and valuable. Later, Marx defined "transform the world" as the purpose of his new philosophy, that is, practical materialism. When it comes to the viewpoint on state, Marx, starting from the rationalist view of state that "Rationality determines the state" and that "The state should be built on the basis of free rationality," criticized the actual autocratic rule of the Prussian state, and condemning the despicable private interests and the infringement on the "rational state". However, no matter how strongly Marx condemned private interests, in real society, private interests still play an irresistible role, and the state has become the private property of the owners of private interests. This is a "distressing question" for Marx. It is this "afflictive question" encountered in theoretical criticism that prompted Marx to re-examine and criticize Hegel's rationalist view of state which he believed in. As a result, he proposed the important idea that it is not that the state determines civil society, but that civil society determines the state and private property determines political state. This new idea led to Karl Marx's "downward" approach to research, that is, by adopting such an approach to study political economy, to find the basis of society. Historical materialism is the direct result of such "downward" approach. For another example, Marx explains the status quo of capitalist society with the theory of alienated labor, elucidating the process of historical development and the inevitability of communist society and the ways of achieving it, which is certainly abstract and speculative, but Marx's idea of labor objectification is exactly a brand-new, extremely important clue to historical materialism. It is from the ideas of labor objectification and alienation that the two most important and well-conceived concepts in historical materialism, namely the productive forces and the production relations, are further extended in due course. There are many more examples of the generation of scientific factors of historical materialism from value-critique methods. In our opinion, it is precisely in this kind of value critique that historical materialism is gradually formed in the interaction between theory and reality.

Second, the "spirit of freedom" and "spirit of practice" inherent in the method of value criticism are the dynamics mechanism for the formation of historical materialism.

As is pointed out earlier, one of the important features of the method of value criticism is passionate criticalness, the essence of which is that it does not acknowledge that the real world is under improvement, and that it is necessary to creatively rearrange the world. This first and foremost reflects a kind of "spirit of freedom" with which Marx fought for the liberation of the proletariat and the freedom of all mankind. At the same time, "criticalness" also reflects his great concern for reality, giving his theory a strong sense of reality and practice, which embodies the "spirit of practice".

The "spirit of freedom" is an important moral support for Marx's exploration of the truth of historical materialism and even his life-long arduous research activities for profound theories. No real profound theory, no faith. One cannot be engaged in well-conceived theoretical research without faith. Marx believes that the primary foundation of philosophical research is the courage and the spirit of freedom.[1] He regards transforming the real world and finding a realistic and reliable path of the liberation for the exploited and oppressed proletariat as his philosophical mission. In our view, this kind of "spirit of freedom" is precisely the firm faith that guided Marx to explore the nature and development law of the social history, and thus to work hard for his whole life on the path of scientific research without fear of any hardship. Without such faith, how could he have kept at his research with such courage and tenacity? In essence, historical materialism is a well-conceived theory that pinpoints

---

[1] Quoted from Марк Моисеевич Розенталь (ed.): История марксистской диалектики (The History of Marxist Dialectics), Chin. ed., Beijing: People's Publishing House, 1986, p.124.

a realistic path for the proletariat to fight for freedom and emancipation. Therefore, in a certain sense, it can be said that historical materialism is nothing more than the theorization of this "spirit of freedom".

The "spirit of practice" makes Marx's theory always open to practice and reality. Because the method of value critique starts from the ideal "obligation", rationally fabricates and formulates an abstract concept, and uses it as a theoretical weapon to criticize reality. Therefore, the contradiction between theory and reality is inevitably caused: when criticizing reality, theory can never achieve a universal and thorough persuasion, let alone many new problems and facts encountered thereby. In this way, it inevitably prompted Marx to continuously revise and improve his understanding, so as to approach the objective truth that profoundly reveals the essence of real society and history and the law of development—historical materialism. It can be seen that the spirit of practice gave Marx's early theory an inherent self-development mechanism.

In addition, precisely because Marx stood on the position of the exploited and oppressed laboring people and the proletariat, taking it as his mission to explore the path of emancipating the laboring people and the proletariat--the representatives of the new productive forces, whose interests, requirements and desires often reflected and represented historical changes, trends and directions of development, the value orientation inherent in the method of value critique is most likely to lead Marx on the path to historical materialism.

Third, the method of value critique has forged Marx's highly abstract thinking ability, which undoubtedly plays an important role in forming the historical materialism as a well-conceived theory.

An important characteristic of the method of value critique is to explain and criticize the reality through abstract conceptual thinking. Different from F. Engels who reached historical materialism mainly through carrying out "economic critique" via direct contact and research on practical issues, what Marx did first is attach importance to "philosophical critique" staying in the realm of abstract theoretical speculation for a long time. What is the result? In our opinion, Marx, after cultivating the theoretical thinking of the method of value critique, has cultivated a kind of thinking ability of rigorous theoretical analysis and synthesis and conceptual reasoning. As we know, the more abstract and logical the theory is, the more profound and rigorous it will be, and thus, the more profound and thorough the analysis of problems and the explanation of things will be. Therefore, the ability of conceptual reasoning, and the analytical and abstract power of thinking are indispensable for the establishment of scientific theories. As such, historical materialism is an abstract summary of the essence of social history and its development laws. This undoubtedly requires the founders of historical materialism to have profound perception and high ability of analysis and abstraction. Only in this way can we perceive the nature of complex and fragmented social and historical phenomena and thereby "extract" and generalize the laws of the development of society and history. Historical facts have proved that one of the important reasons why historical materialism is convincing and persuasive and able to withstand criticism and attacks from all sides is that such theory has a high degree of thinking dominance and a rigorous conceptual logical structure, correctly revealing and grasping the structure and nature of social history and the laws of its development. And this is inseparable from Marx's long-term application of the abstract theoretical thinking method of value critique.

    Of course, there is no doubt that the method of value critique has many limitations. It is not a judicious method. However, we cannot thereby safely dismiss the role of value critique in the formation of historical materialism. Otherwise, we cannot correctly and truly understand the emergence of historical materialism, nor can we truly and thoroughly grasp the characteristics of Marxist theory.

Historical Science on Proletariat and Human Emancipation: On Unity of Scientificity and Value of Marxist Philosophy*

I. What are historical limitations of traditional model of interpretation?

The interpretation of a theory is always associated with the real needs of a given subject. The acceptance and interpretation of Marxism by the Chinese people are also closely linked with the then situation of Chinese society and with anti-imperialism and anti-feudalism struggle and realizing the revolutionary goal of national independence and liberation. Marxist historical materialism was understood mainly as the theories of class struggle, violent revolution, materialist dialectics as rational transformation of the actual order, the core of dialectics, namely the thought of the unity of opposites, as the struggle of contradictions; from the perspective of theoretical source, the textbook system was mainly based on Section Two, Chapter Four of Stalin's *The History of the Communist Party of the Soviet Union*(Bolsheviks) —"Dialectical Materialism and Historical Materialism". With the development of practice and the times, this traditional model of interpretation of Marxist philosophy has increasingly exposed its historical limitations, the main ones of which lie in its ignorance of the fundamental significance of the concept of practice for Marxist philosophy, of the great significance of such issues as the free and well-rounded development of everyone, value and the concept of values for Marxist philosophy, and of the new challenges brought to Marxist philosophy by new changes, new achievements, and new issues which have emerged in the contemporary scientific and technological revolution. It can be said that we have lacked a comprehensive and overall grasp of the system of

---

* Originally published in The *Chinese Academy of social sciences*, 2005-9-8 and the theoretical edition of *Beijing Daily*, 2006-2-5.

Marxist theories for quite some time. In order to embody the "true spirit" of Marxism in the construction of Chinese Marxist philosophy, I think the fundamental thing is to correctly understand and grasp the "general characteristics" of K. Marx's and F. Engels' thoughts, and grasp the thinking mode and the value standpoint embodied in Marxist philosophy, which must be realized from the inherent connection of Marxist theories and that between Marxism and its historical and contemporary practices.

Marxist philosophy cannot be more accurately grasped unless it is interpreted from the perspective of the connection between Marxist philosophy and Marxist holistic theory. For a long time, we have been accustomed to dividing Marxism into three components, or expounding Marxism from three aspects. In fact, the Marxist theory is a whole. It is a science concerning the general laws of historical formation and social development, and also a special science on the laws of capitalist development. Marx initially conducted political and economic studies in order to seek the solutions to the "distress of material interests", during which he exposed and criticized their philosophical beliefs (mainly manifested in the critique of *German Ideology*), discovered the close connection between human perceptual practice and human history, explained social structure and operation mechanism with human perceptual practical activities, revealed the development of human history, found the general laws of the development of human society, and thus created historical materialism—a new philosophy with a new worldview and a new materialism. And then he arduously conducted an in-depth systematic study on the operation and development mechanism of the capitalist mode of production, which mainly manifested itself in the revelation and analysis of the logic of capital governance. Finally, he draws the conclusion of scientific socialism, which shows the ideal of free and well-rounded development of each individual in future society. It can be seen that Marx's thought is the unity of philosophical criticism (criticism of traditional metaphysics), capital criticism and social criticism, and achieves the theoretical integration in the critical analysis of capital. For Marx, philosophy, political economy, scientific socialism, etc., constitute an organic whole of thought. Therefore, if we understand Marx's philosophy only from the perspective of philosophy, we cannot really grasp the "position" of Marx's philosophy, nor can we truly grasp the overall appearance and essence of Marx's thought.

II. What are the embodiments of original and universal ideas of Marxist philosophy

From the perspective of the thinking mode and values, the ideas of Marxist philosophy that is original and of universal significance include:

(1) Marxist philosophy interprets the structure and operation mechanism of society with human perceptual practice, reveals the general laws of the development of human society and the particular laws of capitalist development, and is a kind of science on the mechanism of historical formation and social development. The revelation of historical materialism to the structure and operation of human society is still a great cognitive tool with the strongest explanative capacity in contemporary times, and is also of great significance to analyze and grasp the law of contemporary social development.

(2) Marx's revelation and critique of the logic of capital ruling humanity in commodity society, commodity fetishism, and human independence based on material dependence, his critique of alienated labor, and the profound thought that the highest ideal of human society is the free and well-rounded development of each individual, have extremely important guidance and enlightenment for the analysis and criticism of contemporary capitalism and the sound development of the socialist market economy in contemporary China.

(3) The idea that the basic characteristics of future society should be defined from the dimension of human development. K. Marx and F. Engels paid great attention to the reality, individuals' living circumstances and development future, to the emancipation of the proletariat, and regarded the free and well-rounded development of each individual and the harmonious development of their society as the goal of communist society. As K. Marx and F. Engels pointed out in the "Communist Manifesto", "In place of the old bourgeois society, with its classes and class antagonisms, we shall have an association, in which the free development of each is the condition for the free development of all."[①] F. Engels pointed out in his *Socialism: Utopian and Scientific*: The future society that has abolished capitalism, has thereby eliminated the class rule, and the public power has lost its political nature. The history when man is dominated by alien forces will come to end. There, "man for the first time becomes the real, conscious lord of nature, because he has now become master of his own social organization." "The extraneous objective forces that have, hitherto, governed history, pass under the control of man himself. Only from that time will man himself, more and more consciously, make his own history. It is

---

① Marx, K. & F. Engels: *Selected Works of Marx and Engels*, Vol. 1, Chin. ed., Beijing: People's Publishing House, 1995, p. 294.

the ascent of man from the kingdom of necessity to the kingdom of freedom." Man has finally become the master of his own social organization, thus becoming the lord of nature and becoming his own master — a "free man"— F. Engels calls it "the cause of liberating the world".[①] F. Engels referred to all previous human history as "prehistoric history", and its theoretical form is "scientific socialism". This thought has very important guiding significance for the practice of socialism for the goal of comprehensively and correctly understanding Marxism and understanding socialism.

(4) Many principles of Marxist philosophy are general and universal, and the explanation of the operation and development of human society is still valid today. There are many examples that can be cited in this regard, such as the principle that social existence determines social consciousness, the viewpoint of practice, the idea that people are the creators of human history, the methods of class analysis, etc.

(5) Marxist dialectics provides us with a judicious way of thinking.

The aforementioned five aspects, whether in terms of the judiciousness of their thinking or their value standpoints, in my opinion, have critical and constructive significance for the development of the present-day world and of contemporary China, and can even be said to have value beyond time and space.

III. To clarify contemporary value of Marxism does not mean that Marxism does not need development

From the perspective of theoretical characteristics, Marxist philosophy is an organic combination of criticality and ideality, judiciousness and valuability, theoreticality and practicality, has a rigorous and logical theoretical system (its theoretical logic deeply reflects and thoroughly reveals the practice logic of that time), is an ideal construction based on historical science about the emancipation of the proletariat and of mankind, is a well-conceived theoretical system about the emancipation of the proletariat and all mankind, and is the organic unity of the scientific spirit and humanistic spirit. It is Marx's scientific critique that gives us insight into the secrets of human existence; it is Marx's proposals that man is liberated from the domination of nature and the domination of human social relations, and that individuals achieve their own transcendence and realize their free and comprehensive development that show us the bright prospects of human life. If Marx

---

① Marx, K. & F. Engels: *Selected Works of Marx and Engels*, Vol. 1, Chin. ed., Beijing: People's Publishing House, 1972, p. 441, 443.

is the "Prometheus of the world", Marxism is like a "sacred fire", leading human society to transcend the ignorance of itself and lacerate the darkness of alienation and non-freedom, illuminating the goal of human progress, and giving mankind the hope of life and great motivation for struggle. Both the critique spirit and the ideal spirit are important connotations of Marxism which we should publicize rather than suppress.

Although Marxism was born in the society more than 150 years ago, it is still having a significant impact on the world. Why? Because Marxism reflects the practical logic at that time with the theoretical logic like "iron", showing a strict scientific nature; Marxism, with its profound judiciousness and thorough criticism, has profoundly and enormously influenced and changed the way of capitalism's existence and development and even the entire history of the world. What Marxism shows is the free and well-rounded development of everyone, which has achieved the complete liberation of the proletariat and even the entire mankind, and pointed the direction for mankind to constantly transcend various "darkness" such as alienation. Marx declared the secrets as to how he criticized and exposed the capitalist mode of production, but truth-seeking spirit of science which has made it possible that "he had hardly one personal enemy" and the great personality power of K. Marx and F. Engels invite future generations and even opponents of their ideas to have a sincere respect for them! Marx was rated as the greatest thinker of the millennium in 1999, and recently as the greatest philosopher since ancient times; Sartre thinks Marx's thought marks the unsurpassable peak of philosophy movement, and Derrida issued at the beginning of the new century a slogan: "Pay tribute to Marx." All these have demonstrated great strength and charm of Marx's thought. The profound reason is that Marxist values and values on the internal mechanisms are based on the judicious judgment of laws of history and social development, Marxism has truly achieved the organic and intrinsic unification of science and value.

To clarify the contemporary value of Marxism does not mean that Marxism does not need to develop. Marxism is a product of the transition from liberal capitalism to monopoly capitalism. Contemporary capitalism has developed itself to the stage of transnational capitalism, in which, compared with the Marxist era, science and technology have made considerable progress, the operating mechanism of contemporary capitalism has also undergone great changes, and the concrete practical form of socialism is also not completely consistent with Marx's vision. In fact, the various schools of Western Marxism have enriched and supplemented Marxist theory from different angles and aspects. We must treat Marxism with a

Marxist attitude, that is, a historical dialectical perspective, adhering to and developing Marxism in accordance with the development of the times and specific practices. Marxists in contemporary China need to explore the "Chinese path", sum up "Chinese experience", and develop Sinicized Marxism to guide China's modernization.

Historical Meditation on Theoretical Basis of Historical Materialism*

A correct understanding of the theoretical basis of historical materialism is the key to correctly grasping the essence and system of historical materialism and even the entire Marxist philosophy. However, up to now, people's understandings of the theoretical basis of historical materialism are still widely divided, with each having their own roots. Therefore, making historical analysis and theoretical reflection on the theoretical basis of historical materialism has become an issue of great theoretical significance. This article intends to make a new survey and review on the understanding of the theoretical basis of historical materialism by several important Marxist theorists, namely F. Engels, Plekhanov, Lenin, Stalin and Lukács, so as to deepen the study of historical materialism research.

I

Historical materialism is presented to the world with a fresh look that is completely different from any previous historical philosophy. Regarding its theoretical basis, some people felt puzzled and some have misunderstood. For a long time, historical materialism was called "economic materialism"; and sometimes it was considered "in a position to be combined with many other philosophies", as if historical materialism does not have its own unique theoretical basis, nor is it a complete system, but a simple accumulation of some independent doctrines. In order to defend historical materialism and its theoretical basis, F. Engels wrote in his later years a series of works and letters such as *Anti-Dühring* and *Theses on Feuerbach*. He thought that in these two writings "I have given the most detailed account of

---

* The article is written with the cooperation of Prof. Yang Geng(杨耕), originally published in *Journal of Renmin University of China*, 1988(6).

historical materialism which, as far as I know, exists."[1]

The scientific concept of practice is a microcosm of the entire historical materialism. In this sense, it can be said that explaining the theoretical contribution of Marx's concept of practice is explaining the theoretical contribution of the entire Marxist historical materialism. F. Engels realized the basic status of the concept of practice—especially the viewpoint of labor—in the system of historical materialism and understood human history from labour and from the interaction between man and nature. According to F. Engels, the unity of opposites between man and nature includes not only the naturalization of man in terms of the development the laws of nature, that is, "we, together with our flesh, blood and mind all belong to the nature and exist in the nature," but also include the humanization interfering with nature and affecting it through labor, that is, "our rule over nature". "Naturalism's historical view is one-sided in that it believes that only the natural world acts on man, and that natural conditions determine the historical development of man everywhere. But it forgets that man also acts against the natural world, changes the natural world, and creates new living conditions for himself." Labor created man himself; man created his own history. "The mastery over nature, which begins…with labour, widened man's horizon at every new advance. He was continually discovering new, hitherto unknown, properties of natural objects. On the other hand, the development of labour necessarily helped to bring the members of society closer together."[2] At the same time, the most essential and immediate basis of human thought is precisely the alteration of nature by men, not solely nature as such. "It is in the measure that man has learned to change nature that his intelligence has increased."[3] It is not hard to see that F. Engels regards the most basic form of labor-practice as the basis of the entire human history and regards labor as the basis for human development, as the basis not only for human material existence and development, but also for the development of human social relations and psychic abilities. F. Engels grasped the profound essence of Marx's historical materialism: it is in the process of practice that people transform and understand the natural world, and at the same time transform, create

---

[1] Marx, K. & F. Engels: *Selected Works of Marx and Engels*, Vol. 4, Chin. ed., Beijing: People's Publishing House, 1995, p. 698.
[2] Marx, K. & F. Engels: *Collected Works* of *Marx and Engels*, Vol. 3, Chin. ed., Beijing: People's Publishing House, 2012, p. 991,922, 998.
[3] Marx, K. & F. Engels: *Collected Works of Marx and Engels*, Vol.20, Chin. ed., Beijing: People's Publishing House, 1971, p. 574.

and understand themselves, including their own social relations, body structure and thinking structure.

As Marx put it, "the entire so-called history of the world is nothing but the creation of man through human labor, nothing but the emergence of nature for man."①

Correct understanding of labor and its historical status has given F. Engels a correct basic understanding of the theoretical basis of historical materialism. In F. Engels's view, historical materialism is the science on the reality of human beings and their historical development, and its task is to reveal the general laws of human historical movement. In order to accomplish this task, historical materialism must regard practical theory as its own theoretical basis. Historical materialism "recognized that the key to the understanding of the whole history of society lies in the history of the development of labor".② According to F. Engels, K. Marx's "Theory of Practice"—"The Theses of Feuerbach" —is invaluable as the first document in which is deposited "the brilliant germ of the new world outlook"③ and is "the origin of historical materialism".④ It is for this reason that F. Engels publishes "Theses of Feuerbach" as an appendix to the book *On Feuerbach*, an overview of Marx's conception of history. Our analysis shows that F. Engels essentially regarded practical materialism as the theoretical basis of historical materialism. We agree with F. Engels's view. This view is actually what Marx has always emphasized. According to Marx, social life, in essence, is practical. Therefore, the materialist conception of history expounds the entire process of history standing "on the basis of real history", that is, expounding this conception of history "starting out from the material practice".⑤

We disagree with the viewpoint of "Western Marxism" that F. Engels did not see that the scientific concept of practice is the theoretical basis of historical materialism. However, we cannot fail to see that F. Engels did not explicitly

---

① Marx, K. & F. Engels: *Collected Works of Marx and Engels*, Vol. 42, Chin. ed., Beijing: People's Publishing House, 1979, p. 131.
② Marx, K. & F. Engels: *Collected Works of Marx and Engels*, Vol. 4, Chin. ed., Beijing: People's Publishing House, 1995, p. 258.
③ Ibid, p.213.
④ Ibid, p.721.
⑤ Marx, K. & F. Engels: *Collected Works of Marx and Engels*, Vol. 1, Chin. ed., Beijing: People's Publishing House, 1995, p. 92.

combine labor, production and practice to reveal the deep structure of practice. In *On Feuerbach* that "has given the most detailed account of historical materialism", F. Engels simply summed up practice as "experiment and industry".[①] At the same time, he fully expanded the view that practical materialism is the theoretical basis of historical materialism, even somewhat ignoring the significance of practice as the basic category of historical materialism. For example, in his later years, F. Engels emphasized "the theory of reciprocal action" that historical development is the result of the reciprocal action of many factors such as economy, politics and thought, in order to criticize economic materialism and clarify historical materialism. This undoubtedly has great theoretical significance. However, F. Engels did not further clarify the basis for the unification of historical materialism and historical dialectics. That is, he did not elaborate, based on practice, history and its development from the high perspective of the relation between the subject and object of history. In our opinion, this is one of the reasons why F. Engels's "late communication" failed to stop the spreading of vulgar "economic determinism" in the Second International. As the famous Yugoslavian philosopher Predrag Vranicki fairly remarks, the concept of practice not only overcomes that of contemplation, but also brings about a fundamental historical measure, which F. Engels did not sufficiently emphasize in these works, but which he never completely ignored.[②] It should be said that this evaluation is fair.

We have also noticed that there are also some discordant sounds in the entire symphony of F. Engels expounding the theoretical foundation of historical materialism. In *Anti-Duhring* and his late letters, F. Engels believed that the basic principle of historical materialism is sought not in philosophy, but in economics of the relevant epochs. This means that the theory of "economic inevitability" constitutes the theoretical foundation of historical materialism. We have serious reservations about this. This view of F. Engels cannot be said to be wrong, but at least it is not accurate. If historical materialism relied solely on economic research to establish its own theory of economic inevitability without further progress, then, historical materialism is at best an economic sociology. As a historical philosophy of dialectical materialism, historical materialism certainly is established with the aid of

---

① Marx, K. & F. Engels: *Collected Works of Marx and Engels*, Vol. 4, Chin. ed., Beijing: People's Publishing House, 2012, p. 232.
② Vranicki, Predrag: *History of Marxism*, Vol. 1, Chin. ed., Beijing: People's Publishing House, 1986, p. 244.

economic research, sought "in economics of the relevant epochs", and at the same time, Moe necessarily "in philosophy of the relevant epochs", making a philosophical abstraction and generalization of the research results of economics As historical facts tell us, Marx's view of practice is the product of the organic combination of economic analysis and philosophical critique and is the crystallization of Marx's criticism and inheritance of the labor theory of British classical economics and that of German classical philosophy. Marx starts out from practice and labor to reveal the law of dialectical movement of productivity and production relation, thus establishing the theoretical edifice of historical materialism. In our opinion, the theory of "economic inevitability" is an important viewpoint of historical materialism, while practical materialism is the theoretical foundation of historical materialism. The two are not contradictory, but the "economic inevitability" theory of historical materialism is based on the well-conceived concept of practice. F. Engels emphasis on the importance of "economic inevitability" itself is understandable, but he confuses the theoretical foundation of historical materialism with the important viewpoint of historical materialism establishing itself on this "foundation". How can F. Engels' "theory of reciprocal action", "theory of economic determinism" and "theory of practice as the core" be integrated and thereby work out what is theoretically ideal? It has been an important task for the later generations of Marxists.

II

F. Engels' viewpoints on the theoretical foundation of historical materialism is inherited by Plekhanov. However, Plekhanov pays more attention to F. Engels' second view, namely the theory of "economic inevitability". Of course, he also put forward some unique opinions.

Plekhanov argues that action explains to the dialectical materialist the historical development of rationality of social man, all his philosophy of practice is reduced to action, and dialectical materialism is the philosophy of action; and that when he acts on external nature in order to survive, man changes his own nature—a sentence containing the entire essence of Marx's theory of history. According to Plekhanov, materialism is boring, gloomy, and miserable if it disregards human social practice and specific human actions.[①] These views are incisive. If he had followed this direction

---

① *Selected Philosophical Works of Georgi Plekhanov*, Vol. 1, Chin. ed., Beijing: SDX Joint Publishing Company, 1959, p. 676, 747, 769.

indicated by them, Plekhanov might have revealed the theoretical foundation of historical materialism in a comprehensive and correct manner. Regrettably, however, he failed to treat these views as the theoretical foundation of historical materialism and fully develop these valuable views, but regarded practice as a category of epistemology, and considered, within this scope, practice first and foremost as the criterion for testing truth. Plekhanov's understanding of practice is narrow, and he failed to combine the concept of practice with that of history. Therefore, although he acknowledged the importance of the concept of practice in the historical materialism, it is still out of his field of vision when he discussed historical materialism in detail.

Plekhanov was critical, from the very beginning, of the view that historical materialism is economic materialism. He maintained that economic materialism is nothing more than claiming that economic factors, i.e., economic relations or economic structure, play an essential role in social life, that it is a necessary theoretical ladder for the transition from idealist conception of history to materialist conception of history, without excluding historical idealism. And he even thinks that economic relation itself is a "function" of human nature or human knowledge. In Plekhanov's view, the most important discovery of historical materialism is that economic structure or economic relations are actually determined by the state of productivity, and change due to changes in productivity; before using it to explain historical phenomena, economy itself needs to be explained first. Economy is not the final explanation of history, and "it is the result itself and the 'function' of productive forces." Therefore, historical materialism and economic materialism are essentially different. Plekhanov's critical exposition of economic materialism is precisely to explain the theoretical basis of historical materialism. According to his view, the productive forces are the ultimate explanation of history and historical materialism finds in the state of productivity a reasonable understanding of all historical phenomena, including economic relations and the concept of knowledge. The opportunity of the success of historical materialism lies in "explaining the evolution of social form and human thought, not from psychology, but from the perspective of political economy", "expounding the history of ideas from material conditions of human existence and from economic history".[①] His critique of economic materialism is quite brilliant, and he also has a considerable understanding of the difference between economic materialism and historical

---

[①] *Selected Philosophical Works of Georgi Plekhanov*, Vol. 2, Chin. ed., Beijing: SDX Joint Publishing Company, 1961, p. 186,387,747.

materialism. However, he did not see that the viewpoint of practice is the first and basic viewpoint of historical materialism. He only explained history and ideas from the perspective of economic history, which means that he took the theory of "economic inevitability" for the theoretical foundation of historical materialism.

We do not agree with this view of Plekhanov. Undoubtedly, the productive forces are the determinant of the economic relations, but are not the ultimate explanation of history. According to Marx's point of view, "The productive forces are the result of practical human energy."[1] The basic content of human practical activity is the reciprocal action between man and nature. "Reciprocal action is the true *causa finalis* of things .... Only from this universal reciprocal action do we arrive at the real causal relation."[2] In the conception of history, there is no more fundamental interaction than the reciprocal action between man and nature. This kind of reciprocal action constitutes the most basic practical activity, in which all history exists and develops. All historical phenomena, including the productive forces, come not only from such practical activity as the *"causa finalis"* of human history, but also can be correctly expounded only through this practice. In this sense, the history of historical philosophy cannot far antedate the emergence of the reciprocal action between man and nature, that is, practical activity. Plekhanov failed to understand Marx's point of view profoundly and failed to unify the theory of the productive forces with the well-conceived concept of practice, thus failing to correctly explain the reasons for the movement and development of the productive forces themselves. In order to avoid using the spirit or knowledge to explain the movement and development of the productive forces themselves, Plekhanov turned to geographical determinism and held that "the development of the productive forces themselves are determined by the attributes of the geographical environment surrounding humankind."[3] This shows that although he did not fall into the idealist view of history, he moved towards a naturalistic conception of history. In this way, in Plekhanov, there existed a strange phenomenon in the entire theoretical 'starry sky' of historical materialism: Although the orbit of the sun has been specified, what prevails in the interpretation of the entire

---

[1] Marx, K. & F. Engels: *Collected Works of Marx and Engels*, Vol. 27, Chin. ed., Beijing: People's Publishing House, 1972, p. 477.
[2] Engels, Friedrich: *Dialectics of Nature*, Chin. ed., Beijing: People's Publishing House, 1971, p. 192.
[3] *Selected Philosophical Works of Georgi Plekhanov*, Vol. 2, Chin. ed., Beijing: SDX Joint Publishing Company, 1962, p. 186, 387, 747.

celestial body is still Ptolemy's theory.

Plekhanov is a typical example: Both what he watched closely and what he ignored, both what led to his success and what led to his failure, have jointly proved a basic principle, that is, the theory of practice should be placed to the primary logical position of historical materialism, which is the "absolute command" of historical materialism.

III

When elaborating the principles of historical materialism, Lenin and Plekhanov walked on the same path; while understanding the theoretical foundation of historical materialism, they parted ways. This seems to be a contradiction, but after all, it is a historical fact.

Historical materialism is the application of the basic principle of materialism in the field of social history and the basis of historical materialism is philosophical materialism.[①] This is Lenin's basic thought on the theoretical basis of historical materialism. What are the fundamental characteristics of "philosophical materialism" in question? Lenin made no specific and definite statement about this. However, studying his writings leads us to know that he actually believes that "philosophical materialism" as the theoretical basis of historical materialism is practical materialism. First, he pointed out in his article "Karl Marx" that the fundamental reason why the old materialists including Feuerbach fell into idealism in the field of history was that "they do not grasp the significance of 'revolutionary,' 'practical' activity." This means that without bringing "critique of practice" into the analysis of human history, materialism would never have been "promoted" and implemented into the field of history. Second, he explored "the relationship between Hegel and historical materialism" in *Philosophical Notes* and criticized, extracted and developed Hegel's dialectical concept of practice and analyzed the structure of practice, that is, the process of interaction between the subject and the object through labor instruments as medium, pointing out the important characteristic of practice, namely an active material activity. According to his opinion, Hegel's concept of practice "has already had the germination of historical materialism". "Historical materialism, is the application and development of the seed of genius thought that has been in the state of

---

① *Selected Works of Lenin*, Vol. 2, Chin. ed., Beijing: People's Publishing House, 2012, p.226.

germination in Hegel's thinking."① His views have profound theoretical implications: Marx's concept of practice is the sublation and "development" of Hegelian concept of practice, and historical materialism is based on the materialist dialectical concept of practice.

What needs to be pointed out is that two major works of historical materialism— *Economic and Philosophical Manuscripts of 1844* and *German Ideology*, did not ever come into his sight. However, his insights on the theoretical basis of historical materialism are profound. Facts have proved that these ideas of him are the most energetic and should be conscientiously summarized and developed.

IV

"Familiarity is not necessarily true knowledge." Stalin was very familiar with Lenin, but did not really understand him, did not grasp the profound essence of his viewpoints just literally understanding the view that "historical materialism is the application of the principle of materialism in the field of social history." But Lukács truly understood the profound meaning of Lenin's views, and under Lenin's inspiration, he reexamined the theoretical basis of historical materialism② and showed a broad prospect for a correct understanding of this issue.

According to Stalin's view, historical materialism is the promotion and application of the principle of dialectical materialism in the field of social history. Dialectical materialism is such a theory: "its views on natural phenomena, its methods of studying natural phenomena, and its methods of cognizing these phenomena are dialectical; its explanation of natural phenomena and its understanding of the phenomena of nature, and its related theory are materialistic."③ Then it is not difficult to see that Stalin actually took a so-called dialectical materialist view of nature as the theoretical basis of the dialectical materialist view of history.

We cannot say that Stalin's viewpoint does not make any sense. After all, he has seen the connection between historical materialism and dialectical materialism. However, we cannot agree with his view. Regardless of whether this concept of nature can be regarded as the theoretical basis of the concept of history, this view contains double theoretical mistakes. First, it breaks the internal connection between theory

---

① *Notes on philosophy,* Beijing: People's Publishing House, 1974, p. 202, 348.
② Zhang Bolin(compiled): *Selected Translations of Lukacs' Essays on Philosophy and Aesthetics.* Beijing: China Social Science Press, 1985, p. 21-22.
③ *Selected Works of Stalin*, Vol.2, Chin. ed., Beijing: People's Publishing House, 1979, p.424.

and method. He did not understand that in dialectical materialism there is neither a materialism merely as a "theory" nor a dialectic merely as a method. Materialism is both a theory and a method. Dialectics is both a method and a theory. The integration of theory and method has an incomparably solid theoretical foundation and is deeply rooted in the inherent nature of dialectical materialism. Second, it confuses the essential difference between Marx's materialism and mechanical materialism. When discussing the "basic characteristics of Marxist philosophical materialism", Stalin actually showed us only the common ground between Marxist materialism and mechanical materialism, and failed to see that the essential feature of Marxist materialism is practical materialism. It is this theoretical particularity that distinguishes Marxist materialism from mechanical materialism and other forms of materialism. In *Dialectical Materialism and Historical Materialism*, Stalin quoted the sentence "Thinking and thinking material must not be separated, and material is the subject of all changes" as Marx's words. In fact, this is an obvious misquote. He regarded Marx's retelling of Hobbesian thought as Marx's own, the viewpoint Marx tended to criticize as the one he appreciated. In our opinion, this is not an accidental oversight, which shows that Stalin did not clearly recognize the essential difference between Marxist materialism and mechanical materialism.

In short, the dialectical materialism understood by Stalin is essentially a kind of view of nature in which theory and method are separated, materialism and dialectics are simply put together, displaying a strong color of mechanical materialism. With such a kind of "dialectical materialism" as its theoretical basis, historical materialism will inevitably be rendered "abnormal": There disappears what Marx has paid great attention to between man and nature, namely "material transformation" "energy transformation" and "transformation between material and concept". The development of production methods has become a mysterious movement; and the law of history has become a pre-made "absolute plan", independent of human activity. Stalin attempted to expound historical materialism in a popular way, but he simply understood historical materialism and its theoretical basis, and reached the logic end on this path.

If Stalin's understanding of the theoretical basis of historical materialism has been regarded as the only choice, then Lukacs' understanding of it has aroused heated debate. Before commenting on Lukács' views, we need to clarify two issues. First, is Lukács a Marxist or a "Western Marxist"? To illustrate this, we can cite a passage of "Outline for the Centenary of the Birth of George Lukacs" by the Hungarian

Socialist Workers Party. "Since he became a communist and a Marxist, until the end of his life, Lukács has unswervingly defended and continued to develop the classic legacy of Marxism-Leninism, consolidating and reforming its historical foundation of dialectical materialism." "George Lukács is an outstanding representative of a great Marxist-Leninist thought in the 20th century."[①] We agree with this assertion. In the following discussion, we will consider Lukács as a Marxist. Second, his expositions on the theoretical basis of historical materialism can be divided into early and later periods. Then, which should prevail, his earlier exposition or the later one? In the early days, he adopted the theory of "historical totality" as the theoretical basis of historical materialism. According to him, the so-called category of totality is "the general superiority of the whole to the part", meaning that any part is meaningful only when it is connected with the whole. "Only when the isolated facts in social life are regarded as some aspects of the historical process and included in the totality can the knowledge of the facts become the knowledge of reality." Therefore, "In historical interpretation, what constitutes the decisive difference between Marxism and science on bourgeois is not the principle that economic motivation takes the first place, but the view of totality."[②] This view of Lukács is indeed insightful and meaningful for opposing the vulgarization theory of the Second International. However, he "overcorrected". He criticized the vulgar economic determinism, but exaggerated the role of proletarian consciousness, so that the theory of "historical totality" was shrouded in shadow of idealism. He emphasized historical dialectics but denied dialectics of nature, which made the practical category lack the real content, namely material exchange between man and nature. Since the 1930s, he has repeatedly criticized his mistakes and tried to correct them. He "started everything from scratch" and deeply understood "Marx's discourse on objectivity as the basic material attribute of all things and relations" and restored the reputation for dialectics of nature, taking it as a necessary prerequisite for the historical ontology. His self-criticism is touching, and his insights are quite profound. For this reason, when we comment on Lukács' understanding of the theoretical basis of historical materialism, we use his later exposition as a blueprint.

According to Lukacs, human labor is always teleological—it sets a goal, and

---

① *Research Materials on the History of International Communist Movement* (14). Beijing: People's Publishing House, 1985, p. 86, 87.
② *Lukács,* Georg: *History and Class Consciousness,* Eng. ed., tran. by Rodney Livingstone, The MIT Press, 1972.

this goal is the result of choice. Therefore, human labor expresses human freedom. But the existence of this freedom only manifests itself in setting into motion the objective natural forces which subject themselves to the law of causality of the material world.① That is to say, labor contains the human purpose and there are objective material premises. It is an active, objective material activity that transforms nature. Besides, he also clearly realized that labor is the original form and foundation of practice. Obviously, he has incorporated the material transformation between man and nature and between material and idea into the scope of practice, and has defined practice as actual human activity to transform nature and society, so that the concept of practice begets real content. Lukács' views are completely consistent with Marx's. In "Economic Manuscripts of 1861-63", K. Marx pointed out that labor is a purposeful activity of possessing natural materials.② This definition has been repeated by him more than once and has been written into the final version of *Capital*. He even understood the subjective conditions of production as the labor force displayed purposefully.③ He also combines labor and practice and through analyzing the processes and elements of labor, he reveals the most essential feature of practice, that is, practice as the perceptual material human activity of transforming the objective world. In his view, practice is the basis of how man created himself and historically developed, and of the entire human society. If history is the totality of the interaction between the subject and the object and the process of dialectical movement, then the actual carrier and foundation of such interaction and dialectical movement are practical human activity. Practice is also the totality of history. Lukács' argument reminds us of K. Marx's famous saying: "The coincidence of the changing of circumstances and of human activity or self-change [Selbstveränderung] can be conceived and rationally understood only as revolutionary practice." "All social life is essentially practical."

Because of a correct understanding of practice and its status in social history Lukács strongly emphasized "material practice" and "labor" are the basic categories of historical materialism, and explicitly regarded practical materialism as the theoretical basis of historical materialism, linking society with nature through the category of practice, trying to establish a historical "practical ontology". The concept

---

① *Lukacs' Autobiography*, Beijing: Social Sciences Literature Press, 1986, p. 203, 294.
② Marx, K. & F. Engels: *Collected Works of Marx and Engels*, Vol.47, Chin. ed., Beijing: People's Publishing House, 1979, p. 55.
③ Marx, K. & F. Engels: *Collected Works of Marx and Engels*, Vol.49, Chin. ed., Beijing: People's Publishing House, 1982, p. 38.

of labor is the key to such analysis. Following K. Marx's thinking, Lukács conceived of ontology as philosophy itself, but philosophy based on history ... The essence of human society is the purposeful human actions, that is, labor, which is the most important new category because it includes everything.[①] According to Lukacs's theory, it is K. Marx's creation of a well-conceived concept of practice that made it possible that K. Marx's theoretical work directly follows the theoretical clues left by Hegel, and at the same time, it has realized a revolutionary change in Hegel's philosophy, which finally made the light of materialism shine into the depths of history. The Marxist view of labor has managed to do this because it gives content to the material changes of society and nature, thus giving content to the relationship between labor categories and their natural premises, and also making the changes resulting from the changes in the premises of the social development of labor have content.[②] In this way, Lukács turned back to Marxism and restored the original appearance of the theoretical foundation of historical materialism.

V

So far, we have commented on the understanding of the theoretical basis of historical materialism by F. Engels, Lenin, Stalin, Plekhanov, and Lukács. In the meantime, we also have discussed K. Marx's views on this issue, when necessary. Now, we summarize what we have been after and make the following conclusions:

According to Marx's point of view, activity for itself is "the material practical activity" of human beings to transform the external world. It is practice that provides the ultimate motivation for human self-existence and self-development while providing a realistic basis for him to change, create and truly understand the world of objects. Practice is the basis and foundation for the existence of the entire human world. Intuitive materialism has fallen into idealism in the field of history for the fundamental reason that perception is not understood as practical activity; practical materialism is created and enabled K. Marx to stand on the commanding height of the times. He took practical materialism as the theoretical basis of the conception of history, thereby finally liberating history from the fence of idealism, eliminating the myth of the opposition between mental history and material nature, and filling the gap between humanism and scientism. Social life is essentially practical. If practical

---

① *Lukács' Autobiography*, Chin. ed., Beijing: Social Sciences Literature Press, 1986, p. 203, 294.
② *Lukács' Essays on Literature*, Vol. 1, Chin. ed., Beijing: China Social Sciences Press, 1980, p.432.

problems are restricted only to the scope of epistemology and excluded from history, then this will inevitably lead to a reverse displacement of the materialist conception of history, that is, to economic materialism and finally to historical idealism. Therefore, it is necessary to introduce the concept of practice into the conception of history as the theoretical basis of the latter. Marx defines historical materialism as the expounding of any concept from material practice, that is, starting from material practice, describing the entire process of history and the reciprocal action between various aspects of this process.[①]

It had been a long time before Marx's profound insights attracted people's attention. In his understanding of the theoretical basis of historical materialism, F. Engels is basically correct, but there are still something inaccurate; Plekhanov did have profound points, but he also made an incorrect understanding; Stalin pushed the incorrect understanding to the extreme and totally excluded the concept of practice from historical materialism, thereby abandoning K. Marx's epoch-making contribution to a considerable extent, which is an astonishing theoretical regression in the history of Marxist philosophy. Lenin was sharp-eyed for he foreshadowed the new ideas of solving the problems, though his expositions are rare. Lukacs walked on the path to truth and returned to K. Marx's historical materialism at a high level, which provided us with a broad thinking space for a comprehensive and in-depth understanding of the theoretical basis of historical materialism.

Taking the concept of practice as the theoretical basis of historical materialism does not result from external needs, but from the leading logic of historical materialism itself. It has a solid theoretical and practical basis, deeply rooted in the intrinsic nature of this well-conceived conception of history. "Historical materialism" which excludes the concept of practice or merely uses it as a general view has exposed various difficulties and weaknesses. This has been proved by practice impotent to meet the requirements of the times. For this reason, some scholars have returned to practical materialism and tried to "reconstruct" historical materialism on the basis of a well-conceived concept of practice. What is striking is that this kind of "reconstruction" is in the ascendant, showing great vitality in various "constructions". It can be predicted that historical materialism which is characterized by the well-conceived concept of practice will again become an important topic for philosophers in the near future.

[①] Marx, K. & F. Engels: *Collected Works of Marx and Engels*, Vol. 21, Chin. ed., Beijing: People's Publishing House, 1960, p. 43.

On the Principle of Marxist Subjectivity and Its Practical Significance*

Since the Third Plenary Session of the 11th CPC Central Committee, held from Dec 18 to 22, 1978, the Party has broken through the old rigid mode of thinking, captured the pulsation of the spirit of the times, refined its essence, and tried to create a new mode of thinking characteristic of the times. It is the true exploration and harvest of our philosophical theory in the past ten years, during which great changes have taken place in all fields and aspects of China's social life. One of the important features of the new spirit and new mode of thinking associated with these changes is the reestablishment and implementation of the Marxist principle of subjectivity.

I. Correctly understand Marxist principle of subjectivity

The so-called principle of subjectivity is, in general, the principle of recognizing, valuing and upholding the status and role of the subject in practical and cognitive activity.

The subject and the object are a pair of relational opposites in the objective activity of mankind. There is a kind of "law of correlation" between the two: only when certain objective relations (such as practice and cognition) are formed between human beings and objects and between human beings, can they be the subject and the object. Therefore, the concepts of the subject and the object are meaningless to leave the concrete objective relationship and lose any of them. On this premise, we will naturally ask further questions as follows: Which side is in the guiding and leading position in the interaction between the subject and the object? To put more definitely, what position do the structure, characteristics and function of the subject occupy here? This is the so-called "the problem concerning subjectivity". Different

---

① Originally published in *Academic Journal of Zhongzhou,* 1988(6).

philosophies have different answers to this question, among which the different ways of making positive conclusions about the status and function of the subject constitute the essentially different principle of subjectivity.

The Marxist principle of subjectivity is based on the unification of dialectical materialism and historical materialism—the cornerstone of "practical materialism". Its basic content is most concentrated in K. Marx's theses -- "Theses of Feuerbach", especially in its first article. He pointed out that the understanding of "the thing, reality, sensuousness" in well-conceived "practical materialism" does not focus only on the form of the object or of contemplation, but understand them "as sensuous human activity, practice", "subjectively".[1] Lenin also expressed this principle in the same explicit language: all human practice must be "included in the complete 'definition' of things".[2] Practice is the objective material activity of mankind. In practice, on the one hand, the subject must be geared to the needs of the object, pay attention to the role or effect of the object, and act according to the nature and laws of the object, that is, understand and transform the world according to the true features of the world (including the person as the object); on the other hand, what is more important is that the subject always starts from himself, understands and transforms the object, and the world according to his ability, way, needs and scale. Therefore, in any cognition and practice, there objectively exists a "subjectivity effect". From the former side arises the principle of objectivity; from the latter side arises the principle of subjectivity. Both K. Marx and Lenin did not deny the former, but they emphasized the influence of the latter on the former, reminding people that the understanding and theoretical generalization ("definition") of objects and things cannot be achieved in isolation from the subjective factors, so the principle of subjectivity should be consciously implemented, which has universal significance in epistemology.

To fully grasp the Marxist principle of subjectivity, we should, while drawing a line from previous and current misconceptions, first and foremost fully understand the provisions and requirements as follows:

First, it is a principle that fully recognizes and reveals subjectivity effect. It is a conclusion of true dialectical materialism that things should be understood from the aspects of the subject and of human practice. In this case, it is incompatible

---

[1] Central Translation and Compilation Bureau: *Feuerbach*, Chin. ed., Beijing: People's Publishing House, 1988, p.87.
[2] *Selected Works of Lenin*, Vol.4, Chin. ed., Beijing: People's Publishing House, 1995, p.419.

with a certain traditional prejudice that interprets materialism as "objectivism". This prejudice manifests itself as mistakenly applying the correct basic principle of materialism that "existence is primary and thinking is secondary" is mistakenly applied to the relationship between the subject and the object, and arrived at such a conclusion of fatalism that violates facts as "the object is primary while the subject is secondary, and the object determines the subject." In fact, this is not only far away from Marxist practical materialism, it is also a retrogression or stagnation, compared with the old and general materialism. This kind of "objectivist" prejudice has long restricted the deep inquiry into subjectivity.

Second, it is an objectivity principle. Here in Marxism, subjectivity and objectivity are not antagonistic concepts. The subject, as a real person and his group under various circumstances, is, above all, an objective existence — the social being. It is not that people's social consciousness determines their social existence, but that their social existence determines their consciousness. Therefore, the Marxist principle of subjectivity involves social, historical and objective understanding of human subjectivity. If subjectivity is attributed to human spirit, consciousness, subjectivity, ignoring human social materiality, social existence and the objectivity of their relations, it is not the way of historical materialism or Marxism, but the way of historical idealism.

Third, it is a principle that requires a specific analysis of the subject. "Subject" is not a general abstraction or entity, but a relational category. Therefore, it is necessary to confirm who is the subject in the specific object relation, grasp the concrete structure, function, characteristic and role of the subject, and explore the interrelationship between subjects at different levels, and cannot be abstracted. In theoretical research, there are two extremes as far as generalization of a special subject at a particular relationship level is concerned: one extreme is to treat the category subject-human or group subject-society, class, nation, etc. as the only "subject"; the other is to regard the individual subject—the individual—as the only "subject". If these two extremes are mutually exclusive or alternative, it leads either to obliteration of individuals and individuality, or lead to individualism and liberalism while denying the collective and society, which is contrary to the spiritual essence of the Marxist principle of subjectivity. This principle precisely shows that there are many different levels and aspects of the subject-object relation in the world and in social life, each relation having its own specific subject. Only by correctly and fully understanding the respective characteristics and functions of each subject can we profoundly explain the existence and development of its relation, without confusing or replacing different relations and their subjects.

Fourth, it is a principle that emphasizes the unity of human right and responsibility. To acknowledge the specific status and role of the subject is precisely to judiciously establish the boundaries between power and responsibility that people should and can bear in their own practice and cognition and to rationally unite the two. If one misunderstands the principle of subjectivity as the one which allows people to do whatever they want to do, or to satisfy their greed for power without taking on responsibility, even to the degree of "absolute freedom of will", he or she, at least, is caught in a one-sided imagination. Both power and responsibility come from actual status and role of the subject, and should not be separated from each other. In face of the object, the power of the subject is where the responsibility lies, and vice versa. Therefore, the first enlightenment that any real subject (human, society, class, and individual) can get from the principle of subjectivity is to consciously recognize his power and responsibility and their unity, and not others. In this sense, the principle of subjectivity can also be said to be the principle of unity between strengthening the self-construction of the subject and giving full play to the subject's initiative to transform the world.

Fifthly, Marxism has its own principle of subjectivity, which does not mean that it denies the principle of objectivity. The mutual restriction and mutual complementation between the two can ensure that cognition and practice are fruitful. They have their own focuses and functions, and must be followed in our thinking and work. However, comparatively speaking, especially under the contemporary historical conditions, the principle of subjectivity has a more profound and positive theoretical and practical significance.

II. Establish the profound practical significance of "subjective thinking"

Applying the Marxist principle of subjectivity to think, understand, make decisions, and evaluate means consciously mastering and applying dialectical materialism and historical materialism thinking at a new height. This is of great significance for people who have been fettered by outdated and rigid ideas for a long time to emancipate their minds and change their way of thinking. It is an important spiritual guarantee and ideological weapon for China's current reform and construction.

1.The "theory of the primary stage" is the product of correct self-awareness of social subjects in China

The process from putting forward the question of national condition to answering it is not just a process of understanding "the object", as some people understand. In a more profound substantive sense, it is a real self-awareness of the social subject in China. This can be found by reviewing the history of more than 30 years: Such facts concerning the "objective" aspects of China's national condition— "a long history, vast territory, abundant resources, a large population, poverty and backwardness" — is not the basis that distinguishes the theory of "three red flag"[①] of the 1950s and the theory of "opposing capitalist restoration" between the 1960s and 1970s from the theory of the primary stage of socialism today. The basis that distinguishes today's theory from yesterday's "Left" theory lies in the different answers to the following questions: "Where is our society and our country in the sequence of historical development?" "What kind of society is ours? what kind of people are ours? What do we need? and what can we do and what can we not do now?" and so on. In short, all these questions can be boiled down to a single question: "What are the state, need and capability of our country, society and nation as the subject of the socialist cause?" Having summarized the painful lessons of past mistakes and setbacks, we know that the very reason for such mistakes and setbacks is that in the backward state of poverty and blankness, we once forgot that the country was a society born of semi-feudal and semi-colonial country, and, consequently, took a series of decisions that utterly ignored the reality of the subject, starting out only from the abstract concept that "socialism is more advanced than capitalist only to adopt a series of decisions that transcended the reality of the subject". This just shows us that just knowing how the object is cannot guarantee that we can correctly decide what we should do; Only when we have a deeper and more comprehensive understanding of ourselves as the subject, can we make the right choice. Therefore, without regard for its value in making a correct cognition of national condition, the theory of the primary stage of socialism cannot be truly and profoundly understood and correctly implemented.

This theory has fundamental significance for the current reform in China and the entire process of modernization, which proves the methodological significance

---

[①] In 1958, the CPC put forward the general line of socialist construction, that is, "build socialism through gathering up all forces and striving for the best, so as to achieve greater, faster, better and more economical results, which is commonly known as the "three red flags," together with the "Great Leap Forward" Movement and people's commune. —Tr.

of establishing subjective thinking. Some people may disagree with this, for we can often hear such views that the main reason why the socialist construction in China has suffered twists and turns during the past 30 years is that it has overemphasized human subjectivity and initiative, but has not paid enough attention to and implemented the principle of objectivity. Of course, this view is certainly not wrong, but its summarization of past experience and lessons is not methodologically profound enough, and the conclusion drawn from it thereby is even more negative and reductive. It seems that the reason why we were often frustrated is just how little we knew about the object. Why did we know so little? It obviously involves the factors of us as the subject. Of course, it is right to stress that we should respect the restriction of the object and its nature and laws on human beings. However, the correct treatment of the object is the subject's power and responsibility, so the subject's critical reflection on itself cannot be lacking. In the activities of socialist construction for more than 30 years, there is not so much overemphasis on subjectivity and human initiative as failure to understand subjectivity for a long period of time or as the lack of a clear understanding of the status, role and effect of the subject in the development of things and in all activities, or as inadequacy of talk and understanding of subjectivity. One of the most important reasons why we were frustrated in the past is precisely because we were affected by the concept that "the object determines the subject" and do not recognize or cannot face up to the involvement of us (as the subject) in any understanding of the subject. Instead, we conclude that it was caused only by the object. This provided an excuse for all irresponsible behaviors of "paying tuition fee but not knowing well". At present, China is carrying out a comprehensive reform involving politics, economy, culture and other fields in many aspects. In the final analysis, it is the social subject who transforms and changes its own structure, ability and situation. Therefore, as the social subjects in the primary stage of socialism, we need to have a clear understanding of our own situation, otherwise it will be difficult to surpass ourselves, and actively and creatively engage in the cause of building socialism so as to ensure the steady and rapid development of socialist construction.

2. The essence of socialist democracy is to realize the role of the people as a dominant player

The Marxist principle of subjectivity particularly emphasizes the importance of respecting and promoting the status and role of the dominant player in social development. This, in terms of political and organizational systems of socialism, calls for the establishment of a highly socialist democracy.

Whether it be in the initial stage of socialist society or in its intermediate stage or even in an advanced stage, the people being the masters of the country is one of the fundamental signs. The so-called "being masters of the country", refers to becoming the subject of social possession, management, decision-making, implementation, inspection, supervision and evaluation. Theoretically speaking, the socialist system ended the rule of the minority of exploiters and realized the fundamental equality of the majority of people. Citizens shared and controlled the means of production, thus naturally becoming the dominant player of social politics. In this sense, the socialist democratic system is essentially a new "highest-type" democracy, which is extensive and more authentic than bourgeois democracy. However, there is a big gap between the reality of China and the essence of this theory for two main reasons. At present, the democratic system in which people are the masters of the country has been established, but it is not yet sound enough. Both the breadth of democratic development (the scope of democratic implementation) and its depth (the conditions and extent of the people's management of the country and society) are inadequate. Bureaucracy, excessive concentration of power and patriarchy are still widespread. The democratization of the political life of the Party and the country, the democratization of economic management and of the entire social life have yet to be further developed. One of the main reasons for these two phenomena is that limited by the objective historical conditions of the country, the level of democratic quality is not high. The so-called democratic quality includes two aspects: one referring to the degree of self-consciousness of one's status and role; the other referring to the ability to supervise the political life of the country and society and to participate in political discussions and management. As China had been under the autocratic rule of feudal society for a long time, and lacked democratic tradition, weak democratic consciousness and requirements became a common phenomenon. The weak subjective foundation of democratization determines that China's socialist democratic construction cannot be improved and perfected quickly due to the situation of the subject itself. Changing this situation, that is, improving the quality of the democratized subject and constructing a social foundation suitable for democratization, is the primary prerequisite for the construction of socialist democratization.

The other reason is the subjective error that occurs when the inner contradictions are dealt with in the democratic process. Democracy is actually the power of the members of a certain society or group to handle with its internal affairs. Therefore, the subject of any democratic system is always the union of many individuals within a certain range which is the synthesis of their power, will, and opinions. "The minority obeys the majority" and "bottom-up authorization" are the basic forms of democracy. The objects of democracy, that is, the objects of management through democracy, are the public affairs of society and individuals within the scope of democracy. In this way, individuals may have two different identities under the democratic system: the subject and the object. On the one hand, the citizens of socialist countries are the subjects of democratic system; on the other hand, as the subjects of individual behaviors, they are the target of democratic management, that is, the object. This dual identity of the individual is a contradiction that is inevitably encountered in the construction of democracy in general and the construction of socialist democracy in particular. The purpose of democratic construction is precisely to make these two identities organically and fully unified, that is, to achieve that the people themselves can fully manage themselves.

The fundamental mistake of the past is that in cognition and action, people were often regarded as the target and the object of democracy, which led to the separation and opposition of the two identities. Its main manifestation is: not advocating the people to implement democracy and improving the democratic system, but emphasizing "exercising democracy among the people" from above; not taking concentration as the means and form of democracy (Acting in accordance with "The minority obeys the majority" is the part of concentrating opinions in the democratic process), but taking it for the form of "guidance" higher than democracy. No efficient forms that are conducive to the people's rights to be informed, to participate, to discuss state affairs, and to make decisions, but the means of directly managing and intervening the people's personal thoughts and behaviors which were comparatively effective; administrative power which should be essentially granted by the bottom to the top is actually granted by the top to the bottom, with a *de facto* incoordination between these two ways, and so on. The above-mentioned erroneous handling is related not only to the limitations of specific historical conditions, but also to the failure to fully understand the subjective characteristics of democracy in theory and ideology

It is told by the Marxist principle of subjectivity that the fundamental task and goal of the democratization of socialism lies in fully relying on the people to fully implement their status as the subjects, enabling, through economic, political and other social reforms, the people to become the subject in departments in various fields, with the unity of responsibility, power and interests achieved, not just becoming the object. Only by making people feel that they are the *de facto* subject not only in the fundamental essence but also in the specific form, can they deepen their understanding of subjectivity, democracy, power and responsibility, raise their awareness of the need to participate, execute, supervise and manage, and intensify their legal and moral consciousness, can socialist democracy be made highly sound.

3.Enhancing the consciousness of national subject is the guarantee for the success of China's reform and construction

The Marxist principle of subjectivity not only provides us with methodological principles for understanding the world and formulating guidelines and policies, but also advocates a kind of ethos for transforming the world that is most progressive, vigorous and cohesive, which constitutes an admirable mental condition. Today, we must judiciously and conscientiously foster the spirit of the Chinese nation as the main body of socialist construction, uniting as one, working with one heart, and winning the victory of reform and construction through independent and arduous struggle.

The basis for fostering the spirit of the Chinese nation as the main body of socialist construction consists in consciously and fully realizing that the major force of the country's reform and socialist modernization is a whole including all nationalities, all strata and every citizen in the country, namely the entire Chinese nation, the socialist motherland, not any specific nationality, class, stratum or individual. Any group or individual is qualified to serve as the major force of this cause only if they stand in this position and actually serve the cause of revitalizing the entire nation. Only this major force can undertake this great cause. Therefore, in order to succeed in reform and construction, we must rely on the establishment and development of the awareness of the position of the people as masters of their own destiny.

"Carrying forward the spirit of the Chinese nation as the main body of socialist construction" is not an empty and abstract slogan. It has rich and concrete underlying messages. In the thinking and conduct currently prevailing in the country, there are many manifestations that distorted and undermined this spirit, such as the sense of national inferiority characterized by national traditional cultural nihilism and blind worship of foreign countries; arrogance and conservative attitude characterized by the lack of modern appeal and refusal to criticize tradition; the so-called "love of migratory birds" with which the people involved treat the cause of their motherland as if they were bystanders, in "spectator psychology", unconfident in the face of difficulties, evading reality, to name just a few. It is believed that among them, the most significant and deepest impact at present, and therefore the most noteworthy is the tendency of "decomposition of subjectivity" which has existed in society.

There are mainly two interrelated forms of "decomposition of subjectivity" in thinking and conduct: "individualization of power" and "short-term behavior". The former means that the power originally belonging to the nation and the social subject was changed into the power of individuals or small groups of individuals. Those who should exercise power on behalf of the nation and the social subject in fact exercised power only for individuals or groups of local people, only bearing the responsibility for individual (local) subjects, not for the overall subject (nation and society). It is accompanied by the "short-term" of goals and behaviors: since the actual subjects are individual and limited, the goals and behaviors tend to shift from focusing only on the local interests to only focusing on the immediate interests, not on the long-term interests, especially the long-term interests of the nation and society. The "individualization of power" causes the subject to be spatially decomposed, and "short-term behavior" causes the subject to be temporally decomposed. The inevitable consequence of the "decomposition of subjectivity" is the formation of "subject uncertainty" and "subject displacement" of many social public powers and affairs, which, in fact, has nurtured and strengthened various bad habits and corruption. The "bureaucracy" in manifestation of using public fund for food, drink and travel power to seek personal gain, corruption and bribery, cronyism, relationship-based policy, protectionism of local or small groups and using administrative power to do business, detrimental behaviors such as embezzling public funds for personal use, such as food, drink and travel; the extravagant and wasteful style through keeping up with the joneses; power obsession but irresponsibility; unhealthy tendencies such as "pulling some strings", "doing favors", all these are actually nothing but the result of some people turning the public power in their hand into private power. This is also related to the ideological roots of the malformed "eagerness for quick success and instant benefits", and various short-term behaviors such as "killing chickens to get eggs" and "exhausting the moss to fish" just in order to achieve "brilliant results" during one's tenure.

The phenomenon of "decomposition of subjectivity" arises from the imperfect and unreasonable social system, and from the weakness of people's overall subject consciousness. The superposition and mutual transformation of these two reasons are prone to bring about a certain vicious circle, which will cause serious harm to the great cause of revitalizing China. To fundamentally eliminate and even prevent its harm, it is necessary to manage the economic environment, rectify the economic order, and comprehensively deepen reforms, so that the corresponding powers and responsibilities of the subject can be implemented at various levels, in an effective and balanced manner. At the same time, it is necessary to strengthen the promotion, publicity and education of the consciousness of the whole nation as the principal role.

Speaking of promoting this consciousness, there are still some philosophical and theoretical issues that need to be clarified. For example, in recent years, some comrades in the academic circle have pointed out that in the traditional Chinese feudal culture, there was a sense of "society orientation" and everything was based on "society" (actually a ruling class made up of a small number of people in the name of society), ignoring individuals and denying individuality in social life, which is a backward concept. Today, what should be advocated is the concept of "individual orientation," that is, to achieve social development and progress on the basis of fully liberating individuals and developing individuality. It cannot be denied that some of these ideas contained some reasonable and positive factors, which also produced a certain good influence. However, we believe that simply advocating "substituting the individual orientation for society orientation" is not only one-sided in theory, but also improper in the current historical practice of Chinese society.

In any social life of each historical era, what is "oriented" has been historically and concretely changing, and there is no fixed and eternal absolute formula. The development from the "society-oriented" system in which feudalism uses patriarchal clan system as its essence to deny human of individuality to the "individual-oriented" system in which capitalism takes private economic interests as its essence, is just a social and cultural phenomenon formed under a certain historical condition. From the perspective of the overall development of the entire human history, they are not the only two unique forms of orientation, not the alternative poles from which people can "choose one." In fact, the development of modern society has already broken through a single orientation system that jumps between the two poles, but has moved toward a diversified and multi-polarized "subject-oriented" system, which means, in a multi-level, multi-faceted and multi-relational social life, whoever is the subject in a certain relationship determines the basis of orientation in it, rather than universalizing the status of a particular subject and thus singularizing the orientation of the whole society. It is the same case with the contemporary global issues (ecology, energy, peace, population, etc.) which must be based on humankind in all parts of the world, with the issue of class struggle which can only be class-oriented, with the issue of ethnicity which should be nationality-oriented, and with the issues concerning with individuals which should be individual-oriented. The subjects at different levels and in different sides cannot be confused and replaced. Therefore, "orientation" is not absolutized in a single, unique sense. Facts have proved that intentional or unintentional confusion of different subjects and orientations is just one of the important reasons for decision-making and selection and leading to confusion.

The "subject-oriented" thinking method should first identify the specific subjects in different social relations (this will make it clear that individuals, groups, and society are the subjects of social relations and social activities at different levels), and thus further recognize the status of each subject in their respective levels and scopes. In short, it is a specific analysis of the "ontology", rather than a simple generalization. For example, as for the matters that are purely personal activities and individuality development, respect must be paid to the status of the individual as the subject, who cannot be replaced by others, groups, and society, or even violently interfered. However, when an individual acts merely as a member of a common subject, as one part of a whole, the group subject should be taken as the orientation, not the individual as the orientation. If the leading officials of the state, the civil servants of social organizations, and the workers in specific links of the large-scale industrial production system are all individual-oriented, and are only responsible for personal interests, interest and individuality, but treat the overall power and responsibility as aliens, then what result will it lead to? It is hard to imagine.

Therefore, establishing the concept of "subject orientation" is not only the theoretical basis for emancipating the mind, promoting the diversification of social life, and promoting the liberation of individuality and the free development of individuals, but also strengthening the reasonable social connections and the construction of the wholeness and unity of the country, nation and society, the necessary philosophical premise for judiciously and rationally combining these two aspects. Here, any one-sided or extreme attitude that placed the nation in sharp opposition to the individual is incompatible with the times and the reality. The correct understanding and handling of the relationship between the two is precisely the awareness that revolutionaries and builders of the present age should at least have.

The spirit of the Chinese nation as the main body of socialist construction can be carried forward consciously and effectively unless it is understood judiciously and comprehensively. With the main body of the society as a whole, this spirit requires all members to cooperate closely, have one heart and one mind, and have the will to bear any difficulties and risks as one person; to require the nation as a whole to form its own image, independent and self-reliant. All this is not contradictory to the full development of the vast majority of individuals within the country, the nation and the society, the prosperity of democracy, freedom, science and culture, and the enrichment of people's personalities and health. They are complementary, and mutually reinforcing. Achieving this ideal combination also means the creation of a new type of subject in the approaching middle and high stages of socialism. Therefore, it is of far-reaching historical significance to take the continuous enhancement of the consciousness of the nation as the main body and the carrying-forward of the spirit of the Chinese nation as the main body of socialism as the combination of the necessary condition and the internal goal of the current reform and construction.

Social Transformation and Trend of Chinese Philosophy in the 21st Century*

I. Social transformation and social context of the development of Chinese philosophy in the 21st century

The socialist modernization construction characterized by reform and opening up has brought about tremendous and profound changes in Chinese society. As some scholars have pointed out, since entering the modern history, Chinese society has never been so vigorous as it is today, and the process of the modernization in Chinese society has never progressed as rapidly as it is today, moving forward with each passing day. Moreover, we believe that the practice of today's China aims at building a socialist market system which is by far the most profound and extensive change in Chinese history. Here we use the concept of "social transformation" to properly reflect and summarize the connotation and characteristics of this change. From sociological point of view, the Chinese society in transition has the following characteristics:

First of all, in the period of social transformation, the old and new systems are stuck together. The old economic system and its operating mechanism have not yet lost the subjective and objective conditions for its existence, and will inevitably become a huge obstacle to the establishment and operation of the new system. This contradiction in the economic system not only directly affects economic development, but also affects the development of politics, culture, and even the whole society on a more profound level. Second, during the period of social transformation, the differentiation of interests was revealed. Benefit distribution breaks free from the shackles of a highly centralized traditional planning management system and flows along the law of competition, which results in the adjustment of the interests

---

* Originally published in *Academia Bimestrie* (《学海》), 2000 (2).

of members of the society. Some people, driven by interests, take undue advantage of certain gaps and loopholes in the transition between the old and the new system, grabbing benefits through unfair competition or means, and even appropriate public power to illegally participate in commodity management activities for personal gain, thus resulting in contradictions and conflicts of interests. Such contradictions not only directly affect the actual interests and reform "carrying capacity" of a considerable number of social members, but also profoundly affects the superstructure, particularly the political power system and its operation mechanism, and has a huge impact on social stability and development. Third, in the period of social transformation, value orientation is different. The market economy is turbulent with complex and diverse value pursuits. Social members of different status, different levels, different interests, and different experiences will show different value-judging standards and value goal pursuits for any change. They will show different attitudes towards or responses to the same social phenomenon. Such differences or contradictions in value orientation not only directly affects people's tolerance and adaptability to economic reform, but also more profoundly affects people's recognition and participation in political system reforms and political development, thus affecting political stability and social coordination on a broader level. Fourth, during the period of social transformation, cultural collisions have intensified. Regarding the various events and contradictions in the social transformation, members of society hold different cultural perspectives. The influx of a large number of Western cultures is in harmony with contemporary Chinese culture, but some parts also have sharp contradictions with traditional culture, so there emerges a strong contrast of cultural concepts among some social members. Such contradiction in cultural concepts not only directly affects people's value choices for social transformation and social development, but also may affect national interests.[①]

In general, during the period of social transformation, social conflicts may increase due to changes in the structure of social professional groups, differentiation and conflict of interests, and differentiation and contradictions of interests which have been sharpened by the changes in social and economic systems.

The *status quo* and characteristics of social transformation is inevitably reflected in the evolution of philosophical thought. From a philosophical point of view,

---

① Bao Xinjian(包心鉴): "On the Political Development in the Period of Social Transformation in China" (《论中国社会转型时期的政治发展》), *Xinhua Digest*, 1996(10).

people's concepts and mentality during the period of social transformation are also in unprecedented fission and shock. To accelerate development, we must deepen reforms, which will inevitably mean transforming the old system, mechanism, order and concepts. This will inevitably increase social instability during the social transformation. Therefore, how to properly handle and coordinate the relationship between reform, development and stability is a fundamental one with overall strategic significance in the entire process of social transformation and modernization. The most notable feature of people's ideas during the social transformation is their instability in conflicts and changes, which tends to breed irrationalism such as relativism, non-centrism, and skepticism. In particular, the increase in the intensity of social reforms and the influence of certain external stimuli can easily lead to confusion and blindness, and sometimes even lead to fierce social conflicts, or cause social anomie.

In fact, in the contemporary Chinese philosophical circle, the 1978 debate on truth criterion, as the pioneer of philosophical changes, kicked off the beginning of the transformation of contemporary Chinese society. In the past 20 years, it has experienced several important development periods, such as the great debate on human nature, alienation and humanitarianism, the debate on practical philosophy, the debate on subject and value, and the enduring debate on the relationship between Chinese and Western culture, traditional culture and modernization. In the meantime, although there have been many thoughts and opinions, they have not been separated from the theme of integrating Chinese and Western culture and reconstructing modern Chinese philosophy. The source and turning point for all these controversies lie in the further development of China's reform, which is a philosophical reflection of the "transitional society." We know that society is a systematic structure, so any social reform must be a systematic project. While people are carrying out economic and political reforms, corresponding ideological and cultural reforms must keep pace with them. At present, the country's old economic system has been broken, and political democratization is also expanding. This will inevitably trigger people to explore how to change their mind in order to reconstruct the spirit of contemporary Chinese culture. That is compatible with economic and political modernization.

It is against the background of such social transformation that contemporary Chinese philosophy presents one of the most notable characteristics: a trend of great exchange, communication and integration of Chinese and Western philosophy has emerged. At the current momentum, this trend will continue into the new century.

This is not only because the issues about relations of traditional Chinese philosophy, modern Western philosophy, and the newly-emerging Hong Kong and Taiwan philosophies to Chinese Marxist philosophy need to be deeply discussed and resolved theoretically and academically, but also because, against the background of reform and opening up, the discussion of these issues has increasingly gone beyond the scope of unalloyed academic debates, and has become a profound theoretical movement which will go for a long time, which aims to transform the national thinking mode and cultural psychological structure through new communication and integration, promote social transformation, build a new culture, and develop a new Chinese philosophy.

II. The background of the development of Chinese philosophy in the 21st century

The rapid development of modern science and technology has greatly changed the social life and has become "the first impetus" for social development and progress.

The 20th century is an era in which science and technology advance by leaps and bounds. Since the 1950s, a remarkable new technological revolution has emerged worldwide, which has brought about major changes in various aspects such as the mode of labor, management and organization, the methods of management and people's attitudes toward production and interpersonal relationships. A series of high-tech achievements have been widely applied in the field of social production, integrating science, technology, production, and management into a unified system, changing the entire social structure. The new technological revolution has promoted not only the development of the productive forces, but also tremendous changes in the production relations and even the social superstructure. In the era of highly socialized technology, issues such as human values, attitudes and lifestyles, and the meaning of life are not only for the general public but also for philosophers to rethink.

The development of the new scientific and technological revolution has made society more and more information-based, and the unstoppable trend of social opening and highly-developed information technology has made the connections between different nations and communities around the world much closer. IT application and globalization have become an important feature and trend of contemporary society.

With the widespread use of microelectronics technology, electric energy, and computers in the fields of production, management and living, information has become the object of people's work. Intelligent labor for processing information has gradually taken the place of the "machine + labor" labor mode and has become the main mode of labor, so that the "fourth industry", namely the information industry, has emerged. Some scholars predicted that in the early 21st century, about 86% of employees in the United States would be mainly concentrated in the service industry, nearly half of whom would be engaged in information collection, processing, and dissemination with new labor methods. It is not hard to predict that in the 21st century, the world people face will be an increasingly informatized "information world view".

Thanks to the invention and application of modern communication technologies such as rapid modern transportation and program-controlled telephones, fax telegraphs, information highways, and communication satellites, communication among people has become very simple and easy, and geographical environment, national boundaries and ethnic differences are no longer the boundary of mutual communication. Taking economic activity as an example. The modern economy has surmounted national barriers and moves towards regional collectivization and globalization. Modern economy and science and technology are becoming an international undertaking. The world today has become a big system that is closely linked and inseparable. No nation or country can stay outside of this system. Some people even exclaim that "the earth is getting smaller" and the world is becoming a "global village". Therefore, people's concept of time and space and their way of thinking are bound to change accordingly.

In addition, peace and development are still the main themes of international relations in the world today. The world is increasingly moving toward a multi-polar pattern.

The pattern has been broken in which the post-war confrontation between the United States and the Soviet Union under the Yalta system became the main line of international relations. The pattern of multi-polar power competition and coexistence is reflected in the fact that the United States still strives to maintain its position as the only superpower in the world, but it has to confront with its serious domestic problems and challenges from other rising international forces, which restricts its ability to handle international affairs. Russia, which has lost the strength of a superpower, is striving to restore its status as a major power, and its conflict with the West is increasing. Japan has become an economic super power with a more pronounced propensity to become a political power and strives to establish equal relations with the United States; the European Union has also become the largest economic and trade group in the world and obviously tends to become a major political power. The struggle between the United States, Europe and Russia has become more acute around the central issue of what mechanism should be adopted and who should lead European affairs; the Asia-Pacific region is on the rise. The rapidly developing China has been playing an increasingly important role in promoting peace and development in Asia-Pacific region and even in the world, and its international status and prestige are getting higher and higher. Due to the development of the multi-polar forces, the weakening of the strength of superpowers and the greatly intensified economic and technological competition, the world situation will continue to ease. Therefore, a philosophical spirit of understanding, communication, integration, and coordination has become a strong requirement of the times or it has become the zeitgeist.

In short, the extensive infiltration and profound impact of technological development on social life and the development trend of the times will surely have an important impact on people's values and ways of thinking. Modern scientific and technological achievements require people to master modern ways of thinking, such as control methods, systems methods, information methods and collaborative methods, and put forward higher requirements for comprehensiveness, dynamics, information, and creativity of people's thinking. In the information society of the 21st century, we must have a way of thinking that is compatible with the information age. In addition, due to the popularization of television and the increasingly widespread use of multimedia technology in the family, people's concepts are deeply influenced by the public media. Surrounded by strong public culture, it is increasingly difficult for people to escape the influence of the popularized concepts of value on their concepts and behavior choices, so human autonomy, initiative and creativity are becoming increasingly precious. There is no doubt that the above-mentioned characteristics and trends of the present era will have a profound impact on the direction and content of Chinese philosophy in the 21st century.

III. Philosophical warnings from the experience and lessons of Western modernization

1. Emergence of a serious "value crisis" in Western modernization

According to Daniel Bell, at the beginning of industrialization, there are often two interacting forces, namely the religious impetus and the economic impulse discovered by Weber, the latter mainly manifested as a utilitarian impulse. With the development of industrialization, economic impulse has gradually become the only driving force.① The utilitarian principle has indeed injected some vitality into the development of social economy, but at the same time it has also brought another consequence, namely the formation of a "market orientation" mechanism. Therefore, people tend to shape themselves according to the needs of the market. Their goal seems to be nothing but to successfully sell themselves in the market. So, people are essentially commercialized. This combination of universal commercialization and money worship has led to the loss of subject value, and society seems to be a combination of different commodity atoms that care only about their own interests.

In the process of Western modernization, the over-prominence of individual principles is conducive to individual creativity, individual diversification and the introduction of competition mechanisms, but it will easily lead to the proliferation of individualism and even egoism and actually it has done so. The interaction between individualism and universal commercialization turns people into a relationship of contract, business, and competition. The lack of pure super-utilitarian emotional communication causes alienation, indifference, tension and conflict in interpersonal relationships.

Related to individualism and market-oriented logic, relativism has become a universal trend of thought in modern society. Nowadays, there in Western society also emerges a postmodernist trend characterized by negativity, decentralization, fragmentation, anti-orthodox, anti-tradition, anti-authority, uncertainty, discontinuity, and pluralism.

All these show that Western society did not realize its original belief that "people are the purpose" because of modernization, but fell into a crisis of universal existence and belief. The so-called nihility, absurdity, deterioration of social atmosphere and moral decay are all manifestations of the loss of human meaning and value. Existentialism is a philosophical reflection of this Western "social illness."

2.Western capitalist society exhibits negative effect of restricting the overall development of people brought about by the development of science and technology, namely the effect of technological alienation

---

① Bell, Daniel: *The Cultural Contradictions of Capitalism*, Chin. ed., Beijing: SDX Joint Publishing Company, 1989.

Originally, the development of science and technology has provided more and more material foundations, technical means, and mental and cultural factors for the free and well-rounded development of each individual. However, under the conditions of the capitalist production relations, the priority status of technology has replaced and eliminated the status of people as "purpose". Modern society seems to have become a technological society. The autocracy of technology can be seen everywhere, from the mass production of machines to the operation of political institutions. In a technology-ruled and authoritarian society, people seem to be merely appendages to machines (including industrial machines, political machines, etc.), and they have no choice but to obey technical regulations. As a role of the modern division of labor and industrial assembly lines, people have unique needs and emotions which have been ruthlessly ignored. The relationship between technology and people, between means and ends is reversed. Just as industrialization did not truly realize the belief that man is an end, the manipulation of technology on man does not make man truly independent. The value requirements of man itself have been left out or forgotten.

3. Regarding the relationship between man and nature, prominent problems of modern industrial society are destruction of natural ecological environment and increasingly serious environmental pollution

In terms of the relations between man and nature, the basic orientation of modernization is to conquer and utilize nature, and constantly achieve the domination of nature. In the process of modernization, when the interests of human beings are taken as the only starting point, the connection of the natural objects themselves is outside of the vision of mankind, and nature has become the object of endless grabbing, plundering and possession of human beings. The result is the increasing depletion of natural resources and the deterioration of human living environment, the latter being characterized by pollution of the atmosphere, water resources, and food, as well as ecological imbalance. Due to the uncontrolled plunder of nature, the structure and function of the ecosystem have been destroyed. The desertification of land, the reduction of forest resources, the destruction of the ozone layer and the extinction of certain species have caused unprecedented catastrophes to the ecological environment. The imbalance of the relationship between man and nature and the deterioration of the natural ecological environment have become a global problem that threatens the survival and development of mankind. The emergence of such problem has profoundly exposed the error of the "human-centered concept".

In short, the modernization process in the West is indeed accompanied by many negative phenomena. And this negative phenomenon is actually caused by one-sided misleading of certain values. It should be pointed out that revealing the negative effects of the process of the Western modernization does not mean denying modernization itself but aims to provide lessons for the modernization of post-development countries like ours. For a developing country that is in the process of modernization, how to avoid the problems and/or limit the costs incurred in the process of the Western modernization is a historical problem. Philosophy can do something in this respect.

IV. Trend and characteristics of Chinese philosophy in the 21st century

In the 21st century, what is the trend of Chinese philosophy? What will be its mainstream and research focus? There were lively discussions in the Chinese philosophical circle. At present, there are generally the following views.

Firstly, Chinese philosophy in the 21st century must be a philosophy full of creativity and motivation. This view holds that the creative philosophy of the 21st century will be a continuation of the development of Chinese philosophy today. In the past two decades, the discussions in the Chinese philosophical circle have revolved around such issues as practice as the criterion for testing truth, the essence and function of knowledge, subject and object, human subjectivity and initiative, and practical materialism, in which runs through a main thread, that is, the focus on human creative activity and the creativity of human activity. Following this thread of thought, we will find that the future of Chinese philosophy is creativity philosophy.

Secondly, continuing to promote the Sinicization of Marxism will be the mainstream of the development of Chinese philosophy in the 21st century. The scholars holding this view believe that the mainstream of the development of Chinese philosophy since the 20th century has been the Sinicization of Marxism. To carry out a democratic revolution and build an independent, prosperous, democratic and free New China has been the basic practice of the Chinese people since the 20th century. This practice was achieved on Marxism, first and foremost under its philosophical guidance. Marxist philosophy has been adapted to the Chinese context in this process and has become the guiding principle of the whole nation. However, since the late 1970s, the ideological line of reform and opening up has been based on Marxist philosophy. The continuous development of this cause still must rely on the guidance of Marxist philosophy. Therefore, continuing to promote the Sinicization of Marxism will be the mainstream of the development of Chinese philosophy in the 21st century.

Thirdly, the trend of philosophy development in the 21st century should be the rise of conventionalism. This view holds that the more human society develops, the less the role of natural relationships on humans, and that humans tend to become social beings. The more complicated the social relations of human beings are, the more they are affected by the various social conventions. The tendency of conventionalism will inevitably be reflected in philosophy and will rise to a major topic of contemporary philosophical research. Today, the development of human civilization has reached an astonishing level. At the same time, human beings have also found that their survival is in a comprehensive crisis. Globally coordinated development has become a major issue for human survival. Therefore, various commitments are not only embodied in their respective countries and nations, but also increasingly embodied in international relations. It can be predicted that by the 21st century, conventionalism will develop into a basic trend in philosophy and other fields.

Fourthly, to rebuild people's beliefs and value system will become the theme and leading development trend of Chinese philosophy. Scholars who hold this view believe that with the satisfaction of people's material needs come all kinds of confusion and perplexity that people encounter in the mental realm. People are dazzled by money worship, egoism, and non-moralism. Coupled with the decline of heroism and rationalism, the problem of cultural home has become a common modern physical or mental distress. Therefore, the pursuit of a cross-century cultural home will become the mainstream of future philosophical development

Fifthly, the basic trend of Chinese philosophy in the 21st century is the development of branch philosophy. Relevant scholars believe that it is the basic trend of Chinese philosophy to strengthen the research of branches of philosophy oriented to social change and the development of the times, and making philosophical research concrete and practical. To this end, economic philosophy, philosophy of science, management philosophy, culture philosophy, political philosophy, moral philosophy, legal philosophy, development philosophy should be studied. At present, philosophical research should develop in the direction of modernization and concretization, expand and deepen the points and areas of philosophical research, and find new growth points for philosophy. This is the fundamental way out for the development of Chinese philosophy.

Sixthly, Chinese philosophy in the 21st century will be a double play of philosophy's globalization and individualization. The globalization of philosophical research is the inherent requirement of the nature of philosophy. Nowadays, the globalization of philosophy is more realistic. There are three reasons: (a) It is an inherent requirement of the market economy because the market economy is a kind of world economy. (b) It is the inevitable result of the development of contemporary science, technology, society and civilization. (c) The common problems which mankind faced, such as global problems, development problems, etc., require philosophical research to shift to the global scope of mankind. However, the globalization of philosophical research is not to abolish the individuality of philosophical research, but to highlight individuality. The market economy is essentially an individualized economic system, and philosophical research itself is also individualized, so the Chinese philosophy in the 21st century will be a positive outcome of the globalization and individualization of philosophical research.①

Each of these six kinds of views, we believe, has a certain practical basis, and each has its own rationale. But we agree more with the second and fifth view.

Looking back the history of Chinese philosophy in the 20th century, we find that there have been two fruitful "philosophical climaxes". The first is the period of the new democratic revolution led by the first generation of Chinese Communists with Mao Zedong at the core, which combined the universal truth of Marxism with the concrete reality of China at that time, and gave rise to the Sinicized Marxism—Mao Zedong Thought. Its core content and fundamental foundation is to advocate seeking truth from facts, proceed from reality in everything, integrate theory with practice, and oppose bookish and dogmatic philosophical lines and viewpoints. The main results of this thought are embodied in philosophical (military philosophical) works such as *On Practice, On Contradiction, On Protracted War, The Strategic Issues of the Chinese Revolution*. Mao Zedong Thought judiciously and clearly answered the important questions concerning China's future and destiny, which puzzled people at that time about where China is going and how the road of the Chinese revolution should go, and pointed out the correct path of the Chinese revolution. It was under the guidance of Mao Zedong Thought (most importantly his philosophical thought) that the Chinese revolution was victorious and realized the century-long ideal of national independence and independence that the Chinese people dreamed of since the outbreak of the Opium War. The People's Republic of China (PRC) was founded

---

① See *Macau Daily*, 1996-4-14(17).

in 1949 and a new era was opened up in history. As a result, Mao Zedong Thought, a product of the Sinicization of Marxism, has also become the guiding philosophy of the Party and has become the mainstream ideology. The second "philosophical climax" appeared at the end of the 1970s, starting from the discussion that practice is the only criterion for testing truth. The Chinese Communists represented by Deng Xiaoping inherited Mao Zedong Thought, once again combined the basic principles of Marxism with the development reality of China and the times, thinking about and solving China's development problems, that is, the problem of socialist modernization, and gradually formed contemporary China's Marxism, namely Deng Xiaoping Theory, found a way to build and develop socialism and realize modernization in a country like China, which is relatively backward in economy and culture. The quintessence of Deng Xiaoping Theory is to emancipate the mind and seek truth from facts, and its philosophical basis is the Marxist philosophy of practice: "Insist on seeking truth from facts, proceed from reality in everything, integrate theory with practice, and insist that practice is the criterion for testing truth." Many scholars believe that the philosophy of practical materialism, with practice as the logical starting point, is not only the logical source of Deng Xiaoping Theory, but also the philosophical foundation of this theory. The 15th National Congress of the CPC established Deng Xiaoping Theory as the guiding political principle for the socialist modernization of the Party and the country, and it has thus become a lamp by which the feet of Chinese people are guided. In connection with this, practical materialistic philosophy is bound to show strong vitality.

Based on a summary of the emergence of the aforementioned two philosophical climaxes and the establishment of the two corresponding dominant philosophical forms, we find that there is something in common: these two philosophies (essentially the same) have respectively provided scientific guidance (at the level of worldview and methodology) for exploring and answering fundamental issues related to the rise and fall of the Chinese nation, such as the Chinese revolution and China's development path. Although there are many related views (such as copying the Soviet-Russian revolutionary model theory, total Westernization theory, etc.), they are divorced from the reality of Chinese society and lack a practical basis, and they have been eliminated by history and the times. Mao Zedong Thought and practical materialism, as the sound world view and methodology that revealed the development path of the Chinese revolution and China's modernization, stood out from numerous theoretical trends and became the mainstream philosophical form of Chinese society.

Based on the summary of the experience drawn from the development history of Chinese philosophy in the 20th century, we can see that which philosophy should become the mainstream form of Chinese philosophy in China in the 21st century is not determined by people's subjective will, but objectively determined. We believe that the mainstream form of Chinese philosophy in the 21st century must meet the following conditions:

First, it should guide the Chinese people to move forward in a new direction along the existing correct path, that is, provide scientific and philosophical support for the correct and feasible path of social development and progress. Otherwise, it could hardly make an impact in history, much less become the mainstream form.

Second, it must reflect the characteristics and trends of the development of the times, and also reflect and sublimate the spirit of the times. Otherwise, it would lose its freshness and zeitgeist.

Third, it should become the "home" for people to seek meaning and to become the people's spiritual refuge. Otherwise, it would lose the support of the people and its vitality.

Under the leadership of the third generation of the central collective leadership with Jiang Zemin at the core, the cause of building socialism with Chinese characteristics pioneered and guided by Deng Xiaoping Theory will continue to advance into the 21st century. Practice has proved and will continue to prove that under the guidance of Deng Xiaoping Theory, the cause of building socialism with Chinese characteristics will surely make even greater achievements. Deng Xiaoping Theory, as the product of Marxism being better integrated with the realities of China and keeping abreast with the times, will also continue to be enriched and improved in practice and in the development of the times. This theory and its philosophical, namely practical materialism, thanks to China's prosperity and national rejuvenation, will surely shine brighter on the world stage in the 21st century, and its "mainstream form" status will therefore be more firmly confirmed. Specifically, this mainstream philosophy must emphasize the following characteristics:

First, we should adhere to the concept of respecting practice and seeking truth from facts as a starting point for understanding and solving problems. We should follow this line of philosophical understanding, with no vacillation.

Second, we should give better play to the functions of philosophical reflection and criticism, should be more conscious about resolving problems to identify problems and conflicts in practice, constantly summarizing successful experience in practice, and correcting improper or wrong thinking tendencies in practice, so as to enhance the consciousness and scientific nature of practical activity ,reduce and avoid blindness, and make the cause of building socialism with Chinese characteristics proceed more smoothly and healthily.

Third, we need to show even greater courageousness and broadmindedness. With the changes in the call of our day, peace and development have become the trend of the world, and the trends of multi-polarity, IT application and globalization have been surging forward. The mainstream Chinese philosophy in the 21st century must display the characteristics and trends of development of the times, namely diversity, interrelatedness, interactivity, holism, openness and inclusiveness.

Fourth, we shall pay more attention to the existence and value of individuals, caring about them and serve them in the pursuit of their life goals. When philosophy indeed provides people with spiritual support and psychological consolation, as the cultural home, an invaluable part of their repertory, and even as a source of driving force of life, this kind of philosophy has really entered and taken root in their hearts, and thereby laid its profound and solid foundation to establish itself as a mainstream philosophy. Especially in the current period of social transformation, due to the rapid changes in various aspects, the intensification of social differentiation and differences, and the conflicts of various concepts, people are prone to get disoriented, suffering such mental issues as psychological imbalance, choice conflict, role conflict and split personality. The Chinese philosophy in the 21st century cannot ignore the perplexity and loss of the state and significance of human existence. Instead, it should seek appropriate alliance with psychology, literature, aesthetics, and art, guide people to go beyond confusion to persistence, beyond illusion to reason, beyond absurdity to truth, beyond secular to sublime, and form a value system that is compatible with the socialist market economy and consistent with the essential needs of people. For this reason, the existing philosophical system must have a major change in content and language form.

Fifth, we should fully absorb ideological viewpoints in traditional Chinese philosophy that are conducive to solving the problems that have arisen in the process of modernization. In response to the alienation of interpersonal relationship and of the relationship between man and nature, and the opposition between instrumental rationality and value rationality, which have emerged in the construction of the market economy system, we must achieve harmony between man and nature and between individuals and the general public, on the basis of the development of modern large-scale production and the socialist market economy.

The individual's principal position is highlighted in the market economy. For thousands of years, in Chinese philosophy and culture, the concept of dependence of the individual on the group is too deeply rooted, and the individual's sense of independence is too weak, so it is necessary to learn all the reasonable things contained in the Western individualism and break those concepts of Confucianism which cling to the individual's dependence on the group, but ignore or even deny individual independence. At the same time, however, it is also necessary to prevent individuals, due to emphasis on developing their self-reliance, from developing themselves towards uncaring, group-indifferent individualism, even into the proliferation of extreme individualism, egoism, hedonism, and money worship, or towards nihilism similar to postmodernism. In this regard, China has been convinced since ancient times that the relation between man and nature as well as between individual and group must and can be harmonized. In particular, Confucianism attaches much importance to the group harmony and advocates the lofty moral spirit of individual dedication to the group, which we should critically inherit.[①]

To sum up, with the deepening of the cause of building socialism with Chinese characteristics until the realization of the "three-step strategic goal" in the middle of the 21st century, the strong vitality and leading position of practical materialism philosophy, characterized by the aforementioned five points, will be more definitely proved.

In addition, it can be predicted that in the 21st century, the differentiation trend of philosophy will become more obvious. From the perspective of the development of specific disciplines of philosophy, ethics, life philosophy, thinking science, aesthetics, cultural philosophy, educational philosophy, management philosophy, economic philosophy, development philosophy and other disciplines will be further developed. At the same time, in order to find a better and more powerful way to affect people's daily life and mental consumption, philosophy will establish appropriate modes of cooperation with other disciplines such as literature, art, psychology and public relations, etc., and combine the profoundness and "permeability" of philosophy with the linguistic features and relaxed forms of these disciplines, so as to exert the utmost power of philosophy and realize its value.

While there exists the mainstream form of philosophy, due to the continuous

---

① *Philosophical Trends*, 1995(8):2-3.

differentiation of interests, the diversification of professional subjects, and the intensification of IT application and globalization, diversified philosophical trends are bound to emerge from time to time. The most prominent possibility is that relativism and individualism of anti-authoritarianism and anti-centrism will have a broader and more lasting influence, and will have a certain impact on the mainstream form of philosophy. This will also be inevitable.

Radically Changing World and Mission of Contemporary Marxist Philosophy*

Since the 1990s, the most distinctive and far-reaching characteristics of human society are undoubtedly globalization, IT application, and networking. The human social form, the operation mechanism and the development mechanism are undergoing major changes.

Globalization is the process of the global expansion of capital, the rapid development and widespread application of information technology, which has made the intercourse between different subjects of humankind increasing common and compact, and has realized what K. Marx called "universal intercourse" from "national history" to "world history", which is characterized by rapidity, relevance, interactivity and openness. Information activity has become the basic mode of material movement and social movement, and has greatly promoted the mutual complementation of human production, circulation, and consumption and their respective efficiencies, which indicate the progress of society

A globalized, informatized and networked society is also a technological society. The contemporary social communication and organization structure system is constructed based on a series of modern technologies such as information, satellite, and telecommunications. The objects of people's intercourse, practice, and cognitive activity are becoming increasingly information-based, and social organizations are becoming more and more network-based. The application of high-tech in social production and social life is becoming more and more extensive and in-depth.

Technological society undoubtedly brings about tremendous changes in human productivity and the production relations, but it also has an extremely important impact on human existence and circumstances. "Isn't technological change

---

* Originally published in *Social Sciences in China* (《中国社会科学》), 2004(1).

overthrowing our view of time, our view of distance and space, our description of the world, our relations with life, mind, body, disease, disability, work, and leisure?"① In this new technological society, people not only rely more and more on technology, cannot do without technology, adapt to the requirements of technology, and are dominated by technology, but also tend to live in a world of symbolic artificial scenes.

Postmodernists such as Baudrillard have profoundly revealed the basic characteristics of contemporary society: technologization, virtualization, media-overflow, and consumer-dominance. They point out that human beings are living in a "simulation" world, in which the difference between reality and image has disappeared, and daily life is presented in an aesthetic manner; that is, a simulated world, a post-modern culture, appeared.② With information technology, network technology and electronic media, human beings are living in the transition between the real world and the virtual world. "This step from the printing age to the imagery era was due to the invention of photography."③ If the advent of photography is just the beginning of picturization and visualization of modern culture, the emergence of virtual technology provides a handy technical foundation for image culture. "Digital imagery is not just another new technology in the history of image creation, and it is also a new method of writing, which can be compared with the invention of printing and the creation of the alphabet."④ "The image culture, especially the dynamic image culture, cannot be underestimated because they act on emotion through image, and thus have exerted and will continue to exert a profound influence on the expression and value system."⑤

Habermas once profoundly pointed out that the proliferation of technological rationality and its continuous expansion into people have resulted in the colonization of the life world, that is, the continuous technologization and institutionalization of the life world. In his opinion, the intercourses in daily life operate according to a non-

---

① Scheps, Ruth (ed.): *Le'Empire des Techniques*, Chin. ed., Beijing: SDX Joint Publishing Company, 1999, p. 4.
② Baudrillard, Jean : *The Consumer Society*, Chin. ed., Nanjing: Nanjing University Press, 2000.
③ Mcluhan, Marshall: *Understanding Media*. Chin. ed., Beijing: The Commercial Press, 2000, p. 240.
④ Scheps, Ruth (ed.): *Le' Empire des Techniques,* Chin. ed., Beijing: SDX Joint Publishing Company, 1999, p. 98.
⑤ Ladriere, Jean: *The Challenge Presented to Cultures by Science and Technology,* Chin. ed., Beijing: The Commercial Press, 1997, p. 124.

instrumental principle and there is no need to meet such mandatory requirements of the system as profit, control and efficiency.[①] The system's rule over the life world, the interpersonal relationship, and people's lives are becoming more and more technicalized, instrumentalized, and standardized, and individuals' daily life is increasingly subjected to external mandatory requirements, control and supervision, such as technology, management norms, and laws, and thus technical rationality undermines the normal and harmonious state of interpersonal communication, personal free space is constantly being eroded, the social and humanistic living environment is seriously deteriorating, and the humanistic connotation of the life world is becoming increasingly weak.[②] It can be said that human beings have changed from the previous state of natural man and social man to the current state of "technical man".

The technological society is bound to be a risky society. Just because the information movement has become the basic mode of material movement and social movement, along with the IT application, networking and digitization of human intercourse, the connectivity, interactivity, openness, and immediacy between various social subjects and social things have been greatly enhanced and the uncertainty and fragility of the state of human society have also increased. The uncertainty in contemporary society mainly comes from two aspects: First, social intercourses are increasingly dependent on information technology and the network, and the issues of network security and information security may arise at any time for various reasons, such as hacker attacks and network paralysis that cause the interruption of economic and political exchanges, leading to serious consequences.

Second, due to tremendous changes in the information movement, the technological basis and mechanisms of communication in contemporary society, the connectivity and interactivity and integrity of communication have increased, thus the transmission effect of risk is not only rapid but also more magnified. The information about an emergency is disseminated in a speed which would be unimaginable under traditional social conditions, and which is now likely to cause turbulence or even collapse of a certain sub-system of society and even the social system. The financial turmoil that swept the world at the end of the 20th century, and a series of emergent

---

① Poster, Mark: *The Second Media Age,* Chin. ed., Nanjing: Nanjing University Press, 2001, p. 65.
② J. Habermas, M. Haller: *The Past as Future,* Chin. ed., Hangzhou: Zhejiang People's Publishing House, 2001, p. 182.

crisis events that followed in the 21st century such as the "September 11" and "SARS" outbreaks, and the paralysis of the U.S. power grid system were all spread with their impact being so widely, deeply and swiftly spread that has never happened before in history. These are enough to show the high relevance and dependence of contemporary society, the high efficiency and instantaneity of the transmission effect, as well as the extreme fragility and instability, which clearly shows the of contemporary society. characteristics

To sum up, the present-day society is a globalized society with universal and intensified communication; it is a technologized society with IT application, networking and digitization as a structural mechanism; It is a "risk society" full of uncertainty and risk; it is a transnational society where the sovereignty of a nation-state is being weakened and "the world's public social space" is growing day by day. Human beings are also increasingly becoming "decentralized" and "delocalized" "world historical persons", that is, "world citizens". All these indicate that the human society is undergoing profound changes.

What is the status quo of contemporary Chinese philosophy in the face of a profoundly changing world? What should contemporary Chinese philosophy deal with and where should it go? This is an important subject for contemporary Chinese philosophy researchers.

For a long time, the situation in the field of Chinese philosophy has been that Chinese philosophy, Western philosophy, and Marxist philosophy are separated, lacking communication and dialogue, and even belittling each other. Philosophy, as the wisdom of love, has been dismembered and divided. Philosophers have also become one-sided, "specialized" "philosophical workers". This abnormal phenomenon has been reinforced by the unreasonable and unscientific discipline system, academic evaluation system, and teaching methods. This *status quo* of philosophy obviously cannot respond to the problems of the times, let alone shoulder the mission of guiding people to change the world.

Since the 20th century, human society has undergone drastic and profound changes. While it has created brilliant civilization achievements, mankind is also facing a serious survival crisis. A series of global issues such as environmental pollution, ecological imbalances, ethnic conflicts, regional wars, terrorism, thermonuclear threats, cultural contradictions, and the gap between the rich and the poor have cast a deep shadow on human survival and development in the 21st century. The predicament of survival and development is actually a crisis of the concept of human survival and development. It essentially reflects the crisis of human civilization, which is the so-called "the crisis of modernity".

How can we deal with and resolve these crises and establish a fair and reasonable order of human life? It is not only a subject that today's thinkers and politicians from all over the world have been trying hard to explore, but also a question that global citizens who have a bearing on the future of mankind must face in practice. The massive anti-globalization movement, the green movements, the feminist movements, and even the successive terrorist activities and regional wars are actually direct manifestations of human crises and different ways of resolving crises. Universal ethics, universal values, communicative rationality, cross-cultural understanding and dialogue, returning to the life world, survival philosophy ontology, justice ethics, pursuits of difference, marginalism and pluralism as academic purport, opposition to centralism, essentialism, and foundationalism and many other postmodern thoughts are all manifestations of philosophy's ideological construction aiming to respond to the problems of the times and solve the crises. They are all responses to the philosophical approach to the crises of modern civilization, and thus are the embodiment of human wisdom.

Philosophy is the thinking on what happen in different times. Proposing and constructing, in reflection and criticism, philosophical ideas that reflect the direction of public reason and human public interest is the only way for philosophy to characterize its own existence and realize its own value. The value of philosophy is to provide a philosophical argument for the rational and harmonious order of human life and human society, that is, to provide a cultural home that represents the ideal of human existence, and the corresponding way of thinking. Therefore, how to critically reflect on the dilemma of contemporary human survival and the concepts and models of civilization, and how to shoulder the historic mission of humanity in the new century in solving global problems that threaten the progress of human civilization have become major subjects of philosophical research in the world today.

Now that Marxism has achieved continuous historic and theoretical leaps in adapting Marxism to China's conditions, and has also constantly encountered new challenges in practice and in theory, Marxist philosophy, as the foundation of the conception of history and values, is facing a change in the form of how to reflect the spirit of the times.

Today, we urgently need to pay attention to and study the following issues:

— adhering to and developing Marxism social formation theory. This theory is an important part of materialist conception of history. In contemporary times, due to the rapid development of scientific and technological revolution and the changes in the mode of production and social structure prompted by the wave of globalization, changes have taken place in the nature and characteristics of contemporary social formation, and new characteristics have emerged in the organizational structure and operation mechanisms of contemporary society. How to understand these new changes and characteristics, and how to evaluate various Western social theories (post-industrial society theory, information society theory, knowledge society theory, global society theory, consumer society theory, etc.), there have always been various disputes in academia.

It is undoubtedly a task of great theoretical significance to form an explanatory framework and theoretical paradigm with profound insight into the complex phenomena of human existence and development and to realize the new development of historical materialism in the contemporary era on the basis of correctly grasping the social formation theory of Marxist classical writers and the characteristics of the times. In addition, through the analysis and study of social formation, we can further understand the dynamic system of the historical development of human society, judiciously predict the future of human social development, and provide basic theoretical support for the leap-forward development of late-developing countries. A correct understanding of the evolution of social formation and the basis for its development in the contemporary era will help us to study and grasp the complexity and new characteristics of social existence and movement mechanism, and provide basic theoretical support for scientific, rational and effective solutions to social conflicts, promoting social development, especially the development of the great cause of building socialism with Chinese characteristics, and making our way of thinking, practice and decision-making reflect the new development of social formation.

— Adhering and developing Marxist social production theory. Due to the new characteristics of the scientific and technological revolution since the end of the 20th century, the socialization of science and technology and scientificalization and technologization of society have become the basic facts and trends in the existence and development of human society. Knowledge practice, with knowledge production and knowledge labor as its important parts, has become a leading form of human practice. Knowledge practice is an important form of new differentiation in the development of human practice. It results from the continuous innovation and development of science and technology as well as its widespread penetration and application in social production and social life, which reflects the current Zeitgeist that knowledge becomes the way of human existence. Knowledge practice has become the basic driving force for economic development and human social progress. How to understand the status of this form of practice in the system of human practice and the relationship between this form of practice and the form of material production and intellectual production? It needs to be accurately elucidated in the deepening of the study of Marxist social production theory.

—Adhering to and developing Marxist cultural theory. "The form of culture is first determined by the political and economic form," "Any given culture (as an ideological form) is a reflection of the politics and economics of a given society, and the former in turn has a tremendous influence and effect upon the latter"[①] This is the basic viewpoint of Marxist historical materialism on the relationship between economy, politics, and culture. Due to the rapid development of science and technology and the fierce competition of overall national strength, and the mutual turbulence of various ideologies and cultures worldwide, culture has become more and more prominent in the country's overall national strength, and cultural exchanges and communication have become an important part of the relations between nations. Cultural contradictions and conflicts have also increasingly become an aspect of international competition and conflicts. The current competition between nations is the one between overall national strength, the fundamental difference is the one between national qualities and talents, and in fact it is a competition between national cultures.

Therefore, It is undoubtedly a subject of great theoretical and practical significance how to deeply understand the important position and role of culture in contemporary and future society from the perspective of the historical materialistic theory of social development motivation, and how to deeply understand the dialectical relationship of interdependence and mutual promotion between material civilization construction and mental civilization construction, between cultural construction and economic construction.

—The influence of medialization, visualization and aestheticization of culture on human survival and social development. A prominent change in contemporary social culture is medialization, visualization, living, economicalization of culture, and

---

[①] *Selected Works of Mao Zedong*, Vol. 2, Chin. ed., Beijing: People's Publishing House, 1991, p. 663, 664.

aestheticization of daily social life. A new cultural form with media culture or visual culture as its main part has emerged. Due to the rapid development and extensive use of information technology, network technology, and electronic media, people are increasingly living in a symbolic and visualized social environment and live in a perfect but virtual reality.

As the postmodernists such as Featherstone, Baudrillard, and Jameson pointed out, the environment in which people live today is more and more like a "mirror," which constitutes a space where reality is illusioned; people are living in a "simulation" world, a world of images wrapped in layers of symbols. It is the gradual increase in the production capacity of images and the expansion of the density of images in modern society that have pushed us into a new society. In this society, the difference between reality and images has disappeared. Daily life is presented in an aesthetic way, that is, a simulated world or post-modern culture has appeared.① Bell believes that "Contemporary culture is becoming a visual culture, not a printing culture," and that printing not only emphasizes cognitive and symbolic things, but more importantly also lays stress on the necessary way of conceptual thinking while visual medium-- here it refers to movies and television--imposes speed on the audience, with emphasis on image, rather than words, causing not purification and understanding, but abusive emotions and compassion, that is, the feelings that are quickly exhausted and a false ritual that pretends to be on the scene."② Giddens particularly emphasized the integration of print media and electronic media. "Early newspapers (and all other magazines and periodicals of all kinds) played an important role in separating the space from the location, but after the integration of print and electronic media, this process has become a global phenomenon."③

Media culture and visual culture have been profoundly changing the world. A variety of information, TV literature and art, popular audio and video, pop songs, variety show newspaper and magazine culture and online multimedia and many other popular literary forms have actually become the leading forms of culture. The

---

① See Featherstone, Mike: *Consumer Culture and Postmodernism*, Chin. ed., Nanjing: Yilin Press, 2000; Baudrillard, Jean: *The Consumer Society*, Chin. ed., Nanjing: Nanjing University Press; Jameson, Fredric: *The Cultural Logic of Late Capitalism*, Chin. ed., Beijing: SDX Joint Publishing Company, 1997.
② Bell, Daniel: *The Cultural Contradictions of Capitalism*, Chin. ed., Beijing: SDX Joint Publishing Company, 1989, p156-157.
③ Giddens, Anthony: *Modernity and Self-identity*, Chin. ed., Beijing: SDX Joint Publishing Company, 1998, p. 27.

original paper cultural forms such as novels, poems, proses, dramas, and paintings, and the elite culture such as high art represented by sculpture, music, dance, etc., are replaced by advertisements, pop songs, fashion, TV series and even environmental designing, urban planning, and room decoration and other visual culture and intuitive culture as the leading form of culture. Then, how to correctly understand the impact of this cultural shift on the existence ecology and development trend of human culture, how to correctly understand the impact of this cultural shift on the way of human existence, and how to treat this cultural shift in practice, have entered into the thinking of postmodernist thinkers who proposed and discussed as a subject, but currently we still lack in-depth research. This is indeed a subject of great theoretical and practical significance.

——Adhering to and developing Marxist ethics. Under the conditions of globalization and technological society, the creativity of mankind has been unprecedentedly enhanced, and the scope and effect of human activity have greatly expanded. This is certainly a sign of the growth of man's essential power, and it also highlights the unprecedented great responsibility of mankind. The transformation of social patterns requires not only new concepts and norms in the relationship between man and nature, but also new norms in human activity. Shifting from differences and conflicts to the seeking of dialogue and consensus so as to formulate common regulations has become the basic way to maintain normal and harmonious life order for mankind. Especially in present-day society, people are faced with many global problems that have threatened survival and development, and which have urgently called for the construction of ecological ethics, bioethics, network ethics, the ethics of scientific and technological experts. How to adapt to the requirements of the times and establish a new moral philosophy system and social (political) philosophy theory is obviously also a subject of great theoretical and practical significance.

Others such as K. Marx's theory of class and stratum and his theory of nation-state, the trend of globalization and the development of national culture, the issue of the path to national development under the conditions of globalization and technological society, the connotation of Chinese modernity, etc., are all important topics that need to be studied and answered correctly.

A globalized and technologized society is in an era when there arise a number of global and comprehensive problems that requires various technical experts, more thinkers, especially philosophers, and great wisdom, and which, therefore, is bound to be an era of great achievements in interdisciplinary research. Such an era has put forward an urgent requirement for philosophical research: the integration of knowledge and the fusion of visions.

In such an age of civilizational contradictions and crises, we cannot help but sigh, and also more profoundly understand the incisiveness and profoundness of K. Marx's famous saying, which he pointed out in his era: Philosophers have hitherto only *interpreted* the world in various ways; the point is to *change* it. We believe that philosophy is not only in matters of idea, but also in matters of activity. While attaching importance to text research, philosophy must turn its attention to reality, influence the world, change the world, and provide guidance for human civilization to get rid of crisis and provide an ideal world with its unique vision and profound insight. Therefore, we must break down disciplinary barriers and narrow and shallow opinions, and strengthen debate and dialogue. This is the very way philosophy and philosophers exist.

Therefore, in face of the profoundly changing world and the problems of the times, philosophy must assume the responsibility of guiding people to change the world. Above all, it must actively advocate and promote the exchanges and dialogues among the various disciplines of philosophy to achieve the complementarity and surge of various methods and perspectives, so as to realize the creation and promotion of ideas.

First, ancient and modern philosophical resources and different schools of thought should be integrated, the development of Chinese philosophy research methods should be promoted, and thereby a Chinese philosophy form with Chinese characteristics and connotations should be constructed. This is particularly significant in the context of the intensification of globalization and the dominance of Western culture and academics.

Second, through such promotion and integration, Chinese philosophy can undoubtedly make its due and greater contribution in solving the major problems in contemporary and future human life. China has now fully embarked on the international political, economic and cultural arena. We must put forward our ideas and values that are in line with our national conditions.

Third, we must have a dialogue not only with ancient sages' ideas, but also with various contemporary Western thoughts, and more importantly, strengthen the dialogue and exchanges. We should build more platforms for such dialogue and exchanges, and make our own contribution to the development of Chinese philosophy and Chinese academics.

In order to achieve this goal, we must take Marxist theory as the guidance, have the whole world in view, focus our work in response to changes, be more conscious about resolving problems, keep in mind the themes of the times, and carry out in-depth exchanges, dialogues, and arguments. Only in this way can it be possible to construct a contemporary Chinese philosophical form that showcases not only national characteristics but also the spirit of the times in the context of globalization.

On Construction of Forms of Marxist Philosophy in China Today*

The 20-plus years of reform and opening up has witnessed considerable progress in the study of Chinese Marxist philosophy. The academic accumulation over 20-plus years has laid a solid theoretical foundation for its development and innovation. At the same time, human society that has changed profoundly has posed new issues in the research on Chinese Marxist philosophy. Besides, the research paradigms and methods of Chinese Marxist philosophy are undergoing changes, making a new vital force and energy for its development. And to construct a new form of Sinicized Marxist philosophy is increasingly becoming a common pursuit of people working in the Chinese philosophical circles, which is not only driven by "problem-consciousness" inside the discipline of Marxist philosophy and the theoretical appeal for the development of China's socialist modernization, but also the only way to revive the culture and spirit of the Chinese nation. This article attempts to look into how to construct a new form of Sinicized Marxist philosophy from the perspectives of the true spirit, national characters, and problem consciousness of Marxist philosophy.

Introduction New Trends in the Current Study of Chinese Philosophy

An obvious trend exhibited in the study of contemporary Chinese philosophy is the dialogue and combination between Marxist philosophy, traditional Chinese philosophy, modern and contemporary Western philosophy, and the discussion on how to construct a new form of Chinese philosophy. It is mainly reflected in three research

---

* This article is originally published in *Philosophical Researches*, 2005(7) with the titles of "Contemporary Construction of Sinicized Marxist Philosophy," and in *Journal of Nanjing University* (Philosophy, Humanities, Social Sciences), 2005(6) with the titles of "Rethinking on the Construction of the New Form of Sinicized Marxist Philosophy."

orientations. First, to clarify the principles and viewpoints of classic Marxist philosophy and grasp its essence and approaches. Second, to critically assimilate the essence of Chinese traditional thoughts. Third, to critically absorb the reasonable composition of Western modern philosophy and organically integrate them into contemporary Chinese philosophy. This philosophical form is mainly guided by Marxist philosophy, which aims at realizing the "comprehensive innovation" of "Chinese philosophy, Western philosophy and Marxist philosophy." Since the advent of the new century, there have been at least three large-scale and influential seminars in Chinese philosophical circles closely related to this subject. The first was the "Civilization Conflict and Philosophical Dialogue in the Context of Globalization: Expert Forum of Chinese Philosophy, Western Philosophy, and Marxist philosophy," co-hosted by the China Social Science Magazine and other organizations, held in Guilin, Guangxi, from September 26th to 29th in 2003. The participants have had fruitful discussions on the theme of how to break down the barriers between disciplines and carry out philosophical dialogues to establish a contemporary Chinese philosophy in three academic disciplines — Chinese philosophy, Western philosophy, and Marxist philosophy—in the context of globalization. The second was the academic symposium on "Rewriting Philosophical History and Paradigm Innovation in Chinese Philosophy", held at the People's University of China from March 20th to 21th in 2004. The participants thoroughly discussed the "legitimation" of Chinese philosophy, the philosophical discipline paradigm innovation and the premise and method of rewriting the history of Chinese philosophy from different perspectives, and reached the following consensuses: (a) The paradigms of Chinese philosophy discipline are currently almost all in the mode of "explaining Chinese philosophy with Western theory," which, for all the contributions to the establishment of Chinese philosophy, fails to effectively inherit the quintessence of traditional Chinese culture; (b) The development of Chinese philosophy should still be bound up with those of Western philosophy and Marxist philosophy, given the fact that an important condition for the further development of Chinese philosophy is the combination of these two philosophies. The third was the academic symposium on "Contemporary Value and System Innovation of Marxist Philosophy," organized by the Center for Studies of Values and Culture and the Institute of Marxist Philosophy in Beijing Normal University, held on October 23-24, 2004, in which the participants believed that the tremendous changes in our life brought about by economic globalization and the practice of the construction of socialism with Chinese characteristics have raised new questions to the study of Marxist philosophy, so it is urgent that the system of Marxist philosophy be innovated to demonstrate its contemporary values; and that, in order to innovate Marxist Philosophy System, its relationship with Chinese philosophy and Western philosophy should be handled correctly; that the focus should be laid on the combination of the theory with the actual conditions; and that the prerequisite questions should be answered such as "how to understand philosophy?" "How to understand Marxist philosophy?" and "how to understand Chinese contemporary Marxist philosophy?" It is, therefore, not difficult to find that the construction of a new form of contemporary Chinese philosophy is mainly manifested as "the construction of a new philosophical form of Sinicized Marxist philosophy," a new form of contemporary Chinese philosophy.

How to combine Chinese philosophy, Western philosophy and Marxist philosophy, and how to explore and construct a new form of contemporary Chinese philosophy have become an increasingly heated topic in Chinese philosophy since the turn of the century. That is because it is not only an internal request of philosophy as a discipline, but also a request of the practice of constructing socialism with Chinese characteristics, as well as an objective request made by the tasks of dealing with globalization and Western cultural hegemony, establishing the image of a cultural power and realizing national cultural identity and national rejuvenation, reflecting the cultural pursuit of contemporary Chinese people and their concerns about the future of national culture.

For a long time, there has been a lack of communication and dialogue between Chinese philosophy, Western philosophy and Marxist philosophy, and even despise against each other. In consequence, philosophy [The word literally meaning the "love" (*philo* in Greek) of "wisdom" (*sophia*)] has been disintegrated and split up into various "sub-disciplines of philosophy," and philosophers were also divided into lopsided and "specialized" philosophy workers. This abnormality has been further worsened by the discipline system and academic evaluation system which are not always judiciously and reasonable. Such kind of philosophy, apparently, cannot meet the challenges of the times, let alone shoulder the mission of guiding people to transform the objective world.

The CPC, in the course of leading the national liberation and modernization, combined the basic principles of Marxism with the actual conditions in China, creatively explored a path of new-democratic revolution and the construction of socialism with Chinese characteristics, has achieved three historic leaps of Marxism in China and formed the "three great theoretical fruits" of Mao Zedong Thought, Deng Xiaoping Theory and the important thought of the Three Represents, thus explored a unique road realizing China's modernization in the mode of socialist market economy. But how the in-depth study of "three great theoretical fruits" can be carried out so as to elevate "Chinese experience" from the perspective of philosophy and thus establish the theoretical discourse of Chinese Marxist philosophy? It is an issue of great urgency and significance that has emerged in the construction of a new form of Marxist philosophy in China.

The still-growing globalization has brought about conflicts and integration between the cultures of different nations; thus, the importance of ethnic culture has become more prominent. Under contemporary capitalism, while capital is exported, Western culture is actually expanded and hegemony is under construction at the same time. China's peaceful development needs the support of cultural strength, because culture is quite a precious resource for a nation which is still in the process of progress towards the rest of the world, especially against the background of globalization. So to speak, national culture is an identity card for a nation in the process of globalization and modernization, and philosophy is the soul of this ID card.

The essence of the development of contemporary Chinese philosophy is the awakening and self-construction of national consciousness and national spirit in the process of Chinese modernization in the context of globalization. Creating philosophical theory of the Chinese nation has always been the unswerving pursuit of Chinese philosophers. What Zhang Dainian (张岱年) advocated in his article "On China-centered Cultural Progress" as early as 1935 is "taking the advantages of both China and the Western, adopting the valuable and excellent contributions of the Western while carrying forward China's inherent cultural heritage, and thus integrating them into one and creating a new kind of culture".[①] And Gao Qinghai (高清海) pointed out that to create contemporary Chinese philosophy is in nature to create the "self-consciousness" of the Chinese nation, and that to create contemporary Chinese philosophical theory is the inherent requirement and urgent need of the Chinese people reflecting on the course of their life journey, understanding their living environment, and finding their path to future development. At the commemorative meeting of the 90th anniversary of the Philosophy Department of Peking University in May 2004, Zhao Dunhua (赵敦华), Director of the Philosophy Department of Peking University, delivered a speech on behalf of the philosophers of Peking University: when we advance towards the goal of the rejuvenation of the Chinese nation, the Philosophy Department of Peking University, as the cradle of Chinese philosophers,

---

① Quoted from Fang Keli(方克立): "Zhang Dainian and Chinese philosophy in the 20th century" (《张岱年与二十世纪中国哲学》), *Social Sciences in China*, 2005(1).

is determined to use the philosophy that reflects the spirits of our times and our nation to forge the cultural soul which will help the Chinese nation stand rock-firm in the family of nations. It is also the strong desire of contemporary Chinese philosophy workers.[1] From a global perspective, globalization is irresistible, as well as the peaceful development of socialist modernization with Chinese characteristics, so the contradiction between globalization and nationality is bound to occur throughout the process of building socialist modernization, which determines that to construct a new form of Sinicized Marxist philosophy is in essence to construct a new philosophy of the Chinese nation in the context of modernization, globalization, and informatization.

To prosper and develop Chinese philosophy and social sciences, we should not only set foot on contemporary times but also inherit the tradition, not only proceed from the actual situation of our own country, but also learn from foreign countries. We should vigorously promote the innovation of academic viewpoints, discipline systems, and scientific research methods, thus striving to build a philosophy and social sciences with Chinese characteristics, Chinese style, and Chinese manner.[2] In this incisive exposition, Hu Jintao has pointed out the right direction to constructing a new form of contemporary Chinese Marxist philosophy. It is my overwhelming belief that there are four major problems which need careful consideration and research in constructing a new philosophical form of Marxism in contemporary China.

I. How to embody the "true spirit" of Marxist philosophy

Marxist historical materialism is mainly understood as class struggle and thought about violent revolution, materialist dialectics is mainly seen as the revolution of world order, the core idea of the dialectics—the unification of opposites —is regarded as the struggle of contradictions, which is theoretically mainly derived from Section 2, Chapter 4 of the textbook *History of the Soviet Union Communist Party (Bolshevik)*— "Dialectical Materialism and Historical Materialism".[3] With the development of

---

[1] Zhao Dunhua(赵敦华): "For the Philosophical Development of Chinese Nation" (《为中华民族的哲学腾飞》), www.pku.edu.cn/news/xiao_kan/, 2004-5-10.
[2] This view is stressed by Hu Jintao at the 13th group study session of the Political Bureau of the 16th CPC Central Committee. (See *People's Daily,* 2004-5-29)
[3] Some scholars believe that this model comes from the understanding of Engels's philosophical thoughts of Lenin and Plier Hanov. It is the explanation of Engels of Marx's philosophy, with Lenin's "Materialism and Empirical Criticism" and Engels's "Anti-Dulin Theory" as its direct sources. Marx's philosophy is the "Practical Materialism" summarized in "The Outline of Ferbaha" (see Wu Yuanliang: "Analysis of the Status of Marxist Philosophy and Several theoretical Issues in China," *Dongyue Tribune*, or *Dongyue Lun Cong*《东岳论丛》, 2004(5).

practice and the changes of the times, the traditional mode of interpreting Marxist philosophy has increasingly exposed its historical limitations, which is mainly manifested in its ignoring the fundamental significance which the concept of practice holds for Marxist philosophy, the importance which values and the issue of free and well-rounded development of everyone assume for Marxist philosophy, and the new challenges posed to the Marxist philosophy by the new changes, new achievements and new problems brought about by the contemporary scientific and technological revolution, all of which have affected our overall grasping of Marxist ideology and theoretical essence. How to embody "classicality" and "true spirit" in the construction of a new form of Chinese Marxist philosophy? From my point of view, the most fundamental thing is to correctly understand the "general characteristics" of K. Marx's thought, and grasp the essence of Marxism from, the intrinsic connection between Marxism and its historical practice as well as the intrinsic organic connection of Marxist theory.

First of all, Marxist thought should be interpreted from the perspective of its general characteristics, otherwise Marxist philosophy cannot be really understood.

We have long been accustomed to dividing Marxism into three components and expounding it from three aspects. In fact, Marxist theory is a systematic whole, which is a science about the general laws of historical generation and social development. With the purpose of finding a solution to "the distress of material benefits", K. Marx conducted a study on political economy, in which he exposed and critiqued the related philosophical beliefs (mainly manifested as the critique of *German Ideology*), and in which he discovered the close connection between perceptual human practice and the history of mankind, and used perceptual human practice to explain the structure and operation mechanism of society, which revealed the general laws of the development of human history and fostered a new worldview—historical materialism. And on this basis, he conducted a thorough and systematic study of the operation and development mechanisms of the capitalist mode of production (mainly manifested as the revelation and analysis of the logic of capital domination), which laid the theoretical foundation of scientific socialism and showed the possibility of free and well-rounded development of everyone in future society. It can be seen that Marxist thought is the unification of philosophical critique (traditional metaphysics critique), capital critique and social critique, which has achieved a theoretical fusion in the analysis of capital critique. For his part, K. Marx maintained that philosophy, political economics and scientific socialism constitute an organic whole of thought, and therefore, we cannot understand Marxist philosophy simply from the perspective of philosophy; otherwise, we cannot truly grasp the overall outlook and essence of Marxist thought.

Secondly, we should grasp Marxism from the perspective of the height of world views, values, and methodology as well as the theoretical characteristics of Marxist ideological system.

From the perspective of world views, values, and methodology, Marxism has its guiding significance as follows:

A. Marxism reveals the general laws of the development of human society and the special laws of the development of capitalism, and is a science about mechanisms of history generation and social development. The revelation of historical materialism on the structure and operation mechanism of human society still has explanatory power in the present-day world, and is still of important guidance that is irreplaceable for analyzing and grasping the laws of the development of contemporary society.

B. K. Marx carries out his revelation and critique of commodity society from the perspective of "the logic of capital dominating human beings", commodity fetishism, and such phenomena as man's independence manifested by his dependence on material, the critique of alienated labor, and the exposition of the idea that the highest ideal of human society is to realize free and well-rounded development of everyone. All these are of great significance for the analysis and critique of contemporary capitalism and guidance for the sound development of contemporary Chinese socialist market economy.

C. Marxism defines the basic characteristics of future society rom the value dimension of human development. As K. Marx and F. Engels pointed out in *Manifesto of the Communist Party*, "In place of the old bourgeois society, with its classes and class antagonisms, we shall have an association, in which the free development of each is the condition for the free development of all." [①] In the future society, the rule of the class will be eliminated, the history of people being ruled by alien forces will be ended, and the political nature of the public power will be lost. In *Socialism: Utopian and Scientific*, F. Engels pointed out that in a future society that has done away with capitalism, "man for the first time becomes the real, conscious lord of nature, because he has now become master of his own social organization," and "The extraneous objective forces that have, hitherto, governed history, pass under the control of man

---

① Marx, K. & F. Engels: *Selected Works of Marx and Engels*, Vol. 4, Chin. ed., Beijing: People's Publishing House, 1995, p. 730.

himself. Only from that time will man himself, more and more consciously, make his own history. It is the ascent of man from the kingdom of necessity to the kingdom of freedom." Man, at last the master of his own social organization, becomes at the same time the lord of nature, his own master—a free man. Besides, F. Engels referred to the previous human history as "pre-historic history", enlightening us that the theoretical formation of the "prehistoric" society entering a future "human society" is "scientific socialism". This thought is of great importance in guiding us to correctly and comprehensively understand the practice of Marxism and socialism.

D. Many principles of Marxism are general and universal, whose interpretation of the laws of the operation and development of human society is still valid today. Many examples can be taken in this regard, such as the principle that social existence determines social consciousness, the viewpoint of practice, the view that the people are the creators of history, and the method of class analysis.

E. Marxist dialectics provides us with a scientific thinking mode.

The aforementioned five aspects are of great guidance and even of value beyond time and space, whether in terms of ideological profoundness or in terms of values and standpoint, whether in terms of the development of the present-day world or that of contemporary China.

II. To clarify contemporary value of Marxism does not mean that Marxism does not need development

Marxism, from the perspective of its theoretical characteristic, is a system of thought with rigorous logic, with organic unification of criticalness and realizability, profoundness and valuablity, theoreticality and practicality; an ideal construction based on historical science, a well-conceived ideological system of human liberation, and an organic unification of scientific spirit and humanistic spirit. It is K. Marx's scientific critique that brings to light the secrets of the existence of modern capitalist society; it is Marx's proposals that man be liberated from the rule of Nature and of social relations, that individuals realize transcending themselves, and that individuals realize free and well-rounded development that have shown us the bright future of human life. In this sense, Marx is "Prometheus on earth", and Marxism is a "the gift of fire" which illuminates the goal of human progress and gives mankind the hope to make progress and the great power to struggle. The critical spirit and the ideal spirit are the important connotations of Marxism, which should be carried forward, rather than being cast away.

Marxism has existed for more than 150 years. Why does it still have such a significant impact on the present-day world? That is because its "true spirit" has eternal value: (a) The theoretical logic of Marxism is an objective reflection of the logic of practice and it is of strict profoundness; (b) Marxism has deeply influenced the existence and development models of capitalism and the history of the whole world with its profoundness and criticalness; (c) The free and well-rounded development of people and the actualization of emancipation of the proletariat and all mankind as expounded by Marxism have pointed out the direction for the progress of human society; (d) Marx's scientific truth-seeking spirit and his great charisma make future generations, including their opponents of ideas, sincerely respect them. More than a century after his death, K. Marx was voted as the greatest thinker of the millennium and the greatest philosopher. Jean-Paul Sartre proposed that K. Marx was a horizon that cannot be transcended and Derrida issued the slogan "Pay Homage to K. Marx" at the beginning of the new century. All these has proved that Marxist thought is of great power and charisma.

III. How to prominently exhibit national characters

Although Marxism has been proved to have its contemporary value, it does not mean that there is no need to develop it. Marxism is the product of the transitional stage from non-monopoly capitalism to monopoly capitalism. Contemporary capitalism has run into a stage of transnational capitalism, and its operation mechanism has also undergone great changes. And modern science and technology have made great progress compared with the era in which K. Marx lived. Moreover, the concrete practice of contemporary socialism is also not very consistent with Marx's original imagination. All these indicate that Marxism needs to be developed. Actually, in developed Western countries, various schools of Western Marxism have enriched and supplemented Marxist theory from different perspectives and standpoints, so we must look upon Marxism with a Marxist attitude; that is, to understand Marxism from the perspective of historical dialectics, and develop it according to the changes of the times and specific historical practices. For contemporary Chinese Marxists, it is more important to explore "Chinese path", sum up "Chinese experience" and develop Marxism with Chinese characters so as to guide China's modernization.

It is impossible for us to develop Chinese philosophy without two practical backgrounds, namely, still-growing globalization and modernization of socialism with Chinese characteristics. The global and national contradictions will be basic contradiction all the way to modernization with Chinese characteristics. The most obvious characteristic of the present-day world is economic globalization while economic globalization and the imbalance between social and economic development, to some extent, has worsen the marginalization of disadvantaged nations. The growing economic globalization is "creating a mobile space, an electronic space, a space without center, and a space that can break through any border in the world". Besides, with the development of information technology and global media, cultural communication has broken the boundaries of traditional nation-states and created an increasingly similar global consciousness and global culture. Although we disagree with the term of "cultural globalization", economic globalization and media globalization have broken the connection between culture and territory, and the crisis of identity of national culture (especially the culture of a nation that is in a weak position in the process of economic globalization) has become an increasingly serious problem. In contemporary China, thanks to the development of economy and the enhancement of national power, the cultural identity of the Chinese people has been strengthened. New major challenges, however, have also simultaneously emerged. The construction of socialist market economy will certainly bring about the pluralization of the benefit subjects, which inevitably makes people recognize and promote the heterogeneity of people's thoughts and behaviors, and thereby diversify social culture.

Today, with the development of globalization, in order to realize China's modernization and the great rejuvenation of the Chinese nation, we must attach great importance to national culture and regard the cultivation and promotion of the national spirit as the fundamental way to increase the cohesiveness of the nation so as to provide mental motivation and cultural support for the realization of the modernization with Chinese characteristics and the great national rejuvenation. Since it was introduced into China, Marxism has been developed for more than 100 years and has become the philosophy of the Chinese people, so the essence of constructing contemporary Chinese Marxist philosophy is to cultivate and promote the soul of national spirit. The development of contemporary Chinese Marxist philosophy cannot be separated from the history and cultural tradition of the Chinese nation, which is more than 5,000 years old; contemporary Chinese Marxist philosophy is, above all, "Chinese" philosophy, the philosophy of the Chinese nation, and the one deeply rooted in Chinese national culture and the modernization with Chinese characteristics. To construct the nationality of contemporary Chinese Marxist philosophy, we need to start from three aspects as follows.

1. Absorb the excellent elements of the traditional Chinese culture and enrich its connotation

In general sense, the mainstay of traditional Chinese culture is Confucian culture. It is not only the guiding ideology of the feudal patriarchal society, the instrument of thought for the ruling class of this society, but also the theoretical resource to which intellectuals of this society resorted to restrict the power of the feudal autocracy; meanwhile, it was also the moral principle of ordinary people. It is not only an important part of philosophy, politics, and laws of this society, but also a strong and ever-lasting power of infiltration into literature and art, social psychology, and folk customs. The "mandate of Heaven"[①] theory and the "three cardinal guides"[②] ethics in the classical Confucianism that strengthened the divine authority, monarchical power, paternal authority, and the authority of the husband, are sublated and obsolesced due to its inability to adapt to modern democratic society under the rule of law. But some basic concepts of the Confucian value system, such as benevolence, humanism, supreme hamony, golden mean and integrity, are the mental wealth, which has survived thousands of years of cultural vicissitudes and social practice, and which has been proven to be beneficial to human survival and development and social progress They have not yet gone out of style, but have acquired universality. If they can be guided correctly and endowed with the spirit of the times, not only will it make the national people unite and work in concert, generate great mental power, and form a never-exhausting source of culture, but also are of practical value in promoting moral standards and benefiting the society and people in the process of modernization.

With regard to the relationship between human and nature, Confucianism, according to the ethicized relationship between nature and man, believes that the total value of the world outweighs that of man, and therefore hopes to maintain the harmony between man and nature, thus to achieve the best visionary world in which heaven and man are united as one. The traditional Confucians have the universal feelings and life ideals that "to ordain conscience for Heaven and Earth" and "all people are my brothers and sisters, and all things are my companions", which can make people gain life feelings and mental realm of being integrated with all things

---

① Mandate of Heaven (天命) is a Chinese political and religious doctrine used in ancient times which posited the Emperor is the "son of heaven", and was given the right to rule by divine grace.—Tr.
② Three cardinal guides (三纲) refer to ruler guides subject, father guides son and husband guides wife.—Tr.

on earth. The Confucians comprehend, perceive and pursue the way of Heaven by participating in the continuous reproduction of life of all things on earth. In *The Doctrine of the Mean*, there is a statement of *"cān zàn huà yù,"* in which *"cān zàn"* refers to the influences that man assists in Heaven and Earth; *"huà yù"* refers to the transformative and nourishing power of every and each thing in Nature. If all things in Nature can transform and nourish according to the Heavenly way through man's assistance, a harmonious relationship between man and nature will be established, and an optimal balance of living environment and ecosystem will be achieved. This is an ecological philosophy and ecological ethics peculiar to ancient oriental nations. Although this ecological ideal is based on agricultural society and natural economy and has historical limitations, its basic ideas are of ever-lasting significance, and still can bring us invaluable inspiration.

With regard to dealing with the relationships of groups, societies and states, what Confucianism claims is as follows: "The benevolent love others"; "Harmony is most precious" should be taken as value-orientation and philosophy of life; the golden mean should be observed; "Harmony but not uniformity" should be stressed; common ground on major issues should be sought while minor differences should be looked over; and excessive competition, and vicious confrontation should be opposed so as to avoid the losses for the two parties involved or one swallowing up the other. Currently, with the integration between global economy and information, the development of civilizations all over the world has taken on a tendency of communication, dialogue, infiltration and fusion. At the same time, the so-called theory of "clash of civilizations" has also risen to be a clamour, thus there is no question that the Confucian thoughts of "Harmony but not Sameness" "Help others establish what you yourself wish to establish" and the goals of "peace among all nations", "harmony and peace of the world" are of great practical significance for the correct handling of international relations and the realization of world peace.

With regard to the relationship between individuals and groups, Confucianism expects the two to be in constructive interaction. Based on the idea of "A benevolent person loves others", Confucianism regards mankind as community; and takes the "unity and harmony of oneself and others" and moral harmony as the basic principles of coping with interpersonal relationships from the perspective of coexistence of the same species. And these principles are specifically divided into loyalty, forgiveness, sincerity, integrity, and so forth. Loyalty and forgiveness are extended and developed from "The benevolent love others", respectively from positive and negative sides:

The former is integrity manifesting itself as being considerate of others and a spirit of being ready to help others attain their aims; the latter is a spirit of being able to correlate one's own feelings with those of others and being lenient with others. Sincerity and integrity respectively illustrate truthfulness and honesty in interpersonal intercourse from the intrinsic and extrinsic aspects. Its purpose is to achieve mental communication, ideological understanding, and emotional considerateness, between people of different ages, classes, identities and positions, on the basis of morality, and thereby establish a harmonious interpersonal relationship.

According to Confucianism, much importance is also attached to edification in rites and music. It believes that rites and music are the most prominent symbol of the civilization of human society. The function of "rite" is to determinate one's social identity and normalize one's legalized behavior; and the function of "music" is to cultivate one's temperament and communicate one's emotion. Educating and influencing people through rites and music means realizing the orderliness and harmony of a state's organizations and social relations, and can help to alleviate the various contradictions and conflicts under monarchical hierarchy, thus helping promote national unity and social stability.

With regard to personal moral education and moral cultivation, Confucianism puts on top priority "To be human" and "To be an elitist". "To be human" is to be a cultured person whereas "To be an elitist" is to obtain the ideal personalities that a cultured person should have. Confucian culture is featured by being close to the daily life of human relations, cultivating good human nature, guiding human nature from being subtle to being great, and being skillful in nourishing virtual force, and so on, which plays an extremely important role in moral and ethical normalization of traditional Chinese society establishing Confucian culture as the moral foundation of the traditional Chinese scholars' mental lifeline and the ordinary people's code of conduct and moral basis. If modern transformation and enrichment can be done to these excellent moral resources, it will be highly conducive to carrying forward Chinese culture, passing on the traditional virtues, and cultivating national spirit.

All in all, there are many fine ideas and values in Confucian culture, just as there are many reasonable ideological resources in Buddhism and Taoism. All these should be fully reflected in contemporary Marxist philosophy.

One part of adaptation of Marxism to Chinese conditions is to draw on the excellent traditional culture while the other part, the more important one, is to study the philosophical thoughts contained in the theoretical achievements made since modern China, in particular the CPC's "three great fruits of theoretical innovation", and thus work out the philosophical basis of "Chinese experience" through summarizing and crystalizing.

2. Study philosophical thoughts contained in "three great theoretical fruits"

Mao Zedong Thought, Deng Xiaoping Theory and the important thought of the Three Represents are the "three great theoretical fruits" making three historical leaps in the process of the adaptation of Marxism to Chinese conditions, the theoretical innovation of the CPC, representing the creative achievements of the theoretical thinking of the Chinese nation. To construct new forms of contemporary Marxist Philosophy, we should have an in-depth study of the "three great theoretical fruits" rather than to ignore and eschew them, and further summarize and generalize the philosophical thoughts existing and implied in the "three great theoretical fruits" and elevate them into philosophical discourse.

Not only does Mao Ze-dong Thought have special philosophical works as textual basis, but his other works and revolutionary practice are also rich in philosophical ideas. These works include "Oppose Book Worship", "Problems of Strategy in China's Revolutionary War", "On Practice", "On Contradiction", "On Protracted War", "Reform our Study", "On the Ten Major Relationships", "The Question about Correctly Processing the Contradictions among the People", "Where Do Correct Ideas Come From?", etc. Mao Ze-dong's ideological lines of seeking truth from facts and proceeding from reality are great ideological creation of the first generation of the CPC represented by Mao Zedong by way of combining the basic principles of Marxism with the actual situations of China and the Chinese national culture. It is Marxism adapted to Chinese conditions, with the universal principles of Marxism as the guidance, taking roots in Chinese culture, correctly reflecting China's actual situations and guiding China's path to independence and liberation.

Mao Ze-dong Thought is a new stage in the development of the Chinese culture, especially the proposition of building a new national, scientific, and popular culture. It not only politically explores the "road to liberation" of the Chinese nation to end semi-colonial and semi-feudal rule, but also explores a road of reconstruction of the mental world and the world of meaning for the Chinese nation, which has an invaluable guiding significance for the construction of the contemporary advanced Chinese culture, the development of a new Marxism-guided national, scientific, and popular socialist culture and the strengthening of cultural identity and national cohesiveness.

Mao Ze-dong Thought has strong national characteristics, linguistically or ideologically. It advocates that critically absorbing the essence of the traditional culture of the Chinese nation is a "necessary condition for developing national culture and boosting national self-confidence"; it has absorbed the traditional social ideal of "Great Harmony,"① has set an example of moral personality, and has demonstrated its inheritance of traditional culture, especially Confucianism; its emphasis on nationality is both a manifestation of public opinion in wartime, and an important way of holding people together with culture. In addition, Mao Ze-dong's pursuit of the rational spirit (the unity of subjectivity and objectivity) carries forward the spirit of enlightenment; his emphasis on "the popular" means awareness of democracy. Only the new national, scientific, and popular culture can truly become the basis of the Chinese people's cultural identity. This is one of the main reasons why Mao Ze-dong Thought has enormous charm and has become the intellectual pillar of the rejuvenation of the Chinese nation.

Mao Ze-dong Thought is the original development of Marxist historical materialism, epistemology and dialectic thoughts by the first generation of the CPC represented by Mao Ze-dong by way of combining them with the actual situations in China, especially the actual situations of Chinese revolution and construction. All its philosophical ideas should be embodied in the construction of contemporary Marxist philosophical form adapted to Chinese conditions, which is manifested as follows: the practice-based dynamic, revolutionary theory of reflection; the elucidation of the fundamental laws of cognition(the general line of cognition); the exposition of the concrete and historical unity of subjectivity and objectivity, theory and practice, and knowing and doing; the idea that "social practice is the sole criterion for testing truth"; the quintessence of the issue of contradiction, namely the truth about the relationship between the universality and the specificity of contradiction, and that between the absolute and the relative of contradiction; creative thinking on the contradictions inside a socialist society; the "mass line", a guideline under which CPC officials and members are required to prioritize the interests of the people, rely on them in every task, persist in exercising power for them; a series of dialectical leadership methods and working methods such as "combining the generality and

---

① Great Harmony 大同 is a Chinese utopian vision of the world in which everyone and everything is at peace.—Tr.

particularity", "dissect a 'sparrow'"[1], "learn to 'play the piano'"[2], "advance wave upon wave"[3], "have a head for figures"[4], "allowing for unpredictable circumstances and needs", "being sagacious and resolute" and "deciding in the nick of time".

Deng Xiaoping has no special philosophical works, but he undoubtedly has proposed a ream of brilliant views, all of which are of ingenuity, containing the developed Marxist historical materialism, epistemology and dialectics, and which are manifested as follows: his emphasis on the unification of seeking truth from facts and emancipating the mind, his ideology of the primary stage of socialism; his statement of "Three Favorables" (whether it is favorable for promoting the growth of the productive forces in a socialist society, favorable for increasing the overall strength of the socialist state, and favorable for raising the people's living standards) as a criterion for judging the merits and demerits of all work; his idea that science and technology are the "primary productive forces"; his idea that we must address ourselves to the problem of both material and mental civilization without any letup in the socialist modernization; the theory of step-like development; and social development strategy of driving the overall situation with key points, and so forth.

---

[1] To dissect a "sparrow" is an important method of leadership which refers to conduct an in-depth study on a typical example to find out objective law to solve the problem. —Tr.

[2] "Learn to 'play the piano.' In playing the piano all ten fingers are in motion; it won't do to move some fingers only and not others. But if all ten fingers press down at once, there is no melody. To produce good music, the ten fingers should move rhythmically and in co-ordination. A Party committee should keep a firm grasp on its central task and at the same time, around the central task, it should unfold the work in other fields. At present, we have to take care of many fields; we must look after the work in all the areas, armed units and departments, and not give all our attention to a few problems, to the exclusion of others. Wherever there is a problem, we must put our finger on it, and this is a method we must master. Some play the piano well and some badly, and there is a great difference in the melodies they produce. Members of Party committees must learn to 'play the piano' well." (Cited from Mao Zedong: "Methods of Work of Party Committees, " *Selected Works of Mao Ze-dong:* Volume 4.) –Tr.

[3] "Adopt the policy of advancing in a series of waves to expand the area under the independent regime, and oppose the policy of expansion by adventurist advance." Cited from "Why is It That Red Political Power Can Exist In China?", in *Selected Works of Mao Ze-dong:* Volume 1. –Tr.

[4] "Have a head for figures." That is to say, we must attend to the quantitative aspect of a situation or problem and make a basic quantitative analysis. Every quality manifests itself in a certain quantity, and without quantity there can be no quality. To this day many of our comrades still do not understand that they must attend to the quantitative aspect of things — the basic statistics, the main percentages and the quantitative limits that determine the qualities of things. They have no "figures" in their heads and as a result cannot help making mistakes. Cited from Mao Zedong: "Methods of Work of Party Committees, " *Selected Works of Mao Ze-dong:* Volume 4.) –Tr.

The important thought of the Three Represents and the Scientific Outlook on Development also contain abundant philosophical thoughts. The emphasis on "the benefit of the people" and the new elucidation of the relationship between the Marxist ruling party and the people has highlighted the important position of the issues on values in Marxist theory. The ideological lines of "seeking truth from facts", "emancipating the mind" and "keeping pace with the times" are latest advancement of Marxist epistemology; his view on the status and role of advanced culture construction in social development is an important innovation to historical materialism; the Scientific Outlook on Development and the thought of building a harmonious socialist society are new exploration of the development mode of modern human civilization and new development of Marxist theory of social formation.

3. Summarize and elevate philosophical foundation of "Chinese experience"

Recently, some international personages proposed and positively affirmed the "Chinese Model" and "Beijing Consensus"[①]. I believe that their proposition and discussion are meaningful but not profound enough, for they by no means analyzed and crystalized from a philosophical point of view. The "Chinese Development Model" can be briefly described as the path to the development of the socialist market economy led by the CPC, which is generally referred to as the path to

---

[①] Senior Advisor, a senior consultant on the political and economic issues of the United States, proposed in an article that China's development model is a development way that is in line with China's national conditions and gears to social needs and which seeks justice and high-quality growth. He summarized this development model as "Beijing Consensus," mainly including three aspects: making arduous efforts, boosting active innovation and trying bold experiments; resolutely defending the sovereignty and interests of the country; storing up energy step by step. Among them, innovation and experiments are the soul of the "Beijing Consensus," emphasizing that issues should be addressed flexibly as they actually exist, seeking no unified standard. The "Beijing Consensus" not only focuses on economic development, but also pays attention to social changes, and improves the society through economic development and management improvement. The online version of *International Herald Tribune* carries on May 20, 2004 an article about China's change in its own way, praising China for its promoting the decisive and wise political reform in a gradual way. The *Guardian* carries on May 27, 2004 an article about the experience of China in solving the food and clothing problem for hundreds of millions of people, holding that China's rise provides a reliable choice besides the Western development model. Mexico's *Daily* carries on May 24, 2004 an article entitled "China: Horizon in Asia." believing that the Chinese miracle is the result of the formulation of social and economic policies in accordance with its own situation. These articles approve, *implicitly* or explicitly, the enhancement of China's soft power and its positive impact on the world. [See Liu Guishan 刘桂山: "Summary: Beijing Consensus- success mode of contemporary economic development"《综述:"北京共识"——当代经济发展的成功模式》, *Xinhua Net*, 2004-5-25]

socialism with Chinese characteristics. This path embodies the Marxist world view, values and methodology, combines the outstanding civilization achievements of foreign countries with the actual situations in China, and attaches great importance to organically unifying theory and scheme with practical possibility and practical operability. It is indeed a new modernization model no matter whether in Chinese history or in foreign history. Why can this model work so successfully? The reason was incisively summarized on the 16th National Congress of the CPC as "Ten Pieces of Basic Experience". Here I try to comprehend the reasons for the success of "Chinese path" and "Chinese model" from the perspective of philosophy.

(1) Creatively apply Marxist mode of practical thinking. Seek truth from facts; proceed from China's actual situations; never copy any foreign model of development; never believe in any existing theories and doctrines. Constantly carry out the practice and theoretical exploration of Chinese path of development; attach great importance to theoretical innovation; stick to the principle that practice is the criterion for testing truth and revising theory and policy. In doing so, the Party has gradually formed a correct theory which conforms to China's actual situation and which can guide China to develop successfully, namely, the theory of socialism with Chinese characteristics, and thereby has blazed a unique path of socialist modernization with Chinese characteristics. In practice, the CPC keeps economic development as the central task, firmly gives top priority to development, and is committed to releasing and developing the productive forces.

(2) Highlight the importance of putting people first. The Party always puts the interests of the people, the common prosperity and happiness of the people, the prosperity and civility of the country and the great rejuvenation of the Chinese nation as the supreme pursuit of value in national development, and formulates policies and principles based on the standpoint of the people, which means that the Party sticks to the stand and values of Marxism and therefore wins support from the people, bringing strong support and inexhaustible vitality to the development of the country.

(3) Creatively apply the contradictory dialectics and adherence to dialectical and unified concept of reform and development. Firstly, the Party accurately grasps the "extent" of development and takes the way of incremental reform and development, achieving a leap-forward development of things in the process of "fostering" and enriching the "new characteristics" of things; the Party upholds the strategies of "stable development" and "gradual development", and promotes the development of things based on the law of the unification of opposites instead of

ignoring the other side of the contradiction of things and practicing the strategies of "discontinuous development" and "mutational development". This is creative application of the Marxist dialectics. Secondly, the Party insists on coordinated development: (a)it strikes a balance between reform, development and stability, that is, taking development as the foundation and root, taking reform as the driving force and means, and taking stability as the precondition and goal; (b) it achieves balanced development of material, political and mental civilizations; (c) it works for harmonious development of economy and society; (d) it pushes the coordinated development of human and nature. In a word, "harmonious development" of modernization with Chinese characteristics should be achieved. More than 20 years of exploration of modernization allows us to have a clear understanding and a new theoretical sublimation of it. This is new development of Marxist dialectics and the ideas of "harmony" and "golden mean" of traditional Chinese philosophy. Finally, it adheres to the four cardinal principles and the reform and opening up policy in the process of socialist modernization with Chinese characteristics, which not only draws on the historical experience, but also creatively applies the Marxist principle on the reaction of the production relations to the productive forces and that of superstructure to economic base. This is not only the main characteristic of "Chinese development model", but also the main experience of its achieving great results.

To sum up, the development path of socialism with Chinese characteristics formed since the introduction of the reform and opening - up initiative in 1978 and the economic, political, and cultural institutional structures developed accordingly require Chinese philosophy and social science research to carry out the theoretical in-depth exploration and "legitimacy demonstration". Contemporary Marxist philosophy is supposed to fully study the "Chinese experience" accumulated in the formation of Chinese development path and crystalize philosophical thoughts and propositions with Chinese characteristics.

III. How to display inclusiveness

The theoretical and methodological characteristics of Marxist philosophy determine that it must be a practice-oriented, open-minded ideology. Since the emergence of Marxist philosophy, modern Western philosophy has established a variety of trends and schools of thoughts, among which there are many academic resources that we can draw from, which is of great referential significance for us to judiciously capture and answer the questions of the times. Since the Western Marxism was introduced into the China's academic circle in the 1980s, the study of it has changed from initial introduction to the cultivation of the consciousness to acquire a comprehensive understanding of the Western Marxism, by way of reconsidering the immanent spirit of Marxist philosophy.① Scholars have realized that the theoretical achievements of the Western Marxist philosophy have become a resource which cannot be ignored for the contemporary construction of Marxist philosophy.② The exploration of the Western Marxist philosophy has broken the dogmatic attitude towards Marxist philosophy and rethought its basic theories, trying to develop its spirit in the contemporary historical context, which makes Marxist philosophy an open theory. In the current study, a more in-depth analysis of the Western Marxism and the post-Western Marxism that has emerged since the 1970s is supposed to be conducted; meanwhile, the intrinsic relationship between the Western Marxism and the Marxist philosophy, and in what sense we should reasonably draw on the achievements of the research into the Western Marxist philosophy should be further explored. From this perspective, what I believe is that as far as the construction of the Marxist philosophy in contemporary China is concerned, the Western Marxism, on the basis of carefully identifying and criticizing its misunderstanding and misinterpretation on the Marxist philosophy, has referential significance at least in the following four aspects:

(1) The Western Marxism takes the critical spirit of the Marxist philosophy as the principal factor, and deeply analyzes the politics, economy, and culture of contemporary capitalist society, and adopts research method of capitalism critique, which is of great reference significance for breaking the disciplinary boundaries in Chinese philosophy research and for constructing the forms of contemporary Chinese Marxist philosophy. Confronted with the theoretical texts of Western

---

① In "The Logical Transformation of the Study of Western Marxist Philosophy in China," (《中国西方马克思主义哲学研究的逻辑转换》) published in *Social Sciences in China* (《中国社会科学》), 2004(6), Zhang Yibing (张一兵) and others discusses the overall logical process of the study of Western Marxist philosophy in China and the significance of Western Marxism. It can also be seen from the author's comments that the Chinese Academics' conscious grasp of Western Marxist philosophy has been gradually developed on the level of academic theory.

② Many scholars who study Western Marxism realize that it has been 80 years since Lukács published "History and Class Consciousness" and Korsch published "Marxism and Philosophy" in 1923. A group of theorists and social critics known as "Western Marxism," from Lukács, Bloch, Horkheimer, Adorno to Sartre, Lefebvre, Marcuse, and then Althusser and others, have worked together to explore from different angles the shortcomings of Western civilization and the ways-out, so as to provide some enlightenment for us to understand contemporary capitalism.

Marxist philosophy, we can find that they have actively drawn on the achievements of contemporary philosophical ideology and culture, and striven to achieve the interdisciplinary integration on the basis of the critical spirit of Marxist philosophy. For example, in Lukács' *History and Class Consciousness*, we notice that he integrates Marxist philosophy, German classical philosophy, Weber's political science, sociology and classical economics and other disciplines into a critical theory of an organized capitalist society by adopting the concept of "materialization". Although Lukács has a different theoretical direction from Marx (we can even say that Lukács deviates from Marx), he has promoted the critical spirit of Marxist philosophy. For another example, many scholars of the Frankfurt School have re-interpreted Marx's *Economic and Philosophic Manuscripts of 1844*, and combined his philosophical criticism with psychoanalytic theory, making a deep study of the Fascist personality and a contemporary elaboration of the humanistic thought of Marxist philosophy; Horkheimer and Adorno re-explored the spirit of enlightenment and made a deep theoretical analysis of the roots of the Western culture.

(2) Western Marxism's understanding and grasp of the changes in the stages of development of capitalist society is of great enlightenment for us to have a profound understanding of contemporary capitalism and the law of capitalist development, as well as the intrinsic mechanism of the development of human society, and the construction of contemporary Chinese Marxist philosophy. With the status of Fordism in industrial production established, capitalism has moved into a new stage, that is, the stage of organized capitalism, which not only led to the changes in the capitalist mode of production, but also led to the changes in the relationship between the state and civil society, as well as brought about the cultural and ideological issues. As for this change in capitalist society, Gramsci conducted an in-depth analysis of Marx's theory of state and civil society, ideology and hegemony, and consciously based his own revolutionary strategy on the changes in capitalist society. The concept of "late capitalism" (the new stage of monopolistic capitalism) forms the basis of the philosophy of the Frankfurt School. When Adorno published *Negative Dialectics* in the 1970s, the illusionary rule of capitalism caused by the public media has constituted his important topics, which also formed the realistic premise of the *Negative Dialectics*. This also posed a challenge for us: if we want to understand the Western Marxism, we must simultaneously study the history of capitalist society. Likewise, if we want to develop Marxist philosophy today, these two tasks also need to be carried out at the same time. Only in this way can we truly return to reality.

(3) From the perspective of domestic Marxist philosophy research, Western Marxist research on cultural theory deserves special attention. Western Marxism's thinking on cultural theory is carried out from two important aspects. One is the aspect of cultural philosophy, which is also the metaphysical content of philosophical thinking. Adorno's thinking on enlightenment is one of its important features, and the cultural research in this aspect has been recognized by the academics. The other is the study of popular culture. Benjamin's discussion of mechanical replication technology, and Adorno and Horkheimer's criticism of cultural industry are the issues that are very rare in the domestic study of Marxist philosophy or even do not really attract attention. If this problem does not enter our field of vision, with the electronic media technology developing, the construction of contemporary Marxist philosophy will lack a fresh content which plays a leading role in the current consciousness construction.

(4) Despite that the Western Marxism, including the late "constructive postmodernism" and "ecological Marxist theory" which reveal the negative function of science and technology and the nature of ideology, and thereby realize the criticism of "modernity", is extremely-biased somewhere, it is profoundly and reasonably valuable, especially in acting as a wake-up call for the realization of the harmony between man and nature, of the unification of industrial civilization and ecological civilization, and for the promotion of people's reflection on issues of fairness, equality and justice. So, we should fully absorb its reasonable and valuable thoughts in the construction of the form of contemporary Marxist philosophy adapted to the Chinese context.

In brief, although we are not directly identified with some crucial conclusions of the Western Marxism, it is of great significance for us to understand its basic issues and latest developments, pay attention to the issues raised by Western Marxist scholars in philosophical logic and their criticism of capitalism, and transform these issues into the subjects that we are studying positively. All these will help us uphold and develop Marxist philosophy and the Marxism as a whole.

IV. How to embody epochal character

Marxist philosophy is not only derived from criticism and inheritance of excellent Western cultural achievements, especially the critical inheritance and absorption of German classical philosophy, but also from K. Marx's and F. Engels' answers and solutions to the major problems of their times. It is the quintessence of the spirit of their times. Today, in order to develop Marxist philosophy and construct a new form of Chinese Marxist philosophy, we must accurately capture and solve the problems of the times. This is the fundamental way for the development of Marxist philosophy in the 21st century.

The current major issues of the times include: the relationship between globalization and nationality, the development of contemporary social forms, the role and status of knowledge production, the relationship between the role of culture and diverse civilization systems, universal ethics and communication consensus and rules, the scientific and technological revolution and the ways of human life and development, the national sovereignty, functions and relations in the context of globalization, the path to national development under the social conditions of globalization and IT application, and the issue of modernity, etc.

As for the theory of social form, K. Marx's is the important part of materialist conception of history. In the current era, the rapid development of scientific and technological revolution and the globalization have led to changes in production mode and social structure. How should we understand the new changes brought about by the globalization, IT application, and webfication in the organizational structure and operation mechanisms of our society? How should we understand the trend of development of human society? Some scholars propose that the biggest and most direct question which globalization has posed for us is: Is it possible for "global society" to be the analytical unit of social and historical philosophy? The concept of "global society" is proposed in relation to the traditional "society" with the nation-state as the unit of analysis. Some scholars believe that from the objective trend of the development of human society, globalization will inevitably lead to a global society, and the emergence of the concept and unit of analysis of "global society" is a reflection of this trend. If we can study "global society" as deeply as we study the traditional nation-state-based "society", Marxist historical philosophy will enjoy a new development.[1] Manuel Castells, author of *"The Information Age* trilogy", wrote in his book *The Power of Identity*: "Our world, and our lives, are being shaped by the conflicting trends of globalization and identity. The information technology revolution, and the restructuring of capitalism, have induced a new form of society, the network society. It is characterized by the globalization of strategically decisive economic activities."

---

[1] Research group of Marxist-Leninist Institute of Chinese Academy of Social Sciences: *"Research on Marxism and Several Major Practical Problems," Journal of Chinese Academy of Social Sciences*, 2003-9-26.

How to understand the new changes in and new features of contemporary society? Do globalization, IT application and networking make the form of society enter a new stage? How should we evaluate various theories of social forms in the west (the theories of post-industrial society, information society, knowledge society, global society, consumer society, and so forth)? In the situation that contemporary capitalism has developed into a new stage (transnational capitalism) and assumed new characteristics, how should we view the relationships between capitalism and socialism and between the two social forms? What kind of relationship does the trend of the development of globalization, informatization and networking in contemporary society have with the social form of capitalism and socialism? Or what impact will it have on the development of capitalism and socialism?[①] How should we, on the basis of correctly grasping the Marxist classical writer's theory of social form and the characteristics of the times, summarize the nature and the characteristics of contemporary social form, charting a new interpretation framework and theoretical paradigm for human survival and development, and achieving the new development of historical materialism in the contemporary times? This is undoubtedly an issue of great theoretical significance. Moreover, by analyzing and studying contemporary social forms and correctly understanding the trend of the evolution and development of social forms, we can further understand the power system of the historical development of human society, judiciously predict the future of human social development, and provide theoretical support for the leap-forward development of developing countries, which can help us study the complexity and new features of social existence and movement mechanism, provide a theoretical basis for us to judiciously and effectively solve social conflicts, promote social development, and provide theoretical support for our new ways of thinking, practice, and decision-making to reflect the new development of social form.

As for the theory of production, with the advent of the new characteristics of

---

[①] Some researchers also point out that the relationship between socialism and capitalism should be correctly understood and handled from the perspective of the evolution and replacement of social forms. Although socialism and capitalism exist in the same era as two opposing theories and national systems, the development of the two systems shows a trend of interdependence and complementarity, and this co-existence and interdependence will exist for a long time in the future. However, this does not mean that the two systems are gradually moving towards reconciliation and reunification. No matter what circumstances, the two systems are of fundamental significance. See "Study on Marxism and Several Major Practical Problems," *Journal of Chinese Academy of Social Sciences*, 2003-9-2.

the scientific and technological revolution since the end of the 20th century, the socialization of science and technology and the technologization of society have become the basic facts and trends of the existence and development of today's human society, and knowledge practice with knowledge production and knowledge labor as its important content has become the leading form of human practice. Knowledge practice is an important form emerging from the development of human practice, is the result of the continuous innovation and development and the extensive penetration and application of science and technology in social production and social life, reflecting the current "spirit of the times" that knowledge becomes the way of human existence. Knowledge practice has become the basic driving force for economic development and human social progress. Then, how should we understand the position of this form of practice in the human practice system? How should we understand the relationship between this form of practice and the forms of material and intellectual production forms? These have actually involved the continuance and development of K. Marx's theory of social production in the contemporary era.

As for the theory of culture, "The form of culture is first determined by the political and economic form," and "any given culture (as an ideological form) is a reflection of the politics and economics of a given society, and the former in turn has a tremendous influence and effect upon the latter."[①] This is the basic viewpoint of Marxist historical materialism on the relationship between economy, politics and culture. In the face of the rapid development of science and technology and the fierce competition in comprehensive national power, in the face of the mutual turbulence of various ideologies and cultures around the world, the position of culture in the comprehensive national power is becoming more and more prominent, and the exchange and dissemination of culture has increasingly become an important content of relations between countries. Cultural conflicts have increasingly become an aspect of international competition and international conflicts. The current competition between countries is the one in overall national strength, fundamentally the one in national quality and talent, and essentially the one in national culture. The cultural industry has been recognized as the most dynamic, innovative and profitable industry in the economic field, and its contribution and status in the economy has become increasingly important. So, how to deeply understand the important position and

---

① *Selected Works of Mao Zedong*, Vol. 2, Chin. ed., Beijing: People's Publishing House, 1991, p. 664, 663.

function of culture in contemporary and future society from the height of the social development dynamics theory of historical materialism is undoubtedly an important issue involving the basic theory of historical materialism.

As for the problem of value consensus and universal ethics, under the social conditions of globalization and technologization, human creativity has been unprecedentedly enhanced, and the scope and effect of human activities have greatly expanded. This is certainly a sign of the growth of the essential power of mankind, and it also highlights the unprecedented great responsibility of mankind. In a society where science and technology are highly developed and risks are increasing, human beings need dialogue, communication, negotiation, and consensus more than ever before. It requires not only new concepts and norms for the relationship between man and nature, but also new norms for human activities. How do different civilizations and knowledge systems respect each other, live in harmony, and integrate with each other instead of discriminating against each other or eliminating each other? How do the subjects of different civilizations and interest groups live in harmony with nature? How do the cultural value system of different civilizations change from conflict and divergence to seeking dialogue and consensus, and formulating common norms as the basic way to maintain a normal and harmonious life order of mankind? Especially in the present-day society, human beings are faced with many global problems that have been threatening their survival and development. It is urgent to construct ecological ethics, bioethics, network ethics, the ethics of scientists and technologists, and the political philosophy and humanistic spirit that can embody social justice. How do we adapt ourselves to the requirements of the times and establish a new moral philosophy system? Obviously, it is a subject of great theoretical and practical significance.

As for the issue of modernity and the construction of Chinese modernity, the emergence of a series of global problems, such as environmental pollution, ecological imbalances, ethnic conflicts, regional wars, terrorism, thermonuclear threats, cultural conflicts, and the gap between the rich and the poor, have cast a deep shadow on human survival and development in the 21st century. These problems reflect the crisis of the concept and road to human civilization development, which is essentially the so-called crisis of the "modernity". The issue of modernity requires people to reflect on and reconstruct modernity. In particular, philosophers need to re-understand human beings and their values, human principles of practice, the relationship between human beings and society, the world, and the universe, and study and solve them according to this total and fundamental philosophical thinking and exploration.[①] At the same time, the practice of China's modernization and its further development have exposed and accumulated many deep-seated problems. China's development has been achieved at huge prices, whether in terms of resources and environment or in terms of social justice and stability. The two backgrounds mentioned above are constantly questioning Chinese scholars: What kind of modernity should China construct? And what kind of path should China take to realize the economic, political, cultural, and social development? These questions urgently require academic exploration and argumentation. How should we, proceeding from China's practical exploration of modernization and its unique "experience", from the viewpoints, methods and positions of Marxist philosophy, construct China's modernity and chart a grand blueprint for its future? The question is one of awful moment to the Chinese nation. Thus, it can be seen that the issue of modernity is the central issue not only of world development but also of China's development. In my opinion, globalization, modernization of socialism with Chinese characteristics, modernity and Marxism in Chinese context are the four closely- related practical and theoretical propositions. The process of China's modernization, in theoretical form, is the process of the formation and development of "Sinicized Marxism", and it is manifested in philosophical form as the effort of the integration of Chinese philosophy, Western philosophy and Marxist philosophy, which is essentially the process of constructing and enriching China's modernity. It can be said that this is the internal logic of Chinese scholarship in modern times, including contemporary Chinese philosophy and social sciences.

As for the new philosophical problems brought about by the development of modern science and technology, the development of the information society and the emergence of the "infosphere" have exalted the word "information" to a basic concept that is as important as such basic concepts of "existence" "knowledge" and "meaning". The development of biological sciences and networks has challenged traditional ethical concepts. Some experts believe that the development of contemporary science and technology will have a great impact on basic philosophical concepts, such as virtual reality, artificial life, network structure, and computer modeling in genetic

---

① Research Group of Institute of Philosophy, Chinese Academy of Social Sciences: "Several Academic Orientations of Marxist Philosophy Research," *Journal of Chinese Academy of Social Sciences*, 2003-4-22.

engineering, as well as a series of ethical issues.①

The aforementioned major philosophical issues raised by the times and practices are all we must concentrate our efforts on researching and correctly answering in the process of constructing the form of contemporary Chinese Marxist philosophy. Only in this way can the new form of philosophy have new connotations and indicate that our philosophical thinking has reached a new stage.

The research of Sinicized Marxist philosophy should not only have "text school", but also have "problem-oriented school", "(China's) experience-oriented school" and "tradition-oriented school" (to integrate its relationship between traditional Chinese philosophy and culture). In these kinds of research, we should bear in mind the goal, that is, to develop Marxism in the 21st century and Marxism in China today. So we must integrate the basic principles of Marxism with the characteristics of the times and China's actual situations; we must have the whole world in view; we must constantly summarize "Chinese experience"; we must make comprehensive innovation; we must proceed from China's cultural traditions and practice of modernization; and we must adapt Marxism to the Chinese context in keeping with the times in an ever-changing practice. All these steers to its fundamental orientation the philosophical research into the adaptation of Marxism to China's conditions.

---

① Liu Gang 刘钢: "Philosophy of Information: A New Frontier in Philosophical Exploration," 《信息哲学：哲学探索的新前沿》 *Journal of Chinese Academy of Social Sciences*, 2003-3-4.

On Connotations of Adapting of Marxist Philosophy to the Chinese Context*

Chinese philosophy nowadays has to depend on two major global practical backgrounds: the globalization in the ascendant and the socialist modernization with Chinese characteristics. The contradiction between global and national characters will be a fundamental one running through the whole process of modernization with Chinese characteristics.

The most obvious feature of the present-day world is economic globalization. The growing trend of economic globalization is "creating fluid space, electronic space, space without a center, space that can penetrate borders and the world," "a mobile, electronic and non-central space that can penetrate borders and the world." In particular, the development of information technology and global media has enabled cultural communication to break through traditional territorial boundaries and create an increasingly consistent global culture. The economic globalization and the imbalance of social and economic development have to some extent strengthened the marginalization of disadvantaged nations. Although we do not agree with the term "cultural globalization", the connection between economic and media globalization and territory is indeed clearly broken, and the identity crisis of national culture (especially in those nation-states in an under-privileged position in the process of economic globalization) is increasingly becoming a serious problem. In contemporary China, the Chinese people's cultural identity has been strengthened with economic development and national strength, and at the same time they have encountered new major challenges. The implementation of the socialist market economy will inevitably bring about the diversification of interest subjects, and recognize and even promote the diversification of people's concepts and behaviors, both of which will inevitably

---

* Originally published in *Marxism & Reality,* 2005(5)

lead to the diversification and divergence of social culture.

In an increasingly globalized world, to achieve the modernization of China and the great rejuvenation of the Chinese nation, we must attach great importance to the national culture, take the cultivation and promotion of the national spirit as the fundamental way to enhance national cohesiveness, and provide mental motivation and support for promoting the modernization with Chinese characteristics and achieving the great cause of national rejuvenation. The construction of contemporary Chinese Marxist philosophy is the soul of cultivating and promoting the national spirit. And the contemporary Chinese Marxist philosophy cannot be divorced from the 5,000-year-old cultural tradition of the Chinese nation. It is first of all "Chinese", and the philosophy of "the Chinese nation", that is, the philosophy based on the roots of the Chinese nation's culture.

I. Absorb and clarify outstanding ingredients in traditional culture of the Chinese nation

It is generally believed that the main part of the traditional Chinese culture is Confucian culture. It is not only the leading ideology of the feudal patriarchal society, but also the ideological tool of the ruling class of this society. At the same time, it is also the theoretical resource that restricts the autocratic monarchy by the intellectuals in this society and the moral principle of ordinary people. It is not only an important part of the philosophy, politics, and law of this society, but also has a strong and lasting penetration into literature, art, social psychology, folk customs, and so on. The theory of "the mandate of heaven" and the ethics of three cardinal guides (ruler guides subject, father guides son and husband guides wife) in classical Confucianism that strengthened the theocracy, the monarchy, the patriarchy and the authority of husband are no longer suitable for the needs of the modern democratic society under the rule of law, and are naturally to be discarded and eliminated. However, some basic concepts in the Confucian value system, such as benevolence, humanism, supreme peace, harmony, moderation, and integrity, have been proved to be the mental wealth that has gone through thousands of cultural changes and social practices and has been proven to be beneficial to the survival and development of mankind and social progress. Not only are they not outdated, but also universal. And if properly guided and endowed with the spirit of the times, they will not only produce the most powerful mental strength and the inexhaustible cultural source, but also enable themselves to play a practical role in enhancing morality and benefiting the world's people in the process of the modernization of the contemporary world.

In terms of the relationship between man and nature, traditional Confucian scholars have the universal feeling and ideal of life of "ordaining conscience for heaven and earth*(wei-tian-di-li-xin* 为天地立心)" and "people are my brothers and all things are my kinds(*min-bao-wu-yu*民胞物与)". Such feelings and ideals culturally and ethically lead people to infuse the universe with spiritual content, and produce a sense of life and a mental realm in which man and all things between heaven and earth are integrated into one entity. In *The Doctrine of the Mean,* there is an argument about the principle of "*can-zan-hua-yu*"(参赞化育 meaning "joining in nature")--"*can-zan* (参赞)" refers to the participation and regulation of human beings in the heaven, earth and nature, and "*hua-yu* (化育)" refers to the changes and development of all things in nature. Through "*can-zan*" conducted by human beings, all things in nature will develop themselves ("*hua-yu*") in accordance with the laws of nature and physics, and thus humans and the natural world will naturally establish a coordinated relationship, and the human living environment and ecosystem will naturally form an optimized and balanced state. This ecological ideal is based on agricultural society and natural economy, so it has historical limitations. However, its basic ideas have lasting and universal significance, and they can still provide us with extremely valuable enlightenment.

In dealing with the relationship between groups, society and even the country, Confucianism advocates "the benevolent loves others", takes "Harmony is what matters" as the value orientation and conduct principle, follows the course of the Mean, emphasizes "harmony in diversity", seeking consensus on major issues while preserving differences on minor issues, and opposes excessive competition and vicious antagonism and confrontation which may cause the situations in which neither side gains or one side annexes the other. In the contemporary era, with the integration of the global economy and the integration of information, the development of world civilization has shown a general trend of exchange, dialogue, mutual infiltration and integration. At the same time, the so-called "theory of clash of civilizations" has also been rampant. The Confucian concepts of "harmony in diversity" and "help others secure a footing and succeed if you are to make it yourself" and the idealized goals of "All people under the heaven should enjoy peace" obviously have extremely practical significance for the correct handling of international relations and the realization of world peace.

In terms of the relationship between individuals and groups, Confucianism advocates a healthy interactive relationship between the two. Confucianism starts from the ideological point of "the benevolent loves others", regards human beings as a group, treats interpersonal relationships from the coexistence of the same kind, and regards "People from all over the world comes to live harmoniously with each other" and moral harmoniousness as the basic principles for handling interpersonal relationships. This principle is specifically expanded into many aspects such as loyalty, forgiveness, sincerity, and integrity. The former two—loyalty and forgiveness—extend and develop the concept of "the benevolent loves others" respectively from the positive and negative aspects: "loyalty" refers to the spirit in which people of uprightness are considerate to others and help one to fulfill his wish while "forgiveness" is the spirit in which people treat other people as you would yourself or are more tolerant to others. "Sincerity" and "integrity" explain the truthfulness and honesty in communication respectively from the internal and external aspects. The purpose of being sincere or honest is to achieve psychological communication, ideological exchange and emotional understanding between people on the basis of moral concepts, so as to establish a coordinated and harmonious relationship.

The many afore-mentioned excellent ideas and values contained in Confucian culture, as well as the reasonable resources in traditional culture including Buddhism and Taoism, should be fully reflected in the contemporary Marxist philosophy system.

II. To study philosophical thoughts contained in "three major theoretical achievements"

Mao Zedong Thought, Deng Xiaoping Theory and the important thought of the Three Represents are the "three major theoretical achievements" of the three historic leaps in the Sinicization of Marxism, are the theoretical innovations of the CPC, and represent the creative achievements of the theoretical thinking of the Chinese nation. The construction of contemporary Marxist philosophy should never ignore and set aside these "three major theoretical achievements", but should conduct in-depth studies on them and further summarize the the existing and implicit philosophical thoughts in the "three theoretical achievements" so that they should be upgraded to be philosophical discourses.

First of all, there are not only specialized philosophical works which Mao Zedong Thought is based on, but also many other works of Mao Zedong and his revolutionary practice which contain extremely rich philosophical thoughts, such as "Combat Book Worship", "Strategic Problems of the China's Revolutionary War", "On Practice", "On Contradiction", "On Protracted War", "Reform Our Study", "On the Ten Major Relationships", " On the Correct Handling of the Contradictions among the People", and "Where Do Correct Ideas Come from?" The ideological lines of seeking truth from facts and of all proceeding from the reality of China, which were established by Mao Zedong Thought, are the great ideological creation of the first generation of Chinese Communists represented by Mao Zedong, combining the basic principles of Marxism with the reality of China and the Chinese national culture. Guided by the universal principles of Marxism, taking roots in Chinese culture, it is a Sinicized Marxism that correctly reflects China's actual conditions and points out China's road to independence and liberation against the historical background of a semi-colonial and semi-feudal society.

Mao Zedong Thought marks a new stage in the development of Chinese culture, especially the propositions about building a national, scientific, and popular new culture, not only politically exploring the "road of liberation" for the Chinese nation to get rid of semi-colonial and semi-feudal rule, but also exploring the reconstruction of the order of the mental world and meaning world of the Chinese nation, which has a close bearing on the construction of contemporary advanced Chinese culture, the development of a new national, scientific, and popular socialist culture guided by Marxism, and the strengthening of cultural identity and national cohesion. Mao Zedong Thought embodies strong national characteristics from language form to ideological content. It advocates critically absorbing the essence of the nation's traditional culture, which is necessary condition for developing national culture and enhancing national self-confidence. In particular, it draws on the traditional social ideal of "*da-tong* (大同 Great Harmony)", sets up the model of moral personality, and demonstrates the inheritance of the traditional culture, especially Confucianism. Mao Zedong's emphasis on nationality was not only a manifestation of public opinion in the state of war at that time, but also an important way to unite people's hearts with culture. The pursuit of rationality (the unity of subjectivity and objectivity) carries forward the spirit of enlightenment. And "the popular" means democratic consciousness. Therefore, only the national, scientific and popular new culture can truly become the basis of Chinese cultural identity. For this reason, we can understand why Mao Zedong Thought has infinite intellectual charm and why it has become one of the great mental supports of the rejuvenation of the Chinese nation.

Although Deng Xiaoping does not have a special philosophical work, Deng Xiaoping Theory includes the emphasis of the unification of seeking truth from facts and emancipating the mind, the thought on the primary stage of socialism, the idea of using "three benefits" as the criterion for judging the gains and losses of all works, the thought of "science and technology are the primary productive forces", the thought of "doing material and mental civilization at once and attaching equal importance to each" in the construction of socialist modernization, the "step-wise" approach to and the strategic thinking of social development with key points to promote the overall situation, and so on. All these are the original developments of Marxist historical materialism, epistemology and dialectical thought.

The important thought of the Three Represents and the Scientific Outlook on Development also contain rich philosophical thoughts. First of all, they further emphasize "the interests of the people" and are new interpretation of the relationship between the Marxist ruling party and the people, highlighting even more the importance of value and concepts of value in Marxist theory. The elucidation of the guiding principles of seeking truth from facts, emancipating the mind and keeping pace with the times are the new advancement to Marxist epistemology. The thought on the status and role of building advanced culture in social development is an important innovation to the theory of the culture of historical materialism; and the Scientific Outlook on Development and the thought of building a harmonious socialist society is a new exploration of the development model of human modern civilization and a new development of the theory of Marxist social formation. The important thought of the Three Represents and the Scientific Outlook on Development give a full view of the trend of world civilization, attach great importance to the excellent cultural traditions of their own nation, base themselves on "Chinese practice", and create "Chinese experience", pushing forward the "Chinese Model" of modernization.

III. To summarize and promote philosophical foundation of "Chinese experience"

Recently, some international people have proposed and positively affirmed the "Chinese Model" and the "Beijing Consensus". I believe that the questions and discussions raised by international people are meaningful, but are neither not profound enough nor in line with the reality of the development of "China", let alone analyzed and refined from a philosophical point of view. In my opinion, the "Chinese development model" can be simply put as the road of developing the socialist market economy under the leadership of the CPC or what is commonly called the path of socialism with Chinese characteristics. This path embodies Marxist world outlook, concepts of values and methodology of Marxism, combines the outstanding achievements of foreign civilizations with China's national conditions and reality, and attaches great importance to the organic unification of theory, program and practical possibility and operability. Looking back at Chinese and foreign history, we can find this is indeed a new modernization model. Why has this model achieved great success? The Sixteenth National Congress of the CPC summarizes the "Ten Basic Experiences", which are very incisive and "to the point". Here are the reasons and experience of the success of the "Chinese Model" and "Chinese road" that I have summarized from a philosophical perspective.

(1) China has been adhering to the principle of seeking truth from facts, proceed from the reality of China's development and environment, neither copying any model of foreign development nor blindly believing in any existing doctrinal theologies, but continuing to conduct practical and theoretical exploration of China's development path, attaching great importance to theoretical innovation, so it has not only gradually formed a correct theory which is in line with China's reality and guides China's successful development, that is, the theory of socialism with Chinese characteristics, but also has evolved out of a unique path of modernization, that is, the path to socialism with Chinese characteristics. This is the result of adhering to and creatively applying the world view, epistemology and methodology of Marxist philosophy.

(2) China has persisted in taking economic construction as the central task, firmly taking "development" as the top priority and committing to the liberation and development of the productive forces, which is the result of upholding and applying the basic viewpoints of historical materialism on basic social conflicts and basic driving forces of social development.

(3) China has been regarding as the highest value pursuit of development the interests of the people, the common prosperity and happiness of the people, the prosperity and civilization of the country, and the great rejuvenation of the civilization and the nation. This upholds Marxist concept of value, enables governance and development to receive the greatest power— the support of the people, and provides development with strong support and continuous vitality.

(4) China has adhered to the principle of "degree" of development and taken the path of gradual reform and development, realizing the transition and development of things in the process of "cultivating" and enriching their new quality, adhering to "steady development" and "gradual development", that is, promoting the development

of things while grasping the unity of opposites, rather than ignoring or neglecting the other side of the contradiction of things, and engaging in "fracture development" and "mutation development". This is creative application and development of Marxist dialectics.

(5) China has persisted in coordinated development. First, the relationship between reform, development and stability is properly handled, the "system nature" of things well maintained. "Development" is the basis and the foundation, "reform" is the driving force and the means, and "stability" is the prerequisite and the goal. All these three must be taken into account, or there will be a "loophole" in the ship of modernization. Second, the development of material civilization, political civilization and mental civilization is coordinated. Third, the development of economy and society is coordinated. Fourth, the development of man and nature is coordinated. To sum up, it means realizing modernization with Chinese characteristics and the "harmonious development" of contemporary Chinese society. Regarding this point, after more than 20 years of exploration of modernization roads, we have a clear understanding and sublimation of new theories. This is also the creative application and development of the dialectics of Marxism and the "harmony" and "the golden mean" in traditional Chinese philosophy.

(6) China has integrated the adherence to the Four Cardinal Principles[①] and Reform and Opening Up in the process of the modernization of socialism with Chinese characteristics, which is not only the application of Chinese historical experience but also in line with China's reality, thereby creatively applying the theory of the reaction of the production relations to the productive forces and that of superstructure to economic base. This is not only the main characteristic of "Chinese development model", but also a major experience of the "Chinese development model" achieving great results.

The development path of socialism with Chinese characteristics has been clarified, but this path and the resulting economic, political, cultural system structure still requires Chinese philosophy and social science researchers to continue their academic excavation and make "legitimacy demonstration", and at the same time to deal judiciously and in line with China's national conditions with a large number

---

[①] The "Four Cardinal Principles" were put forward by Deng Xiaoping: adherence to the socialist road; adherence to the people's democratic dictatorship; adherence to the leadership of the CPC; and adherence to Marxism-Leninism and Mao Zedong Thought. They are the fundamental guarantee for the sound development of China's socialist modernization. —Tr.

of new problems and conflicts that have emerged, so as to guide new development. Contemporary Marxist philosophy must fully study the "Chinese experience" accumulated in the Chinese road, and refine philosophical thoughts and propositions with Chinese characteristics.

Main Trends and Issues of Current Studies of Marxist Philosophy in China*

Over the last 20-odd years since the commencement of reform and opening up, great progress has been made in Chinese Marxist philosophical studies while academic accumulation has been achieved to provide a solid theoretical foundation for the development and innovation of Marxist philosophy. However, at the same time, thanks to the rapid development of science and technology as well as the profound changes in human society, many new questions have also been brought to the studies of Marxist philosophy adapted to China's conditions. It is since the late 1990s that Chinese Marxist philosophy has been undergoing great changes in research paradigms, methods and themes, breeding new vigor and vitality for its development.

I. Four trends in current Marxist philosophy studies in China

1. Trend of "text-basedinterpretation"

"Text-based interpretation" is specifically manifested as the following three paths:

The first path is to re-read Marxist philosophy. In the past, constrained and influenced by the incompleteness of materials, distortion of dissemination and historical needs, the interpretation of Marxist philosophy tended to be one-sided, over-simplified and even sometimes incorrect. But now through re-reading Marxist philosophy, some concepts or propositions have been given new exposition, and some issues are proposed, such as whether difference exists between K. Marx's and F.

---

* This article is an academic speech given by the author in some universities and has not been published.

Engels' philosophical thoughts.①

The second path is to re-trace Marxist philosophy. Marxist philosophy has to re-think its relationship with Western philosophical tradition, in particular with German classical philosophy. What is its relationship with Kant's, Hegel's and Feuerbach's philosophical thoughts? Which concepts and aspects of it are influenced? To what extent? How did it "appear on the scene"? (the question of "the route by which it appeared on the scene"); does it belong to the category of early modern philosophy or modern philosophy?②

The third is to take a look back at K. Marx. From the interpretation of the evolution and development of Western Marxist theories, especially the application of Anglo-American Marxist thoughts (post-Marxism) since the 1970s to reflect on Marxist philosophy, to examine in which aspects Western Marxism correctly interprets Marxist philosophy, in which aspects Marxist philosophy has been enriched and developed, and in what aspects Marxist philosophy was deviated or even misinterpreted.③

In the final analysis, the aforementioned studies are still answering the questions: What kind of ideological system is Marxist philosophy? What are its basic principles, viewpoints, methods, and value beliefs?

I cannot agree more with text-based research. There are many new understandings and discoveries through text-based research, which are of great significance for correcting previous misunderstandings of Marxist philosophy and showing what the true Marxist philosophy is. My questions are as follows:

(1) Will text-based interpretation lead to different understandings of the essence of Marxist philosophy? What may attribute to this phenomenon?

(2) In this regard, according to our understandings of Marxist philosophy gained over the past 20 years or so, can we reach consensuses on the following points?

---

① Zhang Yibing 张一兵: *Back to Marx: Changes of Philosophical Discourse in the Context of Economics*《回到马克思——经济学语境中的哲学话语》, Nanjing: Jiangsu People's Publishing House, 1999; Yu Wujin 俞吾金: *A New Understanding of Marx*《重新理解马克思》, Beijing: Beijing Normal University Press, 2005.

② Representative achievements include *From Kant to Marx* by Yu Wujin 俞吾金, Guilin: Guangxi Normal University Press, 2004.

③ For example, Yi Junqing 衣俊卿: "Cultural Critical Theory of New Marxism and Its Enlightenment"《新马克思主义的文化批判理论及其启示》, *Social Sciences in China*, 1997(6); "Criticism of Daily Life in the Process of Modernization"《现代化进程中的日常生活批判》, *Tianjin Social Sciences*, 1991(3). Their internal logic is clear, rigorous and scientific.

—The transcending significance of Marx's new conception of history to previous philosophies. Historical materialism (I call it the conception of practical history) is the analysis of the social structure and the social operation and development mechanisms, the study of the operating and development laws of the capitalist mode of production (capital logic), and the revolutionary and critical practical activities of the sublating of the capitalist system. The internal logic of Marxist thought is clear, rigorous and well-conceived.

　　—K. Marx's revelation and criticism of capital logic are profound, so are his criticism of alienated labor and corresponding solutions.

　　—K. Marx and F. Engels' thoughts on the free and well-rounded development of people in future society. As *The Communist Manifesto* states, "in place of the old bourgeois society, with its classes and class antagonisms, we shall have an association, in which the free development of each is the condition for the free development of all." In the future society where capitalism is sublated, each individual will finally become the master of his/her own social organization, and thus become the lord of the nature, become his own master— "free man". According to F. Engels, such development was called "the cause of liberating the world", and the history prior to this was called the "prehistory" of mankind.

　　—Marxist thought has the characteristic of "totality". K. Marx initially studied political economy in order to seek answers to the "distress of material interests", during which he liquidated and criticized their philosophical beliefs (mainly manifested as a critique of *German ideology*), and discovered the close connection between human "perceptual practical activities" and human history, applying the former to explain the structure and operating mechanism of society, reveal the development of human history, discover the general law of development of human society, and create a practical view of history—historical materialism—a new worldview and a new philosophy.

　　He then conducted arduous research on the operational mechanism of the capitalist mode of production, profoundly revealing and analyzing capital logic, and finally summarized the conclusion of scientific socialism and put forward the ideal of the free and well-rounded development of people in the future society.

　　Thus, it can be seen that Marxist thought is the unity of philosophical critique, capital critique and social critique, and it is an organic whole composed of philosophy, economics, and scientific socialism, etc.

　　Marxism is such an ideological system: it is a science on the general law of historical generation and social development—historical science, and is also a special science on the law of capitalist development; it is a profound ideology on human liberation, and is the ideal construction which is the unity of criticality and constructiveness as well as profoundness and valuablity based on the historical science.

Is the aforementioned understanding valid? Can it become the starting point for further research on Marxist philosophy and serve as a basis to in-depth research on Marxist philosophy?

2. Trend of "problem-oriented research"

Since the mid-1990s, the profound changes in social landscape arising from globalization, technologization and networking have resulted in many new problems to be studied in depth and explained systematically, which did not appear or just sprouted in K. Marx's life. To sum up, the first is the global issues and contemporary issues; the second is the new philosophical issues accompanying the major development of science and technology; the third is the reality issues of contemporary China, such as the theory of social form, the issues of knowledge production status and intellectual power, the issues of cultural theory, value consensus and universal ethics, the issues of sovereignty and function of a nation-state in the context of globalization, the issues of modernity and the construction of Chinese modernity, and new philosophical issues brought about by the development of contemporary science and technology. So, strengthening "problem awareness" and highlighting "problem-oriented research" are what make up the key pivots for the development of contemporary Marxist philosophy and constitute the starting point and foothold of "problem-oriented research" trend.

3. Trend of research on philosophical foundation of "Chinese experience"

Amid the pursuit of modernization since modern times, China has formed its own theoretical programs and practical explorations. And the philosophical foundation contained in them are what need to be summarized and refined.

As the theoretical forms of "Marxist philosophy adapted to China's conditions", Mao Zedong Thought, Deng Xiaoping Theory, the important thought of the Three Represents and the Scientific Outlook on Development, are the theoretical achievements produced out of reflecting, summarizing and elevating the "Chinese experience", which constitute historic landmark achievements of the Sinicization of

Marxist philosophy, is the theoretical innovation of the CPC in exploring China's development path and development model, and is the representative results of the theoretical thinking about the modernization development of the Chinese nation.

The Marxist philosophy adapted to China's conditions should in no way ignore or set aside the theoretical achievements given above; rather, it should undertake in-depth research on them by further summarizing and generalizing the philosophical thoughts contained in them, and integrate these philosophical thoughts into the construction of Chinese-style Marxist philosophy, to which the Chinese contemporary philosophical circle should give due attention.

For example, Mao Zedong Thought has specialized philosophical works as its basis, his many other works and his revolutionary practice also contain extremely rich philosophical thoughts. Mao Zedong Thought is Mao Zedong's innovative development of Marxist materialism, epistemology and dialectics in the practice of Chinese revolution and construction, and should be reflected in the construction of the new form of contemporary Marxist philosophy adapted to China's conditions.

Although Deng Xiaoping did not have any special philosophical works, his thoughts about emancipating the mind and seeking truth from facts, the primary stage of Chinese socialism are original, especially the "three benefits" thoughts, and the thoughts about science and technology as the "primary productive force", etc., and embody the development of Marxist historical materialism, epistemology and dialectics.

The important thought of the Three Represents and the Scientific Outlook on Development also contain rich philosophical thoughts. For example, the greater emphasis on "the interests of the people" and the new exposition on the relationship between the Marxist ruling party and the people, both further highlighted the important positions of value and value concept in Marxist theory; the explanations of the stand and function of constructing advanced culture in social development, can be seen as important innovations of the cultural theory of historical materialism; and the Scientific Outlook on Development and the thought of a harmonious socialist society are the results of new exploration of the development model of modern human civilization, and is the new development of the theory of Marxist social form.

4. Trend of research on "coordinating with traditional Chinese philosophy"

This part is to focus on Chinese traditional philosophical thoughts and their categories, and deal with the modernity, inheritance and sublation of Chinese traditional philosophical thoughts. The specific manifestation is the hitherto existing discussion on "the rewriting of the history of Chinese philosophy", "the issue of the legitimacy of Chinese philosophy", and "the issue of the paradigm shift in the study of Chinese philosophy", which have arisen in the circle of historical study in China.

Some of the basic concepts in the Confucian value system, such as benevolence, humanism, peace, harmony, moderation, and honesty, etc., are cultural wealth that have been proven to be beneficial to human survival, development and social progress after thousands of years of cultural changes and social practice, and which is of great universality. The basic concepts of Confucianism have lasting and universal significance, and can still provide us with extremely valuable enlightenment, such as the ideas that the overall value of the world is higher than that of human beings and "the harmony of Nature and man".

The many excellent ideological values mentioned above contained in Confucian culture and the reasonable number of resources in traditional culture including Buddhism and Taoism, should all be indispensable constituent elements of contemporary Marxist philosophy adapted to China's conditions, which should all be fully utilized and inherited.

II. Studies on some hot issues

1. On contemporary significance of Marxist philosophy

The landmark academic event was the first Marxist Philosophical Forum jointly held from May 26 to 30, 2001 by the magazine agency of *Social Sciences in China*[①] and the Institute of Marxist Philosophy and Chinese Modernization at Sun Yat-sen University in Guangzhou. The forum was themed with "Contemporary Value of Marxist Philosophy", and gathered more than 40 academic leaders from 13 (currently the number has increased to 19) doctoral programs in Marxist philosophy across the country.

One or two years after Karl Marx was voted the greatest thinker of the

---

[①] *Social Sciences in China* is a peer-reviewed journal of the Chinese Academy of Social Sciences. It is published four times a year (in February, May, August and November) by Social Sciences in China Press and Taylor & Francis, an Informa business, 4 Park Square, Milton Park, Abingdon, Oxfordshire OX 14 4RN, UK. —Tr.

millennium in a BBC poll[①], the contemporary value of Marxism has become a hot topic in the theoretical circle, and a large number of related papers have been published. There are still related conferences and related papers published.[②]

The reason why this issue has become a hot issue is related to the profound changes of the times. With the development of globalization, the rapid development of science and technology, the strengthening of the "regulatory function" of capitalism itself, and the collapse of Soviet and Eastern socialism, Marxism fell into silence while the views like Marxism "being over", "being outdated", "being in dilemma" and "being questioned" were growing noisy; and some people in China lost their confidence in Marxism and socialism.

And there are also some scholars who tried to look for inspiration from contemporary Western philosophy and adopted specific concepts of Western philosophy to create all kinds of "absent" Marx.

In this context, how can we enrich and develop the understanding of Marxist philosophy in academic innovation, judiciously respond to the challenges and doubts raised about Marxist philosophy, stand at the height of the times, and show the contemporary significance of Marxist philosophy? It is an important task that cannot be averted by the scholars of Marxist philosophy.

I believe that in present-day world, it is particularly important to highlight and carry forward the zeitgeist of Marxist philosophy. Marxist philosophy embodies the unity of zeitgeist and humanity, as well as that of philosophical rationality and human ideals. To grasp and promote the basic spirit of Marxist philosophy and guide our practice and life is only one of the aspects of realizing the contemporary value of Marxist philosophy. Another important aspect is that we must base

---

① In September 1999, the BBC launched an online poll to find the greatest thinker of the millennium. Karl Marx, a great German philosopher and pioneer of the international communist movement, topped the list, leading Albert Einstein, Isaac Newton and even Charles Darwin with a clear margin. —Tr.

② See more in Sun Zhengyu 孙正聿, "Shaping and Guiding the New Spirit of the Times"《塑造和引导新的时代精神》; Wu Xiaoming 吴晓明, "Theme, Base point and Path: On the Contemporary Significance of Marxist Philosophy"《主题、基点与路径：阐说马克思哲学之当代意义》; Wang Nanti 王南湜, "Three Implications of the Contemporary Nature of Marxist Philosophy"《马克思哲学当代性的三重意蕴》; Xu Junzhong 徐俊忠, "Why Should We Put Forward the Issue of Rereading Marx"《我们何以要提出重读马克思的课题》; Liu Huaiyu 刘怀玉: "Criticism and Reflection on Several Approaches to the Contemporary Interpretation of Marxist Philosophy"《对马克思主义哲学当代性解释若干途径的批评与反思》, in *The Contemporary Significance of Marx's Philosophy*, ed. by Zhao Jianying 赵剑英 & Ye Ruxian 叶汝贤, Beijing: Social Sciences Academic Press, 2006.

ourselves on contemporary social practice to cope with the challenges confronted with Marxist theory in the contemporary era and make the theoretical innovation. Only in this way can we truly realize the contemporary value of Marxist philosophy.

2. On the research into ontology and K. Marx's view of philosophy

The discussion in this part is in essence the one about what kind of philosophy is Marxist philosophy, and about what is the essence and purport of philosophy. In fact, it is the continuation of the discussion on the essence and system of Marxist philosophy in the 1980s and 1990s. Of course, It is done against a new background, that is, in the context in which the contemporary value of Marxist philosophy has been judiciously and powerfully answered.[①]

Huang Nansen(黄楠森), a professor from Peking University, proposed that ontology or existentialism should be given a correct position, so as to blazed a trail to institutionally innovate Marxist philosophy. In Marxist philosophy, what is dominated is materialistic ontology. Discussing K. Marx's thought of ontology is undoubtedly of great significance for getting to the heart of the problem and profoundly understanding Marxist world view.

Gao Qinghai(高清海), a professor of Jilin University, proposed to study the issue of ontological boundary. He believes that the significance of K. Marx's concept of practice is mainly in the transformation of "philosophical thinking mode" rather than the transformation of "ontological form."

Chen Xianda (陈先达), a professor from Renmin University of China, believes that the foothold of the ontology of Marxist philosophy is neither to construct a philosophical system nor to find a basis for the settlement of life, but to establish a philosophy that is different from speculative metaphysical philosophy and that can understand and transform the world.

Sun Zhengyu (孙正聿), a professor of Jilin University, believes that Marxist philosophy is fundamentally different from all old philosophies in the way of representing and reflecting the times and of giving play to its effect. The nature of the old philosophies is to pursue eternal principles, ultimate reality, and absolute truth, so they are fundamentally ontological philosophy, incapable of answering practical

---

[①] For important papers on ontology and Marx's philosophy, see Zhao Jianying & Yu Wujin (ed.): *Marx's Ontology and Its Contemporary Significance* 《马克思的本体论思想及其当代意义》, Beijing: Social Sciences Academic Press, 2006.

questions.

Wu Yuanliang (吴元梁), a researcher from the Institute of Philosophy of the Chinese Academy of Social Sciences, pointed out that there has long existed in theoretical circles various views regarding Marxist philosophical ontology as material ontology, practical ontology, material-practical ontology, social existence ontology, etc. Such views will continue to be discussed, which will contribute to the development of Marxist philosophy. However, various ontological formulations and long-term unresolved disputes over different viewpoints indicate the complexity of this issue.

We might as well change the way of thinking, thinking about the question of what ideas K. Marx put forward that led to revolutionary changes in philosophy and that are still meaningful and valuable today. From this perspective, Marx's idea of the unity between natural existence and social existence on the basis of practice is worth exploring, researching and discussing.

Yu Wujin (俞吾金), a professor of Fudan University, believes that K. Marx's epoch-making contribution to philosophy is the creation of historical materialism, which is the product of the ontological revolution. In other words, historical materialism is Marx's new ontology. This new ontology, in its essence, is the ontology of existentialism, and for Marx, existence is also production, which, in a broad sense, refers to the production and reproduction of the entire society or the entire social life.

Yi Junqing (衣俊卿), a professor of Heilongjiang University, summarized and distinguished two ontological paradigms that embody different dimensions of existence. He believes that there are two basic ontological paradigms in the evolution of philosophy: one is past-oriented, reductionist, and deterministic; the other is future-oriented, open-ended, generative. Between these two basic philosophical ontological paradigms, we see the difference between the "past-oriented" and "future-oriented" dimensions of existence, the difference between closed determinism and open existentialism, and between criticality and non-criticality, between substantiality and non-substantiality, between the value trend of living away from human beings and that of returning to human life world.

Zou Shipeng (邹诗鹏), a professor of Huazhong University of Science and Technology, put forward his thoughts on the contemporariness of Marxist philosophy from the background of the dilemma of human existence and the transformation of contemporary philosophy. He believes that Marxist philosophy does not have an ontological structure in the traditional sense, but this does not mean that Marxist philosophy does not have its own theoretical structure with ontological implications or functions. We can call the theoretical structure of Marxist philosophy that reveals and interprets the comprehensive and rich connotations of human existence and has the meaning of ontological commitment as practical existentialism.

Feng Ziyi (丰子义), a professor of Peking University, focuses on the methodological issues in Marxist theory of ontology. He believes that since any understanding is always connected with its unique method, to grasp the thought of ontology of Marxist philosophy, one must pay attention to the investigation of Marxist methodology of his research on ontological issues. He refined Marxist research methods from four aspects, specifically the conception of relationship, the view of activity and process, the perspective of existentialism, and the conception of human being.

Social Sciences in Chinese published an academic overview of the conference, and a few papers selected by the conference. Other journals have also published related papers one after another, making ontology and Marxist view of philosophy a major hot issue in Marxist philosophy circles, even till today.

3. Tracking research on the new development of Western Marxist theories

The landmark event was the third "Marxist Philosophy Forum" co-organized from October 31 to November 2, 2003 by the *Social Sciences in China* Press, the Department of Philosophy of Nanjing University and the Marxist Social Theory Research Center of Nanjing University. This conference is themed with "Basic Issues and Basic Trends in Contemporary Foreign Studies of Marxist Philosophy," attracts more than 60 academic leaders, distinguished young or middle-aged experts in the studies of Marxist philosophy, Western modern philosophy and foreign Marxism, and receives more than 40 papers.

Many scholars present at the conference believed that through expanding the international perspective of Marxist philosophy research, understanding the basic issues and the latest developments of Western Marxism research, and then conducting academic analysis, dialogue and criticism, we can learn from the experience in adhering to and developing Marxist philosophy, which necessarily contributes to the formation of the Chinese style of Marxist philosophy research.

They believe that critically borrowing the theoretical results of Western Marxism is of indispensable significance for us to adhere to and develop Marxist philosophy and even Marxism as a whole. It can be said that without studying Western Marxism, we would not develop Marxism well, and it is idle to speak of upholding and developing Marxism. For people working in Marxist philosophy in contemporary China, there are various paths for the work of upholding and developing Marxism. There are basically four dimensions: (1) K. Marx's ideological resources; (2) Western Marxist thoughts; (3) methods of human practice and corresponding changes in social form and operating mechanism; (4) the practice of socialism with Chinese characteristics. Among them, Western Marxism is a collection of different ideas based on the characteristics of different stages of the development of human practice. Whether it is correct or not, there is some experience we can learn from in order to adhere to and develop Marxist philosophy. This is the purpose of our study of Western Marxism. The theoretical results of Western Marxism have, in a unique and insightful way, deeply revealed the essence, structure and characteristics of modern society and contemporary society, as well as people's living conditions against such a social background. For example, Georg Lukács' theory of materialization, Gramsci's thoughts on cultural leadership, Habermas's "Communicative Rationality", "technical rationality", "colonization of the life world", and Baudrillard's theory of consumer society, Jameson's "cultural logic of late capitalism", and criticism of scientific and technological rationality, ideological criticism, daily life criticism, popular culture criticism, criticism of modern nation-state, criticism of modernity, etc. These philosophical concepts, these "critical weapons," are the philosophical condensation of the zeitgeist and the symbol of human creative wisdom; the social criticism and cultural criticism made by Western Marxism using these concepts and methods are insightful, powerful and enlightening.

Some scholars believed that, since Georg Lukács published *History and Class Consciousness* in 1923 and Karl Korsch published *Marxism and Philosophy*, Western Marxism has gone through 80 years. In this long historical period, as a kind of intellectual discourse and leftist theory, Western Marxism insisted on uncompromising criticism of capitalist society and bourgeois ideology. A group of theorists and social critics, known as "Western Marxists", from Lukács, Bloch, Horkheimer, Adorno to Sartre, Lefebvre, Marcuse and Althusser, have deeply impressed Chinese researchers, because they have worked together to explore the shortcomings and ways out of Western civilization from different angles, which left a deep impression on researchers, despite the fact that their actual ideological tendencies, political positions and theoretical achievements are different. Therefore, their thoughts are now all utilized as important ideological resources and into today's critical discourse on the ailments of Western civilization, so as to provide some enlightenment for us to understand contemporary capitalism. Although we do not directly agree with some of the key conclusions of Western Marxism, we must pay attention to the problems they put forward from the perspective of philosophical logic, to their innovation in the themes of Marxist philosophy and their exploration of its forms, and to the achievements made in the criticism of capitalism, and then turn these issues into our research subjects.

Today, we are of course faced with more complicated historical and theoretical conditions. Globalization, capital expansion, new global division of labor, ecological issues, and new types of social alienation are no longer the matters of a single region. History requires Marxist philosophy to provide rational analysis of these issues. In theory, various discourses such as postmodernism, postcolonialism, feminism, and the third way have gradually been occupying the leading position of the theory in different ways. Correspondingly, there have emerged "post-Marxist" ideological trend represented by Jean Baudrillard, "post-Marxist" radical discourse represented by Ernesto Laulau, "late Marxism" faction represented by Fredric Jameson, and other feminist or ecological Marxist theories. For example, "ecological Marxism" has been proposed by today's Western Marxists because they were not satisfied with the ecological environment; "post-Marxism" has been proposed because they were not satisfied with the original Western Marxism; and "analytical Marxism" has been proposed because the achievements of modern Western philosophy were absorbed; "alter-globalization and alter-Marxism" have been proposed because they were not satisfied with the control of the global economy by the monopoly capital headed by the United States, and so on. Although they have not fundamentally shaken the ideology of modern capitalism, they have continued to deepen people's understanding of modernity and capitalism, promote their reflection on issues of justice, equality, and fairness, thus actually affecting their value selection and practice process.[①]

4. Research on the construction of modernity and Chinese modernity

Modernity is a central issue encountered in the development of the world and also in the development of China, and it has naturally become the focus issue of today's international academics. Modernization is the unfolded and actualized modernity. The

---

[①] Zhao Jianying & Zhang Yibing (ed.): *Basic Problems of Overseas Marxism*, Beijing: Social Sciences Academic Press, 2006.

emergence of a series of global problems, such as environmental pollution, ecological imbalance, ethnic conflicts, regional wars, terrorism, thermonuclear threats, cultural conflicts and the gap between the rich and the poor, has cast a deep shadow on the survival and development of mankind in the 21st century. Such dilemmas reflect the crisis concerning the hitherto existing concepts and paths of the development of human civilization, and are essentially what is called "modernity" crisis. At the same time, China's modernization practices and its in-depth development have continuously exposed and accumulated many deep-seated problems. China's development has paid a huge price, whether in terms of resources and environment, or in terms of social justice and social stability. The problems arising in the development of the world and China urgently require us to study and answer: What is the origin and connotation of modernity? How did Marx deal with modernity? What kind of modernity should China construct? What kind of path should China take so as to promote economic, political, cultural, and social development? All these urgently need to be explored and demonstrated academically. It can be seen from this that globalization, socialist modernization with Chinese characteristics, modernity, and Marxism adapted to China's conditions are four closely related practical and theoretical propositions. In terms of theoretical form, the process of China's modernization is the process of formation and continuous development of "Marxism adapted to China's conditions"; In terms of philosophical form, it is the pursuit of convergence and integration of Chinese, Western and Marxist philosophy; in terms of connotation, it is the process of construction and enrichment of Chinese modernity. All of these can be considered as the internal logic of Chinese scholarship and contemporary Chinese philosophy and social sciences since the advent of modern times.[①]

In addition, many scholars have also conducted in-depth research on the relationship between the logic of capital and the generation of modernity.

[①] For the study of modernity in Marx's vision, refer to Yu Wujin 俞吾金: "Marx's Diagnosis of Modernity and Its Enlightenment"《马克思对现代性的诊断及其启示》; Zou Shipeng 邹诗鹏: "Chinese Marxist Philosophy and Construction of Chinese Modernity"《马克思主义中国化与中国现代性建构》, *Social Sciences in China*, 2005(1); Lu Pinyue 鲁品越 et al.: "Capital and the Generation of Modernity"《资本与现代性的生成》, *Social Sciences in China*, 2005(3); Feng Ziyi 丰子义: "Contemporary Interpretation of Marx's Modernity Thought"《马克思现代性思想的当代解读》, *Social Sciences in China*, 2005(4); Wu Xiaoming: 吴晓明 "On Marx's Double Criticism of Modernity"《论马克思对现代性的双重批判》, *Academic Monthly*, February 2006; Zheng Hangsheng 郑杭生: "New Modernity and Its Prospects in China"《新型现代性及其在中国的前景》, *Academic Monthly*, February 2006.

5. On construction of a new form of contemporary Sinicized Marxist philosophy

A significant trend in contemporary Chinese philosophical research, I think, is the effort to realize dialogue, communication and integration of Marxist philosophy, traditional Chinese philosophy and Western philosophy, and hence explore how to forge a new form of Chinese philosophy. To forge a new form of contemporary Chinese philosophy, efforts must be made from the following three aspects at the same time: first, to clarify the principles and viewpoints of classic Marxist philosophy, and to grasp its essence and methods;[①] second, to critically absorb the essence of traditional Chinese thought; Third, to critically absorb the reasonable elements of Western modern philosophy and integrate them into the contemporary Chinese philosophy. In my opinion, this philosophical form is based on Marxist philosophy to realize the integration of Marxist philosophy and traditional Chinese philosophy and Western philosophy. Therefore, it can be said that the "construction of contemporary Chinese philosophical form" is mainly manifested as the "construction of Sinicized Marxist philosophical form", and the contemporary Chinese philosophical form is the form of Sinicized Marxist philosophy.

Since the beginning of the new century, there have been at least four large-scale and influential seminars in the philosophical community in the country, all closely related to this topic. The first is the "Civilization Conflict and Philosophical Dialogue in the Context of Globalization: Expert Forum on Chinese Philosophy, Western Philosophy, and Marxist Philosophy" organized by the *Social Sciences in China* Press and other units on September 26-29, 2003. More than 60 young and middle-aged scholars, who engaged themselves in the related research in well-known Chinese universities and research institutions such as Peking University, Renmin University of China, Chinese Academy of Social Sciences, attended the forum. They had productive discussions on how to build a new contemporary Chinese philosophy by breaking down disciplinary barriers between these three branches of philosophy and

---

[①] The implementation of the CPC Central Committee held the project to study and develop Marxist work conference, "the implementation of the project to study and develop Marxist theory is to focus on the changing world, based on the new practice, and to answer which are the basic tenets of Marxism that must be adhered to for a long time, which are the theoretical judgments that need to be enriched and developed in the light of new realities, which are the dogmatic understandings of Marxism that must be abolished, and which are the erroneous views attached to Marxism that must be clarified. We should treat Marxism with a rational attitude." This clearly expresses the academic appeal. See *People's Daily*, 2004,4-29(4).

initiating philosophical dialogues in the context of globalization.

Scholars pointed out that for a long time, the demarcation and distinction between Chinese philosophy, Western philosophy, and Marxist philosophy has made people accustomed to understanding philosophy from a relatively narrow disciplinary standpoint, which makes it difficult to achieve the true form of philosophy. What is called the return to philosophy itself is to transcend the one-sided and knowledge-based understanding of philosophy to reach the true form of philosophy as the thinking of wisdom. It can be said that it is this return that constitutes the intrinsic meaning of philosophical dialogue.

People working in Chinese philosophical circles have never been so avid for an original philosophy. This shows that Chinese philosophy has begun a new period, a period in which Chinese philosophy discovers and re-founds itself, a period in which Chinese philosophy transcends "history of philosophy" to discover "philosophy" and acquires subjectivity. The acquisition of self by Chinese philosophy is an important beginning for Chinese culture to enter another Axial age. Through participating in world dialogue, these people can contribute the value concept of our nation to the world, and reflect on and modify what is currently universal values, reversing the awkward situation between the formal structure of diversified dialogues and the flattened secular cultural life, a situation formed in the wave of globalization, enabling the formal structure of diversified dialogues to obtain substantial content, and making its own unique contribution to the development of world philosophy.

Through this conference, most of the scholars present have fostered a more open-minded research mentality, a broader theoretical vision, a self-consciousness of method, as well as a sense of urgency and mission. Facing the current unique philosophical ecology of China consisting of the three philosophical systems of Chinese philosophy, Western philosophy, and Marxism philosophy, the scholars present believe that through the dialogue and integration of the three disciplines and the self-opening and self-transcendence of the three academic groups, we are on the threshold of a new era in which subjectivity of Chinese philosophy will be restored, its creative dynamics will be reactivated, and thus a new Chinese philosophy will come into being.①

---

① Wei Changbao 魏长宝: "Disciplinary dialogue, visual integration, and creation of contemporary Chinese philosophy: Summary of Academic Symposium of 'Civilization Conflict and Philosophy Dialogue in Context of Globalization'" 《学科对话、视域融合与创建当代中国新哲学——"全球化语境中的文明 冲突与哲学对话"学术研讨会综述》, *Philosophy Research,* 2004(1).

The second is the symposium under the theme of "Rewriting of the History of Philosophy and Paradigm Renovation of Chinese Philosophical Discipline," which was held in Beijing at Renmin University of China and jointly sponsored by the School of Philosophy of RUC, Confucius Research Institute of RUC, *Social Sciences in China* Press, and Journal of RUC during March 20 and 21 of 2004. The symposium attracted about 40 professionals and scholars who were studying Chinese, Western and Marxist philosophies and other related subjects. They believed that, the life of the times calls for a new philosophy, and the development of history calls for a new philosophy. Guided by Marxist philosophy, we should make good use of China's hitherto-obtained philosophical experience and resources while drawing on and absorbing the outstanding achievements of Western philosophy, so as to face and respond to the practical issues that China and the rest of the world have been confronted with; we should carry out interdisciplinary philosophical dialogue and ideological exchange so that the perspectives will converge to give birth to a new contemporary Chinese philosophy that bears the characters of the times and the nation. They have conducted in-depth and fruitful discussions on the "legitimacy" of Chinese philosophy, the paradigm innovation of the discipline of Chinese philosophy, and the prerequisites and methods for rewriting the history of Chinese philosophy, and so on.

Thereby, the following consensuses have been reached: (1) The hitherto-existing paradigm of Chinese philosophical discipline is basically "resolving Chinese problems in Western ways", which has contributed to the establishment of Chinese philosophy, but has not effectively inherited the essence of Chinese traditional culture; (2) The development of Chinese philosophy still cannot disassociate itself from Western philosophy and Marxist philosophy, and an important condition for the further development of Chinese philosophy is to be proficient in Western philosophy and Marxist philosophy; (3) The disciplinary paradigm of the history of Chinese philosophy that discovers and interprets historical data within the framework of Western philosophy can at best be a paradigm of the history of Chinese philosophy with its own characteristic, rather than the one and only paradigm of the history of Chinese philosophy; (4) To write a true history of Chinese philosophy, we must first solve the basic problems of "What kind of philosophy should be established?" "How can we distinguish historical materials?" and "How can we transform ancient Chinese language into modern Chinese language?" and, based on the experience and lessons of our predecessors, make innovations in disciplinary paradigm. These problems may boil down to one thing, namely, rewriting about how Chinese philosophy handles its relationship with Western philosophy, in particular with the viewpoints and methods of Marxist philosophy.

The third one is an academic seminar on "The Contemporary Value of Marxist Philosophy and Its System Innovation" held from October 23 to 24, 2004 by the Value and Cultural Research Center of Beijing Normal University and the Institute of Marxist Philosophy. This seminar mainly discussed the following issues: (1) the historical evolution of and reflection on Marxist philosophy system; (2) the contemporary value of Marxist philosophy; (3) the appellation and main content of Marxist philosophy; (4) the internal structure of Marxist philosophy; (5) the relationship between the scientific system of Marxist philosophy and its teaching system; (6) other issues related to the system innovation of Marxist philosophy; (7) the principles of compiling textbooks of Marxist philosophy. The experts and scholars from Peking University, Renmin University of China, Chinese Academy of Social Sciences and other universities and research institutions believe that since the beginning of the new century, the tremendous changes in the life world brought about by economic globalization, especially the practice of building socialism with Chinese characteristics, have raises new questions for the study of Marxist philosophy, which renders it urgent to carry out system innovation of Marxist philosophy in order to demonstrate the contemporary value of Marxist philosophy. For this end, we must correctly handle the relation of Marxist philosophy to Chinese philosophy and Western philosophy, must focus on the integration of history and theory, and must address such prerequisite questions as "how to understand philosophy" "how to understand Marxist philosophy" and "how to understand contemporary Chinese Marxist philosophy." [①]

At the meeting, Sun Zhengyu (孙正聿), a professor of Jilin University, proposed that a nation that cannot stand up ideologically is a nation that cannot be rejuvenated. Therefore, to realize the great rejuvenation of the Chinese nation, we must regard system innovation as an important task of philosophical development, and achieve development in theoretical thinking. The current research on and the system innovation of Marxist philosophy must be placed in the historical context of

---

① Li Xiaodong 李晓东: "System Innovation as the Research Focus of Current Marxist Philosophy: Urgent Task of Theoretical Innovation"《当前马克思主义哲学的研究焦点——体系创新：理论创新的当务之急》, *China Education News*, 2004-11-16(3).

the Chinese nation, combining its development with the heritage and aspirations of the nation.① Zhang Shuguang (张曙光), a professor of Beijing Normal University pointed out that the system innovation of Marxist philosophy is actually not an innovation of "Marxist philosophy" as a secondary discipline in a narrow sense, but an innovation of contemporary Chinese philosophy.②

In addition, at the symposium of "On Philosophical Innovation in the 21st Century and in Celebration of the 80th Birthday of Prof. Huang Nansen (黄楠森)," held by Peking University on Nov. 29, 2001, the participating experts and scholars also discussed about the development path of Chinese philosophy in the 21st century, believing that the main direction of development of Chinese philosophy in the 21st century is neither the liberalist thought of wholesale Westernization nor the conservative thought of Confucianism restoration, but the thought of integration and innovation for Marxism adapted to China's conditions. It means that Marxist philosophy, Western philosophy and traditional Chinese philosophy are not in opposition to each other but fuse with each other, and that we must integrate the other two under the guidance of Marxist philosophy, so as to achieve the adaption of Marxism to China's conditions and give birth to a new system of Marxist philosophy that bears the characters of our times and our nation. These three philosophies have much in common in their philosophical issues, philosophical wisdom, zeitgeist and civilization trends, with each of them having its own unique language style, expression methods, philosophical categories, and philosophical systems. Only through an arduous and meticulous historical process can these three be integrated innovatively into one.③

To create the Chinese nation's philosophical theory has been always what Chinese philosophers and thinkers have taken an oath to seek. As early as 1935, Zhang Dainian (张岱年)④ advocated in his article "On the Cultural Construction

---

① Li Xiaodong 李晓东: "System Innovation as the Research Focus of Current Marxist Philosophy:Urgent Task of Theoretical Innovation"《当前马克思主义哲学的研究焦点——体系创新:理论创新的当务之急》, *China Education News*, 2004-11-16(3).
② Ibid.
③ The symposium of "On Philosophical Innovation in the 21st Century and in Celebration of the 80th Birthday of Prof. Huang Nansen"《21世纪哲学创新暨庆祝黄楠森教授八十华诞》, held by Peking University, http://www.phil.pku.edu.cn/news, 2001-11-29.
④ Zhang Dainian 张岱年 (1909-2004) was a modern philosopher and historian of philosophy. His research focused mainly on three aspects: interpretation of Chinese history of philosophy, investigation of philosophical questions and discussion of cultural problems. —Tr.

with Chinese Culture as Standard" that "The strengths of both Chinese and Western culture should be combined, China's inherent outstanding cultural inheritance should be carried on while the valuable and excellent cultural contributions produced by the West should be adopted and integrated, thus a new culture will be fostered." Although in Mr. Zhang's late years when he was seriously ill, he said to Chen Lai and Wang Dong who came to visit him: "The work of integration and innovation has to be continued and it now depends on you..."[①]

To create the Chinese nation's own philosophical theory is the lifelong pursuit of the famous contemporary Chinese philosopher Gao Qinghai(高清海), and it is also his philosophical will. In the article "The Future Development of the Chinese Nation Needs Its Own Philosophical Theory", he pointed out that philosophy is the soul of the nation. Philosophy marks the height and depth of a nation's self-consciousness and reflects its level of mental development and maturity. "To create contemporary Chinese philosophy is in essence to create the 'ideological self' of the Chinese nation. To create contemporary Chinese philosophical theory is the innate demand and urgent need of Chinese people to reflect on their own life experience, understand their own living conditions, and seek their own future development path."[②]

In addition to Mr. Zhang and Mr. Gao, Fang Keli (方克立) has also been continuing to explore the "theory of integration and innovation."[③]

At the 90th anniversary of the founding of the Department of Philosophy of Peking University in May, 2004, director of the department Zhao Dunhua（赵敦华）expressed such aspirations on behalf of all philosophy researchers at Peking University: the philosophy is an enterprise which "honors his virtuous nature, and maintains constant inquiry and study, seeking to carry it out to its breadth and greatness, so as to omit none of the more exquisite and minute points which it embraces, and to raise it to its greatest height and brilliancy, so as to pursue the course of the Mean". Philosophers in ancient and modern times, both at home and abroad, are all signs of the civilization of their times. In the era of the great rejuvenation of the

---

① Han Ying 韩莹: "Settling Is Gold: The Last Interview with Zhang Dainian"《沉淀是金：对张岱年最后的访问》, *People*, 2005-1-28.
② Gao Qinghai 高清海: "The Future Development of Chinese Nation Needs Its Own Philosophical Theory"《中华民族的未来发展需要有自己的哲学理论》, *Jilin University Journal Social Sciences Edition*, 2004(2).
③ Fang Keli 方克立: "Zhang Dainian and Chinese philosophy in the 20th century"《张岱年与20世纪中国哲学》 *Social Sciences in China*, 2005(2).

Chinese nation, as the cradle of Chinese philosophers, the Department of Philosophy of Peking University is determined to apply philosophy that reflects our zeitgeist and national spirit to forge the cultural soul of the Chinese nation that can stand among the nations of the world![1] In my opinion, this also expresses the strong desire and common aspirations of people working in contemporary Chinese philosophical circles.

On July 25-26, 2005, the Fifth "Marxist Philosophy Forum" was jointly organized by the magazine agency of *Social Sciences in China*, the Research Center of Philosophical Basic Theory of Jilin University and the School of Philosophy and Sociology of Jilin University. The theme of this forum was "Study on the Forms of Marxist Philosophy in China." The experts present discussed the history and logic of the study of Marxist philosophy in China in the new era; Marx's philosophy and the philosophical path pioneered by K. Marx; the dialogue between Chinese philosophy, Western philosophy and Marxist philosophy and the construction of a form of Marxist philosophy adapted to China's conditions, and so on. It is not difficult to see from this that the construction of a new form of contemporary Chinese philosophy is mainly manifested as the "construction of a new form of Marxist philosophy adapted to China's conditions".

In recent years, Li Jingyuan（李景源）, Li Deshun（李德顺）, and Wu Yuanliang（吴元梁）have proposed and discussed the issue of constructing a new form of Marxist philosophy.[2]

The specific research directions for constructing the new form of contemporary Marxist philosophy adapted to China's conditions are: (1) studies of Marxist classic texts, mainly concentrated in Peking University, Nanjing University, Central Translation and Compilation Bureau, and so on; (2) studies of Foreign Marxism, mainly concentrated in Foreign Marxism Research Center at Fudan University at Fudan University, Marxist Social Theory Research Center at Nanjing University,

---

[1] Zhao Dunhua 赵敦华: "For the Philosophical Development of Chinese Nation"《为中华民族的哲学腾飞》, www.pku.edu.cn/news/xiao_kan/, 2004-5-10.

[2] Li Jingyuan 李景源: "On the Construction of Principles of Socialist Philosophy with Chinese Characteristics"《论建构中国特色社会主义哲学原理》, *Social Science Management and Review*, 2004(3); Li Deshun 李德顺: "The New Form of Marxist Philosophy Facing the 21st Century"《面向21世纪的马克思主义哲学新形态》, *Philosophical Trends*, 2000(2); Wu Yuanliang 吴元梁: "On the Research Status and Some Theoretical Problems of Marxist Philosophy in China"《关于我国马克思主义哲学研究状况及若干理论问题的分析》, *Dongyue Tribune*, 2004(5).

Cultural Research Center at Heilongjiang University and other units; (3) studies of contemporary practical issues and the issues of immediate significance arising in the construction of socialism with Chinese characteristics; (4) discussion on the issue of "the legitimacy of Chinese philosophy" and the "rewriting of the history of Chinese philosophy".

In addition to the scholars in Chinese philosophy, an increasing number of scholars in other directions, especially in Western philosophy and Marxist philosophy, have also begun to pay attention to this issue and participate in discussion. *Academic Monthly* (《学术月刊》) and *Wenhui Readers' Weekly* (《文汇读书周报》) of Shanghai both selected this issue as one of the 2003 top ten academic hot spots in China, which also reflects the general academic and cultural significance of discussing this issue.

New trends are also shown in the methods of Marxist philosophy research:

(1) Practical hermeneutics, specifically, historical interpretation and "historical reduction". By putting a theory back into the historical conditions and context in which it came into being, we can correctly interpret its meaning and thus restore the connotation of the history and times to it. This method features theoretical logic and historical logic, grasping and interpreting the historical connotation reflected by theoretical logic.

(2) The integration of interdisciplinary perspectives or the emerging of the method of overall research. It is firstly because contemporary social practice assumes a holistic nature that if one wants to grasp the essence of an ideological system, he or she must be connected with the economic, political and social development and change which took place at the same time under this ideological system. For example, if one wants to correct understand and grasp various theoretical schools of contemporary Western Marxism and other ideological trends, he or she must connect them with the economic, political and cultural development under contemporary capitalism and even the form of capitalism as a whole. Philosophical analysis cannot be made profoundly unless it is organically connected with economic, political and cultural analysis, and is grasped, probed and criticized in an overall way.

III. Reason and essence of formation of new trends

Why have the integration of "Chinese philosophy, Western philosophy and Marxist philosophy" and the exploration and construction of new forms of contemporary Chinese philosophy gradually become hot topics in Chinese philosophy circles since the turn of the century? They have arisen not only from the inherent requirements of philosophy disciplines--for a long time, Chinese philosophy, Western philosophy, and Marxist philosophy have almost despised each other, without much communication, dialogue, but also from practical requirements for the construction of socialism with Chinese characteristics, and in addition, from the objective requirements for responding to globalization and Western cultural hegemony, reinforcing the cultural image of a major country, enhancing national cultural identity and achieving the great renewal of the Chinese nation, all of which are the reflection of the moral pursuit of the contemporary Chinese people and their concern for the future of national culture. Naturally, the construction of a new form of Marxist philosophy adapted to China's conditions is increasingly becoming a common pursuit of the philosophical circle. The essence of the development trend of contemporary Chinese philosophy is the awakening and self-conscious constructing of national consciousness and national spirit in China's modernization in the era of globalization. Since the trend of globalization and the peaceful development of socialist modernization with Chinese characteristics are irresistible, the conflict between globality and nationality will emerge now and then throughout the acceleration of socialist modernization in China, which determines that the development of Marxist philosophy adapted to China's conditions (namely new development of the philosophy of the Chinese nation in the context of globalization and IT application) is a basic direction for the development of Chinese philosophy in the 21st century.

In the process of leading the national liberation and modernization drive, the CPC has combined the basic principles of Marxism with China's reality, creatively blazed a trail for the new democratic revolution and the development of socialism with Chinese characteristics, and explored a path of achieving China's modernization under the socialist market economy. How can we improve the "Chinese experience" from a philosophical perspective? This requires people working in philosophy and social science circles in China to provide in-depth theoretical excavation into and "legitimacy demonstration" of this path and the resulting economic, political, and cultural system structure, so as to give birth to philosophical thoughts and propositions with Chinese Characteristics, which constitutes an urgent and important subject that Chinese philosophical circles should face when developing a new form of Marxist philosophy.

The globalization still gaining momentum has caused conflicts and fusions between the cultures of different nations, and the importance of national culture has thus become more prominent. When contemporary capitalism exports capital, it is objectively accompanied by the expansion of Western culture and the seeking of hegemony. China's peaceful development needs the support of cultural forces, for culture is a precious resource for a nation in the process of world-oriented development, especially in the context of globalization. It can be said that national culture is an identity card for a nation in the process of globalization and modernization, and philosophy is precisely the soul of this identity card.

From a global perspective, globalization and peaceful development of socialist modernization with Chinese characteristics are irresistible, in which the conflict between globalization and nationality will frequently emerge through the whole course of construction of Chinese socialist modernization, which also determines that the forging of a new form of Marxist philosophy adapted to China's conditions, in essence, is the developing of a new philosophy of the Chinese nation in the context of modernization, globalization and IT application.

IV. A few comments

1. On research paradigm

I strongly agree that we should carry out "text-based research". A deep understanding of the way out of Marxist thought is of great significance for correcting some of the hitherto-existing misunderstandings and misinterpretations of Marxist philosophy, and grasping the nature and characteristics of Marxist thought system and its ideological essence.

There have emerged many new insights and discoveries through text-based research, and the related questions are as follows: (1) What is the possibility space for text interpretation? Or will it lead to a different understanding of the nature of Marxist philosophy? (2) Can the following points concerning Marxist philosophy in the past 20 years become consensuses? Or can these consensuses be established? For example, the transcendental significance of the new conception of history for the previous philosophies, K. Marx's revelation and criticism of capital logic, alienated labor and the corresponding solutions, the thought of free and well-rounded development of people in future society, the theoretical features of Marxist philosophy—scientificalness, revolutionariness (class consciousness), criticality and unification, etc. These are all general consensuses on Marxist philosophy. Will they be "transcended?" This is the question that we should take into consideration if we adopt text-based research method.

In addition, as a whole, compared with the research in the first trend, the research in the latter three trends remains weak. I believe that in order to develop a new form of Marxist philosophy adapted to China's conditions, we must achieve the transformation of the research paradigm of Marxist philosophy, which is inseparable from the aforementioned four research paths. Therefore, while advancing "text-based research," we should pay attention to "problem-oriented research", "philosophical basic research on the path and experience of Chinese modernization", and "research on contemporary value of traditional Chinese philosophical thoughts". None of the aforementioned research directions can be followed without sticking to the goal of constructing the form of Marxist philosophy adapted to China's conditions, namely contemporary Chinese national philosophy, so as to forge the philosophy soul for Chinese modernization and to provide a correct way of thinking and a harmonious cultural home for the Chinese people who have been in multiple variation of globalization, modernization, and marketization. The construction of the form of Marxist philosophy adapted to China's conditions is an arduous and long process that requires joint efforts of the Chinese philosophical circles. The task of constructing "national philosophy" in the pursuit of modernization was proposed in the early 20th century. The older generation of philosophers such as Feng Youlan(冯友兰), Jin Yuelin(金岳霖), Ai Siqi(艾思齐), Li Da(李达), and Zhang Dainian(张岱年) made unremitting and fruitful efforts for it, but there is still much room for development. Now we discuss "constructing the form of Marxist philosophy adapted to China's conditions", which is the continuation of this historic mission. Therefore, it is necessary for us to keep at it.

2.Vigorously deepen "problem-oriented research"—growth point for development and innovation of Marxist philosophy

Marxist philosophy is derived not only from the criticism and inheritance of the excellent Western cultural achievements, especially the criticism, inheritance and absorption of German classical philosophy, but also from the answers and solutions to the major problems of their times which K. Marx and F. Engels have offered, which is the best of the Zeitgeist of their time. Nowadays, in order to develop Marxist philosophy and construct a new form of Marxist philosophy adapted to China's conditions, we must accurately capture and solve the problems most relevant to our times. It is the fundamental way for Marxist philosophy to develop in the 21st century.

The current major issues of the times concern with the following: the relationship between globalization and nationality; the development of contemporary social forms; the role and status of knowledge production; the role of culture and the relationship between diversified civilization systems; universal ethics, the common sense and rules of communication; scientific and technological revolutions and the way of human existence and development; the relationship between the sovereignty, functions and relations of a nation-state in the context of globalization; K. Marx's theory of world history and the current development of globalization; national development path under the social conditions of globalization and IT application; modernity, etc. In addition, the research on the issues of philosophical basis of Chinese experience and the philosophical connotation of the Scientific Outlook on Development has been gradually carried out.

The aforementioned major philosophical issues raised by our era and practice are all that we should concentrate on researching and answering correctly, so as to forge the form of contemporary Marxist philosophy adapted to China's conditions. Only in this way can we claim that our philosophical thinking has been lifted to a new level.[①]

3. On learning style

We should have in-depth theoretical knowledge, deep practical concern and great efforts to achieve the integration of theory and practice. However, there is still much room for us to do in the latter two aspects. Some researchers indulge in admiring themselves for the discourses they have make up by themselves; some are prone to be fettered by old conventions. Also, there are some who even regard Western theories and discourse as the gold standard and thus unconsciously become trumpeters of Western capitalist ideology, far from contributing their own ideas.

---

① [In recent years, *Social Sciences in China*（《中国社会科学》）has made great efforts to promote the research in this field and published the following articles: Chen Xianda 陈先达: "Philosophy in Questions and Problems in Philosophy"《问题中的哲学和哲学中的问题》, *Social Sciences in China*, 2006(3); Zhang Shuguang 张曙光: "The Realism and Transcendence of Marxist Philosophy"《马克思主义哲学应有的现实性和超越性》, *Social Sciences in China*, 2006(4); "The Frontiers of contemporary philosophical Research"《当代哲学研究的前沿问题》, *Social Sciences in China*, 2006(5).

Cultural Issues and Theory of Chinese Socialist Culture

Status and Value of Humanities*

Building up socialist market economic system, for the Chinese people, is a completely new exploration and practice. In this exploration, new problems, new situations and new conflicts have emerged one after another. People who working with theories and who are responsible for making decisions should face up to the new problems in practice, give sound explanations, and formulate corresponding countermeasures. Among them, how to correctly understand the status and role of humanities under market economy is one of the problems that practice urgently needs us to solve.

It is obvious that the role of the natural science technology in promoting economic development and social progress. As for the value of the humanities (including philosophy and social sciences), it is also an indisputable fact. However, under the conditions of market economy, the humanities have encountered challenges.

As we know, the market economy is based on the principle of equal exchange of commodities. Under this principle, the relationship between people is manifested as the relationship between things. Currency is the link between them and the yardstick to measure the value of things. Satisfying the needs of material interests to the greatest extent is an inevitable requirement for people to engage in economic activities under the conditions of market economy. Based on this, some people believe that because it is generally difficult for human science knowledge to directly and obviously display its promotive effect on society and economy, to satisfy people's desire to get rich. Therefore, it has no value in the market economy.

It is precisely under the influence and dominance of this more popular understanding that the humanities and social science research has experienced serious funding shortages, the loss of researchers, the shortage or gap of talents, and the difficulty in publishing academic results. Therefore, a correct understanding of the

---

* Originally published in *Guangming Daily*, 1994-6-15.

status and value of the humanities and social sciences is the first prerequisite for re-energizing the humanities.

The humanities, as a psychic phenomenon accompanying human practice, can exist and endure for a long time. This is testimony to its ability to satisfy certain needs for human survival and development. Such needs are embodied in the following points: Human development is inseparable from theoretical thinking, and the humanities is an important way to nurture, cultivate and train people's quality of thinking. What is more, in a certain sense, humanities research is also a purpose for human beings, and it is out of the need of its inherent nature. The humanities play different roles for different people. For a person who is engaged in a partial, specific or low-level job, its role may not be obvious because he only needs to employ specific empirical thinking. In this case, the value of the humanities is naturally not obvious. But even so, a person's humanistic and scientific attainment directly affects his attitude towards life. For a person who is engaged in overall and holistic work, especially decision-makers and managers, whether he or she has humanities and social science attainment or not has a great influence on the development and effectiveness of his work. Here, rich historical knowledge, holistic thinking, far-sighted vision, the art of observing the world, the ability to coordinate interpersonal relationships, and the dialectical and appropriate working methods have a great bearing on the success or failure of the work. All of these are obtained through the cultivation and forging of humanities and social science attainment. Facts have also proved that many great politicians, scientists and even big industrialists with outstanding achievements in Chinese and foreign history are often savvy about the humanities and social sciences such as philosophy and history, consciously or unconsciously, and have their own clear world view and outlook on life. For a nation, the development status of humanities and social sciences is an important indicator to measure the level of theoretical thinking and the quality of the entire nation, to measure its conscientiousness and maturity in handling human beings themselves and the relationship between man and nature. Specifically, its value is reflected in at least the following aspects:

First, conceptual revolution is the prerequisite and forerunner of social revolution (including economic revolution), and it always originates from the humanities. Judging from historical practice, mankind always sounded the clarion call for emancipating the mind in the field of humanities, thus unveiling the prelude to social revolution. Take philosophy as an example. It is the thinking of human beings on their own existence (including the existence of the relationship between man and nature) and its rationality, and it is also a kind of thinking to trace the source. This kind of thinking is a kind of critical reflective activity. Therefore, philosophy is a conscious activity of human beings. It manifests itself as human beings' critical reflection on the past practical activities, summarizing experiences from successes, drawing lessons from failures, enriching their own essential power, predicting and constructing the rationality of further human practice and making human beings become more and more self-conscious and "purposive" in practice. Obviously, the nature of philosophical reflection and criticism actually reflects the spirit of constantly emancipating the mind and pioneering and innovating. The courage and ability of a political party or nation to reflect and criticize, to a large extent, determines its pace of progress and the degree of pioneering spirit. Here, philosophy is an important way to make human thinking more and more correct and rational in practice so as to reduce deviations and errors which may arise in human practice and thereby enhance effectiveness. Philosophy is the science of thinking and critique via which human beings constantly emancipate their minds and approach the truth. This is the epitome of philosophical value. This value of philosophy indicates that humanities, including philosophy, have values that other disciplines do not have.

Second, the reasonable solution to specific contradictions in human practice needs the wisdom of humanities, especially philosophy. Practical activity is purposive and intentional human activity. Different practical subjects are always active to satisfy their own needs and interests. In this way, it is inevitable that any human practical activity is rife with contradiction, which can be categorized under two headings, namely, the contradiction between different human actors and the contradiction between man and nature. How shall we recognize the types, relations and status of these contradictions and thereby resolve them? This requires philosophical thinking, especially dialectical thinking. How to identify and resolve the main contradictions in practical activities, how to formulate strategic priorities in activities, how to formulate specific plans, methods and steps, how to coordinate the local and global situations, the immediate and long-term goals, economy and politics, economy and society, equity and efficiency, and many other kinds of contradiction between reform and development and stability, all require the guidance of Marxist philosophy. The practice of socialist development in China over the past 40 years has shown that every big mistake and setback is the result of our deviating from the dialectical thinking in our guiding philosophy, the prevalence of idealism and the rampancy of metaphysics.

The role of philosophy and the humanities in this aspect has been summarized as the method value to solve the problems which arise in human practice.

Thirdly, as far as economic development is concerned, values centered on philosophy and other cultural concepts are also one of the important cultural forces that regulate and promote economic development. This effect is strong rather than superficial. Examining the economic development of some regions and countries in the world, we can find that the economic development of these regions and countries has certain models of their own. And behind these different economic development models there are certain values, or it can be said that these development models are the product of certain cultural traditions and values. For example, the American market economy model actually embodies a kind of liberalism and individual-oriented cultural values. The Japanese market economy model emphasizes the role of entrepreneurship and social community, which more clearly embodies the collectivist values of the Confucianism of the East Asia. With regard to the relationship between cultural factors such as that between values and economic development, Max Weber believed that the development of Western capitalism was in essence supported by the Protestant ethical spirit. It is the spirit of dedication and hard work required by Protestant ethics to redeem original sins that has played a normative and dynamic role in the development of Western capitalism. In the process of realizing modernization in China, there is also the question of what kind of model to develop. In how to determine a reasonable and sound development model and development practice, China's traditional cultural resources cannot be ignored. In fact, ignoring its existence and value not only is impossible, but also will inflict a huge cost. Therefore, if there is any economic value of the humanities, the aforementioned normative and dynamic role of the humanities and social sciences in shaping and constructing a model of economic development its economic value.

Fourthly, the value of the humanities and culture must be viewed from the perspective of the driving force that promotes the overall progress of the society and the important indicator to measure such progress. The increase in the level of social material productivity is not only a direct driving force for social progress, but also a fundamental indicator to measure social progress. This is beyond doubt. However, acknowledging this does not mean ignoring the motivating effect of other factors on social progress. The development of the productive forces is the direct driving force of social progress, but it is by no means the only one. In addition, cultural, conceptual and other non-economic factors play an objectively undeniable important role in directing social progress, the breadth and depth of social transformation, and the process of social progress. Besides, because human beings are the most important factor in productivity, and the main participants of production activities, who have grown up in certain cultural contexts and traditions, always with their own consciousness, emotion and will. In this way, the subject of economic activity will inevitably be restricted and affected by their way of thinking, values and other factors. Therefore, human cultural and psychological background, values, ways of thinking, emotion and will and other factors also play a role in the development of productivity. From this point of view, measuring social progress depends not only on the level of material productivity, but also on whether social values, cultural concepts can adapt to and promote the development of the productive forces, and whether they can meet the needs of cultural and psychological human life.

Needless to say, economic determinism (the thought that as long as the economy develops, every other problems can naturally be solved), unconditional economic supremacy (economic activities are above all other activities, and non-economic activities such as culture, education, etc. are all irrelevant and unimportant) and narrow utilitarianism (whatever can meet the needs of one's material interests is useful; otherwise, meaningless.) is extremely one-sided and detrimental. Such values not only violate the objective law of social development, but also are non-dialectical thinking which is one-sided and goes to extremes. If the relationship between economy and culture, between economy and society is dealt with according to such idea, our development is bound to inflict a heavy cost. The CPC Central Committee has repeatedly stressed that the two civilizations should be developed together and with the same efforts. It is indeed a wise initiative. Now, the important issue is to effectively implement this decision in practical work. It can be believed that if we understand and value the status and role of the humanities from the perspective of the importance of cultural civilization construction, we will not only promote the well-rounded development of all our people and improve the "soft environment" for reform and development, but also of great service to the sound development of the humanities.

Exploring a New World of Value in Conflicts and Changes: Mentality and Orientation of the Youth in Contemporary China*

Contemporary Chinese youth, as a cross-century generation that connects the past and the next, will become the backbone of Chinese society in the 21st century. At the turn of the century, their choice of values will inevitably have important historical connotations and influences. So, in the context of present-day social transformation, what is the mentality of Chinese youth? What kind of values, life philosophy, and psychological qualities should they construct and establish to respond to social changes and welcome the advent of the 21st century, so as to fully realize their own value while adapting to and promoting the development of the times?

I. Conflicts and changes

The composition of present-day Chinese youth can basically be divided into two categories in terms of time: one, the youth born during the period between the mid-1950s and the mid-1960s; the other, the youth born in the 1970s. The former received the education of ideological concepts under the political and economic system of the 1950s and 60s during their growth; the latter was more influenced by a series of new ideas since the reform and opening up was started during their growth. With regard to the ideological concepts of Chinese society before and after the implementation of the reform and opening policy, the latter is the inheritance of the former and thus they are somewhat homogeneous, but there also exist many changes and differences. Therefore, there are some common characteristics in the mentality and behavior orientation of Chinese youth of today, but there are also many differences. This article

---

* Originally published in *Open Times*《开放时代》, 1995 (1).

attempts to describe the general characteristics of these two types of youth, and the differences in certain characteristics.

Before the initiation of reform and opening up, in line with the highly centralized economic and political system, strict and unified ideological control was implemented in the field of ideology. The collective and national interests are paramount, and the collective values which claims that individuals are absolutely subordinate to the collective was the core of the social values which gained currency during that period, as well as its entire content and fundamental norms. In addition, there were pan-moralism politicizing morality and the tendency to centralize political values. Such fundamental norm was supposed to be adhered to not only in what people said and what they did, but also in what they thought.

The practice of reform and opening up, especially the implementation of the socialist commodity economy and market economy, has broken the social economic base on which the hitherto existing values had depended, thereby forming a new structure and a new pattern of values, the salient feature of which is that the structure of the hitherto existing unitary values is transformed into a pattern of values with multiple orientations coexisting. This pattern of multiple values has the following main factors: (1) collective values guided by Marxism advocated by the government; (2) traditional ethical and moral values contained in the Chinese culture; (3) the values introduced from Western culture; (4) the values of market economy.

Generally speaking, with less historic burden, young people are often the social group who are keener in perception, more liberated in mind, and more resolute and enterprising in action, and who tend to become advocates and recipients of new ideas and concepts. However, we have also noticed the fact that in social changes, there are always some resistance forces, which consist of not only some elderly people who once have lived in the old historic period for a long time, but also some young people influenced by the ideological education prevailing in the 1950s and 1960s. These people understand, support and actually promote the modernization of social material life, but they are more attached to the traditions in areas such as cultural life and interpersonal relationship. They cannot bear the exchange principle of the market economy invading the field of interpersonal communication, thinking that such exchange with money and other utilitarian things as the content would replace the past interpersonal relationship characteristic of simplicity, gentility, and sincerity. They oppose individualism, egoism, and narrow pragmatism. They do not understand or even despise those trendy ideas, behaviors and fashions, regarding those deeply influenced by the trend as "the beat generation" and "the generation without ideals and responsibilities". These young people have become those who intellectually yearn for modernity and emotionally return to tradition. They become the subject of Factors (1) and (2) in the structure of value system given above. These young people are cultural conservatives during the transitional period of social modernization drive, and are the main factor in the conflict between old and new ideas

However, what has impressed us more deeply is the major change in the values of the youth. The fulfilment of the practice of the reform and opening up and the development of market economy have exerted a huge impact on the original values. For a considerable number of young people (in both categories of youth, mainly in the first one), the original orthodox values and traditional living standards are questioned and doubted, and the ethical dogmas which are separated from the actual social development level and people' actual life was abandoned.

The main manifestation is as follows:

First, the transformation of core values. How to deal with the relationship between the individual and the group can best reflect the core content of values. Under the normalization of the original values, people must unconditionally obey to collective and national requirements. Everything, ranging from life ideal, career orientation and position selection, to personal inner world, hobby and even love and marriage should be reported to the organizations and groups. Any individual was supposed to take collective and national interests as the yardstick to judge the rationality and legitimacy of whatever he or she did, whether in material life or in cultural or psychological life. This view of value is based and centered on society and the collective, where the individual in a true sense disappears. However, the development of market economy and the diversification of interest subjects have gradually allowed the individual's independence and autonomy to be established. Under the conditions of market economy, people engaged in economic activity must choose their own behaviors based on their own interests. People must learn to dynamically design and develop by themselves according to the needs of society and the market. More and more young people face up to and actively pursue their personal value, dignity and interests, and their self-awareness, enterprising spirit, desire for achievement and self-responsibility have increased significantly. According to several related surveys conducted by Institute of Sociology of Chinese Academy of Social Sciences, there are 25%-40% of young people who deny such statements representative of absolute collectivism as "A personal issue, no matter how important, is a minor issue. A state matter, no matter how trivial, is a major matter." "Those who only care about themselves are villains, and those who value others are gentlemen." Instead, such viewpoints which affirm personal needs, such as "Do it subjectively for oneself and objectively for others have been endorsed by many young people. They have doubts about value judgment which absolutely negates personal selfish desires, such as "Selfishness is the root of all evil", and even about one-third of young people agree with the extreme individualism which is embodied in "Every man is for himself, and the devil takes the hindmost."① In addition, the survey also shows that among contemporary youth, only 1.6% of urban youth regard "having a common belief" as the main yardstick for measuring the governance of the country. Only 19.8% of them take "Doing great contribution to society" as their job-selection criteria, while personal needs and value realization are the overwhelming orientation in the job selection criteria.② These survey results can show that the original collective values centered on selfless dedication and unconditional absolute obedience to collective and national interests are waning away, and individualistic values centered on the pursuit of personal interests and the realization of personal self-worth are taking over.

Second, the change from idealistic value orientation to pragmatic value orientation.

"Set one's greatest virtue expound one's ideas in writing; set one's meritorious service" is the basic design of Chinese philosophy concerning the pursuit of human value, among which the accomplishment of a sage's realm of sublime good and supreme beauty is the highest value pursuit of life. The idealistic pursuit of life value is the basic tradition of the Chinese. After the founding of the PRC in 1949, "the struggle for the realization of communism and for the liberation of the proletariat and even mankind" is the highest value norm for the social public. For this reason, it was required that people should sacrifice their personal desires and worldly pleasures, and "tighten their belts" and work hard, work day and night and even contribute their lives to the realization of communism. It should be said that in that era, there was a strong belief among the older generation of proletarian revolutionaries and many officials, workers, peasants, and intellectuals. They fulfilled this belief, created epic deeds, and

---

① *China Youth Perspective*《中国青年大透视》, Beijing: Beijing Publishing House, 1993, p. 14, 43.
② Ibid.

set up many admirable shining examples of heroism for future generations. However, at the present time, the universality and dominance of such values have been greatly weakened. Many young people believe that this kind of ideal is too distant, too grandiose, and too empty, and that personal life in this world is of the most realistic significance. The young people of today are more concerned about their own state and immediate interests, emphasizing that people should first be responsible for themselves, their families, and their life on earth, in this world, and create a practical, beautiful and rich life in their own right. According to a survey on the evolution of young people's values, 51.4% of them basically agree with the statement that "people should enjoy pleasure in good time", the percentage higher by 5.8% than that of those who hold the opposite attitude. Among those who disagree, only 15.3% clearly expressed "opposition".[1] When answering "What is the greatest happiness in life", only 6% (of urban youth) and 10.9% (of rural cousins) chose "contributing to society".[2] An outstanding manifestation of the idea of secularism is the unconcealed and even crazy pursuit of young people for material enjoyment and money. The survey results show that 54.9% of young people agree with the proposition that "work is to make money". The main factors entering the consideration when they choose a career are high income and self-realization. Slogans such as "Seek nothing but profit; care only for money" are widely spread among young people. In this way, the idealistic and heroic personality values which were advocated in the past are retreating from the leading position and are replaced by secularism values that focus on personal, temporal existence and the pursuit of money.

  Third, the change from unitary values and beliefs to diversified values. For a long time, collective-based values have been in a unified and active position in Chinese society. This kind of value measures the value of individual existence by whether an individual obeys to collective interests and collective will, and regulates what people think, say and do. With the deepening of opening up and the development of market economy, the absoluteness and strictness of such values are being shaken. The values of present-day Chinese society are exhibiting the characteristics of relativity and pluralism. The coexistence of multiple values is very prominent among contemporary youth. Some of them believe in the view of life that "the pursuit of ideals is higher than the pursuit of riches, and the value of life lies in dedication" whereas some

---

[1] *China Youth Perspective*, Beijing: Beijing Publishing House, 1993, p.48.
[2] Ibid., p. 16.

believe in money worship; Some believe in the life standard of "All other people serve me and I serve all other people", some of them still believe in selfish and self-interested outlook on life that "Every man for himself, and the devil takes the hindmost"; and some embrace the so-called "rational egoism" which requires agents to always prioritize their self-interest over any competing concerns; some indulged themselves in national cultural nihilism worshipping everything foreign, some are stick to the traditions and the values of benevolence advocated by traditional culture...In short, among present-day Chinese youth, absolute unitary value beliefs no longer exist. Instead, they are replaced by a world vision which is the sum of diversified, undominant, disorderly, and non-integrative values.

It can be seen from the above that the movement from conflict to resistance and to change is the basic trend of values among today's Chinese youth in the context of modern social transformation.

II. Wrong way of the contemporary youth in the choice of values

In the process of conflict, resistance and change, which is the evolution of the values of contemporary Chinese youth, we feel that the contemporary youth embody a strong modern spirit of enterprising pioneering, innovative competition, and vigorous progress, playing the central theme of the spirit of the times. But in this central theme, we also have heard many discordant sounds, heavy sighs and painful shouts out of confusion, perplexity, anxiety and even nihilism. Here is a list of its performance as follows:

First, there is an anti-traditional and anti-cultural nihilism mentality among contemporary youths which manifests itself as being lost in faith and disorganized in personality. In the context of diversified values, some young people have lost their own beliefs and values in life, resulting in mental disorder, anomie of behavior, and loss of self-independence, autonomy and judgment. In addition, the rapid changes in social life, the increasing development of public media and the expansion of information flow have made individuals get an increasingly comprehensive and true grip of the bizarre external world and self, and are increasingly dominated and influenced by the public media. On this occasion, people are even more required to "inquire accurately; reflect carefully; discriminate clearly; practice earnestly". However, at present, some people, especially those who are not deeply involved in the world, and who have strong vanity, are completely influenced by others, their surrounding environment and social fashion, in their self-cognition or behaviors.

They have rooted in market fluctuation their value orientation as well as their ways of and attitudes towards eating, clothing, housing, transportation and entertainment, and think high of themselves as "in line with the trend of the times". They regard their catering to the impetuousness of the society and to the crude, low-grade madness as a sign of success and a manifestation of self-worth. They become the floating grass in the ocean of the life, rising and sinking with the ups and downs of the wave; they are the dust of the times, following the impact of the airflow and falling to the left or the right. Whoever has a lot of money can possess him or her. Whoever has a big fist can control him or her. Whoever has a high pitch can dominate him or her. These people who have lost their self and independent personality are all in very dangerous situations and are prone to juvenile delinquency. The personality conflict and disorganization that occur in social transition may jeopardize the community. So, we should attach great importance to this.

Second, money worship which advocates desperate pursuit of riches by any means has a great impact on contemporary youth. Under the conditions of a market economy, the emphasis on and pursuit of money is an inevitable phenomenon; it is indeed a step forward compared with the traditional values according to which the pursuit of money is something shameful to talk about. However, there are some people who, in order to pursue money, always attempts to obtain it by some opportunistic or even unscrupulous means. In order to reap huge profits, some people can cut corners and even make fake and shoddy products, totally regardless of the interests and life of others; in order to achieve a certain profit target, some can pollute the environment and destroy the ecological balance; in order to get rid of poverty as soon as possible and gain both fame and fortune, some literati can make up their stories and frequently concoct cultural waste products, only to mislead and cause harm to the young men and to pollute the sound civilized atmosphere of society. In order to highlight their political achievements in office, some leading officials can disregard long-term and overall interests and engage in bluffing bubble economy and short-term behaviors of "draining the pond to get all the fish" or "killing the goose that lays the golden eggs." Some officials engage in the abuse of power for personal gain and in a tradeoff of money and power, and cheating and corruption have become a relatively common phenomenon in the current society. All these are the inevitable manifestations and results of money worship and the eagerness for quick success and instant benefit.

Third, there is still an unhealthy mentality, namely hedonism, among contemporary youth. It is natural for man to pursue a prosperous and comfortable life, and the fundamental goal of socialist modernization is to meet the growing material and cultural needs of the people. However, among the "people who get rich first," some spend money extravagantly to the point of eye-popping absurdity. They regard indulging in eating, drinking and pleasure-seeking and pursuing a luxurious life as the entire content of life, and as the highest value of life. They display their values and statuses through perverted and deformed consumption such as flaunting wealth, spending money extravagantly, burying themselves in the alcohol and hotties, wearing brand-name clothing from head to toes, and blatantly seeking publicity. These people would rather squander and waste than dedicate or invest in public undertakings that benefit society and future generations. They despise ideals, beliefs and ideal personalities; they disdain ethics and art. What they pursue is not the highest level of life value, but so-called fullness and pleasure of every minute, namely every gratifying minute. They believe that only sensory pleasure is the most real and practical, and regard themselves completely as nothing but a money-making machine or a pleasure-seeking machine. This upstart-style, low-level and low-style hedonistic mentality not only plays a very bad social role model, but is also a huge waste of social resources. The emergence of such mentality and behavior is really a sadness. After all, China has not yet shaken off poverty!①

Fourth, the spread of speculative and impetuous mentality. During the transition to a market economy, some people's sense of speculation continued to strengthen. Especially in the current situation where there is still no matched policies and normative systems, there are often nouveau riche who succeeded by speculation, and some people who succeed by relying on their luck or on their professional and interpersonal advantages and thus have carved out a niche in society. Because these "overnight-rich" figures indeed easily obtained success, and because they lived luxurious life, they set bad examples among people, especially among the youth who are prone to admire and even envy and at the same time take chance on fortune and take a lucky thinking for their future, attempting to rely on some of his talents instead of hard work to achieve the goal of reaping both fame and fortune. As a result, indolence, job discontent, and opportunism were widespread. This impetuous

---

① The present article was published in 1995. Now China has achieved success in eradicating absolute poverty, and has embarked on vitalizing its rural areas — a task that is central to the nation's modernization drive, which will continue up to midcentury.—Tr.

mentality is rife with irrationality, emotionality and blindness, and it has a huge market among contemporary Chinese youth.

III. Shake off the shadow of confusion and nothingness

In a sense, modernization is also a process of interest differentiation, conflict, and social order reorganization. But in order to accomplish the great cause of modernization, it is undoubtedly necessary to inspire the national spirit, to gather all the efforts of all social strata, and to work together with one heart and one mind. Obviously, many national mentalities that have emerged in the current process of social transformation, especially the unhealthy mentalities and values that have appeared in the young generation who have crossed the century, are not conducive to the integration and invigoration of the national spirit. It is a discrete force. Then, what is the basis for bringing together the majority of the public and different classes and groups so that they can reach a consensus and work together to do their best for national rejuvenation and social development? I think the key lies in fostering a value that is recognized and accepted together. Common values and value goals can be relied on to unite everyone together. Obviously, the value and value goal today cannot the same as those under the traditional economic and political system before the social transformation, and needs to be reconstructed in the new social practice and under the conditions of the times. I believe that the values of contemporary Chinese, especially young people across the century, should have at least the following aspects:

First, contemporary young people should have the modern spirit of forging ahead, deliberate innovation, and active competition required by modern social practices (mainly practices of market economy), as well as distinctive national cultural qualities and personalities. Historical practices have proven that whether it is the "wholesale Westernization" of national cultural nihilism or the closed and arrogant cultural conservatism, they will hamper the realization of China's modernization. Therefore, one of the important historical missions for the generation of young people across the century is to inherit the fine cultural traditions of the Chinese nation, promoting the Chinese nation's unremitting self-improvement, indomitableness, and unobtrusiveness, and carrying forward the spirit of modern practice so as to achieve the organic integration of the two.

Second, contemporary youth must have a social and collective value orientation, and at the same time have a strong self-consciousness of self-molding, self-development, and self-worth realization. At the important historical juncture of social transformation and national modernization, they should first determine their goals according to the needs of the country, society and nation, and realize their self-worth while making significant contributions to society, the country, and the nation. In other words, contemporary youth must put collective, social, state, and national interests over the interests of the individual, have a strong sense of social responsibility and patriotism, and oppose narrow individual-centered values.

Third, as an important part of the market economy, contemporary youth should consciously and actively advocate and construct a cultural spirit that can adapt to and promote the sound development of the market economy. In addition to following a series of norms required by the operation of the market economy, we should also be strong and self-reliant, hardworking, diligent, thrifty, dedicated, dedicated to the cause, and willing to contribute. We should oppose any means of unfair competition to obtain development opportunities, and oppose hedonism and extravagance, oppose radical individualism, oppose money worship that uses wealth as a yardstick for measuring the value of life. In short, they are supposed to have noble sentiments and mental realm, so that the pursuit of this kind of fashion, sentiment and realm of lofty thought will become the mental driving force for the development of the socialist market economy.

Fourth, in handling human relations, the contemporary youth must have a virtuous and charitable heart. Specifically speaking, one should show consideration for others by putting oneself in their place, and understand others by walking in their shoes; one should aim at helping others with good intentions toward others; be strict with oneself and lenient towards others; be upright and above flattery and never be led astray; remain in society by good faith and trustworthiness; think of righteousness on seeing gain; be ready to give up one's life at the critical moment; be ready to do favors for others, to name just a few. In this way, an interpersonal relationship of mutual love, mutual trust and mutual dependence will be nurtured in our society.

Fifth, the contemporary youth should vigorously promote the spirit of science and democracy. In modern society, science and technology have become a huge pillar of social development and become the "primary productive force". Those who do not have knowledge of modern science and technology can neither make great contribution to society nor face the dilemma of survival and development. Any country that has mastered modern cutting-edge science and technology will occupy the commanding height of social development. Besides this, science is always associated with truth and with the emancipation of the mind. Science only obeys to the truth, never and ever succumbing to any authority or believing blindly in any idol or sticking to any dogma. Therefore, attaching importance to science and technology and carrying forward the scientific spirit of seeking truth from facts also means carrying forward democracy and advocating the spirit of freedom. The spirit of science and democracy is undoubtedly of great significance in promoting China's socialist modernization. Therefore, the contemporary youth who are shouldering important historical responsibilities across the centuries should play a role model in advocating and fulfilling the spirit of science and democracy.

Modernity and Chinese People's Cultural Identity Crisis and Reconstruction in Modern Times*

I. Modernity and the emergence of identity crisis

The historical development of China's modernity[①] is driven by the pursuit of modernization. In modern China facing the crisis of national subjugation and extinction, the most direct manifestation of modernization efforts is the absorption of Western technology and the imitation of systems. At the same time, the abolition of the imperial examination system and the collapse of imperial power as the symbol of ethnic cultural value resulted in a huge chasm at the institutional level, namely the replacing of the traditional Chinese *"tianxia"* (天下; literally: "under heaven")

---

* This article is written with the cooperation of Gan Chunsong 干春松.
① Modernity is a very complex concept. The present article's emphasis on the influence of institutional change on Chinese society mainly results from one of Giddens' concept as follows: "I use the term 'modernity' in a very general sense, to refer to the institutions and modes of behaviour established first of all in post-feudal Europe, but which in the twentieth century increasingly have become world-historical in their impact.'Modernity' can be understood as roughly equivalent to 'the industrialised world' …A second dimension is captialism, where this term means a system of commodity production involving both competitive product markets and the commodification of labour power. " (Giddens, Anthony. *Modernity and self-identity*, Polity Press ,1991, p. 14-15) Some people criticized that Giddens's description of modernity does not take into account the cultural issues:" Giddens does not take cultural issues seriously, ... The whole idea that one can justify the contemporary world without discussing issues that arose from the current debates over the politics of politics, cultural capital, cultural differences, cultural homogeneity and heterogeneity, ethnicity, nationalism, race, gender, and so on is unbelievable. "(Roland Robertson. *Globalization: Social Theory and Global Culture*, SAGE Publications Ltd ,1992. Shanghai People's Publishing House, 2000, p. 187) The present article can be said to have been written with reference to this criticism, but always believes that institutional changes are the fundamental and essential element in the emergence of China's cultural identity crisis.

model[1] with a nation-state model, the replacing of the traditional family-based production mode with a free economical model, and the replacing of the almighty rule of imperial power with the political participation of the people. Institutions are the coacervation of culture. In the final analysis, the emergence and continuation of traditional institutions are the gradual stabilization and formation of various customs and rules in the long-term struggles. What these institutions provide people is safety and "efficacy". In modern times, the discussion on a series of military failures in the West and the root causes of these failures, finally became doubts and denials about the "efficacy" of the Confucian concept system. In this way, through in-depth transformation in technology, system and concept, the common foundation of Chinese people's identity with historical and cultural values no longer exists. What's more serious, the conflict between and the combination of strong nationalism and enlightenment have led to people's enthusiasm for system transplantation, which obscured the serious problem of cultural identity that modernity will inevitably raise.

Therefore, the deepest root of the cultural identity crisis[2] is the complete subversion of the view of history and cosmological views, which Chinese people has long relied on to understand the world. The foundation of Chinese traditional historical view is spatial. This China-centered concept of space determines the causes for cultural differences and the logic of development, and thus forms such terms as "*Yi Xia* (夷夏, the ethnic minority and Han nation)" and "Wen Ye(文野 civilization and barbarism)."

But the logic of modernity is temporal, that is, the new replacing the old.[3] With

---

[1] The detailed discussion of the shift of the modern Chinese people's perception of self-image from "culturalism" to "nationalism" can be found in Jin Guangyao: "Chinese nationalism"《中国的民族主义》, in *Modern China's National Image and Identity*《近代中国的国家形象与国家认同》, Shanghai: Shanghai Ancient Books Publishing House, 2003, p. 173-211.

[2] Some people think that Chinese people do not have "identity crisis." Lucian Pye did not acknowledge the identity crisis brought about by institutional changes to the Chinese. "Most other transitional systems usually have a crisis of identity and the Chinese have generally not experienced it." "They almost have no doubt about their Chinese identity." "The more open they are to the outside world, the more they consciously recognize their Chinese identity." [Lucian W. Pye.*The spirit of Chinese Politics: A Psychocultural Study of the Authority Crisis in Politic Development*, pp. 5,6, M. I. T 1968.]

[3] According to Chinese scholar Gan Yang's description, "The logic of modernity is that the new is the good and the newest is the best, so the young necessarily outdo those in old age and the innovative necessarily outshine the old-fashioned." See more in "Political Philosopher Strauss: Classical conservatism (《政治哲人施特劳斯：古典保守主义的兴起》)," in Strauss, Leo: *Natural Right and History*, tran. by Penggan, Beijing: SDX Joint Publishing Company, 2003, p.10.

the spread of the theory of evolution, this concept has been deeply rooted in the hearts of the people, making the concept of modern Chinese culture gradually changing in the 1920s and 1930s from the view of culture focusing on *East-West* comparison to the one focusing on ancient-modern comparison, with its constant coordinates gradually shifting from space to time. The logical extension of such view of history is the tendency that under a framework of cultural determinism, the causes of China's backwardness was attributed to its own cultural traditions, while its positive aspects or its successes were attributed to Western culture, and thus the issues concerning "value" were transformed those concerning "knowledge". The debate on the relationship between "science metaphysics" and "social historical view" which took place in the 1920s further confirmed the historical view with time as its constant coordinate. Ironically, the modern Neo-Confucianism, which regards itself as the inherence of the Confucian tradition has also accepted this new view of space and time.

"Identity" is, in the final analysis, an attitude toward and a recognition of different cultural systems against a common the spatio-temporal background because each and every culture always has its "self-image" with a certain cultural system as the reference background. For those countries which develop later, modernization means their being forcibly thrown into a new cultural reference background against which they need re-identification of themselves. The values and social formation of the Western as the birthplace of the modernization movement have naturally become a standard form of modernization, which has been framed as "advanced" in the concept of evolution, while other social forms are naturally backward and must be changed.

Therefore, this recognition of "modernity" is a practice of identification, in which we inevitably carry out a complete and thorough liquidation of our cultural traditions according to the new (actually the Western) standards. After the Opium War, China's debates over culture can basically be said to be the manifestation of different self-identified cultural "ego". The identity crisis of the Chinese people lies in the fact that the relatively consistent image against the original background is diversified and multi-directional against the new background.

Globalization is "flowing modernity". The intensification of economic globalization has further highlighted the issue of cultural identity as a universal global issue. Globalization, modernity and cultural identity are closely related chains of logical problems. Both theories of "clashes of civilizations" and "the end of history" are based on this crisis of identity, and it is obvious that the local experience of the

West is used as an example of universal experience. Indeed, there has been a clear convergence on the institutional level due to the global expansion of modernization. This convergence is so overwhelming that one believes that the convergence of cultural patterns that accompany it (such as the universalization of individualistic culture) is also inevitable. However, this is not the case, because the cultural adaptation of each nation and country is subjected to its own history and tradition, and this adjustment and adaptation are also different, and diversified forms have thus emerged, which constitute the so-called "multiple modernity". The present article is not trying to propose a new model, but to describe the different responses of Chinese people in the face of this identity crisis through the thinking of Chinese political and intellectual elites on this issue in modern times, to illustrate the close connection between the issue of cultural identity and the political and social changes in modern China, and thus provide a background for us to reflect on the issues of modernity and cultural identity so that we can respond to this issue more correctly.

II. Seeking to solve cultural identity crisis

The core issue of identity crisis is how to resolve the conflicts between the Western-based institutional system and local and national cultures. In China at the beginning of the 20th century, this issue was presented as a sheer doubt about the value of Confucian culture.

Facing the advanced technology and management experience of the Western, those most insightful modern people have emphasized the superiority of Confucianism morality through the "Tao-qi (道器 logos-utensils, namely law-implement)" category, namely the concept of "ethics before skills" in the Confucian tradition, that is, through the slogans such as "Restrict the foreigners with the techniques learnt from them" and "Making Western learning serve for China." However, Kang You-wei and others think more directly about the significance of traditional values in institutional reforms. First of all, he was aware of the inevitability of China's institutional reforms, but he still insisted on exploring the rationality of such reforms from the resources of traditional Confucianism. This is also an important reason why he wrote two books, namely, *Forgeries in the Classics of the Confucian Canon* (Xin Xue Wei Jing Kao 《新学伪经考》) and *A Study of Confucius as a Reformer* (*Kongzi gaizhi kao*, 《孔子改制考》).

Forgeries in the Classics of the Confucian Canon is just of the bases of Kang You-wei's theory of reform. On this basis, he further developed the tradition of literature and wrote a series of works represented by *Commentary to Rites and Etiquette (Li Yun Zhu*《礼运注》, *Recompilation of Dong Zhongshu's 'Rich Dew of Spring and Autumn (Chunqiu Fanlu)*' ① (*Chunqiu dongshi xue,*《春秋董氏学》) and *A Study of Confucius as a Reformer (Kongzi gaizhi kao,*《孔子改制考》). Making use of two main concepts of state and society proposed in *The Gongyangzhuan*②, namely a great unity (*da yi tong* 大一统) and a historical development in three phases (san shi shuo), he put forward a systematic concept of historical evolution, and constructed a theoretical system of "reform depending on ancient political system (*tuogu gaizhi* 托古改制)", which paid close attention to the issue of how to settle Confucianism, an issue inevitably brought about by the institutional reform. Therefore, on the one hand, he emphasized that the imperial examination must be abolished and Western politics and Western learning should be promoted; on the other hand, he sought new growth points for Confucianism in the design of the new system. After summarizing and inspecting the experience of the West, he concluded that the church system in the West is the institutional resource most likely for Confucianism to rely on after the implementation of institutional changes. In 1895, Kang Youwei put forward a new institutionalized method in the "*Gongche Shangshu*（公车上书 The Pubic Petition）"③ to ensure the publicity and influence of Confucianism, so as to reduce people's evil and resist the temptation of "paganism". Specific measures include the building of a Confucian temple, the

---

① Dong Zhongshu 董仲舒, an expert on the Chunqiu who also wrote the sub-classic Chunqiu fanlu (春秋繁露 "Rich Dew of Spring and Autumn.")—Tr.
② The Gongyang zhuan（公羊传）is a commentary to the Confucian Classic Chunqiu（春秋）"Spring and Autumn Annals." It is said to have been written by Gongyang Gao （公羊高）, a disciple of Zixia（子夏）, who was himself a disciple of Confucius. During the reign of Emperor Jing（汉景帝）(r. 157-141 BCE) of the Han period（汉, 206 BCE-220 CE）it was declared a part of the Confucian Canon to be studied in the National University (taixue 太学). The most important professor (boshi 博士 "erudite") for the Gongyang commentary to the Chunqiu classic was Gongsun Hong（公孙弘）who taught during the reign of Emperor Wu（汉武帝, r. 141-87 BCE). No less important was his predecessor Dong Zhongshu（董仲舒）, an expert on the Chunqiu who also wrote the sub-classic Chunqiu fanlu（春秋繁露 "Rich Dew of Spring and Autumn"). —Tr.
③ The 1898 Reform was a political movement launched by Chinese bourgeois reformists, who, following the example of the West, hoped reform the old government institutions. In 1895, during the reign of Qing Emperor Guangxu, the Qing government was defeated in the Fist Sino-Japanese War. Kang Youwei launched the "Gongche Shangshu（The Pubic Petition）Movement" in Bejing. On June 11, 1898, Emperor Guangxu accepted the reformers' suggestions and promulgated an imperial edict, announcing reforms in political, economic, military, cultural and educational fields. However, the reform was opposed by the conservatives led by Empress Dowager Cixi.

rewarding of those who travel overseas to spread the "teachings" of Confucianism.[①] He even linked the survival of "state" with the survival of "religion", proposing the priority of "protection of religion" to "protection of the state", and clearly stating that Confucianism represented by Confucius should be designated as "state religion".

After the 1911 Revolution, Kang Youwei thought it impossible to guarantee the stability of China by completely imitating the political model and mental resources of the West, so he wrote many articles emphasizing the importance of Confucian values for social order. Kang believed that any kind of political design that is deviated from the culture and social reality of a country is enough to cause the collapse of society. Therefore, he continued to try in practice to establish a basis for Chinese cultural identity by establishing Confucianism as the state religion.

However, after the collapse of institutionalized Confucianism, people could acquire knowledge from diversified sources. The theory of evolution with "It is not the strongest of the species that survive, but the one most responsive to change" as its slogan has become a new belief, and for the emerging international students and people who had grown up under the new education system, Confucianism has become a historical relic. They did not fail to see the intrinsic value of Confucianism, but in the new structure with time as its constant coordinate, they naturally deduced that in order to welcome the imaginary new China, they must bid farewell to Confucianism, and *New Youth* (《新青年》) was adapted to this psychological need to a great extent.

The intellectual class represented *by New Youth* first paid attention to the inseparable relationship between Confucius together with his Confucianism and the old system. Therefore, when discussing the proposal to establish Confucianism as the state religion in the Congress, Chen Duxiu (陈独秀), Li Dazhao (李大钊) and others made sharp criticisms of this proposal. After the failure of Zhang Xun (张勋)'s restoration, Chen Duxiu held that honoring Confucianism and restoration were dependent on each other and that "Confucianism and republicanism are such two absolutely incompatible things that when one exists, the other must be abolished, and this is what I have said many times. Zhang and Kang also know this, so advocating that Confucianism must attack the republic. It is just as what I believe: republicanism

---

① Kang Youwei: "The Second Letter to the Qing Emperor," Xie Xialing (selected): *Implement Reform to Seek Peace: Kang Youwei's Anthology,* Shanghai: Shanghai Far East Press, 1997, p. 283.

excludes Confucianism."[1] The political events which had taken place led Chen Duxiu and others to believe that if the questions about values are not resolved, any institutional reform can only be superficial. The radical way of thinking, however, led them to make an either-or choice: On one hand, they regarded Eastern culture and Western culture as two absolutely different systems, and believed that the difference between the East and the West was not a manifestation of diversification, but rather the difference between "ancient and modern" "new and old", namely the difference between the two cultures of different times; on the other hand, they thought that the Chinese culture represented by Confucianism was a backward culture, not suitable for the development of modern civilization and the needs of China to become independent and prosperous, and that it was a culture that should be discarded. Chen believed that there was no room for compromise between Confucian culture and democratic and scientific values. He was unwilling to leave Confucianism with any room for maneuver, thinking that it was meaningless to start a debate about "true Confucius" and "fake Confucius", though many people at that time tried to make the distinction between Confucius and post-Confucianism at that time. Hu Shi, another representative of the Enlightenment, also believed that we must admit that everything we Chinese people had was not so good as what others had.

Under this either-or choice, everything in Chinese tradition should be abandoned, including families, names and classical Chinese; and even Chinese characters should be phoneticized. The so-called simple reason is that these structures and matters are all inseparable from traditional values.

There is no need to go into details here on the significance of the New Culture Movement for modern China. However, it should be pointed out that those Enlightenment thinkers so over-simply looked at tradition that they even attempted to take a kind of ideologicalized "science" and "democracy" as a universal value and thus solve the problems related to modernization and cultural identity, which obviously ignored the internal relationship between institutions and culture. In the traditional Chinese society, the Chinese people have taken Confucian values as undeniable *Tianli* (天理; literally: the laws of heaven—feudal ethics as propounded by the Song Confucianists). Therefore, judging between right and wrong with Confucian conception as the criterion has become the "collective unconsciousness"

---

[1] Chen Duxiu: "Restoration and Honoring Confucianism," in Pangpu, et al (ed.), *Studies of Pre-Qin Confucianism*, Wuhan: Hubei Education Press, 2003, p.114.

of the Chinese people, which provides them with stability and security. However, in order to resolve the conflict between the new system and the cultural conventions, new legitimacy needs to be established. It is in this sense that we cannot ignore the significance of Kang Youwei's efforts to establish the Confucian Churches.

III. Reflections on enlightenment: nationalization and Sinicization in new enlightenment

After the 1911 Republican Revolution, which ended the rule of the Qing Dynasty (1644-1911), China, in terms of political structure, mainly drew on the political framework of the West, but in terms of ideology, it always intersected with the Confucian concepts. The reliance of the Northern Warlords (1912-1927) on Confucianism is self-evident; the *Kuomintang* (National People's Party), which always took "revolution" as the banner, also took "nationalism" as its motto. The "Three Principles of the People"[①] proposed by Sun Yat-sen[②] first of all emphasized "nationalism", for he believed that "universalism" proposed by the powerful countries was only to maintain their monopoly on the oppression of weak and small nations. "They want to maintain this monopoly position forever, and no longer allow weak and small nations to rejuvenate, so they advocate cosmopolitanism every day, saying that the scope of nationalism is too narrow. In fact, the cosmopolitanism they advocate is imperialism in disguise and aggression in disguise."[③] Therefore, although Sun Yat-sen sometimes also thought that the "Three Principles of the People" are consistent with socialism and communism, he fundamentally believed that the "Three Principles of the People" already contains the content of socialism and at the same time he placed a strong emphasis on the inheritance relationship between the "Three Principles of the People" and the Confucian tradition.

After the death of Sun Yat-sen in 1925, Dai Jitao (戴季陶), as the orthodox interpreter of the Prime Minister's will, proved the connection between the "Three

---

① Three Principles of the People, also called Three Great Principles, Chinese (Pinyin) *Sanmin Zhuy*i or (Wade-Giles romanization) *San-min Chu-i*, the theoretical basis of the political program of the Chinese Nationalist leader Sun Yat-sen (1866–1925), championing the principles of nationalism, democracy, and livelihood. —Tr.

② He was also called Sun Zhongshan (1866-1925), leader of the Chinese Nationalist Party (Kuomintang [Pinyin: *Guomindang*]), known as the father of modern China. Influential in overthrowing the Qing dynasty (1911/12), he served as the first provisional president of the Republic of China (1911–12) and later as *de facto* ruler (1923–25). —tr.

③ Sun Yat-sen: *Three Principles of the People*, Chin. ed., Changsha:Yuelu Bookstore, 2000, p. 39.

Principles of the People" and the Confucian tradition. He proposed that "The original purpose of the Three Principles of the People is to regain and recover national confidence." The foundation of this self-confidence lies in Confucian values. "I am convinced that there is something most lofty in Mr. Zhongshan's doctrine: it is he who explained that the moral spirit embracing loyalty, benevolence, faith, and peace is the foundation of national self-confidence."[①]

Chiang Kai-shek(蒋介石) went even further than Dai Jitao in establishing the connection between the "Three Principles of the People" and Confucianism. He even regarded the "Three Principles of the People" as a modern embodiment of Confucianism and Taoism. "The thought of Yat-sen is entirely Chinese orthodoxy, that is, the theory of righteousness and morality which was inherited from Yao and Shun and ended in Confucius and Mencius."[②] He integrated the "Three Principles of the People" and Sun Yat-sen's thoughts in "Plans for National Reconstruction" (*jianguo fanglue*《建国方略》) and his other writings, and proposed the "five major constructions," namely, psychological, ethical, social, political and economic construction, and launched the "New Life Movement",[③] believing that national rejuvenation not only lies in the strength of force, but the key is the nobility of national morals.

However, the identification of the Confucian tradition in the ideology of the Kuomintang is not entirely reflected in its political design. Although the separation of the five powers and the separation of three powers seem to be somewhat different, the Confucian ideals do not really become the ideals of this regime. We are more willing to regard this tendency of Confucianization as a moral factor that strengthens the rallying power that Chinese society provided when approaching the Western political

---

① Department of the History of the CPC at Renmin University of China (complied): *Selection of Dai Jitao's Doctrines*, Beijing: Renmin University of China Press, 1951, p.14, 22.
② Jiang Jieshi: "Philosophical Issues in China's Education," quoted from *Confucianism in Modern China*, Zhengzhou: Zhongzhou Ancient Books Press, 1991, p. 143.
③ The "New Life Movement" initiated by Jiang Jieshi in 1934 holds an important position in the history of KMT of China and has exerted certain influence on the modem and contemporary history of the country. This socio-reform movement lasting for 15 years had multiple causes. Politically speaking it was directed related with the implementation of the policy of "stabilizing internal situation before resisting foreign aggression" in the wake of the September 18th Incident. Ideologically speaking, the cause lay in the rejection of and babed against the May Fourth Moved by the conservative forces represented by Jiang Jieshi. However, the fundamental motivation was that Jiang Jieshi attempted to take advantage of this opportunity to restore the ruling position of the feudalist ethics and mores, by means of which to control people's thinking and maintain his regime. —Tr.

system.

The situation in the field of academic culture seems somewhat different. The "debate on the relationship between science and metaphysics" and the "debate on the nature of society" seem to prove that Confucianism has been so outdated that it could be stored in the museum, and even the position of Neo-Confucianism is very fragile. For example, Neo-Confucianism fully accepted the values of Enlightenment and the historical concept of progress. Liang Shuming (梁漱溟) and Feng Youlan (冯友兰) and others all accepted the view that the difference between China and the West is the difference between the ancient and the modern while Mou Zongsan's[①] thought of conscience self-negation(良知坎陷说) is tantamount to making excuse for why China did not have democracy or freedom at that time. Thus, their demonstration of the Confucian values largely gave up the rationality of the Confucian system design itself, but "purified" Confucianism into a theory of spirituality. They even used the religiousness of Confucianism to prove the transcendence and universality of Confucianism, so as to find some space for the existence of Confucianism through reconstructing Confucianism to be consistent with Western values. Although we can appreciate the good intentions of Neo-Confucianism to "salvage Confucianism in another way around", we must also point out that the way that Neo-Confucianism seeks cultural identity is fundamentally wrong, because it only can reduce Confucianism to a footnote to Enlightenment and it is difficult for Confucianism to fulfill its intervention in society and make contribution to modern systems.

From the 1930s to the 1940s, with the intensification of Japanese imperialist aggression, the Chinese nation was again at a critical juncture of life and death. National salvation and rejuvenation have become the overriding themes of Chinese politics and culture. Thus, as a result, the government-led trend of Confucianization and the conservative stance in the academic field turned into a joint force under the increasing pressure of Japanese aggression in China. The awareness of national danger and salvation would inevitably enhance the understanding of the importance of the mental power of the country, thus leading to a new understanding of China's local value resources, which is manifested in the discussion of "Chinese-centered culture" and the proposal of the adaptation of Marxism to China's conditions. The

---

① Mou Zongsan 牟宗三 (1909-1995) was the theoretical genius behind New Confucianism, a philosophical and cultural movement marking the revival of *Ruxue* 儒学 in Asia and Northern America since the late 1970s.—Tr.

Chinese Communists proposed it, while Zhang Shenfu (张申府) and others proposed that while inheriting the value of Enlightenment, we need to correctly evaluate the ideological resources that conform to the spirit of the times in Chinese traditional culture, need to retrieve cultural values and reconstruct China's cultural identity. Therefore, the "new enlightment" characterized by the reflection on the trend of enlightenment has become a new way of cultural identification.

Historical data show that the "Manifesto of China-centered Cultural Construction"(《中国本位文化的宣言》) published in January 1935 has a certain relationship with the *Kuomintang*'s propaganda strategy at that time. If we regard it as a political gesture, we can think that the *Kuomintang* regime tried to further enrich the content of nationalism, one of the "Three Principles of the People", while weakening the influence of the West and Soviet Russia. However, if it is regarded as a kind of thinking made by the intellectuals in response to the needs of the times, it should be regarded as a rational thinking on cultural development in the context of nationalism. The theory of "Chinese-centered culture" emphasizes the creation of a new civilization based on the reality of China. This view is reasonable and was accepted by Zhang Shenfu(张申府) and Zhang Dainian(张岱年), who had absorbed materialist dialectics and Russell's analytical methods, and who thus put forward the cultural view of "comprehensive innovation."[①]

This line of thinking was developed into the "Neo-enlightenment Movement" by progressive intellectuals who were later influenced by the CPC. The emergence of the Neo-enlightenment, on the surface, was a response to the notions of the restoration of Confucianism that appeared at that time. It was proposed that the task of the May Fourth Enlightenment was not yet completed, and new enlightenment should be carried out for the Chinese people, "the thoughts of democracy and freedom should be applied to fight dogmatic dogma, scientific culture to replace superstition and folly. This is what democracy and the spirit of science call for."[②] Zhang Shenfu, who once participated in the May Fourth Enlightenment Movement, clearly proposed to correct the radical position at the time: "The Neo-enlightenment can be said to

---

① For the cultural views of Zhang Dainian 张岱年 and his elder brother Zhang Songnian 张崧年(later named Zhang Shenfu张申府) in the 1930s, see Gan Chunsong干春松: "The Cultural Outlook of Zhang Dainian in the 1930s"《张岱年30年代的文化观》, *Journal of Tsinghua University*, 2004 (4).
② Ai Siqi艾思奇: "What is Neo-enlightenment Movement?"《什么是新启蒙运动》, in Ding Shouhe (ed.), *Enlightenment Thoughts in Modern China* (Vol.2), Beijing: Social Sciences Academic Press,1999, p.170.

be a nationalist, profound and democratic ideological and cultural movement. It is necessary to sublate what is regarded as one's own tradition. Here the so-called sublation means that some should be discarded, and some should be preserved and carried forward to a higher stage. The Enlightenment during the May Fourth Movement was too childish in some ways. Therefore, in order to correct the slogan of "Knock down with the Confucian Store"("打倒孔家店") I once put forward: "Knock down with the Confucian Store but rescue Confucius," which means that China's true traditional heritage should be re-evaluated in a critical and analytical manner, and the scumbags should be removed and the dross rejected. After that, it is worth accepting and inheriting."[①]

At the same time, the CPC has always attached great importance to the exploration of the "new culture of the Chinese nation". It has been not only politically exploring the "liberation" of the Chinese nation from semi-colonial and semi-feudal rule, but also exploring the reconstruction of the cultural world of the Chinese nation and the meaningful world order. As Mao Zedong pointed out, "For many years we Communists have struggled for a cultural revolution as well as for a political and economic revolution, and our aim is to build a new society and a new state for the Chinese nation. That new society and new state will have not only a new politics and a new economy but also a new culture. In other words, not only do we want to change a China that is politically oppressed and economically exploited into a China that is politically free and economically prosperous, we also want to change the China which is being kept ignorant and backward under the sway of the old culture into an enlightened and progressive China under the sway of a new culture. In short, we want to build a new China. Our aim in the cultural sphere is to build a new Chinese national culture." In a word, we want to establish "a new culture of the Chinese nation".[②]

Guided by the basic principles of Marxism-Leninism, Mao Zedong summarized ancient and modern Chinese culture, and put forward a proposition of building a new national, scientific, and popular culture, and pointed out that only such a new culture can truly become the basis of the national cohesion and cultural identity of the Chinese people.

[①] Zhang Shenfu 张申府: "On Sinicization," in Luo Rongquan 罗荣渠 (ed.), *From "Westernization" to Modernization,* Beijing: Peking University Press, 1990, p.588.
[②] *Selected Works of Mao Zedong,* Vol.2, Chin. ed., Beijing: People's Publishing House, 1991, p.663.

"New-democratic culture is national. It opposes imperialist oppression and upholds the dignity and independence of the Chinese nation. It belongs to our own nation and bears our own national characteristics. It links up with the socialist and new-democratic cultures of all other nations and they are related in such a way that they can absorb something from each other and help each other to develop, together forming a new world culture; but as a revolutionary national culture it can never link up with any reactionary imperialist culture of whatever nation."

"New-democratic culture is scientific. Opposed as it is to all feudal and superstitious ideas, it stands for seeking truth from facts, for objective truth and for the unity of theory and practice."

"New-democratic culture belongs to the broad masses and is therefore democratic. It should serve the toiling masses of workers and peasants who make up more than 90 per cent of the nation's population d should gradually become their very own."[①]

The Chinese Communists, represented by Mao Zedong, gradually realized in their constant practice that Marxist theory must be combined with the practice of the Chinese revolution. Mao Zedong said: "For a hundred years, the finest sons and daughters of the disaster-ridden Chinese nation fought and sacrificed their lives, one stepping into the breach as another fell, in quest of the truth that would save the country and the people. This moves us to song and tears. But it was only after World War I and the October Revolution in Russia that we found Marxism-Leninism, the best of truths, the best of weapons for liberating our nation." However, he emphasized: "We must integrate the universal truth of Marxism-Leninism with the concrete practice of the Chinese revolution. Otherwise, one can only cite odd quotations from K. Marx, F. Engels, Lenin and Stalin in a one-sided manner, and he chops up history, knows only ancient Greece but not China. This subjectivist method which is contrary to science and Marxism-Leninism does a great deal of harm and thus is a formidable enemy of the people and the nation."[②]

Therefore, this "new culture of the Chinese nation", that is, the new democratic culture, is guided by Marxism. It embodies the sound worldview and methodology of Marxism; the interest demands and value tendencies of the proletariat and all

---

① *Selected Works of Mao Zedong*, Vol. 2, Chin. ed., Beijing: People's Publishing House, 1991, p. 706-709.
② *Selected Works of Mao Zedong*, Vol. 3, Chin. ed., Beijing: People's Publishing House, 1991, p. 796.

the people. It critically advocates absorbing the essence of the national traditional culture, which is "a necessary condition for developing national culture and enhancing national self-confidence", and therefore has a strong appeal and rallying power. Compared with the conservative stances of liberalism and neo-Confucianism or official Confucianism at the time, the neo-democratic cultural outlook is more tolerant. Opposing imperialism becomes the ideal of socialism, which conforms to the basic demands of the Chinese people's pursuit of modernity. The emphasis on nationality was not only a manifestation of public opinion in the state of war at that time, but also an important way to unite people's hearts with culture while the pursuit of rationality (the unity of subjectivity and objectivity) carried forward the spirit of enlightenment. And "the popular" means the concealed democratic consciousness. This is why the CPC established Mao Zedong Thought as the guiding thought of the Chinese Communists after the "Yan'an Rectification Movement", and ruled out Wang Ming and others' wrong approach to Marxism with dogmatism, and the new democratic cultural outlook became the leading concept, which is the main reason for the rapid victory of China's national revolution. The victory of Mao Zedong Thought over dogmatism can also be said to be the victory of "reconstructed modernity" over "transplanted modernity", which also shows that "reconstruction" "combination" and "creation" are the only way for the development of modernity in China.

In a broader sense, Mao Zedong Thought, which includes the new democratic cultural outlook, has judiciously pointed out the road to liberation of the oppressed nation (this is an important content of modernity), and represents the "second stage of development" of modernity[①] which also demonstrates the social ideals after "liberation", which is the unity of "truth" and "value". Moreover, Mao Zedong Thought embodies strong national characteristics on many aspects, ranging from language form to ideological content. In particular, it has absorbed the traditional social ideal of "Great Harmony(大同)", established a model of moral personality, and demonstrated its inheritance with traditional culture, especially Confucianism, thus displaying the infinite ideological charm. Therefore, Mao Zedong's thought, including the new democratic cultural outlook, advocates "Make foreign things serve China" and the Sinicization of Marxism is Chinese; it advocates "Make the past serve the present" and critically inherits Chinese traditional culture, thus pushing Chinese

---

[①] Cites from Anthony D. Smith, *Nations and Nationalism in a Global Era*, Chin. ed., Gong Weibin 龚维斌, et al.(translated), Beijing: The Central Compilation and Translation Press, 2002, p. 8.

culture to a new stage. Mao Zedong Thought is a new stage in the development of Chinese culture.

IV. Contemporary Chinese experience and pursuit of cultural identity

The major setbacks encountered in China's modernization drive, especially serious mistakes like the "Cultural Revolution", have further widened the gap between China and Western countries. In a certain sense, it can be said that Mao Zedong's ideal has not been fully realized. Some of Mao Zedong's explorations were not successful. However, such failure has accumulated rich experience. On this basis, Deng Xiaoping creatively proposed the theory of "building socialism with Chinese characteristics", kicked off a new exploration of the path to China's modernity. As a result, the connotation of modernity has been fruitfully advanced in institutional arrangements such as technological development, system reform and democratic construction.

In contemporary China, the Chinese people's cultural identity has been strengthened with economic development and increased national strength, but at the same time has encountered new major challenges. First, to implement market-oriented socialist reform and socialist market economy, to recognize and promote the diversification of interest subjects will inevitably bring about diversification of concepts and behaviors, and thus culture will inevitably present a trend of diversification and differentiation. Second, The growing trend of economic globalization is "creating fluid space, electronic space, dis-centralized space, a space which can penetrate the boundaries and the world".[①] In particular, the development of information technology and global media has enabled cultural dissemination to break through traditional territorial boundaries and create an increasingly consistent global awareness and global culture. Although we do not agree with the term "cultural globalization", the relationship between economic and media globalization and territory is indeed obviously broken, and the identity crisis of national culture (especially the disadvantaged nation-states in the process of economic globalization) is increasingly becoming a serious problem.

For the current world, the most salient feature is economic globalization, but the imbalance between economic globalization and socio-economic development has to some extent intensified the marginalization of the under-privileged nations. Culture

---

① Molly, David, et al: *Identity Space, Chin. ed.*, Nanjing: Nanjing University Press, 2001, p.156.

has, therefore, become an important weapon to resist and reflect on the trend of globalization.

In the second half of the 20th century, the second generation of CPC with Deng Xiaoping at the core proposed to re-understand Mao Zedong Thought, Marxism, socialism and capitalism. China implemented reform and opening up and returned to the path of modernization with a more down-to-earth attitude. The huge economic gap once caused people to deny their own culture, and the then typical discourse was the dichotomous discourse of blue versus yellow and ocean versus loess. But the same is that the attention to the national interests and the local characteristics in the modernization process has led to the affirmation of the national ideology and culture. Therefore, conservative and radical debates became the focus of the Chinese ideological circle in the 1990s and transformed itself into the complex relationship between liberalism and nationalism.

After more than 20 years of reform and opening up, China's economy has achieved unprecedented development and has ranked among the top in the world in terms of total volume. In an increasingly globalized world, China's economic development will obviously strengthen the recognition of Chinese native culture. Our mainstream ideology, under the goal of "the great rejuvenation of the Chinese nation", has also increasingly shown great emphasis on national culture; it has pointed out that national cohesion is an important aspect of comprehensive national strength, and that the cultivation and promotion of national spirit is the fundamental way of strengthening the national cohesion and an important part of national education; it has proposed "advanced culture" to provide mental power and support for the promotion of modernization with Chinese characteristics for the realization of the great cause of national rejuvenation.

The identification of local resources is not and has never been a rebellion against a trend of globalization. Rather, it should be understood as a kind of reflective cultural behavior(for example, re-understanding and re-evaluating traditional values) and selective cultural behavior (such as consciously emphasizing a certain part of the tradition, for example, Neo-Confucianism emphasizes the transcendence of Confucianism in order to provide a reasonable space for adopting Western political systems and democratic concepts), because when we seek a pure "Chineseness", the local resources on which we are based are actually part of the global structure, which means that they have already played a role in the construction of globalization. But what we often see now is that the emphasis on local resources often means the "recollection" of ancient Chinese ideological resources. Another problem brought about by this tendency is to emphasize the characteristics of precedence and realistic pertinence of ancient concepts. In this way, there will subconsciously arise problems similar to the "theory of Western learning being of Chinese origin"(*xixue zhongyuan* 西学中源) in the late Qing dynasty, holding that the ancient Chinese thoughts potentially contain truthful judgments to solve practical problems. One of exemplary thoughts is the idea of "Maintain harmony between man and nature(*tianren heyi* 天人合一)" which was once thought to be able to save mankind. As a matter of fact, responding to the problems concerning cultural identity in this way is fundamentally nothing less than dismissing China's current experience and escaping creative thinking about it.

Therefore, we emphasize "constructive" cultural identity. Of course, we affirm the goal of modernization and the "basic" values of democracy and science, but our specific goal has changed from "the world" into "realizing the great rejuvenation of the Chinese nation". When seeking a basis of legitimacy for the actual social order and a value fulcrum for the Chinese people, we further follow the path of "combining Marxism with Chinese concrete practices", which is manifested by such ideas as "Cross the river by feeling the stones" or "Practice is the only criterion for testing truth." The basis of legitimacy has changed from a static theory to an emphasis on China's particularity and "Chinese experience", and has undergone theoretical sublimation and creation on this basis, the two major achievements of which are Deng Xiaoping Theory and the important thought of the Three Represents.

Deng Xiaoping Theory and the important thought of the Three Represents further take "practice" and "the interests of the people" as the criteria for measuring the significance and value of theory, and while great importance is attached to "Chinese practice" and "Chinese experience", special attention is also paid to absorbing the spirit of the times and the outstanding achievements of civilization in the development of other nation-states. As far as "modernity" is concerned, the attitude or wisdom of contemporary CPC members is characteristic of "integrativity" "creativity" and "constructivity" in the fusion of the cultural essence of Chinese and Western cultures, ancient and modern cultures.

First of all, this kind of identification acknowledges the truth of Marxism, and at the same time implements the process of testing this truth into the life of Chinese people. Second, the simple fantasy of "Westernization" and "return to ancient times" is averted while Chinese people's cultural identity is constructed based on

China's current experience. In this way, the identification and evaluation of the past values will be "constructive" and base itself on actual needs. It is in the context of globalization and modernity from the perspective of construction and development that the main leaders and theorists of the country construct cultural identity, mainly via striving to enhance national cohesion and promoting the national spirit through interpreting the connotations of cultural tradition, describing, in the language adapted to China's conditions, the principles of international relations that reflect the basis of Chinese values.

For example, in the speech delivered at Harvard University in the United States on November 2, 1997, Jiang Zemin elaborated on how to absorb and promote traditional Chinese culture today. He said: "In the prolonged course of its development, China has formed its fine historical and cultural traditions, which have been either developed or sublated with the changes of the times and social progress. These traditions have exerted a profound impact on the values and way of life of the Chinese people today, and on China's road of advance." He made some observations from four aspects, namely, "First, the tradition of solidarity and unity." "Second, the tradition of maintaining independence." "Third, the peace-loving tradition." "Fourth, the tradition of constantly striving to strengthen oneself."[①] Moreover, in his speech delivered at Harvard University on December 10, 2003, the then premier Wen Jiabao emphasized the value of "Harmony without uniformity(和而不同)". He said: "The Chinese nation has rich and profound cultural reserves. 'Harmony without uniformity' is a great idea put forth by ancient Chinese thinkers. It means harmony without sameness, and difference without conflict. Harmony entails co-existence and co-prosperity, while difference conduces to mutual complementation and mutual support. To approach and address issues from such a perspective will not only help enhance relations with friendly countries, but also serve to resolve conflicts which arise in the international community."[②]

The core of cultural identity is to create new values through utilizing the achievements of its own civilization, rather than simply "review" and "return". For modern China, cultural identity is not only a cultural position, but also is of strategic significance. Looking back at the changes in the Chinese people's understanding of cultural traditions and modernization drive since there arose problems of modernity,

---

① *People's Daily*, 1997-11-2.
② *People's Daily*, 2003-12-10.

we can see that we have been constantly seeking a balance between China and the rest of the world, between tradition and modernity. The key to this balance does not lie in proposing compromising solutions such as "Making the Western learning serve for China, with Chinese learning as foundation," but in creating a new value system which takes roots in one's own culture, which closely responds to major issues that have arisen in the development of the times and China, which the Chinese people are willing to accept, which has its charisma and rallying power, and which reflects and absorbs the common interests of mankind. The value factor in this system may come from Confucianism, Taoism or other Chinese ideological resources, undergo "integrative innovation", and thus form a new culture manifesting distinct features of our times.

Emphasizing the value of local culture does not mean denying or rejecting that of global culture. On the contrary, particularity itself is a product of the Chinese people embracing the rest of the world. It was in the process of assimilating Marxism that the Chinese people discovered the importance of Chinese local experience. Similarly, the value of local ideology can be meaningful only if they are related to global problems. In this process, the sources of value are naturally diversified and multi-regional, and the collision between diversified values will lead to more sharing, not exclusivity. We must integrate the essence of Marxism with China's realities; we must proceed from China's realities and have the whole world in view; we must constantly summarize "Chinese experience"; we must make comprehensive innovation; we must, in ever-changing practice, develop "Marxism adapted to China's conditions", that is, the socialist culture with Chinese characteristics, thus forming a new institutional arrangement that reflects the connotation of Chinese modernity, so as to guide new practices in our own way. This is the conclusion drawn from the great and arduous exploration undertaken since the advent of modern times by the Chinese people and Chinese progressives in a bid to pursue modernity and resolve cultural identity crisis.

The Crisis of Cultural Identity and the Urgency of Constructing Basic Social Values*

Cultural identity is formed by the interaction of common language, national origin, religious beliefs, values, ethical and moral systems, historical geography, economic environment and other factors, and it is an important basis for nation-states to establish the legitimacy of their existence whereas cohesion of nation-states is established on the basis of national interests, cultural traditions and relatively consistent social moral values recognized by the whole people. The cultural identity crisis is mainly manifested in the suspicion and criticism of traditional culture and existing social moral and ethical norms, replacing them with foreign ideology and culture.

The current crisis of cultural identity in China is mainly manifested in two aspects, that is, the doubts on the value of Chinese traditional culture and the mainstream values advocated by mainstream ideologies. Therefore, for contemporary China, cultural identity is not only a cultural position and attitude, but also of great strategic significance.

I. Cultural identity crisis not only endangers security of culture, but also inevitably leads to crisis of political legitimacy

Since the 1990s, the most distinctive and far-reaching characteristics of human society are undoubtedly globalization, IT application and networking. The rapid development of globalization based on information and communication technology and modern means of transportation has made human communication increasingly characteristic of rapidity, timeliness, relevance, interaction, and openness, which has caused major changes in contemporary human communication, that is, the subject of communication has changed from single to multi-layered, diversified

---

* Originally published in *Marxism and Reality*, 2005(2).

and multi-dimensional, and the object of communication has changed from being materialized to being informatized and virtualized, the means of communication have changed from mechanization to electronation and intellectualization, the space for communication has changed from regionalization to fluidization and globalization, and the content of communication has changed from economic and trade-orientation to overall communication covering economics, politics, culture, art, technology, education, talents and other aspects. Mankind has truly entered the era of universal communication of what Marx called "national history" and "world history", and has entered a new era in which information dissemination and cultural dissemination are rapid and even synchronized.

The rapid development of globalization, IT application and networking is "creating a fluid electronic space without a center which can infiltrate into the world regardless of the boundaries".[1] In particular, the development of information technology and the global media enabled cultural dissemination to break through traditional territorial boundaries and create an increasingly consistent global consciousness and global culture. Although we do not agree with the term "cultural globalization", the connection of economic globalization and media globalization with territory is indeed clearly broken, and Western lifestyles and Western culture have swept along with the economic activities, making the crisis of national cultural identity becoming an increasingly serious problem.

In contemporary China, the Chinese people's cultural identity has been strengthened along with economic development and national strength enhancement, and at the same time it has encountered new major challenges. First of all, to implement socialist market economy, it is necessary to require and bring about the diversification of interest subjects and of people's concepts and behaviors, and culture will inevitably take on a trend of diversification and difference. Nowadays, ideology and culture have already been diversified, thus there remains difficult issues on how to uphold the guiding position of Marxism in the field of ideology and culture, how to expand the coverage, influence, charisma and attraction of the leading values, so as to reach consensuses in the whole society to the maximum extent possible.

At the same time, marketization, modernization, and globalization will inevitably exert an impact on the national traditional culture and even break it, making the traditional culture drift away from our current social life. The fast-paced lifestyle,

---

[1] Molly, David, et al: *Identity space*, Chin. ed., Nanjing: Nanjing University Press, 2001, p.156.

industrialization, and urbanization have made people increasingly unconscious of protecting traditional culture. Some time ago, South Korea included in its cultural heritage the Dragon Boat Festival, a traditional festival of China, which caused an uproar in the domestic public. In one article titled "'De-traditionalization' Surrenders Cultural Heritage", Han Fudong (韩福东) said thought-provokingly, "China's century-long 'de-traditionalization' movement did not achieve China's prosperity, only to cause the 'fractured generation'—a lost generation who are ignorant of traditional culture.... Because of our indifference to tradition, we are far less able to preserve our traditions than our neighbor nation. We are unwilling, but we really cannot blame others, for we ourselves take the initiative to hand over cultural heritage to others."

Western capitalist countries, led by the United States, have infiltrated China with their developed and powerful cultural industries and exported various cultural products, which have influenced and changed the world view and values of the Chinese people, especially of the youngsters.

The survival of a nation depends on the maintenance of culture. National culture and national spirit are the core and foundation of national cohesion. The crisis of cultural identity will inevitably lead to the separation of national cohesion, which will cause a crisis of the rule of the ruling party and the state. This has been historically proven by all times and all countries.

II. Crisis of cultural identity in modern times and exploration of Its reconstruction

In fact, the cultural identity of the Chinese people has been in crisis since the advent of modern times, and people of insight have been seeking the reconstruction of the Chinese "world of meaning".

1.Occurrence of Chinese cultural identity crisis in modern times

The Opium War in 1840 forced the Chinese people at that time to open their eyes to the world, compare the advantages and disadvantages of China and the West in order and reflect on their own culture. At first, the reason for failure was owed to a less advanced technology, then to a less well-constructed political system. Finally, a full attack was launched on Confucianism after the defeat of the Sino-Japanese War of 1894-1895. All these manifested the psychological logic of the modern Chinese people undergoing the crisis of cultural identity when they were confronted with the aggressive invasion of modern Western countries and the crisis of national subjugation. More seriously, the abolition of imperial examinations and the collapse of imperial power as a symbol of ethnic cultural value order over the millennia led to a huge gap in the system: the nation-state model was adopted to replace the traditional Chinese "*Tianxia*" (天下 land under heaven) model, the free economic model replaced the traditional family-based production method, and the political participation of the people replaced by the omnipotent rule of imperial power. In a word, the absorption of Western technology and the imitation of the system was regarded as the most direct and important thing for China's modernization. Thus, since the advent of modern times, faced with a series of failures in confronting the Western military attacks, people then explored the root causes of these failures, which ultimately led to doubt, criticism and denial of the Confucian system, and the collapse of the common foundation of the Chinese people's identification of historical and cultural values. So, it can be said that the crisis of Chinese cultural identity has arisen since the advent of modern times.

2. Explorations of reconstruction: from people of insight in early modern times to Kang Youwei, new culture movement and Sun Yat-sen

Admiring Western advanced technology and management experience, the insightful people in early modern times used the category of "*Tao-qi* (道器, literally: logos-utensils)", an important philosophical thought in Confucian tradition, to emphasize the superiority of Confucianism when learning Western technologies and experiences. To put it more specifically, they shouted the slogans of "Learn the foreign skills to control foreigners" and "Chinese learning as essence, Western learning as means(*zhongxu weiti, xixue weiyong* 中学为体 西体为用)", which means "Learn from the advanced technologies in the West in order to resist the invasion of the Western powers" and "Chinese learning for the foundation, Western learning for practical use". In the late *Qing* Dynasty, as the nature of China's semi-colonial and semi-feudal society intensified, the people of insight attached more importance to the exploration of revitalizing the Chinese nation by rebuilding identity value of national culture. Their efforts deserve great attention and are of reference and inspiration.

Kang Youwei and others directly thought about the significance of traditional values in institutional reform. He realized the inevitability of China's institutional reform, but he still insisted on exploring the rationality of this reform from traditional Confucian ideological resources. This is the important reason why he wrote *Xinxue weijing kao* (新学伪经考 *Examination of the School of the Xin Dynasty's False Classics*) and *Kongzi gaizhi kao* (孔子改制考 An Examination of Confucius' Institutional Reforms). Kang Youwei's theory of "reform on the basis of tradition" is deeply concerned about the issue of how to settle Confucianism inevitably brought about by the institutional reform. Therefore, on the one hand, he emphasized the need to abolish the imperial examination and promote Western politics and learning; on the other hand, he sought new growth points for Confucianism in the design of the new system. After summing up and inspecting the Western experience, he concluded that the church system in the West is the most likely institutional resource for Confucianism after the implementation of institutional reform.

After the Revolution of 1911, Kang Youwei believed that completely imitating Western political models and cultural resources would not guarantee the stability of China, so he wrote many articles emphasizing the importance of Confucian values to social order. He believed that any kind of political design that is deviated from the cultural and social reality of a country will lead to the collapse of society. Therefore, he tried to find a basis for Chinese cultural identity by establishing Confucianism as the state religion.

The intellectual class represented by *New Youth*《新青年》first paid attention to the inseparable connection between Confucianism and Confucius and the old system. Therefore, when the Congress discussed the Confucianism proposal, Chen Duxiu (陈独秀), Li Dazhao(李大钊) and others made sharp criticisms of the proposal to establish Confucianism as the state religion. After the restoration of Zhang Xun (张勋) failed, Chen Duxiu believed that respecting Confucianism and restoration were "depending on each other", and that if the questions about values are not resolved, any institutional reform can only be superficial. The political events which had taken place led Chen Duxiu and others to believe that if the questions about values are not resolved, any institutional reform can only be superficial. The radical way of thinking, however, led them to make an either-or choice: On one hand, they regarded Eastern culture and Western culture as two absolutely different systems, and believed that the difference between the East and the West was not a manifestation of diversification, but rather the difference between "ancient and modern" "new and old", namely the difference between the two cultures of different times; on the other hand, they thought that the Chinese culture represented by Confucianism was a backward culture, not suitable for the development of modern civilization and the needs of China to become independent and prosperous, and that it was a culture that should be discarded. Under this an either-or choice, everything in the Chinese tradition should be abandoned.

There is no need to go into details here on the significance of the New Culture Movement for modern China. However, it should be pointed out that those Enlightenment thinkers so over-simply looked at tradition that they even attempted to take a kind of ideologicalized "science" and "democracy" as a universal value and thus solve the problems related to modernization and cultural identity, which obviously ignored the internal relationship between institutions and culture. In the traditional Chinese society, the Chinese people have taken Confucian values as undeniable *Tianli* (天理; literally: the laws of heaven—feudal ethics as propounded by the Song Confucianists). Therefore, judging between right and wrong with Confucian conception as the criterion has become the "collective unconsciousness" of the Chinese people, which provides them with stability and security. However, in order to resolve the conflict between the new system and the cultural conventions, new legitimacy needs to be established. It is in this sense that we cannot ignore the significance of Kang Youwei's efforts to establish the Confucian Churches.

With regard to the reconstruction of national cultural identity, we should not forget Dr. Sun Yat-sen's efforts. After the 1911 Republican Revolution, which ended the rule of the Qing Dynasty (1644-1911), China, in terms of political structure, mainly drew on the political framework of the West, but in terms of ideology, it always intersected with the Confucian concepts. The reliance of the Northern Warlords (1912-1927) on Confucianism is self-evident; the *Kuomintang* (National People's Party), which always took "revolution" as the banner, also took "nationalism" as its motto. The "Three Principles of the People" proposed by Sun Yat-sen first of all emphasized "nationalism", for he believed that "universalism" proposed by the powerful countries was only to maintain their monopoly on the oppression of weak and small nations. "They want to maintain this monopoly position forever, and no longer allow weak and small nations to rejuvenate, so they advocate cosmopolitanism every day, saying that the scope of nationalism is too narrow. In fact, the cosmopolitanism they advocate is imperialism in disguise and aggression in disguise."[1] Therefore, although Sun Yat-sen sometimes also thought that the "Three Principles of the People" are consistent with socialism and communism, he fundamentally believed that the "Three Principles of the People" already contains the content of socialism and at the same time he placed a strong emphasis on the

---

[1] Sun Yat-sen: *Three Principles of the People*, Chin. ed., Changsha: *Yuelu* Bookstore, 2000, p. 39.

inheritance relationship between the "Three Principles of the People" and the Confucian tradition.

The 1911 Revolution ended more than two thousand years of feudal dictatorship, established a democratic republic, and opened up a new era in history, but at that time China's military power, military dictatorship, and the collapse of the traditional authoritative value system made the Chinese fall into the crisis of the world of meaning. Chinese society was still in chaos, and Dr. Sun Yat-sen's "modernization strategy" could only be a dream.

After the death of Sun Yat-sen in 1925, Dai Jitao (戴季陶), as the orthodox interpreter of the Prime Minister's will, proved the connection between the "Three Principles of the People" and the Confucian tradition. He proposed that "The original purpose of the 'Three Principles of the People' is to regain and recover national confidence." The foundation of this self-confidence lies in Confucian values. "I am convinced that there is something most lofty in Mr. Zhongshan's doctrine: it is he who explained that the moral spirit embracing loyalty, benevolence, faith, and peace is the foundation of national self-confidence."[①]

III. Contributions of the CPC members to rebuilding Chinese cultural identity, and restoring national cultural self-esteem and self-confidence

At the most elusive moment in the pursuit of national rejuvenation, "the salvoes of the October Revolution brought us Marxism-Leninism." The Chinese progressives studied and disseminated Marxism and combined it with China's labor movements, and there came the CPC under the guidance of Marxism-Leninism. The first generation of the CPC with Mao Zedong at the core combined the basic principles of Marxism with the reality of the Chinese revolution, and they insisted on the principles of integrating theory with practice and seeking truth from facts in the long-term struggle against all dogmatism according to which everything has to be done by the book or based on copying foreign experience, creatively applied and developed Marxism, found the revolutionary path of encircling the cities from the countryside, and thus realized the first historic leap in the integration of Marxism-Leninism with the reality of China. The theoretical result of this leap is Mao Zedong Thought, a sinicized Marxism taking roots in Chinese culture.

---

① Department of the History of the CPC at Renmin University of China (complied): *Selection of Dai Jitao's Doctrines*, Beijing: Renmin University of China Press, 1951, p.14, 22.

The CPC represented by Mao Zedong are not only politically exploring the "road to liberation" of the Chinese nation from semi-colonial and semi-feudal rule, but also exploring the reconstruction of the mental world order of the Chinese nation. Mao Zedong has always attached great importance to the exploration of "the new culture of the Chinese nation." He pointed out: "For many years we Communists have struggled for a cultural revolution as well as for a political and economic revolution... not only do we want to change a China that is politically oppressed and economically exploited into a China that is politically free and economically prosperous, we also want to change the China which is being kept ignorant and backward under the sway of the old culture into an enlightened and progressive China under the sway of a new culture." [1] In short, we want to build a new Chinese national culture.

Under the guidance of the basic principles of Marxism-Leninism, Mao Zedong summarized the ancient and modern Chinese culture, put forward the proposal of building "a new national, scientific and popular culture", and pointed out that only such a new culture can truly become the basis of national cohesion and cultural identity of the Chinese people.

The Chinese Communists represented by Mao Zedong, have come to realize deeply in their constant practice that one must combine Marxist theory with Chinese revolutionary practice. Otherwise, he can only cite odd quotations from K. Marx, F. Engels, Lenin and Stalin in a one-sided manner; he chops up history, knows only ancient Greece but not China. This subjectivist method which is contrary to science and Marxism-Leninism is to harm not only himself, but also others and the revolution, so it a formidable enemy of the people and the nation.[2]

Thus, the "new Chinese national culture", namely, new-democratic culture, embodies the sound worldview and methodology of Marxism, reflects the interest demands and value orientation of the proletariat, and at the same time, advocates that the critical absorption of the essence of traditional national culture is a necessary condition for developing national culture and enhancing national self-confidence. That is why it has such a strong appeal and rallying power. Compared with the liberalism and the conservative position of neo-Confucianism or official Confucianism of the time, the Neo-democratic cultural outlook is more inclusive. It opposes imperialism to become the ideal of socialism and conforms to the basic demands of the pursuit

---

[1] *Selected Works of Mao Zedong*, Vol.2, Chin. ed., Beijing: People's Publishing House, 1991, p. 663.
[2] Ibid., p795-803.

of modernity by the Chinese people. Its emphasis on nationality is not only the expression of public opinion at the time of the war, but also an important way to unite people's hearts by culture. Its pursuit of science and rationality (the unity of subjectivity and objectivity) carries forward the spirit of enlightenment. The phrase "the popular" means "democratic" consciousness. Therefore, with the defeat of the Japanese invaders and the Kuomintang army, this cultural outlook became the leading one. This is the main reason why the CPC established Mao Zedong Thought as the guiding philosophy of the Chinese Communists after the "Yan'an Rectification Movement", which ruled out the dogmatic approach to Marxism adopted by Wang Ming and others, and made China's national revolution quickly achieve a triumph. The victory of Mao Zedong Thought over dogmatism can also be said to be the victory of "reconstructed modernity" over "transplanted modernity", which also shows that "reconstruction" "combination" and "creation" are the only way for the development of modernity in China.

In a broader sense, Mao Zedong Thought, which embodies new-democratic cultural outlook, not only judiciously identifies the path of liberation of the oppressed nations (an important part of modernity), representing the "second development stage" of modernization, but also demonstrates that the social ideal after "liberation" is the unity of "truth" and "value". Moreover, Mao Zedong Thought embodies strong national characteristics, whether in terms of language form or in terms of ideological content, particularly given that it has absorbed the traditional social ideal of "Great Harmony", set up a model of moral personality, and demonstrated the inheritance of traditional culture, especially Confucianism, thus displaying tremendous ideological charm.

Building socialism in a large eastern country with a relatively backward economy and culture like China is a new topic in the history of the development of Marxism. The second-generation CPC leadership group with Deng Xiaoping at the core inherits and carries forward the essence of Mao Zedong Thought, emancipates the mind, seeks truth from facts, opposes the dogmatism of the "Two Whatevers"[①], and emphasizes that practice is the sole criterion for testing truth. At the critical moment when China's socialist modernization drive was on the brink of collapse, Deng Xiaoping, starting

---

[①] On Feb 7, 197,7 People's Daily, Red Flag magazine and Liberation Army Daily published an editorial titled "Master File to Seize the Key Link". It stated: "We will resolutely uphold whatever policy decisions Chairman Mao made, and unswervingly follow whatever instructions Chairman Mao gave". This error inherited the "left" mistakes of Mao Zedong in his later years.—Tr.

by reflecting on what socialism is and how to build socialism proceeding from the new historical conditions, profoundly revealed the essence of socialism. He pointed out: "We must integrate the universal truth of Marxism with the concrete realities of China, blaze a path of our own and build a socialism with Chinese characteristics — that is the basic conclusion we have reached after reviewing our long history."[①] And thereby we have found a way to build socialism with Chinese characteristics, opened up a new phase of socialist modernization, and achieved the second historic leap in the integration of Marxism-Leninism with China's realities. The theoretical result of this leap is Deng Xiaoping Theory. This ideological theory advocates absorbing all the outstanding achievements of human civilization, and opposing the copying of foreign models, but taking the road of socialism with Chinese characteristics. It is on this road that socialism is flourishing, China's modernization drive has made great achievements recognized by the world, and China's international image and international status, as well as the mental outlook of the Chinese people, have undergone fundamental changes.

Thus, it can be seen that in the revolution and modernization drive, the Sinicization of Marxism is neither taking a dogmatic and bookish approach to Marxist theory, nor is it copying the roads of the West and Russia, but taking its own path. Only in this way can "Chinese problems" be resolved, which allows China to embark on the road of independence, prosperity, democracy and civilization. It can be said that this is the greatest contribution of the CPC to Chinese culture.

IV. Some thoughts and suggestions

The many severe challenges and problems in the current ideological and cultural fields show that we are already in a complex and diverse cultural ecological environment, which we must adapt and get used to, and in which we must learn to correctly face and deal with various complex cultural phenomena, and strive to strengthen the ability to build an advanced socialist culture.

1. To realize China's socialist modernization and the great rejuvenation of the Chinese nation, we must attach great importance to the issue of national cultural identity, and must take the cultivation and promotion of national spirit as the fundamental way to strengthen national cohesion and an important part of national education, and implement it in the specific links of education.

---

① *Selected Works of Deng Xiaoping*, Vol. 3, Chin. ed., Beijing: People's Publishing House, 1993, p. 3.

2. Traditional culture is the blood of a nation and the foundation of a nation, many of which are still very precious ideological resources in contemporary times. We should cherish and respect our own national culture, for any nation that does not value or even despise its own traditional culture cannot move towards modernization. Looking back on the Chinese people's understanding of the relationship between cultural tradition and modernization since the strong invasion of Western culture, we can see that in the sore trouble and distress of internal disorder and foreign invasions, we criticized and rejected the traditional culture too much while cleaning up and reflecting on it. For a long time, we did not attach importance to traditional culture from the perspective of art and aesthetics and from the perspective of maintaining national cohesion. The "Cultural Revolution", particularly the elimination of "the four olds"—the old thoughts, old customs, old habits, old traditions, swept traditional Chinese culture into the garbage dump of history. For the generation that grew up in such a social context, as far as their accomplishment of the traditional culture is concerned, must be congenitally deficient and postnatally unbalanced, only to make endless trouble.

3. The core of constructing cultural identity is to make the best use of the achievements of our own civilization to create new values, but not simply to return to traditional culture. When we seek a kind of pure "Chineseness", the local resources on which we are based are in fact part of the globality, which means that they have already played a role in the construction of globalization. Emphasizing the meaning of local cultural values does not mean rejecting global values; on the contrary, particularity itself is a product of the Chinese embracing the world. It was in the process of accepting Marxism that the Chinese people discovered the importance of Chinese local experience. Similarly, the value of local ideology can only be meaningful when they are related to the context of globalization. The collision between diversified cultures leads to more sharing, rather than monopoly or exclusivity. The key task now is to build a new value system on the basis of the view of our own culture, which reflects the major issues which have arisen in the process of development of the times and of China, which can be accepted by the Chinese people, which bears its charisma and rallying power, and which reflects and absorbs the common interests of humanity. The value factors of such a system may be derived from Marxism, Confucianism, Taoism or any other ideological resource. Through a process of integration and innovation, a new culture with the characteristics of the times will be forged.

The content and form of cultural identity must be adapted to the reality that China is still in the primary stage of socialism. We should respect the reality that there exist diversified ideological concepts and values that have a profound socio-economic base, distinguish between "dominated social values of socialism with Chinese characteristics by socialism" and "basic social values of socialism with Chinese characteristics", and dialectically apply them as guide in practice. "Leading values" are the values advocated and guided by the CPC, that is, to carry forward the national spirit with patriotism as the core and the spirit of the times with reform and innovation as the core, and carry forward the ideas of collectivism, socialism and the view of "serving the people heart and soul". The "basic values" are values recognized and accepted by different social groups and classes, such as respect for life, benevolence and mutual assistance, fairness, justice, equality and freedom; racial harmony, freedom of belief, etc. The distinction between these two values is conducive not only to encouraging progress while taking care of the majority, unifying ideas while respecting differences, but also to promoting the formation of a harmonious society.

We must integrate the universal truth of Marxism with China's realities, develop global vision, constantly sum up "Chinese experience", carry out integration and innovation, develop "Sinicized Marxism" in changing practices, and thereby form a new institutional arrangement to guide new practices and take our own path. All these constitute the fundamental conclusion that the Chinese people have drawn from the arduous pursuit of modernization and the resolution of cultural identity crises since modern times, and which we should always remember and follow in practice.

From New-democratic Culture to Socialist Culture with Chinese Characteristics: How the CPC Inherits and Innovates Chinese Culture*

The CPC was established, developed and expanded under the guidance of the advanced culture of Marxism-Leninism. Over the past 80 years of the CPC have combined the universal truths of Marxism-Leninism with China's realities, and continued to carry out theoretical and practical innovations. Mao Zedong Thought and Deng Xiaoping Theory are the two major historical achievements of the theoretical innovation of the CPC. In this process, the Chinese people also have forged two leading forms of modern Chinese culture with national characteristics—the new democratic culture and the socialist culture with Chinese characteristics, and thereby made an important contribution to the development of modern times.

I. Take our own path and rebuild self-confidence in and self-esteem for national culture

Since modern times, the form and trend of Chinese culture are closely related to the future of modern Chinese society. People who involved in all kinds of cultural trends kept trying to answer the question "Where is China going", in hope of making a strategic choice for China's modernization. In order to change the destiny of enduring impoverishment and long-standing debility and to make the country rich and people strong, in modern China, many people of visions have put forward many ideological and cultural propositions of salvaging China and strengthening the country and people. The Opium War of 1840 awakened many Chinese people

---

* Originally published in *Philosophy Research*, 2001 (10).

from the mindless and arrogant dreams of the Celestial Empire. The tragic failure deeply pierced the hearts of Chinese intellectuals. Why was the "Heaven Empire" miserably defeated by the "small barbarians?" People began to think and to seek, trying to find a way to prosper the country and strengthen the army as soon as possible, and to respond effectively to the invasion of Western culture as soon as possible, so as to restore the former glory and status of the Chinese nation. The past 100 years witnessed the emergence of various ideological and cultural trends, ranging from "restricting the foreigners with the techniques learnt from them" and "making Western learning serve for China" to the reform propositions of the Reformers, to Dr. Sun Yat-sen's "Three Principles of the People", as well as Cultural conservatism represented by the Oriental Culture School and the "*Xueheng* School" and "wholesale Westernization theory" in the early 20th century, but all these failed to solve the problems concerning independence and development of the Chinese nation, nor did they change the tragic situation of the Chinese nation which began since modern times. The "wholesale Westernization" theory holds that the fundamental reason for China's backwardness lies in the backwardness of China's traditional ideology and culture and believes that the future of China lies in thoroughly reforming and abandoning the traditional cultural concepts and their corresponding systems and introducing Western ideology, culture and systems. The emergence of such mentality is nothing but the danger and sadness of a nation. The outbreak of World War I exposed the shortcomings and crisis of the Western capitalistic ideology and culture, and thus people's hopes for the West plunged into endless disappointment. To our great surprise, "The sound of the October Revolution brought Marxism-Leninism to China." China's advanced intellectuals learned, studied and spread Marxism-Leninism, and integrated it with the Chinese labor movement, so there came the CPC as faithful representatives of China's advanced culture, which, as a result, brought the Chinese revolution into a completely new stage.

The first-generation CPC leadership group with Mao Zedong at the core combined the basic principles of Marxism with the realities of the Chinese revolution. In the long-term struggle with the right and "left" wrong tendencies, they adhered to the principle of integrating theory with practice, seeking truth from facts. It is the creative application and development of Marxism that there emerged the revolutionary path of encircling the cities from the countryside, and the first historic leap in the integration of Marxism-Leninism with the reality of China was realized. The theoretical result of this leap is Mao Zedong Thought, a Sinicized Marxism taking roots in Chinese culture. Under the guidance of this ideology, after 28 years of arduous struggle, national independence and liberation have been achieved, the great victory of new democracy has been achieved, and the ideal that the Chinese have fought for a hundred years since the Opium War has been realized. This is the victory of Marxism-Leninism and the victory of Mao Zedong Thought.

Building socialism in a large eastern country with relatively backward economy and culture like China is a new topic in the history of the development of Marxism. The second-generation CPC leadership group with Deng Xiaoping at the core inherited and carried forward the essence of Mao Zedong Thought, emancipated the mind, sought truth from facts, opposed the erroneous tendency of "Two Whatevers", emphasized that practice is the only criterion for testing truth, and summarized what had happened since the founding of New China both positive and negative experience, put forward the theory of socialism with Chinese characteristics, created a new situation in the construction of socialist modernization, and thus achieved the second historic leap in the integration of Marxism-Leninism with China's reality. The theoretical result of this leap is Deng Xiaoping Theory. This theory advocates absorbing all the outstanding achievements of human civilization, while opposing to copy foreign models, and advocates exploring the path of socialist construction that suits China's national conditions. This will inevitably form a socialist culture with Chinese characteristics. It is under the guidance of this advanced culture and under the correct leadership of the Party's second and third generations of central leadership that China's reform and opening up for more than 20 years has made major achievements that have attracted worldwide attention. The level of productivity, development, people's living standards, and overall national strength have all been improved and reached a new level, and the Chinese people's mental outlook has also been updated, and fundamental changes have taken place.

Adapting Marxism to China's conditions produces a leading culture guided by Mao Zedong Thought and Deng Xiaoping Theory, which leads China to embark on the path of independence and prosperity. These two major ideological and theoretical achievements have reshaped our self-confidence in and self-esteem for our national culture, and have taken the lead in Chinese modern culture. It can be said that this is the CPC's greatest contribution to Chinese culture.

II. Theoretical innovation of cultural construction

"The form of culture is first determined by the political and economic form." "Any given culture (as an ideological form) is a reflection of the politics and economics of a given society, and the former in turn has a tremendous influence and effect upon the latter. "① These are our fundamental views of the relation of culture to politics and economics and of the relation of politics to economics, according to Marxist historical materialism. The CPC has always insisted on this view to guide the cultural construction in the periods of revolution, construction and reform. It opposed not only economic determinism but also cultural determinism. When talking about the construction of new-democratic culture, Mao Zedong said: "The old politics and economics of the Chinese nation form the basis of its old culture, just as its new politics and economics will form the basis of its new culture." Therefore, to build a new democratic culture, we must get rid of "the old colonial, semi-colonial and semi-feudal politics and economy and the old culture in their service". ②

Since the Third Plenary Session of the 11th CPC Central Committee, held from Dec 18 to 22, 1978, the Party has adhered to the basic view of Marxism, correctly understanding and dealing with the relations between economic and cultural construction, and the relations between material and cultural civilization, proposing building a socialist culture with Chinese characteristics and believing that the construction of socialist culture should center on economic construction. In this regard, there have been painful lessons in the history of our socialist construction. The criteria for judging the success or failure of socialist cultrual civilization and cultural construction are whether it is conducive to liberating and developing the productive forces, improving people's living standard, and to the well-rounded development of everyone. At the same time, economic construction cannot replace cultural construction which can provide powerful mental motivation and intellectual support for economic development and all-round social progress.

In the report to the 15th National Congress of the CPC, it is systematically expounded the cultural program of building socialism with Chinese characteristics in the primary stage of socialism, clearly regarded cultural construction as a basic content of the Party's basic program in the primary stage of socialism, and proposed a society with Chinese characteristics. Socialist culture is an important thesis that is an important symbol of overall national strength. It is believed that it not only reflects

---

① *Selected Works of Mao Zedong*, Vol. 2, Chin. ed., Beijing: People's Publishing House, 1991, p. 663, 664.
② Ibid., p. 664, 665.

the basic characteristics of China's socialist economy and politics, but also plays a huge role in promoting economic and political development.

In the new century, the trend of globalization is growing, with the competition for overall national strength including culture becoming increasingly fierce. The position of culture in the overall national strength has been becoming more and more prominent. The exchange and dissemination of culture has increasingly become one important part of the relationship between countries. Cultural conflicts have increasingly become an aspect of international competition and conflict.

A few developed capitalist countries rely on their economic and political strength to vigorously export their ideologies and values to developing countries. On the issue of human rights, they ignore the sovereignty of developing countries and enforce their concepts of human rights in an attempt to pursue their economic and political interests. Take the cultural export of the United States as an example. The article "American Popular Culture Permeates the World" published in *The Washington Post* made a true depiction which reports that the main export products of the United States are no longer crops in the ground, nor products manufactured in factories, but popular culture produced in mass and batch production, such as movies, TV shows, music, books, and computer software. Thus, the entertainment industry around the world is flooded with American-made products. Some sociologists even call the spread of American popular culture "the latest action in a long series of efforts to achieve global unity."

So that is how it is. It is through the output of this popular culture that American ideology and values influence the thinking and perception of the younger generation in other countries, especially in developing countries. The United States is actually embarking on a strategy of cultural hegemony. It is an integral part of its economic hegemony and political hegemony strategy. It is a clever, more fundamental and more far-reaching hegemony strategy. The fact is also true. It is precisely through such export of popular culture that the ideology and values of the United States have influenced the thinking and concepts of the young generation in other countries, especially in developing countries. The United States is actually pursuing a strategy of cultural hegemony, which is an integral part of its economic and political hegemony strategy. It is a more ingenious, fundamental, and far-reaching hegemony strategy. The Party puts the development of socialist culture with Chinese characteristics to the strategic position related to the success or failure of China's modernization and the rise and fall of the nation. It is indeed an insightful, profound and to-the-point understanding, which will undoubtedly greatly enhance our understanding of the urgency of cultural construction and the consciousness of vigorously promoting cultural construction in practice.

III. Innovation of cultural connotation

1. Creatively elucidating the main content of new democratic culture

Since the "May Fourth Movement," there have been two main lines of thinking about the development of Chinese culture: first, the New Culture Movement and the radical anti-traditional line represented by Chen Xujing (陈序经); and second, the conservative ideological line emphasizing traditional values represented by Neo-Confucianism. The CPC with Mao Zedong at the core advocated combining Marxism with China's historical legacy to form a "national form." They think "we can put Marxism into practice only when it is integrated with the specific characteristics of our country and acquires a definite national form."[1] On the basis of this ideology, the CPC not only got rid of radicalism's nihilistic attitude towards national culture in terms of cultural outlook, but also opposed conservatism's excessive stance that rejected foreign cultures uncritically. Instead, they proposed a new democratic philosophical view of culture. In this regard, Mao Zedong has made a clear statement and regarded this as the cultural program of the coming new society He says, "The new-democratic culture.... In a word, new-democratic culture is the proletarian-led, anti-imperialist and anti-feudal culture of the people."[2] He once said about a national, scientific and popular culture, holding that "New-democratic culture is national."[3] Here, Mao Zedong proposes that as far as cultures of other nations are concerned, it is necessary "to reject its feudal dross and assimilate its democratic essence." He puts forward the proposition that to advocate "wholesale Westernization" is utterly wrong, for, in doing so, foreign things are absorbed in the practice of formalities for formalities' sake. China has suffered a great deal from the mechanical absorption of foreign material. In terms of applying Marxism to China, "Communists of China must fully and properly integrate the universal truth of Marxism with the concrete practice of the Chinese revolution, or in other words, the universal truth of Marxism must be

---

[1] *Selected Works of Mao Zedong*, Vol. 2, Chin. ed., Beijing: People's Publishing House, 1991, p. 534.
[2] Ibid., p. 698.
[3] Ibid., p.708-709.

combined with specific national characteristics and acquire a definite national form if it is to be useful, and in no circumstances can it be applied subjectively as a mere formula." "Chinese culture should have its own form, its own national form."①

New-democratic culture is scientific. "Opposed as it is to all feudal and superstitious ideas, it stands for seeking truth from facts, for objective truth and for the unity of theory and practice."② It holds that for the ancient Chinese culture, it is necessary to "to reject its feudal dross and assimilate its democratic essence," "we should never swallow anything and everything uncritically." It argues that "we can't swallow anything and everything without criticism." This is "a necessary condition for developing our new national culture and increasing our national self-confidence". Therefore, "we must respect our own history and must not lop it off. However, respect for history means giving it its proper place as a science, respecting its dialectical development, and not eulogizing the past at the expense of the present or praising every drop of feudal poison."③

New-democratic culture belongs to all the people and is therefore democratic. "It should serve the toiling workers and peasants who make up more than 90 per cent of the nation's population should gradually become their very own."④

Obviously, new-democratic culture has inherited the spirit of the "May Fourth Movement". But its slogan, "National, scientific and popular" is more tolerant than the cultural liberalism and neo-Confucianism of the 1940s. In addition, the new democratic culture's emphasis on such conceptions as democracy and equality, on ideological and moral cultivation, and on the practice of the Chinese Communists, contrasted sharply with the corruption and cultural autocracy of the Kuomintang, showcasing the charm of the new-democratic culture, so the new democracy grew quickly to become the leading idea. It should be noted that "Because of the leadership of the proletariat, the politics, the economy and the culture of New Democracy all contain an element of socialism, and by no means a mere casual element but one with a decisive role."⑤ Therefore, the construction of new-democratic culture has made necessary and sufficient preparations for socialist cultural construction.

---

① *Selected Works of Mao Zedong*, Vol. 2, Chin. ed., Beijing: People's Publishing House, 1991, p.707.
② Ibid.
③ Ibid., p.707-708.
④ Ibid., p. 698.
⑤ Ibid., p.704.

2. Exploring a correct way to build Chinese socialist culture

In exploring the way to build socialism with Chinese characteristics, Deng Xiaoping always emphasizes that building socialism with Chinese characteristics requires not only a high degree of material civilization but also a high degree of mental civilization, emphasizing that only by doing well in the two civilizations, can we have socialism with Chinese characteristics.

At the meeting celebrating the 80th anniversary of the founding of the CPC on July 1, 2001, Jiang Zemin clearly points out, "In contemporary China, the development of advanced culture means the development of socialist culture with Chinese characteristics and the construction of socialist mental civilization." He emphasizes that "Our party must always represent the direction of China's advanced culture."[①]

To sum up, the main content of the CPC's theory of socialist culture with Chinese characteristics is as follows:

This culture is socialist. Creating common ideal and mental pillar for our society lies at the root of building socialist culture with Chinese characteristics. The common ideal is to build socialism with Chinese characteristics. We should strengthen Marxist beliefs and inculcate the spirit of socialist humanitarianism, guide our people to foster a correct worldview, outlook on life and sense of values, and provide a powerful ideological driving force and strong intellectual support for economic development and all-round social progress. Since the development of a market economy will inevitably lead to the differentiation of interest groups, how to forge a common ideal in the whole society is a difficult subject to be explored.

Second, this kind of culture is scientific, rendering progress of education and science as the foundation project of cultural construction. In today's world, the technological revolution has progressed by leaps and bounds. The competition in overall national strength has increasingly manifested itself in the competition of technology and education. To this end, the Party has put forward the strategy of rejuvenating the nation through science and education, ensured that the development of education and science receive strategic priority, and step up the pace of technological innovation. The Party believes that "intellectuals can become disseminators of advanced ideas; pioneers of science and technology; train people to be citizens with high ideals, moral integrity, a good education and a strong

---

① *Selected Works of Jiang Zemin*, Vol. 3, Chin. ed., Beijing: People's Publishing House, 2006, p. 276.

sense of discipline; produce excellent intellectual works;"① and that they can play an especially important role in the reform, opening up and modernization drive. Therefore, it is necessary to further foster a good practice of respecting knowledge and talents in the entire society. We should step up publicity and education of scientific knowledge, methods, thinking and spirit, so as to provide a strong intellectual support for economic development and all-round social progress.

Third, this kind of culture is geared to the needs of modernization and the future. The goal of cultural construction is to train people to be citizens with high ideals, moral integrity, a good education and a strong sense of discipline, so as to meet the requirements of modernization and the rejuvenation of the Chinese nation. The CPC has profoundly realized that training hundreds of millions of qualified workers and tens of millions of professional personnel suited to the needs of our modernization drive and fully exploiting the advantages of our vast human resources have a direct bearing on the cause of building socialism in the 21st century. In fact, the construction of a socialist culture with Chinese characteristics aims at improving the quality of the people and nurturing successive generations of talents who can adapt to and push the socialist modernization drive in China. This is a foundation project that has a bearing on the overall victory of the rejuvenation of the Chinese nation and the cause of building socialism.

Fourthly, this kind of culture is geared and open to the world. To develop socialist culture, we must fully embody the spirit of the times and creativity, and we must have a global perspective. The CPC has always advocated learning and absorbing advanced foreign culture.

In the revolutionary years, the Communists of China mainly studied and applied Marxism, but also paid attention to absorbing other foreign cultures. In the period of socialist construction, the Chinese people need to absorb foreign culture even more, so the new generation of leaders represented by Deng Xiaoping realized from historical experience that China's development cannot be separated from the world; that the development of China's culture cannot be separated from the common achievements of human civilization; that China cannot develop its culture in isolation from the common achievements of human civilization; that China cannot develop its culture in

---

① Jiang Zemin: *Hold High the Great Banner of Deng Xiaoping Theory and Comprehensively Advance the Cause of Building Socialism with Chinese Characteristic into the 21st Century: The Report to the Fifteenth National Congress of the CPC*, Beijing: People's Publishing House,1997.

isolation from the common achievements of human civilization; ant that adhering to the principle of having Chinese culture as the base but exploiting the advantages of foreign achievements, we need to launch various forms of cultural exchange, drawing on their strengths while introducing China's achievements to the world; and that the Chinese people must resolutely resist the corrosive influence of decadent ideas and cultures.

Fifth, this kind of culture is national, with distinctive national characteristics and styles. The Chinese nation is a great nation with a long history and excellent culture. The nation has gone through the vicissitudes of life, created a splendid Chinese civilization in the history of human development, and formed a traditional culture with strong vitality. When discussing how to build a new democratic culture, Mao Zedong pointed out, "We should sum up our history from Confucius to Dr. Sun Yat-sen and take over this valuable legacy." He proposed to "serve the past for the present and the foreign for the Chinese," advocating the application of Marxist methods to critically summarize, inherit and absorb Chinese traditional culture.

Jiang Zemin pointed out in his speech at the 80th anniversary: "We should make positive efforts to inherit and develop the fine cultural traditions of the Chinese nation, the revolutionary cultural traditions formed among the Party and people since the May 4th Movement (1919), as well as all the advanced civilization achievements mankind has ever created. With regard to the rich cultural legacies left over from China's history of several thousand years, we should select the essence and discard the dross therefrom, and carry forward and develop them in line with the spirit of the times in order to make the past serve the present."① As far as nationalizing foreign cultures based on the excellent cultural tradition of the country is concerned, the CPC can be regarded as a model.

Sixth, this culture is popular. It is aimed at satisfying the needs of the cultural life of the great majority of people and for well-rounded development. It is completely different from the culture that served the feudal emperors and generals in the past, and also from the elite culture that a few people appreciate themselves alone. It serves the people.

3.Incisively summarize and carry forward the essence of Chinese history and culture

The Chinese nation with a cultural history of 5,000 years has a strong sense of

---

① Jiang Zemin: *Selected Works of Jiang Zemin*, Vol. 3, Beijing: People's Publishing House, 2006, p.278.

national identity. And national culture is an important link with national identity. In striving to develop a socialist culture with Chinese characteristics, the Chinese people must inherit and carry forward the essence of national culture, which will undoubtedly further strengthen national unity and condense the wisdom and strength of the entire nation.

On this issue, China has formed fine traditions. These traditions have been sublimated and developed with the changes of the times and social progress, and have a profound impact on the Chinese people's values, lifestyles, and the development path in China today.

First, the tradition of solidarity and unity. The Chinese nation is a big family composed of 56 ethnic groups. Since time immemorial, close-knit political, economic and cultural links have been established in developing the vast land of the country. The time-honored Chinese culture becomes a strong bond for ethnic harmony and national unity. Solidarity and unity are deeply inscribed in the hearts of the Chinese people as part of their national identity. Ethnic harmony and national unity have remained to be an important guarantee for China's development and progress.

Second, the tradition of maintaining independence. Our ancestors always regarded the spirit of maintaining independence as the foundation of a nation. As one of the cradles of human civilization, China has all along maintained its cultural tradition without letup in its history of several thousand years. In modern times, the frequent bullying and humiliation imperialist powers once weakened China. However, after a hundred years' struggle of the entire Chinese nation, China has stood up again as a giant. This fully testifies to the indestructible strength of this independent national spirit of the Chinese people.

Third, the peace-loving tradition. Chinese thinkers of the pre-Qin days (over 2000 years ago) advanced the doctrine "loving people and treating neighbors kindly are most valuable to a country." This is a reflection of the aspiration of the Chinese people for a peaceful world where people of all countries live in harmony.

Fourth, the tradition of constantly striving to strengthen oneself. Through observing the changing nature of the universe and of all things, ancient Chinese philosophers proposed the following doctrine: "Heaven operates vigorously, and gentlemen exert to strengthen themselves unceasingly." This idea has become an important moral force spurring the Chinese people to work hard for change and innovation. The fruits of China's ancient civilization were brought about by the tireless efforts and hard work of the Chinese nation. In the past one hundred years or so, the Chinese people waged arduous struggles to lift themselves from their historical plight under semi-colonial and semi-feudal rule. Under the guidance of Mao Zedong Thought, the CPC led the Chinese people in achieving China's national independence and people's liberation and in building China into a socialist country with initial prosperity. Today, guided by Deng Xiaoping Theory, the Chinese people are firmly pressing ahead with reform and opening-up and have achieved remarkable successes in the modernization drive.

4.Summarize the spirit of the times, enriching and developing the connotation of Chinese socialist culture

The 80-year history of the CPC has successively gone through quite many severe tests in the new democratic revolution, the tempering of the socialist revolution and the socialist modernization, and the test of various risks, thus leading the Chinese people to achieve brilliant victories in revolution, construction and reform. In the course of these 80 years of struggle, the Communists of China and the Chinese people have faced an extremely ferocious and sinister hostile force. They defeated the enemy when they were outnumbered and weaker, overcoming countless difficulties and obstacles, and creating miracles one after another. It also accumulated extremely rich and precious mental resources. The ideological concept system and practice advocated by the CPC have been condensed into a rich and solemn mental foundation, which constitutes an important content of the Chinese traditional culture and the national spirit. It has not only deeply edified the Party members and officials, but also greatly improved the mental realm and outlook of the people of all ethnic groups. It has become a powerful mental pillar and a vigorous driving force for the entire Party and people of all ethnic groups to realize socialist modernization and the great rejuvenation of the Chinese nation. Mao Zedong called on the whole Party to maintain the same vigour, the same revolutionary enthusiasm and the same death-defying spirit we displayed in the years of the revolutionary wars and carry revolutionary work through to the end. Deng Xiaoping repeatedly called on the whole Party to continue in promoting the revolutionary spirit, which inspires people to work tirelessly, observe strict discipline, make sacrifices, act selflessly and put the interests of others first, the spirit that gives people revolutionary optimism and the determination to overwhelm all enemies and surmount all difficulties in order to win victory. And we did win great victories. Under the extremely difficult conditions, we won the great victory in resisting U.S. aggression and aiding Korea, independently accomplished "The Atom Bomb, Superatomic Bomb and Satellite Project", which is well known as the "Two Bombs and One Star" project, established an independent industrial system and national economic system, and achieved great victory in the fight against floods. All these are the concrete manifestations of the spirit of working tirelessly of the Chinese nation. This shows that advanced culture is the source of strength for overcoming difficulties and winning victory.

To respond to the new century, new situation and new tasks, Jiang Zemin proposed that it is particularly necessary to carry out vigorous publicity work among the whole Party and society, promote the spirit of unremitting struggle for the realization of socialist modernization in the whole party and the whole society, which inspires people to emancipate the mind and seek truth from facts, to keep up with the times and courage innovation, to advance in the face of difficulties without hesitation, to work hard for practical results, and to dedicate selflessly and not contend for fame and position. These not only absorb the essence of our traditional culture and its ethics, but also embody the basic spirit of Marxism. At the same time, they reflect the requirements of the times and social practice. They are the precious intellectual wealth of the Party and the state, which are great intellectual motivation and powerful ideological weapons for the Party to overcome countless difficulties and obstacles and advance its great cause.

IV. Innovating cultural guidelines

1.Putting forward "double-hundred" policy of prospering socialist culture

Mao Zedong further systematically discussed the policy of "Let a hundred flowers blossom, let a hundred schools of thought contend" in his speech entitled "On the Correct Handling of Conflicts Among the People" delivered in February 1957 and in his "Speech at the CPC's National Conference on Publication Work" delivered on March 12,1957. He said, "Letting a hundred flowers blossom and a hundred schools of thought contend is the policy for promoting progress in the arts and sciences and a flourishing socialist culture in our land. Different forms and styles in art should develop freely and different schools in science should contend freely. We think that it is harmful to the growth of art and science if administrative measures are used to impose one particular style of art or school of thought and to ban another. Questions of right and wrong in the arts and science should be settled through free discussion in artistic and scientific circles and through practical work in these fields. They should not be settled in an over-simple manner. A period of trial is often needed to determine whether something is right or wrong. Throughout history at the outset new and correct things often failed to win recognition from the majority of people and had to develop by twists and turns through struggle. Often, correct and good things were first regarded not as fragrant flowers but as poisonous weeds."[1] The policy of "letting a hundred flowers blossom and a hundred schools of thought contend" is not only a systematic summary and reference of the pros and cons of the international communist movement, especially the Soviet cultural construction, but also based on the economic, political, and cultural reality of China's socialist society. Since there are inevitably non-socialist and non-Marxist cultural factors in the primary stage of socialism, how to correctly treat these factors has become an important issue for the development and prosperity of socialist culture. In talking about this issue, Mao Zedong emphasized: "What should our policy be towards non-Marxist ideas? As far as unmistakable counter-revolutionaries and saboteurs of the socialist cause are concerned, the matter is easy, we simply deprive them of their freedom of speech. But incorrect ideas among the people are quite a different matter. Will it do to ban such ideas and deny them any opportunity for expression? Certainly not. It is not only futile but very harmful to use crude methods in dealing with ideological questions among the people, with questions about man's mental world."[2] In short, only by implementing the policy of "letting a hundred schools of thought contend" can all kinds of thoughts be fully expressed, and only through sufficient equal and free discussion can people be allowed to distinguish in comparison, can socialist factors be established and developed, with non-socialist factors gradually overcome and eliminated and its positive factors absorbed. After all, the true, the good and the beautiful always exist by contrast with the false, the evil and the ugly, and grow in struggle with them. Socialist countries need to rapidly develop social economy and culture, and need to create higher and richer cultural achievements than capitalism to meet the ever-growing cultural needs of the people. Thus, it is required that scientific and cultural undertakings be vigorated and prospered.

The policy of "Let a hundred flowers blossom and a hundred schools of thought contend" was put forward based on drawing on the experience of academic and cultural development in China's history, not only summarizing the experience and

---

[1] *Selected Works of Mao Zedong*, Vol. 7, Beijing: People's Publishing House, 1999, p.229.
[2] Ibid., p.232.

lessons of the CPC's leadership in science and culture, but also drawing on the experience and lessons of foreign parties' leadership in science and culture. In this respect, this policy conforms to the objective laws of the development of science and culture in a socialist society. Therefore, implementing this policy is not an expedient measure for building socialist culture, but a basic policy that must be adhered to for a long time to prosper socialist culture. This policy broke the long-standing tradition of cultural despotism in China, and also got rid of the influence of the dogmatization of Marxism in the international communist movement since the 1920s and 1930s, and significantly opened up the way for the prosperity of culture and art, and the expansion and improvement of socialist democracy. The policy of "Let a hundred flowers blossom and a hundred schools of thought contend", together with the Party's policy of literature and art serving the people and socialism and other important policies in the field of science, technology and culture, constitutes the fundamental guarantee for the prosperity and progress of China's socialist cultural undertakings.

In the half-century since the founding of New China in 1949, the Party and government have implemented this policy well, except for those very years when the "ultra-left" trend of thought was overwhelming. It has played an extremely important role in the prosperity and development of socialist culture.

2. Put forward "Four Guidelines" to respond to the new situation

In the practice of building a socialist culture with Chinese characteristics, Deng Xiaoping and Jiang Zemin, while adhering to the guiding position of Marxism, effectively implemented the policy of "Let a hundred flowers blossom and a hundred schools of thought contend" to promote scientific progress and cultural prosperity and development, and provided guarantee by formulating specific mechanisms as possible as they could.

What can we do to actively absorb the achievements of the world's outstanding civilizations while effectively resisting the political attempts of international hostile forces to Westernize and divide China, and build socialism with Chinese characteristics with confidence; to give full play to the positive role of market mechanisms while effectively preventing money worship, the growth and spread of hedonism and extreme individualism, helping people strengthen their socialist ideals and convictions and promoting socialist morality? These constitute a major issue of important and realistic significance. In the process of exploring and solving this issue, Jiang Zemin proposed "Four Guidelines": First, to arm people with scientific theories; Second, to guid people with correct public opinion; Third, to shape people with noble spirit; Fourth, to inspire people with excellent works.

This is a specific policy on socialist cultural construction proposed by the CPC in the primary stage of socialism in accordance with the needs of socialist modernization and the laws of cultural construction. This policy makes our cultural construction bear more practicality and operatability, and make the focus and direction of our work more clearly defined, and it has long-term guiding significance for the future cultural construction.

3. Emphasize the central theme and advocate diversity

To emphasize the central theme is to vigorously advocate all ideas and spirits that are conducive to the development of patriotism, collectivism, and socialism under the guidance of the theory of building socialism with Chinese characteristics and the basic line of the Party, to reform, opening up, and modernization construction, to national unity, social progress, and the happiness of the people, and that use honest labor to strive for a better life. Emphasizing the central theme, making our mental products in line with the interests of the people, promoting social progress, and constantly meeting the people's growing mental and cultural needs, is the theme of the development and prosperity of socialist culture. Mental products that reflect the central theme should not only have a sound and progressive ideological content, but also diverse, lively and high-quality artistic expressions, with strong appeal and influence as well as advantage in the cultural market competition.

Emphasizing the central theme and advocating diversity are the concretization of the policy of "Let a hundred flowers blossom and a hundred schools of thought contend". In cultural construction, as long as these two policies are truly implemented, the socialist culture at the primary stage will certainly be able to put on a colorful and prosperous look.

Thus, it can be seen that the CPC has creatively applied Marxism in the practice of the new democratic revolution and the construction of socialism with Chinese characteristics, and formed an original cultural construction policy, by inheriting and drawing on the essence of traditional culture and foreign culture, by the creation of such a practice as building the socialism with Chinese characteristics, the essence of national traditional culture and foreign culture is organically integrated with the fine traditions and revolutionary spirit formed by the long-term revolution and construction of the people under the leadership of the Party, and innovation were constantly achieved on the basis of new practice, thereby forging and developing a socialist culture with Chinese characteristics. This kind of culture fully embodies the unity of being true to our ideals and focused on current issues, and that of being rational, time-sensitive, globe-aware, and Chinese-identity-responsive.

The CPC bears the historical responsibility for the future of the Chinese nation. The 19th century was a century in which the Chinese nation was in decline, and the 20th century was a century in which the Chinese nation rose to struggle and to try to realize rejuvenation. In the meantime, the Chinese nation has experienced much humiliation and bitterness, much desire and pursuit, many ups and downs, many struggles and sacrifices. We can firmly believe that in the 21st century, under the guidance of the advanced socialist culture with Chinese characteristics, The goal of socialist modernization and the rejuvenation of the Chinese nation will surely be achieved.

An Outlook on Development of Chinese Socialist Culture*

I. Proposal of outlook on development of Chinese socialist culture

As for the status and role of culture in the operation and development of economic and social systems, writers of Marxist classics have written a lot. For the first time in the history of human thought, K. Marx and F. Engels freed themselves from the fetters of idealistic conception of history and rationally explained the relationship between matter and consciousness and between economy, politics and culture. In *German Ideology*, Marx states, "We must begin by stating the first premise of all human existence and, therefore, of all history, the premise, namely, that men must be in a position to live in order to be able to 'make history.' But life involves before everything else eating and drinking, a habitation, clothing and many other things. The first historical act is thus the production of the means to satisfy these needs, the production of material life itself."[①] "The production of ideas, of conceptions, of consciousness, is at first directly interwoven with the material activity and the material intercourse of men, the language of real life. Conceiving, thinking, the mental intercourse of men, appear at this stage as the direct efflux of their material behaviour. The same applies to intellectual production as expressed in the language of politics, laws, morality, religion, metaphysics, etc. of a people."[②] They point out that "We set out from real, active men, and on the basis of their real life-process we demonstrate the development of the ideological reflexes and echoes of this life-process. The phantoms formed in the human brain are also, necessarily,

---

* Originally published in *Marxism Research*, 2008(5).
① Marx, K. & F. Engels: *Selected Works of Marx and Engels*, Vol. 1, Chin. ed., Beijing: People's Publishing House, 1995, p.78-79.
② Ibid., p.72.

sublimates of their material life-process, which is empirically verifiable and bound to material premises. Morality, religion, metaphysics, all the rest of ideology and their corresponding forms of consciousness, thus no longer retain the semblance of independence. They have no history, no development; but men, developing their material production and their material intercourse, alter, along with this their real existence, their thinking and the products of their thinking. Life is not determined by consciousness, but consciousness by life."[1] In other words, fundamentally, people's intellectual production and cultural activity are determined by material production.

In affirming this, K. Marx and F. Engels also emphasized the repercussions of mental and cultural activity on material production and economic activity. In a letter to J.W. Bloch, F. Engels criticized the misunderstanding of the materialistic conception of history that economic factor is the only decisive factor, and he points out: "The economic situation is the basis, but the various elements of the superstructure – political forms of the class struggle and its results, to wit: constitutions established by the victorious class after a successful battle, etc., juridical forms, and even the reflexes of all these actual struggles in the brains of the participants, political, juristic, philosophical theories, religious views and their further development into systems of dogmas."[2] Here F. Engels speaks of other elements which have exerted quite an impact on the course of the historical struggle. Though he focuses primarily on the superstructure, it undoubtedly embraces the opinion that culture has great influence on the historical development.

In the early 1940s, Mao Zedong made a well-known definition of new-democratic culture as follows: "Any given culture (as an ideological form) is a reflection of the politics and economics of a given society, and the former in turn has a tremendous influence and effect upon the latter: economics is the base and politics the concentrated expression of economics. This is our fundamental view of the relation of culture to politics and economics and of the relation of politics to economics."[3]

Mao Zedong's definition clearly points out that culture has tremendous adverse effect on social economic and political development. Professor Feng Tianyu (冯天瑜)

---

[1] Marx, K. & F. Engels: *Selected Works of Marx and Engels*, Vol. 1, Chin. ed., Beijing: People's Publishing House, 1995, p. 73.
[2] Marx, K. & F. Engels: *Selected Works of Marx and Engels*, Vol.4, Chin. ed., Beijing: People's Publishing House, 1995, p.696.
[3] *Selected Works of Mao Zedong*, Vol. 2, Chin. ed., Beijing: People's Publishing House, 1991, p. 663-664.

calls the culture interpreted above in a narrow sense the value system of culture: "It adapts to the production mode and life style of a particular nation and constitutes the values and codes of conduct spread in language as symbols. The culture in this concept or mental culture, corresponds to economy and politics, is a reflection of the politics and economics of the society, and gives a tremendous influence and effect upon the economy and politics of the society."[1] Rethinking about the history of human culture, we can find that it is precisely the various cultural creations and cultural spirits generated by mankind in the material production that have been effectively changing mental world, thinking modes, civilization landscape, mental realm and rational cognition of mankind, and hereupon have, as one of the motive forces, been making human history stride forward. For this reason, Raymond Williams proposes that Marxists give culture a high value.[2]

Since the Third Plenary Session of the 11th CPC Central Committee, held from December 18 to 22, 1978, the second-generation leadership with Deng Xiaoping as the core and the third-generation leadership with Jiang Zemin as the core have adhered to the basic viewpoint of Marxism and correctly understood and dealt with the relationship between economic and cultural construction, and between material civilization and mental civilization, and hence proposed to build a socialist culture with Chinese characteristics. What they believe in is as follows: First of all, socialist culture construction must be done with economic construction as the centre. Otherwise, not only will the cultural construction be badly done, but it will also inflict grave damage to economic construction. This has been a hard lesson in the history of socialist construction in China. At the same time, cultural construction cannot be replaced by economic construction, because it can provide powerful mental motivation force and intellectual support for economic development and all-round social progress. In 1979, Deng Xiaoping pointed out: "While working for a socialist civilization which is materially advanced, we should build one which is culturally and ideologically advanced by raising the scientific and cultural level of the whole nation and promoting a rich and diversified cultural life inspired by high ideals."[3]

---

[1] Feng Tianyu 冯天瑜: *Reflections on Chinese Cultural History*, Wuhan: Huazhong University of Science and Technology Press, 1989, p.19.
[2] Williams, Raymond: *Culture and Society*, Chin. Ed., tran. by Wu Songjiang & Zhang Wending, Beijing: Peking University Press, 1991, p. 350.
[3] Deng Xiaoping: *Selected Works of Deng Xiaoping*: Vol. 2, Chin. ed., Beijing: People's Publishing House, 1994, p. 208.

In 1980, he added: "The socialist country that we must construct, must not only have a high-level material civilization, but must also have a high-level of mental civilization. When I speak of a civilization with a high cultural and ideological level, I refer not only to education, science and culture (which are of course indispensable) but also to communist thinking, ideals, beliefs, morality and discipline, as well as a revolutionary stand and revolutionary principles, comradely relations among people, and so on."① At the 12th National Party Congress, Deng Xiaoping emphasized: "Material progress will suffer delays and setbacks unless we promote cultural and ethical progress as well. We can never succeed in revolution and construction if we rely on material conditions alone. In the past, no matter how small and weak the Party was, and no matter what difficulties it faced, we always maintained great combat effectiveness thanks to our faith in Marxism and communism. Because we shared common ideals, we had strict discipline. That is our real strength today as it has been in the past and will be in the future. Some comrades no longer have a clear understanding of this truth. So, it is hard for them to pay close attention to building a society that is advanced culturally and ethically."② In his talks given in Wuchang, Shenzhen, Zhuhai and Shanghai in 1992, Deng Xiaoping pointed out that "Guangdong is trying to catch up with Asia's 'four little dragons' in 20 years, not only in terms of economic growth, but also in terms of improved public order and general social conduct — that is, we should surpass them in both material and ethical progress. Only that can be considered building socialism with Chinese characteristics."③

In the great practice of promoting the building of socialism with Chinese characteristics, the third-generation collective leadership with Jiang Zemin as the core has upheld and developed Deng Xiaoping's thought on how to correctly handle the interrelations between the construction of material civilization and mental civilization, and between the cultural construction and the economic construction. In his speech at the Celebration of the 70th Anniversary of the CPC, Jiang Zemin clearly stated that "socialism with Chinese characteristics is a unified whole of socialist economy, politics and culture." We must not only build socialist

---

① Deng Xiaoping: *Selected Works of Deng Xiaoping*, Vol. 2, Chin. ed., Beijing: People's Publishing House, 1994, p.208.
② Deng Xiaoping: *Selected Works of Deng Xiaoping*, Vol.3, Chin. ed., Beijing: People's Publishing House, 1993, p.144
③ Ibid., p.378.

economy and politics with Chinese characteristics, but also build socialist culture with Chinese characteristics. At the 14th National Congress of the CPC in October 1992, the Third Plenary Session of the 14th CPC Central Committee in November 1993, and the Sixth Plenary Session of the 14th CPC Central Committee in October 1996, he elaborated the issue of attaching importance to the construction of mental civilization and cultural construction. At the 15th National Congress of the CPC, held from September 12 to 18, 1997, Jiang systematically discussed the Party's cultural program of building socialism with Chinese characteristics in the primary stage of socialism, and clearly defined the construction of socialist culture with Chinese characteristics as a basic content of its basic program of the Party in the primary stage of socialism; he put forward the important conclusion that socialist culture with Chinese characteristics is a significant indicator of comprehensive national strength. In the report to the 16th National Congress of the CPC, it is pointed out that "In the present-day world, culture is interactive with economic and political activities, and its status and functions are becoming more and more outstanding in the competition in overall national strength. The power of culture is deeply rooted in the vitality, creativity and cohesion of a nation. All Party members must fully understand the strategic significance of cultural development and make socialist culture develop and flourish."[①] These important judgments have shown that the CPC has fully realized that culture is more and more closely linked to economy and politics, and has profoundly revealed the special position and role of culture in our times.

Since the 16th National Congress, held from Nov 8 to 14, 2002, the CPC Central Committee with Hu Jintao as general secretary has consistently adhered to the guidance of dialectical materialism and historical materialism, in light of the new features and new trends in the development of human practices, has been continuously deepening the status and role of culture in the socialist economic development, and put forward a series of new ideas and new theses on the development of advanced socialist culture, which have further enriched and improved the Scientific Outlook on Development and meanwhile deepened our understanding of the outlook on the development of socialist culture with Chinese characteristics.

As Hu Jintao pointed out, without cultural heritage and continuous cultural

---

① *Historical Documents Since the Sixteenth National Congress of the CPC (I)*, Beijing: People's Publishing House, 2005, p.30.

innovation, it is impossible for a nation to stand proudly in the family of nations. This thesis links cultural construction with cultural innovation and raises national cultural quality, cultural heritage and cultural innovation to the height of realizing the great rejuvenation of the Chinese nation. Ever since, the Party has attached greater importance to cultural construction and took clearer and more effective measures to effectively promote socialist cultural construction. The Third Plenary Session of the 16th CPC Central Committee, held from October 11 to 14, 1978, explicitly included the reform of cultural system in the important task of improving the socialist market economic system and further defined the general idea and goal of deepening cultural system reform. "Decision of the Central Committee of the CPC on Strengthening the Building of the Party's Governance" adopted by the Fourth Plenary Session of the 16th CPC Central Committee puts forward the view of deepening cultural system reform and liberating and developing cultural productive forces. The Fifth Plenary Session of the 16th CPC Central Committee, held from October 8 to 11, 2005, stressed that we should establish a public cultural service system, actively and vigorously develop cultural undertakings and industries and create more excellent cultural products that meet the needs of the people.

"Several Opinions on Deepening Cultural System Reform" issued by the CPC Central Committee and the State Council further put forward the need to "establish a new outlook on cultural development" and pointed out that in the historical process of building a moderately prosperous society in an all-round way and achieving the rejuvenation of the Chinese nation, the development of advanced socialist culture has a status and role of general and strategic significance.

We must fully understand the importance and urgency of reforming the cultural system from the perspective of fully implementing the Scientific Outlook on Development and building a harmonious socialist society, from the perspective of consolidating the guiding ideology of Marxism in China, and from the perspective of strengthening the Party's governing capacity, enhance the sense of responsibility and mission, seize the opportunity of strategic importance, deepen reform, accelerate development, and inject powerful impetus into the construction of advanced socialist culture. As Li Changchun pointed out, "we must persist in emancipating the mind, change concepts, and establish a new outlook on cultural development." He further stressed that "At present, in order to emancipate the mind and change concepts, the most important thing is to grasp comprehensively a series of new ideas and new assertions on the development of advanced socialist culture which the CPC Central Committee has put forward since the 16th CPC National Congress, hence firmly establishing a new outlook of cultural development."①

In the report to the 17th National Congress of the CPC, convened from Oct 15 to 21, 2007, Hu Jintao pointed out more clearly: "In the present era, culture has become a more and more important source of national cohesion and creativity and a factor of growing significance in the competition in overall national strength, and the Chinese people have an increasingly ardent desire for a richer cultural life. We must keep to the orientation of advanced socialist culture, bring about a new upsurge in socialist cultural development, stimulate the cultural creativity of the whole nation, and enhance culture as part of the soft power of our country to better guarantee the people's basic cultural rights and interests, enrich the cultural life in Chinese society and inspire the enthusiasm of the people for progress."②

In order to achieve this goal, four tasks are clearly defined in the "Report": first, to build up the system of socialist core values and make socialist ideology more attractive and cohesive; second, to foster a culture of harmony and cultivate civilized practices; third, to promote Chinese culture and build the common cultural home for the Chinese nation; fourth, to stimulate cultural innovation and enhance the vitality of cultural development.

On January 22, 2008, Hu Jintao stressed at the National Conference on Publicity and Theoretical Work that cultural development should be based on the general requirements of "upholding its political guiding principle, serving the overall interests of the people, serving the people, reforming and innovating", and should, with deeper understanding, broader mind, more efficient policies and more effective measures, focus on building the socialist core value system, strive to consolidate and strengthen the mainstream public opinion, strive to promote reform and innovation, promote the great prosperity and development of socialist culture, and enhance the national cultural soft power so that a good atmosphere can be created for continually emancipating the mind, adhering to the reform and opening up, promoting scientific development, promoting social harmony while a strong ideological and cultural guarantee can be provided for a new victory in the building of a moderately prosperous society at all aspects and a new situation in the cause of building socialism

---

① Li Changchun 李长春: "Fully Implement the Scientific Outlook on Development and Further Promote the Cultural System Reform," *Truth seeking*, 2006 (10).
② Hu Jintao: *Hold High the Great Banner of Socialism with Chinese Characteristics and Strive for New Victories in Building a Moderately Prosperous Society in all Respects - At the 17th National Congress of the CPC*, Beijing: People's Publishing House, 2007, p. 33-34.

with Chinese characteristics.

These aforementioned great conclusions constitute the theoretical framework and essence of the development of socialist culture with Chinese characteristics and are also the guidelines for promoting socialist cultural development in China.

II. Basic connotation of outlook on development of Chinese socialist culture

In the contemporary era, the competition for overall national strength including cultural productivity has become more and more intense. The status of culture in the overall national strength has become increasingly prominent. The exchange and dissemination of culture has increasingly become an important part of the mutual relations among countries. Cultural tension and conflict are also increasingly becoming an aspect of international competition and international conflict. The trend of globalization and IT application driven by the new technological revolution has made culture emerge all of sudden as a new practical force. Cultural productivity is not only a kind of "hard power", which is a certain productive force, but also a kind of "soft power", which is the cohesive force of the nation-state; at the same time, culture is still an innovative force and a powerful driving force for the development of the nation-state. Cultural productivity is injecting a new and more powerful impetus to the social development of contemporary Chinese society, and cultural cohesion is making our economy and society develop in a better, faster and more harmonious manner, making the centripetal force and rallying power of the Chinese nation unprecedentedly strong. Cultural innovation will enable subjectivity and creativity of the country and its people to explode more vigorously. A brand-new understanding of this trait of contemporary culture should become the core and the soul of the outlook on development of socialist culture with Chinese characteristics.

1. Culture is a productive force as well as a hard power

During the long era of human society's agricultural and industrial civilization, the primary industry and the secondary industry constituted real productive forces, while the tertiary industry, including cultural development, did not yet enter the horizon of economic progress. However, with the development of new scientific and technological revolution, the tertiary industry has been playing an increasingly important role in the industrial structure of human society. At the same time, the integration of culture and economy has become more and more profound, and as a result, the production of consumer goods and service activities to meet people's mental and psychological needs has gradually become an industry. Culture has directly become a productive force and gradually become a certain hard power. As a result, there has emerged the cultural industry, a product of close combination of high technology and culture, and an emerging industry that represents the global trend of modern economic, social and cultural development. As UNESCO defined, cultural industry is a series of cultural activities that produce, reproduce, store and distribute cultural goods and services in accordance with industry standards. Since the 1970s, the advent of the "new competitive era" characterized by knowledge, IT application, globalization, intelligentization, internationalization, networking and innovation, has made the development of cultural industry gradually become a global trend. As a rising sunrise industry, the cultural industry has an increasingly important position in the economic development of a country and has become the pillar industry of the economy in developed countries. It can be said that in modern times, the cultural industry is booming day by day, a country's cultural resources and cultural advantages are replacing the advantages of natural resources, which not only directly reflects and gives birth to the productivity and hard power of a nation-state, but also strongly promotes cultural development and prosperity.

China is now in a crucial period of improving the socialist market economic system, comprehensively implementing the Scientific Outlook on Development and building a harmonious socialist society. How can we adapt ourselves to the new situation of world development at this crucial moment of China's reform and development? How can we be invincible in the new round of international competition? The development of cultural industry is crucial.

To free and develop cultural productivity is both the only way to flourish advanced socialist culture and an important way to promote sustainable, stable, rapid and coordinated development of economy. This is a new harvest made by the CPC on the understanding of the status and role of culture. Since the advent of the 1990s, with the establishment and development of China's socialist market economic system, the pace of market-oriented reform in the cultural field has accelerated, so has the development of cultural industry. Since the advent of the 21st century, the development momentum of China's cultural industry has been even greater and its proportion in the economic and social life and its GNP has also become increasingly significant. In October 2000, the "Proposal of the CPC Central Committee on Formulating the Tenth Five-Year Plan for National Economic and Social Development", adopted at the Fifth Plenary Session of the 15th CPC Central

Committee, held from October 9 to 11, 2000, raised the concept of "cultural industry" for the first time in an official document of the Central Committee, which marks China's recognition of the formulation and status of cultural industry, and reflects our increasingly profound understanding of the law of cultural development itself. This is not only the objective requirement of establishing a socialist market economic system for cultural development but also an inevitable requirement of firmly grasping the orientation of advanced socialist culture. At the 16th CPC National Congress held in 2002, for the first time, culture was divided into cultural undertakings and cultural industries, emphasizing the need to actively develop cultural undertakings and cultural industries. In August 2003, the main content of the seventh group study session of the Political Bureau of the 16th CPC Central Committee was "the development situation of the world's cultural industry and the development strategy of China's cultural industry". In November 2003, the "Decision of the CPC Central Government on Certain Issues of Improving the System of Socialist Market Economy", adopted at the Third Plenary Session of the 16th CPC Central Committee in October 2003, clearly put forward the development objectives of the cultural industry, requiring the improvement of cultural industry policies, encouraging the investment of funds in multiple channels, promoting the common development of various types of cultural industry, forming a number of large cultural enterprise groups, and enhancing the overall strength and international competitiveness of cultural industry. In the report to the 17th National Congress of the CPC, further emphasis is attached to the needs to vigorously develop the cultural industry, implement the strategy spearheaded by major cultural industry projects, speed up the construction of cultural industry bases and regional cultural industry clusters, cultivate backbone enterprises and strategic investors in the cultural industry, prosper the cultural markets, and enhance international competitiveness.

2. Culture is a soft power, and is the attraction and cohesion of a nation-state

Culture is not only a direct manifestation of the productive forces, but also as a soft power. It is the concentrated embodiment of the attraction and cohesion of a nation-state. The strength of a nation lies not only in the hard power, including economic output, scientific and technological level, national defense force, and related facilities, but also in the soft power, including core values, national qualities, political and economic system and national image, the proportion of the soft power in the overall national strength continuing to increase. Culture and its influence constitute the most important components of national image and national soft power.

Harvard University Professor Joseph Nye has divided overall national strength into two forms: the hard power and the soft power. The former refers to leading strength, which includes basic resources (such as land, population, and natural resources), military power, economic power and scientific and technological power, whereas the latter is divided into national cohesiveness, universality of cultural identity and engagement in international agencies. Joseph Nye summarized the soft power as the power to guide, attract, and exemplarify, which is an assimilative power, a nation's ideological attractiveness and political orientation. The soft power is extraordinarily expansive and transmissive, transcending time and space and exerting a tremendous influence on human lifestyles and behavior norms. This formulation is very instructive for our understanding of the role of cultural soft power.

Specifically, I think that the cultural soft power is mainly reflected in the following two aspects:

First, the cultural soft power is embodied in its guidance, attractiveness, and exemplariness, an assimilative power as the sign of a nation's ideological appeal and its capacity of political orientation. Culture is the splendor of human subjective world as seen in the objective world, and constitutes the most inspiring and unique brand of a nation-state. Excellent culture can constantly enrich people's spiritual world, enhance their mental strength, and fulfil the special guiding function of sublimating the mind, stimulating the spirit, mellowing the morality, and cultivating the soul. It can not only form a strong attraction and make people intoxicated, fascinated, and linger, but also constitute an exemplary role for the people of other cultures outside the region to learn from, imitate, and absorb. In the long and glorious cultural history, the Chinese culture in the *Tang* Dynasty was just like this. The period of the *Wei, Jin* and Southern and Northern Dynasties (220 A.D.-589 A.D.) witnessed the social turmoil and conflicts and exchanges of diverse and heterogeneous cultures while the *Tang* Dynasty witnessed a magnificent landscape of blossoming and splendor, thanks to the hitherto existing cultural achievements, such as literature and art, music and dance, calligraphy and painting, Buddhist culture, arts and crafts, history and geography. After comparing the *Tang* culture with the Asian and European cultures of the time, the British scholar Herbert George Wells noted: "Throughout the seventh, eighth and ninth centuries, China was the most secure and civilized country in the world... Millions of people indeed were leading orderly, graceful and kindly lives in

China during these centuries when the attenuated populations of Europe and Western Asia were living either in hovels, small walled cities or grim robber fortresses. While the mind of the west was black with theological obsessions, the mind of China was open and tolerant and enquiring."[1] The *Tang* culture not only made the Chinese civilization reach an unprecedented height with its glorious achievements in the previous dynasty, but also spread to other parts of the world with its powerful strength, broad-mindedness, rich connotation and profound meaning, leaving a colorful mark in the history of world culture. At that time, Japanese society absorbed the Chinese culture on an unprecedented scale so that "The more Chinese it was, the more popular it was with the ancient aristocrats." and "Anything from the *Tang* Dynasty had to be brought in as quickly as possible, no matter what."[2] In cultural exchanges with India, the Arab world, and even African countries, the Tang culture, with its guidance, attractiveness, and exemplariness, has also contributed to the dissemination and exchange of Chinese culture around the world.

Under the conditions of economic globalization, the guidance, attractiveness and exemplariness of cultural soft power have become more and more obvious and powerful. Without its own strong culture, a country sooner or later would become a vassal of others. Moreover, the captured culture of a country will penetrate with tremendous power into its economic system, political system, social order and even into the mental world, values, ideals and beliefs of its members, only to reduce itself into a colony of powerful nations. It is in this sense that Qian Mu (钱穆)pointed out in his article "The Evolution of Chinese Cultural Tradition": "Culture is the life of a nation. If a country has no culture, it has no life."[3] Here, from the perspective of "life", the significance and value of culture for a people and a country is highlighted. For this reason, I believe that cultural soft power first and foremost manifests itself as the strong guidance, attractiveness, and exemplariness of a nation-state, which constitutes the charm and charisma of a country's civilization and political orientation.

Second, cultural soft power is also reflected in the power of identity, affinity and cohesion. Culture is a kind of "adhesive" with a high degree of identity, which is the link between human rational cognition and emotional connection, and is also

---

[1] Citation from Feng Tianyu 冯天瑜, etc.: *The History of Chinese Culture*, Shanghai: Shanghai People's Publishing House, 2005, p.494.
[2] *Kiyoshi Inoue: History of Japan,* Chin. ed., Tianjin: Tianjin People's Publishing House, 1975, p.347.
[3] Jiang Yihua 姜义华, etc.(ed.) : *Hong Kong, Taiwan and Overseas Scholars on Chinese Culture* 《港台及海外学者论中国文化》, Shanghai: Shanghai People's Publishing House, 1988, p.1.

the inner condition for a country and a society to be harmonious and stable, and to identify with each other. Generally speaking, cultural identity is formed by the interaction of a shared language, ethnic origin, religious beliefs, values, ethical and moral systems, history, geography, economic environment and other factors, and is an important basis for establishing the legitimacy of the existence of a nation-state. The cohesion of a nation-state is based on nationally shared interests, cultural traditions, and relatively consistent social and moral values. I especially agree with the statement that cultural identity is the "army" capable of "overcoming firmness by gentleness", and is the strongest "national defense".

Cultural soft power also clearly manifests itself as affinity and cohesion. Take Chinese culture as an example: There are many reasons why the Chinese nation has emerged resilient from trials and tribulations. Externally, it was partly because of a stable survival system forged by the interaction between and the constraint of a relatively isolated continental territory, a self-sufficient agrarian economic pattern, and a patriarchal social organizational structure. However, the main cause lies in its internal quality, namely the source of the strong vitality of the Chinese culture which constitutes in the vitality of diversity, the assimilation of uniformity, the convergence of inclusiveness, the affinity of ethicality, the creativity of volatility, and the continuity of national historical consciousness, which constitute what Professor Feng Tianyu (冯天瑜) praised as the vitality and continuity of Chinese culture.

He has said, "What makes Chinese culture most fascinating and admired by the world is not only its antiquity, but also its tenacity and incomparable continuity, and the fact that despite all the vicissitudes and sufferings, it has survived and been inherited. Although Chinese culture has its highs and lows, and has been challenged repeatedly, and has gone through many crisis-filled moments, it has shown time and again its great ability to regenerate, and has become one of the rare ancient cultures in the history of world culture that has never been extinct."[①] In the present-day globalized world, culture is increasingly becoming a country's "business card" and the cultural home that a country upholds and protects. Culture is the root of the nation, and spirit is the soul of the nation. It is for this reason that culture featuring

---

① Feng Tianyu 冯天瑜: *Characteristics of Chinese Culture*《中国文化的特征》, in *Issues of Modern Chinese Culture*《中国近代文化问题》, edited by the Editorial Committee of the Series of Modern Chinese Cultural History, Shanghai: *Zhonghua* Book Company, 1989, p.15.

affinity, identity and cohesion will always shine brightly and is supposed to carry its due weighty responsibility.

In recent years, the Party has deepened its awareness of the significance of cultural soft power and more importance has been attached to its improvement. On November 10, 2006, Hu Jintao proposed at the Seventh National Congress of the Chinese Writers Association and the Eighth National Congress of the Federation of Chinese Literary that "Enhancing the state's soft power is a major and important issue before us." In January 2007, at the 38th group study session of the Political Bureau of the 16th CPC Central Committee, he pointed out again that strengthening the construction and management of network culture is "conducive to enhancing China's soft power". In the report to the Seventeenth National Congress of the CPC, it is clearly stated that it is necessary to "increase the country's cultural soft power".

Therefore, strengthening the construction of advanced socialist culture has been endowed with double meanings. First, cultural construction is of great significance to the construction of a harmonious society. As Hu Jintao pointed out in his speech at a seminar on improving the ability to build a harmonious socialist society, attended by major leading officials at the provincial / ministerial level, whether a society can be harmonious and whether a country can have long-term peace and stability depends to a large extent on the ideological and moral qualities of all its members, and that social harmony cannot be achieved without common ideological beliefs and good moral norms. We should effectively strengthen the construction of advanced socialist culture, and constantly enhance people's mental strength and enrich their mental world. Second, in this new century, cultural soft power has been becoming more and more prominent in the competition of overall national strength, and has become one of important factors of national core competitiveness. With the deepening of economic globalization, the worldwide exchange of ideas and culture has become more widespread, and more and more countries have been taking the improvement of cultural soft power as an important strategy. As a developing socialist country, in order to win the initiative in the fierce international competition and effectively resist the infiltration of Western thoughts and cultures, China must take more effective measures to promote the development and prosperity of socialist culture, continuously enhance the overall strength of China's culture and its international competitiveness, and effectively improve the national cultural soft power.

Socialist ideology is the core of advanced socialist culture, and the socialist core value system is the essential embodiment of socialist ideology. Therefore, vigorously building the socialist core value system has become the fundamental way to continuously enhance the attraction and cohesion of the advanced socialist culture.

3.Culture is an innovative force and a powerful driving force for development of a nation-state

Human society is blazing a trail by constantly resolving the conflicts between man and nature, and between man and society. This process is an ongoing process of innovation. Innovation is the concentrated expression of the essential power of mankind, and human creative activities are the fundamental symbol that distinguishes mankind from the rest of the natural world. Innovation is the basic way for mankind to survive and develop.

The starting point and the symbol of culture are the labor of mankind who makes and uses tools to transform nature in order to satisfy his own life needs. According to Plekhanov, man as a social being is the result of the long-term development of the animal. But only when he was not content to sit back and enjoy the bounty of nature, but began to produce the consumer goods he needed by himself, did the cultural history of man begin.[1] In the practice of human material production and cultural creation, culture actually constitutes a tremendous innovation, which tremendously reforms the knowledge structure and mental outlook of practical subjects and further promotes mankind's transformation of the objective material world. Culture is the concentrated manifestation of human creative activity, is the representation and reflection of the essential strength of mankind and is the fundamental symbol that man is distinguished from nature. There may be more than 200 definitions of culture, but generally speaking, culture refers to the purpose of people and the course of their actions, and it is the integration of human values, modes of thinking and behaviors (lifestyles). It is through such internal integration that the force of the essence of mankind has been strengthened and the way of inventing more powerful ways of transforming the world has been continuously found out. As a result, the process of transformation and assimilation of the subjective world and the objective world has been constantly pushed to a new level.

Zhu Qianzhi (朱谦之) advocated the theory of cultural evolution, believing that "Culture is life in itself. It is not, as the Greek and Roman philosophers and the theologians in the Middle Ages said, something that is constant and still. On the

---

[1] *Selected Works of Plekhanov's Philosophy*, Vol. 2, Chin. ed., tran. by Ru Xin 汝信, Beijing: the Commercial Press, 1959, p.227.

contrary, cultural life is forever in the process of innovation and change. Culture itself is the manifestation of change and movement, and such change is on-going life and evolution. Therefore, culture and evolution are in essence the same thing. On the one hand, it is the accumulation which takes place every minute; on the other hand, it is innovation which crops up every minute. Civilization can preserve the trace of the past culture, but not its spirit. The spirit of the past culture is forever infiltrated into the present."[1] It is in this sense that Zhu Qianzhi proposed that "all cultures are modern cultures,"[2] "Modern culture is a cultural stream that has no beginning and is always new, often creating something and always alive."[3] This shows in fact that culture is a kind of creativity that is constantly undergoing innovation and evolvement. The history of human cultural development is a long history of continuous accumulation, innovation, revolution and metabolism.

The trend of development has increasingly shown that cultural innovation has become the paradigm and foundation of a nation-state's creativity in contemporary times, is a "weak link" that determines its creativity and is related to the overall situation of its national rejuvenation. As Jiang Zemin pointed out, "Innovation is the soul of a nation's progress and an inexhaustible driving force for the prosperity of a country."[4] "We must promote institutional innovation, technological innovation, cultural innovation and other innovations in all fields through theoretical innovation." "This is the way we must administer the Party and the country for a long time."[5] In response to the new phased characteristics of China's development, Hu Jintao clearly put forward the grand goal of its entry into the ranks of innovative countries by 2020. To achieve this goal, he stressed the need to "develop a culture of innovation and strive to cultivate the innovative spirit of the whole society". In the report to the Seventeenth National Congress of the CPC, it is clearly stated that it is necessary to promote the innovation of cultural internal form, institutional mechanism, and communication means from a high starting point of the times to enhance the vitality of cultural development.

---

[1] Zhu Qianzhi 朱谦之: *Cultural Philosophy*, Beijing: The Commercial Press, 1990, p.13.
[2] Ibid.
[3] Ibid., p. 19.
[4] *Historical Documents Since the Sixteenth National Congress of the CPC (I)*, Beijing: People's Publishing House, 2005, p.12.
[5] Jiang Zemin: *Selected Works of Jiang Zemin*, Vol. 3, Beijing: People's Publishing House, 2006, p.103.

In short, in contemporary times, cultural power is a fundamental, permeable, comprehensive and guiding force, and culture is productivity, attraction, cohesion and innovation.

III. Theoretical significance of development of Chinese socialist culture

1. Outlook on development of Chinese socialist culture has enriched the Marxist theory of productive forces

The outlook on the development of socialist culture with Chinese characteristics is based on the new development of human practice and is a creative interpretation and application of the thought of the founders of Marxism on the forms of the productive forces. On the forms of the productive forces, K. Marx has said incisively that all productive forces are material productive forces and intellectual productive forces.① K. Marx and F. Engels refer to human production respectively as "production of one's own life" (production of material life), "production of others' life" and "production of ideas, concepts and consciousness." In my view, there are three forms of generalized production practice: production of material life (material production), human production, and intellectual production. Regarding intellectual production, K. Marx and F. Engels have a detailed description on *German Ideology* that "The production of ideas, of conceptions, of consciousness, is at first directly interwoven with the material activity and the material intercourse of men, the language of real life. Conceiving, thinking, the mental intercourse of men, appear at this stage as the direct efflux of their material behavior. The same applies to intellectual production as expressed in the language of politics, laws, morality, religion, metaphysics, etc., of a people."② "Division of labor is one of the main forces in previous history. Now, division of labor appears in the middle of the ruling class in the form of a division of mental labor and material labor. Because within this class some people emerge as thinkers of that class (They are active, capable thinkers of this class who regard the fabrication of this class's own fantasy as the chief source of their livelihood.)"③

---

① Marx, K. & F. Engels: *Collected Works of Marx and Engels*, Vol. 46 (1), Chin. ed., Beijing: People's Publishing House, 1979, p.173.
② Marx, K. & F. Engels: *Selected Works of Marx and Engels*, Vol. 1, Chin. ed., Beijing: People's Publishing House, 1995, p.72.
③ Marx, K. & F. Engels: *Collected Works of Marx and Engels*, Vol.3, Chin. ed., Beijing: People's Publishing House, 1960, p. 53.

The "Bakunin Abstracts of State Institutions and Anarchy", which was written in late 1874 and early 1875, also raised the issue of "intellectual productivity" with language, literature and technology included as part of such productivity.[①] The aforementioned expositions of K. Marx and F. Engels put forward directly the concepts of intellectual production and intellectual productive forces and revealed the connotation of intellectual production, that is, the activity directly aimed at creating intellectual and cultural products. In a strict sense, intellectual production mainly refers to the intellectual producers who consciously and purposely create various forms of social consciousness (such as science, art, education, morality, religion, politics, law, etc.) and create concepts of practice (policies, plans and programs, etc.), and the distribution, exchange and consumption of intellectual products, namely the relations and processes of mental intercourse. The main part of intellectual production is mainly from mental workers, but not limited to them. Some manual workers are also engaged in intellectual production.

In the contemporary society, in which science and technology have become "primary productive forces", this view of K. Marx has increasingly shown the glorious truth. At present, people's mentally and culturally creative activities are not only an element of material productivity, but have become an independent and important form of production practice. The mentally and culturally creative activities not only serve to create mental life products and satisfy the mental life needs of people and plays an irreplaceable role there but also constitute a strong driving force for creating and developing productive forces and promoting economic development and social progress. Obviously, we can no longer understand the role of spirit and its activities and the relationship between material production and spiritual production through taking spiritual and cultural activities and their functions as a subordinate factor of material production or material productive force. Material production is the basis for the existence and development of human society, and of course it is also the basis for the possibility and existence of mental and cultural creative activities and mental production, which cannot be shaken. But aside from this perspective, from the historical and development trends of the differentiation of human productive practice, we can say that the mental and cultural creation (intellectual production) prominently embodies the essence of mankind as a free and creative existence. It becomes an

---

[①] See Marx, K. & F. Engels: *Collected Works of Marx and Engels*, Vol. 18, Chin. ed., Beijing: People's Publishing House, 1964, p. 682.

important area for human activity, and the more advanced forms of practical activity that human beings pursue relentlessly and actively. For now, culture power is a fundamental, penetrating, comprehensive and guiding force. We have every reason to say that following the pattern of mental productivity, culture has become a new form of productive force.

2. Development of Chinese socialist culture expands the understanding of social motivation from historical materialism

The view of social motivation is an important part of historical materialism. According to the historical materialism, the basic social conflict, that is, the relationship between the productive forces and the production relations, and between the economic base and the superstructure, promotes social progress, in the final analysis. In *The German Ideology*, K. Marx and F. Engels pointed out that the form of social intercourse that is constrained by the productive forces in all historical stages and also restricts the productive forces at the same time is the civil society, that civil society includes individual's all material intercourse at a certain stage of the development and also includes the entire commercial life and industrial life at this stage, and that the social organization forms the foundations of the state and the superstructure of any other conception at all times.[①] The "forms of intercourse" and "civil society" referred here are of the same category as the production relations and the superstructure. In fact, they deal with the contradiction between the productive forces and the production relations, and between the economic base and the superstructure. In the preface to *Critique of Political Economy*, K. Marx expounded this principle more clearly.

However, it should be noted that after K. Marx and F. Engels established the basic idea of social motivation, there has always been a misunderstanding of this idea as an economic determinism. This understanding arose when they were alive. F. Engels made a serious criticism on this in a letter to President Bloch in September 1890. He said "According to the materialist conception of history, the *ultimately* determining element in history is the production and reproduction of real life. Other than this neither Marx nor I have ever asserted. Hence if somebody twists this into saying that the economic element is the *only* determining one, he transforms that

---

① Marx, K. & F. Engels: *Collected Works of Marx and Engels*, Vol. 3, Chin. ed., Beijing: People's Publishing House, 1960, p.40, 41.

proposition into a meaningless, abstract, senseless phrase." [1] If understood this way, the study of historical activities and the account of the evolution of the historical period "would be easier than the solution of a simple equation of the first degree." [2] F. Engels goes on to point out that "The economic situation is the basis, but the various elements of the superstructure—political forms of the class struggle and its results, to wit: constitutions established by the victorious class after a successful battle, etc., juridical forms, and even the reflexes of all these actual struggles in the brains of the participants, political, juristic, philosophical theories, religious views and their further development into systems of dogmas." [3] He here actually affirmed the reaction of the productive relations and the superstructure to the productive forces and the economic base and emphasized the concept of synergy to understand the development of social history.

However, we should admit that for a long period of time we have not had any profound rational grasp of the Marxist view of social motivation in practice, because we have always been emphasizing the fundamental role of the productive forces in promoting economic and social development. This is not wrong in itself, but it is wrong to go so far as to fail in grasping and applying Marxist dialectical culture well. It is always customary to think that culture is something relatively "soft" in relation to economic development, thereby a sector of minor importance. This has led some localities, departments and leaders to set the rank of GDP. They have long marginalized cultural work, thinking that it is "no easy for them to obtain political achievements" through engaging in cultural work. In fact, the separation of culture from economy is one-sided and wrong. Both the one-sided view of performance (behind the values) causes trouble, but also the one-sided view of history is reflected. Thanks to the current rapid development of cultural activities and cultural industries and the promotion of social and economic development, cultural activities, especially cultural innovations, have truly become a powerful driving force for social development. On the basis of inheriting the basic principle of historical materialism, the concept of socialist cultural development with Chinese characteristics has deepened the understanding of the concept of social motive force of the historical

---

[1] Marx, K. & F. Engels: *Selected Works of Marx and Engels*, Vol. 4, Chin. ed., Beijing: People's Publishing House, 1995, p.695-696.
[2] Marx, K. & F. Engels: *Selected Works of Marx and Engels*, Vol. 4, Chin. ed., Beijing: People's Publishing House, 1995, p.696.
[3] Ibid.

materialism. For this very reason, we should firmly grasp the current situation and the characteristics of the times in China's economic and social development to create colorful and contested prosperity of all fields of socialist culture and promote the great prosperity and development of socialist culture.

3.Outlook on development of Chinese socialist culture is an important part of theoretical system of Chinese socialism

The outlook on socialist cultural development with Chinese characteristics is an important theoretical result that the Party has gradually formed in the practice of building socialism with Chinese characteristics since the start of the reform and opening up. It upheld and inherited the basic ideas and views on culture from the classic Marxist writers, upheld and inherited the basic ideas and views on culture in Mao Zedong Thought, and combined the new conditions of the times and the actual construction of socialist modernization so that it gave Marxist cultural development a fresh and vivid element and vividly and concretely developed Marxism. As the major theoretical result of the second historic leap in combining Marxism with the realities of China, the theoretical system of socialism with Chinese characteristics answers three basic questions: (1) what is socialism, how to build it; (2) what kind of party to build, and how to build the party; (3) what kind of development to achieve, and how to develop. The formation of the socialist cultural development with Chinese characteristics is a concentrated answer to what kind of cultural development to achieve and how to develop the socialist culture with Chinese characteristics. It provided the well-conceived guiding principle for developing a wider prospect for the socialist culture with Chinese characteristics with a series of new ideas, new conceptions and new arguments.

Supportive Role of Philosophy and Social Sciences in Construction of Cultural Fronts*

At the outset of 2008, Hu Jintao, the then General Secretary of the Party, regarding how to create a new situation in publicity and theoretical work on the new historic starting point, put forward the general requirement of "upholding its political guiding principle, serving the overall interests of the people, serving the people, reforming and innovating" at the National Publicity and Theoretical Work Conference. The requirements not only judiciously summarize the practical experience of CPC's publicity and theoretical works, but also concludes the basic standards for the Party's publicity and theoretical work since the reform and opening - up process was started in 1978. Philosophy and social sciences constitute an important force to improve the Party's publicity and theoretical work. As is shown by the progress in philosophy and social sciences achieved in China since the introduction of the reform and opening - up initiative, adhering to the correct political orientation, taking Marxism and the great political guiding principles of socialism with Chinese characteristics as the guideline of all the works is the political guarantee for developing and prospering the cause of prospering Philosophy and Social Sciences. The basic way of achieving full-fledged development in philosophy and social sciences is to be centered on the overall situation and serve the people to offer guidance to the endeavors of the Party and the people. Reform and innovation on contents and mechanism are the primary means to prosper philosophy and social sciences. Under the new circumstances, the significance of the Party's publicity and

---

* This article is written with the cooperation of Wu Bo (吴波) and is the project results for the Central Publicity Department. It is originally published in the *Journal of the Chinese Academy of Social Sciences*, 2008-8-14.

theoretical work shall be appreciated by people working in philosophy and social science circles. They shall also profoundly understand the Party's work and its goals proposed by Hu Jintao, the General Secretary, so as to make contribution to the cause of prospering philosophy and social sciences, and open up new prospects for the Party's publicity and theoretical work, in order to achieve a new high in promoting socialist culture.

I. In-depth explanation for the theory of Chinese socialism

A banner can guide our feet; a banner can enable us set our heart. The banner of socialism with Chinese characteristics is the one by which the path for development and progress in contemporary China is guided, and by which all the Party members and the people of all ethnic groups set our heart on endeavoring in unity. Under the new circumstances, people working in philosophy and social science circles should set as their goal the studying, publicizing, and implementing of the spirit of the Seventeenth National Congress. They should expound on the theories and guidelines of socialism with Chinese characteristics, with which the Party members should be armed, with which the solidarity and unity of the people should be maximized, so as to enable them to unswervingly follow the path of socialism with Chinese characteristics.

First, it should be driven home that Deng Xiaoping Theory, the important thought of the Three Represents, and the Scientific Outlook on Development constitute a sound theory that is both in keeping with Marxism-Leninism, Mao Zedong Thought and is in step with the times. Based on the essential characteristics of Marxism, namely inclusiveness, innovation and practicalness, people working in philosophy and social science circles shall clarify the theory of socialism with Chinese characteristics which originates from Marxism-Leninism and Mao Zedong Thought. They shall also, according to the new conditions of the times and the new requirements of practice, elucidate the development and innovation of socialism with Chinese characteristics achieved thorough Marxism-Leninism and Mao Zedong Thought. Based on the dialectical unity of the same origin and keeping up with the times, it is fair to say that "In contemporary China, staying true to socialism essentially means sticking to the path of socialism with Chinese characteristics."

Second, it should be driven home that the Scientific Outlook on Development is an important guideline for China's economic and social development, and a major strategic thought that must be adhered to and implemented in developing socialism with Chinese characteristics. People working in philosophy and social science circles shall fully demonstrate that the Scientific Outlook on Development proposed by the former CPC Central Committee with Hu Jintao as General Secretary is the succession and development of the past three generations of the country's leading groups and is a concentrated expression of Marxist worldview and methodology about development; they should correctly interpret its scientific connotation, essence and basic requirements; they should devote themselves particularly to the exploration of the relationship between implementing the Scientific Outlook on Development and building a socialist harmonious society, between deepening the Reform and Opening-up and strengthening Party building. Only through fully understanding the content and grasping the essence of the Scientific Outlook on Development can people enhance their consciousness and firmness in implementing the Outlook.

Third, it should be driven home that the reform and opening-up has its own historical background, nature, purpose, and achievements, and experience. At its 30th anniversary (1978-2008), people working in philosophy and social science circles should judiciously sum up the experience which has been harvested in the past decades' endeavors. They should make retrospect and reflection on the course of the reform and opening-up and the precious experience. They should understand that the Reform and Opening-up plays a key role in determining the destiny of contemporary China, that it is the only way to develop China's socialism and realize the great rejuvenation of the Chinese nation, that it is only socialism that could save China, that in China, only the reform and opening-up can boost development in aspects of economy, socialism, and Marxism, and that we should be more purposeful and determined in studying and applying the Party's basic theory, line, program and experience.

Fourth, the projects of studying and developing Marxist theory should be further strengthened. We must expand the study on the latest achievements of adapting Marxism to China's conditions, push forward the compilation of Marxist classics and the study of its basic points of views, promote the building of a system of disciplines and teaching materials in an all-round way and add the latest theoretical results of Sinicization of Marxism into the disciplines and textbooks of philosophy and social sciences. By implementing projects of these kinds, we should work to expand and train the teams of Marxist theoretical research and concentrate on the introduction of high-level Marxist theoretical research results, so that Marxist theoretical study and construction projects can play a leading, basic and leading role in upholding the political guiding principles of the CPC.

Fifth, we should work hard to enhance the popular appeal of Marxism in contemporary China. It is important to enable the latest achievements of the adaptation of Marxism to China's conditions to take root in the depth of the hearts of the people and be reflected in the concrete actions of all the people. This is an important political task for people working in the philosophy and social science circles in the new era. They must make great efforts to gear to the multi-level and diversified mental and cultural needs of the people, and work hard to increase the appeal of the theory of socialism with Chinese characteristics. They should go deep into real life, apply popular theoretical language, employ diversified and modern methods of Marxism publicity to answer in an easy-to-understand simple the questions that officials and the people are generally concerned about, analyze things clearly, resolve doubts, dispel doubts, and make the people genuinely believe, study, and apply Marxism.

II. Focus on addressing major practical issues while enhancing theoretical innovation

Now that China's reform and development are at a crucial juncture, a series of major issues concerning the future of socialism with Chinese characteristics urgently need to be resolved by people working in philosophy and social science circles. Under new circumstances, they should set major practical issues as their focus of work in a conscientious fashion, and devote themselves to the sound development of socialism with Chinese characteristics.

First, the research on practical issues of vital importance must be focused on promoting sound development and social harmony. On this journey of promotion, we are faced with a series of major practical problems that urgently need to be resolved, the presentation and resolution of which nearly concern the implementation of the Scientific Outlook on Development, the pursuit of a moderately prosperous society in all respects and the future of socialism with Chinese characteristics. People working in philosophy and social science circles should base themselves on the fundamental reality that we are still in the primary stage of socialism, deeply grasp the new issues and conflicts affecting the country's development, and hold up those problems from the light of economic, political, cultural, and social construction in a view to promote sound development and social harmony, and then rely on the advantages of various disciplines, actively tackle those problems, and strive to provide mental motivation and intellectual support for reform and opening up and socialist modernization.

Second, the theoretical innovation of Marxism should be pushed forward with major practical problems as the main direction. Each and every major theoretical innovation of Marxism is achieved by resolving major practical issues at the time. Integrating the principles of Marxism with the particular reality of the country so as to solve the major practical issues in accordance with the times is the cognition of regularity which had been developed in the Party's adaptation of Marxism to China's conditions. People working in philosophy and social science circles should delve into and solve the issues concerning the overall cause of the Party, the country and the people, and further adapt Marxism to China's conditions, so as to add elements to the socialist theory with Chinese characteristics in terms of its content, subjects and the time.

Third, the research on practical issues of vital importance must be carried out through adhering to the basic Marxist principles of combining theory with practice, and combining the concept of truth with that of value. To carry out the research on such issues through combining theory with practice, people working in philosophy and social science circles should must be close to reality, life and the people, be good at drawing wisdom from the great practice of reform and opening up and from the lively social life, and at promoting the fresh experience accumulated by the Party and the people into theoretical achievements. The research should be carried out through combining the concept of truth with that of value. The development of problem awareness is not only a matter of truth, but also indicates value orientation. The issues raised from different positions are essentially different, and therefore, their solutions also differ significantly. People working in philosophy and social science circles should proceed from the basic stance of the Party and the people. They should properly apply the positions, viewpoints and methods of Marxism, and propose and address the issues on the basis of upholding the unification of concepts of truth and value.

III. Strengthen the construction of system of core socialist values

In this new stage and in this new century, profound changes have taken place in the economic, social, and interest structure, and some setbacks have emerged in the moral construction, which cannot be neglected, and which has rendered unprecedentedly arduous the task to guide social ideology, enhance social integrity, and foster sound social trends. People working in philosophy and social science circles must be keenly aware and alert to potential risks, and hold their accountability consciousness high.

First, delve deeper into the significance of building the system of core socialist values. Building the system of core socialist values is the foundation of socialist cultural construction. In the wake of Western capitalism and its values, if we did not stick to the popularization and development of socialist culture, our unity of socialism would risk being weakened and finally dissolved. As a consequence, the realization of socialist modernization and the rejuvenation of the Chinese nation would fall into empty talks. From this point of view, people working in philosophy and social science circles should illustrate the practical and historical significance of building core socialist values, striving to increase the attractiveness and unity of socialist ideology. They should incorporate the socialist core values into all stages of national education and the entire process of cultural and ethical progress to make them the targets pursued by the people, of their own accord.

Second, the study of the core socialist value system should be deepened. people working in philosophy and social science circles must study in depth the socialist property of the core socialist value system and its essential distinction with other core social value systems, study basic connotations and practical requirements of all the basic elements of the core socialist value system, further study the dialectical relationship among all the basic elements that constitute the core value system, and try to explore the focus of efforts to build the socialist core value system; they must voluntarily set the building of the core socialist value system as their guidance, and strive to carry out their own research in different professional fields; they, standing at the forefront of the times and the society, should endeavor to innovate to nudge the entire nation forward, foster the mental strength of the whole nation to make progress and the mental bond of unity and harmony, and thereby consolidate the common ideological basis for endeavoring in unity of all the Party members and people of all ethnic groups.

Third, the effective ways should be explored to guide social trends of thought with core socialist values. People working in philosophy and social science circles will shoulder their share of responsibility to lead the social trends of thought with core socialist values and fulfill historic mission in the new era. They must properly understand the relationship between "one" and "many". By paying close attention to and carrying out in-depth analysis of the ideological foundation, concrete manifestation and social impact of various social ideological trends, they should clarify the fundamental difference between socialism with Chinese characteristics and social thoughts such as social democracy, neo-liberalism, and cultural conservatism. They need to explore new means to properly handle the problems which has appeared in the ideological and cultural fields. In a bid to seek guidance among values, consensus among diversity, they also need to grasp the ideological orientations of different classes and different groups accurately. With respect and inclusiveness, it is then possible to expand public support and common grounds and bring people of different levels and education backgrounds together to gain development.

IV Continue to enhance national cultural soft power by reform and innovation

Internally, philosophy and social sciences constitute the foundation and core of a nation-state culture, which is of great significance for achieving cultural prosperity. Externally, it is an important part of the national soft power, which is of irreplaceable significance. In present world, as culture becomes more prominent and important, the needs for innovation in this field are imperative.

First, the only way to make philosophy and social sciences prosper is sticking to the orientation of serving the people and socialism and the principle of "letting a hundred flowers blossom and a hundred schools of thought contend" and promoting innovations of discipline system, academic viewpoints and scientific research methods of philosophy and social sciences. Philosophy and social science researchers should study the current new situations, features and problems and promote the formation of new systems, ideas and methods in different fields. As for disciplinary innovation, it is necessary to innovate mechanisms of all important forms including Marxist theory. As far as academic views are concerned, new ideas, opinions and arguments should be put forward to deepen the study of socialism with Chinese characteristics. They must encourage, guide and participate in interdisciplinary research as well as promote the innovation of research methods in this respect.

Second, the administrative mechanism of philosophy and social sciences should be innovated to create a smooth institutional environment for more achievements and talents. It is necessary to further deepen the reform of philosophy and social science research and management system, establishing a talent management system and scientific research system, and allocating social science research resources and integrate research forces to form a joint research force. It is necessary to improve the operation mechanism of philosophy and social sciences, strengthen cooperation and enhance exchange. They need to improve the evaluation and incentive mechanism of philosophy and social sciences, adhere to the principles of quality first and social benefit first, pay attention to originality and actual benefit, and reward the involved workers with outstanding achievements. They need to properly handle the relationship between the macro-management system and the micro-operation mechanism of philosophy and social science construction, properly handle the relation between emphasizing discipline and encouraging creation, so as to mobilize all the wisdom and strength available.

Third, we must implement the strategy of philosophy and social sciences "going out" and promote the outstanding achievements and talents in this field to the world. In the face of the current huge gap between the output and input of culture in the country, more attention should be paid to implement the "going global" strategy. We should establish and improve mechanisms for the exchange of Chinese and foreign scholars, strengthen exchanges and cooperation with influential philosophy and social science institutions in other countries and carry out "academic diplomacy" and "cultural diplomacy", so as to expand the influence of Chinese philosophy and social sciences in the world. We should organize the translation and publication of a series of works that reflect the highest level of contemporary Chinese philosophy and social science research, promote China's outstanding achievements and talents in philosophy and social science to the world, participate in international academic dialogue, so as to showcase China's image as a country with freedom of thought, academic prosperity, democracy, progress, civilization and openness, and enhance the international influence of Chinese culture.

Basic Connotations of the Theory of Chinese Socialist Culture*

China's journey to modernization has taken a unique path for socialism with Chinese characteristics, which focuses on reform and opening up while building socialism with Chinese characteristics, and has formed the theory and system of socialism with Chinese characteristics. The essence of the cultural foundation for socialism with Chinese characteristics involves perspectives on the value and influence of culture, on the connections and relationships of cultural construction to economic, political, social civilization and ecological civilization construction, on how to build a culturally powerful nation with Chinese characteristics, and so on. The socialist culture with Chinese characteristics is not a "heterogeneous culture" born out of nowhere, but is deeply rooted in the long-standing and fine traditional culture of the Chinese people, rooted in the historical logic of social development since modern times and the great creations of the contemporary Chinese people, informed by distinctive nationality, practicality and contemporariness, and is a cultural type or form with unique composition and connotation that has an important influence on the lives of the Chinese people, China's development, and even the development of the world.

I. Historical background of formation of the theory of Chinese socialist culture

Socialist culture with Chinese characteristics has taken shape in conjunction with the history of socio-political reforms along with trends in social thoughts since modern times, and is committed to saving national cultural identity, building a common spiritual home and a world of significance for the Chinese nation, and ultimately achieving the rejuvenation of Chinese culture.

---

* Main content of this article was originally published in *Philosophical Research*, 2014(1).

The Opium Wars opened China's closed doors, and in consequence, Chinese culture was dragooned into world history by capitalist Western powers' overwhelming military might cannons, commodities, production mode, and ideology. Therefore, with the Western culture, which was defined as "advanced culture," making inroads into China, the traditional Chinese culture represented by Confucianism, Buddhism and Taoism was on the wane. At the critical moment when the nation was on the verge of being subjugated, the Chinese people, amidst doubts about traditional culture, gradually fell into a crisis of national cultural identity. What could be done to put an end to such a chaotic reality? Historical propositions and tasks needed to be put forward for the Chinese nation so that the cultural barriers of feudalism could be broken and Chinese culture could be reconstructed, so many dedicated Chinese patriots in different positions and factions, not only explored various paths to save the nation from subjugation and ensured its survival, but also delved into the questions of how to approach traditional culture and what culture should be built.

These dedicated patriots in the recent history of China, under the guidance of the ideological principle "Chinese learning as the essence and Western learning for its utility (*Zhongxue wei ti, xixue wei yong*)", sought to rejuvenate the Chinese nation through studying Western material technology and institutional culture, but all in vain. These failures compelled more radical revolutionaries to take an either-or stance, a tendency that completely exploded in the New Culture Movement. However, this approach, which relied solely on the Western values such as democracy and science and completely abandoned the national culture represented by Confucianism, obviously could not solve the crisis of cultural identity. Although many attempts have ended in failure, they have confirmed a truth: Against the historical background of the collision of Chinese and Western cultures, the construction of new cultural forms will definitely be accomplished by seeking reference to new Western cultural factors and integrating advanced Western cultural factors with Chinese culture. The key to the problem is to identify what kind of Western cultural factors to refer to, and how to combine them with Chinese culture. The Reform Movement of 1898 launched by Kang Youwei and Liang Qichao was only a "minor operation" within feudal culture because it did not touch China's feudal system and could not be understood by the bourgeoisie or even all the people. The "Three Principles of the People" (Nationalism, Democracy and the People's Livelihood) proposed by Dr. Sun Yat-sen overthrew the rule of Qing dynasty, but it also could not fundamentally shake the stubborn feudal system because it could not be understood by the vast majority of peasants.

In the meantime, the CPC integrated Marxism with China's reality, proposing a new culture for the Chinese nation, a new democratic culture that is national, scientific, and belonging to the people. While the CPC was leading the revolution, this new-democratic culture was valued as advanced culture, mobilizing all the people to strive for the country's independence and liberation as well as for their own interests, and thus the outlook of the people was dramatically renewed. This new-democratic culture changed China's destiny of being invaded by capitalist powers since the beginning of the modern times, and helped China achieve national independence and liberation and regain her national cultural self-confidence and self-esteem. Since the founding of the PRC in 1949, the Marxist mainstream ideology has been fully established through ideological and cultural criticism. Marxist ideological views, positions and methods quickly gained dominance in the academic, ideological, and theoretical circles in China. Ideological transformation was carried out among Chinese intellectuals to varying degrees, and the Chinese people also fostered their beliefs in Marxism and communism. However, compared to the monumental historical task of saving the nation from peril, cultural construction in this period obviously seemed inadequate. After its founding in 1949, new China excessively pursued cultural unification, which mainly resulted from practices such as incomplete or even one-sided understanding of Marxist theories, overemphasis on criticism and denial of Chinese traditional culture and Western culture, and inadequate inheritance from traditional culture and absorption of Western culture. These practices resulted in a monotonous, dull and even languishing culture, which otherwise could have been colorful and vigorous. They also caused huge losses in cultural resources, and scientific and technological talents who did not receive the respect and trust they deserved. It could be said that the cultural construction from 1949 to 1976 was no longer able to advance the construction of socialist modernization.

The reform and opening up launched in the late 1970s brought socialist construction back to the path of developing the productive forces, and enabled new opportunities for cultural development. When drawing the grand blueprint of constructing socialism with Chinese characteristics, Deng Xiaoping explicitly put forward the construction of mental civilization, placing great emphasis on developing science and technology and cultivating new socialist citizens with high ideals, moral integrity, good education and a strong sense of discipline. In the more than 30 years after the initiation of the reform and opening-up policy, great progress has been made in science, technology and education in China, which provided a strong intellectual supply and support for the rapid development of socialist modernization. However, during this period, more emphasis was placed on science and technology, with obvious insufficient focus on the construction of humanities and culture. Despite rapid economic and social advancement and significant improvement of the people's quality of material life, serious problems have emerged in the ideological and cultural realm at a national level, mainly manifested as a crisis of faith, trust and moral ethics.

With the continuous deepening of reform, the socialist market economy is developing in depth, beneficiary groups continue to diversify, and the benefit gap is also widening. The diversification of benefits has brought about stratification and ideological differentiation. The exchange principle of the market economy has penetrated all fields, resulting in serious money fetishism, hedonism, extreme individualism, historical nihilism and feudal superstition, and the mainstream ideology and culture of common socialist ideals, beliefs, and morality is in crisis. At the same time, the Western developed capitalist countries started ideological infiltration with their core ideological values, which has brought greater difficulties to the formation of social consensus in socialist China. Considering their own interests and standings, some people inside and outside the CPC, both at home and abroad, put forward various propositions for what path China should follow in the future and what guiding principles it should uphold. Some people advocated the Western liberalist road or democratic socialist road; Others advocated returning to the old way of a highly centralized society modeled after the Soviet Union; some people accused China of taking the path of state capitalism or crony capitalism. To make matters worse, the rise of historical nihilism distorted and maliciously attacked theories, policies and leadership of the CPC, the revolutionary history since modern times, and the history of New China. In addition, marketization, globalization, industrialization, informatization and urbanization have greatly changed people's production methods, lifestyles, and ways of thinking, and have had a great impact on China's traditional culture. The precious resources of traditional Chinese culture have been severely drained. Nowadays, the essence of Chinese traditional culture, such as filial piety, benevolence, trust and justice, is increasingly dismissed. Viewing money as a measurement of value has gained increasing popularity among the Chinese people. Meanwhile, people's sense of faith and morality has been squeezed into a tiny corner and is completely non-existent for some people. Unrighteous phenomena have emerged one after another, such as production and sale of fake products, swindling and abduction. When monetary interests are involved, people's capacity for family affection, friendship and true love are weakened. It could be said that Marxist beliefs have been shaken, Chinese traditional culture has drifted away, and there has been a serious cultural and moral crisis since 1978. A new value system has not yet been established, and socialism with Chinese characteristics is clearly in a state of anomie during this period of social transformation.

Nevertheless, we should also notice that the rapid economic development in China since 1978 has greatly boosted national self-esteem and self-confidence, and that the socialist cultural system with Chinese characteristics based on the socialist theory and system with Chinese characteristics is also developing its own attraction. This is an era when Chinese culture encounters new shocks and challenges, and this is also an era of great opportunities for new development. Put simply, on the one hand, Chinese culture is being creatively reconstructed in the new situation, history, and space, radiating great vitality and building strong national confidence; on the other hand, it is in a state of disunity with the disintegration of mainstream culture and the collapse of faith and morality. For a long time, cultural dimension and cultural construction have not received due attention and research. It will take a significant amount of time to build a strong Chinese culture that reflects the characteristics of traditional Chinese culture, explains and supports China's current experience, and strengthens national identity. It is impossible for us to complete the construction of socialism with Chinese characteristics and the great rejuvenation of the Chinese nation if there is no strong Chinese culture, especially in today's climate of increasingly fierce international competition and cultural confrontation, with great changes and adjustments unprecedented in the history of Chinese society. Obviously, the CPC has fully realized the seriousness and importance of this problem, has put forward a series of new viewpoints on the basis of sifting through and carrying forward the existing thinking and framework of cultural development, and has formed a systematic theory of socialist culture with Chinese characteristics.

II. Pathway of the founding of the theory of Chinese socialist culture

Socialist culture with Chinese characteristics is an important part of the socialist modernization in China. The theory of socialism with Chinese characteristics essentially answers the question of how to modernize China. According to the historical circumstances of China's modernization, the development of the theory of socialist culture with Chinese characteristics can be divided into three stages: brainstorming, ideation and formation. In the brainstorming stage, in the exploration of tapping people's talent and rebuilding national cultural identity, the construction principle of combining Marxism and Chinese native cultural thoughts was gradually formed, namely, "developing a national, scientific and popular socialist culture", which basically established the foundation and future direction of socialist culture with Chinese characteristics. In the stage of ideation, the specific concept of "socialist culture with Chinese characteristics" was formally put forward in the process of exploring the expansion of reform from the economic field to other fields, outlined by the broad strokes of "mental civilization", with socialism with Chinese characteristics as the general outline of the reform. In the stage of formation, with the development of the cause of building socialism with Chinese characteristics, the importance and urgency of cultural construction have become more prominent. In order to gear to the new characteristics of the development of the times and the new international and domestic situations, and respond to the problems in the cultural field, we constantly put forward specific cultural viewpoints and theories, and thus enable the content of the socialist culture with Chinese characteristics to be periodically enriched and improved, and a systematic theory of socialist culture with Chinese characteristics to be formed.

1. Brainstorming: the theory of new-democratic culture

Taking Marxism as the logic reference, Mao Zedong reconstructed the ideology and culture under new historical circumstances, proposed the development of a national, scientific and popular socialist culture, and formed the systemic theory of the cultural propositions of the CPC.

Firstly, he pointed out the importance of building a new culture. And he said: "For many years we Communists have struggled for a cultural revolution as well as for a political and economic revolution, and our aim is to build a new society and a new state for the Chinese nation. That new society and new state will have not only a new politics and a new economy but a new culture."[①] This statement affirms that culture is as important as politics and economy in the revolution and construction of a new country, that is, the rejuvenation of the Chinese nation means not only the achievement of political independence and economic prosperity, but also the elimination of the old feudal culture, the construction of a new culture and the realization of cultural rejuvenation.

---

① *Selected Works of Mao Zedong*, Vol. 2, Chin. ed., Beijing: People's Publishing House, 1991, p. 663.

Secondly, Mao Zedong judiciously and clearly explained the Marxist cultural outlook based on the historical materialism, and put forward the basic principles for constructing a new culture. He said: "Any given culture (as an ideological form) is a reflection of the politics and economics of a given society, and reciprocally, culture has tremendous influence and effect upon the politics and economics; economics is the base and politics the concentrated expression of economics. This is our fundamental view of the relation of culture to politics and economics and of the relation of politics to economics."① Correct understanding and interpreting of Marxist cultural theory is the prerequisite for the construction of a new Chinese culture. At the same time, Mao Zedong also pointed out the way to construct a new culture, that is, to combine Marxism with China's historical traditions and immediate needs to form a "national form". "Chinese communists must fully and properly integrate the universal truth of Marxism with the concrete practice of the Chinese revolution, or in other words, the universal truth of Marxism must be combined with specific national characteristics and acquire a definite national form if it is to be useful, and in no circumstances can it be applied subjectively as a mere formula."② In other words, the construction of Chinese new culture should be based on its culture, history and reality. "China's present new politics and new economy have developed out of her old politics and old economy, and her present new culture, too, has developed out of her old culture."③ And the construction of Chinese new culture should be completed in the cultural collision and exchange with other nations in the world. "China needs to assimilate a good deal of foreign progressive culture to nourish her own culture. Such assimilation of beneficial foreign cultures was not done sufficiently in the past."④

Finally, based on the previous two viewpoints, Mao Zedong put forward the theory of new-democratic culture:

> New-democratic culture is national. It opposes imperialist oppression and upholds the dignity and independence of the Chinese nation. It belongs to our own nation and bears our own national characteristics. It links up with the socialist and new-democratic cultures of all other nations and they are related in such a way that they can absorb something from each other and help each other

---

① *Selected Works of Mao Zedong*, Vol. 2, Chin. ed., Beijing: People's Publishing House, 1991, p.663.
② Ibid., p.707.
③ Ibid., p.708.
④ Ibid., p.706.

to develop, together forming a new world culture; but as a revolutionary national culture it can never link up with any reactionary imperialist culture of whatever nation...

New-democratic culture is scientific. Opposed as it is to all feudal and superstitious ideas, it stands for seeking truth from facts, for objective truth and for the unity of theory and practice...

New-democratic culture belongs to all the people and is therefore democratic. It should serve the toiling masses of workers and peasants who make up more than 90 per cent of China's population, and should gradually become their very own.[①]

Facts prove that the national, scientific and popular new-democratic culture guided by Marxism is the only correct way to realize the cultural transformation of modern China, and it is also a guide to action for the Chinese nation's independence and liberation. It has inspired the national spirit of the Chinese nation and the revolutionary fighting spirit of the people throughout the country, and thus has played a crucial role in the victory of the Chinese revolution. The theory of new-democratic culture has provided the basic stand, principle and framework for developing socialist culture with Chinese characteristics, and has served as a primary foundation for the path of socialist culture with Chinese characteristics, laying the foundation for the formation of the socialist cultural theory with Chinese characteristics.

2. Ideation: from "mental culture" to "Chinese socialist culture"

Before the policy of reform and opening up was introduced, fundamental questions of what socialism is and how to carry out socialist construction were not yet fully understood. Consequently, mistakes were made in the selection of guiding ideology of socialist modernization, causing major setbacks in modernization. In general, cultural development was engulfed in the political struggle and the new-democratic cultural principle proposed by Mao Zedong was not implemented very well. Although the Marxist ideology was established, the fine traditional culture of China was not been properly inherited while the advanced Western culture was also denied and excluded. After the policy of reform and opening up was adopted, Deng

---

① *Selected Works of Mao Zedong*, Vol. 2, Chin. ed., Beijing: People's Publishing House, 1991, p.706-708.

Xiaoping created the theory of socialism with Chinese characteristics on the basis of redefining China's national conditions and the essence of socialism. With the economic construction established as the center, the blueprint has also been drawn for mental civilization construction and cultural construction as an organic part of the theory of socialism with Chinese characteristics.

The reform and opening up policy under the leadership of Deng Xiaoping set right the course of socialism in China, and also kicked off the transformation of cultural construction, focusing on the construction of both mental civilization and economic construction. "The socialist China we are building should have a civilization with a high cultural and ideological level as well as a high material level. When I speak of a civilization with a high cultural and ideological level, I refer not only to education, science and culture (which are of course indispensable) but also to communist thinking, ideals, beliefs, morality and discipline."① Deng Xiaoping emphasized on both material and mental civilization, and pointed out that if we only did a good job in economic construction but failed to improve mental civilization and the people's ideological and moral status had not improved, then it was not socialism with Chinese characteristics.

Since cultural transformation is based on the liberation and development of the productive forces, the focus of cultural construction in this period is science and culture. Under the guidance of Deng Xiaoping's "science and technology is the primary productive force," the development of science and technology has received unprecedented attention. In 1982, Deng Xiaoping definitely proposed to train citizens to be goal-oriented, moral, educated, and disciplined. And intellectuals were more and more respected and given more crucial roles. Fostering new socialist citizens became an important aspect of cultural construction. With the advent of the "knowledge economy", cultural construction has developed into strategy of "cultural innovation". In 1992, Jiang Zemin first mentioned the issue of "innovation" when delivering the speech to the Fourteenth National Congress of the CPC. In 1995, he pointed out in the speech at the national conference on science and technology: "Innovation is the soul of a nation's progress and provides an inexhaustible force for driving a country's prosperity. We will never be able to solve the problem of our country's technological backwardness if we fail to improve our capacity for independent innovation and rely

---

① Deng Xiaoping: *Selected Works of Deng Xiaoping,* Vol. 2, Chin. ed., Beijing: People's Publishing House, 1994, p. 367.

solely on foreign technology. A nation without the ability to innovate can hardly join the ranks of the world's advanced nation."①

As the theory of socialism with Chinese characteristics was initiated and became mature, in the report to the Fifteenth CPC National Congress, it is proposed that "building a socialist culture with Chinese characteristics means taking Marxism as the guidance, aiming at training citizens so that they are goal-orientated, moral, educated and disciplined, and developing a national, scientific and mass socialist culture geared to the needs of modernization, of the world and of the future".② On February 25, 2000, Jiang Zemin put forward the concept of advanced socialist culture when inspecting work in Guangdong Province, and clearly pointed out that the CPC must always represent the direction of advancement of China's advanced culture, indicating that the CPC has a more conscious responsibility for cultural development. This is a major theoretical proposition in the country's cultural construction, and it will provide important guidance for future cultural development.

The socialist culture with Chinese characteristics is the inheritance and development of Mao Zedong's new democratic cultural theory, and it is consistent with Deng Xiaoping's theory of mental civilization construction. As is pointed out in the report to the Fifteenth CPC National Congress, "Socialist culture with Chinese characteristics, as far as its substance is concerned, is identical to socialist ideological and ethical progress we have been promoting since we introduced the reform and opening up. Culture is relative to the economy and politics, while ideological and ethical progress is relative to material progress. Culture in a broad sense refers to the sum of material civilization and mental civilization created by human beings in social and historical practice. The concept of culture, in a broad sense, is the same as that of civilization in a broad sense. In a narrow sense, culture refers to the parallel with economics and politics, that is, the mental content related to human social life such as ideology, morality, literature and art, education, and science."③

The initiation of the concept of "socialist culture with Chinese characteristics" indicates that the main theme and the basic course of the socialist culture with

---

① Jiang Zemin: *Selected Works of Jiang Zemin*, Vol.1, Chinse ed., Beijing: People's Publishing House, 2006, p. 432.]
② Ibid., p. 537.
③ Documentation Research Office of the CPC Central Committee: *Selected Documents Since the Fifteenth National Congress of the CPC*, Vol.1, Chin. ed., *Beijing*: People's Publishing House, 2000, p. 35.

Chinese characteristics has been basically made clear. Culture, as an important sector of the development of socialism with Chinese characteristics, is formally proposed, showcasing the profound internal connection between cultural construction and China's modern economic and political construction. However, a series of viewpoints and theories concerning the content, development path and development goals of the socialist culture with Chinese characteristics are yet to be enriched.

3. Formation: enrichment and integration of content of Chinese socialist culture

After the Fifteenth CPC National Congress convened in 1997 and especially after the Sixteenth CPC National Congress in 2002, with the rapid development of China's economy and society, the problems in the cultural field have become more and more prominent, and so has the backwardness and inadequacy of cultural development. A series of new viewpoints on cultural reform and development are thus spawned and finally integrated into a systematic theory of the development of socialist culture with Chinese characteristics.

First of all, great importance should be attached to the cause of prospering philosophy and social sciences, and regard the development and prosperity of philosophy and social sciences as an extremely important content of cultural construction. In order to consolidate the ideological system guided by Marxism and promote the academic research of philosophy and social sciences, in January 2004, the CPC Central Committee issued the "Opinions on Further Prospering and Developing Philosophy and Social Sciences"; on May 28, 2004, at the thirteenth group study session of the Political Bureau of the 16th CPC Central Committee, Hu Jintao emphasized that we must take the development and prosperity of philosophy and social sciences as a major and urgent strategic task from the strategic perspective of the overall development of the cause of the Party and the country, and earnestly push it into implementation, so as to promote a new and greater development of philosophy and social sciences in China and provide strong ideological guarantee, immaterial motivation and intellectual support for the cause of building socialism with Chinese characteristics.

Based on the refinement of the understanding of the nature of culture under the socialist market economy, in the report to the Sixteenth CPC National Congress, "cultural industries" is proposed and for the first time the distinguishment between cultural undertakings and cultural industries has been made. The Fourth Plenary Session of the 16th CPC Central Committee, held from September 9 to 16, 2004, proposed to uphold the guiding position of Marxism in the field of ideology and continuously improve the ability to build advanced socialist culture; deepen the reform of the cultural system to "liberate and develop cultural productivity." Based on the fact that the overall level of public cultural services in China is still relatively low, and the gap between urban and rural areas and regions is still relatively large, the Fifth Plenary Session of the 16th CPC Central Committee, held from October 8 to 11, 2005, emphasized the need to build a public cultural service system, actively develop cultural undertakings, vigorously develop cultural industries, and create more excellent cultural products that meet the needs of the people. It also proposes to improve the cultural industry policy, and form a cultural industry pattern with public ownership as the main body and multiple ownership systems developing together, and a cultural market pattern with national culture as the main body and absorbing beneficial foreign culture. With the continuous deepening of reforms and the in-depth development of the socialist market economy, there has been a diversification of interests and ideologies, which even resulted in anomie and incredibility in the field of ideology and morality. The Sixth Plenary Session of the 16th CPC Central Committee, held from October 10 to 11, 2006, explicitly states that we should build up the system of core socialist value. As an economic power, China has not yet demonstrated its cultural influence in the world. The Seventeenth CPC National Congress put forth the concept of "cultural soft power" in the Party's documents for the first time. With a new upsurge of cultural development, General Secretary Hu Jintao stated in his speech on July 1st, 2011 that "We must have a keen sense of our own cultural identity, have confidence in our culture" and so on.

More importantly, the issue of major development and great enrichment of socialist culture was discussed in the Sixth Plenary Session of the 17th CPC Central Committee in 2011. It was the first time that the CPC had held a plenary session devoted to a cultural issue. And the "Decision of the CPC Central Committee on Several Major Issues Concerning Deepening the Reform of the Cultural System and Promoting the Great Development and Prosperity of Socialist Culture" (hereinafter referred to as the "Decision") was adopted, which summarized the accomplishments and experience gained from the CPC's practice and theoretical explorations of cultural development during the periods of China's revolution, construction, reform, and put forward some new ideas, forming a new, complete and systematic cultural theory. For the first time, the strategy of "building a strong socialist cultural power" was proposed, and the particular goals for cultural reform and development in 2020 were formulated, and a systematic deployment was made for the current and future period of cultural development. This plenary session and the decisions it made for cultural development reflect the awareness of our ruling party and of the whole society to promote cultural advancement, marking the basic formation of the socialist cultural theory with Chinese characteristics.

Since then, in the boom of cultural construction, the theory of socialist culture with Chinese characteristics has been constantly improved. In the report to the Eighteenth National Congress of the CPC in 2012, socialist core values are further refined. The 2013 National Publicity and Theoretical Work Conference particularly emphasized the extreme importance of doing a good job in ideological work and maintaining cultural security under the new international and domestic complex and changing situation, etc.

III. Basic connotations of Chinese socialist culture

As seen from the process of formation mentioned above, the socialist cultural theory with Chinese characteristics has very rich connotations that need to be interpreted from many different perspectives.

1.About status of culture: as an important part in "five-sphere integrated plan" of Chinese socialism

The CPC has first and foremost understood the status and function of culture from the overall perspective through taking it as one of the important components of the great cause of building socialism with Chinese characteristics, and thus the meaning of socialist culture with Chinese characteristics is first understood through putting it in the overall plan of this great cause. After long-term exploration, the CPC has succinctly generalized economic, political, cultural, social, and ecological progress as what is called "the five-sphere integrated plan" of socialism with Chinese characteristics, with culture as one of its important components.

It is indicated in the report to the Fifteenth CPC National Congress: "Socialist culture with Chinese characteristics is a major force uniting and inspiring the people of all our nationalities, and an important indicator of our overall national strength. This culture originated from the 5,000-year-old civilization of the Chinese nation and is deeply rooted in our endeavor to build socialism with Chinese characteristics. It has distinctive features of the times, representing the basic features of our socialist economy and politics and playing a great role in promoting their development."① As is stated in the "Decision on Several Issues Concerning the Socialist Market Economic System" formulated in the Third Plenary Session of the 16th CPC Central Committee, held from October 11 to 14, 1978, "We must continue to ensure coordinated development of the socialist material well-being, political and ethical civilization. The socialism with Chinese characteristics is a great cause in which socialist market economy, socialist democracy and advanced socialist culture develop coordinately."② Hu Jintao emphasized that "Deepening cultural system reform and coordinately promoting cultural, economic, political and social advancement have been natural elements to achieve sound development."③ The "Decision" passed at the Sixth Plenary Session of the 17th CPC Central Committee, held from October 15 to 18, 2011, indicated that "We must keep economic development as our central task; and we must take cultural prosperity as an important part of development that is regarded as the absolute principle; as the top priority of the Party in governing, and as a essential requirement of thoroughly applying the Scientific Outlook on Development, to further promote the coordinated culture, economy, politics, social and ecological development." ④ It is in the report to the Eighteenth National Congress that economic, political, cultural, social, and ecological progress is generalized as "the five-sphere integrated plan" for building socialism with Chinese characteristics, in which culture is a crucial part. On August 19, 2013, Xi Jinping further stressed the importance of cultural advancement in a speech he delivered at the National Publicity and Theoretical Work Conference: "Economic construction is the Party's central task, and ideological progress is one of its top priorities." The basis for public support and for the Party's governance include material basis of life and mental basis of culture, so we must conscientiously do a good job not only in the central work so as to provide a solid material basis for ideological work, but also in ideological work so as to provide a strong guarantee for the central work.

---

① Jiang Zemin: *Selected Works of Jiang Zemin*, Vol.2, Chin. ed., Beijing: People's Publishing House, 2006, p.33.
② Documentation Research Office of the CPC Central Committee. *Selected Documents Since the Sixteenth National Congress of the CPC*, Vol.1, Beijing: Central Party Literature Press, 2005, p. 481]
③ Hu Jintao: "Speech at the 22nd Group Study Session of the Political Bureau of the 17th CPC Central Committee (July 23, 2010)", *People's Daily*, 2010-7-24.
④ *Decision of the CPC Central Committee on Deepening the Reform of the Cultural System to Promote the Great Development and Prosperity of Socialist Culture*, Beijing: People's Publishing House, 2011, p. 5.

These statements show that the CPC has a clear positioning of the important status of cultural construction in the entire construction of socialism with Chinese characteristics and its relationship with "construction" in other spheres. First and foremost, in the entire process of building socialism with Chinese characteristics, cultural construction should be placed as important as economic, political, social and ecological construction. Next, cultural development should be understood from the perspective of the Scientific Outlook on Development. It means overall, coordinated, and balanced development. Such an outlook follows the laws of social development interpreted by historical materialism; that is, the decisive factor for the development of social history is the productive forces, but the production relations and the superstructure have adverse effects on the productive forces and the economic base. Social development is the result of interaction among economy, politics, culture, geographical environment and other factors. As is shown by the laws disclosed by historical materialism, human history and the realistic practices, we must pay attention to the role of human mind and the power of mental world, especially the values or the great role of cultural development in the socialist modernization drive; we should link culture with politics, economy, society and ecology, so as to achieve the interaction between them and the joint positive development. However, the road, which we often talk about, still has twists and turns when we attempt to apply them into practice. As has been proved by the problems which occurred in the ten-year Cultural Revolution (1966-1976) and in present-day world, we have not really dealt well with the relationship between them in practice.

2.About functions of culture: both soft power and hard power

The socialist culture with Chinese characteristics has strong forces of guidance, cohesion and innovation. As pointed out in the report to the Fifteenth CPC National Congress, "Socialist culture with Chinese characteristics is a major force uniting and inspiring the people of all ethnic groups, and an important indicator of our overall national strength. This culture originated from the 5,000-year-old civilization of the Chinese nation and is deeply rooted in our endeavor to build socialism with Chinese characteristics. It has distinctive features of the times, representing the basic features of our socialist economy and politics and playing a great role in promoting their development."[1] With the deepening of reform and development and the emergence

---

[1] Jiang Zemin: *Selected Works of Jiang Zemin*, Vol.2, Beijing: People's Publishing House, 2006, p.33.

of various problems, the Party has realized that the power of mental culture plays an increasingly prominent role in this era. As pointed out in the report to the Sixteenth CPC National Congress, "In the present-day world, culture is interactive with economic and political activities, and its status and functions are becoming more and more outstanding in the competition in overall national strength. The power of culture is deeply rooted in the vitality, creativity and cohesion of a nation."[①] Hu Jintao addressed that "Nowadays, culture plays an increasingly important role in the competition of comprehensive national strength. Whoever occupies the commanding height of cultural development will be able to take the initiative in the fierce international competition."[②] It is also pointed out in the report to the Seventeenth National Congress that "Culture has become a more and more important source of national cohesion and creativity and a factor of growing significance in the competition in overall national strength, and the Chinese people have an increasingly ardent desire for a richer cultural life."[③] As pointed out in the "Proposal of the CPC Central Committee on Formulating the Twelfth Five-Year Plan for National Economic and Social Development" adopted in the Fifth Plenary Session of the 17th CPC Central Committee in 2010, culture is a nation's spirit and soul, and is a powerful source of strength that develops and revitalizes a country and a nation, so much effort should be made to give full play to the role of culture in guiding and educating people and promoting development, to build a spiritual home for the Chinese nation, to boost cohesion and creativity of the nation. Advanced socialist culture constitutes a guiding political principle of the Marxist political party. All of these documents elaborated on the important status and role of culture, but such elaboration is scattered and incomplete. The "Decision" passed at the Sixth Plenary Session of the 17th CPC Central Committee in 2011 fully and systematically elaborated on the status and function of culture. First, culture to a nation is what blood is to the body, and it is the common spiritual home for the public. The strength of culture, like blood, is deeply rooted in the vitality of a nation, sustaining and supporting the nation's production and development. A nation with a barren mind and a backward culture would sooner

---

① Documentation Research Office of the CPC Central Committee: *Selected Documents Since the Sixteenth National Congress of the CPC*, Vol.1, Beijing: Central Party Literature Press, 2005, p.341.
② Documentation Research Office of the CPC Central Committee. *Selected Documents Since the Sixteenth National Congress of the CPC*, Vol.3, Beijing: Central Party Literature Press, 2005, p.752.
③ Documentation Research Office of the CPC Central Committee: *Selected Documents Since the Seventeenth National Congress of the CPC*, Vol.1, Beijing: Central Party Literature Press, 2009, p.26.

or later become the vassal of others. Second, the CPC summarized the status and role of culture in four aspects: 1) culture has increasingly become an important source of national cohesion and creativity; 2) culture has increasingly become a factor of growing significance in the competition in overall national strength; 3) culture has increasingly become a pivotal support for economic and social development; 4) the Chinese people has increasingly become an ardent desire for a richer cultural life. The elaboration given above shows that the significance of culture understood by the Party has reached a new height, which means culture has been exalted from one area in the superstructure to an important part in "the five-sphere integrated plan"; from the vague concept of "retro-action" to a clear explanation, "guidance of value" and "source of innovation"; and from ideological cognition in mental realm and political discourse of ideology to economic discourse of cultural industry.

Proceeding from the current trend of world development and bearing in mind the overall layout of building socialism with Chinese characteristics, the CPC has profoundly understood the connotations and functions of culture. Culture has become an important field of international competition for a leading strategic position, and cultural soft power contest and confrontation have become more and more fierce, and in contemporary times, culture has come to the fore from a recessive force to an explicit new practical force. First of all, culture is also a kind of "hard power," and is a productive force. With the improvement of people's living standards in China, people's cultural consumption ability has gradually increased. As a new sunrise industry, the cultural industry has become more and more important in the economic development of various countries, and has increasingly become a pillar industry in the economic development of various countries. After 30 years of reform and opening up, the demographic dividend has begun to gradually weakened with the rapid expansion of the extensive economy, so improving the cultural quality of the workers has become an important support for changing the economic growth mode and accelerating economic development. Secondly, culture is a kind of "soft power." Cultural soft power is an important part of overall national strength, which is reflected in its capacity of guidance, attraction, exemplification and radiation. A great culture not only has the guiding power to play in leading ideological trends, sublimating ideas, purifying morality, cultivating souls and strengthening willpower, but also has a powerful radiation on other nations, making them emulate. At the same time, it is embodied as the powers of identification, affinity and cohesion. Culture is an "adhesive" to maintain national sentiments, and is an important factor of gaining national identity and gather national strength. Thirdly, culture is an innovative competence strength and a powerful driving force for the development of a nation-state. Innovation is the basic way for human beings to survive and develop, and cultural innovation has become the paradigm and foundation of the creativity of a nation-state in modern times. The reorientation of the new characteristics and functions of contemporary culture is an important content of basic connotation of the socialist cultural theory with Chinese characteristics.

3. Fostering new citizens in Chinese socialist culture

Culture is essentially rooted in human activities of understanding and transforming the world. It also entails the evaluation of human activities and achievements. As a general term, it encompasses the ways of thinking, values, modes of activity, institutional norms, aesthetic tastes, and human customs. Culture is the result of "becoming human," and in turn, is also a mode of "shaping people." Socialist culture with Chinese characteristics needs to encourage the production of more cultural works that reflect people's life. More importantly, it must pay attention to people and train them in the process of creating a lively culture, and improve people's cultural quality and cultural taste through advanced culture, thus enriching people's mental world and enhancing their mental strength. Great culture is generated in people's practical activities and achieves the purpose of "cultivation" through cultural consumption. Socialist culture with Chinese characteristics places the cultivation of new socialist citizens at the core of cultural construction. Deng Xiaoping once pointed out that "The guarantee to build a socialist civilization is mainly to inculcate ideals, morality, knowledge and discipline in all our people."[1] Jiang Zemin once stated that "Building socialist culture with Chinese characteristics means adopting Marxism as our guide with the goal of training citizens to have high ideals, moral integrity, a good education and a strong sense of discipline."[2] It is emphasized in the report to the Eighteenth National Congress of the CPC that we must enable culture to guide social trends, educate the people, serve society, and boost development.

(a) Ideals and convictions of Marxism and Communism should be adhered to. Marxism is the mainstream ideology of the Party and the state. Strengthening

---

[1] Deng Xiaoping: *Selected Works of Deng Xiaoping*, Vol.2, Chinse ed., Beijing: People's Publishing House,1994, p. 408.
[2] Jiang Zemin: *Selected Works of Jiang Zemin*, Vol.2, Chinse ed., Beijing: People's Publishing House, 2006, p.537.

Marxism and adhering to the ideals and convictions of socialism and communism are the mental characteristics of socialism with Chinese characteristics, and also are the rational methodological guidance, important ideological guarantee and essential characteristics of the CPC leading the people in the drive to modernize.

As Deng Xiaoping pointed out, "From my long political and military experience I have learned that unity is of prime importance and that to achieve unity people must have common ideals and firm convictions. Over the past several decades, we have united the people on the basis of firm convictions that enabled them to struggle for their own interests. Without such convictions, there would have been no cohesion among the people, and we could have accomplished nothing. The highest goal of Communists is to realize communism, but in each historical stage we have a different program of struggle that represents the interests of the overwhelming majority of the people in that particular period. That is why we have been able to unite the people and mobilize them to act with one heart and one mind. With unity like that, we can overcome any difficulty or setback."[1] Jiang Zemin stressed that "Education about our ideal and conviction is the core of the Party's ideological and political work. Only by fostering correct ideals and beliefs firmly among the entire Party membership and the people of all our nations can we continuously enhance the rallying power and combat capability, ensure successive victories for our cause."[2] In the "Speech at the Second Session of the Third Plenary Session of the 17th CPC Central Committee"(October 12, 2008), Hu Jintao pointed out that "We must firmly focus on ideal and conviction, unswervingly arm the whole Party membership with the theory of socialism with Chinese characteristics and use it to educate our people, taking Marxism adapted to contemporary China's conditions to the general public. We must consolidate the guiding position of Marxism in the ideological sphere of our country; we must uphold shared ideal of socialism with Chinese characteristics as well as the common ideological foundation for the concerted endeavor of the people of all ethnic groups."[3] As is showed in the report to the Eighteenth CPC National Congress, we

---

[1] Deng Xiaoping: *Selected Works of Deng Xiaoping,* Vol.3, Chinse ed., Beijing: People's Publishing House,1993, p.190.
[2] Jiang Zemin: *Selected Works of Jiang Zemin,* Vol.3, Chinse ed., Beijing: People's Publishing House, 2006, p.89.
[3] The Publicity Department and the Party Literature Research Center of the CPC Central Committee: *On Cultural Construction: Excerpts of Important Remarks,* Beijing: *Xuexi* Publishing House & Central Party Literature Press, 2012, p. 34.

should unswervingly take the path of socialism with Chinese characteristics, and it declared that we should have every confidence in the socialist path, theory, system and culture with Chinese characteristics. The report also stressed the importance of upholding Communists' ethical pursuing: "Communists' faith in Marxism, socialism and communism is their political soul and sustains them in all tests."[①] General Secretary Xi Jinping, in the speech he delivered on January 5, 2013 at the seminar of the members and alternate members of the newly-elected CPC Central Committee for implementing the guiding principles of the Party's Eighteenth National Congress, judiciously summarized the six development stages of socialism and correctly sorted out the origin, formation and development of socialism with Chinese characteristics; focused on clarifying and answering the four major questions about socialism with Chinese characteristics; acquired a more accurate understanding of the essence of socialism with Chinese characteristics, pointed out the great significance of adhering to Marxism, adhering to socialism and strengthening the ideals and convictions of socialism. In his speech at the National Publicity and Theoretical Work Conference, Xi Jinping also pointed out that Marxist and communist ideals are the lifeblood and soul of communists, and the lack of ideals is an issue that needs to be taken seriously. Our publicity and theoretical work aim to consolidate Marxism as the guiding ideology in China, and cement the shared ideological basis of the whole Party and the people. Lofty beliefs and firm convictions will not arise spontaneously. We must arm our minds with sound theories and continue to build our spiritual home.

Faith serves as a person's mental pillar and life guide, and it is at the core of a person's mental world. A lack of faith will lead to mental slack, while adherence to wrong beliefs will destroy one's life. Adhering to scientific socialism and strengthening the ideals and convictions of socialism are the essential stipulations of the CPC, as well as the mental characteristics and soul of all Chinese people. Only by adhering to these ideals and convictions will the CPC not be mentally slack and degenerate. Similarly, only by educating all the people with socialist ideals and convictions and gathering strength and consensus over the common ideals of socialism with Chinese characteristics can we resist all kinds of erroneous thoughts and propositions, and can socialism with Chinese characteristics achieve great success. In short, belief in Marxism and belief in communism are the mental

---

① The 18th National Congress of the PC Report Document Drafting Team. *The 18th National Congress Report: A Guide Reader*, Beijing: People's Publishing House, 2012, p. 50.

characteristics of socialism with Chinese characteristics.

(b) People's scientific and cultural quality should be improved. Every major change in history has been caused by a scientific and technological revolution. Science and technology have become the primary productive force and the most important factor of overall national strength, and they have also profoundly changed people's way of life. People's scientific and cultural quality directly determines China's scientific and technological innovation, and directly determines the great progress of China's socialist modernization. As Jiang Zemin pointed out, "Only by developing national, scientific and popular socialist culture geared to the needs of modernization, of the world and of the future, can we meet people's ever-increasing needs for culture, continue to promote their ethical, cultural and scientific qualities so as to lead correct direction and provide strong intellectual support for developing economy and productive forces."[①] What needs to be pointed out is that scientific and cultural quality cannot be understood as merely the quality of natural science theory and a certain skill. It also includes humanities and social sciences. Improving the system of national governance and improving national governance capabilities require not only the support of science and technology, but also the guidance of theories of philosophy and social sciences. It is necessary to carry out in-depth study of and have a good mastery of the laws and operating mechanisms of social, economic, and political development to minimize conflicts, effectively allocate resources, and maximize the "collective efforts" of the people. To develop the socialist culture with Chinese characteristics, it is also necessary to construct a system of academic discourse with Chinese characteristics, have an equal dialogue with the Western system of discourse, and demonstrate and expand the influence of Chinese academics in the international arena.

(c) The construction of a socialist moral system and the improvement of people's moral quality should be strengthened. Morality determines people's behavior and value orientation, and is the cornerstone for social harmony; the level of morality is a pivotal symbol of the level of national civilization. Being equally honest with and caring for everyone, young and old, condemning wickedness and commending morality are obligations that everyone who lives in the community should carry out voluntarily. Without the support of moral force, a nation cannot stand strong and

---

① Jiang Zemin: *Selected Works of Jiang Zemin*, Vol.3, Chin. ed., Beijing: People's Publishing House, 2006, p.400.

prosperous.

Morality has been advocated by the Chinese nation since ancient times, and was even regarded by the ancient people as the foundation for people settling down and getting on with their pursuit and as an important strategy for governing the country. It can be said that the Chinese nation has accumulated very rich moral resources for thousands of years. However, in the process of rapid development of the socialist market economy, the nation is facing a dilemma of moral downturn. Venality, transaction between power and money, power-to-power transaction, transaction between power and sex, and connection-based transactions are pervasive, resulting in a lack of faith, a lack of credit, and a lack of respect for the law, belief, nature and others. Corruption among officials is rampant, social morality is deteriorating. Food security, medical security and ecological security are all in crisis, which makes people have no sense of trust and security in their lives. It can be said that the bottom line of social morality, the most basic principles of mankind have been repeatedly challenged. In a nutshell, the root cause is the proliferation of commodity transactions in all fields, and the prevalence of money worship, radical individualism, and power rent-seeking. The structure of social relations is based largely on profit, and all social interactions are vulgar. People have to spend a lot of time, emotion and money on daily study, further education, employment, health care and other things, which sometimes results in power-to-power transaction, and which make the cost of social interactions too high. Therefore, the vast majority of people feel burdened and exhausted, and lack a sense of security and happiness.

In view of China's poor current condition of morality, the construction of a socialist moral system must be taken purposefully as an important feature of the construction of socialist culture with Chinese characteristics. On March 4th, 2006, Hu Jintao set forth the socialist concept of honors and disgrace—"Eight Dos and Don'ts" and made it clear that officials and the public people, especially the vast number of young people should be educated in the socialist concept of honor and disgrace. When meeting with national moral models in September 2007, Hu Jintao emphasized that moral power is an important factor in national development, social harmony, and people's happiness. As is stated in the report to the Eighteenth National Congress of the CPC, "We should integrate the rule of law with the rule of virtue, intensify education in public morality, professional ethics, family virtues, and individual integrity. We should encourage people to willingly meet their statutory duties and obligations to society and family. We should create a social atmosphere in which work is honored and creation is lauded, and cultivate social trends of recognizing honor and disgrace, practicing integrity, encouraging dedication, and promoting harmony."[1] At present, the CPC and the government have given priority to moral governance and development.

(d) The creation of more excellent literary and artistic works should be promoted to enrich people's mental and cultural life. It is the basic requirement of realizing socialism that people can enjoy a rich cultural life, just as is clearly pointed out in the "Decision", "Material poverty is not socialism, nor is spiritual emptiness."[2] As Hu Jintao pointed out, "With the rapid economic and social development, especially with the continuous improvement of people's living standards, China has entered a period that cultural consumption is booming and people aspire for richer culture which has become a significant mark of social civilization and people's quality of life."[3] We need to produce better and more cultural products to meet people's ever-growing cultural needs, enrich their cultural lives, and enhance their mental strength. Literature, film, television, music, dance, photography, art and other literary works that maintain close contact with people's daily lives subtly influence their mental world. To build socialist culture with Chinese characteristics means to create more literary and artistic works that are excellent both ideologically and artistically, giving full play to their role of cultivating sentiment, delighting the body and mind, and teaching in entertaining ways, and thereby enriching people's lives. Literature and art are not created merely for the sake of entertainment, but should be integrated into the system of core socialist values, so vulgar and kitsch works should be resolutely resisted.

4. The core of Chinese socialist culture is the core socialist values

Core values are the concentrated expression of the social nature of a certain social form, are in a leading position in the system of social ideological concepts,

---

[1] Hu Jintao: *Unwaveringly Moving Along the Road of Socialism with Chinese Characteristics and Fighting for a Moderately Prosperous Society in All Respects: The Report to the 18th National Congress of the CPC,* Beijing: People's Publishing House, 2012, p. 32.
[2] *Decision of the Central Committee of the CPC on Deepening the Reform of the Cultural System to Promote the Great Development and Prosperity of Socialist Culture,* Beijing: People's Publishing House, 2011, p. 7.
[3] The Documentation Research Office of the CPC Central Committee: *On Cultural Construction: Excerpts of Important Remarks,* Beijing: Xuexi Publishing House & Central Party Literature Press, 2012, p. 8.

determine the basic principles of social systems and operations, and restrict the basic direction of social development. Therefore, the socialist core value system is the essence of socialist culture with Chinese characteristics, playing a very important leading and commanding role in the social ideological system, and is at the core soul of rejuvenating the nation, determining the developmental direction of socialism with Chinese characteristics.

The "Decision" passed at the Sixth Plenary Session of the 16th CPC Central Committee in 2006 explicitly proposed to build a socialist core value system and foster the mental strength of the whole nation and the mental bond of unity and harmony. The guiding ideology of Marxism, the common ideal of building socialism with Chinese characteristics, China's national character with patriotism and reform and innovation at the core, and the socialist concept of honor and disgrace constitute the basic content of the system of core socialist values. It comprehensively summarizes the essence of socialist culture with Chinese characteristics. After the core socialist value system was proposed, it was generally reported that the value system represented a set of principles, but was not concise and specific, and not easy to spread, so it is necessary to further refine and generalize socialist core values.

The core socialist value system needs further refinement and generalization, and on that basis the socialist core values should be refined and generalized, so that they reflect not only the nature of socialism but also the characteristics of Chinese traditional culture and those of modern practice. The report to the Eighteenth CPC National Congress called for such efforts: "We should promote prosperity, democracy, civility, and harmony, uphold freedom, equality, justice and the rule of law and advocate patriotism, dedication, integrity, and friendship, so as to cultivate and observe core socialist values."[①]

These three sets of core values reflect the value orientations of the nation, institutions, and society, and the internal unity of the country, society, and individuals. They are the mental core of the core socialist value system and the fundamental principles it follows. They unite national strength by shaping the country's image, manifesting the spirit of the system and leading social norms, and specifically answering the question of what the mainstream values of the Chinese people are.

---

① Hu Jintao: *Unwaveringly Moving Along the Road of Socialism with Chinese Characteristics and Fighting for a Moderately Prosperous Society in All Respects: The Report to the 18th National Congress of the CPC,* Beijing: People's Publishing House, 2012, pp. 31-32.

5.Chinese socialist culture is divided into "cultural undertakings" and "cultural industries"

In the report delivered by Jiang Zemin at the Sixteenth National Congress of the CPC on November 8, 2002, it is proposed to "develop cultural undertakings and cultural industries," distinguished cultural undertakings and cultural industries for the first time, and emphasized that "developing cultural industries is an important avenue to enriching socialist culture in the market economy and to meeting the mental and cultural needs of the people." As is proposed in the "Decision on Some Issues Concerning the Improvement of the Socialist Market Economy" adopted at the Third Plenary Session of the 16th CPC Central Committee in 2003, "We should improve policies for cultural industries, encourage fund-raising through multiple channels, promote common development of various cultural industries and create a number of large cultural enterprise groups, so as to enhance the overall strength and international competitiveness of cultural industries."[①] The "Proposal of the CPC Central Committee on Formulating the Eleventh Five-Year Plan for National Economic and Social Development", adopted at the Fifth Plenary Session of the 16th CPC Central Committee in October, 2005, worked out different plans for developing cultural undertakings and cultural industry in accordance with their different characteristics, that is, work to gradually establish a fairly complete system of public cultural services that covers all groups in society, improve policies toward the cultural industry, create a cultural sector in which public ownership is leading and cultural enterprises under diverse forms of ownership develop side by side, and a culture market in which national culture is the backbone and all that is fine in foreign culture should be embraced. We should develop the socialist cultural market and promote cultural industries as one of the pillars of economy. On July 23, 2010, the Political Bureau of the CPC Central Committee conducted the 22nd group study session on deepening the reform of the cultural system. Hu Jintao once again stressed that we should comply with the features and laws of promoting cultural and ethical progress, speed up the reform of the cultural system and establish systems and mechanisms that are conducive to the sound development of culture. As is pointed out in the "Proposal of the CPC Central Committee on Formulating the Twelfth Five-Year Plan for National Economic and Social Development" adopted in the Fifth Plenary Session of the 17th

---

① Documentation Research Office of the CPC Central Committee. *Selected Documents Since the Sixteenth National Congress of the CPC,* Vol.1, Beijing: Central Party Literature Press, 2005, p.478.

CPC Central Committee in 2010, we should promote the cultural industry as a pillar of economy.

Culture has two attributes: intellectuality and commerciality. And it is precisely on the basis of these two attributes that we have made a distinction between non-profit good-will culture ("cultural undertakings") and commercially operational culture ("cultural industries"), and adopted different measures and methods to develop them according to their different nature and characteristics. All of this demonstrates that we have acquired a sober awareness of contradiction and the laws of the internal development of culture, which means that we should neither develop the cultural industry in the way in which we develop cultural undertakings, nor should we develop cultural undertakings in the way in which we develop the cultural industry. In the past, under the planned economy, we entirely ignored the laws of the market and characterized all culture as "undertakings." Since the initiation of the policy of reform and opening up, with the development of the socialist market economy, and especially in the era of knowledge economy, intellectual labor and scientific and technological innovation have increasingly become the driving forces and sources of economic and social development, which shows that culture and economy are increasingly intertwined while economization and industrialization of culture are significantly enhanced. We should follow the laws of the market to deepen the reform of the cultural system, stimulate cultural consumption, boost cultural innovation in science and technology, and encourage cultural productivity. We must give top priority to social effects, to the overall quality of the people and their cultural needs when developing the cultural industry.

6. Vital importance of ideological work necessitates the safeguarding of China's cultural security

Nowadays, peace and development have become the main themes of the times, the struggle in the ideological field has not stopped for a moment, and even has been intensified because, with the acceleration of globalization, informatization and webification, cultural communication has become synchronized and rapid. Therefore, socialist culture with Chinese characteristics should be understood from the perspective of cultural security. As Hu Jintao's "Speech at the National Meeting on Publicity and Theoretical Work" (December 5, 2003) pointed out, "Our country is the world's largest socialist country and will inevitably face the infiltration activities of various hostile forces in the ideological field for a long time. For this reason, all comrades in the Party, especially those on the publicity work and theoretical front, should be vigilant at all times."[1] In the speech delivered at the national meeting on publicity and theoretical work on August 19, 2013, Xi Jinping observed that as all kinds of ideologies and cultures exchanged, mingled and confronted each other more frequently across the world, the struggles of ideology and culture have become profoundly complicated, Western countries regarded our development as a challenge to their values, political systems and models, stepping up ideological and cultural infiltration towards us. The struggle we faced in the ideological field were long-term and sophisticated. Some Western countries are prone to disguise themselves as fighters for justice, vigorously promoting so-called "universal values," slandering the socialist system as so-called bureaucratic capitalism and monopoly capitalism, engaging in historical nihilism and discrediting the history and leadership of the CPC. In essence, they are competing with us for positions, people's hearts, and the support of the people, in an attempt to subvert the government of the CPC.

Although the evolution of thoughts is a long-term process, once the ideological defense line is breached, political turmoil and regime change may occur overnight. There are lessons we can learn from the Soviet Union, Eastern European countries, North Africa and West Asian countries. It should be soberly recognized that since the implementation of the reform and opening-up policy, there have been some good things abroad we have learned and absorbed, but certain values of Western countries, including intentional cultural infiltration by some countries, must be resolutely resisted. They are ostensibly opposed to propaganda, but actually they do in a more vicious way. Nowadays, China's economy and society are developing rapidly, and the people's material living standards are constantly improving. Under such circumstances, we should be vigilant towards Western ideological infiltration. We should consolidate the Party's mass foundation and ruling foundation. To this end, it is not enough to improve material life of the public. After all, expanding the Party's mass foundation and consolidating the Party's ruling position involve two aspects: one is the mental aspect; the other is the material aspect. If the Party loses the mental support from the people, it will get into trouble sooner or later.

We should establish more mental and cultural security mechanisms,

---

[1] The Publicity Department and the Party Literature Research Center of the CPC Central Committee: *On Cultural Construction - Excerpts of Important Remarks,* Beijing: *Xuexi* Publishing House & Central Party Literature Press, 2012, p. 14.

conscientiously developing ideologically and culturally strong immunity, and continuously enhancing the security of our ideological and cultural realm, which is an extremely vital part of our cultural development. Therefore, we should firmly take in hand the leadership, management and initiative of ideological work, and establish our own independent ideological and cultural soul and defense line in the practice of socialism with Chinese characteristics.

7. Enhancing Chinese cultural soft power and promoting Chinese culture to go global

Taking Chinese culture to the global stage is symbolically important and urgently needed for the prosperity and strength of socialist culture with Chinese characteristics, which is related to China's cultural security and is a manifestation of the strong reach and power of Chinese culture. The Seventeenth National Congress of the CPC proposed the concept of "culture as part of the soft power of our country" in the Party's documents for the first time, which clearly stated that promoting Chinese culture to the world and enhancing the soft power of Chinese culture can fully bring out the guiding power, attraction, and radiation of Chinese culture. As Hu Jintao further emphasized in his speech on July, 1st 2011, "We should focus on promoting Chinese culture to the world, forming a cultural soft power that is commensurate with China's international status, and thus increase the international influence of Chinese culture."[1] The Party studied cultural development and further emphasized in the Sixth Plenary Session of the 17th CPC Central Committee in 2011 that Chinese culture should go outside to the rest of the world. At the same time, the National Cultural Development Plan has made specific arrangements for taking Chinese culture to the global stage. As is put forward in the "Outline of the Eleventh Five-Year Plan for Cultural Development", we should be conscientious in implementing major cultural projects, take full advantage of both domestic and international markets and resources, actively participate in international cooperation and competition, strengthen cultural exchanges with foreign countries, expand the international trade of cultural goods and services and the space for cultural development, which can preliminarily change the adverse situation that China's trade deficit in cultural products is relatively wide, foster the cultural pattern of all-round opening in which national culture is taken

---

[1] Hu Jintao: *Speech at the Congress to Celebrate the 90th Anniversary of the Founding of the CPC*, Beijing: People's Publishing House, 2011, p. 24.

as the mainstay and the beneficial elements of foreign culture are absorbed so as to promote Chinese culture overseas. The "Outline of the Twelfth Five-Year Plan for Cultural Development" proposed that "(a)s various ideologies and cultures interact, blend, and clash more explicitly and fight in a more fierce and complex manner, it is more urgent that we should enhance our overall cultural strength, international communication power, influence and competitiveness, resist the cultural infiltration of international hostile forces and safeguard national cultural security." At a meeting on publicity and theoretical work held in August 2013, General Secretary Xi Jinping attached great importance to strengthening external publicity to explain and publicize the special characteristics of modern China. "We should innovate the way of foreign-orientated publicity work, strengthen the construction of the discourse system, focus on creating new concepts and new expressions that connect China with the rest of the world, spread the Chinese voice in telling the Chinese stories"[①] and intensify our international right.

In terms of content, the export of Chinese culture mainly includes the following three aspects:

First, taking the mainstream core values to the global stage. We should show the rest of the world what great achievements China has made in building socialism with Chinese characteristics, enable them to acquire a correct understanding of the problems that have arisen during China's reform and development, expound on the basic meaning of the path, theory and system of socialism with Chinese characteristics, demonstrate tremendous political, economic and social changes that China has undergone, display the national spirit and values, let the people all over the world know more about how rational and effective socialism with Chinese characteristics is and what contribution it has made to the development of human society, so as to enhance their understanding of the development of China's peaceful rise and win more support from the international community and international public opinions.

Second, taking academic achievements to the global stage. Academics, as well as ideology, is the core of cultural soft power. The export of academic achievements is the concentrated expression and dissemination of the Chinese nation's ideas, spirits, wisdom and thoughts in the world, and it is also a significant hallmark of China's

---

① Xi Jinping: *The Governance of China*, Eng. ed., Beijing: Foreign Languages Press, p.156.

prosperity and continuous expansion of her influence in the world. A large number of innovative achievements which are rooted in China's reform and opening-up practice and which embody philosophical and social science research methods, academic views and theoretical systems should be pushed onto the international academic and cultural stage, enter the overseas mainstream high-end academic vision, enable foreign scholars and the general public to understand better and gradually accept China's academic discourse, intellectual framework and way of thinking, form a more objective academic vision and public opinion about China, and thereby enhance Chinese cultural soft power and international influence. Since the initiation of the policy of reform and opening up, China has made remarkable achievements not only in economic development but also in science research, but little translation has been done to introduce the theoretical results and ideological, cultural and artistic works that are of great creativity and that have attracted world attention, even those of great originality. As for many major practical issues, the "Chinese school" scholars have devoted their concern and consideration, but their works or ideas may be not influential enough to be noticed overseas. Those at the academic frontier are basically learning and disseminating Western academic discourse, norms and methodology. Moreover, they are generally in a passive position while having a dialogue with the West, even to the extent that they often lose their collective voice.

Third, taking cultural products to the global stage, that is, developing cultural trade. We must make every effort to build our own cultural brands and accelerate the spread of high-quality literary and artistic works. Cultural products not only act as a means of cultural entertainment, but also embody the core values of a nation; therefore, their going global is crucial to enhancing the international influence of the Chinese culture. Having a cultural brand is the most direct and concrete reflection of a country's overall national strength. American film and media industry, Japanese animation industry, South Korean online-game industry, German's publishing industry and the music industry of the UK, to name a few, have become iconic brands of the international cultural industry.

8.Cultural rejuvenation is the ultimate and root symbol of the great rejuvenation of the Chinese nation

The ultimate goal of the development of socialist culture with Chinese characteristics is to realize the cultural rejuvenation of the Chinese nation, and cultural rejuvenation is the ultimate hallmark and fundamental symbol of the great rejuvenation of the Chinese nation. As pointed out in the report to the Seventeenth National Congress of the CPC, the great rejuvenation of the Chinese nation will definitely be accompanied by a thriving Chinese culture. The theory of socialist culture with Chinese characteristics describes and explains the connotation and process of cultural rejuvenation, from autonomy to self-sufficiency to self-confidence and self-improvement, thus profoundly revealing the importance of cultural rejuvenation for the cultural rejuvenation of the Chinese nation.

First of all, we should achieve cultural autonomy. Autonomous culture is the backbone of a nation's survival and development among the nations of the world. The CPC has been the loyal successor of China's traditional culture and the builder of Chinese autonomous culture. The system of the core socialist values guided by Marxism is the soul of the reinvigoration of the country and nation, and also is an important support in the ethical and cultural fields. This core value system is fundamental to ensuring the socialist nature of China, and is the standard and symbol of the Chinese nation's mental autonomy, without which we may become the ideological appendage of other developed capitalist countries.

Modern Chinese history is a history of humiliation and the Chinese people's inquiry into the causes of the crisis of national survival has gone from the basic logic of "tools" being inferior to others, to the decay of the system, and finally to the cultural backwardness of the feudal system. China's backwardness was ultimately put down to the fact that China had not transformed its institutions and culture of national governance before entering the modern world system. Thus, in the interaction between the process of world history and the transformation of China's internal factors, the old mainstream cultural system collapsed while a new ideology and culture that could integrate national consciousness had not been established. Hence, the whole nation was in a state of disunity like a sheet of loose sand. Marxism, since it was introduced into China, has been combined with the great traditional culture of the Chinese nation, and adapted to the Chinese context, and thus has, for a long time, become the cultural main line of our survival and development, thoroughly stimulating the mental power of the Chinese people, changing our mental outlook, uniting the mental power of hundreds of millions of compatriots, and exploding into an increasingly strong Chinese voice. We have generally shaken off passivity, and the world's perception of the Chinese people has also undergone a fundamental change, from mocking the Chinese people as "sick men of East Asia" to praising the "Chinese path" and "Chinese experience". It can be said that the Chinese miracle has been created largely due to the introspection and autonomy of our cultural spirit.

We need not only cultural autonomy, but also cultural self-sufficiency. The latter means a wealth of richness in mental products and the mental world. Philosophy and social sciences, literature and art, news media and other fields are supposed to produce more high-quality goods to meet the mental needs of the people, enrich their mental world, and make the mental power of the entire nation stronger. If there are no good products, we can only consume Western blockbuster movies or Korean dramas, etc., and passively accept the infiltration of their ideologies and values. Therefore, cultural autonomy needs to be guaranteed by cultural self-sufficiency, and the inadequacy of cultural products will inevitably result in the loss of cultural autonomy. Demonstrating strong Chinese mental and cultural power requires the creation of a large number of outstanding achievements in philosophy and social sciences that represent national standards, have world influence and stand the test of practice and history. Deepening the construction and dissemination of the socialist core value system also requires us to improve the system of public cultural services and create popular intellectual works with higher-end cultural connotations.

Having progressed from cultural autonomy and self-sufficiency to cultural self-reliance and self-confidence, we will ultimately achieve the cultural renewal and the great rejuvenation of the Chinese nation. Over the 30-plus years of reform and opening up, we have embarked on the road of modernization in China, which is the path of development under socialism with Chinese characteristics, and is also the only way to realize the great rejuvenation of the Chinese nation. The remarkable achievements in the economy, social life and all other fields have proven the superiority of the Chinese path and system and demonstrated the independence and self-confidence of Chinese culture. Inspired by these tremendous achievements, we are more than eager to realize national rejuvenation and make the country stronger. The formulation of a strategy to develop a strong socialist culture with Chinese characteristics and the formation of the theory of socialist culture with Chinese characteristics express our aspiration, determination and confidence to realize cultural self-sufficiency, self-reliance, and rejuvenation. Material abundance and national strength are ultimately manifested in cultural self-confidence and self-improvement. The power of ideological culture, namely, cultural hard power and soft power are hallmarks of cultural rejuvenation and also the fundamental symbol of the realization of the great rejuvenation of the Chinese nation. The proposal to develop a strong socialist culture in China profoundly embodies "the awareness of Chinese culture".

The successful experience of Chinese revolution and construction lies in the ability to continuously combine Marxist theories with the practice of Chinese social development, and constantly generate new theories. This process of theoretical construction is not only the adaptation of Marxism to the Chinese context, but also the construction of the theory of socialism with Chinese characteristics. The Party has kept a high level of theoretical self-consciousness and cultural self-consciousness in the long-term practice of cultural construction, conscientiously upheld Marxist theories and methods, studied major issues of cultural reform and development in the process of modernization, continuously summarized the people's lively cultural innovation experience, constantly put forward new viewpoints and thoughts, and gradually formed the theory of socialist culture with Chinese characteristics. It is a process of cultural innovation based on profound Chinese cultural traditions, creative Chinese modernization and Chinese experience. It is the field of the "Olympics" of national competition, and is the real secret to the great rejuvenation of the Chinese nation.

Giving Full Play to the Role of Chinese Socialist Culture: Study Important Remarks by Xi Jinping About Cultural Issues*

Since the 18th National Congress of the CPC, General Secretary Xi has attached great importance to the development of culture. He has made a series of major speeches on the cultural development in the new circumstances, proposing many new visions, new ideas, and new concepts. In his series of major addresses, the socialist culture with Chinese characteristics is repeatedly emphasized, which exhibit his new understanding of the status and role of culture in the new era. As is stressed in "General Secretary Xi Jinping's Speech at Forum on Literature and Art" on October 15, 2014, "After more than 5,000 years of trials and tribulations, China is still here. One of the most important reasons is that generation upon generation of Chinese people have nurtured and developed a unique, broad and profound Chinese culture that has provided a powerful spiritual support for the Chinese nation to overcome difficulties and bring about endless development." When visiting the Temple of Confucius in Qufu, Shandong Province, he said, a nation cannot prosper without morality, just as a person cannot live without it. Prosperous culture is the foundation for either a country or a nation to thrive. And therefore, a vigorous culture is also true for the Chinese nation to gain its great rejuvenation. When talking with the representatives of outstanding young people from all walks of life, he emphasized that it is difficult for a nation without inner strength to be self-reliant, and that a cause that lacks a cultural buttress cannot sustain for long. Under the new circumstances, emphasizing the important supporting role of culture has a very rich connotation of the times.

---

* Originally published in *Chinese Social Sciences* on Mar. 3rd, 2016, with a somewhat different title.

As is well-known, the concept of "pushing for material progress on the one hand and cultural and ethical progress on the other, with great importance attached to both" is the overall design on how to handle the relationship between material and cultural-ethical progress, which consists in Deng Xiaoping's grand blueprint of the Reform and Opening-up. Nonetheless, soon after the adoption of reform and opening up in 1978, Chinese economy and society was backward, and the standards of the people's material lives were low and the main problem was how to meet the people's needs. Therefore, more focus was laid primarily on economic development, and less on culture progress. As the people's anxieties for survival had been to be solved, Deng Xiaoping's promise of "making both economy and culture prosper" were not honored in practice. Nowadays, although China has gained economic and social development, as well as that in its citizens' lives. There still exists the crisis in people's spirit and philosophy, such as a crisis of belief, a crisis of confidence, and moral decline. It is obvious that compared with economic and social development, cultural development is relatively backward. And culture has not played its due role in the practice of building socialism with Chinese characteristics.

The 13th Five-Year Plan period (2016 - 20) is China's economic development is at a stage of shifting the growth rate, restructuring the economy, and addressing the impact of previous stimulus policies. In addition, the world economy has not emerged from a downturn, still in the shadow of the global financial crisis, and there are many uncertain and unstable factors. It is fair to say that in the important breakthrough period for achieving the great rejuvenation of the Chinese nation, how to correctly view the position and role of culture and how to develop and prosper the socialist culture with Chinese characteristics in practice has become very urgent issues before the Party and the country. At a time when we are closer to the goal of the great rejuvenation of the Chinese nation than at any time in modern history, culture must truly play its important supporting role and must not become an area where we fall short and where the great rejuvenation of the Chinese nation is hindered. In the same vein of culture in history, Xi stressed during the Forum on Literature and Art Work that "A great cause needs great spirit...As with numerous high-rise everywhere, the edifice of the Chinese national spirit should stand lofty."

Xi's understanding of the important role of cultural support greatly deepens the connotation of cultural reaction. For instance, culture as a source of inner strength and intellectual support are promoted to culture as "value orientation" and "a source of innovation"; and "heart-warming" and "wisdom-enlightening" cognitive activity is extended to the economic discourse of buttressing economic industry; a domestic vision to satisfy mental and cultural needs of the people is expanded to a global vision to enhance the national cultural soft power. On the whole, the new central collective leadership with Xi Jinping at the core have understood the important role of a socialist culture with Chinese characteristics from a more multi-dimensional perspective which can offer a richer and clearer view. Culture has been at the center of national development strategies and has become a sector which is related to the political sphere. Combining theoretical innovation with policy implementation, we can summarize the important supporting role of the socialist culture with Chinese characteristics in the following aspects:

The first is its leading role, which mainly manifests itself in strengthening ideological work and consolidating the guiding position of Marxism. As General Secretary Xi pointed out, ideological work is of significant importance for the Party. Ideology is the core of a country and a party's political thought, which concern political orientation issues such as what guiding political principles to be uphold, what path to take and what system to adopt. Ideological security is the basis for the stability of the national political system and social security and unity, and it is related to the long -term security of the party and the country. As General Secretary Xi emphasized at the national meeting on publicity and theoretical work on August 19, 2013, "The disintegration of a regime is, more often than not, starting from the sphere of ideology. Political turmoil and regime change may occur overnight, but the ideological evolution is a long-term process. If the ideological defense line is broken, other lines of defense are hard to hold." The important speech made by General Secretary Xi at a symposium on news reporting and public opinion in the same year highlighted the importance of further consolidating our positions and promoting ideological progress. Therefore, against the background of the increasingly fierce international ideological struggle and the increasingly severe ideological division in China, upholding and developing socialism with Chinese characteristics will inevitably give full play to the leading role of socialist ideology and achieve a strong political identity among the majority of the people.

Consolidating the guiding status of Marxism contributes to strengthening theoretical work, which is the mental characteristic of socialism with Chinese characteristics and is also the sound methodological guidance, the correct direction and the important ideological guarantee for the CPC leading the people in carrying out the modernization drive. To uphold the guidance of Marxism, we must first "deepen the study and construction of Marxist theory", which has been written into the outline of the 13th Five-Year Plan. This project should not only sort out the classic Marxist writings, study the basic principles of Marxism, and more importantly, develop Marxism in the 21st- century China. This is put forward by Xi at a group study session of the Political Bureau on dialectical materialism. So far, the Central Political Bureau has collectively studied Marxism twice—first, on historical materialism; second, on dialectical materialism, which has shown the importance attached to Marxism by the new central leadership. The proposition of "developing Marxism in China in the 21st century" is inevitable for the development in the new era and marks the CPC's persistence in and development of Marxism's high political self-confidence and theoretical self-consciousness under the new historical circumstances. The Chinese path is of international significance. Developing Marxism in China in the 21st century is significant not only for better guiding the development of the cause of building socialism with Chinese characteristics, but also for making unique contributions to the diversity of world civilizations.

The second is its cohesive role, which is mainly reflected in putting forward the Chinese dream and cultivating the core socialist values. Marxism holds that the people are the creators of history and the decisive force in promoting social development and social changes. The synergy of the people depends on cohesion which gains its form through culture. The cohesion of China's power relies mainly on the Chinese dream and the socialist core values. General Secretary Xi put forward the idea of the Chinese dream, which possessed strong appeal. The Chinese dream is essentially the dream of the nation, the rejuvenation of the Chinese nation, and the happiness of the people; The dream of realizing the great rejuvenation of the Chinese nation has been a long-cherished dream for more than a hundred years since modern times began, and embodies patriotism of the Chinese people. The core socialist values are the quintessence of the socialist culture with Chinese characteristics, the embodiment of the essential requirements of socialist ideology and the qualitative regulation of the socialist system at the ideological and spiritual level, and is the expression of the value of the path , the theory and the system of socialism with Chinese characteristics. At the thirteenth group study session of the Political Bureau of the 18th CPC Central Committee on February 24□2014, Xi Jinping pointed out that the core socialist values are the soul of cultural soft power and the focus of the building of cultural soft power. Those values are the chief element that determines the nature and orientation of culture. The cultural soft power of a country fundamentally depends on the vitality, cohesion and charisma of its core values. The core socialist values are the reflection of the recognition of the values with the "greatest common denominator" by the people of all ethnic groups, while the Chinese Dream is the common expression of their dreams with the "greatest common denominator". Both of them play a supporting role in uniting the Chinese nation and realizing the great rejuvenation of the Chinese nation.

The third is its motivational role, which is mainly reflected in promoting cultural innovation and implementing philosophy and social science innovation project. Innovation is the primary driving force behind development. The Party and the state have put innovation at the core of the overall national development and constantly promoted innovation in theory, system, science and technology, culture and other aspects. Cultural innovation is an important force in promoting economic and social development. General Secretary Xi pointed out in his speech at the Forum of Art and Literature that "Culture is an important force for the survival and development of the nation. Where is humankind leap and where there is human civilization sublimation, there is cultural historical advance." Emancipating the mind is the precursor to social change. A major social change or progress often stems from the emergence and dissemination of new ideas, new cultures, new knowledge and new ideas. It can be said that cultural innovation capability is the embodiment of a nation and a nation's wisdom and civilization. It is also an important symbol of the overall strength of a nation. The major measures of cultural innovation are first embodied in the implementation of philosophy and social science innovation project. Philosophy and social sciences are the most important part of culture. Building philosophy and social sciences with Chinese characteristics and Chinese style is the basic content of cultural innovation. With the deepening of reform and opening up, new situations and new problems have been cropping up one after another. A series of newly-accumulated practical experience urgently need to be refined and generalized by people working in philosophy and social science circles; a series of new practical topics urgently need to be further researched and answered by them. Cultural innovation means creating cultural products that can meet the requirements of the times. Excellent intellectual and cultural products should reflect the cultural creativity of a state and a nation, and should be the basic criteria for measuring and testing the effectiveness of cultural innovation and development.

The fourth is its decision-making role, which is mainly materialized in China's new-type think-tanks. As General Secretary Xi stressed, we have to pool wisdom and strength from all sides to perform the governance of China. The more formidable the task of economic and social development, the more urgent the need for intellectual supports. The high-end think tanks with international influence should be seen as key projects, and should be specialized. "The Notice on Issuing the Opinions on Strengthening the Construction of New Types of Think Tanks with Chinese Characteristics" issued in January, 2015 by the Central Government suggests that building a new type of think tank with Chinese characteristics is an important support for the Party and government's sound and democratic decision-making in accordance with law; it is an important part of the national governance system and governance capacity modernization; it is a key soft power for a country. The development of think tank reflects the important role of culture in government decision-making. The new think tank with Chinese characteristics is an important support for the sound and democratic decision-making by the Party and the government; it is an important part of the modernization of the state's governing system and governance capacity; and it is an important part of the country's soft power component. The construction of think tanks fully reflects the important role of culture in government decision-making. The new types of think tanks with distinctive Chinese features provide a sound basis for formulating sound public policies and give full play to the role of consultation and counseling; it is committed to resolving the most cutting-edge realities; it is an important force in promoting theoretical innovation; it should disseminate advanced concepts, lead the public to correctly understand public policies and thus create a good social environment for the implementation of policies; it is an important carrier of the country's soft power and has increasingly become an important factor of international competitiveness And has it played an irreplaceable role in its foreign relations.

The fifth is its defining role, which is mainly manifested in accelerating the development of cultural industry and making it the key industry for economy. In the Sixth Plenary Session of the 17th CPC Central Committee, held from October 15 to 18, 2011, the Party suggested that the differences between cultural undertakings and cultural industries should be differentiated, and the latter should be developed to be a pillar of economy. The "Proposal on the 13th Five-Year Plan" once again put forward the idea of promoting cultural industry as a key industry for economy, which reflects the importance the Central Government has attached to its development. With the economic and social development in the country and the improvement of material lives of the people, the rapid growth of cultural consumption and the promising cultural industries have become important parts of emerging industries of strategic importance. It is true that cultural industry is not only an important way of cultural development, but also an important measure to adapt to the new normal China has entered in economic development and speed up the transformation of economic development patterns. The blending of economy and culture can effectively enhance not only the sustainability of economic development, but also the vitality of culture.

The Central Government also introduced two methods for development based on the country's own characteristics and the laws of development. The first is to put social efficiency first and achieve a balance between economic and social efficiency, i.e., to put social efficiency first while pursuing economic returns. When economic returns conflict with social benefits, the latter should be given priority to. It is also emphasized in the speech delivered by General Secretary Xi at the Forum on Literature and Art on October 15, 2014 that literary and art works should not be the slaves to the market and should not bear the stench of money. The second is to develop new forms of business in the cultural sector to promote the integration between traditional media and new types of media. Fundamentally, the development of cultural industry should be on the right path, which requires integration with newly-emerging science and technology.

The sixth is its radiative effect, which is mainly reflected in globally promoting Chinese culture and enhancing culture as part of the soft power of the country. Culture is an important indicator of a country's soft power. Advanced culture has a stronger influence on other countries and nations. Advanced culture embodies the concept of advanced values of a country and a nation and can be appealing to other countries and nations. General Secretary Xi pointed out in his speech at the Forum on Literature and Art that "Human history tells us that the Chinese nation's position and influence in the world have not depended on militarism or external expansion, but on the strong appeal and attraction of the Chinese culture." As General Secretary Xi emphasized at the twelfth group study session of the Political Bureau of the 18th CPC Central Government on December 30, 2013, to improve China's cultural soft power, efforts should be made to spread contemporary Chinese values, that is, the socialist values with Chinese characteristics, which represent the direction of advanced Chinese culture. China has blazed a successful path of socialism with Chinese characteristics. The facts have proved that our path and system, theoretical and social, are successful. More work should be done to refine and explain our ideas, and extend the platform for overseas publicity, so as to enable our culture to be known through international communication and dissemination. We should relate the Chinese Dream to modern Chinese values during our dissemination and explanation; showcase the unique charm of Chinese culture; and build a beautiful image of the country, etc. During his foreign visits, General Secretary Xi also vigorously explained and promoted Chinese culture to demonstrate the confidence and charm of the Chinese national culture. He also particularly emphasized the important role of literature and art in the process of Chinese culture going global. He pointed out that it is far from enough to rely on formal press releases and official introductions to take Chinese culture to the outside world, and it is very limited to rely on foreign people to come to China to understand and experience it personally. In this regard literature and art have an irreplaceable role to play, and can serve as the ideal channel for communication. You are expected to promote splendid Chinese arts globally, introduce foreign audiences to the charm of Chinese culture, and in the course help them develop a better understanding of it.

The seventh is its fundamental role, which is reflected in implementing the project of preserving the traditional Chinese culture, keeping alive the fine traditional Chinese culture. This culture represents the unique cultural identity that distinguishes the Chinese nation from other nations and provides a rich source of strength for the everlasting development of the Chinese nation. General Secretary Xi said in his speech at the Forum on Literature and Art on October 15, 2014 that "Splendid traditional culture is the lifeline of the Chinese nation, an important source of cultivating the socialist core values, and a solid foundation for us to stand firm in the turmoil of world." Chinese civilization is the only one that has not been interrupted and has lasted for more than 5,000 years, and we should make constant development and innovation of it, rather than announcing it; otherwise, the Chinese nation will no longer exist. Since the 18th CPC National Congress, General Secretary Xi have attached importance on many occasions to the development of fine traditional Chinese culture. Among them, the core point is "We should properly handle the relationship between inheritance and innovation, with the focus on transforming and developing the fine traditional Chinese culture in a creative way." The innovation of Chinese traditional culture is, in essence, to combine the fine Chinese traditional culture with the great practice of socialism with Chinese characteristics, and integrate them into the core socialist values of and give full play to its contemporary value. The Proposal also offers a series of measures for the protection and development of the fine traditional culture, such as building an inheritance system for it, strengthening preservation of our cultural heritage, revitalize traditional crafts, and implementation of the project of sorting out Chinese classics.

The 13th Five-Year Plan period (2016-20) is the decisive stage in building a moderately prosperous society in all respects and a critical moment for national rejuvenation. In this period, Whether the socialist culture with Chinese characteristics can flourish and develop, and whether it can play a strong supporting role, is crucial to building a moderately prosperous society in all respects, the great rejuvenation of the Chinese nation, and the realization of the Two Centenary Goals[①]. A series of new ideas and thoughts General Secretary Xi put forward on cultural development have greatly promoted the development of the socialist culture with Chinese characteristics. As General Secretary Xi pointed out in his speech at the Forum of Art and Literature, "The Chinese nation has strong cultural creativity. At every major historical juncture, we can, through culture, feel the changes in the prospects of a nation, stand at the forefront of the times, and air the voices of the times, so as to cheer for hundreds of millions of people and the great motherland." We believe that under the new circumstances, under the guidance of General Secretary Xi Jinping's thought on cultural development, and with the concerted efforts of all walks of life in the field of culture, the Chinese nation will surely stand firm among the nations of the world.

---

① To finish building a moderately prosperous society in all respects by the time the Communist Party of China celebrates its centenary in 2021; and to turn China into a modern socialist country that is prosperous, strong, democratic, culturally advanced, and harmonious by the time the People's Republic of China celebrates its centenary in 2049.

On the Theory of Socialism with Chinese Characteristics

From Decline to Rejuvenation: China's Century-long Pursuit and Prospect of Modernization*

History is a river of time that flows endlessly. Today is the result of yesterday, and future is continuation of today.

We should learn from the past: As we march confidently into the 21st century, we cannot help but look back at the humiliation, pathos and heroism of China's modern history, and reflect on the arduous pursuit of modernization by the Chinese people over the past hundred years.

To understand how modernization has been developing in China can help us more profoundly realize how urgent and historically inevitable it is to rejuvenate the Chinese nation in the 21st century.

I

Rejuvenate China! This has been for centuries not merely the common aspiration and relentless pursuit of numerous public-spirited people, but also an objective requirement of the development of Chinese history, which reflects the objective laws of historical dialectics. Looking back at the modern history of China, we find it is humiliating, frustrating, infuriating, and even more alarming and uplifting. The modern history of China is not only a history of humiliation for the Chinese nation, but also a history of the struggle of the Chinese people to save the country and revive China. In order to save the fate of the fallen nation and the revitalization of the Chinese nation, many public-spirited people, have racked their brains and sacrificed their blood, writing the most thrilling and touching epic of patriotism in the history of the Chinese nation.

---

* Originally published in *Marxist Research* (《马克思主义研究》), 2000(2).

Among the people who made great efforts to rejuvenate the Chinese nation in the 20th century, Sun Yat-sen, Mao Zedong and Deng Xiaoping are the three greatest men who have made the most outstanding contribution.

In order to rejuvenate China, Dr. Sun Yat-sen went hither and thither to call for help and support and set up the United League of China, the first bourgeois political party in China. After a long period of struggle, he also put forward clearly the program of the bourgeois-democratic revolution in China, that is, the "Three Principles of the People" featuring the principles of nationalism, democracy and people's livelihood as the main contents. The Three Principles of the People sought to solve various problems, say, China's national independence, political democracy and the development of social economy. It is the most appropriate way for China's modernization to embark on before Marxism rooted in China in the late 19th and early 20th centuries. It is also the most complete doctrine. If there had been a "modern culture" in China, then Sun Yat-sen's "the Three Principles of the People" would have been the most outstanding representative of it.

Dr. Sun Yat-sen's "Plans for National Reconstruction" marks the fact that his thoughts have already entered the mature stage. In this masterpiece, he brilliantly analyzed the dialectical relationship between democratic politics and socio-economic development and clearly pointed out the way forward for China's future development. It is the first work in the Chinese history that systematically discusses China's mode of modernization, its way forward and its basic principles. Though the ideal was not realized due to various historical constraints, the work did give many important illuminations and inspirations to those who came after it.

Unfortunately, Sun Yat-sen's ideal was not realized. In his article "On the People's Democratic Dictatorship"(*lun renmin minzhu zhuanzheng*, 《论人民民主专政》), Mao Zedong succinctly and pointedly summarized this experience: " From the time of China's defeat in the Opium War of 1840, the Chinese progressives went through untold hardships in their quest for truth from the Western countries. Hong Xiuquan(洪秀全), Kang Youwei, Yen Fu(严复) and Sun Yat-sen were representative of those who had looked to the West for truth before the CPC was born. For them, the only way to save the country is to reform; to reform, the only way is to learn from foreign countries. However, "imperialist aggression shattered the fond dreams of the Chinese about learning from the West. It was very odd —why were the teachers always committing aggression against their pupil? The Chinese learned a good deal from the West, but they could not make it work and were never able to realize their ideals. Their repeated struggles, including such a country-wide movement as the Revolution of 1911, all ended in failure…All other ways have been tried and failed." Not until the founding of the CPC and the founding of Marxism-Leninism, in particular after Mao Zedong established its leadership within the Party, did China set off a new smooth road to modernization through inheriting the revolutionary cause initiated by Dr. Sun Yat-sen. In his article "Commemorating Dr. Sun Yat-sen"[①], Mao Zedong said: "We not only have completed the democratic revolution that Sun Yat-sen did not, but also have turned this revolution into a socialist one."

—In terms of economy, it has put forward a policy of comprehensively promoting economic construction, with industrialization as the main task. It has clearly set out the direction and main task of industrialization, and the need to reform and adjust China's excessively homogeneous economic structure and economic system; it has also formulated a comprehensive, balanced and steadily advancing approach to economic construction.

—I terms of science and technology, the status and role of knowledge and intellectuals in the modernization were fully affirmed.

—In terms of culture, the policy of "letting a hundred flowers bloom and a hundred schools of thought contend" was designed to promote the flourishing of socialist literature, arts and sciences.

—As far as the issue how to treat foreign advanced civilization is concerned, Mao Zedong called on us to comprehensively learn the advanced science and technology and culture of foreign countries by clearly stating "Our policy is to learn from the strong points of all nations and all countries, learn all that is genuinely good in the political, economic, scientific and technological fields and in literature and art." He also emphasized that "In the natural sciences we are rather backward, and here we should make a special effort to learn from foreign countries." He further pointed out: "We must firmly reject and criticize all the decadent bourgeois systems, ideologies and ways of life of foreign countries. But this should in no way prevent us from learning the advanced sciences and technologies of capitalist countries and whatever is rational in the management of their enterprises."

It should be acknowledged that the theory of modernization and the strategy of development formulated by the first generation of collective leadership of the CPC

---

① Speech delivered by Mao Zedong, on March 12, 1938, at the commemoration of the 13th anniversary of the death of Sun Yat-sen and the memorial ceremony for the soldiers killed in the Anti-Japanese War.

with Mao Zedong at the core is more comprehensive, systematic and judicious than Sun Yat-sen's Three Principles of the People. China, under the leadership of the CPC, did make significant progress in modernization in less than 30 years than it had done in the previous several thousand years in the Chinese history, thereby turning the road to capitalist modernization into the one to socialist modernization. In the international community, it successfully realized the national independence which the Chinese people had coveted for several generations. The Chinese people have stood up, despite its bitter experiences during the Century of Humiliation (1839-1949), among the nations of the world, with equanimity. When it comes to domestic politics, democratization has been promoted to a considerable extent and the Chinese people have become the masters of their country. When it comes to economy, in the short span of 30 years, under the leadership of the CPC with Mao Zedong at the core, economy once showed good momentum of sound development, with its foundation growing stronger and its strength growing markedly. When it comes to science and technology, the 30 years witnessed tremendous progress: Needless to say much about the success in the "Two Bombs and One Satellite" project as the core of cutting-edge science and technology for national defense. Even the achievement made in basic sciences was also unprecedented in the Chinese history. In short, despite the fact that there were indeed many mistakes and shortcomings in Mao Zedong era, solid material foundation was laid for the further development of China's modernization.

—On the essence and basic tasks of socialism, Deng Xiaoping concluded that the essence of socialism is liberation and development of the productive forces, elimination of exploitation and polarization, and the ultimate achievement of achieving common prosperity for all people. He reckoned that the most fundamental task at the socialist stage is to develop the productive forces and emphasized that "Poverty is not socialism," and "We must build socialism that can lift the country out of poverty." Therefore, the work focus of the Party and the country must be shifted from taking the class struggle as the key link to socialist modernization with economic construction as the core.

—On the issue of the stage of socialist development, Deng Xiaoping creatively judged that China's socialist construction is still at the primary stage of socialism; that is, China is still at the primary stage of socialism. This is China's biggest national condition. All development plans, guidelines and policies for China's socialist construction must proceed from this basic national condition.

—On the issue of the path of socialist modernization, Deng Xiaoping explicitly proposed to take modernization of socialism with Chinese characteristics as the basic direction. He repeatedly stressed: "The modernization we are striving for is modernization of a Chinese type. The socialism we are building is socialism with Chinese characteristics."

—On the issue of the driving forces for China's socialist modernization, Deng Xiaoping reformed the economic and political systems which did not suit the development of the productive forces in order to make them act as the lever to bring all positive factors into full play and further unleash the enormous potential of productivity. It was put forward clearly that science and technology is a primary source of productivity and it is the progress of science and technology that drives the development of production capacity; education is the basis of scientific and technological progress, more money and effort should be put into developing and expanding education to foster a large number of scientists and technicians, and thereby boost China's global standing in science and technology research the gap in the level of science and technology and as soon as possible shorten the gap in the level of science and technology between China and those advanced countries, and thereby enhance the stamina of China's national economic development.

—On the issue of studying advanced foreign cultures, Deng Xiaoping advocated the full implementation of the policy of opening up to the outside world, learning and introducing advanced foreign cultures and managerial skills, attracting foreign capital, so as to provide the necessary scientific and technological and capital guarantees for accelerating China's economic development. He clearly pointed out: "If we want socialism to achieve superiority over capitalism, we should not hesitate to draw on all advanced methods of operation and techniques of management that reflect the laws governing modern socialized production."

—On the issue of economic system, Deng Xiaoping believed that we can develop a market economy under socialism and market economy is not unique to capitalist society. He explicitly put forward that economy must be dominated by public ownership and must allow the existence and development of various non-public sectors of economy. He insisted that the progress and development of agriculture should be taken as the basis for the overall economic modernization, the realization of industrialization as the overarching goal of economic modernization, the rapid, steady and coordinated development as the regulative principles for economic progress, and the improvement of economic efficiency as the center of economic development.

—On the issue of political system, Deng Xiaoping proposed that we should adhere to the cardinal principle of upholding the people's democratic dictatorship and develop and improve socialist democracy and legal system. He invariably believed that maintaining social stability is an overriding need and the most important prerequisite and prepared environment for China's socialist modernization. Meanwhile, he also stressed on many occasions that the political system of the Party and the country must meet the needs of economic development and restructuring, actively promote the reform of leadership system of the Party and the state and promote the democratization of political activities in China.

——On the issue of cultural system, Deng Xiaoping always believed that we should adhere to the basic principle of the strategic concept of "pushing for material progress on the one hand and cultural and ethical progress on the other , with great importance attached to both" and that building a socialist society with advanced ethical standards should be taken as the main measure to prosper the cultural undertakings and enhance the cultural quality of the people.

——On the issue of socialist modernization, Deng Xiaoping laid out the three-step strategic plan①. He stressed on many occasions that it is necessary to break

---

① As reform and opening up began, the CPC formulated a strategic plan for China's socialist modernization. Unveiled at the 13th CPC National Congress in October 1987, the strategy envisaged three steps for economic development. It drew upon Deng Xiaoping's strategic conclusions. The underlying assumption was that the major challenge in the primary stage of socialism was how to address the inadequate level of development and to satisfy the people's growing material and cultural needs. Aimed at raising the level of development to improve the people's wellbeing, the strategy outlined specific targets for each of the three steps. First, the years from 1981 to the end of the 1980s would see the doubling of the 1980 GNP, thus meeting the most basic needs of the people; second, GNP would double again between 1991 and the end of the 20th century, bringing the people moderate prosperity; third, with the process of modernization basically completed, per capita GNP was expected to reach the level of a moderately developed country by the mid-21st century, further improving the people's wellbeing. At its 15th National Congress held in September 1997, the CPC further modified the third step as: first, to double the 2000 GNP by 2010, bring the people greater prosperity, and build a relatively complete socialist market economy; second, to further develop the economy and have a full range of relevant systems in place by the time the CPC celebrates its centenary in 2021; and third, to accomplish basic modernization and build China into a prosperous, strong, democratic and culturally advanced socialist country by the time the People's Republic celebrates its centenary in 2049. At its 19th National Congress in October 2017, the CPC renewed the development goals for the period between 2020 and 2050. The first step is to realize basic modernization by 2035, and the second step is to further develop China into a great modern socialist country that is prosperous, strong, democratic, culturally advanced, harmonious and beautiful by the mid-21st century. The three-step strategy for development combined a forward-looking vision for building a prosperous China with prudent and careful planning. As a major blueprint guiding the CPC to advance socialism with Chinese characteristics, it combined the courage and ambition of the Party and the Chinese people with a pragmatic approach rooted in a deep understanding of China's existing conditions. ——Tr.

with egalitarianism and with the practice of having everyone "eat from the same big pot", namely, indiscriminate egalitarianism; and that it should be a policy to let some people and some regions prosper before others so that they can bring along the backward regions, and then gradually realize common prosperity and all-round development of Chinese society through the regulation of the country's macroeconomic policies.

Deng Xiaoping's theory of China's modernization reflected and summarized the lessons from China's past experiences and mistakes in seeking socialist modernization over the past decades, drew on historical experience from other socialist countries, reflected and responded to the fundamental trend of the international community, and then, for the first time, systematically answered a series of fundamental questions concerning the future of the Chinese nation, such as how to build socialism in a country like China, where its economy was relatively backward, resources relatively meager, citizens' cultural quality relatively low, and how to consolidate and develop socialism. Precisely under the guidance of this theory, in the past 20 years, tremendous changes have taken place in the Chinese society, with the overall national strength greatly enhanced and the people's living standards improved noticeably. China has enjoyed an unprecedented boost in its international reputation and status. As a result, China has been playing an increasingly important role in international affairs.

The path of socialist modernization with Chinese characteristics initiated by Deng Xiaoping is a great pioneering undertaking in the history of the Chinese nation. The past 20 years has written a glorious chapter in the 5,000 plus years of civilization of the Chinese nation, laying a solid foundation for the great rejuvenation of the Chinese nation. According to the "China in 2020" released by the World Bank in September 1997, "The Chinese economy expanded more than fourfold in the past fifteen years. Between 1978 and 1995 real GDP per capita grew at the blistering rate of 8 percent a year and lifted 200 million Chinese out of absolute poverty."

"Economic reforms, begun in 1978, have advanced China's integration with the world economy, maintained a strong external payments position… liberalized markets for many goods and services, intensified competition in industry, and introduced modern macroeconomic management. Despite concerns about regional disparities, the benefits of growth have been widely shared among China's country-size provincial economies. Although the coastal provinces grew faster than average at 9.7 percent a year, the other provinces also fared well."

Deng Xiaoping is indeed a great person in the history of the Chinese nation. As the core of the second generation of the CPC leadership, he led the Party and the country out of the profound calamity caused by the ten-year Cultural Revolution (1966-1976), and ushered in a new era in the history of reform, opening-up and socialist modernization. He, orienting himself to China's national conditions, the world and the future, conceived and proposed, with his broad vision, a set of strategies for building socialism with Chinese characteristics, and charted a brand-new grand blueprint based on the realities and circumstances of today's China so that the Chinese nation could stand more powerfully in the family of nations. In the two decades under his leadership, China has enjoyed unprecedented progress and development, of which each and every Chinese person is deeply proud. He proved himself worthy of the name of "a fine son of the Chinese people"[①] and stood out as a distinguished national hero.

However, on the eve of Hong Kong's return to its motherland, Deng Xiaoping passed away in 1997, which focused caring eyes of the world on China: Where will China head without Deng Xiaoping? At such a historical juncture, the third generation of the CPC leadership, with Jiang Zemin at the core, were clearly aware of their own historical mission: to develop Deng Xiaoping Theory consistently and creatively, and push the cause of building socialism with Chinese characteristics into full swing in the 21st century so as to realize the all-round rejuvenation of the Chinese nation. This is also a historic mission that the times has endowed the third generation of the CPC leadership.

In his report to the 15th National Congress, Jiang Zemin reviewed the past hundred years of history in China, took a broad view of the overall situation and general trend of the world, took into account China's national conditions, and thereby established the strategy of cross-century development of the Chinese nation and clearly proposed the grand goal of basically realizing modernization in the middle of the 21st century: "Looking into the next century, we have set our goals as follows: In the first decade, the gross national product will double that of the year 2000, the people will enjoy an even more comfortable life and a more or less ideal socialist market economy will have come into being. With the efforts to be made in another

---

[①] Deng Xiaoping once said, "I am a son of the Chinese people. I have a deep love for my people and my country." It was his love for the people that fostered his love for the Party and the country. That is why he said, "My life belongs to the Party and the country." These simple words are a condensed expression of his infinite love for the Party, the country and the people. –Tr.

decade when the Party celebrates its centenary, economy will be more developed and the various systems will be further improved. By the middle of the next century when the People's Republic celebrates its centenary, the modernization program will have been accomplished by and large and China will have become a prosperous, strong, democratic and culturally advanced socialist country."

Jiang Zemin's report to the 15th National Congress of the CPC had more than once mentioned that the all-round rejuvenation of the Chinese nation accords with the "fundamental interests", "common interests" and "common ideal"[①] of the Chinese nation.

In his speech at the closing ceremony of the first session of the 9th National People's Congress (NPC), Jiang Zemin passionately further elaborated his strategic vision and goal for achieving great rejuvenation of the Chinese nation: "By the middle of the next century when the People's Republic celebrates its centenary, the modernization program will have been accomplished by and large and China will have become a prosperous, strong, democratic and culturally advanced socialist country. At that time, China will catch up with the level of moderately developed countries in the world, and the Chinese people will achieve common prosperity on the basis of modernization and realize the great rejuvenation of the Chinese nation." He confidently expressed: "We will certainly triumphantly reach the glorious destination of modernization."

At the 100th anniversary celebration of Peking University, based on recalling the glorious days of the Chinese people's arduous work in the 20th century and looking to the brilliant prospects of the great rejuvenation of the Chinese nation in the 21st century, Jiang Zemin sounded the clarion call for all the people of our whole country, in particular the young generation, to march towards the 21st century: "(I hope all our youth and all the people of our country) unite with one heart and one mind under the guidance of the Party's basic theory and line, boldly break new ground, and progress toward the new century, the glorious goal of modernization, and the great rejuvenation of the Chinese nation."

At the grand celebration of the 50th anniversary of the founding of the PRC in 1949, Jiang Zemin traced the Chinese nation's century-long history of struggle and looked to the prospects of its development in the new century. He solemnly

---

① Documentation Research Office of the CPC Central Committee: *Selected Documents Since the Fifteenth National Congress of the CPC,* Vol.1, Beijing: People's Publishing House, 2000, p.4.

proclaimed to the world: "From the middle of this century to that of the next, the Chinese people, with hard and enterprising work of 100 years, will by and large bring about socialist modernization. The Chinese nation will stand rock-firm in the family of nations." "China will emerge in the East as a prosperous, strong, democratic, culturally advanced and modern socialist country." It declared the confidence and determination with which the CPC leads the people of all ethnic groups in China to strengthen the nation in the new century.

Obviously, Jiang Zemin's "Achieve the great rejuvenation of the Chinese nation" is a clarion call to action, and is the historical mission entrusted by the times to the third generation of the CPC leadership, its sober consensus, and a programmatic slogan highly characteristic of this leadership. This sonorous slogan fully reflected the common aspiration of the people of all ethnic groups across the country and adhered to the dreams and long-cherished aspirations of countless public-spirited people, to which, for more than a hundred years, they have contributed, with their vision, commitment, and even their lives. This resounding slogan will surely further pool the wisdom and strength of the whole Party and the people of all ethnic groups and will inspire the Chinese people to pursue a better life and to strive for the prosperity, democracy and civilization of China.

In order to realize this programme, the third-generation CPC leadership with Jiang Zemin at its core established and formulated a series of guidelines and policies of strategic significance at the juncture of history and the times.

Firstly, the CPC Central Committee with Jiang Zemin at the core has always stressed the importance of upholding Deng Xiaoping Theory, establishing this theory as one of the guiding political principles of the CPC and formally enshrining it into the Party Constitution, and arming with it the entire Party and the people of all China's ethnic groups and adhering to the Party's basic line for 100 years. For the first time, Deng Xiaoping Theory provided for the first time clear systematic answers to several basic questions about how to build, consolidate and develop socialism in China, an economically and culturally underdeveloped country. In contemporary China, only Deng Xiaoping Theory and no other theory can solve the problem of the future and destiny of socialism. Deng Xiaoping Theory is one of the guiding political principles of China's modernization. Therefore, upholding it and establishing it as the Party's guiding political principle and program of action have provided the most credible and fundamental guarantee for the great rejuvenation of the Chinese nation in the 21st century.

Secondly, the third-generation of the CPC leadership with Jiang Zemin at the core, provided systematic summarization of the theoretical achievements and new experiences accumulated since the 13th CPC National Congress, in particular since the 14th National Congress, reiterated that the primary stage of socialism is the paramount reality and the most important national condition in contemporary China, summed up the basic characteristics of the primary stage of socialism, elaborated the basic principles and programs for the primary stage of socialism and answered questions about what socialist economy, politics and culture with Chinese characteristics are and how to build such economy, politics and culture, so that the strategies, principles and policies of China's socialist modernization drive have a solid and sound basis. Thus, we believe that the CPC has been more theoretically and politically mature and has fully possessed the leadership ability to recognize, grasp and control the overall situation.

Thirdly, the third-generation CPC leadership with Jiang Zemin at the core, holding on to the materialist dialectic view of Marxism and targeting the new conflicts and problems which have cropped up in the modernization drive under the conditions of the socialist market economy, profoundly analyzed the twelve major relationships that are of global importance, and believed that the correct handling of the relationship between reform, development and stability is relevant to overall development. As Jiang Zemin pointed out, "Reform is a powerful driving force for economic and social development, which aims to further liberate and develop the productive forces; stability is the premise of development and reform, and development and reform must have a stable political and social environment. Therefore, we need to effectively size up the overall situation, plan carefully, and get a comprehensive grasp of internal relationship between reform, development and stability, so as to ensure they mutually complement and promote each other." "We need to carry forward reform and development while we enjoy political and social stability and ensure long-term political and social stability while pressing ahead with reform and development." This shows that the third-generation leadership has a profound understanding and comprehensive grasp of the overall situation of China's socialist modernization under the new historical conditions and of the laws of building socialism with Chinese characteristics.

Fourthly, as far as the path of economic development and the mode of development are concerned, the third generation of the CPC leadership proposed that China's economic development should be transformed from extensive pattern to intensive one, from denotative development, which is mainly carried out by virtue of increasing investment, launching more projects and pursuing quantity, to connotative development, which is driven by progress in science and technology and in workforce quality and focuses on economic efficiency. It is proposed that we should adopt comprehensive supporting measures in the legal system construction, policy implementation and plan formulation and other aspects, and effectively put the improvement of economic efficiency at the centre of economic work. At the same time, Jiang Zemin, from the perspective of the relationship of economic development with population, resources and environment, also proposed that the strategy of sustainable socio-economic development and the strategy of developing China through science and education should be implemented, that more emphasis should be placed on the implementation of the strategy of sustainable development, and that scientific and technological progress and vigorous development of education and improvement of workforce quality should play a key role in socio-economic development. The proposing and implementation of "Two fundamental changes"① and "Two strategies"② reflect the development concept that the third generation of collective leadership with Jiang Zemin at the core has rationally chosen on the basis of the development of the times and China's national conditions. It is the only way to develop economy and achieve all-round social progress and national rejuvenation.

Fifthly, on the issues of economic reforms, the overarching goal and basic framework of the socialist market economic system have been established and the strategy has been laid out to realize the fundamental transformation from the traditional planned economic system to the socialist market economic system. For the first time, theory of socialist market economy was systematically established. In the report to the 14th National Congress, Jiang Zemin conducted a theoretical analysis based on Deng Xiaoping's thinking that socialism can also engage in market economy, mainly about the relevant discussion in the "South Tour Talk". He clearly put forward the concept of socialist market economy and clearly pointed out that China's goal of economic restructuring is to establish a socialist market economy. "Decision on Issues Concerning the Establishment of a Socialist Market Economic

---

① Two fundamental transformations with overall significance, namely, the transformation of the economic system from the traditional planned economic system to the socialist market economic system, and the transformation of the mode of economic growth from extensive to intensive. –Tr.
② the strategies of reinvigorating China through science and education and strengthening the nation through human resource development. –Tr.

Structure" adopted by the Third Plenum of the 14th Congress of the CPC made further elucidation on the theory of socialist market economy and the guidelines and policies for economic restructuring, and established the basic framework for socialist market economy.

In the 15th National Congress of the CPC, many new theoretical breakthroughs have been made and many new strategic initiatives have been put forward to deepen economic restructuring. For example, "The public sector includes not only the state- and collectively-owned sectors, but also the state-owned and collectively-owned elements in the sector of mixed ownership." "Public ownership can and should take diversified forms. All management methods and organizational forms that mirror the laws governing socialized production may be utilized boldly." "The joint stock system is a form of capital organization of modern enterprises... It can be used both under capitalism and under socialism." "Aiming at improving the state sector of the economy as a whole, we shall effectuate a strategic reorganization of state-owned enterprises by well managing large enterprises while adopting a flexible policy toward small ones." "China needs to develop diverse forms of ownership with public ownership in the leading position." "The non-public sector is an important component part of China's socialist market economy." These new theoretical views are new summarization of the meanings and characteristics of the socialist market economy and that of our understanding about it. They not only serve as powerful theoretical support for continuing to deepen economic reform and others, but also provide a rational guide for action in resolving a series of new conflicts and problems in establishing a socialist market economic system and in developing a socialist market economy.

Sixthly, on the issue of the construction of democratic politics, it has been clearly stated that the Party should take law-based governance and the building of a country of socialist rule of law as a fundamental principle by which the Party leads the people in running the country. In the report to the 15th National Congress, Jiang Zemin pointed out: "Building socialist politics with Chinese characteristics means managing state affairs according to law and developing socialist democracy under the CPC leadership and with the people as the masters of the country. To do this, we should uphold and improve the people's democratic dictatorship led by the working class and based on the worker-peasant alliance. We should uphold and improve the system of people's congresses, the system of multi-party cooperation and political consultation under the leadership of the CPC and the system of regional autonomy in areas inhabited by ethnic minorities. We should promote democracy, improve the legal system and build a socialist country ruled by law."

Managing state affairs according to law and building a country ruled by law serve as symbols of social civilization as well as the fundamental requirements and manifestations of socialist democracy. Managing state affairs according to law and building a socialist country ruled by law should be taken as the basic strategy for the Party to lead the people in governing the country, and thereby the adherence to Party leadership, the development of people's democracy and carrying one's duties in strict accordance with legally specified limits of authority and procedures can be unified, which is important progress in the advancement of the theory of socialist democracy development. Based on the overarching goal of further extending the scope of socialist democracy and improving the socialist legal system, governing the country according to law and making it a socialist country ruled by law, the 15th National Congress of the CPC has also laid out the arrangements for promoting the reform of political structure and improving democracy and the legal system.

Seventhly, on the issue of cultural construction, Jiang Zemin profoundly expounded the programme of developing Chinese socialist culture. As he pointed out, building a socialist culture with Chinese characteristics means taking Marxism as guidance, aiming at training people so that they have high ideals, moral integrity, a good education and a strong sense of discipline, and developing a national, scientific and popular socialist culture geared to the needs of modernization, of the world and of the future. To do this, we should persist in arming the whole Party and educating the people with Deng Xiaoping Theory. We should strive to raise the ideological and ethical standards and the educational, scientific and cultural levels of the whole nation. We should adhere to the orientation of serving the people and socialism and the principle of letting a hundred flowers blossom and a hundred schools of thought contend, laying emphasis on progress and boosting academic activities, art and literature. We should foster socialist ideology and ethics by basing ourselves on China's reality, carrying on the fine cultural traditions handed down from history and drawing on the achievements of other civilizations. Jiang Zemin also pointed out: A socialist culture with Chinese characteristics is a major force in uniting and inspiring the people of all our nationalities, and an important indicator of our overall national strength. This has provided a whole new perspective for the entire Party to attach importance to cultural progress. The process of the modernization drive is largely dependent on the enhancement of the quality of the entire population and the exploitation of intellectual resources, the whole Party must fully understand that cultural advancement is essential and urgent because it plays a great role in developing the cause of building socialism and rejuvenating the nation.

Jiang Zemin also emphasized that in the entire process of socialist modernization, emphasis must always be placed on the development of material civilization, and the center of economic construction must be firmly grasped and not wavered at any time. At the same time, we must firmly attach importance to promoting cultural and ethical advancement, and we absolutely cannot vacillate on this issue. We will never again seek economic growth at the cost of cultural and ethical progress, for socialism with Chinese characteristics is a form of socialism in which material and cultural progresses go hand in hand. Cultural progress should be adapted to economic progress, integrated into the overall plan of economic and social development, and provide a strong mental impetus and intellectual support for economic construction and reform and opening-up.

Eighthly, on the issue of Party building, he proposed pressing ahead with the great new undertaking of Party building, that a contingent of competent officials should be trained, and that the fight against corruption should be raised to the level of a serious political struggle and further intensified. In the report to the 15th National Congress of the CPC, it is pointed out that, in order to advance our cause in an all-round way to the 21st century, it is essential to uphold, strengthen and improve the leadership of the Party. The third generation of the central collective leadership has clearly proposed a "new great undertaking " of Party building in accordance with the new situations and unfamiliar problems which the Party encountered under the conditions of market economy, i.e., to build the Party into a Marxist political party that is armed with Deng Xiaoping Theory, wholeheartedly serving the people, consolidated in the aspects of theoretical and political education, and political and organizational affairs, enabled to withstand all trials and tribulations, always ahead of the times in its historic journey. To achieve this goal, the third generation of the central collective leadership emphasized that the Party's political philosophical and organizational strength and the advantage of its close ties with the people should be given full play to; and that the Party should run itself with strict discipline to maintain its progressive nature and its integrity.

Party building means training a contingent of officials. Adapting itself to the requirements of the times, the new development and the actual situation of the training of a contingent of officials, the third generation of the central collective leadership clearly proposed that it is a strategic task to train and select a large number of excellent young officials who can shoulder cross-century important tasks. Senior leading officials are required to become Marxist politicians. It is an issue of strategic significance whether we can build such a contingent of officials, whether we can guarantee that leadership at all levels in the Party and the country is holden by those who are loyal to Marxism, which is critical to the prospects of the Party.

In the new circumstances, it is a vital issue for our officials, especially Party and government leaders, to respond to the challenges of governance, reform and opening up , and the market economy. Jiang Zemin pointed out: Whether we can fight corruption effectively is related to whether we can maintain the Party's good image among its people, and whether we can continue to maintain and develop the Party's close ties with its people, which, as a result, become a fundamental issue in Party building. The third generation of the central collective leadership with Jiang Zemin at the core put the anti-corruption struggle to the height of the serious political struggle that is critical to the survival of the Party and the country, and reinforce efforts in practice to combat corruption.

In addition, the third generation of the central collective leadership put forward a series of new theories and views on agricultural development and rural reform, intensification of reform and opening up to the outside world, the reform of political structure, the strengthening of national defense and armed forces in the new era, diplomatic relations, the policy of "peaceful reunification and one country, two systems", and the establishment of a new international economic and political order, to name a few. It shows that the third generation of central collective leadership, with Jiang Zemin at its core, has gained a deeper and more profound understanding of the laws of building socialism with Chinese characteristics.

As historical comparison and realistic analysis have shown, it is not only possible for the Chinese nation to achieve great rejuvenation in the 21st century, but is also an urgent requirement for the development of the times.

That the Chinese nation will surely achieve its great rejuvenation in the 21st century has a most important theoretical support and moral assurance, namely the establishment of Deng Xiaoping Theory by the CPC which has been taken as the Party's guiding ideology and enshrined in the Party Constitution.

Deng Xiaoping Theory is the result of a thorough review of lessons learned from the world socialist movement and that from China's socialist modernization. The reason why, since reform and opening up started about 20 years ago, unprecedented changes have taken place in China lies in the guidance of Deng Xiaoping Theory. No theory but Deng Xiaoping Theory alone can settle the issues concerning the development of China, which is a historical conclusion drawn by the Party from history and reality, which we shall never abandon. This theory is a guiding political principle of China's modernization and a valuable cultural wealth and a guide to action for realizing the great rejuvenation of the Chinese nation. Only by upholding and applying Deng Xiaoping Theory in practice and by identifying and responding to unfamiliar problems and new situations which may arise in the modernization drive, can the CPC and its people go from victory to victory on the path of modernization.

The most profound source and tremendous impetus for the Chinese nation to achieve its great rejuvenation in the 21st century come from the Chinese people's pursuit of happiness and the goal of prosperous, democratic, and civilized modernization. The people's pursuit of personal happiness is consciously and harmoniously united with the realization of the great rejuvenation of the whole nation.

The practice of reform and opening up has witnessed profound changes in China and in the way of thinking and values of contemporary the Chinese people. They have more profoundly realized the mistakes they have made in what they thought and did at the previous stages and have gained more understanding of the advanced cultures in the world. The Chinese people have emerged from the misunderstanding of their previous unrealistic socialist outlook on development and the practice of divorcing from their lives and other people, and have come to realize the close relationship between modernization and national revitalization and their own lives. The desire for a better life through their own efforts has become the strong will the Chinese people. This is "awakened desire" of the historical subject. It is in the people's pursuit of their own interests and a better life that the great rejuvenation of the Chinese nation can be realized.

Another favorable condition for the Chinese nation to realize its great rejuvenation in the 21st century is that it has accumulated rich experience in its 21 years of reform and opening up as well as its modernization drive, which has provided valuable experience for the great development and national rejuvenation in the 21st century.

The 21 years of reform and opening up is the process of China's modernization in full swing. The contradictions and problems faced by China's modernization have been and are being exposed. Regarding how to deal with and solve them, we have made much exploration, during which we have reviewed China's positive and negative experience in modernization and learned from the gains and losses. This is undoubtedly a very valuable asset for fully and profoundly understanding the legal system of China's modernization drive, enhancing the consciousness and scientific nature of modernization drive, overcoming blindness and deviation, and enhancing the ability to steered the modernization drive on the right course.

The Chinese nation also has laid a solid material foundation for its great rejuvenation in the 21st century.

The practice of China's reform and opening up and modernization has greatly improved China's overall national strength. From 1993 to 1997, China's gross domestic product (GDP) enjoyed an average annual increase of 11%, at comparable prices. It was one of the countries and regions with the fast-growing economic growth in the world in the same period. In 1996, the ranking of China's GDP rose from the tenth place in 1991 to the seventh place. The gross national product had a quadruple increase on the basis of 1980. In 1999, the GDP exceeded US$ 1 trillion. China's output of grain, cotton, coal, steel, electricity, petroleum and other major industrial and agricultural products were among the highest in the world, with the import and export volume totaling more than US$ 360 billion, for which China ranks high among the world's major trading nations. Over the years, China's scientific capacity and education have been improved significantly, as well as infrastructure. Over 200 million Chinese people have bid farewell to extreme poverty. What is more favorable is, a large domestic market with a population of 1.2 billion will bring enormous potential and a vast space for economic development. In addition, the order of the socialist market economy in China has been taking form, and the institutional conditions for economic development tends to mature, all of which are favorable basic conditions for the Chinese nation to rapidly develop in the 21st century.

To achieve the great rejuvenation of the Chinese nation in the 21st century is also an urgent request of present-day world and the development of the times.

Peace and development remain the main themes of the times. The world is moving towards multi-polarity, with the tendency of economic globalization, regionalization and conglomeration intensified, which provides an opportunity—and a challenge—for the Chinese nation, who must seize opportunities and respond to challenges with concrete actions, so as to realize its all-round rejuvenation. The favorable factors of the world trend and the world pattern will enable our nation to focus its energies on modernization drive in a relatively long peacetime with developed countries optimistic about China's vast market and economic development prospects, which provides the possibility of further expanding economic and technological cooperation and exchange with foreign countries. In addition, with modern science and technology develop rapidly worldwide, China can better leverage its latecomer advantage to achieve the leapfrogging development in certain fields of science and technology. However, compared with the development of developed countries and the current rapid development of the scientific and technological revolution, China is still facing severe challenges and enormous pressure of development. In the overall national strength competition in which high technology takes a leading role, China is still in a vulnerable position.[①] With the economic regionalization, conglomeration and trade protectionism intensifying, economic friction may escalate. Some Western powers are reluctant to see the rise of China and even intend to create a series of obstacles to curb China's development.

Mankind has experienced the era of agricultural economy and industrial economy, and has now entered the information age. Science and technology have become the cornerstone of modern civilization and the decisive factors in promoting sustained economic and social progress. The innovation, dissemination and application of knowledge have become the inexhaustible resources and impetus for future economic and social development. Human beings are about to enter the age of knowledge economy. In the world today, the competition among various countries is increasingly manifested in the competition of science and technology and of talents. The development of science and technology, as well as the innovation of knowledge, continue to determine the development of a country and a nation. Innovation is the soul of a nation's progress. Without innovation, it is hard for a nation to stand firm among the nations of the world. Fundamentally, innovation means education promotion and talent cultivation. Therefore, cultivating a great number of talented people who can adapt to the requirements of the times and of modernization is a grand plan for the future development of the Chinese nation. Otherwise, China's standing would crumble in the world and the Chinese nation would fail to keep up with the pace of the development of the times, and once again face the situation of being abused for lagging behind. The general trend of the world and the external environment urgently demand that the Chinese nation should no longer lose its opportunities and that it should seize every opportunity to respond to challenges and

---

① This essay was first published in 2000. –Tr.

develop itself.

China has a civilization of over 5,000 years, and it was the most powerful nation in the world until the end of the 18th century, which, gradually moved towards debility due to the shortsighted arrogant self-conservative feudal dictatorship clinging to "*Huaxia*-nationality[①] centrism", adopting a policy of closing the country to outside contact. At the same time, the Western countries were carrying on the industrial revolution and moving toward industrial civilization, so when the Opium War broke out, there came stark contrast between weak and backward China and the mighty advanced Western nations. But it was hard to fill the gap instantly. From then on, China was reduced to being beaten and abused, and thus began the tragedy of modern China.

The 19th century was the century when the Chinese nation started to decline. The beginning of the 20th century witnessed shameful occupation by the Allied Forces of the Eight-Power in Beijing with the Summer Palace destroyed in the raging fire. From the middle of the 19th century to the 20th century, the Chinese nation has never ceased its fight against its backwardness, impoverishment, and the foreign bully, or relaxed its effort to achieve its rejuvenation. The torch of modernization in China has been kept aloft and the relay baton of rejuvenating the Chinese nation have been historically passed on to the third generation of the CPC leadership with Jiang Zemin at the core. The "third generation" is a generation that has inherited the past success and opened up the future in the history of China's modernization and the rejuvenation of the Chinese nation and is the first cross-century CPC leadership since its establishment. The "third generation" fully shoulders the weighty responsibility entrusted to them by the times with a profound sense of history and a clear sense of mission. It takes upholding Deng Xiaoping Theory as the most fundamental and most important strategy for China's modernization and the great rejuvenation of the Chinese nation. It is insisted that we should apply it to our entire cause and all our undertakings. In the meantime, Deng Xiaoping Theory should be creatively applied in practice to explore, answer and solve new major issues and new conflicts which have emerged constantly in the reform, opening up and modernization drive. In

---

[①] The former of *Han* nationality. The origin of *Huaxia* was *Jiangji* tribal alliance with the leaders of Emperor *Yan* and Emperor *Huang*. Emperors *Yan* and *Huang* opened up common districts with main departments of the central plains, created common economics with main department of millet agriculture, and founded common psychology with characteristics of hero\ancestor worship, so they have respected "original ancestor of *Huaxia* nationality" for thousands of years. –Tr.

theory, a series of new ideas have been put forward and new breakthroughs have been made in practice. The Chinese people are striding toward the 21st century, with pride and enthusiasm, under the strong leadership of the third generation of collective leadership and courageously marching toward the great rejuvenation of the Chinese nation.

As history has told us, the Chinese nation is a great nation; it has been through hardships and adversity but remains indomitable. The Chinese people are a great people; they possess boundless wisdom and strength. Now on the eve of the 21st century, I often hear the indomitable and magnificent melody of Yellow River Cantata , which is the most vivid symbol of the spirit of the Chinese nation. We can be absolutely certain that under the new circumstances, it will more powerfully encourage the Chinese people to pool the wisdom and strength for reaching the goal of bringing about prosperity, democracy and civilization and realizing the new glory of the Chinese nation in the 21st century!

Theoretical Attribute, Philosophical Basis and Cultural Essence of the Important Thought of the Three Represents*

Marked by the publication of Hu Jintao's speech at a theoretical seminar on the important thought of the Three Represents[①], namely the "Outline for the Study of the Important Thought of the Three Represents", in June, 2003, an unprecedented tide of the interpretation of the "Three Represents" has taken shape among the entire Party members. It is manifested in the following three aspects:

I. New Revelation of the theme of the important thought of the Three Represents

Hu Jintao, at the theoretical seminar on the theory of the important thought of the Three Represents, delivered a speech which stipulates that "The important thought of the Three Represents is a model for upholding Marxism and for the development of Marxism". Why did he say so? To my understanding, "This is because the important thought of the Three Represents closely revolves around the historical theme of the constructing of socialism with Chinese characteristics in contemporary China; based on Deng Xiaoping Theory, further answers the question of what socialism is and how to build it and creatively answers the question about what kind of party to build and how to build a party." This sound theory has achieved fruitful results on

---

* Speech delivered at the seminar of the important thought of the Three Represents held by the Chinese Academy of Social Sciences.

① The Three Represents, namely, that the Party must always represent the development trend of China's advanced productive forces, the orientation of China's advanced culture and the fundamental interests of the overwhelming majority of the Chinese people, is the crystallization of the Party's collective wisdom and a guiding principle the Party must follow for a long time to come, Jiang said in his report. —Tr.

such major issues as guideline, development path, development stage, development strategy, fundamental tasks, developing impetus, reliable forces, international strategy, leadership force and fundamental purpose of building socialism with Chinese characteristics. In a nutshell, the important thought of the Three Represents is a series of closely-connected and inter-connected new ideas, new viewpoints and new theories with regard to reform, development and stability, internal affairs, foreign affairs, national defense, and governance of the Party and the country creatively proposed by the contemporary CPC members mainly represented by Jiang Zemin, based on, since the Fourth Plenary Session of the 13th CPC Central Committee, held from June 23 to 24, 1989, upholding Deng Xiaoping Theory, accurately grasping the characteristics of the times, and judiciously judging which development stage the Party is in, which shows that the Party's understanding of the laws of communist party governing, socialism construction and human society development has reached a new theoretical height and opened up a new realm for the development of Marxism. Therefore, I think it is possible to draw the conclusion that the important thought of the Three Represents is the rational crystallization of the Party's long-term exploration of the laws of governing and rejuvenating the country, and is the unity of the theory of ruling party building and the theory of China's social development.

We should understand the important thought of the Three Represents from the perspective of the historical process of building socialism with Chinese characteristics, so as to deeply understand its theoretical attributes and historical status. As the ruling party, the CPC is the strong leadership core of the great cause of building socialism with Chinese characteristics. It shoulders the noble historical responsibility of leading the development of socialism, advancing modernization, and, based on this, realizing the great rejuvenation of the Chinese nation. The key to running China's affairs well lies in the Party. In contemporary China, the Party's own efforts to strengthen itself through raising its governing capabilities and bolstering its position as the governing party, developing socialism with Chinese characteristics, and fully realizing China's modernization and social progress, are three closely related major issues. After the 1990s, how can the Party meet the development needs of our times and properly deal with the profound and complicated changes which have taken place in the world, the Chinese society, and within the Party, and continuously push forward the cause of building socialism with Chinese characteristics? This is a deep-seated problem that will inevitably be encountered in the process of practicing Deng Xiaoping Theory and advancing the great cause of building socialism with Chinese characteristics. In other words, in the face of profound changes in governance conditions and social environment, what kind of party shall be built? how shall we build the party, strengthen and improve party building, raise the party's leadership and governance level? All these constitutes the inevitable requirement and prerequisite for the development of socialism and the advancing of socialist modernization. The answers to the questions about "what kind of party should the CPC be", "how to build the CPC" provide a sure way to answer in practice the questions about "what is socialism", " how to build socialism ". These two pairs of questions constitute the two fundamental issues closely related to the development of socialism with Chinese characteristics. At the critical moment of building socialism with Chinese characteristics, the important thought of "Three Represents" has seized on and made great efforts to solve the key issue of Party building, which concerns the overall situation of strategic significance; judiciously explained the relationship between Party building and socialist modernization, between the leadership of the Party and the administration of the state, between the leadership of the Party and the people; profoundly reveal the intrinsic relationship between the governance over the Party and the governance over the country and the intrinsic relationship between the economy, politics, and culture of socialism with Chinese characteristics; and judiciously crystallized the arduous exploration of the laws of the ruling party building and socialist progress, the law of human social development and the relationship between each other. Therefore, the important thought of the Three Represents is not only the innovation and development of Marxist theory of party building, but also has developed Marxist historical materialism, political economy, and scientific socialism with new perspectives on a series of issues. The "Three Represents" is not only in line with Marxism-Leninism, Mao Zedong Thought, and Deng Xiaoping Theory, but also reflects the new requirements of the development and changes of the contemporary world and China with regard to the work of the Party and the state. It is the latest achievement in adapting Marxism to China's conditions.

We should also understand the important thought of the Three Represents from the perspective of the development of modern Chinese history, so as to deeply understand the theoretical attributes and historical status of this thought. Modern Chinese history is a history of being bullied and humiliated, a history of rising up and fighting, and a history of making people rich and powerful. Making the people rich and the country strong is the practical theme of modern Chinese history. From Wei Yuan's "learning from the barbarians to develop skills to control the barbarians", the Self-Strengthening Movement, the Hundred Days' Reform, and Dr. Sun Yat-sen's Three Principles of the People, to Mao Zedong's theory of the new democratic revolution, all these are all different theoretical reflections and theoretical strategies of the Chinese people and the Chinese nation in their making the people rich and the country strong. After the CPC won the revolution and took power, the Chinese Communists represented by Mao Zedong, were soberly aware of the tests and challenges posed by the change in the position of the Party. According to Mao Zedong, the journey from Xibaipo (西柏坡)① to Beijing could be vividly likened to "coming to Beijing for exams(进京赶考)②", and pointed out that winning the revolution is only the first step in the Long March, and the road ahead is longer, greater, and tougher. Mao Zedong first led the CPC to successfully complete the transition from the new-democratic revolution to the socialist revolution, and then carried out inspiring explorations on how to consolidate and develop socialism after gaining power to bolster the position of the Party as the governing party, but such exploration has paid a heavy price. The fundamental reason is that the Party made a mistake about what its guiding philosophy should be; that is, it took, as the guide to action, the following two theories: the theory that the productive forces can be promoted through constantly transforming the production relations; the theory that revolution shall be continued under the dictatorship of the proletariat. Such mistake almost brought the Party and the country to the brink of collapse.

Under the historical conditions in which peace and development have become the central theme of the times, Deng Xiaoping summarized the experience and lessons for socialist development at home and abroad, adhered to the basic results of the theory and practice of scientific socialism, and gasped the fundamental issue of "what is socialism", "how to build socialism", profoundly revealing its essence, raising

---

① Hebei village, the former headquarters of the Party and residence of its leaders including Chairman Mao. On March 23, 1949, Mao Zedong and other revolutionaries packed up and left Xibaipo, a sacred place for the then 28-year-long Communist struggle, which paved the way for the founding of the People's Republic of China in 1949, their destination being Beijing, a war-ravaged city more than 350 kilometers away. —Tr.

② "Going to Beijing to rush for an exam" is a proper term for the imperial examination system in ancient China. At that time, students from all over the country had to pass the township examination, and then pass the prefectural and county examinations to be admitted to the *Juren*（举人）before they were eligible to enter Beijing for the *Jinshi*（进士）examination. Since the time for each examination for *Jinshi* is fixed, and the place for the examination is mostly in the capital where the emperor is located, there is a saying of "going to Beijing to rush for an exam." Here it is used as a metaphor. —Tr.

the cognition of socialism to a new rational level, opening up a path of socialism with Chinese Characteristics and pointing the right direction for China's socialist modernization.

Since the 1990s, contemporary Chinese Communists represented by Jiang Zemin have upheld Deng Xiaoping Theory, closely integrated it with the constantly changing situation, accurately grasped the characteristics of the times, judiciously judged which development stage the Party is in, and made in-depth exploration of the law of the governance party building and the law of the progress of socialism with Chinese characteristics and hence formed the important thought of the Three Represents, which correctly answers the question about how the CPC will rally and lead the people of all ethnic groups in China to accelerate socialist modernization and fulfil the historical mission of the great rejuvenation of the Chinese nation and the making of greater contribution to the cause of advancing human progress on the path to socialism with Chinese characteristics when human society has crossed the threshold of the 21st century, profound changes have taken place in the international situation, and China has entered a new stage of development to build a moderately prosperous society in all respects and accelerate socialist modernization. It is a rational sublimation of the theory of Marxist political parties' state governance and national rejuvenation, and is the fundamental guideline for the CPC' governing, prospering of the country, and realization of the goal of building China into a modern socialist country that is prosperous, strong, democratic, and culturally advanced, and the great rejuvenation of the Chinese nation.

II. From ideation to formation of practical method

The clear and in-depth explanation of the essence of the important thought of the Three Represents has made "Three Represents" a form of "the concept of practice" that not only has profound connotation, but also combines knowledge and practice. In the second stage of the study and implementation of the important thought of the Three Represents, from July 2001 to November 2002, Jiang Zemin, on behalf of the CPC Central Committee, delivered an important speech at the celebration of the 80th anniversary of the founding of the Party, systematically expounding the rational connotation and basic content of the important thought of the Three Represents, "proposing that with regard to fully implementing the important thought of the Three Represents, "The key is to persist in advancing with the times, the core is to adhere to the progressive nature of the Party, and the essence is to adhere to governing the country for the people." The 16th National Congress of the CPC has established the important thought of the Three Represents, together with Marxism-Leninism, Mao Zedong Thought, and Deng Xiaoping Theory, as the guiding philosophy that the Party must uphold for a long time, and set forth the plans and requirements for the study and implementation of the "Three Represents".

In Hu Jintao's speech at the seminar on the theory of the important thought of the Three Represents, the essence of this thought is specifically and systematically expounded. As is pointed out, its essence is to build the Party for the public and govern the country for the people and its fundamental purpose and outcome is to realize the shared aspirations of the Chinese people, meet their needs, and safeguard their interests; for the Marxist governing party, it is always essential that the Party should be built for the public and the country be governed for the people, that we should continue to fulfill, uphold and develop the fundamental interests of all the people, and that we should give full play to the enthusiasm of all the people to develop advanced productive forces and advanced culture; the future and destiny of a political party and government depend on popular support. Only when the theories, lines, guidelines, policies, and all the work involved are supported by the people, can a Marxist political party stand in an invincible position for good. As is emphasized, "We should study, understand and implement the important thought of the Three Represents, and firmly grasp the principle of building the Party and governing the country for the people. This is the most important indicator of whether we have truly understood and sincerely implemented the important thought of the Three Represents." In order to uphold this principle, we must implement it in all the work concerning the Party and state formulating and enforcing the guidelines and policies; officials at all levels should keep in alignment with it in the way of thinking and in actions; in the work of solving the people's problems in work and life. As is required, leading officials at all levels must observe the Party's fundamental purpose of wholeheartedly serving the people and being responsible to the people, ensuring that they keep in mind the interests of the people, bear in mind whatever the people are concerned about, rely on the people in their work, and do everything for the people. We must insist on exercising power for the people, care about their feelings, and make benefit for them, sincerely do practical things for them, do one's utmost to solve their problems, persevere in doing good things for them, and emphasize that the interests of the people are nothing trivial. The Party's commitment to serving the public good and exercising power in the interests of the people is a ringing slogan; it is about addressing their gravest needs and problems, and solve their most pressing concerns and those that are essential to their immediate interests, and strive to unify the achievement of the long-term strategic goals of economic and social development and the improvement of the people's lives, and combine the realization of the people's long-term interests with the addressing of their immediate concerns.

The important thought of the Three Represents is an extensive and profound scientific system, but truth is always simple and concrete, and its value ultimately lies in becoming a powerful weapon that guides people to transform the world. The summarization of the essence of the important thought of the Three Represents as the Party's commitment to serving the public good and exercising power in the interests of the people actually simplifies this philosophical system as the fundamental approach and method for guiding all Party members to strengthen the building of the governing party, promote the great cause of building socialism with Chinese characteristics, and realize the great rejuvenation of the Chinese nation.

The important thought of the Three Represents itself contains profound theoretical implications, but it also has a concise language form of practical significance. It not only contains a certain idea, but also expresses a kind of behavior orientation and requirements. The so-called nature is the internal basis on which a thing being distinguished for itself from other things. If one grasps the nature of a thing, he or she grasps its essence. The revelation of the essence of the important thought of the Three Represents as the Party's commitment to serving the public good and exercising power in the interests of the people, makes the trend, requirements and characteristics of the application of this thought more definite, making it "conceptualized" and easier to be applied, to function as the guide of the thinking and actions of the Party members and officials. In a nutshell, such revelation renders the "Three Represents" more feasible, and hence makes the important thought of the Three Represents become a form of theory that not only has profound connotations, but also integrate knowledge with practice.

III. Fundamental characteristic of important thought of the Three Represents lies in practicality

All theories originate from practice and in turn guide new practice and accept practice as the criterion and hence are to be developed and improved. Marx once declared that his philosophy was not only to explain the world, but more importantly, to transform the world. Only when it is mastered by the people and becomes a strong material force in the creative activities of hundreds of millions of people to transform the world, can theory realize its own value and purpose. The important thought of the Three Represents is the result of a thorough review of lessons learned from the past experience of the CPC in leading the people to carry out China's revolution, construction and development over the past 80 years, especially since the 1990s, and is the latest theoretical achievement in adapting Marxism to China's conditions. Therefore, it is the fundamental guideline for strengthening the building of the governing party, advancing the great cause of building socialism with Chinese characteristics, and realizing the long-term stability of the Party and the country and the great rejuvenation of the Chinese nation. Theory must realize its value and continue to develop after guiding new practice. Therefore, Hu Jintao emphasized the practicality of the important thought of the Three Represents. As was pointed out, "The purpose of studying the important thought of the Three Represents is to apply." "Only by applying the important thought of the Three Represents to guide practice can we dig deep into the theories to understand it in full." In order to study, understand and implement the important thought of the Three Represents, we must closely connect it with the realities of reform, opening up and modernization, and with actual work in our respective regions and departments, applying it to solve problems, promote work efficiency, implement the Party's commitment to serving the public good and exercising power in the interests of the people in various tasks, embody it in the work of the Party organizations at all levels and in the actions of the Party members, and hence make it be a powerful mental driving force to promote the cause to achieve new development and create a new situation. At the same time, we must closely connect it with the reality of our own thinking, apply it to guide the transformation of the subjective world, and establish a correct worldview, outlook on life, and values; otherwise, if the problems related to the outlook on power, status, and interests, and is not solved, it is impossible to transform the objective world in a good fashion.

In short, whether the important thought of the Three Represents can be implemented in practice has a bearing on the overall work of the Party and the state, the achievement of the grand goal of building a moderately prosperous society in all respects, the great rejuvenation of the Chinese nation, and the long-term development of the cause of building socialism with Chinese characteristics. As Hu Jintao emphasized, the Party members must be more active and resolute in studying, understanding and applying the important thought of the Three Represents, take it as the guiding principle in the Party work, and consciously apply it to guide their thinking and actions. In his speech at the opening ceremony of the theoretical seminar on the implementation of the important thought of the Three Represents, held on September 3, 2003, attended by major leading officials at the provincial / ministerial level, Hu Jintao also emphasized that it is a fundamental guideline for the work of the Party and state in the new era and in a new stage and if we want to further deepen the new upsurge of studying, understanding and implementing it, we must be more active in doing so, applying it to guide practice and strengthening the transformation of the subjective world. So, it can be seen that the practicality of the important thought of the Three Represents is highly valued and particularly emphasized by the new central leadership group--practicality is its fundamental characteristic.

On Characteristics of a Progressive Theory: Unity of Zeitgeist, Regularity and Affinity to the People

The progressive nature is the lifeblood of a Marxist political party. As Deng Xiaoping said, if a political party or a nation becomes rigid in its thinking, its life will cease. Hu Jintao once profoundly analyzed and judiciously summarized the lessons learned from the loss of the ruling status of some big parties and long-established parties that had been in power for many years, particularly the Communist Parties of the Soviet Union and Eastern European countries, and pointed out that the reason why these parties lost their governing status is in essence that they "lost their progressive nature in the heart of the people" "The progressive nature is the fundamental characteristic of a Marxist party." "The strengthening of the progressive nature of the CPC is of fundamental importance for the survival and development of a Marxist political party, and for its self-improvement." "If a political party attempts to maintain its progressive nature, it must conscientiously, actively and incessantly press ahead with the strengthening of its progressive nature." These important expositions on the strengthening of a political party's progressive nature fully demonstrate how significant it is for a Marxist party to strengthen its progressive nature.

Thoughts and theories are like a lighthouse which guides direction for a navigator on a sea voyage. The philosophical and theoretical programs of a governing party is more related to the development direction of a nation-state. Therefore, it can be said that ideological and theoretical construction is the most fundamental of the most fundamental for a party's strengthening of its progressive nature. As K. Marx and F. Engels once pointed out, the advantage of communists over other proletarian people is that they understand the conditions, processes, and general results of the proletarian movement. To do this, a political party must have a proletarian worldview as its theoretical basis. As Lenin once pointed out, only the political party guided by progressive theories can function as a progressive fighter. As Stalin pointed out, "No revolutionary theory, no revolutionary actions." As Jiang Zemin pointed out, "For a party, a country, and a nation, particularly for a big political party, a big country, and a nation with a large population like ours, if not guided by correct theories, if there is no strong intellectual support based on correct theories, then the party, country, and nation will be thrown into an unimaginable situation. It will fall into a mess, no allying power, no combat capability and no creativity, no bright future." He also once pointed out: "The main criterion for judging the nature of a political party is its theories and programs. If they are Marxist and represent the correct orientation of social development and the fundamental interests of the majority of the people, the party is a progressive one and the vanguard of the working class." Hu Jintao pointed out in his speech at the Central Committee's Work Conference on Marxist Theory Research and Construction Projects that philosophical and theoretical construction is the foundation of Party building. A Marxist political party can formulate correct lines, principles, and policies and pool the strength of the entire Party and the people to fight for noble ideals and goals only if it adheres to the guidance of sound theories.

This shows that a party's philosophical and theoretical construction is the key to strengthening a party's progressive nature. As the history of the CPC since its establishment has proved, if the Party's philosophies, theories, political programs, guidelines, and policies formulated accordingly can correctly reflect the characteristics of the times and China's conditions, and reflect the expectations of the people, then the Party will be able to lead its members and all the people to realize the goals of revolution and development; if the Party's philosophical and theoretical errors occur, the cause of the Party and the development of a nation-state will encounter major setbacks. Only by keeping abreast with the times and keeping the progressiveness of its theories can the Party rally the majority of the Party members and the people and lead the constant progress of the Chinese society.

Then, how can the progressive nature of a political party's ideas and theories be retained for good?

To retain the progressive nature of its ideas and theories for good, a Marxist political party must keep abreast with the times and continue to make theoretical innovation. Therefore, how to ensure the correct direction of theoretical innovation has become a key issue concerning whether the party's progressive nature can be retained for good.

I believe that insisting on theoretical innovation under the principle of unifying Marxist conception of history and values is a basic experience in upholding and developing the progressive nature of a party.

Marxism reveals the general laws of the development of human society and the special laws of the development of capitalist societies; the historical materialism is "the science of real men and of their historical development".[1] At the same time, Marxism is an ideological doctrine on the proletariat and on human liberation, and the essential characteristic of the system of Marxist theories is the unity of scienticity, class character and human trait.

The theoretical innovation must unswervingly adhere to Marxist conception of history.

The historical materialism believes that the creative material production activities of human beings are the basis of human history and the fundamental driving force for the development of human society, the ultimate determinant of which is the development of productive forces; that social existence determines social consciousness, and superstructure and ideology have a huge counter-effect on social existence; that social development is also a process of natural history, which has its inner objective laws; that the people are the creators of history and the main actors of historical development; and that truth is discovered, tested and developed in practice—that is, truth should be sought from facts; to name but a few. These are all the basic connotations of Marxist conception of history, which judiciously reveal the development mechanism and laws of social movement. Theoretical innovation of Marxist political parties must be carried out based on adhering to these correct viewpoints that have been proven in practice and on the combination of the ever-changing international, national and Party situations. In this way, these viewpoints can be applied innovatively and guide the overall development of society. The CPC's theories should reflect the characteristics of the times and grasp the laws of building socialism with Chinese characteristics in the context of the current era; otherwise, strategic mistakes might be made in the economic and social development of China, which will cause huge setbacks.

Theoretical innovation must be explored based on Marxist values. K. Marx and F. Engels laid special stress on the living conditions and the development direction

---

[1] Marx, K. & F. Engels: *Selected Works of Marx and Engels*, Vol. 4, Chin. ed., Beijing: People's Publishing House, 1995, P. 241.

of real individuals, and regarded the emancipation of the proletariat and the free and well-rounded development of everyone and the harmonious development of society as the goal of the communist society. In the "Communist Manifesto", K. Marx and F. Engels pointed out their visions for the future society: "In place of the old bourgeois society, with its classes and class antagonisms, we shall have an association, in which the free development of each is the condition for the free development of all." Almost half a century later, F. Engels still believed that only this passage can summarize the spirit of the new era in the future and accurately and concisely express his and Marx's basic ideas about the future socialist era. In *Das Kapital*, Marx also pointed out that the new society in the future is "a social form based on the basic principle of the well-rounded and free development of each". Mao Zedong pointed out that "The Communist Party is a political party which works for the interests of the nation and the people and which has absolutely no private ends to pursue", and that "Serving the people wholeheartedly" is the abiding mission of the CPC. As Deng Xiaoping pointed out, "If what the Party members mean to do or their tasks are put in a nutshell, there are just two: serve the people wholeheartedly; put the interests of the people first in doing everything." And he also proposed that "The chief criterion for making that judgement should be whether it promotes the growth of the productive forces in a socialist society, increases the overall strength of the socialist state and raises people's livelihoods." With regard to the question about how to judge whether theoretical principles and policies are correct or not, he takes whether people approve them or not, whether people agree on them or not, and whether they please the people or not as the fundamental basis. The important thought of the Three Represents states that "Our Party must always represent the interests of the people" and that "We must always consider the fundamental interests of the people when we think about problems and handle matters." The authors of Marxist classics and the leaders of the CPC have clearly expounded the value orientation and the theoretical stance of Marxist parties' programs. If a political party's theories and its corresponding principles and policies just serve the interests of a few people or of the ruler's alliance, then the people's faith in this political party's leadership will eventually be shaken. Therefore, the theoretical stance that people should always be put first is the prerequisite and important connotation of the theoretical progressiveness of a Marxist party, which gives people a sense of belonging and points out the future of the party.

The Scientific Outlook on Development embodies the unity of Marxist conception of history and values. At present and in the future, whether it can be implemented in all aspects of socialist economic, political, cultural, and social construction is the most important criterion for evaluating the CPC's progressive nature.

The Scientific Outlook on Development characterized by people-first principle, comprehensiveness, coordination, and sustainability is the latest achievement that the CPC has made through summarizing the experience and lessons of domestic and foreign development practices, and absorbing progressive human civilization, under the guidance on Deng Xiaoping Theory and the important thought of the Three Represents, based on the fundamental principles of Marxist dialectical materialism and historical materialism, in light of the historical lessons we have learned and the needs of the current times, and from the height of the situations at home and abroad. It provides rational answers to the major questions about why, for whom and how to develop China in the new stage in the new century, and reveal the objective laws of the current economic and social development, is the unity of the worldview, values, and methodology that guide development, is the CPC's latest understanding of the issues concerning development, is the new development of the guiding principle of socialist modernization, and is a major achievement in the innovation of Marxist theories in the Chinese context.

The Scientific Outlook on Development emphasizes that its essence is to achieve better and faster economic and social development. Development is of top priority, economic progress will be under any circumstances firmly taken as the center, and the sustainable, rapid, coordinated and sound development of economy will be unswervingly promoted. It can be seen that the Scientific Outlook on Development firmly adheres to the basic viewpoint of historical materialism that the productive forces play a decisive role in social development.

The Scientific Outlook on Development, with "people-first" principle as its essence and core, adheres to Marxist values. What is "people-first"? Hu Jintao pointed out: "To adhere to 'people-first' is to aim at achieving the well-rounded development of all people, to seek development and promote it from the fundamental interests of the people, to continuously meet the people's growing material and cultural needs, and to effectively guarantee the people's economic, political and cultural rights, so that the fruits of development benefit all people." For the first time in the CPC's history, the Scientific Outlook on Development regards "people" and the free and well-rounded development of people as the highest goal of socialist development to guide and regulate social development. This is an important theoretical contribution.

The Scientific Outlook on Development is neither a unilateral and reductive approach to economic development nor a unilateral and abstract approach to human development, but emphasizes the internal unity of the people-first concept and economic-progress orientation. Only on the basis of economic development can ever-growing material and cultural needs of the people be constantly satisfied and the free and well-rounded development of people be promoted; "people-first" is the goal of development, and economic-progress orientation is the means to achieve this goal. Without the guidance and regulation of the value target of "the free and well-rounded development of people", development would be nothing more than economic growth, with value connotation and quality excluded. The Scientific Outlook on Development dialectically unifies in practice the two basic indicators of historical development, namely, the development of the productive forces and the free and well-rounded development of people.

At present and in the future, to uphold and develop the Party's progressive nature, the Scientific Outlook on Development as a major achievement of Marxist theoretical innovation should be first and foremost adopted to arm the minds of all the Party members, particularly of leading officials at all levels, through firmly establishing and fully implementing the Scientific Outlook on Development, taking development as top priority. We must always insist on taking economic progress as the center, concentrate on progress, and wholeheartedly seek development; we must constantly release and develop the productive forces through deepening reform.

To uphold and develop the Party's progressive nature, we must implement the Scientific Outlook on Development to steer the path of the economic and social development, and realize the coordinated development between economy and society, between urban and rural areas, and between different regions; we must, on the basis of economic development, promote the all-round progress of society and the well-rounded development of people, promote the coordinated development of socialist material civilization, political civilization, and mental civilization. In particular, we must adhere to the value principle of doing everything for the people, relying on the people, and sharing the fruits of development with them, and resolve their most immediate and most realistic issues. In response to many imbalances in China's development, the Scientific Outlook on Development has included a series of policies and measures to resolve development imbalances and gaps. It emphasizes coordinated and comprehensive development. It is necessary to correctly reflect and take into account the interests of the people from different sectors and correctly handle the relations of the people's interests. The conflicts among the people and other social conflicts must be properly handled, and the interest relationships between different regions and different groups must be properly coordinated, so that the fundamental interests of the great majority of the people can be realized, maintained and developed, and that the fruits of reform and development can be shared by the people. This is an important content for realizing the well-rounded and common development of people, and it is an inevitable requirement for implementing Marxist values on the issue of development.

In short, in the practice of development, the Marxist conception of history and values should be integrated, and the development of the productive forces and the free and well-rounded development of people should be dialectically unified. This is the guiding principle of the CPC's political and theoretical progress, on the basis of which theoretical innovation can be vigorously promoted. Only in this way can the CPC stand in the forefront of the times via its theory, line, guidelines, and policies, and always function as the strong leadership core to build socialism with Chinese characteristics. This is the key to building the Party's progressive nature.

Unity of Development of Productive Forces and Free, Well-rounded Development of People: Reflections on Philosophical Connotations of Scientific Outlook on Development*

Adhering to the concept of development featured by people-orientation, comprehensiveness, coordination and sustainability is a major strategic thought formulated by the CPC proceeding from the overall situation of the cause of the development of the Party and the State in the new stage in this new century, under the guidance of Deng Xiaoping Theory and the important thought of the Three Represents. The Scientific Outlook on Development summarizes the experience of the success of China in the reform, opening up and modernization over the past 20 years, learns the lessons from the development course of other countries, reveals the objective laws of economic and social development, and reflects the Party's new understanding of development issues.[1]

Just as Premier Wen Jiabao pointed out, based on the fundamental principles of Marxist dialectical and historical materialism, the Scientific Outlook on Development summarizes the experience and lessons of both China and other countries on the issues concerning development, absorbs the new achievements of human civilization, keeps abreast with the trend of the times and history, makes it clear the major theoretical and practical questions that cropped up in the new stage in the new century, such as whether China can achieve development, why China should achieve it and how to achieve it. It is a significant development for the guiding principle

---

* Originally published in *Studies on Marxism*. 2006(4).
[1] Hu Jintao: "Speech at the Central Symposium on Population, Resources and Environment," *People's Daily*, 2004-4-5.

of socialist modernization and a great achievement of the Party's emancipating mind, seeking truth from facts, moving forward with the times and advancing innovation in theory. The researcher of the present article believes that the Scientific Outlook on Development is in keeping with the important development theories of Mao Zedong, Deng Xiaoping and Jiang Zemin; that it is a Marxist outlook on development keeping pace with the times, a new answer to the problems that China has confronted in the new era, a new plan for China's path of development in future and a great achievement of the theoretical innovation of dynamic Marxism adapted to the Chinese context.[①] As a new philosophy on development, the Scientific Outlook on Development contains profound philosophical thoughts and fully embodies the worldview, values and methodology capable of guiding development.

I. Integrating productive force development and free and well-rounded human development, Marxist concept of history and values to grasp essence and goals of socialism

There are two fundamental yardsticks adopted in Marxist historical materialism to investigate into the historical development of mankind—one is the development of the productive forces; the other is the free and well-rounded development of people. First, historical materialism holds that human creative activity in material production is both the foundation and the fundamental impetus for the development of human history. The development of the productive forces is the final decisive force for the development of human society. Second, social development is also a natural course of history with its intrinsic objective laws. Third, the people are the principal part of historical development. The emancipation of the proletariat and of all mankind is the ultimate goal of human historical development. All the three points given above are the basic connotations of Marxist concept of history.

The Scientific Outlook on Development emphasizes that development must be given top priority if we want to achieve better and faster development of economy and society. Without development, the outlook on development will make no sense. China is still in the primary stage of socialism and will long remain so. The competition in overall national strength is increasingly fierce nowadays. Under this circumstance,

---

① Wen Jiabao: "Deepen the Understanding, Unifying the Thinking to Firmly Establish and Earnestly Implement the Scientific Outlook on Development: A Speech at the Graduation Ceremony of the Special Seminar for Major Leading Officials at the Provincial and Ministerial levels on 'Establishing and Implementing the Scientific Outlook on Development'," *People's Daily*, 2004-3-1.

in order to accelerate modernization, it is of great strategic significance for China, a major developing country, to take economic progress as the central task, firmly grasp and effectively utilize important strategic opportunities as well as vigorously promote the productive forces. Therefore, we must pursue economic progress as the central task and concentrate on it with every determination. Only by taking economic progress as the central task and continuously enhancing overall national strength can we lay up a solid material foundation for the all-round and coordinated development. And only by doing so can we better resolve the problems and challenges on our road ahead and fulfill the grand goal of achieving socialist modernization and building a moderately prosperous society in all respects. Hence, under any circumstances and at any time, we must be highly focused on economic progress and unwaveringly promote the sustained, coordinated, rapid and healthy economic development.① It can be seen that the Scientific Outlook on Development firmly upholds the fundamental view of historical materialism that the productive forces play a decisive role in social development.

The Scientific Outlook on Development unswervingly adheres to another fundamental yardstick which historical materialism employs to study human historical development—the free and well-rounded development of everyone. One prominent contribution of the Scientific Outlook on Development is that for the first time "people-first" and "free and well-rounded development of everyone" were set by the CPC as the highest goal of socialist development so as to lead and regulate social development.

In his writing *German Ideology*, K. Marx and F. Engels indicate that "the first premise of all human history is, of course, the existence of living human individuals." "Our starting point is those people who engage in practical activities." The "people" mentioned here does not refer to the "people" in Feuerbach's philosophy which they criticized, but the "people in realistic history" ② who engage in practical activities in a specific, material, social, and historical context. Marx believes that the essence of man is not the inherent abstraction of an individual. Instead, it is in fact the sum of all social relations. People's social history has always been the history of individual development regardless of whether they realize it or not; the material relations,

---

① Hu Jintao: "Speech at the Central Symposium on Population, Resources and Environment," *People's Daily*, 2004-4-5.
② The quotes given above cited in *Marx-Engels Selected Works*, Vol. 1, Chin. ed., Beijing: People's Publishing House, 1995, p. 67, 73.

serving as the cornerstone for all the other relations, are but a necessary form to achieve people's material and individual activities.①

K. Marx and F. Engels paid great attention to the living situation and development direction of individuals in reality and is concerned about the emancipation of the proletariat, taking each person's free and all-round development and the society's harmonious development as the goals of communism. In *Communist Manifesto*, K. Marx and F. Engels set forth the vision of a future society: "In place of the old bourgeois society, with its classes and class antagonisms, we shall have an association in which the free development of each is the condition for the free development of all."②

Nearly half a century later, F. Engels still believed that only these words can "summarize the spirit for the new era in the future"③ and can accurately yet succinctly convey his basic idea as well as Marx's for the future of socialism. Marx also points out in *Das Kapital* that the new society in the future is "a social form taking the free and well-rounded of everyone as the basic principle."④ In the book *Socialism: Utopian and Scientific*, F. Engels says that in a future society sublating the capitalism, class domination ends, public rights cut off its relations with politics, and the history that man being ruled by the dissident power is over. There, "man for the first time becomes the real, conscious lord of nature, because he has now become master of his own social organization," that is, "become the master of himself—a free man." "It is the ascent of man from the kingdom of necessity to the kingdom of freedom." F. Engels calls it "a cause of liberating the world" ⑤. In that case, the previous human history is only "pre-historic history".

In my opinion, what K. Marx and F. Engels emphasize more is to define the future society through the development of human beings. *Communist Manifesto* defines socialism through "the free development of every person", which profoundly explains the essential characteristics of socialism and fundamentally distinguishes

---

① Marx, K. & F. Engels: *Selected Works of Marx and Engels*, Vol. 4, Chin. ed., Beijing: People's Publishing House, 1995, p. 532.
② Ibid, p. 730.
③ Ibid, p.731.
④ Marx, K. & F. Engels: *Marx and Engels: Collected Works*, Vol. 23, Chin. ed., Beijing: People's Publishing House, 1972, p. 649.
⑤ Marx, K. & F. Engels: *Selected Works of Marx and Engels*, Vol. 3, Chin. ed., Beijing: People's Publishing House, 1995, p. 758, 760.

socialism from the old society. In the view of K. Marx and F. Engels, as for social progress, the liberation of mankind and the free and well-rounded development of human beings are the ultimate goal for the development of the productive forces. This is not only the real spirit of Marxist philosophy, but also the essential and core proposition of the entire Marxist theoretical system and the highest value pursuit of Marxist theory. This thought is of vital guiding significance for us to comprehensively and correctly understand Marxism, to understand the goal of socialism and to construct socialism with Chinese characteristics.

The Scientific Outlook on Development, with the concept of "people first" at its core and essence, embodies the basic Marxist views on the essential characteristics of the future society. What we undertake is a great cause of building socialism with Chinese characteristics. We must put people first. So, what is "putting people first"? General Secretary Hu Jintao indicated: "Upholding the 'people-first' principle means that, in the fundamental interests of the people, we should take the all-round development of mankind as our goal to pursue and promote development, to continually meet the ever-growing material and cultural needs of the people and to effectively guarantee the people's rights of economy, politics and culture so that the fruits of development can benefit all the people."[①]

According to Marxist historical materialism and the CPC Central Committee's exposition of the Scientific Outlook on Development, the author thinks that we should understand the meaning of "people first" from two aspects: For one thing, "people first" implies that all is done for the sake of the people and all relies on the people yet all the benefits are shared by the people. For another, if one does not take into consideration the living individuals in concrete reality, his or her understanding of "the people" may fall into abstraction. According to the domestic and international history, when in the name of "the people" with the same "identity", it is easy to neglect and obliterate the respect for the realistic individual and the tolerance of "difference". Therefore, when implementing the people-first concept, we must count it as the proper meaning that we should respect every specific individual of their life, dignity, values, and respect their fundamental rights to politics, economy, and culture. "The State respects and preserves human rights" has been enshrined into the Constitution and has become the philosophy for state building and development,

---

① Hu Jintao: "Speech at the Central Symposium on Population, Resources and Environment," *People's Daily*, 2004-4-5.

which is a very important manifestation of the "people-first" concept. The "people" is a "concrete abstraction" consisting of myriad concrete individuals. The meanings in these two aspects should be integrated.

The Scientific Outlook on Development is neither a unilateral and reductive approach to economic development nor a unilateral and abstract approach to human development, but emphasizes the internal unity of the people-first concept and economy progress orientation.[1] Only on the basis of economic development can the ever-growing material and cultural needs of the people be constantly satisfied and the free and well-rounded development of people be promoted;[2] people-first is the goal of development, while economy progress orientation is the means to achieve this goal. Without the guidance and regulation of the value goal of "the free and well-rounded development of people", development would become simple economic growth without value connotation and quality. The Scientific Outlook on Development dialectically unifies in practice the two basic measures of historical development, namely, the development of the productive forces and the free and well-rounded development of people. Only with the continuous increase of social wealth and the continuous progress of social civilization can the needs of the people be better satisfied and the free and comprehensive development of people be further realized. Thus, in practice, the Scientific Outlook on Development dialectically unifies the two basic dimensions of historical development, namely, the development of productive forces and the free and well-rounded development of human beings.

Upholding the principle of putting people first is consistent with the internal requirements of implementing Deng Xiaoping Theory and the important thought of the Three Represents.

Upholding the "people-first" principle is consistent with the implementation of Deng Xiaoping Theory and the requirement inherent in the important thought of the Three Represents, is accordance with the essential requirement of adhering to the Party's commitment to serving the public good and exercising power in the interests of the people, and is an inheritance and further development of Deng Xiaoping Theory and the important thought of the Three Represents.

---

[1] Zeng Qinghong: "Leading officials Should Take the Lead in Establishing and Implementing the Scientific Outlook on Development," *People's Daily*, 2004-2-17.

[2] Hu Jintao: "A Speech at the Special Seminar for Major Leading Officials at the provincial and ministerial levels on Improving the Ability of Building a Harmonious Socialist Society," *People's Daily*, 2005-6-27.

II. Providing a new answer to how to balance relationship between nature, man and society in new space-time context

Theoretical innovation can never be like water without a source, or a tree without roots; on the contrary, it is to sublate and surpass the existing achievements. Many propositions and categories of the philosophy and social sciences have been proposed early in the history of human thought. However, human practice is ever evolving in a way that new problems which crop up in the new practices are resolved and thus new interpretations are formulated. That is what is called innovation. It is the same case with Marxist theory, which achieves innovation and development through ever-changing practice. Marxist philosophy, including its outlook on nature, history and values, offers rational explanations on the relationships between man and nature, between individuals, and between the individual and society. As for China's current plans and actions for development, the Scientific Outlook on Development, integrating the needs and characteristics of the times with the development of China's modernization drive, is the new answers and solutions to these problems, which are sharply pertinent and thus innovative.

In terms of the relationship between man and nature, there is a profound revolution taking place in contemporary science and technology. Man is more adept at transforming nature with a series of new scientific and technological achievements, making nature increasingly become "humanized nature". The great power of science and technology, the rapid development of economy and society, and the huge consumption of resources have even further intensified the conflict between man and nature.

The concept of nature included in Marxist philosophy holds that nature is a material premise of human survival and production. Man and nature are closely linked as a whole. Human beings, just like animals and plants, are objective existence which is natural, physical, and emotional. Thus, we cannot rid ourselves of the internal and external dependence on nature. As Marx noted, "Nature is man's inorganic body – nature, that is, insofar as it is not itself human body. Man lives on nature – means that nature is his body, with which he must remain in continuous interchange if he is not to die."[①] "All production is appropriation of nature on the part of an individual within

---

① Marx, K. & F. Engels: *Marx and Engels: Collected Works*, Vol. 42, Chin. ed., Beijing: People's Publishing House, 1979, p. 95.

and through a specific form of society."①

The concept of nature included in Marxist philosophy supposes that nature has existed long before, that humanity is the product of long-term development of nature, that nature has priority over man, and that the objectivity of the laws of nature's survival and development is independent from human will. F. Engels has long since warned mankind: "We should not indulge in our victories over nature, because for every such victory, nature will retaliate against us. Every victory, in the first stage, achieves what we expect indeed. However, it turns out to be a completely different and unexpected result in the second and third stage, which often erases the original achievements. Residents in Mesopotamia, Minor Asia, Greece and elsewhere destroyed forests in order to get more farmland. They never expected that those lands would become therefore barren land. It is because their depriving of forests, the center and reservoir of water accumulation."② "We must keep in mind that we should govern Nature but never in the way like the conquerors ruling alien nations, yet never behave like an outsider with no relation to nature. Conversely, human beings, together with our flesh, blood and mind, all belong to nature and exist in nature."③ Unfortunately, F. Engels' stark warning did not attract people's attention. It seems that mankind's unceasing and unrestrained possession and enslavement of nature have become more powerful with the support of ever-changing science and technology. Not surprisingly, nature is groaning painfully, and human beings are constantly being retaliated by nature.

Needless to say, for some time, we did not properly handle our relations with nature in our sought of development. For the sake of economic growth, some localities and enterprises carried out predatory development of nature, such as excessive grazing, predatory mining, destructive logging and other acts of plundering and destroying nature. What they did is alarming: They just took from nature, but never invested for it; they just harnessed nature, but never constructed it. In addition, with the conflict between population growth and natural resource shortage becoming increasingly prominent, the wasting of natural resources was rampant due to the extensive growth model. Even now, in some places, there still exist some problems, such as unauthorized use and expropriation of arable land and unauthorized mining

---

① Marx, K. & F. Engels: *Marx and Engels: Collected Works*, Vol. 46 (1), Chin. ed., Beijing: People's Publishing House, 1972, p.24.
② Engels, F. *Dialectics of Nature*, Chin. ed., Beijing: People's Publishing House, 1984, p.304-305.
③ Ibid.

of mineral resources. The overall deterioration of the ecological environment has not been fundamentally reversed; meanwhile, some mineral resources related to people's livelihood, particularly oil, are in desperate shortage; the flood control system of large rivers is not perfect, and the rural infrastructure of water conservancy is relatively poor; the imbalance between supply and demand of water resources is very acute. Resources have become a prominent restrictive factor affecting economic and social development and people's livelihood. The Scientific Outlook on Development draws the lessons from the past practices and proposes that, in the future, China's development must respect the objective existence and laws of nature; must stay in harmony with nature; must coexist with nature; and must maintain a sound, dynamic and dialectical unity with nature. Only in this way, sustainable development can be realized. Otherwise, human beings would be stuck into an untenable situation. Compared with the development achieved in the past, the formulation and implementation of the Scientific Outlook on Development, undoubtedly, has its backwash effect, and is a wake-up call and an innovation.

The development imbalances between economy and society, between urban and rural areas, between different regions, and between different groups are mainly the imbalance of interests among different groups, which, in a philosophical sense, are the conflicts between individuals and between man and nature. The Scientific Outlook on Development was therefore formulated in light of the conflicts and problems which have become prominent in China's social and economic development at the new stage in the new century. Now in face of the continuous development of China's industrialization, urbanization, marketization and continuous expansion of its exchange with the outside world, we should understand and grasp the features of different phases in China's economic and social development [1], which mainly include: the ever-widening wealth gap between urban and rural areas, between regions, and between residents; the pressure on employment and social security; the sluggish development of social undertakings such as education, health care and culture; the intensifying contradiction between population growth, economic development, ecological environment and natural resources; the backward economic growth model, the low overall quality and competitiveness of the economy.

In the Scientific Outlook on Development, a series of measures and policies are formulated to address development imbalance, to coordinate the interests of all the

---

[1] *People's Daily*, 2005-4-17.

parties involved, to resolve the contradiction, and thereby to bring about a "harmonious socialist society" featured by democracy, the rule of law, justice and equality, honesty, friendliness, vitality, stability, orderliness, and harmonious existence between man and nature.

To further deepen reform and opening up is the fundamental requirement of fully implementing the Scientific Outlook on Development. For this purpose, "We should, in accordance with the requirements of coordinating the development pattern of urban and rural areas, of different regions, of economic and social sectors and of man and nature, and of coordinating the national development and the opening-up to the outside world." Among these five aspects, in fact, the first three calls for making the demands heard on the interests of all sectors and handling the relationship between them in the process of reform.

Coordinating the development of economic and social sectors means eliminating the imbalance between economic and societal development, developing social undertakings in all directions, improving people's living standards, realize the coordinated economic and social development and all-round progress, so as to satisfy the people's ever-growing needs of health care, security and culture, and to ensure that the people live and work in peace and contentment.

Coordinating the development of urban and rural areas means transforming the separate urban-rural structures to build a new socialist countryside: more- developed production, better-off farmers, social etiquette and civility, a clean environment, and democratic administration, enabling 800 million rural people to live a moderately prosperous life and narrow the too huge urban-rural gap currently existing in China. If rural people cannot live a moderately prosperous life, it is impossible for all people to do so, much less to achieve common prosperity.

Coordinating the development of different regions means gradually reversing the trend of widening the gap between different regions, promoting coordinated development between regions and thereby realizing common development. According to the actual situations of China's regional development and the requirements for comprehensively promoting modernization, the Central Government of China has put forward an overall strategy—to reach a new stage in the large-scale development of the western region ; deepen reform to accelerate the revitalization of old industrial bases in the northeast and other parts of the country; help the central region rise by tapping into local strengths; and support the eastern region in taking the lead in pursuing optimal development through innovation, so as to forge a new pattern allowing us to thoroughly unlock the potential for cooperation among the eastern, central, and western regions and achieve mutual complementarity in the interest of our common development and prosperity. To implement the regional development strategy, we can take, in accordance with the "Eleventh Five-year Plan" (2007-12), take the following three ways: First, improve the regional coordination and interaction mechanism including market mechanism, cooperation mechanism, reciprocal mechanism and support mechanism. The State will continue to step up the support for the central and western region in terms of economic policies, capital investment and industrial development so as to speed up economic and social development in the old revolutionary base areas, the areas with large ethnic minority populations, border areas, and poor areas. Second, clarify the functions and positions of different regions. Based on the population, resources, carrying capacity of environment and development potential of each region, the State should decide whether and where development need to be optimized, prioritized, restricted, or forbidden. Third, promote the sound development of urbanization. We should actively yet prudently promote urbanization in accordance with the principle of going for steady and incremental progress, conserving the land, pursuing efficient development and laying out a balanced plan for the strategic key areas, so as to accelerate the development in the underdeveloped areas and improve life for the people living in those areas.

From the above, it can be learnt that the Scientific Outlook on Development highlights the coordinated and overall development, which means correctly reflecting and balancing the interests of the people from different sectors, correctly handling the contradictions among the people them and other social contradictions, and well coordinating the relationship of interests between different regions and different groups. Thus, the Scientific Outlook on Development plays an important role in realizing the well-rounded and equal development of people.

III. Adhering to historical dialectics by applying social organism thought of Marxist philosophy, and views of universal connection and development of things

When criticizing Proudhon, K. Marx said, "In constructing the edifice of an ideological system by means of the categories of political economy, the limbs of the social system are dislocated. The different limbs of society are converted into so many separate societies, following one upon the other. How, indeed, could the single logical formula of movement, of sequence, of time, explain the structure of society, in which all relations coexist simultaneously and support one another?"① Marx added: "the present society is no solid crystal, but an organism capable of change, and is constantly changing."② He also said that "Society does not consist of individuals, but expresses the sum of interrelations, the relations within which these individuals stand."③ Marx's concept of social organism shows that the formation and development of human society originated from people's practice of production and communication. It is an organic whole consisting of various social factors and relations which interact, inter-depend, and interconnect. It is the practice and communication that integrate people into an organic whole. While emphasizing the viewpoint that productivity plays a decisive role in social development, historical materialism also underlines the importance of politics (institution) and culture.

F. Engels made outstanding contributions in his later years to upholding and developing the historical materialism. He criticized the tendency of misinterpreting Marxism as metaphysical "mechanical determinism" and "economic determinism" and he indicated: "According to the materialist conception of history, the *ultimately* determining element in history is the production and reproduction of real life. Other than this neither Marx nor I have ever asserted. Hence if somebody twists this into saying that the economic element is the *only* determining one, he transforms that proposition into a meaningless, abstract, senseless phrase."④ He also stressed that "Political, juridical, philosophical, religious, literary, artistic, etc., development is based on economic development. But all these react upon one another and also upon the economic base. It is not that the economic position is the cause and alone active, while everything else only has a passive effect."⑤

F. Engels also believes that superstructures and ideologies in different nations and states are relatively independent and do not correspond exactly to the economic base. Instead, they have their own characteristics and special development rules. "E(e)

---

① Marx, K. & F. Engels: *Selected Works of Marx and Engels*, Vol. 1, Chin. ed., Beijing: People's Publishing House, 1995, p. 143.
② Marx, K. & F. Engels: *Selected Works of Marx and Engels*, Vol. 2, Chin. ed., Beijing: People's Publishing House, 1995, p. 102.
③ Marx, K. & F. Engels: *Marx and Engels: Collected Works*, Vol. 30, Chin. ed., Beijing: People's Publishing House, 1995, p. 221.
④ Marx, K. & F. Engels: *Selected Works of Marx and Engels*, Vol. 4, Chin. ed., Beijing: People's Publishing House, 1995, p. 695.
⑤ Ibid., p.732.

conomically backward countries can still play first fiddle in philosophy."[1]

F. Engels also creatively proposed the theory of "resultant" on historical development. He said: "H(h)istory is made in such a way that the final result always arises from conflicts between many individual wills, of which each in turn has been made what it is by a host of particular conditions of life. Thus, there are innumerable intersecting forces, an infinite series of parallelograms of forces which give rise to one resultant—the historical event. This may again itself be viewed as the product of a power which works as a whole *unconsciously* and without volition."[2]

One of prominent features of the Scientific Outlook on Development is its attention attached to the organic and integral nature of social development and the interaction of multiple factors in social development. The Scientific Outlook on Development underlines "overall development", "coordinated development" and "sustainable development", which embody organic and integral characteristics of social development. They not only uphold the decisive role of the productive forces in social development, but also attach importance to utilizing the great influence and reactions of superstructure (including political restructuring, social construction and social administration, etc.), ideology and cultural factors on social life and development, so they adhere to historical dialectics.

Hu Jintao said, "To realize the overall development, we must take economic construction as the central task and promote economic, political and cultural development in all respects so as to achieve the overall progress of economy and society. To propel the coordinated development, we should, coordinate the development of urban and rural areas, of different regions, of economic and social sectors and of man and nature, and of coordinating the national development and the opening-up to the outside world. We also need to coordinate the productive forces and the production relations, the economic base and the superstructure, and all parts of economy, politics and culture in every aspect. To realize the sustainable development is to promote the harmony between man and nature, to balance the development of economy with that of population, resources and environment, to keep to the path of sustainable development featuring increased production, higher living standards and a sound ecological environment so that we can achieve lasting and sustainable

---

[1] Marx, K. & F. Engels: *Selected Works of Marx and Engels*, Vol. 4, Chin. ed., Beijing: People's Publishing House, 1995, p.704.
[2] Ibid., p.697.

development of the Chinese nation."①

The Scientific Outlook on Development underlines that, at present, when development contradictions are readily apparent in China, government should not only take economic development as the central task, but also avoid stressing one to the neglect of the others. It must correctly handle the relationship between economic development and social development, between urban and rural development, between different regions, between different groups of interests, between economic growth, resources, and environment, between reform, development and stability, between socialist material, political and cultural civilization, and between domestic development and the opening to the outside world.② On the basis of economic progress, it must promote comprehensive social progress and people's well-rounded development, and carry forward the coordinated development of socialist material, political and cultural civilization. Economic progress, political progress, cultural progress and people's well-rounded development are interrelated and interactional. Without the continuous political and cultural progress and the well-rounded development of each one, the pure pursuit of economic growth will not only make economic development unsustainable but will also make it hard to advance. We need to comprehensively promote socialist material progress, political progress and ethical progress in case that development should be restricted by unbalanced development; otherwise, there would be problems such as the widening gap between the rich and the poor, the increasing unemployment, the growing disparity between urban and rural areas and between regions, the aggravating social conflicts, and the deterioration of ecological environment, which may lead to the long-term stagnation of economic and social development or even social turmoil and retrogression .

IV. Expanding Marxism's connotation on social structure and development

One of the fundamental views on historical materialism is to explain the historical formation and social structure through material production activity. According to K. Marx and F. Engels, material production to meet the needs of people

---

① Hu Jintao: "Speech at the Central Symposium on Population, Resources and Environment," *People's Daily*, 2004-4-5.
② Wen Jiabao: "Deepen the Understanding, Unifying the Thinking to Firmly Establish and Earnestly Implement the Scientific Outlook on Development: A Speech at the Graduation Ceremony of the Special Seminar for Major Leading Officials at the Provincial and Ministerial levels on 'Establishing and Implementing the Scientific Outlook on Development'," *People's Daily*, 2004-3-1.

for material life is "the material production of life itself" which is also called "the first historical activity".① All social life is essentially practical. "So much is this activity, this unceasing sensuous labour and creation, this production, the basis of the whole sensuous world as it now exists."② In K. Marx's and F. Engels's opinion, social structures and nations always generate from the process of a certain individual's life. They said: "The fact is, therefore, that definite individuals who are productively active in a definite way enter into these definite social and political relations. Empirical observation must in each separate instance bring out empirically, and without any mystification and speculation, the connection of the social and political structure with production. The social structure and the State are continually evolving out of the life-process of definite individuals."③

In *The Preface to A Contribution to the Critique of Political Economy*, K. Marx makes a classic discourse on the structure of human society: "In the social production of their existence, men inevitably enter into definite relations, which are independent of their will, namely relations of production appropriate to a given stage in the development of their material forces of production. The totality of these relations of production constitutes the economic structure of society, the real foundation, on which arises a legal and political superstructure and to which correspond definite forms of social consciousness. The mode of production of material life conditions the general process of social, political and intellectual life. It is not the consciousness of men that determines their existence, but their social existence that determines their consciousness."④ In K. Marx's view, the totality of the production relations which accommodate to the development of productivity at a certain stage constitutes the economic structure of society, the foundation of society: the political superstructure constitutes the political structure, which is the control system of society; the social ideology constitutes the concept of social structure, which is the intellectual and cultural system of society. Human society is mainly composed of three parts: economy, politics and culture.

Deng Xiaoping pointed out that in the course of building socialism with Chinese

---

① Marx, K. & F. Engels: *Selected Works of Marx and Engels*, Vol. 1, Chin. ed., Beijing: People's Publishing House, 1995, p. 79.
② Ibid, p.77.
③ Ibid, p.71.
④ Marx, K. & F. Engels: *Selected Works of Marx and Engels*, Vol. 2, Chin. ed., Beijing: People's Publishing House, 1995, p. 32.

characteristics, the strategic concept of "pushing for material progress on the one hand and cultural and ethical progress on the other, with great importance attached to both" should be adopted; and that political restructuring is a crucial task in this course. One of important theoretical contributions made by the third generation of the central collective leadership with Jiang Zemin at its core is that it, for the first time, set forth the idea of "political progress" on the basis of Deng Xiaoping Theory, taking pushing for political progress as an important part of building socialism with Chinese characteristics. The "two progresses" has thus been developed into the "three progresses". In the meantime, the view was put forward that culture is a significant component of overall national strength and much more importance has been attached to the construction of advanced culture in social development.

With the further development of socialist market economy, the diversification of people's occupations, the growing needs of people's communication, and the development of communication means (science and technology), various non-governmental organizations have come into being. Playing an increasingly important role in social life, these organizations has led to the rapid advancement of China's civil society. At the same time, however, the contradictions of interests in social life have become increasingly sharp and diversified and many problems regarding social stability and security are to be resolved. The CPC Central Committee with Hu Jintao at its core, with a keen forward-looking vision and a deep theoretical insight, timely proposed that building a harmonious socialist society is a major task for building a moderately prosperous society in all respects and socialism with Chinese characteristics. The Central Committee believed that the building of a harmonious socialist society should be integrated with the construction of socialist material, political, cultural, and ethical civilization. We must continuously consolidate the material foundation of the construction of a harmonious society by developing the productive forces, strengthen the political guarantee by developing the socialist democracy, and reinforce the mental prop by developing advanced socialist culture. Meanwhile, through the construction of a harmonious society, we can provide favorable social conditions for the development of socialist material, political, cultural and ethical progress so that we can promote the all-round development of the socialist material, political, cultural and ethical progress, and the construction of a harmonious society.

Thus, it can be said that, in the CPC's theoretical view, "With the continuous development of China's economy and society, the overall plan of the cause of building socialism with Chinese characteristics has more clearly developed from the three-sphere integrated plan (namely, socialist economic, political, and cultural construction) to the four-sphere integrated plan(namely, socialist economic, political, cultural, and social construction."[1] The "four-sphere integrated plan" will facilitate the holistic development and progress of socialism with Chinese characteristics, and "social construction" will be an important part of the cause of building socialism with Chinese characteristics. Hu Jintao said: "Only by establishing a social system compatible with the socialist economic, political and cultural systems can we foster a social order that is in harmony with the economic, political and cultural orders. In order to take social construction and management to a new level, we must be good at combining the fulfilling of this task with the promotion of coordinated economic and social development, with the satisfaction of the diverse living needs of the people, with the promotion of community-level democracy, and with the strengthening of the Party's governance capability."[2] This is not only a major advance made by the Party in understanding the theory of scientific socialism, but also a continuation and development of K. Marx's theory of social structure and development.

The Scientific Outlook on Development takes social structure, social progress and social management together into consideration, and regards the strengthening of social progress and social management as the main part of social development, which enriches the Marxist theory of social structure and social development. Hu Jintao suggests that, with the change of social structure, it is necessary to comprehensively analyze, grasp and strengthen social progress and management, so as to lay a solid foundation for policy formulation and government work; that it is necessary to strengthen the investigation into and research on the development of and changes in the social structure, so as to acquire an in-depth understanding and analysis of the development, changes and trends of the structure of social groups, urban-rural structure, regional structure, population structure, employment structure, social organization structure, etc., which is of great service to deepening the understanding of the characteristics and laws of China's social development under the conditions of developing the socialist market economy and opening to the outside world, and thereby better promoting social progress and management; it is necessary to

---

[1] Hu Jintao: "A Speech at the Special Seminar for Major Leading Officials at the provincial and ministerial levels on Improving the Ability of Building a Harmonious Socialist Society," *People's Daily*, 2005-6-27.
[2] Ibid.

strengthen the investigation into and research on the changes in the evolution of the relationship of social interest, so as to further deepening the understanding and analysis of the changes and trends in China's development of social interest structure and interest relationship, which is of great service to improving policies and measures and to better coordinating the interest relations and interest requirements of all parties; and it is necessary to step up the investigation into and research on maintaining social stability, and deepen the understanding and analysis of changes and trends in the development of public security and social order, so as to create a sound mechanism to safeguard social stability and to ensure that the Chinese people will live and work in peace and contentment. He also suggests that it is necessary to adapt to the advancement of the socialist market economy and the great changes in social structure, to thoroughly study the laws of social management, to update the concept of social management, and to promote the reform and innovation of social progress and management, so as to forge a more effective management system to meet the requirements of social development and the needs of the people as quickly as possible.[1]

The Scientific Outlook on Development also puts forward specific approaches on how to strengthen social progress and improve the social management system in building a harmonious socialist society: improve the social governance model under which Party committees exercise leadership, government assumes responsibility, non-governmental actors provide assistance, and the public get involved; taking expanding employment, improving the social security system, clearly defined distribution relationship, and developing social undertakings as the focus of efforts, properly handle the relations between different interest groups and earnestly address the most pressing and most immediate issues that concern the people the most. Besides, it is also necessary to strengthen the building of harmonious communities, villages and towns, to advocate the harmony among the people so as to consolidate the foundation of social harmony. It is necessary to properly handle the contradictions within the people under the new circumstances, open up the channels for public complaint and oversight, and develop a sound mechanism for mediating and settling social contradictions and disputes. It is necessary to improve the system

---

[1] "Strengthen Investigation and Research, Strive to Improve Working Skills, and Fully Execute All Tasks for the Construction of a Harmonious Society," *People's Daily*, 2005-2-23.

of early warning, the mechanism for public mobilization and emergency rescue, and the capability to properly handle emergencies. It is necessary to strengthen the comprehensive maintenance of public order, improve the system for maintenance of law or order, continue the Peaceful China initiative, advance the fight against crime and illegal activities in accordance with the law to protect people's lives and property, ensure social stability, and safeguard national security. All the above are new practical and theoretical exploration.

In conclusion, the Scientific Outlook on Development which means putting people first and aiming at comprehensive, coordinated and sustainable development is the CPC's rational answer to the readily apparent issues which have cropped up in China's economic and social development at the new stage in the new century, namely, why China should achieve development, who China shall achieve it for, and how to achieve it, revealing the objective laws of economic and social development through following the guidance of Deng Xiaoping Theory and the important thought of the Three Represents, making alive the basic tenets of Marxist dialectical and historical materialism, standing at a new historic starting point, summarizing all positive and negative experiences in the development of China itself and many other countries in the world, and thereby absorbing the new achievements of human civilization. It is the CPC's new understanding of the issues concerning development, a significant development for the guiding principle of socialist modernization, and a great achievement of theoretical innovation of Marxism to respond to China's conditions; it is the combination of the world outlook, values and methodology concerning development, a new development philosophy. It will surely exert a profound and far-reaching influence on China's future and even the world's development.

Only Through Reform and Opening Up Can We Develop China, Socialism and Marxism: Studying the Report to the 17th National Congress of the CPC*

Hu Jintao's important report to the Seventeenth National Congress of the CPC, guided by Deng Xiaoping Theory and the important thought of the Three Represents, is the thorough implementation of the Scientific Outlook on Development, analyzing the new changes in the international and domestic situations, and reviewing the new progress in various undertakings carried forward since the 16th National Congress of the CPC in 2002, summarizing the new experience obtained since the initiation of the reform and opening up policy, putting forward the new requirements for achieving the goal of building a moderately prosperous society in all respects, and making the overall deployment for China's socialist economic progress, political progress, cultural progress, and social progress, and party building, thus pointing out the direction for us the further development of the Party and the state.

I. will focus on what I have learned from the second part of this report.

The second part of the report summarizes the great historical process and valuable experience of reform and opening up, highly appraises the historical status of the great practice of reform and opening up, and incisively explains the internal relationship between reform and opening up and the path of socialism with Chinese characteristics and the theory of socialism with Chinese characteristics. Magnificently and majestically, it encapsulates the theoretical strength and charm of Marxist

---

* Speech at the Symposium on studying the report to the 17th National Congress of the CPC held by the Chinese Academy of Social Sciences.

documents as the unity of the concept of history and value. Such reading is indeed quite enriching.

First of all, it is pointed out in the report that the decision to launch reform and opening up is vital to the destiny of contemporary China, that reform and opening up are the only way of developing socialism with Chinese characteristics and rejuvenating the Chinese nation, that only socialism can save China, and that only reform and opening up can develop China, socialism and Marxism.

Secondly, it is pointed out that reform and opening up have generated historic change to people's lives, the country, and the Party. In 1978, the Party held the Third Plenary Session of the 11th CPC Central Committee, which ushered in the new historical period of reform and opening up.

In 1978, the Party convened the Third Plenary Session of the 11th CPC Central Committee of great historical significance, ushering in a new era in China's development. Since then, the CPC members have led the Chinese people to epic accomplishments through the Chinese nation's self-improvement, with an indomitable courage and in a creative way, and thus brought about the improvement of the Chinese people's life, the advancement of our socialist country, the progress of our Party.

Finally, it is pointed out that reform and opening up represent a great new revolution carried on by the people under the Party's leadership in a new era

In the final analysis, the historical significance of reform and opening up is manifested in two aspects: First, in practice, the policy of reform and opening up has blazed a path to consolidate, improve and develop socialism, and created a new path to socialist modernization, namely the path of socialism with Chinese characteristics; second, in theory, it has innovated Marxism and the theory of socialism, and has thus forged the theory of socialism with Chinese characteristics. It is in the new practical exploration of reform and opening up that we have gradually embarked on a unique path of socialist development, namely the path of socialism with Chinese characteristics, and gradually formed a theory of socialism with Chinese characteristics; it is in the new practical exploration of reform and opening up that the self-improvement and self-development of China's socialist system has been promoted, with strong vitality injected into socialism. It is precisely since the policy of reform and opening up was introduced in 1978 that the CPC members and the Chinese people, with their enterprising spirit and magnificent innovativeness, have written a brilliant chapter of the Chinese nation's self-improvement and tenacious struggle. As a result, the Party, the country, and the people have changed in ways without precedent.

Reform and opening up have forged the extraordinary capacity of the CPC to govern under the new historical conditions and with its firm belief and determination to promote socialism with Chinese characteristics. Therefore, Hu Jintao pointed out that "Reform and opening up constitute a strategic choice that has shaped the course of development of today's China, the only way of developing socialism with Chinese characteristics and rejuvenating the Chinese nation. Only socialism can save China, and only reform and opening up can develop China, socialism and Marxism." It is a natural choice made by the Chinese people in their 30 years of spectacular innovation, a choice that can stand the test of time, and a truth that shows the way to the future. We must not lose our faith and confidence in socialism with Chinese characteristics just because of some problems which have cropped up in some phase of the reform and opening up. Just as Hu Jintao pointed out, reform and opening up constitute a great new revolution. It cannot be completed overnight, nor will it be plain sailing. Essentially, they accord with the aspirations of the Party membership and the people and keep up with the trend of the times. The orientation and path of reform and opening up are entirely correct, and their merits and achievements can never be negated. To stop or reverse reform and opening up would only lead to a blind alley. This is a wise and correct evaluation of the great practice of reform and opening up from the perspective of historical development. we should clearly understand our basic national condition, that is, China is still in the primary stage of socialism, and will remain so for a long time to come.

The report incisively summarizes the connotation of the path of building socialism with Chinese characteristics, that is, we should, under the leadership of the CPC and bearing in mind China's basic national conditions, pursue economic progress as the central task, adhere to the Four Cardinal Principles, be committed to the reform and opening-up policy, release and develop the productive forces, strengthen and improve the socialist system, promote the socialist market economy, socialist democracy, an advanced socialist culture, and a harmonious socialist society, and make China a prosperous, strong, democratic, culturally advanced and harmonious modern socialist country. The main reason why this path is completely correct and can lead China to development and progress is that we have adhered to the basic tenet of scientific socialism and in the meantime added to them distinct Chinese characteristics in light of China's conditions and the features of the times. In contemporary China, the very purpose of staying true to socialism is to keep to the path of socialism with Chinese characteristics.

The report clearly elaborated the connotation of the theory of socialism with Chinese characteristics, which incorporates Deng Xiaoping Theory, the important thought of the Three Represents, and the Scientific Outlook on Development and other major strategic thoughts. This theory has inherited, continued and creatively developed Marxism - Leninism and Mao Zedong Thought. It is the result of the concerted efforts of all our people and the wisdom of several generations of the CPC members. It is the latest achievement in adapting Marxism to China's conditions, the Party's invaluable political and intellectual asset, and the common ideological foundation for the concerted endeavor of the people of all ethnic groups. It is an open system that keeps developing. In contemporary China, the very purpose of staying true to Marxism is adhering to Marxism.

The fundamental reason behind all our achievements and progress since the reform and opening up policy was introduced can be boiled down to one idea: We have blazed a path of socialism with Chinese characteristics and established the theory of socialism with Chinese characteristics. Essentially, the very purpose of adhere to socialism with Chinese characteristics is to keep to this path and uphold this theory.

In short, General Secretary Hu Jintao, in this report, has judiciously answered the important questions, such as what guiding political principles the CPC should uphold in the decisive stage of reform and development, what path to follow, in what mental status, and what goals of development it shall move forward. This report is a programmatic document that accords with the aspirations of the Party membership and the people and keeps up with the trend of the times. It is of great significance to dispel the mist clouding our practice of reform and opening up, unswervingly carry it out, and press ahead with the work of building socialism with Chinese characteristics.

Unswervingly Take the Path of Chinese Socialism: Study the Report to the 18th CPC National Congress*

The 18th National Congress of the CPC was successfully held and attracted worldwide attention. It is a meeting of special historical significance, making the future course of China's development more well-defined, and further strengthening the confidence of the Party and the people of all ethnic groups across the country in keeping to the path of socialism with Chinese characteristics.

I. Solemn Declaration of Future Course of China's development

In this report, Hu Jintao pointed out: "Throughout the past 30-plus years of continuous exploration for reform and opening up, we have upheld socialism with Chinese characteristics and rejected both the old and rigid closed-door policy and any attempt to abandon socialism and take an erroneous path. The path of socialism with Chinese characteristics, the system of theories of socialism with Chinese characteristics and the socialist system with Chinese characteristics are the fundamental accomplishments made by the Party and people in the course of arduous struggle over the past 90-plus years. We must cherish these accomplishments, uphold them all the time and continue to enrich them." This is a solemn declaration about the CPC, China, and the future course of the Chinese nation. It is related to the future of the contemporary China. It also determines the course of development in the following five, ten years, and beyond.

After more than 30 years of reform and opening up, China's socialist market economy has been gradually improved, and great achievements have been made

---

* Originally published in *Chinese Social Sciences Today* (《中国社会科学报》), 2012-12-10.

in all aspects. China's international standing continued to rise, and its international environment has also undergone substantial change. Multiple change including globalization, informatization, networking, marketization, industrialization, and urbanization have all overlapped in the same space and, at the same time, forming a complex environment for development that tests the CPC's governance capacity. From a domestic perspective, the reform is in a critical stage. China is currently being plagued by many difficult problems in the economic, political, social, and ethical and cultural fields, which need to be addressed through deepening and advancing the reforms. At the same time, for the part of the researcher, China is currently facing division of interests, division class, and division understanding. It is undeniable that there are different interest groups in today's society, which belong to different social strata, and thus have different understandings. such divisions are intertwined to form different voices and expectations, and different views on some major theoretical and practical issues. Internationally, some countries or international public opinion have questioned the value of Chinese path, and even do not want to see China become more and more successful in its construction, labeling Chinese path as "national capitalism", or put forward the "China threat theory" and "China collapse theory". It is against such a background that, in the report to the 18th National Congress of the CPC, it is once again clearly declared that it is essential that socialism with Chinese characteristics be uphold and lead the whole Party and the people of all ethnic groups across the country to take the path of socialism with Chinese characteristics. Hu Jintao emphasized in the report that "The issue of what path we follow is of vital importance for the survival of the Party, the future of China, the future of the Chinese nation, and the wellbeing of the people."

It is an extremely arduous task to explore the path of national rejuvenation in a socially and economically underdeveloped Eastern country like China as it was back then. For more than nine decades, the Party has closely relied on the people, combined the basic principles of Marxism with China's reality and the characteristics of the times, and blazed its path independently. The great victory of reform created and developed socialism with Chinese characteristics and fundamentally changed the future of the Chinese people and the Chinese nation. In this sense, the path of building socialism with Chinese characteristics is a natural choice for the development of Chinese society in modern times, a choice made by the people. This path has not come easily and ought to be doubly cherished!

II. Promoting theoretical and practical innovation of Chinese socialism in solving problems, and realizing the essence of socialism in an all-round way

In the report to the 18th National Congress of the CPC, it is pointed out that to achieve new victory for socialism with Chinese characteristics and open up a new situation under new historical conditions, we must have a firm grasp of the following eight basic requirements: We must uphold the position of the people as the principal actors in the country; we must continue to release and develop the productive forces; we must continue on the path of reform and opening up; we must safeguard social fairness and justice; we must pursue common prosperity; we must promote social harmony; we must pursue peaceful development; we must uphold the leadership of the Party. Among these, the upholding of the people's position as the principal actors in the country, the safeguarding of social fairness and justice, and the pursuit of common prosperity, and the promotion of social harmony have been given special emphasis for the first time under the framework of the connotations of socialism with Chinese characteristics in response to the readily apparent contradictions and problems that have cropped up. It is a theoretical innovation.

In particular, it needs to be emphasized that unswervingly upholding socialism with Chinese characteristics means neither following the old and rigid closed-door policy nor taking erroneous paths through abandoning socialism. In my opinion, "old and rigid closed-door policy" refers to the path taken in the era of highly centralized planned economy, as a result of rigid, closed and one-sided understanding of socialism, which has been proved to be unworkable by the huge price paid for 30 years of exploration since the founding of the People's Republic of China and which, worse, violated the basic theories of Marxism, the laws of socialist development and the laws of the development of human society. The "erroneous paths through abandoning socialism", I think, mainly include the following three paths: the path of free capitalism, the path of state capitalism or crony capitalism, and the path of democratic socialism. These three erroneous paths are all impassable, and if they were taken, they would even cause the collapse of the Party and the fall of the state. In this regard, it is specifically emphasized in the report that "We should give full play to the superiority of the socialist political system in China" and that "We should not mechanically copy the political systems of Western countries."

In the report to the 18th National Congress of the CPC, the rich connotation of the path of building socialism with Chinese characteristics is profoundly explained. Taking the path of socialism with Chinese characteristics means that we must, under the leadership of the CPC and basing ourselves on China's realities, take economic progress as the central task and adhere to the Four Cardinal Principles and the policy of reform and opening up. It means that we must release and develop the productive forces, develop the socialist market economy, socialist democracy, an advanced socialist culture and a harmonious socialist society, and promote socialist ecological progress. It also means that we must promote the well-rounded development of people, achieve prosperity for all over time, and make China a modern socialist country that is prosperous, strong, democratic, culturally advanced and harmonious. Economic, political, cultural, social, and ecological civilization progress have enriched the content of the building of socialism Chinese characteristics, with the goal of realizing the all-round progress of society and the well-rounded development of people. This will be a pioneering initiative that has no precedent. We need to fully realize and demonstrate the essence of socialism through such major progress in the great practice of building socialism with Chinese characteristics.

The path of socialism with Chinese characteristics has been opened up, and the fundamental system has been established. At the same time, we need to continue to improve it in practice and constantly enrich it in theory. I believe that special attention should be paid to the existing "three forms of existence" of socialism as follows.

The first is socialist values. Keeping to the path of socialism with Chinese characteristics is inseparable from acquiring a correct, comprehensive, and profound understanding of socialism. Mao Zedong began to think about this issue in his later years. In the new historical period of reform and opening up, Deng Xiaoping clearly put forward a theory on the essence of socialism. After decades of exploration, we now have obtained a deeper understanding of socialism. The second is socialist system. System is the way of existence and basic structure of social organism. At present, we have formed a set of fundamental theories in economic, political, cultural and social and other construction, which have laid a solid foundation for the building of socialism with Chinese characteristics. The third is socialist public policy. Compared with the first two forms given above, this one has not been paid enough attention. Socialism has changed from being a utopia to being a science, then to being a practical movement, and finally to being establish as a system of institutions. It is not only a real journey of the development of history, but also logically unalterable. However, in addition to this, I believe that there should be and must be a series of subtle and complex systems of public policies to reflect the superiority of the system. For quite a long time, socialism as China's basic system had not been well refined and concretized into public policies, resulting in the superiority of this system not being well reflected. This is what we should make up for today. This has in fact deeply embodied by the "Five-sphere Integrated Plan", namely, China's overall plan for building socialism with Chinese characteristics, that is, to promote coordinated progress in the economic, political, cultural, social and eco-environmental fields, reflecting the concretization and refinement of the all-round social progress and the well-rounded development of people in the socialist system.

III. Being firm in ideals and convictions and remain true to faith of CPC

The key to building socialism with Chinese characteristics is to strengthen the building of the CPC itself. In the final part of the report delivered at the 18th National Congress of the CPC, it is clearly stated that we must comprehensively enhance the level of Party building. Only by building the Party well and keeping its political qualities forever will the path of building socialism with Chinese characteristics be broadened.

It is pointed out in the report that communists' faith in Marxism, socialism and communism is their political soul and sustains them in all tests. Therefore, the CPC must hold up the banner of ideals and convictions. As a political party with a history of more than 90 years, the CPC has been guided by Marxism since it was founded in 1921. It is a Marxist political party whose purpose is to serve the people wholeheartedly and has firm ideals and convictions. Especially at present, in such complicated and ever-changing international and domestic situation and confronted by such complex problems, the CPC as the ruling party must unwaveringly hold up the banner of ideals and convictions. This is a powerful instrument for ensuring that the essence of the Party will never change its nature or betray its colors. However, it should be noted that currently there are some Party members and officials who neither learn nor believe in Marxism, but pursue money worship, hedonism, individualism, obsess over feudal superstition, or advocate Western universal values, and who do not care about common people but ghosts and gods. If such bad practice was allowed to easily flourish, the CPC would exist only in name, betraying its colors. The report also emphasized that the principal position of the people must be upheld. The CPC is a political party endeavoring for the well-being of the people, and its purpose is to serve the people. The faith in Marxism and its putting people first are the mental characteristics of the Party. Without these two qualities, socialism with Chinese characteristics would lose its characteristics and connotations. In his report to the 18th National Congress of the CPC, Hu Jintao emphasized that the whole Party must strengthen its confidence in the path, theory, and system of socialism with Chinese characteristics, which are derived from the Party's history of struggle and the achievements it has harvested in development. More than 90 years of unremitting exploration and more than 30 years of reform and opening up have laid a solid foundation for the realization of the great revival of the Chinese nation and made people have firmer faith. As long as we can keep to the path of building socialism with Chinese characteristics, which has never been walked before, we will be able to solve all the problems relating to reform and development, and China, an ancient Eastern country, will be alive with great vitality, with the great rejuvenation of the Chinese nation getting closer than ever.

On Necessity and Innovation of the Path of Chinese Socialism*

The Eighteenth National Congress of the CPC on Nov 8, 2012 is the one of great importance held when China has entered the decisive stage of completing the building of a moderately prosperous society in all respects. It has five major achievements.

First, it has profoundly expounded the theoretical and historical status of the Scientific Outlook on Development, and proposed that the Scientific Outlook on Development is the latest development of theoretical system of socialism with Chinese characteristics. It, together with Marxism-Leninism, Mao Zedong Thought, Deng Xiaoping Theory, and the important thought of the Three Represents, has been established as the theoretical guidance to which the Party must adhere for a long time. This is an important historical achievement of the 18th CPC National Congress.

Second, it has solemnly announced to the people both within and outside the Party and both in China and abroad what banner China will hold up and what path it will take in the future.

Third, it has made a major arrangements for China's deepening reform and development and other major issues in the next five or even in the ten years.

Fourth, it has profoundly elaborated the basic connotation of socialism with Chinese characteristics, and proposed that we should have every confidence in our path, theory and system, never vacillate in or relax our efforts or act recklessly, and forge ahead with tenacity and resolve, which is of great significance for unifying ideas, boosting confidence, forging strength, and promoting the great cause of

---

* Originally published in *Thirty Famous Scholars on the 18th National Congress of the CPC*, ed. by the Department of Marxism at the Chinese Academy of Social Sciences. Beijing: China Social Sciences Press, 2013.

building socialism with Chinese characteristics and building a moderately prosperous society in all respects.

Fifth, a new Central Committee has elected, the succession of the new leaders to the old has been successfully realized and a new central leadership collective has been elected with Xi Jinping as general secretary. This new leadership collective will surely lead the Party and the Chinese nation from a new starting point to make new great achievements in building a moderately prosperous society in all respects and in realizing the great rejuvenation of the Chinese nation.

Therefore, it is indeed a meeting which calls for upholding the CPC's guiding political principles, carrying forward its cause and forging ahead. It is a meeting aimed to boost the morale of the Party, the people and the army, inspire their fighting spirit, promote China's socialist modernization construction and realize the great rejuvenation of the nation at a new starting point, and pool common understanding and strength for building a moderately prosperous society in all respects.

I. Taking the path of Chinese socialism is an inevitable choice for the development of China's history in modern times

The 18th CPC National Congress proposed that we must unswervingly follow the path of socialism with Chinese characteristics and reject both the old and rigid closed-door policy and any attempt to abandon socialism and take an erroneous path. This is very important. Just as Xi Jinping has stated, it is a proclamation of China's future direction, which is particularly concerned by the people both within and outside the Party and both in China and abroad: We should unswervingly follow the path of socialism with Chinese characteristics.

As we all know, after 1840, China, a previously great country, suffered repeated invasions and bullying by Western capitalist powers, and gradually reduced itself to a country of poverty and weakness, almost on the verge of national subjugation, which triggered a profound reflection among the then Chinese people of vision on why China had been so backward, At first, they thought that the first reason lied in the inferiority in weapon and technology. Later, they gradually realize that the very reason lied in the inferiority in institution. The failure of the Reform Movement of 1898, or *Wu Xu* political reform, made them think that a more profound reason behind the inferiority in institution was that culture lagged behind Western culture. Therefore, up to the May 4th movement, they questioned, criticized and denied the value of Chinese traditional culture. This kind of understanding and mentality continued for a long time, and some Chinese people, especially intellectuals and people of vision, lost confidence in Chinese culture. This problem is particularly fatal. As a result of losing self-confidence in one's own culture, one has actually lost self-respect for the whole Chinese nation, which means that one was deprived of mental foundation, "not enjoy that independence for long", and that one's spirit has collapsed.

At that time, progressive intellectuals began to seek the path of national independence and prosperity. After the May 4th Movement, they introduced Marxism-Leninism into China and founded the CPC in 1921. In this process, the Party combined the basic principles of Marxism with the concrete conditions in China. In such a process, two major theoretical and political achievements have been produced. The first is Mao Zedong Thought, which, combining the basic tenets of Marxism with the concrete practice of the Chinese revolution, answers the question of what path the Chinese revolution should follow and, in fact, puts forward a rational guiding principle for the national liberation. Of course, Mao Zedong Thought also made an important contribution to China's construction. Valuable experience has been accumulated in the exploration. It is the CPC members who combine the basic tenets of Marxism with the practice of China. Then under the guidance of Mao Zedong Thought, China has achieved national independence and liberation and established a socialist system that has fundamentally changed the future of the Chinese nation since the advent of modern times. After the founding of the PRC in 1949, under the guidance of Mao Zedong Thought, the Party has also explored the path to socialist construction. We have abandoned the Soviet model and explored our own path of development. However, as we all know, during our exploration of building socialism with Chinese characteristics, we have accumulated a wealth of experience, but at a heavy historical price. Deng Xiaoping incisively remarked at the opening ceremony of the 12th CPC National Congress: Take a path of our own and build socialism with Chinese characteristics. This is the basic conclusion drawn by the Party in summing up long-term historical experience. Under the leadership of the second generation of collective leadership with Deng Xiaoping at the core, we have initiated the path of socialism with Chinese characteristics. Deng Xiaoping Theory has its rich connotation, under the guidance of which China's socialist construction has entered a new historical stage and China's reform and opening up and socialist modernization have made remarkable achievements.

For sure, the theoretical system of socialism with Chinese characteristics has been constantly enriched and improved, and later there emerged two other theoretical achievements: the important thought of the Three Represents and the Scientific

Outlook on Development. China has become the second largest economy in the world through over 30 years of reform and opening up and the building of socialism with Chinese characteristics. Overall national strength, cultural soft power and international influence have risen sharply. China can already stand firm and strong in the East. The achievements shows that there is a historical necessity in taking the path of socialism with Chinese characteristics, which is the inevitable result of the development in modern China. In a context obviously characterized by the encirclement of the Western imperialist powers, it is impossible for China to take the path of capitalism, for it can only make China become a vassal of the Western capitalist powers, which many theorists of the Party, like Hu Shen (胡绳), have profoundly elaborated. The feasibility of following the Soviet style has been denied by the Party's exploration from the early days of the founding of the PRC in 1949 to the 1950s. Therefore, the Party had taken many detours and paid a high price in such theoretical and practical exploration before embarking on the path of socialism with Chinese characteristics, which, as the thirty years of reform and opening up and the socialist modernization drive have demonstrated, has changed China and the future of the Chinese nation over the past century and more. China has been standing rock-firm in the East as one of major countries in the world, and the Chinese nation has burnished its image, and the international influence of Chinese culture has increased significantly. The people's confidence in the Chinese nation, especially in Chinese culture, including the confidence in the theory of socialism with Chinese characteristics and the CPC, has been enhanced, which has never happened since the advent of modern times. Therefore, in retrospect, we can say that the path of socialism with Chinese characteristics is a natural choice for the development of Chinese society in modern times, and a choice of the Chinese people. It is a Chinese path to prosperity and the people's wellbeing. It is not only the path we should take but also a successful one for realizing the great rejuvenation of the Chinese nation, which is a basic conclusion we can draw as long as we review our history. Therefore, Xi Jinping's speech at the press conference on November 15, 2012 and when he visited the exhibition "Road to Rejuvenation" are of deep historical connotation and wonderful profundity.

II. Chinese Socialism: unity of value form, institutional form and public policy form

The rational connotation of the path of socialism with Chinese characteristics is vividly summarized in the report to the 18th National Congress of the CPC. As pointed out in the report, taking the path of socialism with Chinese characteristics means that we must, under the leadership of the CPC, take economic progress as the central task, adhere to the Four Cardinal Principles and the policy of reform and opening up. It means that we must release and develop the productive forces, develop the socialist market economy, socialist democracy, an advanced socialist culture and a harmonious socialist society, and promote socialist ecological progress. It also means that we must promote the well-rounded development of people, achieve common prosperity, and develop China into a great modern socialist country that is prosperous, strong, democratic, culturally advanced, and harmonious. This path actually embodies its connotation at three levels:

We should, under the leadership of the CPC and bearing China's basic conditions in mind, pursue economic progress as the central task, uphold the Four Cardinal Principles, be committed to the reform and opening up policy. This is the basic line of the CPC. Then, the Speech goes on to deal with the issues with regard to releasing and developing the productive forces, including the building of the socialist market economy, socialist democracy, an advanced socialist culture, a harmonious society, and a sound ecological environment, all these constituting the five major layouts and the basic framework for the path with Chinese socialism. To promote the well-rounded development of people, achieve common prosperity, and make China a modern socialist country that is prosperous, strong, democratic, culturally advanced and harmonious, is the goal of the path of socialism with Chinese characteristics. As Deng Xiaoping said, the essence of socialism is to release and develop the productive forces, eliminate exploitation, eliminate polarization and ultimately achieve common prosperity. This summary of the path of socialism with Chinese characteristics fully embodies the essence of socialism.

An important feature of the path of socialism with Chinese characteristics is the socialist market economy, which is the original creation of the CPC. The market economy has long existed and the Western capitalist countries are also engaged, but this is not something unique to capitalism. Jiang Zemin elaborated the basic framework for the socialist market economy in the Party's 14th National Congress. As he said, adding the word "socialist" to the front of the phrase "market economy" is not insignificant, but a finishing touch, which means we must integrate the basic principles of socialism and the essential requirements of socialism with the mechanisms and rules of the market economy, so as to constitute the essence of the path of socialism with Chinese characteristics. This means that, first and foremost, what we are engaging in is not a free market economy or unalloyed marketism, and that we should combine macro-control with a market economy. On the one hand, we must improve the macro-control system, and at the same time, give full play to the fundamental role of market in the allocation of resources to a greater extent and in a wider scope. In this case, it also includes improving the basic economic system, in which public ownership is the mainstay of the economy, economic entities of diverse ownership develop together; and improving the system of income distribution, in which distribution according to work is the main form that coexists with other forms of distribution.

In the report to the 18th National Congress of the CPC, it is also pointed out that, in order to promote the economic restructuring, what is essential is that we should properly handle the relationship between the government and the market, and that we must see that the market plays the decisive role in resource allocation, the government plays its role better. These expositions are still centered on the issue of how to improve the socialist market economy, because it is created by the CPC.

The connotation of the path of socialism with Chinese characteristics that is also expounded in this report, also covers socialist democracy, an advanced socialist culture, a harmonious socialist society, and socialist ecological conservation, all of which are the rich connotation of socialism with Chinese characteristics, which can be prescribed from the other dimensions. Then what is its goal? That is to promote all-round social progress and the well-rounded development of people and achieve common prosperity. This shows the basic principles and basic views on scientific socialism, developed by K. Marx and F. Engels. In the Marxist interpretation of the essence and the goals of socialism, the highest goal is to promote the common development of people and achieve the well-rounded development of people and common prosperity. Therefore, the elaboration of the path of socialism with Chinese characteristics in the report to the 18th National Congress of the Communist Party of China, which is based on the national conditions of contemporary China and adheres to the basic tenets and views of Marxism, especially scientific socialism, is a kind of adherence to and innovation of Marxism. Therefore, this elaboration, in fact, is the grasping and stipulation of the connotation and orientation of socialism with Chinese characteristics from the unity of three dimensions, namely, the productive forces, the production relations and the free and well-rounded development of people.

The report also made a new analysis of the socialist system with Chinese characteristics, pointing out that this system includes Deng Xiaoping Theory, the important thought of the Three Representsand and the Scientific Outlook on Development; that recognition of the Scientific Outlook on Development as the latest achievement of the theory of socialism with Chinese characteristics, the enshrinment of it into the Party Constitution, and the establishment of it, together with Marxism-Leninism, Mao Zedong Thought, Deng Xiaoping Theory and the important thought of the Three Represents, as the theoretical guidance that the Party must adhere to for a long time, constitute one of the major historic achievements of the 18th National Congress of the CPC. With regard to the socialist system with Chinese characteristics, the 18th National Congress of the CPC also conducted a judicious and accurate summary. The theory of socialism with Chinese characteristics includes the following: the system of people's congresses as China's fundamental political system; the basic political systems of multi-party cooperation and political consultation under the leadership of the CPC, of regional ethnic autonomy, and of community-level self-governance; other systems and mechanisms such as the system of socialist laws with Chinese characteristics, the basic economic system in which public ownership is the mainstay and economic entities of diverse ownership develop together.

The report also profoundly expounded the relationship between the path, the theory and system of socialism with Chinese characteristics, pointed out that the path of socialism with Chinese characteristics is the way to reach the goal, the theory of socialism with Chinese characteristics offers a guide to action, and the system with socialism with Chinese characteristics provides the fundamental guarantee, these three functioning as an integral whole in the great practice of building socialism with Chinese characteristics. This is the salient feature of the long-term endeavors of the CPC leading the people in building socialism. Therefore, the report to the18th National Congress of the CPC is a reveiw of the work over the past decade and even a thorough review of China's experience of over 30 years of reform and opening up in exploring and advancing the theory of socialism with Chinese characteristics, focusing on the path we have taken and the theories concerned and the issue of how we can achieve such brilliant achievements, offering a particularly clear generalization of the relationship between these three aspects, which reflects the Party's strong theoretical consciousness.

The elaboration of the report to the 18th National Congress of the CPC on the relationship between the path, theory and system of socialism with Chinese characteristics also gave us a profound inspiration: we can also understand from another perspective the nature of socialism with Chinese characteristics. The earliest human ideal on socialism took shape long ago, and utopian socialism has been discussed in many ways. K. Marx and F. Engels transformed utopian socialism into scientific socialism, into a practice and into a movement. Lenin and Mao Zedong really established the socialist system. The movement from an ideal form of good values about the development of human society to the fact that K. Marx, F. Engels, Lenin and Mao Zedong regarded it as a scientific theory, as a practice and movement, and established socialist system constitutes the historical process of socialism. However, If we just stay at these two levels, we can not fully demonstrate socialism in practice. This has been proven by history. We once had such a bright ideal as socialism and communism, for which we also established the corresponding political system and economy system, etc., but we had no corresponding rational public policies in line with the then realities to fully realize the values, ideals and advantages of socialism. Therefore, when we read the report to the 18th National Congress of the CPC, we can find that the Party has specific policies and measures for promoting socialism with Chinese characteristics in the new phase and in the new circumstance, in terms of economy, livelihood, social progress and culture. Therefore, we can say that the Party has gained a good understanding of building socialism with Chinese characteristics, which has entered a new stage and a new realm, that is to say, to regard socialism with Chinese characteristics as the unity of socialist values, socialist system and public policy, with these three forms being interdependent and indispensable.

III. Contemporary China rejects both the old and rigid closed-door policy and any attempt to abandon socialism and take an erroneous path

In the report to the 18th National Congress, it is mentioned that "contemporary China rejected both the old and rigid closed-door policy and any attempt to abandon socialism and take an erroneous path." This remark is rich in connotation and is a declaration of the future direction of China. With the deepening of globalization and the reform and opening up, many achievements have been made in economic, political, cultural , social , ecological and other forms of progress. The overall national strength and cultural soft power have greatly enhanced China's international influence, but it cannot be evaded that in the process of deepening the reform and opening wider to the outside world and promoting the great cause of building socialism with Chinese characteristics, a series of conflicts and problems have cropped up or will do so, such as a widening gap between rich and poor and a large income disparity between the residents of different social strata--in other words, inequitable distribution, as well as serious corruption of some officials, high resource consumption for which huge price has been paid for development as far as ecological environment is concerned. In addition, in the process of development, ideas are diversified, which, to a certain extent, have gone astray; to a certain extent, this means that people have doubt about their ideals and convictions, that their moral standards need to be raised, and that the issue of integrity is pressing. These issues should be addressed in the process of deepening reform and promoting development. However, regarding these issues, different voices have been indeed heard inside and outside the Party, at home and abroad. These conflicts and problems can be summed up as four Divisions: division of rich and poor, division of classes, division of interests, and division of ideas. People of different walks of life and different groups naturally have different positions, interest demands, ideas and views. Therefore, it is increasingly difficult to reach a consensus on what path China shall follow in the future, what guiding political principle it shall uphold and where it shall head.

These conflicts and problems invite a question: Given that there is such division between rich and poor, such serious corruption, such morality downturn and such serious environmental pollution, does that mean that there is something wrong with the reform and development, and that the traditional socialist model was better? This sort of doubt seems to have been creeping over some community-level people. However, in the 18th National Congress report, it is pointed out that this old path cannot be taken any longer. What is called the erroneous path can take on the following trends: One is that the capitalist path guided by neo-liberalism is the economic and political model of complete marketization, complete privatization and multi-party system. People who held such view believe that such problems as mentioned above arise from incomplete reform in China. We do admit that such problems need to be solved in the course of reform, but the exponents of this trend are trying to lead us towards neo-liberal capitalism, which is an erroneous path. Some people claim that China should follow the path of democratic socialism advocated by the Western Social Democratic Party, given the lagging development of socialist democratic politics in the country, the lack of sound social welfare policies, and the polarization between rich and poor. Also there are some people at home and abroad who have pointed out that the current reforms in China have encountered various problems, so we must be alert to the risks of state monopoly capitalism and crony capitalism, in which involves excessive concentration of political power and the overmighty public power, the oversize monopoly industries, and the excessive power intervention by political power in the market economy, to the detriment of China's development.

Therefore, in summary, according to the report to the 18th National Congress of the CPC, we cannot abandon socialism to take an erroneous path, whether it may be free capitalism, or democratic socialism, or the so-called state capitalism or crony capitalism.

In the report to the 18th National Congress of the CPC, it is especially emphasized that we will never follow the Western development model, which means that, proceeding from its national conditions, China "does not engage in multi-party rotation in power, in diversification of theoretical guidance, in the separation of powers and the two-chamber system, and in federalism and privatization" so that all power of the country can be ensured in the hands of the people, which the central government of China has requently emphasized.

Finally, China must frequently take the path of peaceful development. Historically, the Western capitalist countries, in order to rise as great powers, have taken the path of invading other countries by force and plundering resources in a colonial way. In the report to the 18th National Congress of the CPC, it is pointed out that we must take the path of peaceful development and will realize peaceful development in international relations of equality, mutual trust and mutual benefit. We will never follow the old path of the rise of the great powers as Western capitalist countries. This should also be included in what means by not taking an erroneous path.

Therefore, regarding the future direction of China, in the report to the 18th National Congress of the CPC, a clear declaration is made that the path and theory and system with Chinese characteristics are the fundamental direction of the contemporary China's development and progress. Only the socialism with Chinese characteristics can develop China. It is the only way and the successful path to the great rejuvenation of the Chinese nation. Therefore, the 18th CPC National Congress accurately states that we should forge ahead with tenacity and resolve, instead of vacillating in or relaxing our efforts or acting recklessly, on the path to socialism with Chinese characteristics, and that this path has been the crystallization of the collective wisdom of the CPC and the Chinese people in their exploration since the founding of modern China in 1949, and is the choice of history, and of the people. So we must cherish what has been accomplished and never deviate from it but rather continue to enrich it.

IV. Keep confidence in the path and theories and system of socialism with Chinese characteristics

In the report to the 18th CPC National Congress, it is emphatically and incisively expounded that the whole Party should have full confidence in the theory, path and system of socialism with Chinese characteristics. This idea is made very impressively and very necessarily. Over the past 30 years of reform and opening up, we have made tremendous achievements. Under the guidance of the theoretical system of socialism with Chinese characteristics, we have made many historic achievements on the path of socialism with Chinese characteristics. We should have such confidence. Despite the many problems that still exist in the current process of development, we should never lose confidence. At present, given the problems in our development, some people, both within and outside the Party, both at home and abroad, even question the effectiveness and prospects of Chinese path. Given the corruption, the polarization of rich and poor and environmental problems, there are some people who suggest taking the old path, or other paths. All these are manifestations of the loss of confidence in Chinese path. Therefore, it is of high relevance to highlight the importance of fostering stronger confidence in the path, theory, system, and culture of socialism with Chinese characteristics.

In the report to the 18th National Congress of the CPC, it is made clear that in the face of these problems, we must continue to carry out theoretical and practical innovation, not only upholding but also advancing the theoretical system of socialism with Chinese characteristics, and then solve them. We should have confidence in solving them and about the future of China. Some international public opinion in the West is questioning the effectiveness of Chinese path, thinking that China's economic construction has been successful, but political restructuring is lagging behind and is not imitable to other countries; in other words, that they acknowledge China's economic progress, but do not acknowledge China's political restructuring and institution building, as well as human rights, human development and other issues. This statement is utterly wrong, or is made with ulterior motives. I think our current stage of development is a crucial time. Now that China is at the cruicial stage of development, the report to the 18th National Congress of CPC holds that the whole Party should have every confidence in our path, theory and system, which is to allow us to increase consensus and cohesion on the basis of the self-confidence in what we have achieved, to carry out theoretical and practical innovation on these issues, and to formulate some new policies to solve these problems so that we can gain more self-confidence and steadily widen the path of socialism with Chinese characteristics. Therefore, confidence and determination are the most essential. Now, we have walked more than half the journey, so if these problems are resolved, the rationality and effectiveness of the socialist economic system and political system with Chinese characteristics in China will be truly established. In other words, at that time, the dissidents in the West will also have to acknowledge the Chinese path, thinking that Chinese system is a new model of the modernization of human society and opens up a new path for the modernization of human society. As we know, the path of modernization that has been considered the most effective is the path dominated by Western capitalism, consisting of its political system, economic system, and universal values. At that time, there emerged the final conclusion of history that the path of socialism is unworkable, with the economy not boosted at all, and politics centralized. China's development has now demonstrated the effectiveness of this system, but if the problems mentioned above can not be solved, China is likely to retreat or remain stagnant. So this path cannot be said to be completely successful. We must try to solve the middle-income trap, and then to take a step forward to a moderately prosperous society in all respects. In this case, a dynamic situation will been created. The effectiveness and profundity of the Chinese system will be acknowledged by those dissidents, both within and outside the Party, at home and abroad. Therefore, the whole Party having every confidence in our path, in our theory and in our system is particularly pertinent, for they are especially important things to boost confidence, build consensus and cohesion to solve these problems, promote development, achieve the overall victory of socialist construction, and realize the rejuvenation of the Chinese nation.

V. Highlights and innovations of the report to the 18th CPC National Congress: upholding the principal position of the people, safeguarding social fairness and justice, and striving for common prosperity

In the process of deepening the reform and opening up and advancing socialism with Chinese characteristics, some problems have cropped up. In the report to the 18th CPC National Congress, it is stated that China is now at a critical stage of building a moderately prosperous society in all respects. Our development and more than 30 years of exploration has laid a very solid material foundation, and has made historic achievements in economic, social and cultural progress, as well as enhancing international influence and cultural soft power. But there are still many problems confronting us. What should we do? If we continue to deepen the reform and move forward, then we will, as is mentioned in the report, achieve the grand goal of building a moderately prosperous society in all respects by 2020, the 100th anniversary of the founding of the CPC in 1921. However, if we did not have corresponding theoretical and practical innovations to solve these problems, we would be entangled in these problems, and China would stagnate or even regress. China is now at a very critical juncture in the process of building a moderately prosperous society in all respects and realizing the great rejuvenation of the Chinese nation. It is the dawn before the great rejuvenation. Whether these problems can be solved depends on the determination and innovation of the CPC. Judging from what is said in the report to the 18th National Congress of the CPC, the Party has a very clear understanding of the current problems. In every part of the report, comprehensive arrangements have been made for solving these problems and corresponding policies have been formulated; in a nutshell, the "Eight Upholds" has been proposed in the report, which have enriched the connotation of the theoretical system and path of socialism with Chinese characteristics. Hu Jintao particularly emphasized that in order to win new victories in socialism with Chinese characteristics under new historical circumstances, we must fulfill with firm determination the following requirements: we must uphold the position of the people as the principal actors in the country; we must continue to release and develop the productive forces; we must persevere in reform and opening up; we must safeguard social fairness and justice; we must resolutely pursue common prosperity; we must promote social harmony; we must pursue peaceful development; and we must uphold the leadership of the Party. These eight requirements together constitute a new expression, at least three of which have never been definitely stated, which are of great originality.

First, it is made clear that we must uphold the position of the people as the principal actors in the country. To my understanding, there invlove three basic points: First, according to the historical materialism and the basic principles of Marxism, the people are the basic motive force for promoting social and historical progress. This is the basic Marxist view of social development. Second, the power of the CPC as a Marxist party comes from the people. Third, the purpose of the CPC is to serve the people wholeheartedly and to govern for the people, all its development goals being for the people, to promote the well-rounded development of people, and to pursue common prosperity. Therefore, this point has been proposed in the report to the 18th National Congress of the CPC when the principle of people first is mentioned.

Second, it is made clear that we must safeguard social fairness and justice, it is proposed that we should promote equal rights, equal opportunities and fair rules for all, and that the upholding of social fairness and justice be the special connotation of socialism with Chinese characteristics. All these are extremely targeted.

Third, it is emphasized that we must resolutely pursue common prosperity. This is the fundamental principle of socialism with Chinese characteristics. We should adhere to the basic socialist economic system and the socialist income distribution system. We should adjust the pattern of national income distribution, tighten its regulation by secondary distribution and work hard to narrow income gaps so that all the people can share in more fruits of development in a fair way and move steadily toward common prosperity.

The afore-mentioned three requirements mean what the Party and the country will focus on through making greatest efforts in advancing the great cause of building socialism with Chinese characteristics. This is an enrichment of the theoretical system of socialism with Chinese characteristics.

VI. Be firm in ideals and convictions, and People-first principle, maintain the ethos and political integrity of the CPC

As the governance party, the CPC shoulders the leadership responsibility of advancing the great cause of reform and opening up and the socialism with Chinese characteristics. Therefore, the key to China's problems is to improve and strengthen Party building; strengthen intra-party building is fundamental. With regard to Party building, what has been most impressive in the report to the 18th National Congress of the CPC includes the following two points: First, the CPC Central Committe upholds ideals and convictions, emphasizing that the CPC must strengthen their ideals and convictions, namely, the faith in Marxism, socialism and communism, and that this is the soul and cultural traits of the CPC. This is very pertinent. We cannot look over the fact that although the CPC now has more than 80 million Party members, but a small number of Party members and officials have lost the political soul of a party member, do not learn or believe in Marxism, and have no faith in socialism and communism. What is the CPC? It must first have ideal requirements, namely, ideals and cultural pursuit. The 18th National Congress of the CPC pointed out that it is particularly important to emphasize this point in intensifying education to maintain its progressive nature and its integrity. We must promote the cultural pursuit of the CPC members. We join the Party because we believe in Marxism, so we must strengthen our faith in socialism and communism, and endeavor for such ideal and conviction in our actions and work; in other words, a Party member devoid of ideals lacks an essential quality. Moreover, in such a stage, so many problems have cropped up among the ranks of Party members and officials. So, it is very necessary to uphold ideals and convictions of the Party members. Much importance should be attached in these respects.

With regard to strengthening Party building, there is another point in the report that deserves our special attention. In this report, emphasis is laid on the CPC's people-first principle through expounding the principle of the people's principal position, especially the need to put people first, exercise governance for the people and always maintain close ties with them; it proposes that serving the people is the fundamental purpose of the Party, and putting people first and exercising governance for the people is the ultimate yardstick for judging all the Party's performance in this regard, and that at all times we must put the people's interests above and rely on them to propel history forward. Therefore, this report actually clarified such a simple truth that the CPC comes from the people. The power of the CPC as the ruling party comes from the people. Its concept of governance is that everything should be done for the happiness of the people and the prosperity of the country. Over decades, from its very founding to its exploration of the road of revolution, construction, and development, the CPC has focused its efforts on the same theme: the happiness of the Chinese peole. The founding and development of the CPC have been based on relying on the people and serving them, and every victory of the Party depends on the people and serve them. This is the basic law of the long-term governance of the CPC. So it is very dangerous for the Party members and officials to forget the people, become distanced from them or to seek interests only for a few people or interest groups, which may result in the collapse of the Party and even the subjugation of the nation. Therefore, the emphasis of this report on the Party's people-first principle is of profound meaning and high pertinence.

In addition, regarding strengthening Party building, this report is deeply impressive in that it proposed that we must unswervingly combat corruption and preserve the Communists' political integrity, emphasized that combating corruption and promoting political integrity, which is a major political issue of great concern to the people, is a clear-cut and long-term political commitment of the Party, so if we fail to handle this issue well, it could prove fatal to the Party, and even cause the collapse of the Party and the fall of the State; it is proposed that we must make unremitting efforts to combat corruption, promote integrity and stay vigilant against degeneration. It is also proposed that we must see to it that officials are honest, the government is clean, and political integrity is upheld, which conforms to the people's and the Party's aspirations, and which displays the Party's determination to combat corruption. With such determination and corresponding deployment, the Party can achieve self-purification, self-improvement, and self-development, so that the Communists can keep clean and honest, which will ensure the Party its integrity and progressive nature. Therefore, this report is innovative in its elaboration on combating corruption so as to preserve Communists' political integrity, demonstrate their strong determination to achieve our ideals. Therefore, we should have every reason to be optimistic.

In this report, Hu Jintao said that as long as we stay true to our ideal, are firm in our conviction, never vacillate in or relax our efforts or act recklessly, and forge ahead with tenacity and resolve, we will surely have every confidence in our path, in our theories and in our system and truly take the development path of socialism with Chinese characteristics. At that time, what Thatcher once said about China will not be justified any longer—she allegedly said in a book that China can never be a superpower and that "China today exports television sets. Not ideas." As a matter of fact, not only can we export material products, but also our system which is also effective, at least effective for China, and the philosophical and the theoretical innovation behind the system is also correct. It is a new trail blazed for human development, posing a challenge for the existing capitalist system, as another system that can compete with it. This is a manifestation of the soft power of Chinese culture.

Therefore, I think this report has a very high starting point and a very broad vision, elaborating the path, theory and system of socialism with Chinese characteristics from the laws of the governance of the CPC, of socialist development, and of human development, so we must have such a mind and vision. The CPC is engaged in a great undertaking. It has opened up a new path to modernization, that is, the path of socialism with Chinese characteristics. This is not only the path which the Chinese people have followed and managed to turn the poor and backward old China into an increasingly prosperous and powerful new China, but also the path which they continue to follow to realize modernization and national rejuvenation. It may also provide reference for other underdeveloped countries to achieve modernization.

Therefore, at that time, the CPC and the Chinese people can truly be proud. At that time, China is definitely a major country, not only an economic super-power, but also a political super-power, a cultural super-power, and a socially harmonious country at the same time.

This report has a very strong sense of history, hardship consciousness, and innovation consciousness. It clearly embodies the firmness and high degree of consciousness and self-confidence in upholding socialism with Chinese characteristics and taking the path of socialism with Chinese characteristics. It is very important for China, which is currently at a critical stage of reform and development.

Chinese Socialism as a New Social Form: its Value and Significance*

After more than 30 years of reform and opening up, China's socialist market economy has developed in depth, and great achievements have been made in all aspects. Its international status has been continuously improved, and the international environment we face has also undergone major changes. Multiple changes such as globalization, informatization, cyberization, marketization, industrialization and urbanization, have all overlapped in the same space and at the same time, forming a complex environment for development. The development of domestic society is faced with the differentiation of interests, classes, and understanding; the Western anti-China forces have stepped up their ideological infiltration in the country. As a result, there have been different opinions and expectations in the understanding of socialism with Chinese characteristics within and outside the Party, at home and abroad. For this reason, in the report to the 18th National Congress of the CPC, the CPC Central Committe put forward that we should have every confidence in Chinese path, theory and system. As Xi Jinping, China's current General Secretary, clearly pointed out in the "Speech at the Seminar of the Members and Alternate Members of the Newly-elected CPC Central Committee for Implementing the Guiding Principles of the Party's 18th National Congress", "Socialism with Chinese characteristics is the dialectical unity of the theoretical logic of scientific socialism and the historical logic of Chinese social development. It is a scientific socialism rooted in China's land, reflecting the wishes of the Chinese people, adapting to the requirements of China's development and progress…" The issue of choosing a path is crucial for a party and a country. It is pointed out in the report to the 18th National Congress of the CPC, convened from November 8 to 14, 2012, that "The issue of what path we follow is

---

* Originally published in *Marxist Studies*, 2013(9).

of vital importance to the survival of the Party, the future of China, the destiny of the Chinese nation, and the wellbeing of the people." Xi Jinping also stresses: "It is the most important question that is related to the success or failure of the Party, and which path to take decides the life of the Party." From the perspective of a Marxist theory of social formation and of comparison with other social formations, and based on studying the report to the 18th National Congress of the CPC and a series of important speeches by General Secretary Xi Jinping, we can deeply understand the extraordinariness, originality and great significance of socialism with Chinese characteristics.

I. Socialist Formation with Chinese Characteristics: Unity of Path, Theory and System

We should understand the great significance of socialism with Chinese characteristics from the Marxist theory of social formation. According to the viewpoints of historical materialism, the social formation is the unity of economic base and the superstructure based on a certain number of productive forces. Propelled by the contradictions between the productive forces and the relations of production, and between the economic base and the superstructure, social formation can continue to develop and change successively one after another. The unity and universality of the development of social formation lies in the fact that the movement of the contradictionbetween the economic base and the superstructure promotes the development and evolution of human society from a low-level form to a high-level form in the basic path of primitive society—slave society—feudal society—capitalist society—communist society (the primary stage of which is socialist society). Marxism also holds that the universality and unity (typicality) of the social formation development do not exclude diversity and particularity, because the actual social formations and their development are complex and diverse. And more often than not, there is a transitional formation between any two social formations. The same social formation has the common essence and can exist in different countries and ethnic groups, and at the same time it also has different characteristics in terms of economic base and superstructure. In addition, the historical materialism also holds that the evolution and development of social formation are also the unity of sequentiality and asynchrony of successive replacement. As a result, a complex situation in which multiple social formations coexist in the same era has taken shape. However, the diversity of multiple social formations coexisting in different spaces in the same era is just another manifestation of the asynchrony of the replacement of social formation. These different social formations, which do not exist in the same time but exist in the same space, influence and restrict each other, and show the direction and mainstream of historical development in various differences.

According to the basic view of historical materialism, it can be believed that socialism with Chinese characteristics, viewed from the vertical dimension of Chinese history, has developed itself from a semi-colonial and semi-feudal society through new-democratic revolution to a new democratic society, and then through socialist revolution to a socialist society of socialism, socialism at the primary stage. It is different from the traditional and rigid socialist model. Viewed from a horizontal dimension, Chinese socialism is also different from the socialist formations of other countries, such as the Soviet model and the Cuban model. Of course, it is fundamentally different from the various social formations of capitalism, such as democratic socialism, liberal capitalism, and state monopoly capitalism. General Secretary Xi Jinping pointed out that we must let the people of the rest of the world know that there are such a group of Chinese people who are doing such a thing and who are doing it quite well.

We believe that socialism with Chinese characteristics is the socialist formation produced in the process of seeking national independence, liberation, construction and development in modern China. It is a new type of socialism reflecting not only the theoretical logic of scientific socialism but also China's national conditions. It is a new type of institutional civilization that coexists with other social formations of capitalism in the context of globalization, fundamentally different from them, struggling against and cooperating with them, and constantly showing its obvious strength.

Only when we understand the path, theory and system of socialism with Chinese characteristics based on the Marxist theory of social formation can we have a deeper understanding of the extraordinariness and uniqueness of socialism with Chinese characteristics and a more profound understanding of its vicissitudes and its richness in national connotation and world historical significance. Socialism with Chinese characteristics is the original creation of the CPC and has been a natural choice for the development of Chinese society in modern times. The unity of the path, theory, and system of socialism with Chinese characteristics is exactly the social formation of socialism with Chinese characteristics.

II. Chinese socialism is socialism, not any other 'ism'

General Secretary Xi Jinping pointed out clearly: "Socialism with Chinese characteristics is socialism, not any other 'ism.' The foundational principles of scientific socialism cannot be abandoned; only if they are abandoned would our system no longer be socialist."① This is a prescriptive explanation of the essence of socialism with Chinese characteristics and an answer to its nature and direction. Socialism with Chinese characteristics is socialism precisely because it adheres to the values and fundamental principles of scientific socialism, that is, highly developed forces of production, realization of common prosperity and the free and well-rounded development of people, the three points which summarize the core essence of the normative concept of scientific socialism.

K. Marx and F. Engels created scientific socialism on the premise and basis of correctly understanding and revealing the laws of social development. In *Preface to a Contribution to the Critique of Political Economy*, they made a classic description of the historical materialism: "In the social production of their existence, men inevitably enter into definite relations that are independent of their will, namely relations of production appropriate to a given stage in the development of their material forces of production. The totality of these relations of production constitutes the economic structure of society, the real foundation, on which arises a legal and political superstructure and to which correspond definite forms of social consciousness. The mode of production of material life conditions the general process of social, political and intellectual life. It is not the consciousness of men that determines their existence, but their social existence that determines their consciousness." ②The relationships between the productive forces and the relations of production and between the economic base and the superstructure constitute the basic contradiction and fundamental motive force of social development, in which the productive forces are the ultimate determinant, and is the measure of all social progress. The relations of production shall be appropriate to the development of their productive forces. The relations of production appropriate to a given stage in the development of their material forces of production constitute the economic structure and the real foundation of a given social form, and define the main characteristics of a social form.

---

① Xi Jinping: *The Governance of China*, Eng. ed., Beijing: Foreign Language Press, 2014, p.22.
② Marx, K. & F. Engels: *Selected Works of Marx and Engels*, Vol. 2, Chin. ed., Beijing: People's Publishing House, 1995, p. 32.

K. Marx and F. Engels also described and explained the basic principles and realization conditions of communist society on the basis of the critique of capitalist society from the height of the unity of historical outlook and values. In his letter to the magazine editorial office of *Annals of the Fatherland*[1] in 1877, K. Marx summarized that humankind "may ultimately arrive at the form of economy which will ensure, together with the greatest expansion of the productive powers of social labour, the most complete development of man." At the same time, K. Marx also clearly pointed out that it is a society "securing for every member of society." In his view, the existence of such a society means being "not only fully sufficient materially, and becoming day-by-day fuller, but an existence guaranteeing to all the free development and exercise of their physical and mental faculties."[2]

On the basis of historical materialism, combining the principles of the productive forces with those of common prosperity and those of the free and well-rounded development of people, K. Marx and F. Engels expounded the essence of scientific socialism, in which the principle of the productive forces is the foundation, just as K. Marx pointed out in *Capital*, only the highly developed productive forces "under such a condition, can create a practical foundation for a social form with the free and well-rounded development of every person as its basic principle."[3] Meanwhile, the development of the productive forces will aim at prosperity for all people and their free and well-rounded development. So scientific socialism is neither the "average wealth" under very low level of the productive forces nor the "polarization between rich and poor" under the conditions of developed productive forces.

In the process of creating and developing socialism with Chinese characteristics, the CPC has deeply understood and grasped the essential connotation of scientific socialism, that is, always regarding the liberation and development of the productive forces, the realization of prosperity for all, and the realization of the well-rounded development of people as the core concept and the principles guiding modernization.

After the Third Plenary Session of the 11th CPC Central Committee, Deng Xiaoping put forward the important theoretical and practical issues of understanding

---

[1] Otechestvennye Zapiski, variously translated as "Annals of the Fatherland", "Patriotic Notes", "Notes of the Fatherland", etc.—Tr.
[2] Marx, K. & F. Engels: *Collected Works of Marx and Engels*, Vol. 3, Chin. ed., Beijing: People's Publishing House, 2009, p. 563-564.
[3] Marx, K. & F. Engels: *Marx and Engels: Collected Works*, Vol. 23, Chin. ed., Beijing: People's Publishing House, p. 649.

what socialism is and how to build socialism. After summarizing the experience and lessons of socialist construction practices at home and abroad, he gave clear answers: "The essence of socialism is liberation and development of the productive forces, elimination of exploitation and polarization, and the ultimate achievement of prosperity for all." [1] Later, Jiang Zemin and Hu Jintao emphasized the well-rounded development of people on the basis of Deng Xiaoping Theory about the essence of socialism. Jiang Zemin said in his speech on July 1st, 2001: "All undertakings to build socialism with Chinese characteristics, and in fact, everything that we do should aim not just at meeting people's immediate material and cultural needs, but also at improving the qualities of the people or an all-round development of the people. This is the essential requirement of Marxism regarding the building of a new socialist society." At the Third Plenary Session of the 16th CPC Central Committee in 2003, Hu Jintao put forward the Scientific Outlook on Development, taking putting people first and promoting the well-rounded development of people as the core of the Outlook. From the perspective of the unity of path, theory and system, based on the nearly 500-year-old socialist development, and in response to various misunderstandings and doubts about Chinese socialism, General Secretary Xi Jinping profoundly explained the basic connotation of Chinese socialism from both the positive and negative aspects, further guiding and regulating the theory and practice of socialism with Chinese characteristics.

III. Chinese socialism is a socialism of reform and opening up, rather than the closed and rigid traditional socialism

Chinese Socialism was first initiated by Deng Xiaoping in the period of reform and opening up. It is socialism that continues to reform and open up, not a traditional socialism that is closed and rigid. In the report to the 18th National Congress of the CPC, it is clearly pointed out that we should reject the old and rigid closed-door policy.

K. Marx and F. Engels gave us their account of the foundational principle of scientific socialism simply from the perspective of value form, and did not provide ready answers for socialist construction. The People's Republic of China, in the first thirty years after its founding in 1949, confronted the new problem about how to

---

[1] *Selected Works of Deng Xiaoping*, Vol. 3, Chin. ed., Beijing: People's Publishing House, 1993, p. 373.

understand and grasp socialism in practice. At first, the CPC learned and copied the experience of the Soviet Union, with socialism talked about in abstraction without regard for the productive forces and the requirements for the development of the productive forces, with the public ownership of the means of production and the common prosperity overly emphasized, with more public and unalloyed relations of production blindly pursued on a larger scale. Due to the Party's "leftist" error in its guiding ideology, the political system and social management had become rigid. Besides, the capitalist technology and management experience as well as the excellent traditional culture of China were rejected in the field of ideology and culture; the idea of "preferring socialist weeds to capitalist seedlings" prevailed. Nevertheless, practice has proved that the old and rigid closed-door policy did not and will not work.

Deng Xiaoping understood the shortcomings of the closed and rigid traditional socialism, and on this basis, he rethought about the issue of how to build socialism in China, an economically and culturally underdeveloped country. Under the guidance of the ideological line of "freeing up the mind and seeking truth from facts", he successfully solved the problem and created socialism with Chinese characteristics, which, compared with the traditional socialism, is characterized by reform and opening up. The very purpose of reform is to change the various relations of production and management systems and mechanisms that are not appropriate for the development of the productive forces; The very purpose of opening up is to conform to the trend of the times of globalization, actively participate in the international division of labor, strengthen exchanges and cooperation with other countries in the world, and make full use of the world's outstanding civilization achievements. Therefore, General Secretary Xi Jinping said: "If our Party had not decisively decided to implement the policy of reform and opening up in 1978, and unswervingly promoted it, and firmly grasped its correct direction, socialist China would not be what it is today, and it might have been plagued by serious crises."[①]

Socialism with Chinese characteristics recognizes that Chinese socialism has developed itself in a particular historical context, at a certain time and at a certain place, so it cannot be divorced from its existing objective conditions. Xi Jinping said: "What doctrine a country may choose is based on whether it can resolve the historical

---

[①] *The Important Speeches Made by Secretary-General Xi Jinping: A Reader*, Beijing: Xuexi Publishing House & People's Publishing House, 2014, p. 18.

problems that confront the country."① Therefore, only through constantly reforming and opening up can we better resolve the new problems which have cropped up in the process of the development of the times. If we have remained stagnant, we would be laughed at for taking foolish actions without regard for the changing environment—what we do is a lot less considered than the marking of the boat in order to find a lost sword.

IV. Chinese socialism is socialism putting people first, not new bureaucratic capitalism that only meets interests of minorities

Socialism with Chinese characteristics is guided by the Marxist concept of the history of the people, insists that the people are the principal actors in the country or in the history, and regards safeguarding the fundamental interests of all the people and realizing the well-rounded development of people as its fundamental goals.

Putting the interests of the people first is the principle and purpose that the CPC has always adhered to. Mao Zedong put forward the idea of "Serving the people wholeheartedly" at the memorial service held for Zhang Side(张思德), and the "Seventh National Congress"② of the Party enshrined it in the Party Constitution as the purpose of the CPC, which has been developed into the mass line of doing everything for the people, relying on them in every task, carrying out the principle of "from the masses, to the masses". Deng Xiaoping said in the preface to the *Selections of Deng Xiaoping*: "I am the son of the Chinese people. I deeply love my motherland and people." Jiang Zemin regarded the view that the Party should "always represent the fundamental interests of the overwhelming majority of the people in China" as one of the contents of his important thinking of the Three Represents.③ Hu Jintao took the principle of putting people first as the core of the Scientific Outlook on Development.

In the report to the 18th National Congress of the CPC, it is made clear that "We must uphold the position of the people as the principal actors in the country." In the

---

① Xi Jinping: *The Governance of China*, Eng. ed., *Beijing:* Foreign Language Press, 2014, p.22.
② The Seventh National Congress of the Party was held in Xi'an, China, from April 23 to June 11, 1945. It is mainly held to discuss the strategies about the War of Chinese People's Resistance Against Japanese Aggression.—Tr.
③ It is a guiding socio-political theory credited to Jiang Zemin, which can be interpreted as CPC represents advanced the productive forces; Represents the progressive course of China's advanced culture stands for cultural development; Represents the fundamental interests of the majority. —Tr.

political field, we should adhere to people's democracy, improve the system of the people's congresses, the system of multiparty cooperation and political consultation under the leadership of the Party and the system of community-level self-governance, develop socialist democracy and guarantee the people as the masters of the country. In the economic field, we should endeavor to raise the living standards of people, adhere to the basic socialist economic system and socialist system of income distribution, adjust the pattern of national income distribution, tighten its regulation by secondary distribution and work hard to narrow income gaps so that all the people can share more fruits of development in a fair way and move steadily toward common prosperity. In the cultural field, we should enrich people's intellectual and cultural lives and protect people's basic cultural rights and interests. In the field of social development, we are supposed to strengthen the management and safeguard social fairness and justice. Recently, in order to better achieve the goal set at the 18th National Congress of the CPC, General Secretary Xi Jinping has fully deployed the Party's program of mass line education and practice to further improved the Party's work style. The people are to the Party is what water is to fish, flesh to blood, waters to boats, the earth to the seeds. Coming from the people and taking root among them, the Party serves the people, and therefore people are the life of the Party and the foundation of the Party's invincible position. The Party would lose its vitality if it becomes disengaged from the people, undermines the interests of people. Only by being dedicated to improving people's wellbeing, solving pressing problems of major concern to the people, upholding the fundamental interests of all the people and maintaining close ties with the people, can we maintain the Party's progressive nature and integrity and consolidate its foundation and position as the ruling party.

The development of socialism with Chinese characteristics for more than 30 years has greatly improved the material and cultural life of the people, and various rights and interests, such as political participation, education rights, health care rights, and development rights, have been better protected. However, in recent years, China's economic development has also witnessed some bad phenomena: power rent-seeking, corruption, which in turn leads to the capitalization of power, the interweaving of capital and power, using their power to allocate social resources, the restriction on market access and the suppression of competition, and seeking private profit for a particular group. Some scholars refer to this phenomenon as crony capitalism or new bureaucratic capitalism. Such phenomenon we should keep vigilant with all the time, for it can be said that cronies or vested interest groups are increasingly becoming malignant tumors that corrode the sound development of society, a strong resistance to reform, and an obstacle to maintaining social fairness and justice and achieving common prosperity. But this is not a prerequisite for socialism with Chinese characteristics, but something caused by corruption as a result of the internal defects of the operating mechanism of public-owned enterprises and the political and democratic system in the primary stage of socialism. It is a phenomenon of power alienation, which, with the continuous improvement of the socialist system with Chinese characteristics, will inevitably be eradicated.

V. Chinese socialism is socialist market economy system, rather than state capitalism

Under socialism with Chinese characteristics, the socialist market economy is implemented. The socialist market economy is an economic form that combines the ideal value of socialism with the means of market regulation. While adhering to the basic regulatory role of the market, it gives full play to the state's ability to maintain adequate control and regulation in key market areas and market links. This is the Party's experience and lessons learned from world economic development, summed up in the long-term practice and exploration of socialist construction, and it is also "China's original creation" based on China's basic national conditions. It overcomes the drawbacks of planning guidance, full liberalization and market-oriented regulation, and better deals with the relationship between fairness and efficiency. It can not only ensure rapid economic development, but also ensure that it does not deviate from the socialist orientation of fairness, justice and common prosperity.

After the outbreak of the world financial crisis, only China's economic development has remained sound. When summarizing China's successful experience, some Westerners labeled China as "state capitalism", accusing China and other emerging economies of gaining unfair competitive advantages through government support. It is said that China's macro-control has stifled market efficiency and vitality, and state-owned enterprises are inefficient, monopolizing major resources and most of the market share, and causing severe disruption to the market economic order characterized by fair competition. They advocated market omnipotence, desperate to promote neoliberalism in the name of globalization. They stood for absolute liberalization, complete privatization and complete marketization, and opposed any kind of state economic intervention and regulation.

The accusation of "state capitalism" is totally untenable. First of all, the nature of Chinese economy is socialism. The basic economic system, in which public ownership is the mainstay of the economy and economic entities of diverse ownership develop together, ensures that the state controls the "lifeline" of economy, thereby realizing the fundamental interests of the people and reflecting the value goal of socialist common prosperity. State monopoly capitalism, however, refers to a system where Western monopoly capital controls the economy and the entire country with the overall assistance and support by the country to satisfy the big capitalists' purpose of exploiting and plundering wealth. Therefore, there is a fundamental difference between these two systems. Second, since the end of the Second World War, almost all the countries in the world have more or less strengthened state intervention and government control. That is, government-led or macroeconomic regulation and control is something every country has, and even those countries that claim to be liberalized, privatized, and market-oriented could not function well without government supervision and control. Therefore, we cannot deny the status of market economy just because our government controls the "lifeline" of economy. Third, those Western countries that proclaim neoliberalism have not developed well, their relaxation of financial debt supervision has led to a serious financial crisis, which has not yet ended. Some Western scholars promoted those tricks that have failed in their own countries and have caused crises to other countries that have developed better than their own. What is their intention? Their profound intention is to resort to the big stick of national capitalism to weaken the role of sovereign states in economic regulation, in an attempt to maintain the favorable position that they have always occupied under the rules of the global game. Finally, in international trade and economic competition, China actively participates in economic globalization, adheres to the principle of independence, and follows international economic rules and international practices to implement internal and external openness and fair competition in domestic and foreign markets. We will not take improper means to gain more competitive advantages, and we will never discriminate against foreign companies in the domestic market.

VI. Chinese socialism is socialism with core socialist values as ideological feature, rather than socialism that "accepts universal values"

In terms of ideology, socialism with Chinese characteristics adheres to Marxism-Leninism, Mao Zedong Thought, and social theory with Chinese characteristics as the guidance, strengthens the ideals and convictions of socialism and communism, and actively builds core socialist value system. In the report to the 18th National Congress of the CPC, it is pointed out that the core socialist values[①] are the soul of the Chinese nation and serve as the guide for building socialism with Chinese characteristics. We should carry out thorough study of and education in these values and employ them to guide social trends of thought and forge public consensus. Here "soul" refers to the interllectual trait. If the "soul" of the core socialist values were lost, socialism with Chinese characteristics would lose its socialist nature.

In recent years, some people have promoted "universal values". The so-called universal values are essentially Western values, such as freedom, democracy, and human rights. They claimed that "Western values are the mainstream of human civilization", "China can embrace a bright future only if it accepts the universal values of the West", and "Reform and opening up is the process of gradually accepting universal values." These remarks are obviously deliberately opposing, discrediting, and showing hatred for Marxism-Leninism, Mao Zedong Thought, and the theory of socialism with Chinese characteristics, and thus disrupting the ideology of the Party and the state and the beliefs of people. General Secretary Xi Jinping said: "Why did the Soviet Union collapse? Why did the Communist Party of the Soviet Union collapse? One important reason is that it completely denied the history of the Soviet Union and the CPSU, denied the theory of Lenin and Stalin, engaged in the movement of history of nihilism, and clutched up its thought."[②]

Universal values are not purely the topic of academic debate. From a theoretical point of view, mankind's yearning for beautiful things should be interlinked. We should promote prosperity, democracy, civility, and harmony; uphold freedom, equality, justice and the rule of law and advocate patriotism, dedication, integrity, and friendship. Obviously, these are similar to the values advocated by the West. However, the formation of the mainstream values of a society has its own specific historical background, and is integrated with its institutional form and mainstream ideology. The universal values advocated by the Western countries led by the United

---

① The core socialist values are prosperity, democracy, civility, harmony, freedom, equality, justice, the rule of law, patriotism, dedication, integrity and friendship. They were first mentioned in the political report delivered in November 2012 to the 18th National Congress, titled, "Firmly March on the Path of Socialism with Chinese Characteristics and Strive to Complete the Building of a Moderately Prosperous Society in All Respects."
② *The Important Speeches Made by Secretary-General Xi Jinping: A Reader,* Beijing: *Xuexi* Publishing House & People's Publishing House, 2014, p.19-20.]

States are not the concepts of freedom, democracy and human rights proposed by enlightenment thinkers of the 18th century, but the new rhetoric which emerged in their attempt to "remake the world" after the end of the Cold War. This point has been revealed very clearly by Samuel Huntington, a famous American scholar, in his book *The Clash of Civilizations and the Remaking of World Order*, stating that "The concept of a universal civilization is a distinctive product of Western civilization... At the end of the twentieth century the concept of a universal civilization helps justify Western cultural dominance of other societies and the need for those societies to ape Western practices and institutions. Universalism is the ideology of the West for confrontations with non-Western cultures."[1]

Obviously, there is an essential difference between core socialist values and universal values. The former is the ideological feature of socialism with Chinese characteristics and serves the construction of the socialism with Chinese characteristics that aims to realize the prosperity of country, the happiness of people and the rejuvenation of the nation. The latter essentially defends the hegemonism of Western countries headed by the United States. If universal values were taken as the "soul", socialism would cease to exist except in name, and the essence of it would be changed. Therefore, the preaching of universal values is essentially intent on misleading China to deviate from the path of socialism and toward the path of capitalism.

VII. Chinese socialism is socialism adhering to peaceful development, instead of relying on aggression and plundering other countries to develop hegemonism

Chinese socialism adheres to the path of peaceful development. As Deng Xiaoping said, the Chinese people concentrate on production, "realize the four modernizations, and never seek hegemony"[2] Since the founding of New China in 1949, China has advocated the Five Principles of Peaceful Coexistence, and has always emphasized independence and win-win cooperation in the socialist modernization drive, advocating respect for the right of other countries to choose their own paths, and never succumbing to hegemonism in all its manifestations. "We must respect the way the Parties and peoples of different countries deal with their

---

[1] Huntington, Samuel. P.: *The Clash of Civilizations and the Remaking of the World Order*, NY: Simon Schuster Inc., 1996, p. 66.
[2] Deng Xiaoping: *Selected Works of Deng Xiaoping*, Vol. 2, Chin. ed., Beijing: People's Publishing House, 1994, p. 111.

own affairs. They should be left to find their own paths by themselves and explore ways to solve their own problems. No Party should act like a patriarchal party and issue orders to others. We object to being ordered about and we, for our part, will never issue orders to others. This should be regarded as an important principle."①

Historically, the Western capitalist powers have realized their dream of becoming as great powers, dominating the world, by following the path of invading other countries and plundering resources. Therefore, due to China's remarkably enhanced comprehensive strength after more than 30 years of development and accumulation, some Western forces have advocated the "China Threat Theory", which is an excuse for hostile forces to block China and hinder it from rising and becoming more powerful. In the report to the 18th National Congress of the CPC, it is stated that China calls for promoting equality and mutual trust, inclusiveness and mutual learning, and mutually beneficial cooperation in international relations and making joint efforts to safeguard international fairness and justice. During his meeting with Obama during his visit to the United States, Xi Jinping emphasized: "China will unswervingly follow the path of peaceful development, unswervingly deepen reforms and expand opening up, strive to realize the Chinese dream of the great rejuvenation of the Chinese nation, and strive to advance the noble cause of advancing peace and development of mankind." All this shows that the path to the rise of great powers in Western capitalist countries is abandoned by socialism with Chinese characteristics.

VIII. Chinese socialism is a socialism basically established but not yet firmly established, still developing and improving

As a social formation, socialism with Chinese characteristics is a process of gradual formation and continuous development and improvement. It is advancing in the great exploration of reform and opening up. Facing the complicated and changeable situation at home and abroad, China has continuously solved economic, political, cultural, social, ecological and other problems encountered in development, and has formed a series of theories, systems and policies on governance, internal affairs and foreign affairs. The path of socialism with characteristics has become increasingly salient, and the socialist formation with Chinese characteristics has basically taken shape. During his inspection tour of southern China in 1992, Deng

---

① Deng Xiaoping: *Selected Works of Deng Xiaoping*, Vol. 2, Chin. ed., Beijing: People's Publishing House, 1994, p.319.

Xiaoping pointed out, "It will probably take another thirty years for us to develop a more mature and well-defined system in every field. The principles and policies to be applied under each system will also be more firmly established."①

We think that through more than 30 years of reform and opening up and socialist modernization, we have formed the path, theory and system of socialism with Chinese characteristics, achieved brilliant achievements that have attracted worldwide attention, and greatly improved China's overall national strength and international status. We have enough reasons to say: The three aspects of socialism with Chinese characteristics, namely, the path, the theory and the system, have been integrated to constitute the socialist formation with Chinese characteristics, which has basically been established. The path of socialism with Chinese characteristics is a way to reach the goal, the theory of socialism with Chinese characteristics offers a guide to action, and the system of socialism with Chinese characteristics provides a fundamental guarantee. All three serve the great cause of building socialism with Chinese characteristics. This great practice also constitutes the socialist formation with Chinese characteristics, which has rich and specific connotations. In the report, the CPC Central Committe made a preliminary summary: The path of socialism with Chinese characteristics is followed under the leadership of the CPC, based on the basic national conditions, by focusing on economic construction, by adhering to the Four Cardinal Principles, by persisting in reform and opening up, by emancipating and developing the productive forces, by building socialist market economy, socialist democratic politics, advanced socialist culture, socialist harmonious society, socialist ecological civilization, by promoting the well-rounded development of everyone, by achieving prosperity for all people over time, and thus building a prosperous, democratic, civilized and harmonious socialist modernization nation. The theoretical system of socialism with Chinese characteristics is a sound theoretical system that includes Deng Xiaoping Theory, the important Thought of the Three Represents, and the Scientific Outlook on Development. It is an adherence to and development of Marxism-Leninism and Mao Zedong Thought. The socialist system with Chinese characteristics includes the following: the system of people's congresses as China's fundamental political system; the basic political systems of multi-party cooperation and political consultation under the leadership of the CPC, of regional ethnic

---

① Deng Xiaoping: *Selected Works of Deng Xiaoping*, Vol. 2, Chinse ed., Beijing: People's Publishing House, 1993, p.372.

autonomy, and of community-level self-governance; other systems and mechanisms such as the system of socialist laws with Chinese characteristics, the basic economic system in which public ownership is the mainstay and economic entities of diverse ownership develop together. General Secretary Xi Jinping emphasized: "These are the manifestations of the basic principles of scientific socialism under the new historical conditions; only if they are abandoned would our system no longer be socialist."[1]

This summary shows that the Party's understanding and grasp of socialism with Chinese characteristics has reached an unprecedented height. General Secretary Xi Jinping said: "Socialism with Chinese characteristics is the integration of the theory of scientific socialism and social development theories of Chinese history. Socialism has taken root in China. It reflects the wishes of the people and meets the development needs of the country and the times. It is a sure route to success in building a moderately prosperous society in all respects, and in the acceleration of socialist modernization, and in the great renewal of the Chinese nation."[2] The tremendous achievements made in China's development over the past 30 years have also proved that socialism with Chinese characteristics has shown superior vitality and effectiveness than other social systems in the same period, and has been basically established as a new social formation.

However, as General Secretary Xi Jinping said, "Marxism will not remain stagnant. It will certainly keep up with the times, the progress of our practice and the advance of science. Socialism too always advances through practice."[3] "Our understanding of socialism, our mastery of the laws governing socialism with Chinese characteristics, has reached an unprecedented height. There is no doubt about this. At the same time, we must also realize that our country's socialism is still in its primary stage, and we are still facing many problems and issues which need to be defined and resolved. Our understanding and handling of many major issues are still in the process of deepening. There is also no doubt about this. It will take time for us to understand a thing. We have worked on socialism only for decades, so what we have known about it is still very limited. All this requires us to boldly explore new

---

[1] *The Important Speeches Made by Secretary-General Xi Jinping: A Reader*, Beijing: Xuexi Publishing House & People's Publishing House, 2014, p.16.
[2] Xi Jinping. *The Governance of China*, Eng. ed., Beijing: Foreign Languages Press Co. Ltd, 2014, p.23.
[3] Ibid., p.25.

ways to deepen the development."① At present, we are still in the primary stage of socialism, with economic development in a transitional period. Problems such as the polarization between the rich and the poor, lack of faith, moral decline, corruption, ecological destruction, and waste of resources have become increasingly serious. As a result, there have been some doubts about socialism with Chinese characteristics. In fact, these are the problems that must be faced when a new stage is ushered in for socialism with Chinese characteristics. This is also the case with other countries at the new stage of development. We must be confident in the path, the system of theories and the system of socialism with Chinese characteristics, adhere to the basic tenets of scientific socialism, persist in innovation in practice, theory and institutional building, and continue to deepen our understanding of many major issues in the practice of reform and opening up, and solve these problems. Only in this way can we continuously improve the path, theories, and the system of socialism with Chinese characteristics.

We firmly believe that, just as General Secretary Xi Jinping pointed out, "As socialism with Chinese characteristics progresses, our institutions will undoubtedly mature, the strength of our system will become self-evident, and our development path will assuredly become wider."② We can "realize a moderately prosperous society by the centenary of the CPC in 2021" "turn China into a prosperous, democratic, culturally advanced and harmonious modern socialist country by the centenary of the PRC in 2049." In other words, socialism with Chinese characteristics as a new type of system civilization that is different from rigid traditional socialism and from all kinds of capitalism is truly established, as a new social formation of socialism with Chinese characteristics. The effectiveness and rationality of the system will be fully demonstrated. Then, those conceited or arrogant people who oppose and question socialism with Chinese characteristics may let out a sigh of disappointment. At that time, the great rejuvenation of the Chinese nation, the great ideal that the Chinese nation constantly pursues, will be truly realized.

---

① *The Important Speeches Made by Secretary-General Xi Jinping: A Reader*, Beijing: Xuexi Publishing House & People's Publishing House, 2014, p.16.
② Ibid.

A Comprehensive and Incisive Interpretation of Marxism: Study Important Remarks by General Secretary Xi Jinping on Marxism*

Marxism is the fundamental guiding thought for the establishment of the CPC and the founding of the People's Republic of China in 1949. Since the 18th National Congress of the CPC, General Secretary Xi Jinping has published a series of important expositions on Marxism. Recently, in his speech to celebrate the 95th anniversary of the founding of the Party on July 1, 2016 and his speech at Seminar on Philosophy and Social Sciences, focusing on the issues relating to Marxism, he has comprehensively and incisively expounded such questions as "Why we must adhere to the guidance of Marxism?" "How do we understand and grasp Marxism?" "How shall we uphold and develop Marxism?" He put forward many new viewpoints, and provide judicious guidance for our accurate understanding and correct development of Marxism.

I. Unwaveringly Uphold guiding status of Marxism

On July 1, 2016, General Secretary Xi Jinping delivered a speech at a ceremony marking the 95th anniversary of the founding of the CPC and he pointed out: "Marxism is the fundamental guiding thought for the establishment of the Party and our country. Departing from or abandoning Marxism, the Party would lose its soul and direction. On the issue of Marxism as the fundamental guiding thought, we shall not waver under any circumstances."① On this issue, he highlighted two key words: one is "fundamental"; the other is "unwavering". Adherence to taking Marxism as the

---

* Originally published in *Chinese Social Sciences Today*, July 28, 2016.
① Xi Jinping. *The Governance of China*, Chin. ed., Beijing: Foreign Languages Press, 2017, p.33.

guiding ideology has a bearing on the future of the Party and the state, as well as the great rejuvenation of the Chinese nation.

Why is it necessary to unwaveringly uphold the guiding status of Marxism? Xi Jinping once made a systematic elaboration in his speeches at the Seminar of the Members and Alternate Members of the Newly-elected CPC Central Committee for Implementing the Guiding Principles of the Party's 18th National Congress, at the Seminar on Philosophy and Social Sciences, and in the celebration of the 95th anniversary of the founding of the Party, he once again expounded on this issue, mainly in the following aspects:

First, in his elaboration, General Secretary Xi Jinping points out the rationality of Marxism from a theoretical point of view. He pointed out: "Marxism and its development in China have always been a sound guideline for handling the affairs of the Party and our people, and a foundation for unity in the Party and between people of all ethnicities."[1] K. Marx and F. Engels realized the great transformation of socialism from fantasy to science based on the grasping of the laws of human social development (historical materialism) and the special laws of capitalism (the theory of surplus value). Xi has repeatedly emphasized that Marxism is not out of date. No matter how the times change and how science progresses, Marxism still showcases the power of scientific thought and still occupies the commanding height of truth and morality. He also criticized the misunderstanding that Marxism is not a science. Some believed that Marxism is outdated, and that what China is doing now is not Marxism; some said that Marxism is just an ideological preaching without academic rationality and systematicness. We must not just regard Marxism as an ideology and deny its scientific nature. Deng Xiaoping put it well when he said: "I am convinced that more and more people will come to believe in Marxism, because it is a science."[2]

Second, it points out the powerful intellectual force of Marxism from the perspective of belief. Marxism is the belief of the CPC and a powerful intellectual force that supports the Party in overcoming difficulties and setbacks. General Secretary Xi Jinping pointed out: "The guiding philosophy is the intellectual beacon of a party. Over the past 95 years, the CPC has accomplished so many tasks which were thought to be impossible by other political forces. The reason for this has been

---

[1] Xi Jinping: *The Governance of China*, Eng. ed., Beijing: Foreign Languages Press, 2017, p.33.
[2] Deng Xiaoping: *Selected Works of Deng Xiaoping*, Vol. 3, Chin. ed., Beijing: People's Publishing House, 1993, p. 382.

precisely attributed to our adoption of Marxism as our guide of action, while the theories of Marxism have then been further developed. This has allowed the Party to free itself from the limitations of all previous political forces, which focused on pursuing their own special interests. This has enabled us to hold on to the materialist dialectic view and selflessly lead China's revolution, development and reform, whilst sticking to the truth and correcting the mistakes we made. The Party has never wavered in its belief in Marxism either in favorable or unfavorable circumstances."① He also stressed the importance of upholding the ideals and convictions of communism in the new situation. In his important speech at the opening ceremony of the seminar of the members and alternate members of the newly-elected CPC Central Committee for implementing the guiding principles of the Party's 18th National Congress, he pointed out that the Party members, particularly Party officials, should maintain a firm belief in lofty communist ideals, along with the common ideal of building socialism with Chinese characteristics, and pursue them with dedication. Our revolutionary ideals are of the greatest importance. A party member devoid of ideals lacks an essential quality—as does one who engages in empty talk about lofty ideal without doing anything. In his speech celebrating the 95th anniversary of the founding of the CPC, General Secretary Xi Jinping emphasized once again that in order to strengthen the shared ideal of communism and socialism with Chinese characteristics, "The wavering of one's faith and ideal is the most dangerous risk."

Third, it points out the effectiveness of taking Marxism as the guidance from the perspective of historical facts and practice. It is under the guidance of Marxism that the CPC has led the Chinese people to achieve one victory after another in their revolution and construction and has blazed a new path of development that is different from those of Western countries, namely, the path of socialism with Chinese characteristics, and formed the theoretical framework and established the system of Chinese socialism, "allowing China to keep abreast with the times, and bringing about a leap forward whereby the Chinese people have gone from regaining dignity to becoming prosperous and strong." Socialism with Chinese characteristics exhibits strong confidence in the path, theories, system and culture. General Secretary Xi Jinping pointed out: "The great victory of the Chinese people, achieved under the leadership of the CPC put the Chinese nation, the curator of a 5,000-year-old civilization, well on the way to modernization, infusing new

---

① Xi Jinping: *The Governance of China*, Eng. ed., Beijing: Foreign Languages Press, 2017, p.33.

vigor into Chinese civilization. This great victory placed the tenets of socialism, which go back 500 years, on a highly realistic, feasible, and correct path in the world's most populous country, allowing scientific socialism to display renewed vigor in the 21st century. Moreover, this great victory enabled the PRC, founded more than 60 years ago, to captivate the world with its achievements in development. In little more than 30 years, China, the world's largest developing country, has shaken off poverty and risen to become the world's second largest economy. Guaranteeing its own survival, it has performed an earth-shaking miracle in the history of human development, and infused the Chinese nation with new vitality."

Fourth, it points out from the perspective of development that Marxism exhibits great vitality. As General Secretary Xi Jinping pointed out, "Facing the new characteristics of our era and the demands of new realities, Marxism also needs to be better integrated with the realities of China, keep abreast with the times, and respond to the need of the Chinese people. Marxism does not put a lid on truth but opens a path to truth."[①] "What we build is socialism with Chinese characteristics, and nothing else. History has not ended and will not end. To judge whether socialism with Chinese characteristics is good or not, we should look to the facts and listen to the voices of the Chinese people—not to the subjective judgment of those who look at China through a distorted lens. The CPC and the Chinese people are more than confident that we can offer the Chinese solution to the human society for people to explore for a better social system." It can be said that both the development of Marxism in China and socialism with Chinese characteristics have displayed great vitality and vigor.

II. Incisive Summarization of Basic Meanings of Marxism

General Secretary Xi Jinping emphasized that Marxism have wide-ranging contents, covers many domains and is a complete theoretical system. It is imperative to fully grasp the basic tenets of Marxism as a whole. In his speech at the symposium on philosophy and social sciences—"Speed up the construction of philosophy and social sciences with Chinese characteristics"—on May 17, 2016,[②] he pointed out: "The writers of Marxist classics have a broad vision and rich knowledge. The theoretical system and knowledge system of Marxism have a broad sphere,

---

① Xi Jinping: *The Governance of China*, Eng. ed., Beijing: Foreign Languages Press, 2017, p.33.
② Ibid., p.366.

nature, human society, and human thinking, including history, economics, politics, culture, society, eco-environment, science and technology, the military, and Party development." "The tenets of Marxism on the laws of the materiality of the world and its development, human society and its development, the essence of knowledge and its development, etc., provide us with a basic worldview and methodology for our study and grasp of various disciplines and various domains of philosophy and social sciences." Here, it fully reveals the Marxist worldview (ontology), the profound conception of history, and the Marxist epistemology. In terms of theoretical logic, Marxism is a complete theoretical system that includes worldview, epistemology, methodology, and values, and it must be grasped as a whole. In terms of worldview, through critique of philosophy and political economics, it has opened up a new worldview based on human practical activity, and constructed the laws of the materiality of the world and its development, the laws of human society and its development, the laws of the nature of knowledge and its development, and other basic principles. In terms of epistemology, as Xi Jinpin put it, "Marxism reveals the nature, internal connection and the laws of the development of the matter. It is a 'great instrument of understanding' and a powerful ideological weapon for people to observe the world and analyze problems." In terms of methodology, materialist dialectics is a judicious method of analyzing the objective world. General Secretary Xi Jinping made a brief summarization: "We must persevere in looking at problems from the perspective of connected, strengthen strategic and systematic thinking, distinguish between essence and phenomenon, mainstream and tributary, look at both hitherto existing problems and their development trends, look at both the local and the overall situation, put forward views and conclusions thus made should be objective, accurate, able to withstand tests, and, on the basis of a comprehensive and objective analysis, supposed to reveal the big logical trend of social development in our country and the development of human society."① In terms of values, Marxism points out the correct way to achieve the complete liberation and the free and well-rounded development of people through the elimination of private ownership and of classes, and the establishment of a communist society. When he was in middle school, K. Marx made up his mind to choose "the profession that can work best for the welfare of mankind". The great theoretical system of Marxism was researched and

---

① One of the main points of the speech at a symposium with the Workers in the fields of philosophy and social sciences in May 2016. —Tr.

constructed by K. Marx and F. Engels revolving around how to free the proletariat and all mankind from exploitation, oppression and alienation.

Marxism exists as a whole that contains three internally-linked components, namely, Marxist philosophy, political economics and scientific socialism. General Secretary Xi Jinping attached great importance to these three basic components, and made important elaboration respectively. With regard to Marxist philosophy, he once presided over the eleventh and twentieth group study session of the Political Bureau of the 18th CPC Central Committee, at which historical materialism and dialectical materialism were studied respectively in 2013 and 2015. He briefly explained the basic tenets and methodology of Marxist philosophy, such as the dialectical relationship between social existence and social consciousness, between the productive forces and the relations of production, between economic base and superstructure; the principle that the world is unified in matter and that matter determines consciousness; the theory of the movement of opposites in the development of things; the dialectical relationship between knowledge and practice; Marxist views on practice and the people, and materialist dialectics, etc.; and it is pointed out that studying and applying philosophy is a good tradition and a key skill of the Party, and we must uphold Marxist philosophy education and arm the whole Party. With regard to political economics, General Secretary Xi Jinping emphasized when presiding over the 28th group study session of the Political Bureau of the 18th CPC Central Committee on November 23, 2015 that Marxist political economics is an important part of Marxism, and it is also a required course for our upholding and development of Marxism. Since the Third Plenary Session of the Eleventh CPC Central Committee, held from December 18 to 22, 1978, the Party has combined the basic principles of Marxist political economics with the new practice of reform and opening up, constantly enriched and developed Marxist political economics, and formed many important theoretical results of contemporary Chinese Marxist political economics, which are political economics adapted to China's national conditions and characteristics of the times in contemporary China, not only working well in guiding the country's economic development, but also opening up new realms of Marxist political economics. In his speech at the Symposium on Philosophy and Social Sciences on May 17, 2016, he pointed out: "Some people say that Marxist political economics is outdated, and *Capital* is outdated. This statement is arbitrary. Take the international financial crisis as an example. Many Western countries underwent the continued economic downturn, increased polarization, and the deepening of social conflicts, which indicate that the inherent contradiction between the socialization of production and the private ownership of the means of production still exists in capitalism, but its manifestations and characteristics are different." When he attended the symposium with experts analyzing the country's current economic situation on July 8, 2016, Xi Jinping once again pointed out: "Upholding and developing the political economy of socialism with Chinese characteristics means that we must take Marxist political economy as the guide to summarize and refine the experience of China's great practice of reform, opening up, and socialist modernization, and at same time draw on the beneficial elements of Western economics. Socialist political economics with Chinese characteristics can only be enriched and developed in practice, and must be tested by practice and then guide practice. It is necessary to strengthen related research, exploration, and the summarization of what we have known about the law of development, constantly improve the theoretical system of socialist political economics with Chinese characteristics, and promote the construction of economic disciplines that should display salient Chinese features and style."

With regard to scientific socialism, in his speech at the seminar of the members and alternate members of the newly-elected CPC Central Committee for implementing the guiding principles of the Party's 18th National Congress sorted out and analyzed the history of socialist thought, which is divided into 6 phrases from its being proposed to the present development, especially the historical process and great practice of the Party's exploration of socialism with Chinese characteristics; systematically and profoundly expounded on several major theoretical issues that need to be grasped in adhering to and developing socialism with Chinese characteristics; concluded that "Socialism with Chinese characteristics is the integration of the theory of scientific socialism and social development theories of Chinese history"[①] and pointed out that it is necessary to continue with the great cause of upholding and developing socialism with Chinese characteristics.

In short, Marxism is a logically rigorous ideological system which integrate criticality and ideality, profundity and value, theoreticality and practicality. To understand Marxism, we must grasp its "true spirit" as a whole, deeply understand its lofty realms, rational connotations, and cultural essence, and adhere to the integrity of its content system, of its logic and of its history. The issue of Marxism's integrity/totality is an important issue that the theoretical and academic circles have always

---

① Xi Jinping: *The Governance of China*, Eng. ed., Beijing: Foreign Languages Press, 2017, p.23.

paid attention to. General Secretary Xi Jinping gave an affirmative answer to this, which has very important guiding significance.

III. Marxism takes as its mission the realization of the free and well-rounded development of people and the emancipation of all mankind

Realizing the emancipation of the proletariat through the establishment of a communist society and thereby realizing the free and well-rounded development of everyone is the highest ideal of Marxism. It was the first time that General Secretary Xi Jinping very clearly proposed it at the Seminar on Philosophy and Social Sciences. He said: "Marxism adheres to the position of realizing the liberation of the people and safeguarding the interests of the people, and takes the realization of the free and well-rounded development of people and the liberation of all mankind as its own responsibility, reflecting the beautiful vision of mankind for an ideal society." Realizing the free and well-rounded development of everyone is the most fundamental feature of the ideal society of mankind in the future envisioned by K. Marx and F. Engels—communist society, and it is the highest philosophical proposition of Marxism. In 1894, in his reply letter to Giuseppe Canepa, F. Engels summed up the spirit of the future communist society in the most concise terms: "I have found nothing except the following passage taken from the *Communist Manifesto* (Italian edition of Critica Sociale,p.35): '*Al posto della vecehia societa borghesedivisa in class; cozzanti fra loro, subenta un'associazione, nella quale illibero sviluppo di ciascumo e la condizione per il libero sviluppo di tutti*'."[①]

Marx, in his *Capital*, described communism as "a more advanced social form with the full and free development of everyone as its basic principle."

The free and well-rounded development of people means the development in which people are put first, that is, handling well the relationship between man and nature and the relationship between people, liberate man from dependence on things and on man, and eliminate man's alienation. To achieve the liberation of people, on the one hand, we must vigorously develop the productive forces and achieve great material wealth; on the other hand, we must achieve fairness and justice, and safeguard personal rights and interests. Over the past 30 years of reform and opening up, China

---

① English version: In place of the old bourgeois society, with its classes and class antagonisms, we shall have an association, in which the free development of each is the condition for the free development of all. —Tr.

has made tremendous achievements in economic and social development and people's living standards have greatly improved, but the issue of fairness and justice has not been resolved. Therefore, at the Third Plenary Session of the 18th CPC Central Committee, held from November 9 to 12, 2013, it is proposed that the comprehensive deepening of reforms should take the promotion of social fairness and justice and the improvement of people's well-being as the starting point and the objective... to achieve more development results and benefit all people more equitably. This requires on the one hand to divide the "cake" well after it gets bigger, and on the other hand to protect the rights of the people, promote the construction of a society under the rule of law, strengthen the Party' work style and fight against corruption, and handle the relationship between public power and individual rights. General Secretary Xi Jinping pointed out in the article "Conscientiously integrate our thoughts into the spirit of the Third Plenary Session of the 18th CPC Central Committee": "Through innovative institutional arrangements, we should strive to overcome the phenomenon of violating fairness and justice caused by human factors, and ensure the people's equal rights to participate and develop. We should take social fairness and justice and the living standards of the people as a mirror to examine our systems, mechanisms, policies and regulations in all respects, and introduce reforms accordingly by focusing on areas where the problems of injustice and inequality are most prevalent." Therefore, General Secretary Xi Jinping once again explained the idea of the free and well-rounded development of people in the new situation, which is very profound and targeted.

IV. A critical attitude is the most valued quality of Marxism

General Secretary Xi Jinping pointed out: "We must analyze and assess foreign theories, concepts, discourses, and methods, taking in what suits us and discarding what does not. Philosophy and social science researchers must adopt a critical attitude, the most valued quality of Marxism."[1] General Secretary Xi Jinping clearly pointed out the critical inclination of Marxism, so we must accurately understand the concept of the critical nature of Marxism and reflect it in the process of developing Marxism.

To grasp and showcase this feature, we need to grasp the following points: First, the concept of the critical nature of Marxism is the criticism based on historical facts and historical laws, and the theoretical criticism based on the revealing of the inherent

---

[1] Xi Jinping: *The Governance of China*, Vol.2, Eng. ed., Beijing: Foreign Languages Press, 2017, p.369.

contradictions of the development of human society and the particular contradictions of capitalist society. At present, the CPC has been carrying out criticism in the exploring and grasping of the laws that underlie governance by a communist party , the development of socialism , and the evolution of human society. Second, we must adhere to the unity of practical criticism and theoretical criticism. Practical criticism is higher than theoretical criticism, and theoretical criticism is realized through practical criticism, which is based on and guides practical criticism. K. Marx said in the introduction of "Hegel's Critique of Philosophy of Law": "The weapon of criticism cannot, of course, replace criticism of the weapon, material force must be overthrown by material force; but theory also becomes a material force as soon as it has gripped the masses. Theory is capable of gripping the masses as soon as it demonstrates *ad hominem*, and it demonstrates *ad hominem* as soon as it becomes radical. To be radical is to grasp the root of the matter. But, for man, the root is man himself." "As philosophy finds its material weapon in the proletariat, so the proletariat finds its intellectual weapon in philosophy." Third, criticism is "sublation", not absolute denial. In the postscript to the second edition of the first volume of *Capital* in 1872, K. Marx made a classic elaboration on the dialectical method used in *Capital*: "it [Dialectic] includes in its comprehension and affirmative recognition of the existing state of things, at the same time also, the recognition of the negation of that state, of its inevitable breaking up; because it regards every historically developed social form as in fluid movement, and therefore takes into account its transient nature not less than its momentary existence; because it lets nothing impose upon it, and is in its essence critical and revolutionary." Last, criticism is the driving force for philosophical development and social progress. Criticism is the prerequisite for seeking truth and for innovation. Without a critical attitude, K. Marx and F. Engels would not have been able to create Marxism. Similarly, without a critical attitude, Mao Zedong would not have been able to establish the revolutionary road of encircling cities from the countryside; without a critical attitude, Deng Xiaoping would not have been able to open up the situation of reform and opening up; in the same way, without a critical attitude, our reforms would have been stagnant. We must adhere to the critical nature of Marxism, have the courage and capability to question, and adhere to problem orientation. General Secretary Xi Jinping pointed out: "Focusing on solving problems is a distinctive feature of Marxism. Problems are the starting point and the source of innovative power. Only by listening to the voices of the times, responding to the call of the times, and earnestly studying and solving major and urgent problems can we truly grasp the historical context, find the law of development, and promote theoretical innovation." A problem - solving approach is the embodiment of critical spirit and scientific spirit.

V. Realize theoretical innovation of Marxism in the process of Sinicization, modernization and popularization of Marxism

General Secretary Xi Jinping pointed out: "As a theory, Marxism develops with the times. It is an open theoretical system that continues to develop with the times, practice, and sound development. It does not put a lid on truth but opens a path to truth... Adherence to Marxism means the integration of it with the development of Marxism, so as to constantly make theoretical innovation in conjunction with new practice. That is the very reason why Marxism maintains its vigor and vitality." Upholding Marxism requires continuous development of Marxism. Without developing and innovating Marxism, we cannot truly adhere to it. General Secretary Xi Jinping proposed that only by the integration of upholding and development can we realize the innovation of Marxist, which means promoting the Sinicization, modernization, and popularization of Marxism in accordance with the development of the times. At its most important, we should construct Marxism in the 21st-century China. During the twentieth group study session of the Political Bureau of the 18th CPC Central Committee on January 23, 2015, he emphasized that we must, in accordance with the changes of the times and the development of practice, continuously deepen understanding, constantly sum up experience, and constantly realize the benign interaction between theoretical innovation and practical innovation, and develop Marxism of the 21st Century China in this integration and interaction. At a symposium on philosophy and social sciences, General Secretary Xi Jinping also pointed out: "Tremendous achievements have been made in adapting Marxism to the Chinese context, but it is far from over. An important task for Chinese philosophy and social science researchers is to continue to promote the Sinicization, modernization and popularization of Marxism, and to develop Marxism in the 21st century and Marxism in modern China." In his speech celebrating the 95th anniversary of the founding of the CPC, he pointed out: "If our understanding of the theory is not thorough, we cannot convince others. We should broaden our horizon to review the prevailing conditions and practical need of Marxism in today's development. We must focus on identifying and resolving problems, and focus our attention on what we are doing. We should listen to the voices of our era and further boost the integration of Marxism and the circumstances and realities of Chinese development today. We should open a new chapter for Marxism in the 21st century and allow it to shine brighter in modern China."①

To develop Marxism in the 21st century and Marxism in contemporary China is a proposition which is inevitable for the development of the practice of building socialism with Chinese characteristics, and marks that the Party has a high degree of theoretical consciousness to uphold and develop Marxism under the new historical circumstances. Since the start of reform and opening up in 1978, China has made great achievements in economic and social development, embarked on a unique path of development, forged unique experience of development, and encountered some more prominent problems, which constitute the basis of practice of innovating China's Marxist theory in the 21st century. Since the 18th National Congress of the CPC, General Secretary Xi Jinping has delivered a series of important speeches on new issues in the new situation, and put forward a series of new ideas, concepts, conclusions, and demands, which constitute theoretical connotations of China's Marxist theory in the 21st century. We must take Marxism as the guiding philosophy and socialism with Chinese characteristics as the practical basis, sort out and summarize the spirit which is encapsulated in a series of important speeches delivered by General Secretary Xi Jinping, and develop Marxism in the 21st-century China, which is different from Western models and Western values. This not only responds to the development needs of China's social economy, but also is a contribution to world civilization.

We must unwaveringly uphold Marxism as the fundamental guiding thought for the establishment of the Party and the state, accurately understand it, and adapt it to the conditions of the 21st-century China, which has a great bearing on the future of the Party and the state, and is of great significance to the sound development of socialism with Chinese characteristics. General Secretary Xi Jinping clearly pointed out the importance of adhering to Marxism as the guiding thought, fully grasped the basic principles of Marxism, emphasized the ideality and critical nature of Marxism, and judiciously pointed out the direction of innovating Marxism. His important exposition on Marxism comprehensively and incisively explained Marxism, which has important guiding significance for the correct understanding and developing of Marxism.

---

① Xi Jinping: *The Governance of China*, Vol.2, Eng. ed., Beijing: Foreign Languages Press, 2017, p.34.

Afterword

I am very happy that my book *Shidai de Zhexue Huisheng*(时代的哲学回声) can be translated into English. First of all, I would like to thank Paths International Ltd for its support. At the same time, I would also like to express my gratitude to Ms. Chen Fengjiao, the translator of this book, without whose devotion and painstaking efforts this English edition could not have been realised.

In 1982, four years after China's adoption of reform and opening-up policy in 1978, I entered the philosophy department of Renmin University of China and began to learn and study philosophy. After I obtained Bachelor and Master degrees at Renmin University of China, I joined the Chinese Academy of Social Sciences, working first for the *Social Sciences in China* journal and currently for the China Social Science Press, mainly engaged in researching Marxist philosophy, the theory of socialism with Chinese characteristics, etc., as well as editing and publishing academic journals and academic works.

Previously published articles on contemporary Chinese philosophy, which I have worked out after many years of efforts, are reprinted here in this book. They are what I have achieved through pondering over, and delving into, the important philosophical issues of the extensive and profound economic and social changes that have taken place with China's reform and opening up, and to some extent are also the reflection of the philosophical issues and the outlook of research development which have been achieved in this historical period in China.

In 1978, the great debate on "Criterion for Testing Truth"[①] was carried out, and thus has turned a new page in the history of China by implementing China's reform and opening-up policy, which has made it urgent for the philosophical community to deepen the research on the basic issues of practice. In this process, I mainly explored the concept, form, subject, logic and operation mechanism of practice. These reflections and studies on the issues of practice have expanded and deepened the understanding of the scientific conclusion that "Practice is the sole criterion for testing truth" and provided theoretical support for promoting the ideological emancipation movement at the initial launch of reform and opening up, such as highlighting human subjectivity and the measure of value, how to grasp the laws of practical activities, and how to achieve the success of practical activities, etc. These are the new exploration and elucidation of Marx's thought of "free and well-rounded development of an individual" in the process of reform and opening up, which has not been highlighted in the previous study of Chinese Marxist philosophy, and on the basis of which, I have also conducted in-depth discussions on the form of Marxist philosophy and contemporary development, the theoretical essence of Marxist philosophy, the contemporary construction of the form of Marxist philosophy with Chinese characteristics, and put forward the direction and pathway of the development of contemporary Chinese Marxist philosophy, to name a few.

In view of the prominent problems such as materialism supremacy, loss of faith, and moral decline that once occurred in the course of reform and opening up, I have conducted in-depth research on values and cultural identity, as well as the theory of socialist culture with Chinese characteristics, analyzed major issues such as cultural identity crisis that emerged after China adopted reform and opening-up policy in 1978, summarized the achievements of the CPC in attaching importance to promoting ethical and cultural progress of socialism, systematically explained the theory of socialist culture with Chinese characteristics, and expounded the great

---

[①] In May 1978, the internal journal of the Party School of the CPC Central Committee, *Theoretical Dynamics*, published an article entitled "Practice is the sole criterion for testing truth". On May 11, *Guangming Daily* forwarded this article under the signature of a special commentator, which caused a strong response. Since then, a great debate on the criterion for testing truth has been held in China. This great debate has fully affirmed the view that "Practice is the sole criterion for testing truth", criticized the "left" ideological error of "Two Whatevers" (i.e. "We will resolutely uphold whatever policy decisions Chairman Mao made, and unswervingly follow whatever instructions Chairman Mao gave"), promoted the extensive and profound ideological liberation movement in Chinese society, and made ideological preparations for China's reform and opening up.

significance of cultural self-confidence and strengthening cultural progress for China's modernization. These studies have played an important role in promoting the theoretical research and practical development of Chinese culture. Through more than 40 years of reform and opening up, China has realized two miracles of rapid economic development and long-term social stability, embarking on the path of Chinese-style modernization, that is, the path of building socialism with Chinese characteristics, and formulated the theory of socialism with Chinese characteristics, namely, the theoretical form of Chinese-style modernization path. I have paid close attention to the theoretical innovation of the CPC, namely, the development of the theory of socialism with Chinese characteristics, delved into the logic of history, theory, and practice of the rejuvenation of the Chinese nation, the rich implications of the path of building Socialism with Chinese characteristics, the innovation of the important thought of the Three Represents, the philosophical basis of the Scientific Outlook on Development, and General Secretary Xi Jinping's comprehensive and incisive explanation of Marxism, and revealed and demonstrated the historical necessity, scientificity and effectiveness of the path of building socialism with Chinese characteristics.

Over the past 40 years, China's great achievements in reform and opening up have attracted the attention of the international community, and foreign scholars have been exploring the secret to China's success in building socialism with Chinese characteristics from different perspectives. This book attempts to make philosophical reflections on the great changes which have taken place in contemporary China. If it can provide reference and inspiration for you, I will feel very honored and happy. If there should be any mistake or omission, please feel free to let me know.

Zhao Jianying
February 9, 2023, a day with spring snowflakes dancing in the sky
on the north bank of Houhai, Beijing

This book is the result of a co-publication agreement between China Social Sciences Press (China) and Paths International Ltd (UK)

Title: Echoes of the Times in Philosophy
Collected Works of Zhao Jianying
Author: Zhao Jianying
Translated by Chen Fengjiao
ISBN: 978-1-84464-783-5
Ebook ISBN: 978-1-84464-784-2

Copyright © 2023 by Paths International Ltd, U.K. and by China Social Sciences Press, China

All rights reserved. No part of this publication may be reproduced, translated, stored in a retrieval system, or transmitted in any form or by any means, electronic, mechanical, photocopying or otherwise, without the prior permission of the publisher.

The copyright to this title is owned by China Social Sciences Press, China. This book is made available internationally through an exclusive arrangement with Paths International Ltd of the United Kingdom and is permitted for sale outside China.

Paths International Ltd
www.pathsinternational.com
Published in the United Kingdom

Printed in the USA
CPSIA information can be obtained
at www.ICGtesting.com
LVHW081227090724
784400LV00004B/65